BYRON'S POETRY

AUTHORITATIVE TEXTS
LETTERS AND JOURNALS
CRITICISM
IMAGES OF BYRON

➤➤ A NORTON CRITICAL EDITION ◄◄

BYRON'S POETRY

AUTHORITATIVE TEXTS
LETTERS AND JOURNALS
CRITICISM
IMAGES OF BYRON

➤➤◄◄

Selected and Edited by

FRANK D. McCONNELL
NORTHWESTERN UNIVERSITY

➤➤ ◄◄

W · W · NORTON & COMPANY · INC · *New York*

Library of Congress Cataloging in Publication Data
Byron, George Gordon Noël Byron, Baron, 1788–1824.
  Byron's poetry.
  Bibliography: p.
  1. Byron, George Gordon Noël Byron, Baron, 1788–1824—Addresses,
essays, lectures. 2. Poets, English—19th century—Biography—Addresses,
essays, lectures.
I. McConnell, Frank D., 1942–   II. Title.
PR4352.M28   1978   821'.7   78–4902
ISBN 0–393–04452–1
ISBN 0–393–09152–X pbk.

Contents

Preface   xi

The Texts of the Poems   1
  A Note on the Texts   2

  From *Hours of Idleness* (1807)   3
  To M.S.G.   3
  To a Beautiful Quaker   3
  To a Lady Who Presented to the Author a Lock
    of Hair Braided with His Own, and Appointed
    at a Night in December to Meet Him in the
    Garden   5
  On a Distant View of the Village and School
    of Harrow on the Hill, 1806   6
  I Would I Were a Careless Child   7
  To Edward Noel Long, Esq.   8
  From *Hebrew Melodies* (1815)   11
  She Walks in Beauty   11
  The Harp the Monarch Minstrel Swept   11
  My Soul Is Dark   12
  The Destruction of Sennacherib   12
  Other Lyrics   13
  Written After Swimming from Sestos to Abydos   13
  To Thyrza   14
  Prometheus   15
  Epistle to Augusta   17
  Darkness   20
  So We'll Go No More A-Roving   22
  Versicles   22
  On This Day I Complete My Thirty-Sixth Year   23
Childe Harold's Pilgrimage   24
  Canto the First (1812)   25
  Canto the Third (1816)   50
  Canto the Fourth (verses 1–10, 164–86) (1818)   76
The Giaour (1812)   84
The Prisoner of Chillon (1816)   115

Manfred (1817)   124

The Vision of Judgment (1822)   159

Don Juan (1819–24)   182

     Fragment on the Back of the Ms. of Canto the First   183

     Dedication   183

     Canto the First   187

     Canto the Second (verses CXLI–CCXVI)   231

     Canto the Fifth   246

     Canto the Ninth   277

     Canto the Sixteenth   294

Byron's Letters and Journals   321

To His Mother, May 1, 1803   323

To Francis Hodgson, November 3, 1808   324

To William Harness, March 18, 1809   324

To Henry Drury, May 3, 1810   325

To Francis Hodgson, September 3, 1811   326

To John Murray, September 5, 1811   327

To Lady Caroline Lamb, May 1, 1812   328

From His Journal, November 1813–April 1814   329

To Lady Melbourne, January 7, 1815   330

To Lady Byron, February 8, 1816   331

To John Murray, September 15, 1817   331

To Thomas Moore, February 2, 1818   332

To John Cam Hobhouse and the Honorable
Douglas Kinnaird, January 19, 1819   333

To the Honorable Douglas Kinnaird, October 26, 1819   334

From His "Detached Thoughts,"
October 1821 to May 1822   334

To the Honorable Augusta Leigh, September 12, 1823   336

To Mr. Mayer, English Consul at Prevesa, undated   337

Criticism   339

Bergen Evans · Lord Byron's Pilgrimage   341

John D. Jump · Byron: The Historical Context   351

Michael G. Cooke · Byron and the Romantic Lyric   360

Francis Berry · The Poet of *Childe Harold*   376

After Giaour

Robert F. Gleckner · *The Giaour* as Experimental
   Narrative   389

Don Juan

{ James R. Thompson · Byron's Plays and *Don Juan*   404
{ Frank D. McConnell · Byron as Antipoet   418
✓ Leslie A. Marchand · Byron in the Twentieth Century   431
✓ E. D. Hirsch, Jr. · Byron and the Terrestrial Paradise   442

whenever

Images of Byron   459

Francis Jeffrey · From the *Edinburgh Review*
   (April 1814)   461
Lady Caroline Lamb · From *Glenarvon* (1816)   462
Thomas Love Peacock · From *Nightmare Abbey* (1818)   462
Robert Southey · From *A Vision of Judgment* (1821)   463
Johann Wolfgang von Goethe · From *Conversations
   with Eckermann* (1822–1832)   464
Stendhal · Memories of Lord Byron (1829)   465
Thomas Carlyle · From *Sartor Resartus* (1838)   467
Gustave Flaubert · From His Letters (1838 and 1845)   467
Ralph Waldo Emerson · Thoughts on Modern
   Literature (1840)   468
Harriet Beecher Stowe · From *Uncle Tom's Cabin*
   (1850)   468
Matthew Arnold · [Byron] (1881)   469
Oscar Wilde · From *The Soul of Man Under Socialism*
   (1891)   470
George Bernard Shaw · Dedicatory Letter to *Man and
   Superman* (1903)   471
James Joyce · From *A Portrait of the Artist as a Young
   Man* (1916)   471
Virginia Woolf · From *A Writer's Diary*
   (Wednesday, August 7, 1918)   472
William Butler Yeats · From *A Vision* (1922)   473
T. E. Lawrence · From *Seven Pillars of Wisdom* (1926)   474
Charles Du Bos · Byron and the Need of Fatality (1931)   474
Mario Praz · From *The Romantic Agony* (1933)   475

T. S. Eliot · Byron (1937)   475
Albert Camus · From *The Rebel* (1951)   476
Vladimir Nabokov · From *Lolita* (1955)   476
W. H. Auden · Byron: The Making of a Comic
   Poet (1966)   477
Angus Wilson · Evil in the English Novel (1967)   477
Anthony Lewis · At Last Lord Byron Gets Place
   in Poets' Corner in Westminster (1968)   478

Chronology   479

Selected Bibliography   483

Preface

Lord Byron during his lifetime was the most internationally famous poet England had produced, and long after his death continued to be one of the most influential, widely imitated, and widely reviled personalities of his age. A complex man, and fond of describing his own complexity, he made the adjective "Byronic" synonymous, during the nineteenth century, with one very important strain of Romantic sensibility: the image of the artist as a mysterious, mocking, perhaps sinful, and certainly outcast figure. Indeed, by the early twentieth century interest in the man's personality seemed far to outweigh the interest in his poems themselves. A common attitude, even of scholars and critics of Romanticism, was that Byron's poetry—except of course for his masterpiece, *Don Juan* —is of an inferior (if not adolescent) quality, and that his real contribution to the cultural history of Europe was solely the force of his extraordinary instinct for self-dramatization and self-advertisement. More recently, however, his poetic reputation has begun another pendulum swing toward the positive side. Contemporary critics and scholars, without diminishing the sheerly personal power Byron exerted over his age, have begun to recognize in his poetry a purely literary power and self-consciousness which makes him appear, not only one of the greatest Romantic poets, but perhaps the most "modern" of that group.

This book is designed to present a picture of Byron, of the range of his accomplishment, and of his complex reputation in the history of English literature. The reader will find here Byron's most permanently-established "classics"—*Childe Harold* canto III, *The Prisoner of Chillon*, and *Don Juan*—and also works whose critical reputation is more arguable: *The Giaour*, for example, and the complete text of *Childe Harold* canto I. Byron's more innocent readers have always been puzzled by the apparent contradiction between his morose, Gothic Romanticism and his high-spirited, often bawdy satire. *Manfred*, at least in the eyes of many readers, seems his most Romantic work, while *The Vision of Judgment*, even more than *Don Juan*, may be taken as his most purely, exuberantly malicious satire (although this tension can be seen as existing in Byron's sensibility even from the earliest of his lyrics). The selection of Byron's letters and miscellaneous prose, besides providing the essential background of the life out of which the poems were written, represents the spontaneous wit and quick intelligence which make him one of his age's masters of informal prose.

The selection of critical essays is intended to give the reader an overview of the most important directions of recent Byron criticism, particularly of that revaluation of the poet *as poet* which has been taking place for the last two decades. And the short selections entitled "Images of Byron" attempt to adumbrate the continuing pressure Byron exerts over important writers and thinkers who have come after him.

This collection is dedicated to my wife, and to the late Professor Bergen Evans of Northwestern University.

FRANK D. MCCONNELL

The Texts of
The Poems

A Note on the Texts

The text of the poems is based on the E. H. Coleridge edition, *The Works of Lord Byron, Poetry,* 7 volumes, 1898–1904. This is the edition of John Murray, Ltd.—a name that has continued to be of value to all students of Byron. Occasional corrections have been introduced based on the Oxford Standard Authors Edition, revised in 1970 by John D. Jump.

The text of the letters and journals is that of the Rowland E. Prothero edition, *The Works of Lord Byron, Letters and Journals,* 6 volumes, 1898–1901 (John Murray, Ltd.).

From *Hours of Idleness* (1807)[1]

To M.S.G.[2]

1

When I dream that you love me, you'll surely forgive;
    Extend not your anger to sleep;
For in visions alone your affection can live,—
    I rise, and it leaves me to weep.

2

Then, Morpheus![3] envelop my faculties fast,   5
    Shed o'er me your languor benign;
Should the dream of to-night but resemble the last,
    What rapture celestial is mine!

3

They tell us that slumber, the sister of death,
    Mortality's emblem is given;   10
To fate how I long to resign my frail breath,
    If this be a foretaste of Heaven!

4

Ah! frown not, sweet Lady, unbend your soft brow,
    Nor deem me too happy in this;
If I sin in my dream, I atone for it now,   15
    Thus doom'd, but to gaze upon bliss.

5

Though in visions, sweet Lady, perhaps you may smile,
    Oh! think not my penance deficient!
When dreams of your presence my slumbers beguile,
    To awake, will be torture sufficient.   20

To a Beautiful Quaker[4]

Sweet girl! though only once we met,
That meeting I shall ne'er forget;
And though we ne'er may meet again,

1. Byron's first volume of poetry was published in a private edition circulated among his friends, when he was an undergraduate at Cambridge (*Fugitive Pieces*, 1806). The poems from *Fugitive Pieces*, and others, were published in 1807 in a volume whose full title is *Hours of Idleness, a Series of Poems, Original and Translated, by George Gordon, Lord Byron, a Minor*. The last part of the title is significant; for in the Preface to *Hours of Idleness* Byron claims public indulgence for the badness of some of the poems on the basis of both his noble birth and his youth. Critics, especially the influential *Edinburgh Review*, were quicker to notice the annoying tone of that preface than they were to evaluate the merits of the poems, and panned *Hours of Idleness* thoroughly and energetically. Byron, never a great turner of the other cheek, retaliated in 1809 with his satire, *English Bards and Scotch Reviewers*, and by leaving England on the tour that was to produce his first major success, *Childe Harold's Pilgrimage*.
2. "M.S.G." is not a name, but a substitution. The manuscript is titled "G.G.B. to E.P."—that is, George Gordon Byron to Elizabeth Pigot, a girl with whom Byron had fallen in love.
3. The classical deity of sleep and forgetfulness.
4. The language of this poem is filled with terms from Quaker theology—"meeting," "spirit," etc.—to which Byron gives a wryly amorous meaning.

Remembrance will thy form retain;
I would not say, "I love," but still,   5
My senses struggle with my will:
In vain to drive thee from my breast,
My thoughts are more and more represt;
In vain I check the rising sight,
Another to the last replies: 10
Perhaps, this is not love, but yet,
Our meeting I can ne'er forget.

What, though we never silence broke,
Our eyes a sweeter language spoke;
The tongue in flattering falsehood deals,   15
And tells a tale it never feels:
Deceit, the guilty lips impart,
And hush the mandates of the heart;
But soul's interpreters, the eyes,
Spurn such restraint, and scorn disguise.   20
As thus our glances oft convers'd,
And all our bosoms felt rehears'd,[5]
No *spirit*, from within, reprov'd us,
Say rather, " 'twas the *spirit mov'd* us."
Though, what they utter'd, I repress,   25
Yet I conceive thou'lt partly guess;
For as on thee, my memory ponders,
Perchance to me, thine also wanders.
This, for myself, at least, I'll say,
Thy form appears through night, through day;   30
Awake, with it my fancy teems,
In sleep, it smiles in fleeting dreams;
The vision charms the hours away,
And bids me curse Aurora's[6] ray
For breaking slumbers of delight,   35
Which make me wish for endless night.
Since, oh! whate'er my future fate,
Shall joy or woe my steps await;
Tempted by love, by storms beset,
Thine image, I can ne'er forget.   40

Alas! again no more we meet,
No more our former looks repeat;
Then, let me breathe this parting prayer,
The dictate of my bosom's care:
"May Heaven so guard my lovely quaker,   45
That anguish never can o'ertake her;
That peace and virtue ne'er forsake her,
But bliss be aye her heart's partaker!
Oh! may the happy mortal, fated
To be, by dearest ties, related,   50

5. Spoke.   6. Dawn's.

For *her*, each hour, *new joys* discover,
And lose the husband in the lover!
May that fair bosom never know
What 'tis to feel the restless woe,
Which stings the soul, with vain regret,   55
Of him, who never can forget!"

To a Lady Who Presented to the Author a Lock of Hair Braided with His Own, and Appointed at a Night in December to Meet Him in the Garden

These locks, which fondly thus entwine,
In firmer chains our hearts confine,
Than all th'unmeaning protestations
Which swell with nonsense, love orations.
Our love is fix'd, I think we've proved it;   5
Nor time, nor place, nor art have mov'd it;
Then wherefore should we sigh and whine,
With groundless jealousy repine;
With silly whims, and fancies frantic,
Merely to make our love romantic?[7]   10
Why should you weep, like *Lydia Languish*,[8]
And fret with self-created anguish?
Or doom the lover you have chosen,
On winter nights to sigh half frozen;
In leafless shades, to sue for pardon,   15
Only because the scene's a garden?
For gardens seem, by one consent,
(Since Shakespeare set the precedent;
Since Juliet first declar'd her passion)
To form the place of assignation.   20
Oh! would some modern muse inspire,
And set her by a *sea-coal* fire;
Or had the bard at Christmas written,
And laid the scene of love in Britain;
He surely, in commiseration,   25
Had chang'd the place of declaration.
In Italy, I've no objection,
Warm nights are proper for reflection;
But here our climate is so rigid,
That love itself, is rather frigid: 30
Think on our chilly situation,
And curb this rage for imitation.
Then let us meet, as oft we've done,
Beneath the influence of the sun;

7. "Romantic," for the late eighteenth and early nineteenth centuries, had strong connotations of the sentimental, the overblown, the (for some) absurdly passionate—e.g. midnight meetings in a garden, even at the dead of winter.
8. A lugubrious, "romantic" character in Richard Brinsley Sheridan's (1751–1816) comedy, *The Rivals*. Sheridan later became a friend of Byron's.

Or, if at midnight I must meet you,   35
Within your mansion let me greet you:
There, we can love for hours together,
Much better, in such snowy weather,
Than plac'd in all th' Arcadian[9] groves,
That ever witness'd rural loves;   40
Then, if my passion fail to please,
Next night I'll be content to freeze;
No more I'll give a loose to laughter,
But curse my fate, for ever after.

On a Distant View of the Village and School of Harrow on the Hill, 1806[1]

Oh! mihi praeteritos referat si Jupiter annos.[2]
—VERGIL

1

Ye scenes of my childhood, whose lov'd recollection
    Embitters the present, compar'd with the past;
Where science first dawn'd on the powers of reflection,
    And friendships were form'd, too romantic to last;

2

Where fancy, yet, joys to retrace the resemblance   5
    Of comrades, in friendship and mischief allied;
How welcome to me your ne'er fading remembrance,
    Which rests in the bosom, though hope is deny'd!

3

Again I revisit the hills where we sported,
    The streams where we swam, and the fields where we fought;   10
The school where, loud warn'd by the bell, we resorted,
    To pore o'er the precepts by Pedagogues taught.

4

Again I behold where for hours I have ponder'd,
    As reclining, at eve, on yon tombstone I lay;
Or round the steep brow of the churchyard I wander'd,   15
    To catch the last gleam of the sun's setting ray.

5

I once more view the room, with spectators surrounded,
    Where, as Zanga, I trod on Alonzo[3] o'erthrown;
While, to swell my young pride, such applauses resounded,
    I fancied that Mossop[4] himself was outshone.   20

6

Or, as Lear, I pour'd forth the deep imprecation,
    By my daughters, of kingdom and reason depriv'd;

9. A classical name for the ideal pastoral, romantic landscape.
1. Harrow, near London, is one of the great English public schools. Byron attended Harrow between 1802 and 1805, before entering Cambridge.
2. "Oh, that God would give back to me the years I have lost!" *Vergil*: Publius

Vergilius Maro, 70–19 B.C., Rome's great epic poet, author of the *Aeneid*.
3. Zanga, Alonzo: characters in *The Revenge*, a tragedy by Edward Young (1683–1765).
4. Henry Mossop (1729–73), an actor famous for his performance as Zanga.

Till, fir'd by loud plaudits and self-adulation,
    I regarded myself as a *Garrick*[5] reviv'd.

7

Ye dreams of my boyhood, how much I regret you!   **25**
    Unfaded your memory dwells in my breast;
Though sad and deserted, I ne'er can forget you:
    Your pleasures may still be in fancy possest.

8

To Ida[6] full oft may remembrance restore me,
    While Fate shall the shades of the future unroll!
Since Darkness o'ershadows the prospect before me,   **30**
    More dear is the beam of the past to my soul!

9

But if, through the course of the years which await me,
    Some new scene of pleasure should open to view,
I will say, while with rapture the thought shall elate me,
    "Oh! such were the days which my infancy knew."   **35**

I Would I Were a Careless Child

I would I were a careless child,
    Still dwelling in my Highland cave,
Or roaming through the dusky wild,
    Or bounding o'er the dark blue wave;
The cumbrous pomp of Saxon pride   **5**
    Accords not with the freeborn soul,
Which loves the mountain's craggy side,
    And seeks the rocks where billows roll.

Fortune! take back these cultured lands,
    Take back this name of splendid sound!   **10**
I hate the touch of servile hands,
    I hate the slaves that cringe around.
Place me among the rocks I love,
    Which sound to Ocean's wildest roar;
I ask but this—again to rove   **15**
    Through scenes my youth hath known before.
Few are my years, and yet I feel
    The world was ne'er design'd for me:
Ah! why do dark'ning shades conceal
    The hour when man must cease to be?   **20**
Once I beheld a splendid dream,
    A visionary scene of bliss:
Truth!—wherefore did thy hated beam
    Awake me to a world like this?

5. David Garrick (1717–79), the foremost Shakespearean actor of his time.
6. Mount Ida, in Greek mythology, was a sacred mountain from which the gods observed human affairs. Byron was fond of imagining Harrow Hill, on which the school is situated, as his own "Mount Ida." See "To Edward Noel Long, Esq.," line 21.

I loved—but those I loved are gone;   25
    Had friends—my early friends are fled:
How cheerless feels the heart alone,
    When all its former hopes are dead!
Though gay companions o'er the bowl
    Dispel awhile the sense of ill;   30
Though pleasure stirs the maddening soul,
    The heart—the heart—is lonely still.

How dull! to hear the voice of those
    Whom rank or chance, whom wealth or power,
Have made, though neither friends nor foes,   35
    Associates of the festive hour.
Give me again a faithful few,
    In years and feelings still the same,
And I will fly the midnight crew,
    Where boist'rous joy is but a name.   40

And woman, lovely woman! thou,
    My hope, my comforter, my all!
How cold must be my bosom now,
    When e'en thy smiles begin to pall!
Without a sigh would I resign   45
    This busy scene of splendid woe,
To make that calm contentment mine,
    Which virtue knows, or seems to know.

Fain would I fly the haunts of men—
    I seek to shun, not hate mankind;   50
My breast requires the sullen glen,
    Whose gloom may suit a darken'd mind.
Oh! that to me the wings were given
    Which bear the turtle to her nest!
Then would I cleave the vault of heaven,   55
    To flee away, and be at rest.

To Edward Noel Long, Esq.[7]

Nil ego contulerim jucundo sanus amico.
—HORACE.[8]

Dear Long, in this sequester'd scene,
    While all around in slumber lie,
The joyous days, which ours have been

    Come rolling fresh on Fancy's eye;
Thus, if, amidst the gathering storm,   5
While clouds the darken'd noon deform,
Yon heaven assumes a varied glow,
I hail the sky's celestial bow,

7. Long was a classmate of Byron's at both Harrow and Cambridge. He entered the Guards, fought in the Napoleonic Wars (the "gathering storm" of line 5) and was drowned in 1809.

8. Literally, "I, when I am rational, can add nothing to (i.e. think of nothing more complete than) a congenial friend." Horace: Quintus Horatius Flaccus, 65–8 B.C., greatest of the Roman lyric poets.

Which spreads the sign of future peace,
And bids the war of tempests cease.   10
Ah! though the present brings but pain,
I think those days may come again;
Or if, in melancholy mood,
Some lurking envious fear intrude,
To check my bosom's fondest thought,   15
  And interrupt the golden dream,
I crush the fiend with malice fraught,
  And, still, indulge my wonted theme.
Although we ne'er again can trace,
  In Granta's[9] vale, the pedant's lore,   20
Nor through the groves of Ida[1] chase
  Our raptured visions, as before;
Though Youth has flown on rosy pinion,
And Manhood claims his stern dominion,
Age will not every hope destroy,   25
But yields some hours of sober joy.
  Yes, I will hope that Time's broad wing
Will shed around some dews of spring:
But, if his scythe must sweep the flowers
Which bloom among the fairy bowers,   30
Where smiling Youth delights to dwell,
And hearts with early rapture swell;
If frowning Age, with cold control,
Confines the current of the soul,
Congeals the tear of Pity's eye,   35
Or checks the sympathetic sigh,
Or hears, unmov'd, Misfortune's groan,
And bids me feel for self alone;
Oh! may my bosom never learn
  To soothe its wonted heedless flow;   40
Still, still, despise the censor stern,
  But ne'er forget another's woe.
Yes, as you knew me in the days,
O'er which Remembrance yet delays,
Still may I rove untutor'd, wild,   45
And even in age, at heart a child.

Though, now, on airy visions borne,
  To you my soul is still the same.
Oft has it been my fate to mourn,
  And all my former joys are tame: 50
But, hence! ye hours of sable hue!
  Your frowns are gone, my sorrows o'er:
By every bliss my childhood knew,
  I'll think upon your shade no more.

Thus, when the whirlwind's rage is past,   55

---

9. Cambridge.
1. See "On a Distant View of the Village and School of Harrow on the Hill,"
stanza 8, line 1.

And caves their sullen roar enclose,
We heed no more the wintry blast,
   When lull'd by zephyr to repose.

Full often has my infant Muse
   Attun'd to love her languid lyre;   60
But, now, without a theme to choose,
   The strains in stolen sighs expire.
My youthful nymphs, alas! are flown;
   E—— is a wife, and C—— a mother,
And Carolina sighs alone,   65
   And Mary's given to another;
And Cora's eye, which roll'd on me,
   Can now no more my love recall—
In truth, dear LONG, 'twas time to flee—
   For Cora's eye will shine on all.   70
And though the Sun, with genial rays,
His beams alike to all displays,
And every lady's eye's a *sun*,
These last should be confin'd to one.
The soul's meridian don't become her,   75
Whose Sun displays a general *summer*!
Thus faint is every former flame,
And Passion's self is now a name;
As, when the ebbing flames are low,
   The aid which once improv'd their light,   80
And bade them burn with fiercer glow,
   Now quenches all their sparks in night;
Thus has it been with Passion's fires,

   As many a boy and girl remembers,
While all the force of love expires,   85
   Extinguish'd with the dying embers.

   But now, dear LONG, 'tis midnight's noon,
And clouds obscure the watery moon,
Whose beauties I shall not rehearse,
Describ'd in every stripling's verse;   90
For why should I the path go o'er
Which every bard has trod before?
Yet ere yon silver lamp of night
   Has thrice perform'd her stated round,
Has thrice retrac'd her path of light,   95
   And chas'd away the gloom profound,
I trust, that we, my gentle Friend,
Shall see her rolling orbit wend,
Above the dear-lov'd peaceful seat,
Which once contain'd our youth's retreat;   100
And, then, with those our childhood knew,
We'll mingle in the festive crew;
While many a tale of former day

Shall wing the laughing hours away;
And all the flow of souls shall pour   105
The sacred intellectual shower,
Nor cease, till Luna's waning horn
Scarce glimmers through the mist of Morn.

From *Hebrew Melodies* (1815)[2]

She Walks in Beauty[3]

1

She walks in Beauty, like the night
    Of cloudless climes and starry skies;
And all that's best of dark and bright
    Meet in her aspect and her eyes:
Thus mellowed to that tender light   5
    Which Heaven to gaudy day denies.

2

One shade the more, one ray the less,
    Had half impaired the nameless grace
Which waves in every raven tress,
    Or softly lightens o'er her face;   10
Where thoughts serenely sweet express,
    How pure, how dear their dwelling-place.

3

And on that cheek, and o'er that brow,
    So soft, so calm, yet eloquent,
The smiles that win, the tints that glow,   15
    But tell of days in goodness spent,
A mind at peace with all below,
    A heart whose love is innocent!

The Harp the Monarch Minstrel Swept[4]

1

The harp the monarch minstrel swept,
    The King of men, the loved of Heaven,

2. *Hebrew Melodies* was published in 1815. It was literally a collection of melodies, with lyrics by Byron and music by Isaac Nathan (1792–1864), a former Rabbinical student turned composer. Byron's friend and banker Douglas Kinnaird (1788–1830) had originally suggested the collaboration, and Byron generously gave the young Nathan copyright to the lyrics of the songs. Nathan's attempt, in writing the music for the songs, was to recreate the spirit of Hebrew folk song; and many, though not all, of Byron's lyrics deal with themes from the Old Testament.

3. On June 11, 1814, Byron attended a party at Lady Sitwell's, and there for the first time saw his young cousin, Lady Wilmot Horton, who had appeared at the party in a mourning dress. Byron was struck by the girl's beauty and by the somber dress in which that beauty was on this evening framed and, returning home. wrote this poem in a single night.

4. The "monarch minstrel" of the title is King David, greatest of the kings of ancient Israel. David is celebrated not only for his heroism, but also as a composer and singer of religious songs, and is traditionally identified as the author of the Book of Psalms.

Which Music hallow'd while she wept
 O'er tones her heart of hearts had given,
 Redoubled be her tears, its chords are riven!   5
It soften'd men of iron mould,
 It gave them virtues not their own;
No ear so dull, no soul so cold,
 That felt not, fired not to the tone,
 Till David's lyre grew mightier than his throne!   10

2

It told the triumphs of our King,
 It wafted glory to our God;
It made our gladden'd valleys ring,
 The cedars bow, the mountains nod;
 Its sound aspired to heaven and there abode!   15
Since then, though heard on earth no more,
 Devotion and her daughter Love
Still bid the bursting spirit soar
 To sounds that seem as from above,
 In dreams that day's broad light can not remove.   20

My Soul Is Dark

1

My soul is dark—Oh! quickly string
 The harp I yet can brook to hear;
And let they gentle fingers fling
 Its melting murmurs o'er mine ear.
If in this heart a hope be dear,   5
 That sound shall charm it forth again:
If in these eyes there lurk a tear,
 'Twill flow, and cease to burn my brain.

2

But bid the strain be wild and deep,
 Nor let thy notes of joy be first: 10
I tell thee, minstrel, I must weep,
 Or else this heavy heart will burst;
For it hath been by sorrow nursed,
 And ached in sleepless silence long;
And now 'tis doom'd to know the worst,   15
 And break at once—or yield to song.

The Destruction of Sennacherib[5]

1

The Assyrian came down like the wolf on the fold,
And his cohorts were gleaming in purple and gold;

5. Sennacherib, King of Assyria (the "Assyrian"), who attacked Judah under the reign of King Hezekiah only to have his whole army smitten by the Lord before they could give battle (II Kings, 19).

And the sheen of their spears was like stars on the sea,
When the blue wave rolls nightly on deep Galilee.

2

Like the leaves of the forest when Summer is green,   5
That host with their banners at sunset were seen:
Like the leaves of the forest when Autumn hath blown,
That host on the morrow lay withered and strown.

3

For the Angel of Death spreal his wings on the blast,
And breathed in the face of the foe as he passed;   10
And the eyes of the sleepers waxed deadly and chill,
And their hearts but once heaved—and for ever grew still!

4

And there lay the steed with his nostril all wide,
But through it there rolled not the breath of his pride;
And the foam of his gasping lay white on the turf,   15
And cold as the spray of the rock-beating surf.

5

And there lay the rider distorted and pale,
With the dew on his brow, and the rust on his mail:
And the tents were all silent—the banners alone—
The lances unlifted—the trumpet unblown.   20

6

And the widows of Ashur[6] are loud in their wail,
And the idols are broke in the temple of Baal;[7]
And the might of the Gentile, unsmote by the sword,
Hath melted like snow in the glance of the Lord!

Other Lyrics

Written After Swimming from Sestos to Abydos

1

If, in the month of dark December,
    Leander,[8] who was nightly wont
(What maid will not the tale remember?)
    To cross thy stream, broad Hellespont!

2

If, when the wintry tempest roared,   5
    He sped to Hero, nothing loth,
And thus of old thy current poured,
    Fair Venus! how I pity both!

6. Assyria.
7. God of the Assyrians.
8. In legend, Leander, the lover of Hero, swam the Hellespont from the Asian coast (Sestos) to the European (Abydos) every night to visit her, until one night he drowned in a storm. Byron and a friend had made the same swim six days before this poem was written. Byron, whose malformed foot prevented him from participating in many sports, excelled and reveled in his prowess as a swimmer.

3

For *me*, degenerate modern wretch,
    Though in the genial month of May,   10
My dripping limbs I faintly stretch,
    And think I've done a feat to-day.

4

But since he crossed the rapid tide,
    According to the doubtful story,
To woo, —and—Lord knows what beside,   15
    And swam for Love, as I for Glory;

5

'Twere hard to say fared the best:
    Sad mortals! thus the Gods still plague you!
He lost his labour, I my jest:
    For he was drowned, and I've the ague.   20

May 9, 1810; published 1812

To Thyrza[9]

Without a stone to mark the spot,
    And say, what Truth might well have said,
By all, save one, perchance forgot,
    Ah! wherefore art thou lowly laid?
By many a shore and many a sea   5
    Divided, yet beloved in vain;
The Past, the Future fled to thee,
    To bid us meet—no—ne'er again!
Could this have been—a word, a look,
    That softly said, "We part in peace,"   10
Had taught my bosom how to brook,
    With fainter sighs, thy soul's release.
And didst thou not, since Death for thee
    Prepared a light and pangless dart,
Once long for him thou ne'er shalt see,   15
    Who held, and holds thee in his heart?
Oh! who like him had watched thee here?
    Or sadly marked thy glazing eye,
In that dread hour ere Death appear,
    When silent Sorrow fears to sigh,   20
Till all was past? But when no more
    'Twas thine to reck of human woe,
Affection's heart-drops, gushing o'er,
    Had flowed as fast—as now they flow.
Shall they not flow, when many a day   25
    In these, to me, deserted towers,

---

9. This is one of a series of poems Byron wrote on the death of a lover whom he calls "Thyrza." There has been much speculation about the identity of the subject. It now seems certain that "Thyrza" was John Edleston, a choirboy of Trinity College, Cambridge (see lines 39–40), who died in 1811, shortly after Byron returned from his tour of the Mediterranean area.

Ere called but for a time away,
    Affection's mingling tears were ours?
Ours too the glance none saw beside;
    The smile none else might understand;   30
The whispered thought of hearts allied,
    The pressure of the thrilling hand;
The kiss, so guiltless and refined,
    That Love each warmer wish forbore;
Those eyes proclaimed so pure a mind,   35
    Ev'n Passion blushed to plead for more.
The tone, that taught me to rejoice,
    When prone, unlike thee, to repine;
The song, celestial from thy voice,
    But sweet to me from none but thine;   40
The pledge we wore—*I* wear it still,
    But where is thine?—Ah! where art thou?
Oft have I borne the weight of ill,
    But never bent beneath till now!
Well hast thou left in Life's best bloom   45
    The cup of Woe for me to drain.
If rest alone be in the tomb,
    I would not wish thee here again:
But if in worlds more blest than this
    Thy virtues seek a fitter sphere,   50
Impart some portion of thy bliss,
    To wean me from mine anguish here.
Teach me—too early taught by thee!
    To bear, forgiving and forgiven:
On earth thy love was such to me;   55
    It fain would form my hope in Heaven!

October 11, 1811; published 1812

Prometheus[1]

1

Titan! to whose immortal eyes
    The sufferings of mortality,
    Seen in their sad reality,
Were not as things that gods despise;
What was thy pity's recompense?   5
A silent suffering, and intense;
    The rock, the vulture, and the chain,

1. Prometheus, greatest of the Titans of classical mythology, came to represent for many of the Romantic poets—Shelley and Keats as well as Byron—the archetype of the visionary, revolutionary mind. It was Prometheus who first gave man the gift of fire, stealing it from Zeus and the Olympian gods, and it was Prometheus (whose name means "far-seeing") who knew the secret of Zeus's eventual defeat. To punish him for his theft of the fire, and to coerce the secret out of him, Zeus chained Prometheus to a mountain where, every day, a vulture was sent to consume his entrails. He never capitulated, though, and was eventually liberated by Hercules.

All that the proud can feel of pain,
The agony they do not show,
The suffocating sense of woe,   10
    Which speaks but in its loneliness,
And then is jealous lest the sky
Should have a listener, nor will sigh
    Until its voice is echoless.

great capacity for suffering

2

Titan! to thee the strife was given   15
    Between the suffering and the will,
    Which torture where they cannot kill;
And the inexorable Heaven,
And the deaf tyranny of Fate,
The ruling principle of Hate,   20
Which for its pleasure doth create
The things it may annihilate,
Refused thee even the boon to die:
The wretched gift Eternity
Was thine—and thou hast borne it well.   25
All that the Thunderer wrung from thee
Was but the menace which flung back
On him the torments of thy rack;
The fate thou didst so well foresee,
But would not to appease him tell;   30
And in thy Silence was his Sentence, ?
And in his Soul a vain repentance,
And evil dread so ill dissembled,
That in his hand the lightnings trembled.

3

Thy Godlike crime was to be kind,   35
    To render with thy precepts less
    The sum of human wretchedness,
And strengthen Man with his own mind;
And baffled as thou wert from high, (*by Gods*)
Still in thy patient energy,   40
In the endurance, and repulse
    Of thine impenetrable Spirit,
Which Earth and Heaven could not convulse,
    A mighty lesson we inherit:
Thou art a symbol and a sign   45
    To Mortals of their fate and force; *not merely clay*
Like thee, Man is in part divine,
    A troubled stream from a pure source;
And Man in portions can foresee
His own funereal destiny;   50
His wretchedness, and his resistance,
And his sad unallied existence:
To which his Spirit may oppose
Itself—and equal to all woes,
    And a firm will, and a deep sense,   55

Which even in torture can descry
   Its own concenter'd recompense,
Triumphant where it dares defy,
And making Death a Victory.

Diodati, July 1816

Epistle to Augusta[2]

1

My Sister! my sweet Sister! if a name
Dearer and purer were, it should be thine.
Mountains and seas divide us, but I claim
No tears, but tenderness to answer mine:
Go where I will, to me thou art the same—   5
A loved regret which I would not resign.
There yet are two things in my destiny—
A world to roam through, and a home with thee.

2

The first were nothing—had I still the last,
It were the haven of my happiness;   10
But other claims and other ties thou hast,
And mine is not the wish to make them less.
A strange doom is thy father's son's,[3] and past
Recalling, as it lies beyond redress;
Reversed for him our grandsire's fate[4] of yore,—   15
He had no rest at sea, nor I on shore.

3

If my inheritance of storms hath been
In other elements, and on the rocks
Of perils, overlooked or unforseen,
I have sustained my share of worldly shocks,   20
The fault was mine; nor do I seek to screen
My errors with defensive paradox;
I have been cunning in mine overthrow,
The careful pilot of my proper woe.

4

Mine were my faults, and mine be their reward.   25
My whole life was a contest, since the day

2. The "Epistle" was written in the summer of 1816 at the Villa Diodati, where Byron was living—on the shore of Lake Geneva, Switzerland. It was not published until 1830, however, since Augusta (Augusta Byron Leigh, his half sister) refused permission for its publication. Byron had left England in self-imposed exile on April 25, 1816, amid the scandal of his separation from his wife (Lady Anne Isabella Milbanke) and widespread rumors of his incestuous affair with Augusta. The veneration of nature in this lyric—and in *Childe Harold* III, on which Byron was also working at the time—marks a new stage in his poetry, perhaps influenced by his new friendship with Shelley and his reexamination (at Shelley's urging) of the poetry of Wordsworth.
3. Genealogically precise: Byron and Augusta were children of the same father by different wives.
4. Byron's grandfather, Admiral Byron (nicknamed "Foul-weather Jack") was celebrated for never making a sea voyage that did not encounter a tempest.

That gave me being, gave me that which marred
The gift,—a fate, or will, that walked astray;[5]
And I at times have found the struggle hard,
And thought of shaking off my bonds of clay: 30
But now I fain would for a time survive,
If but to see what next can well arrive.

5

Kingdoms and Empires in my little day
I have outlived, and yet I am not old;
And when I look on this, the petty spray   35
Of my own years of troubles, which have rolled
Like a wild bay of breakers, melts away:
Something—I know not what—does still uphold
A spirit of slight patience;—not in vain,
Even for its own sake, do we purchase Pain.   40

6

Perhaps the workings of defiance stir
Within me—or, perhaps, a cold despair
Brought on when ills habitually recur,—
Perhaps a kinder clime, or purer air,
(For even to this may change of soul refer,   45
And with light armour we may learn to bear,)
Have taught me a strange quiet, which was not
The chief companion of a calmer lot.

7

I feel almost at times as I have felt
In happy childhood; trees, and flowers, and brooks,   50
Which do remember me of where I dwelt,
Ere my young mind was sacrificed to books,
Come as of yore upon me, and can melt
My heart with recognition of their looks;
And even at moments I could think I see   55
Some living thing to love—but none like thee.

8

Here are the Alpine landscapes which create
A fund for contemplation;—to admire
Is a brief feeling of a trivial date;
But something worthier do such scenes inspire: 60
Here to be lonely is not desolate,
For much I view which I could most desire,
And, above all, a Lake[6] I can behold
Lovelier, not dearer, than our own of old.

9

Oh that thou wert but with me!—but I grow   65
The fool of my own wishes, and forget
The solitude which I have vaunted so

5. Both Byron's innermost sense of his predestined damnation and also, literally, the deformity of his foot which gave him a mincing gait and caused him continual, sometimes obsessive embarrassment.
6. Lake Geneva (or, as in stanza 10, line 3, Lake Leman).

Has lost its praise in this but one regret;
There may be others which I less may show;—
I am not of the plaintive mood, and yet   70
I feel an ebb in my philosophy,
And the tide rising in my altered eye.

10

I did remind thee of our own dear Lake,
By the old Hall which may be mine no more.
Leman's is fair; but think not I forsake   75
The sweet remembrance of a dearer shore:
Sad havoc Time must with my memory make,
Ere that or thou can fade these eyes before;
Though, like all things which I have loved, they are
Resigned for ever, or divided far.   80

11

The world is all before me; I but ask
Of Nature that with which she will comply—
It is but in her Summer's sun to bask,
To mingle with the quiet of her sky,
To see her gentle face without a mask,   85
And never gaze on it with apathy.
She was my early friend, and now shall be
My sister—till I look again on thee.

12

I can reduce all feelings but this one;
And that I would not;—for at length I see   90
Such scenes as those wherein my life begun—
The earliest—even the only paths for me—
Had I but sooner learnt the crowd to shun,
I had been better than I now can be;
The Passions which have torn me would have slept;   95
I had not suffered, and *thou* hadst not wept.

13

With false Ambition what had I to do?
Little with Love, and least of all with Fame;
And yet they came unsought, and with me grew,
And made me all which they can make—a Name.   100
Yet this was not the end I did pursue;
Surely I once beheld a nobler aim.
But all is over—I am one the more
To baffled millions which have gone before.

14

And for the future, this world's future may   105
From me demand but little of my care;
I have outlived myself by many a day;
Having survived so many things that were;
My years have been no slumber, but the prey
Of ceaseless vigils; for I had the share   110
Of life which might have filled a century,
Before its fourth in time had passed me by.

15

And for the remnant which may be to come
I am content; and for the past I feel
Not thankless,—for within the crowded sum   115
Of struggles, Happiness at times would steal,
And for the present, I would not benumb
My feelings farther.—Nor shall I conceal
That with all this I still can look around,
And worship Nature with a thought profound.   120

16

For thee, my own sweet sister, in thy heart
I know myself secure, as thou in mine;
We were and are—I am, even as thou art—
Beings who ne'er each other can resign;
It is the same, together or apart,   125
From Life's commencement to its slow decline
We are entwined—let Death come slow or fast,
The tie which bound the first endures the last!

Darkness[7]

I HAD a dream, which was not all a dream.
The bright sun was extinguished, and the stars
Did wander darkling in the eternal space,
Rayless, and pathless, and the icy Earth
Swung blind and blackening in the moonless air;   5
Morn came and went—and came, and brought no day,
And men forgot their passions in the dread
Of this their desolation; and all hearts
Were chilled into a selfish prayer for light:
And they did live by watchfires—and the thrones, 10
The palaces of crownéd kings—the huts,
The habitations of all things which dwell,
Were burnt for beacons; cities were consumed,
And men were gathered round their blazing homes
To look once more into each other's face;   15
Happy were those who dwelt within the eye
Of the volcanos, and their mountain-torch:
A fearful hope was all the World contained;
Forests were set on fire—but hour by hour
They fell and faded—and the crackling trunks   20
Extinguished with a crash—and all was black.
The brows of men by the despairing light
Wore an unearthly aspect, as by fits
The flashes fell upon them; some lay down

7. This poem was written in 1816 and published the same year, in the volume *The Prisoner of Chillon*, which included the poem by that name. Its theme, the end of human life on earth, is one that caught the imagination of many Romantic and later nineteenth century writers; but Byron's "Darkness" itself is probably inspired by an anonymous book, *The Last Man*, published in 1806.

And hid their eyes and wept; and some did rest   25
Their chins upon their clenchéd hands, and smiled;
And others hurried to and fro, and fed
Their funeral piles with fuel, and looked up
With mad disquietude on the dull sky,
The pall of a past World; and then again   30
With curses cast them down upon the dust,
And gnashed their teeth and howled: the wild birds shrieked,
And, terrified, did flutter on the ground,
And flap their useless wings; the wildest brutes
Came tame and tremulous; and vipers crawled   35
And twined themselves among the multitude,
Hissing, but stingless—they were slain for food:
And War, which for a moment was no more,
Did glut himself again:—a meal was bought
With blood, and each sate sullenly apart   40
Gorging himself in gloom: no Love was left;
All earth was but one thought—and that was Death,
Immediate and inglorious; and the pang
Of famine fed upon all entrails—men
Died, and their bones were tombless as their flesh;   45
The meagre by the meagre were devoured,
Even dogs assailed their masters, all save one,
And he was faithful to a corse, and kept
The birds and beasts and famished men at bay,
Till hunger clung[8] them, or the dropping dead   50
Lured their lank jaws; himself sought out no food,
But with a piteous and perpetual moan,
And a quick desolate cry, licking the hand
Which answered not with a caress—he died.
The crowd was famished by degrees; but two   55
Of an enormous city did survive,
And they were enemies: they met beside
The dying embers of an altar-place
Where had been heaped a mass of holy things
For an unholy usage; they raked up,   60
And shivering scraped with their cold skeleton hands
The feeble ashes, and their feeble breath
Blew for a little life, and made a flame
Which was a mockery; then they lifted up
Their eyes as it grew lighter, and beheld   65
Each other's aspects—saw, and shrieked, and died—
Even of their mutual hideousness they died,
Unknowing who he was upon whose brow
Famine had written Fiend. The World was void,
The populous and the powerful was a lump,   70
Seasonless, herbless, treeless, manless, lifeless—
A lump of death—a chaos of hard clay.

8. Shriveled.

The rivers, lakes, and ocean all stood still,
And nothing stirred within their silent depths;
Ships sailorless lay rotting on the sea,   75
And their masts fell down piecemeal: as they dropped
They slept on the abyss without a surge—
The waves were dead; the tides were in their grave,
The Moon, their mistress, had expired before;
The winds were withered in the stagnant air,   80
And the clouds perished; Darkness had no need
Of aid from them—She was the Universe.

So We'll Go No More A-Roving[9]

1

So we'll go no more a-roving
    So late into the night,
Though the heart be still as loving,
    And the moon be still as bright.

2

For the sword outwears its sheath,   5
    And the soul wears out the breast,
And the heart must pause to breathe,
    And Love itself have rest.

3

Though the night was made for loving,
    And the day returns too soon,   10
Yet we'll go no more a-roving
    By the light of the moon.

February 28, 1817

Versicles[1]

I read the "Christabel;"
    Very well:
I read the "Missionary;"
    Pretty—very:
I tried at "Ilderim;"   5
    Ahem!
I read a sheet of "Marg'ret of *Anjou;*"
    Can you?;

9. This poem contains a special irony. On the surface a lovely, melancholy little meditation on mortal transience, it was written in a letter of Byron's to his friend Thomas Moore, describing Byron's hangover after the Mardi Gras revels in Venice.

1. Actually, this versified joke is a piece of tongue-in-cheek Byronic literary criticism. Coleridge's *Christabel* appeared in 1816; W. L. Bowles's *The Missionary of the Andes* in 1815; H. Gally Knight's *Ilderim* in 1816; Margaret Holford's *Margaret* in 1816; J. W. Webster's *Waterloo* in 1816; and Wordsworth's *The White Doe of Rylstone* in 1815. But the point of the joke is Lady Caroline Lamb's novel, *Glenarvon* (1816), written after the end of her famous and scandalous love affair with Byron, which was transparently her portrait of Byron.

I turned a page of Webster's "Waterloo;"
    Pooh! Pooh!   10
I looked at Wordsworth's milk-white "Rylstone Doe;"
    Hillo!
I read "Glenarvon," too, by Caro Lamb;
    God damn!

March 25, 1817; published 1830

On This Day I Complete My Thirty-Sixth Year[2]

1
'Tis time this heart should be unmoved,
    Since others it hath ceased to move:
Yet, though I cannot be beloved,
    Still let me love!

2
My days are in the yellow leaf;   5
    The flowers and fruits of Love are gone;
The worm, the canker, and the grief
    Are mine alone!

3
The fire that on my bosom preys
    Is lone as some Volcanic isle;   10
No torch is kindled at its blaze—
    A funeral pile.

4
The hope, the fear, the jealous care,
    The exalted portion of the pain
And power of love, I cannot share,   15
    But wear the chain.

5
But 'tis not *thus*—and 'tis not *here*—
    Such thoughts should shake my soul, nor *now*
Where Glory decks the hero's bier,
    Or binds his brow.   20

6
The Sword, the Banner, and the Field,
    Glory and Greece, around me see!
The Spartan, borne upon his shield,
    Was not more free.

7
Awake! (not Greece—she *is* awake!)   25
    Awake, my spirit! Think through *whom*
Thy life-blood tracks its parent lake,
    And then strike home!

2. This is the last poem Byron wrote. He had arrived at Missolonghi on January 5, 1824, to take charge of the "army of liberation" he intended to lead for Greece against the Turks, and he died of a fever on April 19.

8

Tread those reviving passions down,
Unworthy manhood!—unto thee   30
Indifferent should the smile or frown
Of Beauty be.

9

If thou regret'st thy youth, *why live?*
The land of honourable death
Is here:—up to the Field, and give   35
Away thy breath!

10

Seek out—less often sought than found—
A soldier's grave, for thee the best;
Then look around, and choose thy ground,
And take thy Rest.   40

Missolonghi, January 22, 1824; published 1824

Childe Harold's Pilgrimage [1]

A Romaunt (Romance)

In 1809 Byron, with his friend John Cam Hobhouse, left England for a tour of Portugal, Spain, Malta, Albania, Greece, and Turkey. When he returned in 1811 he had completed two cantos of a long, semiautobiographical poem he called "Childe Burun's Pilgrimage." His distant relative R. C. Dallas urged him to publish the poem with the important bookseller, John Murray; and in 1812, after prepublication copies had been carefully circulated among influential members of the nobility and other tastemakers, the two cantos, retitled *Childe Harold's Pilgrimage*, appeared. As Byron said, he awoke one morning to find himself famous. On the strength of *Childe Harold*, and then of the "Oriental" romances he published rapidly in the next three years, Byron from 1812 to 1815 enjoyed an almost unprecedented celebrity in the literary and social world of England. Men and women alike wept at public readings of *Childe Harold*, popular illustrations of the gloomy exile Harold (usually looking exactly like Byron and

1. The title "Childe" does not mean "child" in our sense, but is rather a medieval term for a squire on the point of taking his vows of knighthood. And as the use of that term and frequent other archaic locutions indicates, Byron attempts throughout the "first" *Harold* (cantos I and II), to write a self-consciously "literary" work in self-consciously, and sometimes ludicrously, "literary" language: thus also his selection, for *Harold*, of the "Spenserian Stanza," the verse form of Edmund Spenser's great Elizabethan epic, *The Faerie Queene*. Byron insisted, in the preface to the original poem, that it was not autobiographical: "Harold is the child of imagination." But his disclaimers were not taken seriously by the reading public, and the identification of Harold with Byron was indeed largely responsible for the immense celebrity (and notoriety) into which the poem's publication thrust him. And the original working title for the poem, which Byron composed during his tour of the Mediterranean and the Near East (1809–11), was "Childe Burun"—"Burun" being an archaic form of "Byron."

often contemplating a gravestone) abounded. Not since Goethe's 1774 novel of sentiment and despair, *The Sorrows of Young Werther*, had a book caught so precisely the tone of the age.

In 1815–16, however, Byron's immense popularity veered toward immense notoriety. Smarting from his disastrous marriage, socially ostracized because of his rumored liaison with his half sister, Augusta Byron Leigh, Byron left England in 1816, never to return. And in the first two years of his self-imposed exile he completed the poem that had brought him his initial success, publishing canto III of *Childe Harold* in 1816 and canto IV in 1818. The two later cantos have seemed to many critics more powerful, more deeply honest in their articulation of despair, than the first two. And certainly, under the influence of his newly acquired friend Percy Bysshe Shelley, *Childe Harold* canto III represents Byron's closest approach to the prophetic strain of Romantic poetry. But a reexamination of the often maligned first canto of the poem shows it, too, to be poetry of a very high—if idiosyncratic—order.

The story of the progress of *Childe Harold*, however, is not simply the story of Byron's own fortunes and reversals. Throughout his life Byron was an obsessive and voracious reader of history, and *Harold* is deeply imbued, throughout its course, with a sense of the events which were shaping the future of Europe as Byron wrote. In 1808 Napoleon, in an attempt to strangle Britain's foreign markets, had attempted to occupy Portugal, a long-standing British ally, and had met with unexpected resistance from the Portugese, as well as with a newly efficient British army. Napoleon then removed the Spanish king from his throne, installing his own brother Joseph—and found himself faced with a Spanish revolution of real ferocity. Thus began the "Peninsular War," which lasted from 1808 to 1814, and which signaled the turning of the tide of conquest against Napoleon. Napoleon's defeat came in 1815 at Waterloo. But the aftermath of that defeat, the reconsolidation of the old European monarchies (symbolized by the return of the Bourbons to the throne of France) was, to many libertarians and revolutionaries a grimmer threat to freedom than the unified Europe of Napoleon's dream. So the "deepening of tone" readers have found in the last two cantos of *Harold*, however intimately related it may be to Byron's own life, is also a result of the added complexity, melancholy, and even grudging admiration the events of 1815–16 forced upon the poet's conception of the flawed but titanic character of Napoleon.

CANTO THE FIRST

I

Oh, thou! in Hellas[2] deemed of heavenly birth,
    Muse! formed or fabled at the Minstrel's will!
    Since shamed full oft by later lyres on earth, MUSE
ʟʏʀᴇ Mine dares not call thee from thy sacred Hill: ABUSED
    Yet there I've wandered by thy vaunted rill;
        Yes! sighed o'er Delphi's[3] long deserted shrine,

2. Greece.
3. The Greek shrine of Apollo, god of poetry, and site of his famous oracle.

Where, save that feeble fountain, all is still;
Nor mote[4] my shell[5] awake the weary Nine[6]
To grace so plain a tale—this lowly lay of mine.

II

Whilome[7] in Albion's[8] isle there dwelt a youth
Who ne in Virtue's ways did take delight;
But spent his days in riot most uncouth,
And vexed with mirth the drowsy ear of Night.
Ah me! in sooth he was a shameless wight,
Sore given to revel and ungodly glee;
Few earthly things found favour in his sight
Save concubines and carnal companie,
And flaunting wassailers of high and low degree.

Chaucer

III

Childe Harold was he hight:[9]—but whence his name
And lineage long, it suits me not to say;
Suffice it, that perchance they were of fame,
And had been glorious in another day:
But one sad losel[1] soils a name for ay,
However mighty in the olden time;
Nor all that heralds rake from coffined clay,
Nor florid prose, nor honied lies of rhyme,
Can blazon evil deeds, or consecrate a crime.

reputation or fame

IV

Childe Harold basked him in the Noontide sun,
Disporting there like any other fly;
Nor deemed before his little day was done
One blast might chill him into misery.
But long ere scarce a third of his passed by,
Worse than Adversity the Childe befell;
He felt the fulness of Satiety:
Then loathed he in his native land to dwell,
Which seemed to him more lone than Eremite's[2] sad cell.

V

For he through Sin's long labyrinth had run,
Nor made atonement when he did amiss,
Had sighed to many though he loved but one,
And that loved one, alas! could ne'er be his.
Ah, happy she! to 'scape from him whose kiss
Had been pollution unto aught so chaste;
Who soon had left her charms for vulgar bliss,
And spoiled her goodly lands to gild his waste,
Nor calm domestic peace had ever deigned to taste.

VI

And now Childe Harold was sore sick at heart,
And from his fellow Bacchanals[3] would flee;

4. Might.
5. The lyre of the epic bard.
6. The nine Muses, goddesses of the forms of art.
7. Once upon a time.
8. England's.

9. Called.
1. Wretch.
2. Hermit's.
3. Worshipers of Bacchus, Roman god of wine and revelry.

'Tis said, at times the sullen tear would start,
But Pride congealed the drop within his ee:
Apart he stalked in joyless reverie,
And from his native land resolved to go,
And visit scorching climes beyond the sea;
With pleasure drugged, he almost longed for woe,
And e'en for change of scene would seek the shades below.

VII

The Childe departed from his father's hall:
It was a vast and venerable pile;[4]
So old, it seeméd only not to fall,
Yet strength was pillared in each massy aisle.
Monastic dome! condemned to uses vile!
Where Superstition once had made her den
Now Paphian[5] girls were known to sing and smile;
And monks might deem their time was come again,
If ancient tales[6] say true, nor wrong these holy men.

*condemning
Itself,
debauchery
& monks
alleged
sins*

VIII

Yet oft-times in his maddest mirthful mood
Strange pangs would flash along Childe Harold's brow,
As if the Memory of some deadly feud
Or disappointed passion lurked below:
But this none knew, nor haply cared to know;
For his was not that open, artless soul
That feels relief by bidding sorrow flow,
Nor sought he friend to counsel or condole,
Whate'er this grief mote be, which he could not control.

IX

And none did love him!—though to hall and bower
He gathered revellers from far and near,
He knew them flatterers of the festal hour,
The heartless Parasites of present cheer.
Yea! none did love him—not his lemans[7] dear—
But pomp and power alone are Woman's care,
And where these are light Eros[8] finds a feere;
Maidens, like moths, are ever caught by glare,
And Mammon[9] wins his way where Seraphs[1] might despair.

X

Childe Harold had a mother—not forgot,
Though parting from that mother he did shun;
A sister whom he loved, but saw her not
Before his weary pilgrimage begun:
If friends he had, he bade adieu to none.

4. Newstead Abbey, Byron's estate where he was wont to dress in friar's robes with his friends and play "dissolute monk."
5. From Paphos, island sacred to Aphrodite, goddess of beauty and love. Hence, "Paphian girls" are prostitutes. See stanza LXVI.
6. Byron alludes to the long tradition of tales about secret licentiousness in mon-asteries. This traditional libel had been revived in the Gothic novels of the Romantic period, particularly *The Monk* (1796) by Byron's friend Matthew G. Lewis.
7. Lovers.
8. Greek god of passionate love.
9. In medieval tradition, the demon of material wealth.
1. One of the nine orders of angels.

Yet deem not thence his breast a breast of steel:
Ye, who have known what 'tis to dote upon
A few dear objects, will in sadness feel
Such partings break the heart they fondly hope to heal.

XI

His house, his home, his heritage, his lands,
   The laughing dames in whom he did delight,
   Whose large blue eyes, fair locks, and snowy hands,
   Might shake the Saintship of an Anchorite,[2]
And long had fed his youthful appetite;
   His goblets brimmed with every costly wine,
   And all that mote to luxury invite,
   Without a sigh he left, to cross the brine,
And traverse Paynim[3] shores, and pass Earth's central line.

XII

The sails were filled, and fair the light winds blew,
   As glad to waft him from his native home;
   And fast the white rocks[4] faded from his view,
   And soon were lost in circumambient foam:
And then, it may be, of his wish to roam
   Repented he, but in his bosom slept
   The silent thought, nor from his lips did come
   One word of wail, whilst others sate and wept,
And to the reckless gales unmanly moaning kept.

XIII

But when the Sun was sinking in the sea
   He seized his harp, which he at times could string,
   And strike, albeit with untaught melody,
   When deemed he no strange ear was listening:
And now his fingers o'er it he did fling,
   And tuned his farewell in the dim twilight;
   While flew the vessel on her snowy wing,
   And fleeting shores receded from his sight,
Thus to the elements he poured his last "Good Night."

CHILDE HAROLD'S GOOD NIGHT

1

"Adieu, adieu! my native shore
   Fades o'er the waters blue;
The night-winds sigh, the breakers roar,
   And shrieks the wild sea-mew.
Yon Sun that sets upon the sea
   We follow in his flight;

---

2. Religious hermit.
3. Medieval word for "pagan."
4. The famous white cliffs of Dover, traditionally the traveler's last sight of England.

Farewell awhile to him and thee,
　　My native Land—Good Night!

2

"A few short hours and He will rise
　　To give the Morrow birth;
And I shall hail the main and skies,
　　But not my mother Earth.
Deserted is my own good Hall,
　　Its hearth is desolate;
Wild weeds are gathering on the wall;
　　My Dog howls at the gate.

3

"Come hither, hither, my little page!
　　Why dost thou weep and wail?
Or dost thou dread the billows' rage,
　　Or tremble at the gale?
But dash the tear-drop from thine eye;
　　Our ship is swift and strong:
Our fleetest falcon scarce can fly
　　More merrily along."

4

"Let winds be shrill, let waves roll high,
　　I fear not wave nor wind:
Yet marvel not, Sir Childe, that I
　　Am sorrowful in mind;
For I have from my father gone,
　　A mother whom I love,
And have no friend, save these alone,
　　But thee—and One above.

5

"My father blessed me fervently,
　　Yet did not much complain;
But sorely will my mother sigh
　　Till I come back again."—
"Enough, enough, my little lad!
　　Such tears become thine eye;
If I thy guileless bosom had,
　　Mine own would not be dry.

6

"Come hither, hither, my staunch yeoman,
　　Why dost thou look so pale?
Or dost thou dread a French foeman?
　　Or shiver at the gale?"—
"Deem'st thou I tremble for my life?
　　Sir Childe, I'm not so weak;
But thinking on an absent wife
　　Will blanch a faithful cheek.

7

"My spouse and boys dwell near thy hall,
　　Along the bordering Lake,

And when they on their father call,
 What answer shall she make?"—
"Enough, enough, my yeoman good,
 Thy grief let none gainsay;
But I, who am of lighter mood,
 Will laugh to flee away.

8

cynical

"For who would trust the seeming sighs
 Of wife or paramour?
Fresh feeres will dry the bright blue eyes
 We late saw streaming o'er.
For pleasures past I do not grieve,
 Nor perils gathering near;
My greatest grief is that I leave
 No thing that claims a tear.

9

"And now I'm in the world alone, *Ancient Mariner*
 Upon the wide, wide sea:
But why should I for others groan,
 When none will sigh for me?
Perchance my Dog will whine in vain,
 Till fed by stranger hands;
But long ere I come back again,
 He'd tear me where he stands.

10

"With thee, my bark, I'll swiftly go
 Athwart the foaming brine;
Nor care what land thou bear'st me to,
 So not again to mine.
Welcome, welcome, ye dark-blue waves!
 And when you fail my sight,
Welcome, ye deserts, and ye caves!
 My native Land—Good Night!"

XIV

On, on the vessel flies, the land is gone,
 And winds are rude in Biscay's[5] sleepless bay.
Four days are sped, but with the fifth, anon,
 New shores descried make every bosom gay;
And Cintra's[6] mountain greets them on their way,
 And Tagus[7] dashing onward to the Deep,

---

5. The bay of Biscay is the traveler's entry into the waters of Spain and Portugal.
6. Cintra (now Sintra) is a Portugese town near Lisbon, and site of the infamous "Convention of Cintra" (1808) where England, after helping the Portugese repel a French invasion, agreed to give the French Army safe conduct out of the country. Byron, like the other Romantics, felt that England's behavior was a betrayal of the nascent spirit of revolutionary nationalism—for while the English would aid their satellite, Portugal, in resisting Napoleon's attempt to isolate England economically from the European Continent, they would not allow the victorious Portugese to carry their triumph to the point of real national independence from foreign policies.
7. Portugal's central river, which according to legend carried gold particles in its depths.

His fabled golden tribute bent to pay;
    And soon on board the Lusian[8] pilot's leap,
And steer 'twixt fertile shores where yet few rustics reap.

XV

Oh, Christ! it is a goodly sight to see
    What Heaven hath done for this delicious land!
    What fruits of fragrance blush on every tree!
    What goodly prospects o'er the hills expand! *Eden*
    But man would mar them with an impious hand:
    And when the Almighty lifts his fiercest scourge
    'Gainst those who most transgress his high command,
    With trebel vengeance will his hot shafts urge
Gaul's locust host,[9] and earth from fellest foemen purge.

XVI

What beauties doth Lisboa first unfold!
    Her image floating on that noble tide,
    Which poets vainly pave with sands of gold,
    But now whereon a thousand keels did ride   *ships man marrying nature*
    Of mighty strength, since Albion was allied,
    And to the Lusians did her aid afford:
    A nation swoln with ignorance and pride,
    Who lick yet loathe the hand that waves the sword
To save them from the wrath of Gaul's unsparing lord.

XVII

But whoso entereth within this town,
    That, sheening far, celestial seems to be,
    Disconsolate will wander up and down,
    'Mid many things unsightly to strange ee;
    For hut and palace show like filthily:
    The dingy denizens are reared in dirt;
    Ne personage of high or mean degree
    Doth care for cleanness of surtout[1] or shirt,
Though shent with Egypt's plague[2], unkempt, unwashed, unhurt.

XVIII

Poor, paltry slaves! yet born 'midst noblest scenes—
    Why, Nature, waste thy wonders on such men?
    Lo! Cintra's glorious Eden intervenes
    In variegated maze of mount and glen.
    Ah, me! what hand can pencil guide, or pen,
    To follow half on which the eye dilates
    Through views more dazzling unto mortal ken
    Than those whereof such things the Bard[3] relates,
Who to the awe-struck world unlocked Elysium's[4] gates.

---

8. Portugese, from "Lusitania," an ancient name for Portugal.
9. The French Army which had invaded Portugal.
1. Overcoat.
2. Reference to the debilitating plagues with which God punished Egypt in the Book of Exodus.
3. Probably Vergil, who in the sixth book of the *Aeneid* describes the life of the blessed in Elysium.
4. Elysium is the Paradise of Roman mythology.

XIX

The horrid crags, by toppling convent crowned,
  The cork-trees hoar that clothe the shaggy steep,
  The mountain-moss by scorching skies imbrowned,
  The sunken glen, whose sunless shrubs must weep,
  The tender azure of the unruffled deep,
  The orange tints that gild the greenest bough,
  The torrents that from cliff to valley leap,
  The vine on high, the willow branch below,
Mixed in one mighty scene, with varied beauty glow.

XX

Then slowly climb the many-winding way,
  And frequent turn to linger as you go,
  From loftier rocks new loveliness survey,
  And rest ye at "Our Lady's house of Woe;"[5]
  Where frugal monks their little relics show,
  And sundry legends to the stranger tell:
  Here impious men have punished been, and lo!
  Deep in yon cave Honorius[6] long did dwell,
In hope to merit Heaven by making earth a Hell.

XXI

And here and there, as up the crags you spring,
  Mark many rude-carved crosses near the path:
  Yet deem not these Devotion's offering—
  These are memorials frail of murderous wrath:
  For wheresoe'er the shrieking victim hath
  Pour'd forth his blood beneath the assassin's knife,
  Some hand erects a cross of mouldering lath;
  And grove and glen with thousand such are rife
Throughout this purple land, where Law secures not life.

XXII

On sloping mounds, or in the vale beneath,
  Are domes where whilome kings did make repair;
  But now the wild flowers round them only breathe:
  Yet ruined Splendour still is lingering there.
  And yonder towers the Prince's palace[7] fair:
  There thou too, Vathek[8]! England's wealthiest son,
  Once formed thy Paradise, as not aware
  When wanton Wealth her mightiest deeds hath done,
Meek Peace voluptuous lures was ever wont to shun.

XXIII

Here didst thou dwell, here schemes of pleasure plan,
  Beneath yon mountain's ever beauteous brow:

---

5. The convent of Nossa Señora da Peña, "Our Lady of Sorrow," near Lisbon. Monasteries and convents frequently served as way-stations for exhausted travellers.

6. A historical personage (died 1596), a religious hermit who lived a life of total seclusion and self-denial in a cave near the convent of Our Lady of Sorrow.

7. Probably the Palace of Cintra, the "Marialva" of stanza XXV.

8. William Beckford, author of *Vathek* (1787), one of the most famous and influential of Gothic novels. Much of Beckford's life was spent in a fantastic attempt to construct an architecture equivalent to his own romantic dreams, and his English home, Fonthill Abbey, is one of the most striking of eighteenth century neo-Gothic buildings.

But now, as if a thing unblest by Man,
  Thy fairy dwelling is as lone as Thou!
  Here giant weeds a passage scarce allow
  To Halls deserted, portals gaping wide:
  Fresh lessons to the thinking bosom, how
  Vain are the pleasaunces on earth supplied;
Swept into wrecks anon by Time's ungentle tide!

            XXIV

Behold the hall[9] where chiefs were late convened!
  Oh! dome displeasing unto British eye!
  With diadem hight Foolscap, lo! a Fiend,
  A little Fiend that scoffs incessantly,
  There sits in parchment robe arrayed, and by
  His side is hung a seal and sable scroll,
  Where blazoned glare names known to chivalry,
  And sundry signatures adorn the roll,
Whereat the Urchin points and laughs with all his soul.

            XXV

Convention is the dwarfish demon styled
  That foiled the knights in Marialva's[1] dome:
  Of brains (if brains they had) he them beguiled,
  And turned a nation's shallow joy to gloom.
  Here Folly dashed to earth the victor's plume,
  And Policy regained what arms had lost:
  For chiefs like ours in vain may laurels bloom!
  Woe to the conquering, not the conquered host,
Since baffled Triumph droops on Lusitania's coast.

            XXVI

And ever since that martial Synod[2] met,
  Britannia sickens, Cintra! at thy name;
  And folks in office at the mention fret,
  And fain would blush, if blush they could, for shame.
  How will Posterity the deed proclaim!
  Will not our own and fellow-nations sneer,
  To view these champions cheated of their fame,
  By foes in fight o'erthrown, yet victors here,
Where Scorn her finger points through many a coming year?

            XXVII

So deemed[3] the Childe, as o'er the mountains he
  Did take his way in solitary guise:
  Sweet was the scene, yet soon he thought to flee,
  More restless than the swallow in the skies:
  Though here awhile he learned to moralise,
  For Meditation fixed at times on him;
  And conscious Reason whispered to despise

9. The Convention of Cintra.
1. The Convention of Cintra was signed in the palace of the Marchese Marialva.
2. Assembly.
3. The first instance of what will become a characteristic of Byron's practice throughout *Harold*. Having suspended the story for his own meditations on history and fate, Byron has to remind himself that he is, indeed, telling a tale in the third person.

His early youth, misspent in maddest whim;
But as he gazed on truth his aching eyes grew dim.

XXVIII

To horse! to horse! he quits, for ever quits
    A scene of peace, though soothing to his soul:
Again he rouses from his moping fits,
    But seeks not now the harlot and the bowl.
Onward he flies, nor fixed as yet the goal
    Where he shall rest him on his pilgrimage;
And o'er him many changing scenes must roll
    Ere toils his thirst for travel can assuage,
Or he shall calm his breast, or learn experience sage.

XXIX

Yet Mafra[4] shall one moment claim delay,
    Where dwelt of yore the Lusians' luckless queen;[5]
And Church and Court did mingle their array,
    And Mass and revel were alternate seen;
Lordlings and freres[6]—ill-sorted fry I ween!
    But here the Babylonian Whore[7] hath built
A dome, where flaunts she in such glorious sheen,
    That men forget the blood which she hath spilt,
And bow the knee to Pomp that loves to varnish guilt.

XXX

O'er vales that teem with fruits, romantic hills,
    (Oh, that such hills upheld a freeborn race!)
Whereon to gaze the eye with joyaunce fills,
    Childe Harold wends through many a pleasant place.
Though sluggards deem it but a foolish chase,
    And marvel men should quit their easy chair,
The toilsome way, and long, long league to trace,
    Oh! there is sweetness in the mountain air,
And Life, that bloated Ease can never hope to share.

XXXI

More bleak to view the hills at length recede,
    And, less luxuriant, smoother vales extend:
Immense horizon-bounded plains succeed!
    Far as the eye discerns, withouten end,
Spain's realms appear whereon her shepherds tend
    Flocks, whose rich fleece right well the trader knows—
Now must the Pastor's arm his *lambs* defend:
    For Spain is compassed by unyielding foes,[8]
And *all* must shield their *all*, or share Subjection's woes.

4. A town just north of Lisbon.
5. Maria I of Portugal (1734–1816), who went mad after the death of her husband and one of her sons. From 1799 till her death she was queen in name only, with her son Maria José Luis acting as regent.
6. Monks.
7. The "whore of Babylon" of St. John's *Revelations* was taken by many Protestants to represent the Catholic Church.
8. In 1808 Napoleon had forced Charles IV to abdicate the Spanish throne, and had placed his own brother, Joseph, as king in Spain. The Spanish resented and violently resisted French occupation of their country throughout the Peninsular War 1808–14. (See the Introduction to *Childe Harold's Pilgrimage*.)

XXXII

Where Lusitania and her Sister meet,
  Deem ye what bounds the rival realms divide?
Or ere the jealous Queens of Nations greet,
  Doth Tayo interpose his mighty tide?
  Or dark Sierras rise in craggy pride?
  Or fence of art, like China's vasty wall?—
  Ne barrier wall, ne river deep and wide,
  Ne horrid crags, nor mountains dark and tall,
Rise like the rocks that part Hispania's land from Gaul:

XXXIII

But these between a silver streamlet glides,
  And scarce a name distinguisheth the brook,
  Though rival kingdoms press its verdant sides:
  Here leans the idle shepherd on his crook,
  And vacant on the rippling waves doth look,
  That peaceful still 'twixt bitterest foemen flow;
  For proud each peasant as the noblest duke:
  Well doth the Spanish hind the difference know
'Twixt him and Lusian slave, the lowest of the low.

XXXIV

But ere the mingling bounds have far been passed,
  Dark Guadiana[9] rolls his power along
  In sullen billows, murmuring and vast,
  So noted ancient roundelays[1] among.
  Whilome upon his banks did legions throng
  Of Moor and Knight, in mailéd splendour drest:
  Here ceased the swift their race, here sunk the strong;
  The Paynim turban and the Christian[2] crest
Mixed on the bleeding stream, by floating hosts oppressed.

"noble war"

XXXV

Oh, lovely Spain! renowned, romantic Land!
  Where is that standard which Pelagio bore,
  When Cava's traitor-sire first called the band
  That dyed thy mountain streams with Gothic gore?[3]
  Where are those bloody Banners which of yore
  Waved o'er thy sons, victorious to the gale,
  And drove at last the spoilers to their shore?
  Red gleamed the Cross, and waned the Crescent pale,
While Afric's echoes thrilled with Moorish matrons' wail.

XXXVI

Teems not each ditty with the glorious tale?
  Ah! such, alas! the hero's amplest fate!
  When granite moulders and when records fail,
  A peasant's plaint prolongs his dubious date.

9. Spanish river flowing into Portugal.
1. Songs.
2. "Paynim" and "Christian" refer to the wars of liberation of the Spaniards from Moorish occupation.

3. Count Julian of Ceuta (Cava) in 711 aided the Moslem invasion of Spain. This invasion was resisted heroically by the Christian king Pelagio (Pelayo) who ruled 718–37.

*pride
of
Ozymandias*

Pride! bend thine eye from Heaven to thine estate,
See how the Mighty shrink into a song!
Can Volume, Pillar, Pile preserve thee great?
Or must thou trust Tradition's simple tongue,
When Flattery sleeps with thee, and History does thee wrong.

XXXVII

Awake, ye Sons of Spain! awake! advance!
Lo! Chivalry, your ancient Goddess, cries,
But wields not, as of old, her thirsty lance,
Nor shakes her crimson plumage in the skies:
Now on the smoke of blazing bolts she flies,
And speaks in thunder through yon engine's roar:
In every peal she calls—"Awake! arise!"
Say, is her voice more feeble than of yore,
When her war-song was heard on Andalusia's[4] shore?

XXXVIII

Hark!—heard you not those hoofs of dreadful note?
Sounds not the clang of conflict on the heath?
Saw ye not whom the reeking sabre smote,
Nor saved your brethren ere they sank beneath
Tyrants and Tyrants' slaves?—the fires of Death,
The Bale-fires flash on high:—from rock to rock
Each volley tells that thousands cease to breathe;
Death rides upon the sulphury Siroc,[5]
Red Battle stamps his foot, and Nations feel the shock.

XXXIX

Lo! where the Giant[6] on the mountain stands,
His blood-red tresses deepening in the Sun,
With death-shot glowing in his fiery hands,
And eye that scorcheth all it glares upon;
Restless it rolls, now fixed, and now anon
Flashing afar,—and at his iron feet
Destruction cowers, to mark what deeds are done;
For on this morn three potent Nations meet,
To shed before his Shrine the blood he deems most sweet.

XL

By Heaven! it is a splendid sight to see *in war*
(For one who hath no friend, no brother there)
Their rival scarfs of mixed embroidery, *no
longer
glorious
up close*
Their various arms that glitter in the air!
What gallant War-hounds rouse them from their lair,
And gnash their fangs, loud yelling for the prey!
All join the chase, but few the triumph share;
The Grave shall bear the chiefest prize away,
And Havoc scarce for joy can number their array.

XLI

Three hosts combine to offer sacrifice;
Three tongues prefer strange orisons[7] on high;

---

4. A province of Spain.
5. The Sirocco, the hot southern wind of the Mediterranean area.

6. Both a cannon and, figuratively, the gigantic power of Napoleonic France.
7. Prayers.

Three gaudy standards flout the pale blue skies;
The shouts are France, Spain, Albion, Victory!
The Foe, the Victim, and the fond Ally
That fights for all, but ever fights in vain,
Are met—as if at home they could not die—
To feed the crow on Talavera's[8] plain,
And fertilise the field that each pretends to gain.

XLII

There they shall rot—Ambition's honoured fools!
Yes, Honour decks the turf that wraps their clay!
Vain Sophistry! in these behold the tools,
The broken tools, that Tyrants cast away
By myriads, when they dare to pave their way
With human hearts—to what?—a dream alone.
Can Despots compass aught that hails their sway?
Or call with truth one span of earth their own,
Save that wherein at last they crumble bone by bone?

XLIII

Oh, Albuera![9] glorious field of grief!
As o'er thy plain the Pilgrim[1] pricked his steed,
Who could forsee thee, in a space so brief,
A scene where mingling foes should boast and bleed!
Peace to the perished! may the warrior's meed[2]
And tears of triumph there reward prolong!
Till others fall where other chieftains lead
Thy name shall circle round the gaping throng,
And shine in worthless lays, the theme of transient song.

XLIV

Enough of Battle's minions! let them play
Their game of lives, and barter breath for fame:
Fame that will scarce reanimate their clay,
Though thousands fall to deck some single name.
In sooth 'twere sad to thwart their noble aim
Who strike, blest hirelings! for their country's good,
And die, that living might have proved her shame;
Perished, perchance, in some domestic feud,
Or in a narrower sphere wild Rapine's path pursued.

XLV

Full swiftly Harold wends his lonely way
Where proud Sevilla triumphs unsubdued:
Yet is she free? the Spoiler's wished-for prey!
Soon, soon shall Conquest's fiery foot intrude,
Blackening her lovely domes with traces rude.
Inevitable hour! 'Gainst fate to strive
Where Desolation plants her famished brood

---

8. Talavera de la Reina is a town of central Spain which was the scene of a bloody battle between French and English troops in 1809.
9. A Spanish town where the French Army was defeated by the English in 1811.
1. Harold. Again Byron brings himself back from meditation to narration.
2. Reward.

Is vain, or Ilion,[3] Tyre might yet survive,
And Virtue vanquish all, and Murder cease to thrive.

don't resist inevitable Time

XLVI

But all unconscious of the coming doom,
    The feast, the song, the revel here abounds;
    Strange modes of merriment the hours consume,
    Nor bleed these patriots with their country's wounds:
    Nor here War's clarion, but Love's rebeck[4] sounds;
    Here Folly still his votaries inthralls;
    And young-eyed Lewdness walks her midnight rounds:
    Girt with the silent crimes of Capitals,
Still to the last kind Vice clings to the tott'ring walls.

Nobles' pleasures

XLVII

Not so the rustic—with his trembling mate
    He lurks, nor casts his heavy eye afar,
    Lest he should view his vineyard desolate,
    Blasted below the dun hot breath of War.
    No more beneath soft Eve's consenting star
    Fandango twirls his jocund castanet:
    Ah, Monarchs! could ye taste the mirth ye mar,
    Not in the toils of Glory would ye fret;
The hoarse dull drum would sleep, and Man be happy yet!

Simple living

XLVIII

How carols now the lusty muleteer?
    Of Love, Romance, Devotion is his lay,
    As whilome he was wont the leagues to cheer,
    His quick bells wildly jingling on the way?
    No! as he speeds, he chants "Vivā el Rey!"[5]
    And checks his song to execrate Godoy,[6]
    The royal wittol Charles, and curse the day
    When first Spain's queen beheld the black-eyed boy,
And gore-faced Treason sprung from her adulterate joy.

XLIX

On yon long level plain, at distance crowned
    With crags, whereon those Moorish turrets rest,
    Wide-scattered hoof-marks dint the wounded ground;
    And, scathed by fire, the greensward's darkened vest
    Tells that the foe was Andalusia's guest:
    Here was the camp, the watch-flame, and the host,
    Here the bold peasant stormed the Dragon's nest;
    Still does he mark it with triumphant boast,
And points to yonder cliffs, which oft were won and lost.

3. Ilium, or Troy. Tyre was another splendid ancient city whose fall has been the subject of countless moralizing reflections. Byron, totally within the spirit of his age, delights in speculating on the perishability of human effort.
4. An ancient stringed musical instrument.
5. "Long live the king." After Napoleon had replaced Charles IV with his brother, Joseph Buonaparte, Spanish resistance to French occupation centered around loyalty to the rightful and exiled king, Charles's son Ferdinand VII.
6. Emanuel Godoy, Spanish diplomat under Charles IV and the queen's lover. It was Godoy who first persuaded Charles (the "wittol" or fool) to join in European resistance to the French Revolution in 1793, and who in 1807–8 was instrumental in furthering French occupation of Spain.

L

And whomsoe'er along the path you meet
 Bears in his cap the badge[7] of crimson hue,
 Which tells you whom to shun and whom to greet:
 Woe to the man that walks in public view
 Without of loyalty this token true:
 Sharp is the knife, and sudden is the stroke;
 And sorely would the Gallic foeman rue,
 If subtle poniards, wrapt beneath the cloke,
Could blunt the sabre's edge, or clear the cannon's smoke.

LI

At every turn Morena's[8] dusky height
 Sustains aloft the battery's iron load;
 And, far as mortal eye can compass sight,
 The mountain-howitzer, the broken road,
 The bristling palisade, the fosse o'erflowed,
 The stationed bands, the never-vacant watch,
 The magazine in rocky durance stowed,
 The holstered steed beneath the shed of thatch,
The ball-piled pyramid, the ever-blazing match,

LII

Portend the deeds to come:—but he whose nod
 Has tumbled feebler despots from their sway,
 A moment pauseth ere he lifts the rod;
 A little moment deigneth to delay:
 Soon will his legions sweep through these their way;
 The West must own the Scourger of the world.
 Ah! Spain! how sad will be thy reckoning-day,
 When soars Gaul's Vulture, with his wings unfurled,
And thou shalt view thy sons in crowds to Hades hurled.

LIII

And must they fall? the young, the proud, the brave,
 To swell one bloated Chief's unwholesome reign?
 No step between submission and a grave?
 The rise of Rapine and the fall of Spain?
 And doth the Power that man adores ordain
 Their doom, nor heed the suppliant's appeal?
 Is all that desperate Valour acts in vain?
 And Counsel sage, and patriotic Zeal—
The Veteran's skill—Youth's fire—and Manhood's heart of steel?

LIV

Is it for this the Spanish maid, aroused,
 Hangs on the willow her unstrung guitar,
 And, all unsexed, the Anlace[9] hath espoused,
 Sung the loud song, and dared the deed of war?
 And she, whom once the semblance of a scar
 Appalled, an owlet's 'larum chilled with dread,

---

7. The red cockade, in Spain a mark of
loyalty to Ferdinand VII.
8. The mountain chain, chief bastion of
the city of Seville's resistance to French
siege.
9. A long, tapering dagger.

Now views the column-scattering bay'net jar,
The falchion[1] flash, and o'er the yet warm dead
Stalks with Minerva's step where Mars[2] might quake to tread.

LV

Ye who shall marvel when you hear her tale,
Oh! had you known her in her softer hour,
Marked her black eye that mocks her coal-black veil,
Heard her light, lively tones in Lady's bower,
Seen her long locks that foil the painter's power,
Her fairy form, with more than female grace,
Scarce would you deem that Saragoza's[3] tower
Beheld her smile in Danger's Gorgon[4] face,
Thin the closed ranks, and lead in Glory's fearful chase.

LVI

Her lover sinks—she sheds no ill-timed tear;
Her Chief is slain—she fills his fatal post;
Her fellows flee—she checks their base career;
The Foe retires—she heads the sallying host:
Who can appease like her a lover's ghost?
Who can avenge so well a leader's fall?
What maid retrieve when man's flushed hope is lost?
Who hang so fiercely on the flying Gaul,
Foiled by a woman's hand, before a battered wall?

LVII

Yet are Spain's maids no race of Amazons,[5]
But formed for all the witching arts of love:
Though thus in arms they emulate her sons,
And in the horrid phalanx dare to move,
'Tis but the tender fierceness of the dove,
Pecking the hand that hovers o'er her mate:
In softness as in firmness far above
Remoter females,[6] famed for sickening prate;
Her mind is nobler sure, her charms perchance as great.

LVIII

The seal Love's dimpling finger hath impressed
Denotes how soft that chin which bears his touch:
Her lips, whose kisses pout to leave their nest,
Bid man be valiant ere he merit such:
Her glance how wildly beautiful! how much
Hath Phoebus[7] wooed in vain to spoil her cheek,

---

1. A broad sword.
2. Minerva is goddess of wisdom and Mars the war god.
3. Saragossa, capital of the province of Aragon in Spain. In 1808 the citizens, including the women, successfully held off an invading French army.
4. In classical mythology the Gorgons were female monsters whose gaze turned men to stone.
5. The famous woman warriors, virginal and ferocious, of classical myth.

6. Primarily, of course, English ladies whose "prate" (vapid chatter) Byron detested all his life and whom he satirized viciously in the last cantos of *Don Juan*.
7. Apollo in his role as sun god. He has tried in vain to darken the skin of the ladies of Spain, for their darkness only enhances their seductiveness. This is Byron in another of his most famous postures, the international connoisseur of women.

Which glows yet smoother from his amorous clutch!
Who round the North for paler dames would seek?
How poor their forms appear! how languid, wan, and weak! [England]

LIX

Match me, ye climes! which poets love to laud; [poet speaking about Harold in Spain (where Harold was)]
  Match me, ye harems of the land! where now[8] [heavenly harems]
  I strike my strain, far distant, to applaud
  Beauties that ev'n a cynic must avow;
  Match me those Houris, whom ye scarce allow
  To taste the gale lest Love should ride the wind,
  With Spain's dark-glancing daughters—deign to know,
  There your wise Prophet's[9] Paradise we find,
His black-eyed maids of Heaven, angelically kind.

LX

Oh, thou Parnassus[1]! whom I now survey, [interruption]
  Not in the phrensy of a dreamer's eye,
  Not in the fabled landscape of a lay,
  But soaring snow-clad through thy native sky,
  In the wild pomp of mountain-majesty! [Muses don't work any more]
  What marvel if I thus essay to sing?
  The humblest of thy pilgrims passing by
  Would gladly woo thine Echoes with his string,
Though from thy heights no more one Muse will wave her wing.

LXI

Oft have I dreamed of Thee! whose glorious name [creativity = divine]
  Who knows not, knows not man's divinest lore:
  And now I view thee—'tis, alas, with shame
  That I in feeblest accents must adore.
  When I recount thy worshippers of yore [Past poets]
  I tremble, and can only bend the knee;
  Nor raise my voice, nor vainly dare to soar,
  But gaze beneath thy cloudy canopy
In silent joy to think at last I look on Thee!

LXII

Happier in this than mightiest Bards have been,
  Whose Fate to distant homes confined their lot,
  Shall I unmoved behold the hallowed scene,
  Which others rave of, though they know it not? [echo of gentle Spirit left]
  Though here no more Apollo haunts his Grot,
  And thou, the Muses' seat, art now their grave,
  Some gentle Spirit still pervades the spot,
  Sighs in the gale, keeps silence in the Cave,
And glides with glassy foot o'er yon melodious wave. [gonna finish off Byron's Harold "past"]

LXIII

Of thee hereafter.—Ev'n amidst my strain
  I turned aside to pay my homage here;

---

8. This stanza was written in Turkey.
9. Muhammad, who in the Koran promised to the faithful, among other joys, a harem of houris—angelic concubines—after death.

1. The Greek mountain sacred to the Muses and to the god of poetry, Apollo.

Forgot the land, the sons, the maids of Spain;
Her fate, to every freeborn bosom dear;
And hailed thee, not perchance without a tear.
Now to my theme—but from thy holy haunt
Let me some remnant, some memorial bear;
Yield me one leaf of Daphne's[2] deathless plant,
Nor let thy votary's hope be deemed an idle vaunt.

LXIV

But ne'er didst thou, fair Mount! when Greece was young,
See round thy giant base a brighter choir,
Nor e'er did Delphi, when her Priestess sung
The Pythian[3] hymn with more than mortal fire,
Behold a train more fitting to inspire
The song of love, than Andalusia's maids,
Nurst in the glowing lap of soft Desire:
Ah! that to these were given such peaceful shades
As Greece can still bestow, though Glory fly her glades.

LXV

Fair is proud Seville; let her country boast
Her strength, her wealth, her site of ancient days;
But Cadiz, rising on the distant coast,
Calls forth a sweeter, though ignoble praise.
Ah, Vice! how soft are thy voluptuous ways!
While boyish blood is mantling, who can 'scape
The fascination of thy magic gaze?
A Cherub-Hydra[4] round us dost thou gape,
And mould to every taste thy dear delusive shape.

LXVI

When Paphos[5] fell by Time—accurséd Time!
The Queen who conquers all must yield to thee—
The Pleasures fled, but sought as warm a clime;
And Venus, constant to her native Sea,
To nought else constant, hither deigned to flee,
And fixed her shrine within these walls of white:
Though not to one dome circumscribeth She
Her worship, but, devoted to her rite,
A thousand Altars rise, for ever blazing bright.

LXVII

From morn till night, from night till startled Morn[6]
Peeps blushing on the Revel's laughing crew,
The Song is heard, the rosy Garland worn;

2. Daphne, pursued by Apollo, was saved by being transformed into a laurel tree.
3. From Pythios, an older name of Apollo's sacred grove, Delphi; hence, sacred to Apollo.
4. Cadiz, city of vice, is imagined by Byron as a combination of beautiful boy (cherub) and mythic, many-headed serpent. This is an arresting image, particu-

larly in view of recent studies of Byron's pathological love and loathing of sexuality.
5. Island sacred to Venus, goddess of love, the "Queen" of the next line.
6. In *Paradise Lost* I (742–43) Milton describes the fall of the devil Mammon from Heaven: "From Morn/To Noon he fell, from Noon to dewy Eve."

Devices quaint, and Frolics ever new,
Tread on each other's kibes.[7] A long adieu
He bids to sober joy that here sojourns:
Nought interrupts the riot, though in lieu
Of true devotion monkish incense burns,
And Love and Prayer unite, or rule the hour by turns.

LXVIII

The Sabbath comes, a day of blessed rest:
What hallows it upon this Christian shore?
Lo! it is sacred to a solemn Feast:
Hark! heard you not the forest-monarch's[8] roar?
Crashing the lance, he snuffs the spouting gore
Of man and steed, o'erthrown beneath his horn;
The thronged arena shakes with shouts for more;
Yells the mad crowd o'er entrails freshly torn,
Nor shrinks the female eye, nor ev'n affects to mourn.

LXIX

The seventh day this—the Jubilee of man!
London! right well thou knows't the day of prayer
Then thy spruce citizen, washed artisan,
And smug apprentice gulp their weekly air:
They coach of hackney, whiskey, one-horse chair,
And humblest gig through sundry suburbs whirl,
To Hampstead, Brentford, Harrow make repair;
Till the tired jade the wheel forgets to hurl,
Provoking envious gibe from each pedestrian churl.

LXX

Some o'er thy Thamis[9] row the ribboned fair,
Others along the safer turnpike fly;
Some Richmond-hill ascend, some scud to Ware,
And many to the steep of Highgate hie.
Ask ye, Boeotian[1] Shades! the reason why?
'Tis to the worship of the solemn Horn,[2]
Grasped in the holy hand of Mystery,
In whose dread name both men and maids are sworn,
And consecrate the oath with draught, and dance till morn.

LXXI

All have their fooleries—not alike are thine,
Fair Cadiz, rising o'er the dark blue sea!
Soon as the Matin bell proclaimeth nine,
Thy Saint-adorers count the Rosary:
Much is the VIRGIN teased to shrive them free
(Well do I deem the only virgin there)

[handwritten marginal notes: "cuckhold?", "phallic?", "hypocrisy on every level", "praying on way to obscene bullfight"]

---

7. Boils or blisters on the feet.
8. The bull in the ring.
9. The river Thames in London—along with Richmond, etc., of the following lines, a popular London scene of Sunday recreation.
1. Site of ancient Thebes, city of Oedi-

pus, and renowned for its prophet Tiresias (one of the "shades" asking the question).
2. The reference is to a popular English drinking game of the eighteenth and early nineteenth centuries, "swearing on the horn."

From crimes as numerous as her beadsmen be;
    Then to the crowded circus forth they fare:
Young, old, high, low, at once the same diversion share.

LXXII

The lists are oped, the spacious area cleared,
    Thousands on thousands piled are seated round;
    Long ere the first loud trumpet's note is heard,
    Ne vacant space for lated wight is found:
    Here Dons, Grandees, but chiefly Dames abound,
    Skilled in the ogle of a roguish eye,
    Yet ever well inclined to heal the wound;
    None through their cold disdain are doomed to die,
As moon-struck bards complain, by Love's sad archery.

LXXIII

Hushed is the din of tongues—on gallant steeds,
    With milk-white crest, gold spur, and light-poised lance,
    Four cavaliers[3] prepare for venturous deeds,
    And lowly-bending to the lists advance;
    Rich are their scarfs, their chargers featly prance:
    If in the dangerous game they shine to-day,
    The crowd's loud shout and ladies' lovely glance,
    Best prize of better acts! they bear away,
And all that kings or chiefs e'er gain their toils repay.

LXXIV

In costly sheen and gaudy cloak arrayed,
    But all afoot, the light-limbed Matadore
    Stands in the centre, eager to invade
    The lord of lowing herds; but not before
    The ground, with cautious tread, is traversed o'er,
    Lest aught unseen should lurk to thwart his speed:
    He arms a dart, he fights aloof, nor more
    Can Man achieve without the friendly steed—
Alas! too oft condemned for him to bear and bleed.

LXXV

Thrice sounds the Clarion; lo! the signal falls,
    The den expands, and Expectation mute
    Gapes round the silent circle's peopled walls.
    Bounds with one lashing spring the mighty brute,
    And, wildly staring, spurns, with sounding foot,
    The sand, nor blindly rushes on his foe:
    Here, there, he points his threatening front, to suit
    His first attack, wide-waving to and fro
His angry tail; red rolls his eye's dilated glow.

LXXVI

Sudden he stops—his eye is fixed—away—
    Away, thou heedless boy! prepare the spear:

3. The picadors who prepare the bull for the matador, by taunting and enraging the bull from horseback. Byron's precise description of the cermonial of the bull-fight is perhaps the most famous passage in *Harold* I.

Now is thy time, to perish, or display
The skill that yet may check his mad career!
With well-timed croupe[4] the nimble coursers veer;
On foams the Bull, but not unscathed he goes;
Streams from his flank the crimson torrent clear:
He flies, he wheels, distracted with his throes;
Dart follows dart—lance, lance—loud bellowings speak his woes.

LXXVII

Again he comes; nor dart nor lance avail,
Nor the wild plunging of the tortured horse;
Though Man and Man's avenging arms assail,
Vain are his weapons, vainer is his force.
One gallant steed is stretched a mangled corse;
Another, hideous sight! unseamed appears,
His gory chest unveils life's panting source;
Though death-struck, still his feeble frame he rears;
Staggering, but stemming all, his Lord unharmed he bears.

LXXVIII

Foiled, bleeding, breathless, furious to the last,
Full in the centre stands the Bull at bay,
Mid wounds, and clinging darts, and lances brast,[5]
And foes disabled in the brutal fray:
And now the Matadores around him play,
Shake the red cloak, and poise the ready brand:
Once more through all he bursts his thundering way—
Vain rage! the mantle quits the conynge[6] hand,
Wraps his fierce eye—'tis past—he sinks upon the sand!

LXXIX

Where his vast neck just mingles with the spine,
Sheathed in his form the deadly weapon lies.
He stops—he starts—disdaining to decline:
Slowly he falls, amidst triumphant cries,
Without a groan, without a struggle dies.
The decorated car appears—on high
The corse is piled—sweet sight for vulgar eyes—
Four steeds that spurn the rein, as swift as shy,
Hurl the dark bulk along, scarce seen in dashing by.

LXXX

Such the ungentle sport that oft invites
The Spanish maid, and cheers the Spanish swain.
Nurtured in blood betimes, his heart delights
In vengeance, gloating on another's pain.
What private feuds the troubled village stain!
Though now one phalanxed host should meet the foe,
Enough, alas! in humble homes remain,
To meditate 'gainst friend the secret blow,

4. Horse's hindquarters.   6. Cunning.
5. Broken.

For some slight cause of wrath, whence Life's warm stream must
flow.

LXXXI

But Jealousy has fled: his bars, his bolts, *[all hope gone]*
  His withered Centinel, Duenna[7] sage!
And all whereat the generous soul revolts,
Which the stern dotard deemed he could encage,
Have passed to darkness with the vanished age.
Who late so free as Spanish girls were seen,
(Ere War uprose in his volcanic rage,)
With braided tresses bounding o'er the green,
While on the gay dance shone Night's lover-loving Queen?

LXXXII

[NARR.] Oh! many a time and oft, had Harold loved,
  Or dreamed he loved, since Rapture is a dream; *[unreal]*
But now his wayward bosom was unmoved,
For not yet had he drunk of Lethe's[8] stream;
And lately had he learned with truth to deem *[best things about love is that it flies away]*
Love has no gift so grateful as his wings:
How fair, how young, how soft soe'er he seem,
Full from the fount of Joy's delicious springs
Some bitter o'er the flowers its bubbling venom flings.

LXXXIII

Yet to the beauteous form he was not blind,
  Though now it moved him as it moves the wise;
Not that Philosophy on such a mind
E'er deigned to bend her chastely-awful eyes:
But Passion raves herself to rest, or flies;
And Vice, that digs her own voluptuous tomb,
Had buried long his hopes, no more to rise:
Pleasure's palled Victim! life-abhorring Gloom *[life in death "unnamed horror"]*
Wrote on his faded brow curst Cain's[9] unresting doom.

LXXXIV

Still he beheld, nor mingled with the throng; *[Byronic hero]*
  But viewed them not with misanthropic hate:
Fain would he now have joined the dance, the song; *[jadedness "love doesn't last" "Beauty passes" won't allow himself to feel (demon in him)]*
But who may smile that sinks beneath his fate?
Nought that he saw his sadness could abate:
Yet once he struggled 'gainst the Demon's sway,
And as in Beauty's bower he pensive sate,
Poured forth his unpremeditated lay,
To charms as fair as those that soothed his happier day.

---

7. The traditional escort, an aged female, for a Spanish lady of high birth.
The term has become proverbial for sexual repression or prudery.
8. The river of forgetfulness in the classical underworld.
9. Here for the first time Byron identifies Harold (and himself) with Cain, in
one of his most important analogies. As
Cain was condemned to wander the
earth, marked forever as a sinner for his
murder of Abel, so Byron frequently imagined himself and his heroes as modern
Cains, whose guilt was almost too prime-
val, too deep to be named.

poet responds to Beauty

fights Demon by creating Beauty (Poem)

TO INEZ

1

Nay, smile not at my sullen brow;
　　Alas! I cannot smile again:
Yet Heaven avert that ever thou
　　Shouldst weep, and haply weep in vain.

2

And dost thou ask what secret woe
　　I bear, corroding Joy and Youth?
And wilt thou vainly seek to know
　　A pang, ev'n thou must fail to soothe?

3

It is not love, it is not hate,
　　Nor low Ambition's honours lost,
That bids me loathe my present state,
　　And fly from all I prized the most:

4

It is that weariness which springs
　　From all I meet, or hear, or see:
To me no pleasure Beauty brings;
　　Thine eyes have scarce a charm for me.

5

It is that settled, ceaseless gloom
　　The fabled Hebrew Wanderer bore;[1]
That will not look beyond the tomb,
　　But cannot hope for rest before.

6

What Exile from himself can flee?
　　To zones though more and more remote,
Still, stilll pursues, where'er I be,
　　The blight of Life—the Demon Thought.[2]

(self-consciousness ruins everything)

7

Yet others rapt in pleasure seem,
　　And taste of all that I forsake;
Oh! may they still of transport dream,
　　And ne'er—at least like me—awake!

8

Through many a clime 'tis mine to go,
　　With many a retrospection curst;
And all my solace is to know,
　　Whate'er betides, I've known the worst.

unknown crime

9

What is the worst? Nay do not ask—
　　In pity from the search forbear:

1. The "wandering Jew" of medieval legend—an infidel who, for cursing Christ at the crucifixion, was condemned to wander the earth for all time seeking the gift of death and peace.
2. Byron identifies consciousness, or *self*-consciousness, as the primary despoiler of man's Paradise on earth. This stanza is a reminiscence of Satan's statement in *Paradise Lost* IV (75), "Which way I fly is Hell; myself am Hell."

Smile on—nor venture to unmask
Man's heart, and view the Hell that's there.

LXXXV

Adieu, fair Cadiz! yea, a long adieu!
Who may forget how well thy walls have stood?
When all were changing thou alone wert true,
First to be free and last to be subdued:
And if amidst a scene, a shock so rude,
Some native blood was seen thy streets to dye,
A Traitor only fell beneath the feud:
Here all were noble, save Nobility;
None hugged a Conqueror's chain, save fallen Chivalry!

LXXXVI

Such be the sons of Spain, and strange her Fate!
They fight for Freedom who were never free,
A Kingless people for a nerveless state;
Her vassals combat when their Chieftains flee,
True to the veriest slaves of Treachery:
Fond of a land which gave them nought but life,
Pride points the path that leads to Liberty;
Back to the struggle, baffled in the strife,
War, war is still the cry, "War even to the knife!"[3]

LXXXVII

Ye, who would more of Spain and Spaniards know
Go, read whate'er is writ of bloodiest strife:
Whate'er keen Vengeance urged on foreign foe
Can act, is acting there against man's life:
From flashing scimitar to secret knife,
War mouldeth there each weapon to his need—
So may he guard the sister and the wife,
So may be make each curst oppressor bleed—
So may such foes deserve the most remorseless deed!

LXXXVIII

Flows there a tear of Pity for the dead?
Look o'er the ravage of the reeking plain;
Look on the hands with female slaughter red;
Then to the dogs resign the unburied slain,
Then to the vulture let each corse remain,
Albeit unworthy of the prey-bird's maw;
Let their bleached bones, and blood's unbleaching stain,
Long mark the battle-field with hideous awe:
Thus only may our sons conceive the scenes we saw!

LXXXIX[4]

Nor yet, alas! the dreadful work is done;

3. "War to the knife? Palafox's answer to the French general at the seige of Saragoza." [*Byron's note*.]
4. An important if confusing stanza. Francisco Pizarro, the sixteenth-century conqueror of Peru, led the Incas ("Quinto's sons") into bondage. Now Spain herself is in bondage while America (Columbia) is thriving, liberated from European rule. Byron's use of the theological term "retribution," to describe this set of events signals two important aspects of his thought: his inescapably moralistic, Protestant viewpoint on world history, and his insistence—highly Romantic—that political liberation is possible only in the form of worldwide, total liberation of the oppressed.

Fresh legions pour adown the Pyrenees:
  It deepens still, the work is scarce begun,
  Nor mortal eye the distant end foresees.
  Fall'n nations gaze on Spain; if freed, she frees
  More than her fell Pizarros once enchained:
  Strange retribution! now Columbia's ease
  Repairs the wrongs that Quito's sons sustained,
While o'er the parent clime prowls Murder unrestrained.

xc

Not all the blood at Talavera shed,
  Not all the marvels of Barossa's fight,
  Not Albuera lavish of the dead,
  Have won for Spain her well asserted right.
  When shall her Olive-Branch be free from blight?
  When shall she breathe her from the blushing toil?
  How many a doubtful day shall sink in night,
  Ere the Frank robber turn him from his spoil,
And Freedom's stranger-tree grow native of the soil!

[margin note: Spain is slaved to her own vices as well as to France.]

xci

And thou, my friend!⁵—since unavailing woe
  Bursts from my heart, and mingles with the strain—
  Had the sword laid thee with the mighty low,
  Pride might forbid e'en Friendship to complain:
  But thus unlaurelled to descend in vain,
  By all forgotten, save the lonely breast,
  And mix unbleeding with the boasted slain,
  While Glory crowns so many a meaner crest!
What hadst thou done to sink so peacefully to rest?

xcii

Oh, known the earliest, and esteemed the most!
  Dear to a heart where nought was left so dear!
  Though to my hopeless days for ever lost,
  In dreams deny me not to see thee here!
  And Morn in secret shall renew the tear
  Of Consciousness awaking to her woes,⁶
  And Fancy hover o'er thy bloodless bier,
  Till my frail frame return to whence it rose,
And mourned and mourner lie united in repose.

[margin note: Bafflement in face of uncertainty writes poem.]

xciii

Here is one fytte⁷ of Harold's pilgrimage:
  Ye who of him may further seek to know,
  Shall find some tidings in a future page,
  If he that rhymeth now may scribble moe.
  Is this too much? stern Critic! say not so:
  Patience! and ye shall hear what he beheld

5. John Wingfield, who died in 1811 as *Harold* I was being prepared for Murray. Byron's mother had died a month earlier and his beloved Cambridge chorister John Edleston (subject of the "Thyrza" lyrics) died in the same year.
6. A crucial line for Byron's lifelong sense that consciousness itself—memory of loss and foreknowledge of death—is mankind's great curse.
7. Medieval word for "canto" or "section." At the end of the poem, Byron reverts heavily to the labored "poetic diction" of the opening stanzas.

In other lands, where he was doomed to go:
Lands that contain the monuments of Eld,[8]
Ere Greece and Grecian arts by barbarous hands[9] were quelled.

CANTO THE THIRD

I

Is thy face like thy mother's, my fair child!
ADA[1]! sole daughter of my house and heart?
When last I saw thy young blue eyes they smiled,
And when we parted,—not as now we part,
But with a hope.—[2]

     Awaking with a start,
The waters[3] heave around me; and on high
The winds lift up their voices: I depart,
Whither I know not; but the hour's gone by,
When Albion's lessening shores could grieve or glad mine eye.

II

Once more upon the waters! yet once more!
And the waves bound beneath me as a steed
That knows his rider. Welcome to their roar!
Swift be their guidance, wheresoe'er it lead!
Though the strained mast should quiver as a reed,
And the rent canvass fluttering strew the gale,
Still must I on; for I am as a weed,
Flung from the rock, on Ocean's foam, to sail
Where'er the surge may sweep, the tempest's breath prevail.

III

In my youth's summer I did sing of One,[4]
The wandering outlaw of his own dark mind;
Again I seize the theme, then but begun,
And bear it with me, as the rushing wind
Bears the cloud onwards: in that Tale I find
The furrows of long thought, and dried-up tears,
Which, ebbing, leave a sterile track behind,
O'er which all heavily the journeying years
Plod the last sands of life,—where not a flower appears.

IV

Since my young days of passion—joy, or pain—
Perchance my heart and harp have lost a string—
And both may jar[5]: it may be, that in vain
I would essay as I have sung to sing;
Yet, though a dreary strain, to this I cling;

---

8. Olden time.
9. The Turks.
1. Augusta Ada Byron, born to Byron and Lady Byron December 10, 1815.
2. Byron's hope for a reconciliation with his estranged wife, a hope which was never to be realized.
3. On April 25, 1816, Byron sailed from

England ("Albion") never to return.
4. Harold.
5. Sound out of tune. Byron here acknowledges his freer use of the Spenserian stanza in *Harold* III, and also the darker, more bitter tone which his reflections on human fate have taken since his triumph of 1812.

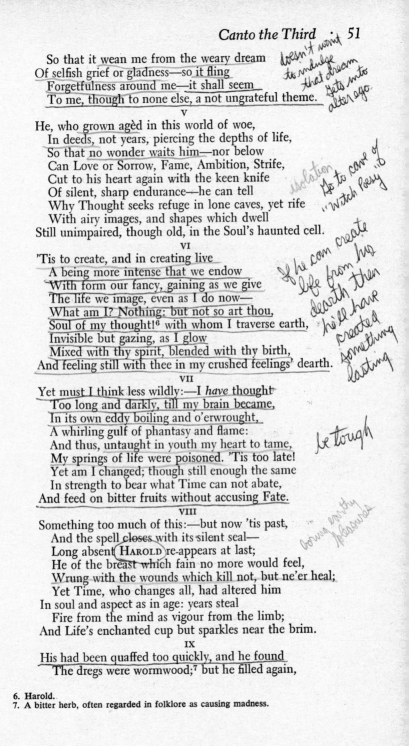

So that it wean me from the weary dream
Of selfish grief or gladness—so it fling
Forgetfulness around me—it shall seem
To me, though to none else, a not ungrateful theme.

V

He, who grown agèd in this world of woe,
In deeds, not years, piercing the depths of life,
So that no wonder waits him—nor below
Can Love or Sorrow, Fame, Ambition, Strife,
Cut to his heart again with the keen knife
Of silent, sharp endurance—he can tell
Why Thought seeks refuge in lone caves, yet rife
With airy images, and shapes which dwell
Still unimpaired, though old, in the Soul's haunted cell.

VI

'Tis to create, and in creating live
A being more intense that we endow
With form our fancy, gaining as we give
The life we image, even as I do now—
What am I? Nothing: but not so art thou,
Soul of my thought![6] with whom I traverse earth,
Invisible but gazing, as I glow
Mixed with thy spirit, blended with thy birth,
And feeling still with thee in my crushed feelings' dearth.

VII

Yet must I think less wildly:—I *have* thought
Too long and darkly, till my brain became,
In its own eddy boiling and o'erwrought,
A whirling gulf of phantasy and flame:
And thus, untaught in youth my heart to tame,
My springs of life were poisoned. 'Tis too late!
Yet am I changed; though still enough the same
In strength to bear what Time can not abate,
And feed on bitter fruits without accusing Fate.

VIII

Something too much of this:—but now 'tis past,
And the spell closes with its silent seal—
Long absent HAROLD re-appears at last;
He of the breast which fain no more would feel,
Wrung with the wounds which kill not, but ne'er heal;
Yet Time, who changes all, had altered him
In soul and aspect as in age: years steal
Fire from the mind as vigour from the limb;
And Life's enchanted cup but sparkles near the brim.

IX

His had been quaffed too quickly, and he found
The dregs were wormwood;[7] but he filled again,

6. Harold.
7. A bitter herb, often regarded in folklore as causing madness.

And from a purer fount, on holier ground,
And deemed its spring perpetual—but in vain!
Still round him clung invisibly a chain
Which galled for ever, fettering though unseen,
And heavy though it clanked not; worn with pain,
Which pined although it spoke not, and grew keen,
Entering with every step he took through many a scene.

X

Secure in guarded coldness, he had mixed
    Again in fancied safety with his kind,
    And deemed his spirit now so firmly fixed
    And sheathed with an invulnerable mind,
    That, if no joy, no sorrow lurked behind;
    And he, as one, might 'midst the many stand
    Unheeded, searching through the crowd to find
    Fit speculation—such as in strange land
He found in wonder-works of God and Nature's hand.

XI

But who can view the ripened rose, nor seek
    To wear it? who can curiously behold
    The smoothness and the sheen of Beauty's cheek,
    Nor feel the heart can never all grow old?
    Who can contemplate Fame through clouds unfold
    The star which rises o'er her steep, nor climb?
    Harold, once more within the vortex, rolled
    On with the giddy circle, chasing Time,
Yet with a nobler aim than in his Youth's fond[8] prime.

XII

But soon he knew himself the most unfit
    Of men to herd with Man, with whom he held
    Little in common; untaught to submit
    His thoughts to others, though his soul was quelled
    In youth by his own thoughts; still uncompelled,
    He would not yield dominion of his mind
    To Spirits against whom his own rebelled,
    Proud though in desolation—which could find
A life within itself, to breathe without mankind.

XIII

Where rose the mountains, there to him were friends;
    Where rolled the ocean, thereon was his home;
    Where a blue sky, and glowing clime, extends,
    He had the passion and the power to roam;
    The desert, forest, cavern, breaker's foam,
    Were unto him companionship; they spake
    A mutual language, clearer than the tome
    Of his land's tongue, which he would oft forsake
For Nature's pages glassed by sunbeams on the lake.

8. Optimistic, foolish.

XIV

Like the Chaldean,[9] he could watch the stars,
  Till he had peopled them with beings bright
As their own beams; and earth, and earth-born jars,
And human frailties, were forgotten quite:
Could he have kept his spirit to that flight
He had been happy; but his clay will sink
Its spark immortal, envying it the light
  To which it mounts, as if to break the link
That keeps us from yon heaven which woos us to its brink.

[margin: leaving human world]
[margin: "wanting" impossible]
[margin: still has body & heart]

XV

But in Man's dwellings he became a thing
  Restless and worn, and stern and wearisome,
Drooped as a wild-born falcon with clipt wing,
To whom the boundless air alone were home:
Then came his fit again, which to o'ercome,
As eagerly the barred-up bird will beat
His breast and beak against his wiry dome
  Till the blood tinge his plumage—so the heat
Of his impeded Soul would through his bosom eat.

[margin: Frenetic activity good if you can control it]
[margin: wants to soar]

XVI

Self-exiled Harold wanders forth again,
  With nought of Hope left—but with less of gloom;
The very knowledge that he lived in vain,
That all was over on this side the tomb,
Had made Despair a smilingness assume,
Which, though 'twere wild,—as on the plundered wreck
When mariners would madly meet their doom
  With draughts intemperate on the sinking deck,—
Did yet inspire a cheer, which he forbore to check.

[margin: Total Despair]
[margin: Harold through — not for Byron]

XVII

Stop!— for thy tread is on an Empire's dust!
  An Earthquake's spoil is sepulchred below!
Is the spot marked with no colossal bust?
Nor column trophied for triumphal show?
None; but *the moral's truth* tells simpler so.—
As the ground was before, thus let it be;—
How that red rain hath made the harvest grow!
  And is this all the world has gained by thee,
Thou first and last of Fields! king-making Victory?[1]

XVIII

And Harold stands upon this place of skulls,
  The grave of France, the deadly Waterloo![2]

9. Ancient Semitic people who founded the city of Babylon. The Chaldeans were renowned for their astrological and astronomical knowledge.
1. The defeat and exile of Napoleon not only returned the Bourbon monarchy to the throne of France, but strengthened the power and confidence of national monarchies throughout Europe.
2. The site in Belgium where on June 18, 1815, the Duke of Wellington met and routed Napoleon's army. It was the final defeat for Napoleon and for his dream of a united Europe under his despotic control.

How in an hour the Power which gave annuls
Its gifts, transferring fame as fleeting too!—
In "pride of place" here last the Eagle[3] flew,
Then tore with bloody talon the rent plain,
Pierced by the shaft of banded nations through;
Ambition's life and labours all were vain—
He wears the shattered links of the World's broken chain.[4]

XIX

Fit retribution! Gaul may champ the bit
And foam in fetters;—but is Earth more free?
Did nations combat to make *One* submit?
Or league to teach all Kings true Sovereignty?
What! shall reviving Thraldom again be
The patched-up Idol of enlightened days?
Shall we, who struck the Lion down, shall we
Pay the Wolf homage? proffering lowly gaze
And servile knees to Thrones? No! *prove*[5] before ye praise!

XX

If not, o'er one fallen Despot boast no more!
In vain fair cheeks were furrowed with hot tears
For Europe's flowers long rooted up before
The trampler of her vineyards; in vain, years
Of death, depopulation, bondage, fears,
Have all been borne, and broken by the accord
Of roused-up millions: all that most endears
Glory, is when the myrtle[6] wreathes a Sword,
Such as Harmodius[7] drew on Athens' tyrant Lord.

XXI

There was a sound of revelry by night,
And Belgium's Capital[8] had gathered then
Her Beauty and her Chivalry—and bright
The lamps shone o'er fair women and brave men;
A thousand hearts beat happily; and when
Music arose with its voluptuous swell,
Soft eyes looked love to eyes which spake again,
And all went merry as a marriage bell;
But hush! hark! a deep sound strikes like a rising knell!

XXII

Did ye not hear it?—No—'twas but the Wind,
Or the car rattling o'er the stony street;
On with the dance! let joy be unconfined;
No sleep till morn, when Youth and Pleasure meet

---

3. Napoleon. " 'Pride of place' is a term of falconry, and means the highest pitch of flight.' [*Byron's note.*]
4. Reference to Napoleon's final imprisonment and exile on the island of St. Helena.
5. Test, examine carefully.
6. Tree sacred to Venus, and therefore symbol of love.

7. Sixth century B.C. Athenian patriot who attempted to assassinate the tyrant Hipparchus.
8. Brussels. On June 15, 1815, the eve of the battle of Quatre-bras (itself a prelude to the battle of Waterloo), the Dutchess of Richmond gave a lavish ball in Brussels.

To chase the glowing Hours with flying feet—
But hark!—that heavy sound breaks in once more,
As if the clouds its echo would repeat;
And nearer—clearer—deadlier than before!
Arm! Arm! it is—it is—the cannon's opening roar!

XXIII

Within a windowed niche of that high hall
Sate Brunswick's fated Chieftain;[9] he did hear
That sound the first amidst the festival,
And caught its tone with Death's prophetic ear;
And when they smiled because he deemed it near,
His heart more truly knew that peal too well
Which stretched his father[1] on a bloody bier,
And roused the vengeance blood alone could quell;
He rushed into the field, and, foremost fighting, fell.

XXIV

Ah! then and there was hurrying to and fro—
And gathering tears, and tremblings of distress,
And cheeks all pale, which but an hour ago
Blushed at the praise of their own loveliness—
And there were sudden partings, such as press
The life from out young hearts, and choking sighs
Which ne'er might be repeated; who could guess
If ever more should meet those mutual eyes,
Since upon night so sweet such awful morn could rise!

XXV

And there was mounting in hot haste—the steed,
The mustering squadron, and the clattering car,
Went pouring forward with impetuous speed,
And swiftly forming in the ranks of war—
And the deep thunder peal on peal afar;
And near, the beat of the alarming drum
Roused up the soldier ere the Morning Star;
While thronged the citizens with terror dumb,
Or whispering, with white lips—"The foe! They come! they
come!"

XXVI

And wild and high the "Cameron's Gathering"[2] rose!
The war-note of Lochiel, which Albyn's[3] hills
Have heard, and heard, too, have her Saxon foes:—
How in the noon of night that pibroch[4] thrills,
Savage and shrill!   But with the breath which fills
Their mountain-pipe, so fill the mountaineers

9. Frederick William, German Duke of Brunswick, who fell at Quatre-bras.
1. The Duke of Brunswick's father, Charles William Ferdinand, a passionate opponent of Napoleon, had died in 1806 at the battle of Auerbach.
2. Battle song of the Camerons, a Scottish clan.
3. The ancient home ground of the Clan Cameron. *Albyn* is another name for Scotland (cf. *Albion* for England).
4. Any of a number of military tunes and cadences for bagpipe.

With the fierce native daring which instils
The stirring memory of a thousand years,
And Evan's—Donald's[5] fame rings in each clansman's ears!

XXVII

And Ardennes[6] waves above them her green leaves,
Dewy with Nature's tear drops, as they pass—
Grieving, if aught inanimate e'er grieves,
Over the unreturning brave,—alas!
Ere evening to be trodden like the grass
Which now beneath them, but above shall grow
In its next verdure, when this fiery mass
Of living Valour, rolling on the foe
And burning with high Hope, shall moulder cold and low.

XXVIII

Last noon beheld them full of lusty life;—
Last eve in Beauty's circle proudly gay;
The Midnight brought the signal-sound of strife,
The Morn the marshalling in arms,—the Day
Battle's magnificently-stern array!
The thunder-clouds close o'er it, which when rent
The earth is covered thick with other clay
Which her own clay shall cover, heaped and pent,
Rider and horse,—friend,—foe,—in one red burial blent!

XXIX

Their praise is hymned by loftier harps than mine;
Yet one[7] I would select from that proud throng,
Partly because they blend me with his line,
And partly that I did his Sire some wrong,
And partly that bright names will hallow song;
And his was of the bravest, and when showered
The death-bolts deadliest the thinned files along,
Even where the thickest of War's tempest lowered,
They reached no nobler breast than thine, young, gallant Howard!

XXX

There have been tears and breaking hearts for thee,
And mine were nothing, had I such to give;
But when I stood beneath the fresh green tree,
Which living waves where thou didst cease to live,
And saw around me the wide field revive
With fruits and fertile promise, and the Spring
Come forth her work of gladness to contrive,
With all her reckless birds upon the wing,
I turned from all she brought to those she could not bring.

XXXI

I turned to thee, to thousands, of whom each

---

5. Two heroes of the Clan Cameron.
Sir Evan Cameron (1629–1719) had
fought against Cromwell, and Donald
Cameron (1695–1748), Evan's grandson,
had supported James Stuart, the "Young
Pretender," in his claim to the British
throne.
6. The forest in Belgium and northern
France.
7. Frederick Howard, son of the Earl of
Carlisle. Byron had attacked Howard in
English Bards and Scotch Reviewers.

And one as all a ghastly gap did make
  In his own kind and kindred, whom to teach
  Forgetfulness were mercy for their sake;
  The Archangel's trump,[8] not Glory's, must awake
  Those whom they thirst for; though the sound of Fame
  May for a moment soothe, it cannot slake
  The fever of vain longing, and the name
So honoured but assumes a stronger, bitterer claim.

                  XXXII

They mourn, but smile at length—and, smiling, mourn
  The tree will wither long before it fall;
  The hull drives on, though mast and sail be torn;
  The roof-tree sinks, but moulders on the hall
  In massy hoariness; the ruined wall
  Stands when its wind-worn battlements are gone;
  The bars survive the captive they enthral;
  The day drags through though storms keep out the sun;
And thus the heart will break, yet brokenly live on:

                  XXXIII

Even as a broken Mirror, which the glass
  In every fragment multiplies—and makes
  A thousand images of one that was,
  The same—and still the more, the more it breaks;
  And thus the heart will do which not forsakes,
  Living in shattered guise; and still, and cold,
  And bloodless, with its sleepless sorrow aches,
  Yet withers on till all without is old,
Showing no visible sign, for such things are untold.

                  XXXIV

There is a very life in our despair,
  Vitality of poison,—a quick root
  Which feeds these deadly branches; for it were
  As nothing did we die; but Life will suit
  Itself to Sorrow's most detested fruit,
  Like to the apples on the Dead Sea's shore,[9]
  All ashes to the taste: Did man compute
  Existence by enjoyment, and count o'er
Such hours 'gainst years of life,—say, would he name threescore?

                  XXXV

The Psalmist[1] numbered out the years of man:
  They are enough; and if thy tale be *true*,
  Thou, who didst grudge him even that fleeting span,
  More than enough, thou fatal Waterloo!
  Millions of tongues record thee, and anew
  Their children's lips shall echo them, and say—
  "Here, where the sword united nations drew,

8. The trumpet which the Archangel shall sound at the end of the world, according to *Revelations*, to signal the resurrection of the dead.
9. "The (fabled) apples * * * were said to be fair without, and, within, ashes." [*Byron's note.*]
1. King David, traditional author of the Psalms.

Our countrymen were warring on that day!"
And this is much—and all—which will not pass away.

XXXVI

There sunk the greatest, nor the worst of men,[2]
Napoleon Whose Spirit, antithetically mixed,
One moment of the mightiest, and again
On little objects with like firmness fixed;
Extreme in all things! hadst thou been betwixt,
Thy throne had still been thine, or never been;
For Daring made thy rise as fall: thou seek'st
Even now to re-assume the imperial mien,
And shake again the world, the Thunderer of the scene!

XXXVII

Removed Conqueror and Captive of the Earth art thou!
She trembles at thee still, and thy wild name
Was ne'er more bruited in men's minds than now
That thou art nothing, save the jest of Fame,
Who wooed thee once, thy Vassal, and became
The flatterer of thy fierceness—till thou wert
A God unto thyself; nor less the same
To the astounded kingdoms all inert,
Who deemed thee for a time whate'er thou didst assert.

XXXVIII

Oh, more or less than man—in high or low—
Battling with nations, flying from the field;
Now making monarchs' necks thy footstool, now
More than thy meanest soldier taught to yield;
An Empire thou couldst crush, command, rebuild,
can't control himself But govern not thy pettiest passion, nor,
However deeply in men's spirits skilled,
Look through thine own, nor curb the lust of War,
Nor learn that tempted Fate will leave the loftiest Star.

XXXIX

Yet well thy soul hath brooked the turning tide
With that untaught innate philosophy,
Which, be it Wisdom, Coldness, or deep Pride,
Is gall and wormwood to an enemy.
"good loser" When the whole host of hatred stood hard by,
To watch and mock thee shrinking, thou hast smiled
With a sedate and all-enduring eye;—
When Fortune fled her spoiled and favourite child,
He stood unbowed beneath the ills upon him piled.

XL

Sager than in thy fortunes; for in them
Ambition steeled thee on too far to show
That just habitual scorn, which could contemn
Men and their thoughts; 'twas wise to feel, not so
To wear it ever on thy lip and brow,
And spurn the instruments thou wert to use
don't let men know that you hate them

2. The reference is to Napoleon.

Till they were turned unto thine overthrow:
'Tis but a worthless world to win or lose;
So hath it proved to thee, and all such lot who choose.

XLI

If, like a tower upon a headlong rock,
    Thou hadst been made to stand or fall alone,
    Such scorn of man had helped to brave the shock;
    But men's thoughts were the steps which paved thy throne,
    Their admiration thy best weapon shone;
    The part of Philip's son was thine—not then
    (Unless aside thy Purple had been thrown)
    Like stern Diogenes to mock at men:[3]
For sceptred Cynics Earth were far too wide a den.

XLII

But Quiet to quick bosoms is a Hell,
    And *there* hath been thy bane; there is a fire
    And motion of the Soul which will not dwell
    In its own narrow being, but aspire
    Beyond the fitting medium of desire;
    And, but once kindled, quenchless evermore,
    Preys upon high adventure, nor can tire
    Of aught but rest; a fever at the core,
Fatal to him who bears, to all who ever bore.

XLIII

This makes the madmen who have made men mad
    By their contagion; Conquerors and Kings,
    Founders of sects and systems, to whom add
    Sophists, Bards, Statesmen, all unquiet things
    Which stir too strongly the soul's secret springs,
    And are themselves the fools to those they fool;
    Envied, yet how unenviable! what stings
    Are theirs! One breast laid open were a school
Which would unteach Mankind the lust to shine or rule:

XLIV

Their breath is agitation, and their life
    A storm whereon they ride, to sink at last,
    And yet so nursed and bigoted to strife,
    That should their days, surviving perils past,
    Melt to calm twilight, they feel overcast
    With sorrow and supineness, and so die;
    Even as a flame unfed, which runs to waste
    With its own flickering, or a sword laid by,
Which eats into itself, and rusts ingloriously.

XLV

He who ascends to mountain-tops, shall find
    The loftiest peaks most wrapt in clouds and snow;

3. Philip's son was Alexander the Great (356–23 B.C.), conqueror of the ancient world; Diogenes was a Greek philosopher of the fourth century B.C., one of the "Cynic" school who claimed distrust of all human pretensions to honesty or nobility. Alexander is reported to have said that if he had not been a king (hence a wearer of the royal purple), he would have wished to be Diogenes.

He who surpasses or subdues mankind,
Must look down on the hate of those below.
Though high *above* the Sun of Glory glow,
And far *beneath* the Earth and Ocean spread,
Round him are icy rocks, and loudly blow
Contending tempests on his naked head,
And thus reward the toils which to those summits led.

XLVI

Away with these! true Wisdom's world will be
Within its own creation, or in thine,
Maternal Nature! for who teems like thee,
Thus on the banks of thy majestic Rhine?
There Harold gazes on a work divine,
A blending of all beauties; streams and dells,
Fruit, foliage, crag, wood, cornfield, mountain, vine,
And chiefless castles breathing stern farewells
From gray but leafy walls, where Ruin greenly dwells.

XLVII

And there they stand, as stands a lofty mind,
Worn, but unstooping to the baser crowd,
All tenantless, save to the crannying Wind,
Or holding dark communion with the Cloud
There was a day when they were young and proud;
Banners on high, and battles passed below;
But they who fought are in a bloody shroud,
And those which waved are shredless dust ere now,
And the bleak battlements shall bear no future blow.

XLVIII

Beneath these battlements, within those walls,
Power dwelt amidst her passions; in proud state
Each robber chief upheld his arméd halls,
Doing his evil will, nor less elate
Than mightier heroes of a longer date.
What want these outlaws conquerors should have
But History's purchased page to call them great?
A wider space—an ornamented grave?
Their hopes were not less warm, their souls were full as brave.

XLIX

In their baronial feuds and single fields,
What deeds of prowess unrecorded died!
And Love, which lent a blazon to their shields,
With emblems well devised by amorous pride,
Through all the mail of iron hearts would glide;
But still their flame was fierceness, and drew on
Keen contest and destruction near allied,
And many a tower for some fair mischief won,
Saw the discoloured Rhine beneath its ruin run.

L

But Thou, exulting and abounding river!
Making thy waves a blessing as they flow

Through banks whose beauty would endure for ever
Could man but leave thy bright creation so,
Nor its fair promise from the surface mow
With the sharp scythe of conflict,—then to see
Thy valley of sweet waters, were to know
Earth paved like Heaven—and to seem such to me,
Even now what wants thy stream?—that it should Lethe[4] be.

LI

A thousand battles have assailed thy banks,
But these and half their fame have passed away,
And Slaughter heaped on high his weltering ranks:
Their very graves are gone, and what are they?
Thy tide washed down the blood of yesterday,
And all was stainless, and on thy clear stream
Glassed, with its dancing light, the sunny ray;
But o'er the blackened Memory's blighting dream
Thy waves would vainly roll, all sweeping as they seem.

LII

Thus Harold inly said, and passed along,
Yet not insensible to all which here
Awoke the jocund birds to early song
In glens which might have made even exile dear:
Though on his brow were graven lines austere,
And tranquil sternness, which had ta'en the place
Of feelings fiercer far but less severe—
Joy was not always absent from his face,
But o'er it in such scenes would steal with transient trace.

LIII

Nor was all Love shut from him, though his days
Of Passion had consumed themselves to dust.
It is in vain that we would coldly gaze
On such as smile upon us; the heart must
Leap kindly back to kindness, though Disgust
Hath weaned it from all wordlings: thus he felt,
For there was soft Remembrance, and sweet Trust
In one fond breast,[5] to which his own would melt,
And in its tenderer hour on that his bosom dwelt.

LIV

And he had learned to love,—I know not why,
For this in such as him seems strange of mood,—
The helpless looks of blooming Infancy,
Even in its earliest nurture; what subdued,
To change like this, a mind so far imbued
With scorn of man, it little boots to know;
But thus it was; and though in solitude
Small power the nipped affections have to grow,
In him this glowed when all beside had ceased to glow.

LV

And there was one soft breast, as hath been said,

---

4. The river of forgetfulness in the classical underworld.

5. Augusta, the poet's half sister.

Which unto his was bound by stronger ties
Than the church links withal; and—though unwed,
That love was pure—and, far above disguise,
Had stood the test of mortal enmities
Still undivided, and cemented more
By peril, dreaded most in female eyes;
But this was firm, and from a foreign shore
Well to that heart might his these absent greetings pour!

1

The castled Crag of Drachenfels[6]
Frowns o'er the wide and winding Rhine,
Whose breast of waters broadly swells
Between the banks which bear the vine,
And hills all rich with blossomed trees,
And fields which promise corn and wine,
And scattered cities crowning these,
Whose far white walls along them shine,
Have strewed a scene, which I should see
With double joy wert *thou* with me.

2

And peasant girls, with deep blue eyes,
And hands which offer early flowers,
Walk smiling o'er this Paradise;
Above, the frequent feudal towers
Through green leaves lift their walls of gray;
And many a rock which steeply lowers,
And noble arch in proud decay,
Look o'er this vale of vintage-bowers;
But one thing want these banks of Rhine,—
Thy gentle hand to clasp in mine!

3

I send the lilies given to me—
Though long before thy hand they touch,
I know that they must withered be,
But yet reject them not as such;
For I have cherished them as dear,
Because they yet may meet thine eye,
And guide thy soul to mine even here,
When thou behold'st them drooping nigh,
And know'st them gathered by the Rhine,
And offered from my heart to thine!

4

The river nobly foams and flows—
The charm of this enchanted ground,
And all its thousand turns disclose
Some fresher beauty's varying round:
The haughtiest breast its wish might bound
Through life to dwell delighted here;
Nor could on earth a spot be found

6. Ancient castle on the Rhine.

To Nature and to me so dear—
Could thy dear eyes in following mine
Still sweeten more these banks of Rhine!

LVI

By Coblentz,[7] on a rise of gentle ground,
There is a small and simple Pyramid,
Crowning the summit of the verdant mound;
Beneath its base are Heroes' ashes hid—
Our enemy's—but let not that forbid
Honour to Marceau![8] o'er whose early tomb
Tears, big tears, gushed from the rough soldier's lid,
Lamenting and yet envying such a doom,
Falling for France, whose rights he battled to resume.

celebrates Heroes on Earth

LVII

Brief, brave, and glorious was his young career,—
His mourners were two hosts, his friends and foes;
And fitly may the stranger lingering here
Pray for his gallant Spirit's bright repose;—
For he was Freedom's Champion, one of those,
The few in number, who had not o'erstept
The charter to chastise which she bestows
On such as wield her weapons; he had kept
The whiteness of his soul—and thus men o'er him wept.

hero

LVIII

Here Ehrenbreitstein,[9] with her shattered wall
Black with the miner's blast, upon her height
Yet shows of what she was, when shell and ball
Rebounding idly on her strength did light:—
A Tower of Victory! from whence the flight
Of baffled foes was watched along the plain:
But Peace destroyed what War could never blight,
And laid those proud roofs bare to Summer's rain—
On which the iron shower for years had poured in vain.

LIX

Adieu to thee, fair Rhine! How long delighted
The stranger fain would linger on his way!
Thine is a scene alike where souls united (in death)
Or lonely Contemplation thus might stray;
And could the ceaseless vultures cease to prey
On self-condemning bosoms, it were here,
Where Nature, nor too sombre nor too gay,
Wild but not rude, awful yet not austere,
Is to the mellow Earth as Autumn to the year.

Harold's

Prometheus & Prisoner

LX

Adieu to thee again! a vain adieu!
There can be no farewell to scene like thine;

---

7. German city on the Rhine.
8. French general killed in 1796 defending revolutionary France against the reactionary forces of the European monarchs.

9. Rhine fortress, reputedly one of the strongest in Europe, captured by the French in 1799 and blown up by them in 1801. The French captured it by literally starving the defenders out.

The mind is coloured by thy every hue;
And if reluctantly the eyes resign
Their cherished gaze upon thee, lovely Rhine!
'Tis with the thankful glance of parting praise;
More mighty spots may rise—more glaring shine,
But none unite in one attaching maze
The brilliant, fair, and soft,—the glories of old days.

LXI

The negligently grand, the fruitful bloom
Of coming ripeness, the white city's sheen,
The rolling stream, the precipice's gloom,
The forest's growth, and Gothic walls between,—
The wild rocks shaped, as they had turrets been,
In mockery of man's art; and these withal
A race of faces happy as the scene,
Whose fertile bounties here extend to all, (of trees)
Still springing o'er thy banks, though Empires near them fall.

LXII

But these recede. Above me are the Alps,
The Palaces of Nature, whose vast walls
Have pinnacled in clouds their snowy scalps,
And throned Eternity in icy halls
Of cold Sublimity, where forms and falls
The Avalanche—the thunderbolt of snow!
All that expands the spirit, yet appals,
Gather around these summits, as to show
How Earth may pierce to Heaven, yet leave vain man below.

LXIII

But ere these matchless heights I dare to scan,
There is a spot should not be passed in vain,—
Morat![1] the proud, the patriot field! where man
May gaze on ghastly trophies of the slain,
Nor blush for those who conquered on that plain;
Here Burgundy bequeathed his tombless host,
A bony heap, through ages to remain,
Themselves their monument; the Stygian[2] coast
Unsepulchred they roamed, and shrieked each wandering ghost.

LXIV

While Waterloo with Cannæ's[3] carnage vies,
Morat and Marathon[4] twin names shall stand;
They were true Glory's stainless victories,
Won by the unambitious heart and hand
Of a proud, brotherly, and civic band,

1. Site where in 1476 Swiss patriots defeated a much larger invading army from Burgundy. The Burgundian dead were left unburied, and even in 1816 a pile of their bones remained at the scene —some of which Byron carried off as souvenirs.

2. Beside the River Styx in the classical underworld.
3. Site of a bloody battle between Rome and Carthage, 216 B.C.
4. Site of the famous battle in 490 B.C. where the Greeks defeated a much larger invading army from Persia.

All unbought champions in no princely cause
Of vice-entailed Corruption; they no land
Doomed to bewail the blasphemy of laws
Making Kings' rights divine, by some Draconic[5] clause.

LXV

By a lone wall a lonelier column rears
A gray and grief-worn aspect of old days;
'Tis the last remnant of the wreck of years,
And looks as with the wild-bewildered gaze
Of one to stone converted by amaze,
Yet still with consciousness; and there it stands
Making a marvel that it not decays,
When the coeval[6] pride of human hands,
Levelled Aventicum, hath strewed her subject lands.[7]

LXVI

And there—oh! sweet and sacred be the name!—
Julia[8]—the daughter—the devoted—gave
Her youth to Heaven; her heart, beneath a claim
Nearest to Heaven's, broke o'er a father's grave.
Justice is sworn 'gainst tears, and hers would crave
The life she lived in—but the Judge was just—
And then she died on him she could not save.
Their tomb was simple, and without a bust,
And held within their urn one mind—one heart—one dust.

LXVII

But these are deeds which should not pass away,
And names that must not wither, though the Earth
Forgets her empires with a just decay,
The enslavers and the enslaved—their death and birth;
The high, the mountain-majesty of Worth
Should be—and shall, survivor of its woe,
And from its immortality, look forth
In the sun's face, like yonder Alpine snow,
Imperishably pure beyond all things below.

LXVIII

Lake Leman[9] woos me with its crystal face,
The mirror where the stars and mountains view
The stillness of their aspect in each trace
Its clear depth yields of their far height and hue:
There is too much of Man here, to look through
With a fit mind the might which I behold;
But soon in me shall Loneliness renew
Thoughts hid, but not less cherished than of old,
Ere mingling with the herd had penned me in their fold.

5. Draco, an Athenian statesman of the late seventh century B.C. was famous for the harshness of his laws.
6. Built at the same time.
7. The column at which Harold/Byron gazes has survived the other buildings of the Roman city of Adventicum, once the Roman capital of Switzerland.
8. Julia Alpinula, a young priestess, died of grief soon after her father was executed in 69 A.D. for leading a rebellion against the emperor.
9. Lake Geneva.

LXIX

To fly from, need not be to hate, mankind:
  All are not fit with them to stir and toil,
  Nor is it discontent to keep the mind
  Deep in its fountain, lest it overboil
  In the hot throng, where we become the spoil
  Of our infection, till too late and long
  We may deplore and struggle with the coil,[1]
  In wretched interchange of wrong for wrong
Midst a contentious world, striving where none are strong.

LXX

There, in a moment, we may plunge our years
  In fatal penitence, and in the blight
  Of our own Soul turn all our blood to tears,
  And colour things to come with hues of Night;
  The race of life becomes a hopeless flight
  To those that walk in darkness: on the sea
  The boldest steer but where their ports invite—
  But there are wanderers o'er Eternity
Whose bark drives on and on, and anchored ne'er shall be.

LXXI

Is it not better, then, to be alone,
  And love Earth only for its earthly sake?
  By the blue rushing of the arrowy Rhone,
  Or the pure bosom of its nursing Lake,
  Which feeds it as a mother who doth make
  A fair but froward infant her own care,
  Kissing its cries away as these awake;—
  Is it not better thus our lives to wear,
Than join the crushing crowd, doomed to inflict or bear?

LXXII

I live not in myself, but I become
  Portion of that around me; and to me
  High mountains are a feeling, but the hum
  Of human cities torture: I can see
  Nothing to loathe in Nature, save to be
  A link reluctant in a fleshly chain,
  Classed among creatures, when the soul can flee,
  And with the sky—the peak—the heaving plain
Of Ocean, or the stars, mingle—and not in vain.

LXXIII

And thus I am absorbed, and this is life:—
  I look upon the peopled desert past,
  As on a place of agony and strife,
  Where, for some sin, to Sorrow I was cast,
  To act and suffer, but remount at last
  With a fresh pinion; which I feel to spring,
  Though young, yet waxing vigorous as the Blast

1. The mortal body.

Which it would cope with, on delighted wing,
Spurning the clay-cold bonds which round our being cling.

LXXIV

And when, at length, the mind shall be all free
    From what it hates in this degraded form,
    Reft of its carnal life, save what shall be
    Existent happier in the fly and worm,—
    When Elements to Elements conform,
    And dust is as it should be, shall I not
    Feel all I see less dazzling but more warm?
    The bodiless thought? the Spirit of each spot?
Of which, even now, I share at times the immortal lot?

[margin note: Shellian: abstruse & ethereal Byron does not want to throw of mortal coil. It is Byron exploring]

LXXV

Are not the mountains, waves, and skies, a part
    Of me and of my Soul, as I of them?
    Is not the love of these deep in my heart
    With a pure passion? should I not contemn
    All objects, if compared with these? and stem
    A tide of suffering, rather than forego
    Such feelings for the hard and worldly phlegm
    Of those whose eyes are only turned below,
Gazing upon the ground, with thoughts which dare not glow?

[margin note: condemn non-soarers?]

LXXVI

But this is not my theme; and I return
    To that which is immediate, and require
    Those who find contemplation in the urn,
    To look on One,[2] whose dust was once all fire,—
    A native of the land where I respire
    The clear air for a while—a passing guest,
    Where he became a being,—whose desire
    Was to be glorious; 'twas a foolish quest,
The which to gain and keep, he sacrificed all rest.

LXXVII

Here the self-torturing sophist, wild Rousseau,
    The apostle of Affliction, he who threw
    Enchantment over Passion, and from Woe
    Wrung overwhelming eloquence, first drew
    The breath which made him wretched; yet he knew
    How to make Madness beautiful, and cast
    O'er erring deeds and thoughts, a heavenly hue
    Of words, like sunbeams, dazzling as they past
The eyes, which o'er them shed tears feelingly and fast.

LXXVIII

His love was Passion's essence—as a tree
    On fire by lightning; with ethereal flame
    Kindled he was, and blasted; for to be
    Thus, and enamoured, were in him the same.

2. Jean-Jacques Rousseau (1712–78), the great French philosopher and novelist who was one of the first and most pow- erful of Romantic thinkers; Rousseau was born at Geneva.

But his was not the love of living dame,
Nor of the dead who rise upon our dreams,
But of ideal Beauty, which became
In him existence, and o'erflowing teems
Along his burning page, distempered though it seems.

LXXIX

This breathed itself to life in Julie,[3] *this*
Invested her with all that's wild and sweet;
This hallowed, too, the memorable kiss[4]
Which every morn his fevered lip would greet,
From hers, who but with friendship his would meet;
But to that gentle touch, through brain and breast
Flashed the thrilled Spirit's love-devouring heat;
In that absorbing sigh perchance more blest
Than vulgar minds may be with all they seek possest.

LXXX

His life was one long war with self-sought foes,
Or friends by him self-banished; for his mind
Had grown Suspicion's sanctuary, and chose,
For its own cruel sacrifice, the kind,
'Gainst whom he raged with fury strange and blind.
But he was phrensied,—wherefore, who may know?
Since cause might be which Skill could never find;
But he was phrensied by disease or woe,
To that worst pitch of all, which wears a reasoning show.

LXXXI

For then he was inspired, and from him came,
As from the Pythian's mystic cave[5] of yore,
Those oracles which set the world in flame,[6]
Nor cease to burn till kingdoms were no more:
Did he not this for France? which lay before
Bowed to the inborn tyranny of years?
Broken and trembling to the yoke she bore,
Till by the voice of him and his compeers,
Roused up to too much wrath which follows o'ergrown fears?

LXXXII

They made themselves a fearful monument!
The wreck of old opinions—things which grew,
Breathed from the birth of Time: the veil they rent,
And what behind it lay, all earth shall view.
But good with ill they also overthrew,
Leaving but ruins, wherewith to rebuild
Upon the same foundation, and renew

3. The passionate heroine of Rousseau's
novel, *La Nouvelle Héloise*.
4. A reference to Rousseau's own unre-
quited love for the Comtesse d'Houditot,
narrated in his *Confessions*.
5. The shrine of Apollo at Delphi ("Pythios" is an older name for Delphi); the
priestesses of Delphi were renowned for
their gift of prophecy in the ancient
world.
6. Rousseau's writings were—and still
are—regarded as an important part of
the intellectual background of the
French Revolution.

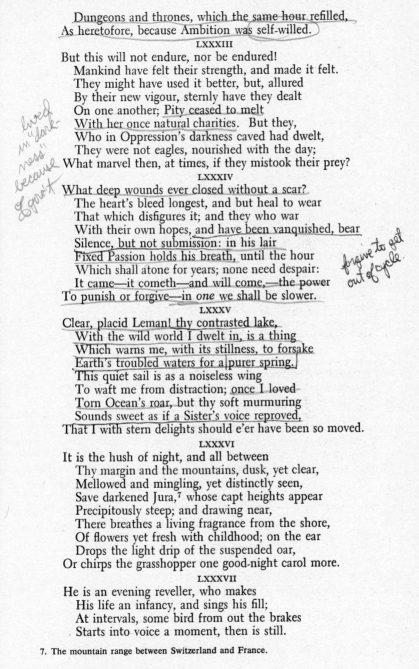

Dungeons and thrones, which the same hour refilled,
As heretofore, because Ambition was self-willed.

LXXXIII

But this will not endure, nor be endured!
　　Mankind have felt their strength, and made it felt.
　　They might have used it better, but, allured
　　By their new vigour, sternly have they dealt
　　On one another; Pity ceased to melt
　　With her once natural charities. But they,
　　Who in Oppression's darkness caved had dwelt,
　　They were not eagles, nourished with the day;
What marvel then, at times, if they mistook their prey?

lived "in darkness" because of spirit

LXXXIV

What deep wounds ever closed without a scar?
　　The heart's bleed longest, and but heal to wear
　　That which disfigures it; and they who war
　　With their own hopes, and have been vanquished, bear
　　Silence, but not submission: in his lair
　　Fixed Passion holds his breath, until the hour
　　Which shall atone for years; none need despair:
　　It came—it cometh—and will come,—the power
To punish or forgive—in *one* we shall be slower.

forgive to get out of cycle.

LXXXV

Clear, placid Leman! thy contrasted lake,
　　With the wild world I dwelt in, is a thing
　　Which warns me, with its stillness, to forsake
　　Earth's troubled waters for a purer spring.
　　This quiet sail is as a noiseless wing
　　To waft me from distraction; once I loved
　　Torn Ocean's roar, but thy soft murmuring
　　Sounds sweet as if a Sister's voice reproved,
That I with stern delights should e'er have been so moved.

LXXXVI

It is the hush of night, and all between
　　Thy margin and the mountains, dusk, yet clear,
　　Mellowed and mingling, yet distinctly seen,
　　Save darkened Jura,[7] whose capt heights appear
　　Precipitously steep; and drawing near,
　　There breathes a living fragrance from the shore,
　　Of flowers yet fresh with childhood; on the ear
　　Drops the light drip of the suspended oar,
Or chirps the grasshopper one good-night carol more.

LXXXVII

He is an evening reveller, who makes
　　His life an infancy, and sings his fill;
　　At intervals, some bird from out the brakes
　　Starts into voice a moment, then is still.

7. The mountain range between Switzerland and France.

There seems a floating whisper on the hill,
But that is fancy—for the Starlight dews
All silently their tears of Love instil,
Weeping themselves away, till they infuse
Deep into Nature's breast the spirit of her hues.

LXXXVIII

Ye Stars! which are the poetry of Heaven!
If in your bright leaves we would read the fate
Of men and empires,—'tis to be forgiven,
That in our aspirations to be great,
Our destinies o'erleap their mortal state,
And claim a kindred with you; for ye are
A Beauty and a Mystery, and create
In us such love and reverence from afar,
That Fortune,—Fame,—Power,—Life, have named themselves
        a Star.

LXXXIX

holy feeling

All Heaven and Earth are still—though not in sleep,
But breathless, as we grow when feeling most;
And silent, as we stand in thoughts too deep:—
All Heaven and Earth are still: From the high host
Of stars, to the lulled lake and mountain-coast,
All is concentered in a life intense,
Where not a beam, nor air, nor leaf is lost,
But hath a part of Being, and a sense
Of that which is of all Creator and Defence.

XC

out of critical point

Then stirs the feeling infinite, so felt
In solitude, where we are *least* alone;
A truth, which through our being then doth melt,
And purifies from self: it is a tone,
The soul and source of Music, which makes known
Eternal harmony, and sheds a charm
Like to the fabled Cytherea's zone,[8]
Binding all things with beauty;—'twould disarm
The spectre Death, had he substantial power to harm.

XCI

Not vainly did the early Persian[9] make
His altar the high places, and the peak
Of earth-o'ergazing mountains, and thus take
A fit and unwalled temple, there to seek
The Spirit, in whose honour shrines are weak
Upreared of human hands.   Come, and compare
Columns and idol-dwellings—Goth or Greek—
With Nature's realms of worship, earth and air— *infinite worship*
Nor fix on fond abodes to circumscribe thy prayer!

8. The belt of Venus (Cytherea), goddess of love, which endowed its wearer
with the power of instailling love in others.

9. Byron refers to the ziggurats—artificial mountains—used by the Babylonians
as places of worship.

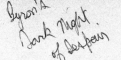

XCII

The sky is changed!—and such a change! Oh Night,
  And Storm, and Darkness, ye are wondrous strong,
  Yet lovely in your strength, as is the light
  Of a dark eye in Woman! Far along,
  From peak to peak, the rattling crags among
  Leaps the live thunder! Not from one lone cloud,
  But every mountain now hath found a tongue,
  And Jura answers, through her misty shroud,
Back to the joyous Alps, who call to her aloud!

XCIII

And this is the Night:—Most glorious Night!
  Thou wert not sent for slumber! let me be
  A sharer in thy fierce and far delight,—
  A portion[1] of the tempest and of thee!
  How the lit lake shines, a phosphoric sea,
  And the big rain comes dancing to the earth!
  And now again 'tis black,—and now, the glee
  Of the loud hills shakes with its mountain-mirth,
As if they did rejoice o'er a young Earthquake's birth.

XCIV

Now, where the swift Rhone cleaves his way between
  Heights which appear as lovers who have parted
  In hate, whose mining depths so intervene,
  That they can meet no more, though broken-hearted:
  Though in their souls, which thus each other thwarted,
  Love was the very root of the fond rage
  Which blighted their life's bloom, and then departed;—
  Itself expired, but leaving them an age
Of years all winters,—war within themselves to wage:

XCV

Now, where the quick Rhone thus hath cleft his way,
  The mightiest of the storms hath ta'en his stand:
  For here, not one, but many, make their play,
  And fling their thunder-bolts from hand to hand,
  Flashing and cast around: of all the band,
  The brightest through these parted hills hath forked
  His lightnings,—as if he did understand,
  That in such gaps as Desolation worked,
There the hot shaft should blast whatever therein lurked.

XCVI

Sky—Mountains—River—Winds—Lake—Lightnings! ye!
  With night, and clouds, and thunder—and a Soul
  To make these felt and feeling, well may be
  Things that have made me watchful; the far roll
  Of your departing voices, is the knoll[2]

---

1. Cf. Shelley's 1819 "Ode to the West Wind," line 61: "Be thou me, impetuous one!"

2. Mistake for "knell," the tolling sound of a bell.

Of what in me is sleepless,—if I rest.
But where of ye, O Tempests! is the goal?
Are ye like those within the human breast?
Or do ye find, at length, like eagles, some high nest?

XCVII

Could I embody and unbosom now
That which is most within me,—could I wreak
My thoughts upon expression, and thus throw
Soul—heart—mind—passions—feelings—strong or weak—
All that I would have sought, and all I seek,
Bear, know, feel—and yet breathe—into *one* word,
And that one word were Lightning, I would speak;
But as it is, I live and die unheard,
With a most voiceless thought, sheathing it as a sword.

XCVIII

The Morn is up again, the dewy Morn,
With breath all incense, and with cheek all bloom—
Laughing the clouds away with playful scorn,
And living as if earth contained no tomb,—
And glowing into day: we may resume
The march of our existence: and thus I,
Still on thy shores, fair Leman! may find room
And food for meditation, nor pass by
Much, that may give us pause, if pondered fittingly.

XCIX

Clarens! sweet Clarens[3] birthplace of deep Love!
Thine air is the young breath of passionate Thought;
Thy trees take root in Love; the snows above,
The very Glaciers have his colours caught,
And Sun-set into rose-hues sees them wrought
By rays which sleep there lovingly: the rocks,
The permanent crags, tell here of Love, who sought
In them a refuge from the worldly shocks,
Which stir and sting the Soul with Hope that woos, then mocks.

C

Clarens! by heavenly feet thy paths are trod,—
Undying Love's, who here ascends a throne
To which the steps are mountains; where the God
Is a pervading Life and Light,—so shown
Not on those summits solely, nor alone
In the still cave and forest; o'er the flower
His eye is sparkling, and his breath hath blown,
His soft and summer breath, whose tender power
Passes the strength of storms in their most desolate hour.

CI

All things are here of *Him*; from the black pines,
Which are his shade on high, and the loud roar
Of torrents, where he listeneth, to the vines

---

3. Town on Lake Geneva, where the action of *La Nouvelle Héloise* takes place.

Which slope his green path downward to the shore,
Where the bowed Waters meet him, and adore,
Kissing his feet with murmurs; and the Wood,
The covert of old trees, with trunks all hoar,
But light leaves, young as joy, stands where it stood,
Offering to him, and his, a populous solitude.

CII

A populous solitude of bees and birds,
And fairy-formed and many-coloured things,
Who worship him with notes more sweet than words,
And innocently open their glad wings,
Fearless and full of life: the gush of springs,
And fall of lofty fountains, and the bend
Of stirring branches, and the bud which brings
The swiftest thought of Beauty, here extend
Mingling—and made by Love—unto one mighty end.

CIII

He who hath loved not, here would learn that lore,
And make his heart a spirit; he who knows
That tender mystery, will love the more;
For this is Love's recess, where vain men's woes,
And the world's waste, have driven him far from those,
For 'tis his nature to advance or die;
He stands not still, but or decays, or grows
Into a boundless blessing, which may vie
With the immortal lights, in its eternity!

CIV

'Twas not for fiction chose Rousseau this spot,
Peopling it with affections; but he found
It was the scene which Passion must allot
To the Mind's purified beings; 'twas the ground
Where early Love his Psyche's[4] zone unbound,
And hallowed it with loveliness: 'tis lone,
And wonderful, and deep, and hath a sound,
And sense, and sight of sweetness; here the Rhone
Hath spread himself a couch, the Alps have reared a throne.

CV

Lausanne! and Ferney![5] ye have been the abodes
Of Names which unto you bequeathed a name;
Mortals, who sought and found, by dangerous roads,
A path to perpetuity of Fame:
They were gigantic minds, and their steep aim
Was, Titan-like, on daring doubts to pile
Thoughts which should call down thunder, and the flame

4. Greek name for the soul. In the myth of Cupid and Psyche (Love and the Soul), Psyche, a young girl, was beloved of Cupid, the god of love, who "unbound her zone" or undressed her, discovering her naked beauty.
5. Lausanne was the French home of Edward Gibbon (1737–94), author of *The Decline and Fall of the Roman Empire*, one of the greatest English historians and skeptics. Ferney was the home of Voltaire—François Marie Arouet (1694–1778)—the brilliant French satirist and rationalist.

Of Heaven again assailed—if Heaven, the while,
On man and man's research could deign do more than smile.

CVI

The one[6] was fire and fickleness, a child
    Most mutable in wishes, but in mind
    A wit as various,—gay, grave, sage, or wild,—
    Historian, bard, philosopher, combined;
    He multiplied himself among mankind,
    The Proteus[7] of their talents: But his own
    Breathed most in ridicule,—which, as the wind,
    Blew where it listed, laying all things prone,—
Now to o'erthrow a fool, and now to shake a throne.

CVII

The other,[8] deep and slow, exhausting thought,
    And hiving wisdom with each studious year,
    In meditation dwelt—with learning wrought,
    And shaped his weapon with an edge severe,
    Sapping a solemn creed[9] with solemn sneer;
    The lord of irony,—that master-spell,
    Which stung his foes to wrath, which grew from fear
    And doomed him to the zealot's ready Hell,
Which answers to all doubts so eloquently well.

CVIII

Yet, peace be with their ashes,—for by them,
    If merited, the penalty is paid;
    It is not ours to judge,—far less condemn;
    The hour must come when such things shall be made
    Known unto all,—or hope and dread allayed
    By slumber, on one pillow, in the dust,
    Which, thus much we are sure, must lie decayed;
    And when it shall revive, as is our trust,
'Twill be to be forgiven—or suffer what is just.

CIX

But let me quit Man's works, again to read
    His Maker's, spread around me, and suspend
    This page, which from my reveries I feed,
    Until it seems prolonging without end.
    The clouds above me to the white Alps tend,
    And I must pierce them, and survey whate'er
    May be permitted, as my steps I bend
    To their most great and growing region, where
The earth to her embrace compels the powers of air.

CX

Italia too! Italia! looking on thee,
    Full flashes on the Soul the light of ages,

---

6. Voltaire.
7. The old man of the sea in Greek mythology, capable of changing his shape at will; thus our word "protean" to describe a multifaceted, versatile intelligence.
8. Gibbon.
9. Christianity—which Gibbon, like Voltaire, held in contempt as a relic of superstition.

Since the fierce Carthaginian[1] almost won thee,
To the last halo of the Chiefs and Sages
Who glorify thy consecrated pages;
Thou wert the throne and grave of empires; still,
The fount at which the panting Mind assuages
Her thirst of knowledge, quaffing there her fill,
Flows from the eternal source of Rome's imperial hill.

CXI

Thus far have I proceeded in a theme *Byron, Harold, all*
Renewed with no kind auspices:—to feel
We are not what we have been, and to deem
We are not what we should be,—and to steel
The heart against itself; and to conceal,
With a proud caution, love, or hate, or aught,—
Passion or feeling, purpose, grief, or zeal,—
Which is the tyrant Spirit of our thought,
Is a stern task of soul:—No matter,—it is taught.

CXII

And for these words, thus woven into song,
It may be that they are a harmless wile,—
The colouring of the scenes which fleet along,
Which I would seize, in passing, to beguile
My breast, or that of others, for a while.
Fame is the thirst of youth,—but I am not
So young as to regard men's frown or smile,
As loss or guerdon[2] of a glorious lot;—
I stood and stand alone,—remembered or forgot.

CXIII

I have not loved the World, nor the World me;
I have not flattered its rank breath, nor bowed
To its idolatries a patient knee,
Nor coined my cheek to smiles,—nor cried aloud
In worship of an echo; in the crowd
They could not deem me one of such—I stood
Among them, but not of them—in a shroud
Of thoughts which were not their thoughts, and still could,
Had I not filed[3] my mind, which thus itself subdued.

CXIV

I have not loved the World, nor the World me,—
But let us part fair foes; I do believe,
Though I have found them not, that there may be
Words which are things,—hopes which will not deceive,
And Virtues which are merciful, nor weave
Snares for the failing; I would also deem
O'er others' griefs that some sincerely grieve—
That two, or one, are almost what they seem,—
That Goodness is no name—and Happiness no dream.

there is some good

1. Hannibal (247–183 B.C.), Rome's most   2. Prize.
dangerous adversary in the Punic Wars   3. Defiled.
with Carthage.

CXV

My daughter! with thy name this song begun!
  My daughter! with thy name thus much shall end!—
  I see thee not—I hear thee not—but none
  Can be so wrapt in thee; Thou art the Friend
  To whom the shadows of far years extend:
  Albeit my brow thou never should'st behold,
  My voice shall with thy future visions blend,
  And reach into thy heart,—when mine is cold,—
A token and a tone, even from thy father's mould.

CXVI

To aid thy mind's development,—to watch
  Thy dawn of little joys,—to sit and see
  Almost thy very growth,—to view thee catch
  Knowledge of objects,—wonders yet to thee!
  To hold thee lightly on a gentle knee,
  And print on thy soft cheek a parent's kiss,—
  This, it should seem, was not reserved for me—
  Yet this was in my nature:—as it is,
I know not what is there, yet something like to this.

CXVII

Yet, though dull Hate as duty should be taught,
  I know that thou wilt love me: though my name
  Should be shut from thee, as a spell still fraught
  With desolation, and a broken claim:
  Though the grave closed between us,—'twere the same,
  I know that thou wilt love me—though to drain
  My blood from out thy being were an aim,
  And an attainment,—all would be in vain,—
Still thou would'st love me, still that more than life retain.

CXVIII

The child of Love! though born in bitterness,
  And nurtured in Convulsion! Of thy sire
  These were the elements,—and thine no less.
  As yet such are around thee,—but thy fire
  Shall be more tempered, and thy hope far higher!
  Sweet be thy cradled slumbers! O'er the sea
  And from the mountains where I now respire,
  Fain would I waft such blessing upon thee,
As—with a sigh—I deem thou might'st have been to me!

CANTO THE FOURTH

I

I STOOD in Venice, on the "Bridge of Sighs";[1]
  A Palace and a prison on each hand:
  I saw from out the wave her structures rise

1. A covered bridge between the Palace   Prison of San Marco.
of the Doge or Duke of Venice and the

As from the stroke of the Enchanter's wand:
A thousand Years their cloudy wings expand
Around me, and a dying Glory smiles
O'er the far times, when many a subject land
Looked to the wingéd Lion's[2] marble piles,
Where Venice sate in state, throned on her hundred isles!

II

She looks a sea Cybele,[3] fresh from Ocean,
Rising with her tiara[4] of proud towers
At airy distance, with majestic motion,
A Ruler of the waters and their powers:
And such she was;—her daughters had their dowers
From spoils of nations, and the exhaustless East
Poured in her lap all gems in sparkling showers.
In purple was she robed, and of her feast
Monarchs partook, and deemed their dignity increased.

III

In Venice Tasso's[5] echoes are no more,
And silent rows the songless Gondolier;
Her palaces are crumbling to the shore,
And Music meets not always now the ear:
Those days are gone—but Beauty still is here.
States fall—Arts fade—but Nature doth not die,
Nor yet forget how Venice once was dear,
The pleasant place of all festivity,
The Revel of the earth—the Masque[6] of Italy!

IV

But unto us she hath a spell beyond
Her name in story, and her long array
Of mighty shadows, whose dim forms despond
Above the Dogeless[7] city's vanished sway;
Ours is a trophy which will not decay
With the Rialto; Shylock and the Moor,
And Pierre,[8] can not be swept or worn away—
The keystones of the Arch! though all were o'er,
For us repeopled were the solitary shore.

V

The Beings of the Mind are not of clay:
Essentially immortal, they create
And multiply in us a brighter ray
And more beloved existence: that which Fate

---

2. The emblem of St. Mark the Evangelist, patron saint of Venice.
3. In Greek mythology, the mother of all the gods.
4. Crown.
5. Torquato Tasso (1544–95), Venetian poet and author of the Renaissance epic, *Jerusalem Delivered*. Until the end of the eighteenth century Venetian gondoliers commonly sang alternate stanzas of *Jerusalem Delivered* to each other as their boats passed.
6. A highly ceremonial, elegant court entertainment, common especially during the early seventeenth century.
7. The last Doge of Venice was deposed by Napoleon in 1797. In 1817 Venice was under Austrian rule.
8. A character in Thomas Otway's play, *Venice Preserved* (1682). Shylock is Shakespeare's *Merchant of Venice*, and the Moor is *Othello*.

Prohibits to dull life in this our state
Of mortal bondage, by these Spirits supplied,
First exiles, then replaces what we hate; (english society)
Watering the heart whose early flowers have died,
And with a fresher growth replenishing the void.

VI

Such is the refuge of our youth and age—
The first from Hope, the last from Vacancy;
And this wan feeling peoples many a page—
And, may be, that which grows beneath mine eye:
Yet there are things whose strong reality
Outshines our fairy-land; in shape and hues
More beautiful than our fantastic sky,
And the strange constellations which the Muse
O'er her wild universe is skilful to diffuse:

VII

I saw or dreamed of such,—but let them go,—
They came like Truth—and disappeared like dreams;
And whatsoe'er they were—are now but so:
I could replace them if I would; still teems
My mind with many a form which aptly seems
Such as I sought for, and at moments found;
Let these too go—for waking Reason deems
Such over-weening phantasies unsound,
And other voices speak, and other sights surround.

VIII

I've taught me other tongues—and in strange eyes
Have made me not a stranger; to the mind
Which is itself, no changes bring surprise;
Nor is it harsh to make, nor hard to find
A country with—aye, or without mankind;
Yet was I born where men are proud to be,—
Not without cause; and should I leave behind
The inviolate Island of the sage and free,
And seek me out a home by a remoter sea,

IX

Perhaps I loved it well; and should I lay
My ashes in a soil which is not mine,
My Spirit shall resume it—if we may
Unbodied choose a sanctuary. I twine
My hopes of being remembered in my line
With my land's language: if too fond and far
These aspirations in their scope incline,—
If my Fame should be, as my fortunes are,
Of hasty growth and blight, and dull Oblivion bar

X

My name from out the temple where the dead
Are honoured by the Nations—let it be—
And light the Laurels on a loftier head!

And be the Spartan's epitaph[9] on me—
"Sparta hath many a worthier son than he."
Meantime I seek no sympathies, nor need—
The thorns which I have reaped are of the tree
I planted,—they have torn me,—and I bleed:
I should have known what fruit would spring from such a seed.

* * *

CLXIV

But where is he, the Pilgrim of my Song,[1]
The Being who upheld it through the past?
Methinks he cometh late and tarries long.
He is no more—these breathings are his last—
His wanderings done—his visions ebbing fast,
And he himself as nothing:—if he was
Aught but a phantasy, and could be classed
With forms which live and suffer—let that pass—
His shadow fades away into Destruction's mass,

CLXV

Which gathers shadow—substance—life, and all
That we inherit in its mortal shroud—
And spreads the dim and universal pall
Through which all things grow phantoms; and the cloud
Between us sinks and all which ever glowed,
Till Glory's self is twilight, and displays
A melancholy halo scarce allowed
To hover on the verge of darkness—rays
Sadder than saddest night, for they distract the gaze,

CLXVI

And send us prying into the abyss,
To gather what we shall be when the frame
Shall be resolved to something less than this—
Its wretched essence; and to dream of fame,
And wipe the dust from off the idle name
We never more shall hear,—but never more,
Oh, happier thought! can we be made the same:—
It is enough in sooth that *once* we bore
These fardels[2] of the heart—the heart whose sweat was gore.

CLXVII

Hark! forth from the abyss a voice proceeds,
A long low distant murmur of dread sound,
Such as arises when a nation bleeds
With some deep and immedicable wound;—
Through storm and darkness yawns the rending ground—
The gulf is thick with phantoms, but the Chief

9. This was said by the mother of Brasidas, a Spartan general, to strangers who praised her late son's bravery.
1. By the time of these concluding stanzas of the poem, Harold has come to Rome.
2. Burdens.

Seems royal still, though with her head discrowned,
  And pale, but lovely, with maternal grief—
She clasps a babe, to whom her breast yields no relief.

CLXVIII

Scion[3] of Chiefs and Monarchs, where art thou?
  Fond Hope of many nations, art thou dead?
  Could not the Grave forget thee, and lay low
  Some less majestic, less belovéd head?
  In the sad midnight, while thy heart still bled,
  The mother of a moment, o'er thy boy,
  Death hushed that pang for ever: with thee fled
  The present happiness and promised joy
Which filled the Imperial Isles so full it seemed to cloy.

CLXIX

Peasants bring forth in safety.—Can it be,
  Oh thou that wert so happy, so adored!
  Those who weep not for Kings shall weep for thee,
  And Freedom's heart, grown heavy, cease to hoard
  Her many griefs for ONE; for she had poured
  Her orisons for thee, and o'er thy head
  Beheld her Iris.[4]—Thou, too, lonely Lord,
  And desolate Consort—vainly wert thou wed!
The husband of a year! the father of the dead!

CLXX

Of sackcloth[5] was thy wedding garment made;
  Thy bridal's fruit is ashes: in the dust
  The fair-haired Daughter of the Isles is laid,
  The love of millions! How we did entrust
  Futurity to her! and, though it must
  Darken above our bones, yet fondly deemed
  Our children should obey her child, and blessed
  Her and her hoped-for seed, whose promise seemed
Like stars to shepherd's eyes:—'twas but a meteor beamed.

[handwritten margin note: dreams seemed cancelled but hope remains]

CLXXI

Woe unto us—not her—for she sleeps well:
  The fickle reek of popular breath, the tongue
  Of hollow counsel, the false oracle,
  Which from the birth of Monarchy hath rung
  Its knell in princely ears, till the o'erstung
  Nations have armed in madness—the strange fate
  Which tumbles mightiest sovereigns, and hath flung
  Against their blind omnipotence a weight
Within the opposing scale, which crushes soon or late,—

CLXXII

These might have been her destiny—but no—
  Our hearts deny it: and so young, so fair,
  Good without effort, great without a foe;

---

3. Child or heir. The word here refers to the Princess Charlotte, daughter of George IV, a rebellious but widely loved girl who died in 1817.
4. Rainbow.
5. The cloth of funeral garments.

But now a Bride and Mother—and now *there*!
How many ties did that stern moment tear!
From thy Sire's to his humblest subject's breast
Is linked the electric chain of that despair,
Whose shock was as an Earthquake's, and opprest
The land which loved thee so that none could love thee best.

CLXXIII

Lo, Nemi![6] navelled in the woody hills
So far, that the uprooting Wind which tears
The oak from his foundation, and which spills
The Ocean o'er its boundary, and bears
Its foam against the skies, reluctant spares
The oval mirror of thy glassy lake;
And calm as cherished hate, its surface wears
A deep cold settled aspect nought can shake,
All coiled into itself and round, as sleeps the snake.

CLXXIV

And near, Albano's[7] scarce divided waves
Shine from a sister valley;—and afar
The Tiber[8] winds, and the broad Ocean laves
The Latian[9] coast where sprung the Epic war,
"Arms and the Man,"[1] whose re-ascending star
Rose o'er an empire:—but beneath thy right
Tully[2] reposed from Rome;—and where yon bar
Of girdling mountains intercepts the sight
The Sabine farm[3] was tilled, the weary Bard's delight.

CLXXV

But I forget.—My Pilgrim's shrine is won,
And he and I must part,—so let it be,—
His task and mine alike are nearly done;
Yet once more let us look upon the Sea;
The Midland Ocean[4] breaks on him and me,
And from the Alban Mount we now behold
Our friend of youth, that Ocean, which when we
Beheld it last by Calpe's rock[5] unfold
Those waves, we followed on till the dark Euxine[6] rolled

CLXXVI

Upon the blue Symplegades:[7] long years—
Long, though not very many—since have done
Their work on both; some suffering and some tears
Have left us nearly where we had begun:

6. A village not far from Rome, famous for its ancient grove sacred to the goddess of virginity, Diana.
7. River near Rome. See stanza CLXXV, line 6.
8. The river which runs through Rome.
9. The southeast coast of Italy where—according to the great epic poem of Rome, the *Aeneid* of Vergil (70–19 B.C.)—Aeneas landed after the Trojan War to found the empire of Rome.
1. "*Arma virumque,*" the first words of

the *Aeneid.*
2. Marcus Tullius Cicero (106–43 B.C.), the great orator of the Roman Republic.
3. The Sabine area was north of Rome. Horace (65–8 B.C.), Rome's greatest lyric poet—the "weary Bard"—owned a farm there.
4. The Mediterranean.
5. Gibraltar.
6. The Black Sea.
7. Rocks between the Black Sea and the Bosporus.

Yet not in vain our mortal race hath run—
We have had our reward—and it is here,—
That we can yet feel gladdened by the Sun,
And reap from Earth—Sea—joy almost as dear
As if there were no Man to trouble what is clear.

CLXXVII

Oh! that the Desert were my dwelling-place,
With one fair Spirit[8] for my minister,
That I might all forget the human race,
And, hating no one, love but only her!
Ye elements!—in whose ennobling stir
I feel myself exalted—Can ye not
Accord me such a Being? Do I err
In deeming such inhabit many a spot?
Though with them to converse can rarely be our lot.

CLXXVIII

There is a pleasure in the pathless woods,
There is a rapture on the lonely shore,
There is society, where none intrudes,
By the deep Sea, and Music in its roar:
I love not Man the less, but Nature more,
From these our interviews, in which I steal
From all I may be, or have been before,
To mingle with the Universe, and feel
What I can ne'er express—yet can not all conceal.

CLXXIX

Roll on, thou deep and dark blue Ocean—roll!
Ten thousand fleets sweep over thee in vain;
Man marks the earth with ruin—his control
Stops with the shore;—upon the watery plain
The wrecks are all thy deed, nor doth remain
A shadow of man's ravage, save his own,
When, for a moment, like a drop of rain,
He sinks into thy depths with bubbling groan—
Without a grave—unknelled, uncoffined, and unknown.

CLXXX

His steps are not upon thy paths,—thy fields
Are not a spoil for him,—thou dost arise
And shake him from thee; the vile strength he wields
For Earth's destruction thou dost all despise,
Spurning him from thy bosom to the skies—
And send'st him, shivering in thy playful spray
And howling, to his Gods, where haply lies
His petty hope in some near port or bay,
And dashest him again to Earth:—there let him lay.

CLXXXI

The armaments which thunderstrike the walls
Of rock-built cities, bidding nations quake,

8. Probably Augusta, his half-sister.

And Monarchs tremble in their Capitals,
The oak Leviathans,[9] whose huge ribs make
Their clay creator the vain title take
Of Lord of thee, and Arbiter[1] of War—
These are thy toys, and, as the snowy flake,
They melt into thy yeast of waves, which mar
Alike the Armada's pride or spoils of Trafalgar.[2]

CLXXXII

Thy shores are empires, changed in all save thee—
Assyria—Greece—Rome—Carthage—what are they?
Thy waters washed them power while they were free,
And many a tyrant since; their shores obey
The stranger, slave, or savage; their decay
Has dried up realms to deserts:—not so thou,
Unchangeable save to thy wild waves' play,
Time writes no wrinkle on thine azure brow—
Such as Creation's dawn beheld, thou rollest now.

CLXXXIII

Thou glorious mirror, where the Almighty's form
Glasses itself in tempests; in all time,
Calm or convulsed—in breeze, or gale, or storm—
Icing the Pole, or in the torrid clime
Dark-heaving—boundless, endless, and sublime—
The image of Eternity—the throne
Of the Invisible; even from out thy slime
The monsters of the deep are made—each Zone
Obeys thee—thou goest forth, dread, fathomless, alone.

CLXXXIV

And I have loved thee, Ocean! and my joy
Of youthful sports was on thy breast to be
Borne, like thy bubbles, onward: from a boy
I wantoned with thy breakers—they to me
Were a delight; and if the freshening sea
Made them a terror—'twas a pleasing fear,
For I was as it were a Child of thee,
And trusted to thy billows far and near,
And laid my hand upon thy mane—as I do here.

CLXXXV

My task is done—my song hath ceased—my theme
Has died into an echo; it is fit
The spell should break of this protracted dream.
The torch shall be extinguished which hath lit
My midnight lamp—and what is writ, is writ,—
Would it were worthier! but I am not now
That which I have been—and my visions flit

9. Sea beasts or monsters. Byron is speaking of battleships.
1. Judge.
2. The Spanish Armada attacking England in 1588 and the French navy at the battle of Trafalgar in 1805 were both severely damaged by storms before they could engage in battle.

Less palpably before me—and the glow
Which in my Spirit dwelt is fluttering, faint, and low.
                    CLXXXVI
Farewell! a word that must be, and hath been—
A sound which makes us linger;—yet—farewell!
Ye! who have traced the Pilgrim to the scene
Which is his last—if in your memories dwell
A thought which once was his—if on ye swell
A single recollection—not in vain
He wore his sandal-shoon, and scallop-shell;
Farewell! with *him* alone may rest the pain,
If such there were—with *you*, the Moral of his Strain.[3]

The Giaour[1]

Until recently it was a critical truism that none of Byron's romances
(except *The Prisoner of Chillon*) were worth reading except as historical
curios. This is an odd judgment, since the romances—especially the "Oriental" tales of sin and swashbuckling, *The Giaour* and *The Bride of Abydos*
(1812) and *The Corsair* and *Lara* (1813)—were the poems which more
than any others consolidated Byron's greatest and happiest period of celebrity, 1812–15, and which gave the image of the "Byronic" hero its most
striking articulation. Modern critics of Byron, indeed, have discovered in
these tales a richness and a complexity which redeems them from their long
obscurity, especially in the case of *The Giaour*.

No breath of air to break the wave[2]
That rolls below the Athenian's grave,
That tomb[3] which, gleaming o'er the cliff,

3. At the end of the manuscript Byron
wrote:
Laus Deo! [Praise be to God!]
BYRON.
July 19, 1817.
La Mira, near Venice.
1. Published in 1813. The original edition was less than seven hundred lines,
to which Byron added in subsequent editions. In his advertisement to the poem,
he refers to it as the "disjointed fragments" of a tale he no longer cares to
complete; and indeed the plot is difficult
to follow at a first reading, supporting
the impression of fragmentation which
many critics have echoed with regard to
the tale. But deliberately fragmented narrative is a common and subtle device in
Romantic—and later—writing, used at
various times by Wordsworth, Coleridge,
Shelley, and the Gothic novelists. It is
arguable, then, that the multiple speakers
of *The Giaour* represent a complex and
experimental technique Byron did not
wish to acknowledge, as ill in keeping

with his public pose as a gifted amateur
of poetry.
    Giaour is an Arabic word meaning
"infidel" (i.e., non-Moslem) and shares
the same root as the Hebrew word *goi*
("gentile"): a singularly appropriate
term for the alienated Byronic hero, the
man without country, caste, or cause.
2. The first six lines pose the question
Byron asks himself in this and other
romances: whether heroism is possible in
the modern world. See Francis Jeffrey's
remarks on Byron in the "Images of
Byron" section, and *Don Juan* I: "I
want a hero."
3. "A tomb above the rocks on the promontory, by some supposed to be the sepulchre of Themistocles." [*Byron's
note.*] Themistocles was the fifth century
B.C. leader of Athens during the Persian
wars; in line 5 he is said to have saved
his native land "in vain" since, in the
early nineteenth century, Greece was
under the hegemony of the Ottoman Empire.

First greets the homeward-veering skiff
High o'er the land he saved in vain;
When shall such Hero live again?

———

Fair clime! where every season smiles
Benignant o'er those blesséd isles,
Which, seen from far Colonna's height,[4]
Make glad the heart that hails the sight,   10
And lend to loneliness delight.
There mildly dimpling, Ocean's cheek
Reflects the tints of many a peak
Caught by the laughing tides that lave
These Edens of the eastern wave: 15
And if at times a transient breeze
Break the blue crystal of the seas,
Or sweep one blossom from the trees,
How welcome is each gentle air
That wakes and wafts the odours there!   20
For there the Rose, o'er crag or vale,
Sultana of the Nightingale,[5]

The maid for whom his melody,
His thousand songs are heard on high,
Blooms blushing to her lover's tale: 25
His queen, the garden queen, his Rose,
Unbent by winds, unchilled by snows,
Far from the winters of the west,
By every breeze and season blest,
Returns the sweets by Nature given   30
In softest incense back to Heaven;
And grateful yields that smiling sky
Her fairest hue and fragrant sigh.
And many a summer flower is there,
And many a shade that Love might share,   35
And many a grotto, meant for rest,
That holds the pirate for a guest;
Whose bark in sheltering cove below
Lurks for the passing peaceful prow,
Till the gay mariner's guitar   40
Is heard, and seen the Evening Star;
Then stealing with the muffled oar,
Far shaded by the rocky shore,
Rush the night-prowlers on the prey,
And turn to groans his roundelay.[6]   45

———

4. Colonae was an ancient city of Asia
Minor, northeast across the Aegean Sea
from the Greek mainland. Byron's
speaker gazes at the Greek isles (the
"Edens of the eastern wave," line 15)
from this promontory.

5. Sultana: queen or lover. "The attachment of the nightingale to the rose is a
well-known Persian fable." [*Byron's
note.*]
6. Song, ballad.

Strange—that where Nature loved to trace,
As if for Gods, a dwelling place,
And every charm and grace hath mixed
Within the Paradise she fixed,
There man, enamoured of distress,   50
Should mar it into wilderness,
And trample, brute-like, o'er each flower
That tasks not one laborious hour;
Nor claims the culture of his hand
To bloom along the fairy land,   55
But springs as to preclude his care,
And sweetly woos him—but to spare!
Strange—that where all is Peace beside,
There Passion riots in her pride,
And Lust and Rapine wildly reign   60
To darken o'er the fair domain.
It is as though the Fiends prevailed[7]
Against the Seraphs they assailed,
And, fixed on heavenly thrones, should dwell
The freed inheritors of Hell;   65
So soft the scene, so formed for joy,
So curst the tyrants that destroy!

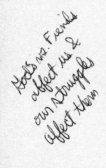

He who hath bent him o'er the dead
Ere the first day of Death is fled,
The first dark day of Nothingness,   70
The last of Danger and Distress,
(Before Decay's effacing fingers
Have swept the lines where Beauty lingers,)
And marked the mild angelic air,
The rapture of Repose that's there,   75
The fixed yet tender traits that streak
The languor of the placid cheek,
And—but for that sad shrouded eye,
 That fires not, wins not, weeps not, now,
 And but for that chill, changeless brow,   80

Where cold Obstruction's apathy
Appals the gazing mourner's heart,
As if to him it could impart
 The doom he dreads, yet dwells upon;
 Yes, but for these and these alone,   85
Some moments, aye, one treacherous hour,
He still might doubt the Tyrant's power;
So fair, so calm, so softly sealed,
The first, last look by Death revealed!
Such is the aspect of this shore;   90

7. Byron imagines man's despoiling of the islands as the triumph of the devils over the angels (seraphs) of God, again striking his theme from *Harold* I: the human destruction of the earthly Paradise.

Freedom

'Tis Greece, but living Greece no more!
So coldly sweet, so deadly fair,
We start, for Soul is wanting there.
Hers is the loveliness in death,
That parts not quite with parting breath;   95
But beauty with that fearful bloom,
That hue which haunts it to the tomb,
Expression's last receding ray,

Freedom

A gilded Halo hovering round decay,
The farewell beam of Feeling past away!   100
Spark of that flame, perchance of heavenly birth,
Which gleams, but warms no more its cherished earth!

    Clime of the unforgotten brave!
Whose land from plain to mountain-cave
Was Freedom's home or Glory's grave!   105
Shrine of the mighty! can it be,
That this is all remains of thee?
Approach, thou craven crouching slave:
Say, is not this Thermopylæ?[8]
These waters blue that round you lave,—   110
    Oh servile offspring of the free—
Pronounce what sea, what shore is this?
The gulf, the rock of Salamis![9]
These scenes, their story not unknown;
Arise, and make again your own;   115
Snatch from the ashes of your Sires
The embers of their former fires;
And he who in the strife expires
Will add to theirs a name of fear
That Tyranny shall quake to hear,   120
And leave his sons a hope, a fame,
They too will rather die than shame:
For Freedom's battle once begun,
Bequeathed by bleeding Sire to Son,
Though baffled oft is ever won.   125
Bear witness, Greece, thy living page!
Attest it many a deathless age!
While Kings, in dusty darkness hid,
Have left a nameless pyramid,
Thy Heroes, though the general doom   130
Hath swept the column from their tomb,
A mightier monument command,
The mountains of their native land!
There points thy Muse to stranger's eye
The graves of those that cannot die!   135
'Twere long to tell, and sad to trace,

recapture Old Glory

fought for freedom

glory not pyramids

8. Scene of the heroic resistance by
Spartan soldiers to a Persian invasion,
480 B.C.

9. Scene of Themistocles' naval victory
over the Persian fleet, 480 B.C.

Each step from Splendour to Disgrace;
Enough—no foreign foe could quell
Thy soul, till from itself it fell;
Yet! Self-abasement paved the way   140
To villain-bonds and despot sway.

What can he tell who treads thy shore?
  No legend of thine olden time,
No theme on which the Muse might soar
High as thine own days of yore,   145
  When man was worthy of thy clime.
The hearts within thy valleys bred,
The fiery souls that might have led
  Thy sons to deeds sublime,
Now crawl from cradle to the Grave,   150
Slaves—nay, the bondsmen of a Slave,
  And callous, save to crime;
Stained with each evil that pollutes
Mankind, where least above the brutes;
Without even savage virtue blest,   155
Without one free or valiant breast,
Still to the neighbouring ports they waft
Proverbial wiles, and ancient craft;
In this the subtle Greek is found,
For this, and this alone, renowned.   160
In vain might Liberty invoke
The spirit to its bondage broke
Or raise the neck that courts the yoke:
No more her sorrows I bewail,
Yet this will be a mournful tale,   165
And they who listen may believe,
Who heard it first had cause to grieve.

Far, dark, along the blue sea glancing,
The shadows of the rocks advancing
Start on the fisher's eye like boat   170
Of island-pirate or Mainote;[1]
And fearful for his light caïque,
He shuns the near but doubtful creek:
Though worn and weary with his toil,
And cumbered with his scaly spoil,   175
Slowly, yet strongly, plies the oar,
Till Port Leone's[2] safer shore

---

1. The Mainotes were inhabitants of the Peloponnesus, the southern section of Greece around Sparta. Anticipating the general Greek revolution against the Turks by fifty years, the Mainotes had begun a bloody and ruthless campaign against their Turkish overlords in 1770, and by 1779 had established their territory as a virtually independent state. Thus the anonymous Turkish fisherman who opens the action of the poem is quite right to be frightened at the possibility of meeting one of the fierce and nationalistic Mainotes.
2. The medieval name of the harbor of Cantharus, southwest of Athens.

Receives him by the lovely light
That best becomes an Eastern night.

———

FISHERMAN:
Who thundering comes on blackest steed,[3]   180
With slackened bit and hoof of speed?
Beneath the clattering iron's sound
The caverned Echoes wake around
In lash for lash, and bound for bound;
The foam that streaks the courser's side   185
Seems gathered from the Ocean-tide:
Though weary waves are sunk to rest,
There's none within his rider's breast;
And though to-morrow's tempest lower,
'Tis calmer than thy heart, young Giaour!   190
I know thee not, I loathe thy race,
But in thy lineaments I trace
What Time shall strengthen, not efface:
Though young and pale, that sallow front
Is scathed by fiery Passion's brunt;   195
Though bent on earth thine evil eye,
As meteor-like thou glidest by,
Right well I view and deem thee one
Whom Othman's sons[4] should slay or shun.

On—on he hastened, and he drew   200
My gaze of wonder as he flew:
Though like a Demon of the night
He passed, and vanished from my sight,
His aspect and his air impressed
A troubled memory of my breast,   205
And long upon my startled ear
Rung his dark courser's hoofs of fear.
He spurs his steed; he nears the steep,
That, jutting, shadows o'er the deep;
He winds around; he hurries by;   210
The rock relieves him from mine eye;
For, well I ween, unwelcome he
Whose glance is fixed on those that flee;
And not a star but shines too bright
On him who takes such timeless flight.   215
He wound along; but ere he passed
One glance he snatched, as if his last,
A moment checked his wheeling steed,
A moment breathed him from his speed,
A moment on his stirrup stood—   220
Why looks he o'er the olive wood?

3. The first narrator of the poem speaks, an anonymous Turkish fisherman who has just put his boat to shore at Port Leone, and witnesses the Giaour's flight along the seashore.
4. Turks, after the name of the thirteenth-century founder of the Turkish (Ottoman) Empire.

The Crescent glimmers on the hill,
The Mosque's high lamps are quivering still
Though too remote for sound to wake
In echoes of the far tophaike,[5]   225
The flashes of each joyous peal
Are seen to prove the Moslem's zeal.
To-night, set Rhamazani's[6] sun;
To-night, the Bairam[7] feast's begun;
To-night—but who and what art thou   230
Of foreign garb and fearful brow?
And what are these to thine or thee,
That thou shouldst either pause or flee?

[margin: excluded from ceremony]

He stood—some dread was on his face,
Soon Hatred settled in its place: 235
It rose not with the reddening flush
Of transient Anger's hasty blush,
But pale as marble o'er the tomb,
Whose ghastly whiteness aids its gloom.
His brow was bent, his eye was glazed;   240
He raised his arm, and fiercely raised,
And sternly shook his hand on high,
As doubting to return or fly;
Impatient of his flight delayed,
Here loud his raven charger neighed—   245
Down glanced that hand, and grasped his blade;
That sound had burst his waking dream,
As Slumber starts at owlet's scream.
The spur hath lanced his courser's sides;
Away—away—for life he rides: 250
Swift as the hurled on high jerreed[8]
Springs to the touch his startled steed;
The rock is doubled, and the shore
Shakes with the clattering tramp no more;
The crag is won, no more is seen   255
His Christian crest[9] and haughty mien.
'Twas but an instant he restrained
That fiery barb[1] so sternly reined;
'Twas but a moment that he stood,
Then sped as if by Death pursued;   260
But in that instant o'er his soul
Winters of Memory seemed to roll,
And gather in that drop of time
A life of pain, an age of crime.

[margin: Dares not Remember Past]

5. Turkish musket. Its firing was used to announce the beginning of the Bairam feast.
6. Ramadan, the Moslem month of expiation and fasting.
7. The feast succeeding the abstinence of Rhamazani. Byron carefully excludes the Giaour from the life of the culture around him.
8. A Turkish spear.
9. Presumably a design—perhaps a family emblem—upon the Giaour's helmet.
1. The Giaour's steed, a Barbary or Arabian stallion.

O'er him who loves, or hates, or fears, 265
Such moment pours the grief of years:
What felt *he* then, at once opprest
By all that most distracts the breast?
That pause, which pondered o'er his fate,
Oh, who its dreary length shall date! 270
Though in Time's record nearly nought,
It was Eternity to Thought!
For infinite as boundless space
The thought that Conscience must embrace,
Which in itself can comprehend 275
Woe without name, or hope, or end.

The hour is past, the Giaour is gone;
And did he fly or fall alone?
Woe to that hour he came or went!
The curse for Hassan's sin was sent 280
To turn a palace to a tomb;
He came, he went, like the Simoom,[2]
That harbinger of Fate and gloom,
Beneath whose widely-wasting breath
The very cypress droops to death— 285
Dark tree, still sad when others' grief is fled,
The only constant mourner o'er the dead!

The steed is vanished from the stall;
No serf is seen in Hassan's hall;
The lonely Spider's thin gray pall 290
Waves slowly widening o'er the wall;
The Bat builds in his Haram bower,
And in the fortress of his power
The Owl usurps the beacon-tower;
The wild-dog howls o'er the fountain's brim, 295
With baffled thirst, and famine, grim;
For the stream has shrunk from its marble bed,
Where the weeds and the desolate dust are spread.
'Twas sweet of yore to see it play
And chase the sultriness of day, 300
As springing high the silver dew
In whirls fantastically flew,
And flung luxurious coolness round
The air, and verdure o'er the ground.
'Twas sweet, when cloudless stars were bright, 305
To view the wave of watery light,
And hear its melody by night.
And oft had Hassan's Childhood played
Around the verge of that cascade;
And oft upon his mother's breast 310

2. "The blast of the desert, fatal to every-   eastern poetry." [*Byron's note*.]
thing living, and often alluded to in

That sound had harmonized his rest;
And oft had Hassan's Youth along
Its bank been soothed by Beauty's song;
And softer seemed each melting tone
Of Music mingled with its own.   315
But ne'er shall Hassan's Age repose
Along the brink at Twilight's close:
The stream that filled that font is fled—
The blood that warmed his heart is shed!
And here no more shall human voice   320
Be heard to rage, regret, rejoice.
The last sad note that swelled the gale
Was woman's wildest funeral wail:
That quenched in silence, all is still,
But the lattice that flaps when the wind is shrill: 325
Though raves the gust, and floods the rain,
No hand shall close its clasp again.
On desert sands 'twere joy to scan
The rudest steps of fellow man,
So here the very voice of Grief   330
Might wake an Echo like relief—
At least 'twould say, "All are not gone;
There lingers Life, though but in one"—
For many a gilded chamber's there,
Which Solitude might well forbear;   335
Within that dome as yet Decay
Hath slowly worked her cankering way—
But gloom is gathered o'er the gate,
Nor there the Fakir's[3] self will wait;
Nor there will wandering Dervise[4] stay,   340
For Bounty cheers not his delay;
Nor there will weary stranger halt
To bless the sacred "bread and salt."[5]
Alike must Wealth and Poverty
Pass heedless and unheeded by,   345
For Courtesy and Pity died
With Hassan on the mountain side.
His roof, that refuge unto men,
Is Desolation's hungry den.
The guest flies the hall, and the vassal from labour,   350
Since his turban was cleft by the infidel's sabre!

———————

I hear the sound of coming feet,[6]
But not a voice mine ear to greet;
More near—each turban I can scan,

3. A mendicant monk of the Moslem religion.
4. A dervish, member of a Moslem ascetic order.
5. A Moslem pledge of hospitality to strangers.

6. The narrative becomes a dialogue between an anonymous boatman and Hassan, a flash back to the Emir's disposal of the corpse of Leila, whom he has killed because of her love for the Giaour.

And silver-sheathèd ataghan;[7]   355
The foremost of the band is seen
An Emir[8] by his garb of green:
"Ho! who are thou?"—"This low salam
Replies of Moslem faith I am.
The burthen ye so gently bear,   360
Seems one that claims your utmost care,
And, doubtless, holds some precious freight—
My humble bark would gladly wait."

    "Thou speakest sooth:[9] thy skiff unmoor,
And waft us from the silent shore;   365
Nay, leave the sail still furled, and ply
The nearest oar that's scattered by,
And midway to those rocks where sleep
The channelled waters dark and deep.
Rest from your task—so—bravely done,   370
Our course has been right swiftly run;
Yet 'tis the longest voyage, I trow,
That one of—

            ———————

    Sullen it plunged, and slowly sank,
The calm wave rippled to the bank;   375
I watched it as it sank, methought
Some motion from the current caught
Bestirred it more,—'twas but the beam
That checkered o'er the living stream:
I gazed, till vanishing from view,   380
Like lessening pebble it withdrew;
Still less and less, a speck of white
That gemmed the tide, then mocked the sight;
And all its hidden secrets sleep,
Known but to Genii[1] of the deep,   385
Which, trembling in their coral caves,
They dare not whisper to the waves.

            ———————

    As rising on its purple wing[2]
The insect-queen[3] of Eastern spring,
O'er emerald meadows of Kashmeer   390
Invites the young pursuer near,
And leads him on from flower to flower
A weary chase and wasted hour,
Then leaves him, as it soars on high,
With panting heart and tearful eye: 395

7. Turkish saber.
8. A title of honor for one of the direct descendants of Mohammed. Emirs traditionally wore green.
9. Truth.
1. Nature spirits of Arabian folklore and literature.

2. In this and the following fragment (422–38), Byron himself speaks as a reflective, third-person narrator.
3. "The blue-winged butterfly of Kashmeer, the most rare and beautiful of the species." [*Byron's note.*]

So Beauty lures the full-grown child,
With hue as bright, and wing as wild:
A chase of idle hopes and fears,
Begun in folly, closed in tears.
If won, to equal ills betrayed,   400
Woe waits the insect and the maid;
A life of pain, the loss of peace;
From infant's play, and man's caprice:
The lovely toy so fiercely sought
Hath lost its charm by being caught   405
For every touch that wooed its stay
Hath brushed its brightest hues away,
Till charm, and hue, and beauty gone,
'Tis left to fly or fall alone.
With wounded wing, or bleeding breast,   410
Ah! where shall either victim rest?
Can this with faded pinion soar
From rose to tulip as before?
Or Beauty, blighted in an hour,
Find joy within her broken bower?   415
No: gayer insects fluttering by
Ne'er droop the wing o'er those that die,
And lovelier things have mercy shown
To every failing but their own,
And every woe a tear can claim   420
Except an erring Sister's shame.

The Mind, that broods o'er guilty woes,
    Is like the Scorpion[4] girt by fire;
In circle narrowing as it glows,
The flames around their captive close,   425
Till inly searched by thousand throes,
    And maddening in her ire,
One sad and sole relief she knows—
The sting she nourished for her foes,
Whose venom never yet was vain,   430
Gives but one pang, and cures all pain,
And darts into her desperate brain:
So do the dark in soul expire,
Or live like Scorpion girt by fire;
So writhes the mind Remorse hath riven,   435
Unfit for earth, undoomed for heaven,
Darkness above, despair beneath,
Around it flame, within it death!

Black Hassan from the Haram flies,[5]
Nor bends on woman's form his eyes;   440
The unwonted chase each hour employs,

4. Byron alludes to the ancient legend that the scorpion, when surrounded by fire, stings itself to death in a rage.

5. The narrator is once again a nameless Turk who gives us the details of Leila's betrayal of Hassan.

Yet shares he not the hunter's joys.
Not thus was Hassan wont to fly
When Leila dwelt in his Serai.[6]
Doth Leila there no longer dwell?   445
That tale can only Hassan tell:
Strange rumours in our city say
Upon that eve she fled away
When Rhamazan's last sun was set
And flashing from each Minaret   450
Millions of lamps proclaimed the feast
Of Bairam through the boundless East.
'Twas then she went as to the bath,
Which Hassan vainly searched in wrath;
For she was flown her master's rage   455
In likeness of a Georgian page,[7]
And far beyond the Moslem's power
Had wronged him with the faithless Giaour.
Somewhat of this had Hassan deemed;
But still so fond, so fair she seemed,   460
Too well he trusted to the slave
Whose treachery deserved a grave:
And on that eve had gone to Mosque,
And thence to feast in his Kiosk.[8]
Such is the tale his Nubians[9] tell,   465
Who did not watch their charge too well;
But others say, that on that night,
By pale Phingari's[1] trembling light,
The Giaour upon his jet-black steed
Was seen, but seen alone to speed   470
With bloody spur along the shore,
Nor maid nor page behind him bore.

———

Her eye's dark charm 'twere vain to tell,[2]
But gaze on that of the Gazelle,
It will assist thy fancy well;   475
As large, as languishingly dark,
But Soul beamed forth in every spark
That darted from beneath the lid,
Bright as the jewel of Giamschid.[3]
Yea, *Soul*[4] and should our prophet say   480
That form was nought but breathing clay,
By Alla! I would answer nay;

6. Seraglio, the apartments in which the members of a Sultan's harem lived.
7. A Georgian is a native of the southern Caucasus. It is interesting that Lady Caroline Lamb, with whom Byron was involved in a notorious and violent love affair in 1813, frequently affected the dress of a page boy.
8. An open pavilion or summerhouse.
9. Black slaves from the area of the Sudan, often used as harem eunuchs.

1. The moon.
2. The narrative now appears to be a reminiscence, by Hassan, of the extraordinary beauty of Leila.
3. The fabled ruby of the Sultan Giamschid.
4. According to the Koran, women did not have souls. Hassan, remembering Leila, finds this impossible to accept. The "prophet" is Mohammed.

Though on Al-Sirat's[5] arch I stood,
Which totters o'er the fiery flood,
With Paradise within my view,   485
And all his Houris[6] beckoning through.
Oh! who young Leila's glance could read
And keep that portion of his creed
Which saith that woman is but dust,
A soulless toy for tyrant's lust?   490
On her might Muftis[7] gaze, and own
That through her eye the Immortal shone;
On her fair cheek's unfading hue
The young pomegranate's blossoms strew
Their bloom in blushes ever new;   495
Her hair in hyacinthine flow,
When left to roll its folds below,
As midst her handmaids in the hall
She stood superior to them all,
Hath swept the marble where her feet   500
Gleamed whiter than the mountain sleet
Ere from the cloud that gave it birth
It fell, and caught one stain of earth.
The cygnet nobly walks the water;
So moved on earth Circassia's daughter,[8]   505
The loveliest bird of Franguestan![9]
As rears her crest the ruffled Swan,
   And spurns the wave with wings of pride,
When pass the steps of stranger man
   Along the banks that bound her tide;   510
Thus rose fair Leila's whiter neck:—
Thus armed with beauty would she check
Intrusion's glance, till Folly's gaze
Shrunk from the charms it meant to praise.
Thus high and graceful was her gait;   515
Her heart as tender to her mate;
Her mate—stern Hassan, who was he?
Alas! that name was not for thee!

————

Stern Hassan hath a journey ta'en[1]
With twenty vassals in his train,   520
Each armed, as best becomes a man,
With arquebuss[2] and ataghan;
The chief before, as decked for war,
Bears in his belt the scimitar

5. The razor-thin bridge leading to the Moslem paradise.
6. Female spirits who, according to the Koran, entertained the blessed Moslems in Paradise.
7. Moslem religious judges.
8. Leila, a native of the northern Caucasus, called Circassia. Leila's situation—she is a European in thralldom to the Turk—is a deliberate parallel to the situation of enslaved Greece, with reference to which Byron begins *The Giaour*.
9. Circassia.
1. The narrator is now, again, an anonymous Turk, a spectator of the coming battle.
2. Arquebus: Turkish long rifle.

Stained with the best of Arnaut[3] blood,   525
When in the pass the rebels stood,
And few returned to tell the tale
Of what befell in Parne's vale.[4]
The pistols which his girdle bore
Were those that once a Pasha[5] wore,   530
Which still, though gemmed and bossed with gold,
Even robbers tremble to behold.
'Tis said he goes to woo a bride
More true than her who left his side;
The faithless slave that broke her bower,   535
And—worse than faithless—for a Giaour!

    The sun's last rays are on the hill,
And sparkle in the fountain rill,
Whose welcome waters, cool and clear,
Draw blessings from the mountaineer: 540
Here may the loitering merchant Greek
Find that repose 'twere vain to seek
In cities lodged too near his lord,
And trembling for his secret hoard—
Here may he rest where none can see,   545
In crowds a slave, in deserts free;
And with forbidden wine[6] may stain
The bowl a Moslem must not drain.

    The foremost Tartar's[7] in the gap
Conspicuous by his yellow cap;   550
The rest in lengthening line the while
Wind slowly through the long defile:
Above, the mountain rears a peak,
Where vultures whet the thirsty beak,
And theirs may be a feast to-night,   555
Shall tempt them down ere morrow's light;
Beneath, a river's wintry stream
Has shrunk before the summer beam,
And left a channel bleak and bare,
Save shrubs that spring to perish there: 560
Each side the midway path there lay
Small broken crags of granite gray,
By time, or mountain lightning, riven
From summits clad in mists of heaven;
For where is he that hath beheld   565
The peak of Liakura[8] unveiled?

---

3. Albanian. Albania, in the western Balkan peninsula, was also under Turkish domination in the early nineteenth century.
4. The valley of Mount Parnes, northwest of Athens.
5. An honorary term added to the name of any Moslem of high rank.
6. The Koran forbids Moslems to drink alcoholic beverages.
7. Turks of the Siberian region, famous for their ferocity.
8. An alternate name for Mount Parnassus in central Greece.

They reach the grove of pine at last;
"Bismillah!⁹ now the peril's past;
For yonder view the opening plain,
And there we'll prick our steeds amain:"   570
The Chiaus¹ spake, and as he said,
A bullet whistled o'er his head;
The foremost Tartar bites the ground!
  Scarce had they time to check the rein,
Swift from their steeds the riders bound;   575
  But three shall never mount again:
Unseen the foes that gave the wound,
  The dying ask revenge in vain.
With steel unsheathed, and carbine bent,
Some o'er their courser's harness leant,   580
  Half sheltered by the steed;
Some fly beneath the nearest rock,
And there await the coming shock,
  Nor tamely stand to bleed
Beneath the shaft of foes unseen,   585
Who dare not quit their craggy screen.
Stern Hassan only from his horse
Disdains to light, and keeps his course
Till fiery flashes in the van
Proclaim too sure the robber-clan   590
Have well secured the only way
Could now avail the promised prey;
Then curled his very beard with ire,
And glared his eye with fiercer fire;
"Though far and near the bullets hiss,   595
I've scaped a bloodier hour than this."
And now the foe their covert quit,
And call his vassals to submit;
But Hassan's frown and furious word
Are dreaded more than hostile sword,   600
Nor of his little band a man
Resigned carbine or ataghan,
Nor raised the craven cry, Amaun!²
In fuller sight, more near and near,
The lately ambushed foes appear,   605
And, issuing from the grove, advance
Some who on battle-charger prance.
Who leads them on with foreign brand
Far flashing in his red right hand?
"'Tis he! 'tis he! I know him now;   610
I know him by his pallid brow;
I know him by the evil eye

---

9. "In the name of God," a common
pious Moslem ejaculation. This phrase
begins each chapter of the Koran.

1. A Turkish messenger.
2. Arabic for "Mercy," a cry of surrender.

That aids his envious treachery;
I know him by his jet-black barb;
Though now arrayed in Arnaut garb,   615
Apostate from his own vile faith,
It shall not save him from the death:
'Tis he! well met in any hour,
Lost Leila's love—accurséd Giaour!"

   As rolls the river into Ocean,   620
In sable torrent wildly streaming;
   As the sea-tide's opposing motion,
In azure column proudly gleaming,
Beats back the current many a rood,
In curling foam and mingling flood,   625
While eddying whirl, and breaking wave,
Roused by the blast of winter, rave;
Through sparkling spray, in thundering clash,
The lightnings of the waters flash
In awful whiteness o'er the shore,   630
That shines and shakes beneath the roar;
Thus—as the stream and Ocean greet,
With waves that madden as they meet—
Thus join the bands, whom mutual wrong,
And fate, and fury, drive along.   635
The bickering sabres' shivering jar;
   And pealing wide or ringing near
   Its echoes on the throbbing ear,
The deathshot hissing from afar;
The shock, the shout, the groan of war,   640
   Reverberate along that vale,
   More suited to the shepherd's tale:
Though few the numbers—theirs the strife,
That neither spares nor speaks for life!
Ah! fondly youthful hearts can press,   645
To seize and share the dear caress;
But Love itself could never pant
For all that Beauty sighs to grant
With half the fervour Hate bestows
Upon the last embrace of foes,   650
When grappling in the fight they fold
Those arms that ne'er shall lose their hold:
Friends meet to part; Love laughs at faith;
True foes, once met, are joined till death!

———

   With sabre shivered to the hilt,   655
Yet dripping with the blood he spilt;
Yet strained within the severed hand
Which quivers round that faithless brand;
His turban far behind him rolled,

And cleft in twain its firmest fold;   660
His flowing robe by falchion[3] torn,
And crimson as those clouds of morn
That, streaked with dusky red, portend
The day shall have a stormy end;
A stain on every bush that bore   665
A fragment of his palampore;[4]
His breast with wounds unnumbered riven,
His back to earth, his face to Heaven,
Fall'n Hassan lies—his unclosed eye
Yet lowering on his enemy,   670
As if the hour that sealed his fate
Surviving left his quenchless hate;
And o'er him bends that foe with brow
As dark as his that bled below.

———

"Yes, Leila sleeps beneath the wave,[5]   675
But his shall be a redder grave;
Her spirit pointed well the steel
Which taught that felon heart to feel.
He called the Prophet, but his power
Was vain against the vengeful Giaour: 680
He called on Alla—but the word
Arose unheeded or unheard.
Thou Paynim[6] fool! could Leila's prayer
Be passed, and thine accorded there?
I watched my time, I leagued with these,   685
The traitor in his turn to seize;
My wrath is wreaked, the deed is done,
And now I go—but go alone."

———

The browsing camels' bells are tinkling:
His mother[7] looked from her lattice high—   690
   She saw the dews of eve besprinkling
The pasture green beneath her eye,
   She saw the planets faintly twinkling:
" 'Tis twilight—sure his train is nigh."
She could not rest in the garden-bower,   695
But gazed through the grate of his steepest tower.
"Why comes he not? his steeds are fleet,
Nor shrink they from the summer heat;
Why sends not the Bridegroom his promised gift?
Is his heart more cold, or his barb less swift?   700
Oh, false reproach! yon Tartar now
Has gained our nearest mountain's brow,
And warily the steep descends,

3. A broad curved sword.
4. Flowered shawl worn by Moslems of high rank.
5. In this short passage, the Giaour him- self speaks for the first time in the poem.
6. Pagan.
7. Hassan's mother.

And now within the valley bends;
And he bears the gift at his saddle bow—   705
How could I deem his courser slow?
Right well my largess shall repay
His welcome speed, and weary way."

only
Tartar
returns

The Tartar lighted at the gate,
But scarce upheld his fainting weight!   710
His swarthy visage spake distress,
But this might be from weariness;
His garb with sanguine spots was dyed,
But these might be from his courser's side;
He drew the token from his vest—   715
Angel of Death! 'tis Hassan's cloven crest!
His calpac[8] rent—his caftan red—
"Lady, a fearful bride thy Son hath wed:
Me, not from mercy, did they spare,
But this empurpled pledge to bear.   720
Peace to the brave! whose blood is spilt:
Woe to the Giaour! for his the guilt."

A Turban carved in coarsest stone,[9]
A Pillar with rank weeds o'ergrown,
Whereon can now be scarcely read   725
The Koran verse that mourns the dead,
Point out the spot where Hassan fell
A victim in that lonely dell.
There sleeps as true an Osmanlie[1]
As e'er at Mecca[2] bent the knee;   730
As ever scorned forbidden wine,
Or prayed with face towards the shrine,
In orisons resumed anew
At solemn sound of "Alla Hu!"[3]
Yet died he by a stranger's hand,   735
And stranger in his native land;
Yet died he as in arms he stood,
And unavenged, at least in blood.
But him the maids of Paradise
  Impatient to their halls invite,   740
And the dark heaven of Houris' eyes
  On him shall glance for ever bright;
They come—their kerchiefs green they wave,
And welcome with a kiss the brave!
Who falls in battle 'gainst a Giaour   745
Is worthiest an immortal bower.

deserves
heavenly
reward

---

8. "The calpac is the solid cap or centre part of the headdress; the shawl is wound round it, and forms the turban." [*Byron's note.*]
9. The speaker is again a Turk, contrast-ing the fates of Hassan and the Giaour.
1. Turk.
2. The sacred city of Islam.
3. The last words of the Moslem call to prayer.

[margin: about Giaour]

But thou, false Infidel! shall writhe[4]
Beneath avenging Monkir's[5] scythe;
And from its torments 'scape alone
To wander round lost Eblis'[6] throne; 750
And fire unquenched, unquenchable,
Around, within, thy heart shall dwell;
Nor ear can hear nor tongue can tell
The tortures of that inward hell!
But first, on earth as Vampire[7] sent, 755
Thy corse shall from its tomb be rent:
Then ghastly haunt thy native place,
And suck the blood of all thy race;
There from thy daughter, sister, wife,
At midnight drain the stream of life; 760
Yet loathe the banquet which perforce
Must feed thy livid living corse:
Thy victims ere they yet expire
Shall know the demon for their sire,
As cursing thee, thou cursing them, 765
Thy flowers are withered on the stem.
But one that for thy crime must fall,
The youngest, most beloved of all,
Shall bless thee with a *father's* name—
That word shall wrap thy heart in flame! 770
Yet must thou end thy task, and mark
Her cheek's last tinge, her eye's last spark,
And the last glassy glance must view
Which freezes o'er its lifeless blue;
Then with unhallowed hand shalt tear 775
The tresses of her yellow hair,
Of which in life a lock when shorn
Affection's fondest pledge was worn,
But now is borne away by thee,
Memorial of thine agony! 780
Wet with thine own best blood shall drip
Thy gnashing tooth and haggard lip;
Then stalking to thy sullen grave,
Go—and with Gouls and Afrits[8] rave;
Till these in horror shrink away 785
From Spectre more accursed than they!

———

[margin: FISHERMAN (LATER)]

"How name ye yon lone Caloyer?[9]
His features I have scanned before

4. The same speaker continues his reflection upon the contrasting fates of Hassan and the Giaour, now uttering a violent curse against the Giaour.
5. One of the two Moslem judges of the dead.
6. Ruler of the Moslem underworld.
7. Except for an incomplete novel, this is the only mention in Byron of the myth of the vampire, the doomed soul who cannot die and feeds on the blood of the living. Nevertheless, Byron has been frequently associated with the literature of vampirism as an expression of Romantic despair.
8. Moslem demons.
9. The first speaker of the narrative, the Turkish fisherman, sees the Giaour years later, now become a "caloyer" or religious recluse.

In seclusion

In mine own land: 'tis many a year,
   Since, dashing by the lonely shore,   790
I saw him urge as fleet a steed
As ever served a horseman's need.
But once I saw that face, yet then
It was so marked with inward pain,
I could not pass it by again;   795
It breathes the same dark spirit now,
As death were stamped upon his brow.

Monk

   " 'Tis twice three years at summer tide[1]
     Since first among our freres[2] he came;
And here it soothes him to abide   800
     For some dark deed he will not name.
But never at our Vesper[3] prayer,
Nor e'er before Confession chair
Kneels he, nor recks[4] he when arise
Incense or anthem to the skies,   805
But broods within his cell alone,
His faith and race alike unknown.
The sea from Paynim land he crost,
And here ascended from the coast;
Yet seems he not of Othman race,   810
But only Christian in his face:
I'd judge him some stray renegade,
Repentant of the change he made,
Save that he shuns our holy shrine,
Nor tastes the sacred bread and wine.   815
Great largess to these walls he brought,
And thus our Abbot's favour bought;
But were I Prior,[5] not a day
Should brook such stranger's further stay,
Or pent within our penance cell   820
Should doom him there for aye to dwell.
Much in his visions mutters he
Of maiden whelmed beneath the sea;
Of sabres clashing, foemen flying,
Wrongs avenged, and Moslem dying.   825
On cliff he hath been known to stand
And rave as to some bloody hand
Fresh severed from its parent limb,
Invisible to all but him,
Which beckons onward to his grave,   830
And lures to leap into the wave."

money talks

—————

Dark and unearthly is the scowl

---

1. A monk of the monastery where the
Giaour is sequestered speaks.
2. Monks.
3. The evening prayer.

4. Cares.
5. Byron may be satirizing here the
proverbial bickering of monks among
themselves.

That glares beneath his dusky cowl:[6]
The flash of that dilating eye
Reveals too much of times gone by;   835
Though varying, indistinct its hue,
Oft will his glance the gazer rue,
For in it lurks that nameless spell,
Which speaks, itself unspeakable,
A spirit yet unquelled and high,   840
That claims and keeps ascendancy;
And like the bird whose pinions quake,[7]
But cannot fly the gazing snake,
Will others quail beneath his look,
Nor 'scape the glance they scarce can brook.   845
From him the half-affrighted Friar
When met alone would fain retire,
As if that eye and bitter smile
Transferred to others fear and guile:
Not oft to smile descendeth he,   850
And when he doth 'tis sad to see
That he but mocks at Misery.
How that pale lip will curl and quiver!
Then fix once more as if for ever;
As if his sorrow or disdain   855
Forbade him e'er to smile again.
Well were it so—such ghastly mirth
From joyaunce ne'er derived its birth.
But sadder still it were to trace
What once were feelings in that face: 860
Time hath not yet the features fixed,
But brighter traits with evil mixed;
And there are hues not always faded,
Which speak a mind not all degraded
Even by the crimes through which it waded: 865
The common crowd but see the gloom
Of wayward deeds, and fitting doom;
The close observer can espy
A noble soul, and lineage high:
Alas! though both bestowed in vain,   870
Which Grief could change, and Guilt could stain,
It was no vulgar tenement
To which such lofty gifts were lent,
And still with little less than dread
On such the sight is riveted.   875
The roofless cot, decayed and rent,
   Will scarce delay the passer-by;
The tower by war or tempest bent,

[handwritten margin note: It is not because of joy he smiles]

6. Monk's hood. The Giaour, though a lay resident in the monastery, could nevertheless dress in monastic habit.
7. Byron alludes to the legend that snakes can mesmerize birds. Cf. the reference to the Giaour as "Gorgon" at line 896.

While yet may frown one battlement,
    Demands and daunts the stranger's eye;   880
Each ivied arch, and pillar lone,
Pleads haughtily for glories gone!

"His floating robe around him folding,[8]
    Slow sweeps he through the columned aisle;
With dread beheld, with gloom beholding   885
    The rites that sanctify the pile.
But when the anthem shakes the choir,
And kneel the monks, his steps retire;
By yonder lone and wavering torch
His aspect glares within the porch;[9]   890
There will he pause till all is done—
And hear the prayer, but utter none.
See—by the half-illumined wall
His hood fly back, his dark hair fall,
That pale brow wildly wreathing round,   895
As if the Gorgon[1] there had bound
The sablest of the serpent-braid
That o'er her fearful forehead strayed:
For he declines the convent oath,
And leaves those locks unhallowed[2] growth,   900
But wears our garb in all beside;
And, not from piety but pride,
Gives wealth to walls that never heard
Of his one holy vow nor word.
Lo!—mark ye, as the harmony   905
Peals louder praises to the sky,
That livid cheek, that stony air
Of mixed defiance and despair!
Saint Francis, keep him from the shrine!
Else may we dread the wrath divine   910
Made manifest by awful sign.
If ever evil angel bore
The form of mortal, such he wore;
By all my hope of sins forgiven,
Such looks are not of earth nor heaven!"   915

    To Love the softest hearts are prone,[3]
But such can ne'er be all his own;
Too timid in his woes to share,
Too meek to meet, or brave despair;
And sterner hearts alone may feel   920

8. The speaker is again a monk of the abbey, puzzled and frightened at the Giaour's presence.
9. That is, during holy services the Giaour retires to the central enclosed patio area of the monastery.
1. The Gorgons in Greek mythology were monsters whose gaze could turn a man to stone.
2. A true monk would have undergone a ritual shaving of the head (tonsure) to signal his entry into monastic discipline.
3. The speaker is again Byron as reflective narrator.

The wound that Time can never heal.
The rugged metal of the mine
Must burn before its surface shine,
But plunged within the furnace-flame,
It bends and melts—though still the same;   925
Then tempered to thy want, or will,
'Twill serve thee to defend or kill—
A breast-plate for thine hour of need,
Or blade to bid thy foeman bleed;
But if a dagger's form it bear,   930
Let those who shape its edge, beware!
Thus Passion's fire, and Woman's art,
Can turn and tame the sterner heart;
From these its form and tone are ta'en,
And what they make it, must remain,   935
But break—before it bend again.

————

If solitude succeed to grief,
Release from pain is slight relief;
The vacant bosom's wilderness
Might thank the pang that made it less.   940
We loathe what none are left to share:
Even bliss—'twere woe alone to bear;
The heart once left thus desolate
Must fly at last for ease—to hate.
It is as if the dead could feel[4]   945
The icy worm around them steal,
And shudder, as the reptiles creep
To revel o'er their rotting sleep,
Without the power to scare away
The cold consumers of their clay!   950
It is as if the desert bird,[5]
    Whose beak unlocks her bosom's stream
    To still her famished nestlings' scream,
Nor mourns a life to them transferred,
Should rend her rash devoted breast,   955
And find them flown her empty nest.
The keenest pangs the wretched find
    Are rapture to the dreary void,
The leafless desert of the mind,
    The waste of feelings unemployed.   960
Who would be doomed to gaze upon
A sky without a cloud or sun?
Less hideous far the tempest's roar,
Than ne'er to brave the billows more—

4. The image of remorse as a kind of live burial is one instance of Byron's importance for such later writers as Baudelaire and Poe.

5. The pelican, reputed in legend to feed her young from the blood of her own breast.

Thrown, when the war of winds is o'er,   965
A lonely wreck on Fortune's shore,
'Mid sullen calm, and silent bay,
Unseen to drop by dull decay;—
Better to sink beneath the shock
Than moulder piecemeal on the rock!   970

———

GIAOUR: "Father! thy days have passed in peace,[6]
'Mid counted beads, and countless prayer;
To bid the sins of others cease,
Thyself without a crime or care,
Save transient ills that all must bear,   975
Has been thy lot from youth to age;
And thou wilt bless thee from the rage
Of passions fierce and uncontrolled,
Such as thy penitents unfold,
Whose secret sins and sorrows rest   980
Within thy pure and pitying breast.
My days, though few, have passed below
In much of Joy, but more of Woe;
Yet still in hours of love or strife,
I've 'scaped the weariness of Life: 985
Now leagued with friends, now girt by foes,
I loathed the languor of repose.
Now nothing left to love or hate,
No more with hope or pride elate,
I'd rather be the thing that crawls   990
Most noxious o'er a dungeon's walls,
Than pass my dull, unvarying days,
Condemned to meditate and gaze.
Yet, lurks a wish within my breast
For rest—but not to feel 'tis rest.   995
Soon shall my Fate that wish fulfil;
And I shall sleep without the dream
Of what I was, and would be still,
Dark as to thee my deeds may seem:
My memory now is but the tomb   1000
Of joys long dead; my hope, their doom:
Though better to have died with those
Than bear a life of lingering woes.
My spirit shrunk not to sustain
The searching throes of ceaseless pain;   1005
Nor sought the self-accorded grave
Of ancient fool and modern knave:

6. At this point the Giaour himself speaks again. His "confession" to the aged Friar is not so much a retelling of the story as we have already pieced it together from its multiple narrators, as it is a new version of the tale, now told from within the consciousness of the self-tormented, "Byronic" hero. This long passage constitutes Byron's last addition to the poem as it was originally published.

Yet death I have not feared to meet;
And in the field it had been sweet,
Had Danger wooed me on to move   1010
The slave of Glory, not of Love.
I've braved it—not for Honour's boast;
I smile at laurels won or lost;
To such let others carve their way,
For high renown, or hireling pay: 1015
But place again before my eyes
Aught that I deem a worthy prize—
The maid I love, the man I hate—
And I will hunt the steps of fate,
To save or slay, as these require,   1020
Through rending steel, and rolling fire:
Nor needst thou doubt this speech from one
Who would but do—what he *hath* done.
Death is but what the haughty brave,
The weak must bear, the wretch must crave;   1025
Then let life go to Him who gave;
I have not quailed to Danger's brow
When high and happy—need I *now*?

———

"I loved her, Friar! nay, adored—
    But these are words that all can use—   1030
I proved it more in deed than word;
There's blood upon that dinted sword,
    A stain its steel can never lose:
'Twas shed for her, who died for me,
    It warmed the heart of one abhorred: 1035
Nay, start not—no—nor bend thy knee,
    Nor midst my sin such act record;
Thou wilt absolve me from the deed,
For he was hostile to thy creed!
The very name of Nazarene[7]   1040
Was wormwood[8] to his Paynim spleen.
Ungrateful fool! since but for brands
Well wielded in some hardy hands,
And wounds by Galileans[9] given—
The surest pass to Turkish heaven—   1045
For him his Houris still might wait
Impatient at the Prophet's gate.
I loved her—Love will find its way
Through paths where wolves would fear to prey;
And if it dares enough, 'twere hard   1050
If Passion met not some reward—
No matter how, or where, or why,
I did not vainly seek, nor sigh:
Yet sometimes, with remorse, in vain

7. Christian, from Jesus' home, Naza-   8. Plant with an extremely bitter taste.
reth.   9. Christians.

I wish she had not loved again.   1055
She died—I dare not tell thee how;
But look—'tis written on my brow!
There read of Cain[1] the curse and crime,
In characters unworn by Time:
Still, ere thou dost condemn me, pause;   1060
Not mine the act, though I the cause.
Yet did he but what I had done
Had she been false to more than one.
Faithless to him—he gave the blow;
But true to me—I laid him low: 1065
Howe'er deserved her doom might be
Her treachery was truth to me;
To me she gave her heart, that all
Which Tyranny can ne'er enthrall;
And I, alas! too late to save!   1070
Yet all I then could give, I gave—
'Twas some relief—our foe a grave.
His death sits lightly; but her fate
Has made me—what thou well mayst hate.
    His doom was sealed—he knew it well,   1075
Warned by the voice of stern Taheer,[2]
Deep in whose darkly boding ear
The deathshot pealed of murder near,
    As filed the troop to where they fell!
He died too in the battle broil,   1080
A time that heeds nor pain nor toil;
One cry to Mahomet for aid,
One prayer to Alla all he made:
He knew and crossed me in the fray—
I gazed upon him where he lay,   1085
And watched his spirit ebb away:
Though pierced like pard[3] by hunter's steel,
He felt not half that now I feel.
I searched, but vainly searched, to find
The workings of a wounded mind;   1090
Each feature of that sullen corse
Betrayed his rage, but no remorse.
Oh, what had Vengeance given to trace
Despair upon his dying face!
The late repentance of that hour   1095
When Penitence hath lost her power
To tear one terror from the grave,
And will not soothe, and cannot save.

———

"The cold in clime are cold in blood,
Their love can scarce deserve the name;   1100
But mine was like the lava flood

1. The Giaour condemns himself for Lei-   Cf. *Harold* I, LXXXIII.
la's death in terms of the myth of Cain,   2. Hassan's soothsayer.
so important for Byron's imagination.   3. Leopard.

That boils in Aetna's[4] breast of flame.
I cannot prate in puling strain *whimpering*
Of Ladye-love, and Beauty's chain:
If changing cheek, and scorching vein,   1105
Lips taught to writhe, but not complain,
If bursting heart, and maddening brain,
And daring deed, and vengeful steel,
And all that I have felt, and feel,
Betoken love—that love was mine,   1110
And shown by many a bitter sign.
'Tis true, I could not whine nor sigh,
I knew but to obtain or die.
I die—but first I have possessed,
And come what may, I *have been* blessed.   1115
Shall I the doom I sought upbraid?
No—reft of all, yet undismayed
But for the thought of Leila slain,
Give me the pleasure with the pain,
So would I live and love again.   1120
I grieve, but not, my holy Guide!
For him who dies, but her who died:
She sleeps beneath the wandering wave—
Ah! had she but an earthly grave,
This breaking heart and throbbing head   1125
Should seek and share her narrow bed.
She was a form of Life and Light,
That, seen, became a part of sight;
And rose, where'er I turned mine eye,
The Morning-star of Memory!   1130

"Yes, Love indeed is light from heaven;
  A spark of that immortal fire
With angels shared, by Alla given,
  To lift from earth our low desire.
Devotion wafts the mind above,   1135
But Heaven itself descends in Love;
A feeling from the Godhead caught,
To wean from self each sordid thought;
A ray of Him who formed the whole;
A Glory circling round the soul!   1140
I grant *my* love imperfect, all
That mortals by the name miscall;
Then deem it evil, what thou wilt;
But say, oh say, *hers* was not Guilt!
She was my Life's unerring Light;   1145
That quenched—what beam shall break my night?
Oh! would it shone to lead me still,
Although to death or deadliest ill!

4. The unpredictable volcano of Greece.

Why marvel ye, if they who lose
   This present joy, this future hope,   1150
   No more with Sorrow meekly cope;
In phrensy then their fate accuse;
In madness do those fearful deeds
   That seem to add but Guilt to Woe?
Alas! the breast that inly bleeds   1155
   Hath nought to dread from outward blow:
Who falls from all he knows of bliss,
Cares little into what abyss.
Fierce as the gloomy vulture's now
   To thee, old man, my deeds appear: 1160
I read abhorrence on thy brow,
   And this too was I born to bear!
'Tis true, that, like that bird of prey,
With havock have I marked my way:
But this was taught me by the dove,[5]   1165
To die—and know no second love.
This lesson yet hath man to learn,
Taught by the thing he dares to spurn:
The bird that sings within the brake,
The swan that swims upon the lake,   1170
One mate, and one alone, will take.
And let the fool still prone to range,
And sneer on all who cannot change,
Partake his jest with boasting boys;
I envy not his varied joys,   1175
But deem such feeble, heartless man,
Less than yon solitary swan;
Far, far beneath the shallow maid
He left believing and betrayed.
Such shame at least was never mine—   1180
Leila! each thought was only thine!
My good, my guilt, my weal, my woe,
My hope on high—my all below.
Earth holds no other like to thee,
Or, if it doth, in vain for me: 1185
For worlds I dare not view the dame
Resembling thee, yet not the same.
The very crimes that mar my youth,
This bed of death—attest my truth!
'Tis all too late—thou wert, thou art   1190
The cherished madness of my heart!

"And she was lost—and yet I breathed,
   But not the breath of human life:
A serpent round my heart was wreathed,

---

5. According to legend, the dove is monogamous, and dies of grief when its
mate dies.

And stung my every thought to strife.　　　1195
Alike all time, abhorred all place,
Shuddering I shrank from Nature's face,
Where every hue that charmed before
The blackness of my bosom wore.
The rest thou dost already know,　　　1200
And all my sins, and half my woe.
But talk no more of penitence;
Thou seest I soon shall part from hence:
And if thy holy tale were true,
The deed that's done canst *thou* undo?　　　1205
Think me not thankless—but this grief
Looks not to priesthood for relief.[6]
My soul's estate in secret guess:
But wouldst thou pity more, say less.
When thou canst bid my Leila live,　　　1210
Then will I sue thee to forgive;
Then plead my cause in that high place
Where purchased masses proffer grace.
Go, when the hunter's hand hath wrung
From forest-cave her shrieking young,　　　1215
And calm the lonely lioness:
But soothe not—mock not *my* distress!

"In earlier days, and calmer hours,
　　When heart with heart delights to blend,
Where bloom my native valley's bowers,　　　1220
　　I had—Ah! have I now?—a friend!
To him this pledge I charge thee send,
　　Memorial of a youthful vow;
I would remind him of my end:
　　Though souls absorbed like mine allow　　　1225
Brief thought to distant Friendship's claim,
Yet dear to him my blighted name.
'Tis strange—he prophesied my doom,
　　And I have smiled—I then could smile—
When Prudence would his voice assume,　　　1230
　　And warn—I recked not what—the while:
But now Remembrance whispers o'er
Those accents scarcely marked before.
Say—that his bodings came to pass,
　　And he will start to hear their truth,　　　1235
　　And wish his words had not been sooth:
Tell him—unheeding as I was,
　　Through many a busy bitter scene
　　Of all our golden youth had been,
In pain, my faltering tongue had tried　　　1240

6. "The monk's sermon is omitted. It seems to have had so little effect upon the patient, that it could have no hopes from the reader." [*Byron's note*.]

To bless his memory—ere I died;
But Heaven in wrath would turn away,
If Guilt should for the guiltless pray.
I do not ask him not to blame,
Too gentle he to wound my name;   1245
And what have I to do with Fame?
I do not ask him not to mourn,
Such cold request might sound like scorn;
And what than Friendship's manly tear
May better grace a brother's bier?   1250
But bear this ring, his own of old,
And tell him—what thou dost behold!
The withered frame, the ruined mind,
The wrack by passion left behind,
A shrivelled scroll, a scattered leaf,   1255
Seared by the autumn blast of Grief!

"Tell me no more of Fancy's gleam,
No, father, no, 'twas not a dream;
Alas! the dreamer first must sleep,
I only watched, and wished to weep;   1260
But could not, for my burning brow
Throbbed to the very brain as now:
I wished but for a single tear,
As something welcome, new, and dear:
I wished it then, I wish it still;   1265
Despair is stronger than my will.
Waste not thine orison, despair
Is mightier than thy pious prayer:
I would not, if I might, be blest;
I want no Paradise, but rest.   1270
'Twas then—I tell thee—father! then
I saw her; yes, she lived again;
And shining in her white symar
As through yon pale gray cloud the star
Which now I gaze on, as on her,   1275
Who looked and looks far lovelier;
Dimly I view its trembling spark;
To-morrow's night shall be more dark;
And I, before its rays appear,
That lifeless thing the living fear.   1280
I wander—father! for my soul
Is fleeting towards the final goal.
I saw her—friar! and I rose
Forgetful of our former woes;
And rushing from my couch, I dart,   1285
And clasp her to my desperate heart;
I clasp—what is it that I clasp?
No breathing form within my grasp,
No heart that beats reply to mine—

Yet, Leila! yet the form is thine!　　　　　1290
And art thou, dearest, changed so much
As meet my eye, yet mock my touch?
Ah! were thy beauties e'er so cold,
I care not—so my arms enfold
The all they ever wished to hold.　　　　　1295
Alas! around a shadow prest
They shrink upon my lonely breast;
Yet still 'tis there! In silence stands,
And beckons with beseeching hands!
With braided hair, and bright-black eye—　　1300
I knew 'twas false—she could not die!
But *he* is dead! within the dell
I saw him buried where he fell;
He comes not—for he cannot break
From earth;—why then art *thou* awake?　　1305
They told me wild waves rolled above
The face I view—the form I love;
They told me—'twas a hideous tale!—
I'd tell it, but my tongue would fail:
If true, and from thine ocean-cave　　　　1310
Thou com'st to claim a calmer grave,
Oh! pass thy dewy fingers o'er
This brow that then will burn no more;
Or place them on my hopeless heart:
But, Shape or Shade! whate'er thou art,　　1315
In mercy ne'er again depart!
Or farther with thee bear my soul
Than winds can waft or waters roll!

"Such is my name, and such my tale.
　Confessor! to thy secret ear　　　　　1320
I breathe the sorrows I bewail,
　And thank thee for the generous tear
This glazing eye could never shed.
Then lay me with the humblest dead,
And, save the cross above my head,　　　　1325
Be neither name nor emblem spread,
By prying stranger to be read,
Or stay the passing pilgrim's tread."

He passed—nor of his name and race
He left a token or a trace,　　　　　　1330
Save what the Father must not say[7]
Who shrived him on his dying day:
This broken tale was all we knew
Of her he loved, or him he slew.

7. According to the ritual of the confessional, anything the Friar heard would
be a sacred trust, to be broken under no
circumstances.

The Prisoner of Chillon[1]

The Prisoner of Chillon, published in 1816, during Byron's last exile from England, has always been one of his most widely read and admired poems, perhaps because its passages of near delirium and absolute despair seem more "confessional," or more conventionally Romantic (in the line of Wordsworth and Shelley), than do the earlier verse tales of adventure.

Sonnet on Chillon[2] (opposite of poem)

ETERNAL Spirit of the chainless Mind!
   Brightest in dungeons, Liberty! thou art:
   For there thy habitation is the heart— (imprison)
The heart which love of thee alone can bind;
And when thy sons to fetters are consigned—   5
   To fetters, and the damp vault's dayless gloom,
   Their country conquers with their martyrdom,
And Freedom's fame finds wings on every wind.
Chillon! thy prison is a holy place,
   And thy sad floor an altar—for 'twas trod,   10
Until his very steps have left a trace
   Worn, as if thy cold pavement were a sod,
By Bonnivard!—May none those marks efface!
   For they appeal from tyranny to God.

I

My hair is grey, but not with years,
Nor grew it white
   In a single night,
As men's have grown from sudden fears:
My limbs are bowed, though not with toil,   5
   But rusted with a vile repose,
For they have been a dungeon's spoil,
   And mine has been the fate of those
To whom the goodly earth and air
Are banned, and barred—forbidden fare;   10
But this was for my father's faith,
   I suffered chains and courted death;
Instead That father perished at the stake
For tenets he would not forsake;
And for the same his lineal race   15
In darkness found a dwelling place;

1. Written and published in 1816 after Byron and Shelley had visited the Castle of Chillon in Switzerland. François Bonivard (1496–1570) was a brilliant Genevese priest whose democratic sentiments caused Duke Charles III of Savoy, then dictator of Geneva, to imprison him in the Castle of Chillon from 1530 till 1536. Byron was struck not only with the image of Bonivard as a revolutionary spirit but also by the theme of solitary confinement, isolation, and mania—a particularly brutal version of the Byronic theme of the self-tortured mind. 2. The Sonnet was written after the completion of the *Prisoner*. Here, as in the "Epistle to Augusta" and *Manfred*, Byron reveals his debt, during this phase of his career, to the revolutionary mysticism of his friend Shelley.

We were seven[3]—who now are one,
  Six in youth, and one in age,
Finished as they had begun,
  Proud of Persecution's rage;   20
One in fire, and two in field,
Their belief with blood have sealed,
Dying as their father died,
For the God their foes denied;—
Three were in a dungeon cast,   25
Of whom this wreck is left the last.

II

There are seven pillars of Gothic mould,
In Chillon's dungeons deep and old,
There are seven columns, massy and grey,
Dim with a dull imprisoned ray,   30
A sunbeam which hath lost its way,
And through the crevice and the cleft
Of the thick wall is fallen and left;
Creeping o'er the floor so damp,
Like a marsh's meteor lamp: 35
And in each pillar there is a ring,
  And in each ring there is a chain;
That iron is a cankering thing,
  For in these limbs its teeth remain,
With marks that will not wear away,   40
Till I have done with this new day,
Which now is painful to these eyes,
Which have not seen the sun so rise
For years—I cannot count them o'er,
I lost their long and heavy score   45
When my last brother drooped and died,
And I lay living by his side.

III

They chained us each to a column stone,
And we were three—yet, each alone;
We could not move a single pace,   50
We could not see each other's face,
But with that pale and livid light
That made us strangers in our sight:
And thus together—yet apart,
Fettered in hand, but joined in heart,   55
'Twas still some solace in the dearth
Of the pure elements of earth,
To hearken to each other's speech,
And each turn comforter to each
With some new hope, or legend old,   60
Or song heroically bold;
But even these at length grew cold.

3. The historical Bonivard had only two brothers, neither of whom seems to have shared his imprisonment.

Our voices took a dreary tone,
An echo of the dungeon stone,
   A grating sound, not full and free,   65
   As they of yore were wont to be:
   It might be fancy—but to me *missing*
They never sounded like our own. *something*

IV

I was the eldest of the three,
   And to uphold and cheer the rest   70
   I ought to do—and did my best— *SOFT*
And each did well in his degree.
   The youngest, whom my father loved,
Because our mother's brow was given
To him, with eyes as blue as heaven—   75
   For him my soul was sorely moved:
And truly might it be distressed
To see such bird in such a nest;
For he was beautiful as day— *old days*
   (When day was beautiful to me   80
   As to young eagles, being free)—
   A polar day, which will not see
A sunset till its summer's gone,
   Its sleepless summer of long light,
The snow-clad offspring of the sun: 85
   And thus he was as pure and bright,
And in his natural spirit gay,
With tears for nought but others' ills,
And then they flowed like mountain rills,
Unless he could assuage the woe   90
Which he abhorred to view below.

V

The other was as pure of mind,
But formed to combat with his kind; *TOUGH*
Strong in his frame, and of a mood
Which 'gainst the world in war had stood,   95
And perished in the foremost rank
   With joy:—but not in chains to pine:
His spirit withered with their clank,
   I saw it silently decline—
   And so perchance in sooth did mine: 100
But yet I forced it on to cheer
Those relics of a home so dear.
He was a hunter of the hills,
   Had followed there the deer and wolf
   To him this dungeon was a gulf,   105
And fettered feet the worst of ills.

VI

   Lake Leman[4] lies by Chillon's walls:
A thousand feet in depth below

4. Lake Geneva.

Its massy waters meet and flow;
Thus much the fathom-line was sent   110
From Chillon's snow-white battlement,
    Which round about the wave inthralls:
A double dungeon wall and wave
Have made—and like a living grave.
Below the surface of the lake   115
The dark vault lies wherein we lay:
We heard it ripple night and day:
    Sounding o'er our heads it knocked;
And I have felt the winter's spray
Wash through the bars when winds were high   120
And wanton in the happy sky;
    And then the very rock hath rocked,
    And I have felt it shake, unshocked,
Because I could have smiled to see
The death that would have set me free.   125

VII

I said my nearer brother pined,
I said his mighty heart declined,
He loathed and put away his food;
It was not that 'twas coarse and rude,
For we were used to hunter's fare,   130
And for the like had little care:
The milk drawn from the mountain goat
Was changed for water from the moat,
Our bread was such as captives' tears
Have moistened many a thousand years,   135
Since man first pent his fellow men
Like brutes within an iron den;
But what were these to us or him?
These wasted not his heart or limb;
My brother's soul was of that mould   140
Which in a palace had grown cold,
Had his free breathing been denied
The range of the steep mountain's side;
But why delay the truth?—he died.
I saw, and could not hold his head,   145
Nor reach his dying hand—nor dead,—
Though hard I strove, but strove in vain,
To rend and gnash my bonds in twain.
He died—and they unlocked his chain,
And scooped for him a shallow grave   150
Even from the cold earth of our cave.
I begged them, as a boon, to lay
His corse in dust whereon the day
Might shine—it was a foolish thought,
But then within my brain it wrought,   155
That even in death his freeborn breast
In such a dungeon could not rest.

I might have spared my idle prayer—
They coldly laughed—and laid him there:
The flat and turfless earth above   160
The being we so much did love;
His empty chain above it leant,
Such Murder's fitting monument!

VIII

But he, the favourite and the flower,
Most cherished since his natal hour,   165
His mother's image in fair face,
The infant love of all his race,
His martyred father's dearest thought,
My latest[5] care, for whom I sought
To hoard my life, that his might be   170
Less wretched now, and one day free;
He, too, who yet had held untired
A spirit natural or inspired—
He, too, was struck, and day by day
Was withered on the stalk away.   175
Oh, God! it is a fearful thing
To see the human soul take wing
In any shape, in any mood.
I've seen it rushing forth in blood,
I've seen it on the breaking ocean   180
Strive with a swoln convulsive motion,
I've seen the sick and ghastly bed
Of Sin delirious with its dread:
But these were horrors—this was woe
Unmixed with such—but sure and slow: 185
He faded, and so calm and meek,
So softly worn, so sweetly weak,
So tearless, yet so tender—kind,
And grieved for those he left behind;
With all the while a cheek whose bloom   190
Was as a mockery of the tomb,
Whose tints as gently sunk away
As a departing rainbow's ray;
An eye of most transparent light,
That almost made the dungeon bright;   195
And not a word of murmur—not
A groan o'er his untimely lot,—
A little talk of better days,
A little hope my own to raise,
For I was sunk in silence—lost   200
In this last loss, of all the most;
And then the sighs he would suppress
Of fainting Nature's feebleness,
More slowly drawn, grew less and less:
I listened, but I could not hear;   205

5. Last.

I called, for I was wild with fear;
I knew 'twas hopeless, but my dread
Would not be thus admonishéd;
I called, and thought I heard a sound—
I burst my chain with one strong bound,   210
And rushed to him:—I found him not,
I only stirred in this black spot,
I only lived, I only drew
The accursed breath of dungeon-dew;
The last, the sole, the dearest link   215
Between me and the eternal brink,
Which bound me to my failing race,
Was broken in this fatal place.
One on the earth, and one beneath—
My brothers—both had ceased to breathe: 220
I took that hand which lay so still,
Alas! my own was full as chill;
I had not strength to stir, or strive,
But felt that I was still alive—
A frantic feeling, when we know   225
That what we love shall ne'er be so.
    I know not why
    I could not die,[6]
I had no earthly hope—but faith,
And that forbade a selfish death.   230

IX

What next befell me then and there
    I know not well—I never knew—
First came the loss of light, and air,
    And then of darkness too:
I had no thought, no feeling—none—   235
Among the stones I stood a stone,
And was, scarce conscious what I wist,[7]
As shrubless crags within the mist;
For all was blank, and bleak, and grey;
It was not night—it was not day;   240
It was not even the dungeon-light,
So hateful to my heavy sight,
But vacancy absorbing space,
And fixedness—without a place;
There were no stars—no earth—no time—   245
No check—no change—no good—no crime—
But silence, and a stirless breath
Which neither was of life nor death;
A sea of stagnant idleness,
Blind, boundless, mute, and motionless!   250

---

6. Compare with this the line in Coleridge's *Rime of the Ancient Mariner* (IV,
262): "And yet I could not die." Byron
was a great admirer of Coleridge's
poem.
7. Knew.

X

A light broke in upon my brain,—
  It was the carol of a bird;
It ceased, and then it came again,
  The sweetest song ear ever heard,
And mine was thankful till my eyes   255
Ran over with the glad surprise,
And they that moment could not see
I was the mate of misery;
But then by dull degrees came back
My senses to their wonted track;   260
I saw the dungeon walls and floor
Close slowly round me as before,
I saw the glimmer of the sun
Creeping as it before had done,
But through the crevice where it came   265
That bird was perched, as fond and tame,
  And tamer than upon the tree;
A lovely bird, with azure wings,
And song that said a thousand things,
  And seemed to say them all for me!   270
I never saw its like before,
I ne'er shall see its likeness more:
It seemed like me to want a mate,
But was not half so desolate,
And it was come to love me when   275
None lived to love me so again,
And cheering from my dungeon's brink,
Had brought me back to feel and think.
I know not if it late were free,
  Or broke its cage to perch on mine,   280
But knowing well captivity,
  Sweet bird! I could not wish for thine!
Or if it were, in wingéd guise,
A visitant from Paradise;
For—Heaven forgive that thought! the while   285
Which made me both to weep and smile—
I sometimes deemed that it might be
My brother's soul come down to me;
But then at last away it flew,
And then 'twas mortal well I knew,   290
For he would never thus have flown—
And left me twice so doubly lone,—
Lone—as the corse within its shroud,
Lone—as a solitary cloud,
  A single cloud on a sunny day,   295
While all the rest of heaven is clear,
A frown upon the atmosphere,
That hath no business to appear
  When skies are blue, and earth is gay.

XI

A kind of change came in my fate,   300
My keepers grew compassionate;
I know not what had made them so,
They were inured to sights of woe,
But so it was:—my broken chain
With links unfastened did remain,   305
And it was liberty to stride
Along my cell from side to side,
And up and down, and then athwart,
And tread it over every part;
And round the pillars one by one,   310
Returning where my walk begun,
Avoiding only, as I trod,
My brothers' graves without a sod;
For if I thought with heedless tread
My step profaned their lowly bed,   315
My breath came gaspingly and thick,
And my crushed heart felt blind and sick.

XII

I made a footing in the wall,
    It was not therefrom to escape,
For I had buried one and all,   320
    Who loved me in a human shape;
And the whole earth would henceforth be
A wider prison unto me:
No child—no sire—no kin had I,
No partner in my misery;   325
I thought of this, and I was glad,
For thought of them had made me mad;
But I was curious to ascend
To my barred windows, and to bend
Once more, upon the mountains high,   330
The quiet of a loving eye.

XIII

I saw them—and they were the same,
They were not changed like me in frame;
I saw their thousand years of snow
On high—their wide long lake below,   335
And the blue Rhone in fullest flow;
I heard the torrents leap and gush
O'er channelled rock and broken bush;
I saw the white-walled distant town,
And whiter sails go skimming down;   340
And then there was a little isle,
Which in my very face did smile,
    The only one in view;
A small green isle, it seemed no more,
Scarce broader than my dungeon floor,   345

But in it there were three tall trees,
And o'er it blew the mountain breeze,
And by it there were waters flowing,
And on it there were young flowers growing,
   Of gentle breath and hue.   350
The fish swam by the castle wall,
And they seemed joyous each and all;
The eagle rode the rising blast,
Methought he never flew so fast
As then to me he seemed to fly;   355
And then new tears came in my eye,
And I felt troubled—and would fain
I had not left my recent chain;
And when I did descend again,
The darkness of my dim abode   360
Fell on me as a heavy load;
It was as is a new-dug grave,
Closing o'er one we sought to save,—
And yet my glance, too much opprest,
Had almost need of such a rest.   365

XIV

It might be months, or years, or days—
   I kept no count, I took no note—
I had no hope my eyes to raise,
   And clear them of their dreary mote;
At last men came to set me free;   370
   I asked not why, and recked not where;
It was at length the same to me,
Fettered or fetterless to be,
   I learned to love despair.
And thus when they appeared at last,   375
And all my bonds aside were cast,
These heavy walls to me had grown
A hermitage—and all my own!
And half I felt as they were come
To tear me from a second home: 380
With spiders I had friendship made,
And watched them in their sullen trade
Had seen the mice by moonlight play,
And why should I feel less than they?
We were all inmates of one place,   385
And I, the monarch of each race,
Had power to kill—yet, strange to tell!
In quiet we had learned to dwell;
My very chains and I grew friends,
So much a long communion tends   390
To make us what we are:—even I
Regained my freedom with a sigh.

Manfred[1]

In the last seven years of his life, Byron—besides completing *Childe Harold* and writing *Don Juan*—produced more dramas than all the other major English Romantics combined: *Manfred* in 1817; *Marino Faliero, Cain, Sardanapalus,* and *The Two Foscari* in 1821; *Werner* in 1822; *Heaven and Earth* in 1823; and *The Deformed Transformed* in 1824. This output seems even more remarkable when we consider that Byron insisted, both in letters and in prefaces to his plays, that they were never intended for performance on the stage, and that the last thing he desired was for any actor, anytime, to speak his lines. And history, with a few lapses, has satisfied his dramatic ambitions—or lack of them.

Indeed, Byron, like his fellow Romantics, appears to have thought of his experiments in drama mainly as "closet drama"—an internalized, obsessively private act of the theater of the mind, rather than the theater of proscenium arch, footlights, and audiences. As idolaters of the unapproachable greatness of Shakespeare and heirs of the brittle comedy of the eighteenth-century stage, the Romantics generally faced the drama as a challenge they knew they would fail, but nevertheless had to try. And not even the most ardent admirer of Romanticism would claim that Wordsworth's *The Borderers*, Shelley's *The Cenci,* or Keats's *Otho the Great* represent their most characteristic or triumphant moments.

But Byron, even in his contempt for actual dramatic performance, achieved a curious theatrical power that his contemporaries missed. Too self-conscious and analytical (like any good Romantic, or modern) to be able to represent the actual transformation of passion and thought in his dramas, he nevertheless articulated a kind of frozen, impotent rage against the immutability of fate which makes him the greatest, perhaps the only, Romantic tragedian. Unlike the plays of Shakespeate or the great Greek tragedians, each of Byron's tragedies opens *after* the definitive catastrophe of its hero: the worst has already happened before the opening line is spoken. And as we watch these Byronic protagonists struggle, not against the possibility but against the inevitable recognition of their own downfall, we might almost be witnessing the birth of the dramaturgy which appeals to the modern mind, the first approach to the theater of the absurd.

Dramatis Personæ

MANFRED
CHAMOIS HUNTER
ABBOT OF ST. MAURICE
MANUEL
HERMAN

---

1. Written and published in 1817. *Manfred,* the most popular and celebrated of Byron's dramas, has frequently been regarded as his version of that most central of Romantic myths, the Faust legend. The greatest treatment of the myth, Goethe's *Faust* (Part One), had appeared in 1808, and Goethe himself, in an article on *Manfred,* assumed that Byron's drama was derived from his own. But there are important differences: Manfred, unlike Faust, does not sell his soul to the Devil; rather, he defies the power of the underworld, and controls that power through his own indomitable will.

WITCH OF THE ALPS
ARIMANES
NEMESIS
THE DESTINIES
SPIRITS, ETC

*The Scene of the Drama is amongst the Higher Alps—partly in the
Castle of Manfred, and party in the Mountains.*

Act I.

SCENE I.—MANFRED *alone.—Scene, a Gothic Gallery.—Time, Midnight.*

Man. The lamp must be replenished, but even then
It will not burn so long as I must watch:
My slumbers—if I slumber—are not sleep,
But a continuance of enduring thought,
Which then I can resist not: in my heart   5
There is a vigil, and these eyes but close
To look within; and yet I live, and bear
The aspect and the form of breathing men.
But Grief should be the Instructor of the wise;
Sorrow is Knowledge: they who know the most   10
Must mourn the deepest o'er the fatal truth,
The Tree of Knowledge is not that of Life.
Philosophy and science, and the springs
Of Wonder, and the wisdom of the World,
I have essayed, and in my mind there is   15
A power to make these subject to itself—
But they avail not:[2] I have done men good,
And I have met with good even among men—
But this availed not: I have had my foes,
And none have baffled, many fallen before me—   20
But this availed not:—Good—or evil—life—
Powers, passions—all I see in other beings,
Have been to me as rain unto the sands,
Since that all-nameless hour. I have no dread,
And feel the curse to have no natural fear,   25
Nor fluttering throb, that beats with hopes or wishes,
Or lurking love of something on the earth.
Now to my task.—
                    Mysterious Agency!
Ye Spirits of the unbounded Universe!
Whom I have sought in darkness and in light—   30
Ye, who do compass earth about, and dwell
In subtler essence—ye, to whom the tops
Of mountains inaccessible are haunts,

2. These lines are a paraphrase of the   Christopher Marlowe's Elizabethan *Trag-*
opening of Goethe's *Faust,* as well as of   *edy of Dr. Faustus.*

And Earth's and Ocean's caves familiar things—
    I call upon ye by the written charm   35
Which gives me power upon you—Rise! Appear!

                        [*A pause.*]

They come not yet.—Now by the voice of him
Who is the first[3] among you—by this sign,
Which makes you tremble—by the claims of him
Who is undying,—Rise! Appear!——Appear!   40

                        [*A pause.*]

If it be so.—Spirits of Earth and Air,
Ye shall not so elude me! By a power,
Deeper than all yet urged, a tyrant-spell,
Which had its birthplace in a star condemned,
The burning wreck of a demolished world,   45
A wandering hell in the eternal Space;
By the strong curse which is upon my Soul,
The thought which is within me and around me,
I do compel ye to my will,—Appear!
[*A star is seen at the darker end of the gallery: it is stationary; and
    a voice is heard singing.*]

First Spirit

Mortal! to thy bidding bowed,   50
From my mansion in the cloud,
Which the breath of Twilight builds,
And the Summer's sunset gilds
With the azure and vermilion,
Which is mixed for my pavilion;   55
Though thy quest may be forbidden,
On a star-beam I have ridden,
To thine adjuration bowed:
Mortal—be thy wish avowed!

Voice of the Second Spirit

Mont Blanc[4] is the Monarch of mountains;   60
    They crowned him long ago
On a throne of rocks, in a robe of clouds,
    With a Diadem of snow.
Around his waist are forests braced,
    The Avalanche in his hand;   65
But ere it fall, that thundering ball

---

3. Arimanes or Ahriman, ruler of evil
and earthbound spirits in the mythology
of Zoroastrianism, the Persian religion
from which Byron takes the machinery
of *Manfred*. Manfred will meet Arimanes in Act II, scene iv.
4. Mont Blanc, on the border between
France and Italy, is the highest of the
Alps, and a crucial scene for Romantic
poetry. Shelley's lyric, "Mont Blanc"
(1816), Mary Shelley's *Frankenstein*
(1818), and *Manfred* all utilize this im-
pressive, glacier-capped peak as an essential feature of their visions of human
striving against an alien, impassive cos-
mos.

Must pause for my command.
The Glacier's cold and restless mass
  Moves onward day by day;
But I am he who bids it pass,   70
  Or with its ice delay.
I am the Spirit of the place,
  Could make the mountain bow
And quiver to his caverned base—
  And what with me would'st *Thou*?   75

Voice of the THIRD SPIRIT

In the blue depth of the waters,
  Where the wave hath no strife,
Where the Wind is a stranger,
  And the Sea-snake hath life,
Where the Mermaid is decking   80
  Her green hair with shells,
Like the storm on the surface
  Came the sound of thy spells;
O'er my calm Hall of Coral
  The deep Echo rolled—   85
To the Spirit of Ocean
  Thy wishes unfold!

FOURTH SPIRIT

Where the slumbering Earthquake
  Lies pillowed on fire,
And the lakes of bitumen[5]   90
  Rise boilingly higher;
Where the roots of the Andes
  Strike deep in the earth,
As their summits to heaven
  Shoot soaringly forth;   95
I have quitted my birthplace,
  Thy bidding to bide—
Thy spell hath subdued me,
  Thy will be my guide!

FIFTH SPIRIT

I am the Rider of the wind,   100
  The Stirrer of the storm;
The hurricane I left behind
  Is yet with lightning warm;

5. Volcanic rock; here in its molten form, as an image of the Fourth Spirit's violence.

To speed to thee, o'er shore and sea
   I swept upon the blast: 105
The fleet I met sailed well—and yet
   'Twill sink ere night be past.

SIXTH SPIRIT

My dwelling is the shadow of the Night,
Why doth thy magic torture me with light?

SEVENTH SPIRIT

The Star which rules thy destiny 110
Was ruled, ere earth began, by me:
It was a World as fresh and fair
As e'er revolved round Sun in air;
Its course was free and regular,
Space bosomed not a lovelier star. 115
The Hour arrived—and it became
A wandering mass of shapeless flame,
A pathless Comet, and a curse,
The menace of the Universe;
Still rolling on with innate force, 120
Without a sphere, without a course,
A bright deformity on high,
The monster of the upper sky!
And Thou! beneath its influence born—
Thou worm! whom I obey and scorn— 125
Forced by a Power (which is not thine,
And lent thee but to make thee mine)
For this brief moment to descend,
Where these weak Spirits round thee bend
And parley with a thing like thee— 130
What would'st thou, Child of Clay! with me?

The SEVEN SPIRITS

Earth—ocean—air—night—mountains—winds—thy Star,
   Are at thy beck and bidding, Child of Clay!
Before thee at thy quest their Spirits are—
   What would'st thou with us, Son of mortals—say? 135
   Man. Forgetfulness——
   First Spirit.   Of what—of whom—and why?
   Man. Of that which is within me; read it there—
Ye know it—and I cannot utter it.
   Spirit. We can but give thee that which we possess:
Ask of us subjects, sovereignty, the power 140
O'er earth—the whole, or portion—or a sign
Which shall control the elements, whereof

We are the dominators,—each and all,
These shall be thine.
   Man.   Oblivion—self-oblivion!
Can ye not wring from out the hidden realms   145
Ye offer so profusely—what I ask?
   Spirit. It is not in our essence, in our skill;
But—thou may'st die.
   Man.   Will Death bestow it on me?
   Spirit. We are immortal, and do not forget;
We are eternal; and to us the past   150
Is, as the future, present. Art thou answered?
   Man. Ye mock me—but the Power which brought ye
     here
Hath made you mine. Slaves, scoff not at my will!
The Mind—the Spirit—the Promethean[6] spark,
The lightning of my being, is as bright,   155
Pervading, and far darting as your own,
And shall not yield to yours, though cooped in clay!
Answer, or I will teach you what I am.
   Spirit. We answer—as we answered; our reply
Is even in thine own words.
   Man.   Why say ye so?   160
   Spirit. If, as thou say'st, thine essence be as ours,
We have replied in telling thee, the thing
Mortals call death hath nought to do with us.
   Man. I then have called ye from your realms in vain;
Ye cannot, or ye will not, aid me.
   Spirit.   Say—[7]   165
What we possess we offer; it is thine:
Bethink ere thou dismiss us; ask again;
Kingdom, and sway, and strength, and length of days—
   Man. Accurséd! what have I to do with days?
They are too long already.—Hence—begone!   170
   Spirit. Yet pause: being here, our will would do thee
     service;
Bethink thee, is there then no other gift
Which we can make not worthless in thine eyes?
   Man. No, none: yet stay—one moment, ere we part
I would behold ye face to face. I hear   175
Your voices, sweet and melancholy sounds,
As Music on the waters; and I see
The steady aspect of a clear large Star;
But nothing more. Approach me as ye are,

6. In Greek mythology, the Titan Prometheus stole the fire of Zeus to give it
to mankind. He is thus an image, for
the Romantics, of the revolutionary
spirit which brings new light, new truth,
to men.
7. According to the manuscript, this is
part of the Spirit's speech, although logi-
cally it seems to belong to Manfred, as
his command to the Spirits to explain
themselves. It is conceivable that Byron
intended the command to be ambiguous,
since, as the Spirit has already said to
Manfred at lines 159–160, "our reply/Is
even in thine own words."

Or one—or all—in your accustomed forms.   180
   Spirit. We have no forms, beyond the elements
Of which we are the mind and principle:
But choose a form—in that we will appear.
   Man. I have no choice; there is no form on earth
Hideous or beautiful to me. Let him,   185
Who is most powerful of ye, take such aspect
As unto him may seem most fitting—Come!
   *Seventh Spirit (appearing in the shape of a beautiful
       female figure)*. Behold!
   Man.   Oh God! if it be thus, and *thou*
Art not a madness and a mockery,
I yet might be most happy. I will clasp thee,   190
And we again will be——

                [The figure vanishes.]
       My heart is crushed!
            *[*MANFRED *falls senseless.]*

   A voice is heard in the Incantation which follows.

     When the Moon is on the wave,
       And the glow-worm in the grass,
     And the meteor on the grave,
       And the wisp on the morass;   195
     When the falling stars are shooting,
     And the answered owls are hooting,
     And the silent leaves are still
     In the shadow of the hill,
     Shall my soul be upon thine,   200
     With a power and with a sign.

     Though thy slumber may be deep,
     Yet thy Spirit shall not sleep;
     There are shades which will not vanish,
     There are thoughts thou canst not banish;   205
     By a Power to thee unknown,
     Thou canst never be alone;
     Thou art wrapt as with a shroud,
     Thou art gathered in a cloud;
     And for ever shalt thou dwell   210
     In the spirit of this spell.

     Though thou seest me not pass by,
     Thou shalt feel me with thine eye
     As a thing that, though unseen,
     Must be near thee, and hath been;   215
     And when in that secret dread
     Thou hast turned around thy head,
     Thou shalt marvel I am not
     At thy shadow on the spot,

And the power which thou dost feel   220
Shall be what thou must conceal.

And a magic voice and verse
Hath baptised thee with a curse;
And a Spirit of the air
Hath begirt thee with a snare;   225
In the wind there is a voice
Shall forbid thee to rejoice;
And to thee shall Night deny
All the quiet of her sky;
And the day shall have a sun,   230
Which shall make thee wish it done.

From thy false tears I did distil
An essence which hath strength to kill;
From thy own heart I then did wring
The black blood in its blackest spring;   235
From thy own smile I snatched the snake,
For there it coiled as in a brake;
From thy own lip I drew the charm
Which gave all these their chiefest harm;
In proving every poison known,   240
I found the strongest was thine own.

By the cold breast and serpent smile,
By thy unfathomed gulfs of guile,
By that most seeming virtuous eye,
By thy shut soul's hypocrisy;   245
By the perfection of thine art
Which passed for human thine own heart;
By thy delight in others' pain,
And by thy brotherhood of Cain,
I call upon thee! and compel   250
Thyself to be thy proper Hell![8]

And on thy head I pour the vial
Which doth devote thee to this trial;
Nor to slumber, nor to die,
Shall be in thy destiny;   255
Though thy death shall still seem near
To thy wish, but as a fear;
Lo! the spell now works around thee,
And the clankless chain hath bound thee;
O'er thy heart and brain together   260
Hath the word been passed—now wither!

---

8. As in *Harold* I, "To Inez," stanza 6, line 4, a reminiscence of Satan in *Para-dise Lost* IV (75): "Which way I fly is Hell; myself am Hell."

SCENE II.—*The Mountain of the Jungfrau.*[9]—*Time,*
Morning.—MANFRED *alone upon the cliffs.*

Man. The spirits I have raised abandon me,
The spells which I have studied baffle me,
The remedy I recked of tortured me;
I lean no more on superhuman aid;
It hath no power upon the past, and for   5
The future, till the past be gulfed in darkness,
It is not of my search.—My Mother Earth!
And thou fresh-breaking Day, and you, ye Mountains,
Why are ye beautiful? I cannot love ye.
And thou, the bright Eye of the Universe,   10
That openest over all, and unto all
Art a delight—thou shin'st not on my heart.
And you, ye crags, upon whose extreme edge
I stand, and on the torrent's brink beneath
Behold the tall pines dwindled as to shrubs   15
In dizziness of distance; when a leap,
A stir, a motion, even a breath, would bring
My breast upon its rocky bosom's bed
To rest for ever—wherefore do I pause?
I feel the impulse—yet I do not plunge;   20
I see the peril—yet do not recede;
And my brain reels—and yet my foot is firm:
There is a power upon me which withholds,
And makes it my fatality to live,—
If it be life to wear within myself   25
This barrenness of Spirit, and to be
My own Soul's sepulchre, for I have ceased
To justify my deeds unto myself—
The last infirmity of evil. Aye,
Thou winged and cloud-cleaving minister,   30

                              [*An Eagle passes.*]

Whose happy flight is highest into heaven,
Well may'st thou swoop so near me—I should be
Thy prey, and gorge thine eaglets; thou art gone
Where the eye cannot follow thee; but thine
Yet pierces downward, onward, or above,   35
With a pervading vision.—Beautiful!
How beautiful is all this visible world!
How glorious in its action and itself!
But we, who name ourselves its sovereigns, we,
Half dust, half deity, alike unfit   40
To sink or soar, with our mixed essence make
A conflict of its elements, and breathe
The breath of degradation and of pride,
Contending with low wants and lofty will,

---

9. One of the tallest of the Swiss Alps.

Till our Mortality predominates, 45
And men are—what they name not to themselves,
And trust not to each other. Hark! the note,
          [*The Shepherd's pipe in the distance is heard.*]
The natural music of the mountain reed—
For here the patriarchal days are not
A pastoral fable—pipes in the liberal air, 50
Mixed with the sweet bells of the sauntering herd;
My soul would drink those echoes. Oh, that I were
The viewless[1] spirit of a lovely sound,
A living voice, a breathing harmony,
A bodiless enjoyment—born and dying 55
With the blest tone which made me!

        Enter from below a CHAMOIS HUNTER

   Chamois Hunter.   Even so
This way the Chamois[2] leapt: her nimble feet
Have baffled me; my gains to-day will scarce
Repay my break-neck travail.—What is here?
Who seems not of my trade, and yet hath reached 60
A height which none even of our mountaineers,
Save our best hunters, may attain: his garb
Is goodly, his mien manly, and his air
Proud as a free-born peasant's, at this distance:
I will approach him nearer.
     Man. (*not perceiving the other*). To be thus— 65
Grey-haired with anguish, like these blasted pines,
Wrecks of a single winter, barkless, branchless,
A blighted trunk upon a curséd root,
Which but supplies a feeling to Decay—
And to be thus, eternally but thus, 70
Having been otherwise! Now furrowed o'er
With wrinkles, ploughed by moments, not by years
And hours, all tortured into ages—hours
Which I outlive!—Ye toppling crags of ice!
Ye Avalanches, whom a breath draws down 75
In mountainous o'erwhelming, come and crush me!
I hear ye momently above, beneath,
Crash with a frequent conflict; but ye pass,
And only fall on things that still would live;
On the young flourishing forest, or the hut 80
And hamlet of the harmless villager.
     C. Hun. The mists begin to rise from up the valley;
I'll warn him to descend, or he may chance
To lose at once his way and life together.
     Man. The mists boil up around the glaciers; clouds 85

---

1. The word was coined by William
Wordsworth and during the early nineteenth century was strongly associated
with the Romantic yearning for ecstatic
assimilation into nature.
2. Mountain antelope (pronounced
"shammy").

Rise curling fast beneath me, white and sulphury,
Like foam from the roused ocean of deep Hell,
Whose every wave breaks on a living shore,
Heaped with the damned like pebbles.—I am giddy.
  C. Hun. I must approach him cautiously; if near,   90
A sudden step will startle him, and he
Seems tottering already.
  Man.   Mountains have fallen,
Leaving a gap in the clouds, and with the shock
Rocking their Alpine brethren; filling up
The ripe green valleys with Destruction's splinters;   95
Damming the rivers with a sudden dash,
Which crushed the waters into mist, and made
Their fountains find another channel—thus,
Thus, in its old age, did Mount Rosenberg[3]—
Why stood I not beneath it?
  C. Hun.   Friend! have a care,
Your next step may be fatal! for the love
Of Him who made you, stand not on that brink!
  Man. (*not hearing him*). Such would have been for
     me a fitting tomb;
My bones had then been quiet in their depth;
They had not then been strewn upon the rocks   105
For the wind's pastime—as thus—thus they shall be—
In this one plunge.—Farewell, ye opening Heavens!
Look not upon me thus reproachfully—
You were not meant for me—Earth! take these atoms!
  [As MANFRED *is in act to spring from the cliff, the*
     CHAMOIS HUNTER *seizes and retains him with a*
     sudden grasp.]
  C. Hun. Hold, madman!—though aweary of thy life,   110
Stain not our pure vales with thy guilty blood:
Away with me——I will not quit my hold.
  Man. I am most sick at heart—nay, grasp me not—
I am all feebleness—the mountains whirl
Spinning around me——I grow blind——What art thou? 115
  C. Hun. I'll answer that anon.—Away with me——
The clouds grow thicker——there—now lean on me—
Place your foot here—here, take this staff, and cling
A moment to that shrub—now give me your hand,
And hold fast by my girdle—softly—well—
The Chalet will be gained within an hour:
Come on, we'll quickly find a surer footing,
And something like a pathway, which the torrent
Hath washed since winter.—Come, 'tis bravely done—
You should have been a hunter.—Follow me.   125
  [As *they descend the rocks with difficulty, the scene*
     closes.]

---

3. Mount Rossberg, in Switzerland, was the scene of a massive and disastrous avalanche on September 2, 1806.

Act II

SCENE I.—A *Cottage among the Bernese Alps.*—MANFRED
and *the* CHAMOIS HUNTER.

>   *C. Hun.* No—no—yet pause—thou must not yet go
>   forth:
> Thy mind and body are alike unfit
> To trust each other, for some hours, at least;
> When thou art better, I will be thy guide—
> But whither?
>   *Man.*   It imports not: I do know   5
> My route full well, and need no further guidance.
>   *C. Hun.* Thy garb and gait bespeak thee of high
>   lineage—
> One of the many chiefs, whose castled crags
> Look o'er the lower valleys—which of these
> May call thee lord? I only know their portals;   10
> My way of life leads me but rarely down
> To bask by the huge hearths of those old halls,
> Carousing with the vassals; but the paths,
> Which step from out our mountains to their doors,
> I know from childhood—which of these is thine?   15
>   *Man.* No matter.
>   *C. Hun.*   Well, Sir, pardon me the question,
> And be of better cheer. Come, taste my wine;
> 'Tis of an ancient vintage; many a day
> 'T has thawed my veins among our glaciers, now
> Let it do thus for thine—Come, pledge me fairly!   20
>   *Man.* Away, away! there's blood upon the brim!
> Will it then never—never sink in the earth?
>   *C. Hun.* What dost thou mean? thy senses wander
>   from thee.
>   *Man.* I say 'tis blood—my blood! the pure warm
>   stream
> Which ran in the veins of my fathers, and in ours
> When we were in our youth, and had one heart,
> And loved each other as we should not love,[4]
> And this was shed: but still it rises up,
> Colouring the clouds, that shut me out from Heaven,
> Where thou art not—and I shall never be.   30
>   *C. Hun.* Man of strange words, and some half-
>   maddening sin,
> Which makes thee people vacancy, whate'er
> Thy dread and sufferance be, there's comfort yet—
> The aid of holy men, and heavenly patience——

---

4. E. H. Coleridge notes, in the John Murray Edition, "The critics of the day either affected to ignore or severely censured . . . the allusions to an incestuous passion between Manfred and Astarte." The reference of this passage to Byron's own relationship with his half-sister Augusta would have been scandalously obvious to the contemporary public.

Man. Patience—and patience! Hence—that word
  was made   35
For brutes of burthen, not for birds of prey!
Preach it to mortals of a dust like thine,—
I am not of thine order.
    C. Hun.   Thanks to Heaven!
I would not be of thine for the free fame
Of William Tell;[5] but whatsoe'er thine ill,   40
It must be borne, and these wild starts are useless.
    Man. Do I not bear it?—Look on me—I live.
    C. Hun. This is convulsion, and no healthful life.
    Man. I tell thee, man! I have lived many years,
Many long years, but they are nothing now   45
To those which I must number: ages—ages—
Space and eternity—and consciousness,
With the fierce thirst of death—and still unslaked!
    C. Hun. Why, on thy brow the seal of middle age
Hath scarce been set; I am thine elder far.   50
    Man. Think'st thou existence doth depend on time?
It doth; but actions are our epochs: mine
Have made my days and nights imperishable,
Endless, and all alike, as sands on the shore,
Innumerable atoms; and one desert,   55
Barren and cold, on which the wild waves break,
But nothing rests, save carcasses and wrecks,
Rocks, and the salt-surf weeds of bitterness.
    C. Hun. Alas! he's mad—but yet I must not leave him.
    Man. I would I were—for then the things I see   60
Would be but a distempered dream.
    C. Hun..   What is it
That thou dost see, or think thou look'st upon?
    Man. Myself, and thee—a peasant of the Alps—
Thy humble virtues, hospitable home,
And spirit patient, pious, proud, and free;   65
Thy self-respect, grafted on innocent thoughts;
Thy days of health, and nights of sleep; thy toils,
By danger dignified, yet guiltless; hopes
Of cheerful old age and a quiet grave,
With cross and garland over its green turf,   70
And thy grandchildren's love for epitaph!
This do I see—and then I look within—
It matters not—my Soul was scorched already!
    C. Hun. And would'st thou then exchange thy lot for
  mine?
    Man. No, friend! I would not wrong thee, nor
  exchange   75
My lot with living being: I can bear—

(Handwritten margin note: pleasant & primitive: manfred knows too much to accept this.)

---

5. The legendary Swiss patriot, forced by   off his son's head.
an Austrian governor to shoot an apple

However wretchedly, 'tis still to bear—
In life what others could not brook to dream,
But perish in their slumber.
    C. Hun.   And with this—
This cautious feeling for another's pain,   80
Canst thou be black with evil?—say not so.
Can one of gentle thoughts have wreaked revenge
Upon his enemies?
    Man.   Oh! no, no, no!
My injuries came down on those who loved me—
On those whom I best loved: I never quelled   85
An enemy, save in my just defence—
But my embrace was fatal.
    C. Hun.   Heaven give thee rest!
And Penitence restore thee to thyself;
My prayers shall be for thee.
    Man.   I need them not,
But can endure thy pity. I depart—   90
'Tis time—farewell!—Here's gold, and thanks for thee—
No words—it is thy due.—Follow me not—
I know my path—the mountain peril's past:
And once again I charge thee, follow not!

                              [*Exit* MANFRED.]

    SCENE II.—A *lower Valley in the Alps.*—A *Cataract*

             Enter MANFRED.

It is not noon—the Sunbow's rays still arch
The torrent with the many hues of heaven,
And roll the sheeted silver's waving column
O'er the crag's headlong perpendicular,
And fling its lines of foaming light along,   5
And to and fro, like the pale courser's tail,
The Giant steed, to be bestrode by Death,
As told in the Apocalypse. No eyes
But mine now drink this sight of loveliness;
I should be sole in this sweet solitude,   10
And with the Spirit of the place divide
The homage of these waters.—I will call her.
    [MANFRED *takes some of the water into the palm of his hand*
          and flings it into the air, muttering the adjuration. After a
          pause, the WITCH OF THE ALPS *rises beneath the arch of*
          the sunbow of the torrent.]
Beautiful Spirit! with thy hair of light,
And dazzling eyes of glory, in whose form
The charms of Earth's least mortal daughters grow   15
To an unearthly stature, in an essence
Of purer elements; while the hues of youth,—
Carnationed like a sleeping Infant's cheek,
Rocked by the beating of her mother's heart,

Or the rose tints, which Summer's twilight leaves   20
Upon the lofty Glacier's virgin snow,
The blush of earth embracing with her Heaven,—
Tinge thy celestial aspect, and make tame
The beauties of the Sunbow which bends o'er thee.
Beautiful Spirit! in thy calm clear brow,   25
Wherein is glassed serenity of Soul,
Which of itself shows immortality,
I read that thou wilt pardon to a Son
Of Earth, whom the abstruser powers permit
At times to commune with them—if that he   30
Avail him of his spells—to call thee thus,
And gaze on thee a moment.
    Witch.   Son of Earth!
I know thee, and the Powers which give thee power!
I know thee for a man of many thoughts,
And deeds of good and ill, extreme in both,   35
Fatal and fated in thy sufferings.
I have expected this—what would'st thou with me?
    Man. To look upon thy beauty—nothing further.
The face of the earth hath maddened me, and I
Take refuge in her mysteries, and pierce   40
To the abodes of those who govern her—
But they can nothing aid me. I have sought
From them what they could not bestow, and now
I search no further.
    Witch.   What could be the quest
Which is not in the power of the most powerful,   45
The rulers of the invisible?
    Man.   A boon;—
But why should I repeat it? 'twere in vain.
    Witch. I know not that; let thy lips utter it.
    Man. Well, though it torture me, 'tis but the same;
My pang shall find a voice. From my youth upwards   50
My Spirit walked not with the souls of men,
Nor looked upon the earth with human eyes;
The thirst of their ambition was not mine,
The aim of their existence was not mine;
My joys—my griefs—my passions—and my powers,   55
Made me a stranger; though I wore the form,
I had no sympathy with breathing flesh,
Nor midst the Creatures of Clay that girded me
Was there but One who——but of her anon.
I said with men, and with the thoughts of men,   60
I held but slight communion; but instead,
My joy was in the wilderness,—to breathe
The difficult air of the iced mountain's top,
Where the birds dare not build—nor insect's wing
Flit o'er the herbless granite; or to plunge   65
Into the torrent, and to roll along

On the swift whirl of the new-breaking wave
Of river-stream, or Ocean, in their flow.
In these my early strength exulted; or
To follow through the night the moving moon, 70
The stars and their development; or catch
The dazzling lightnings till my eyes grew dim;
Or to look, list'ning, on the scattered leaves,
While Autumn winds were at their evening song.
These were my pastimes, and to be alone; 75
For if the beings, of whom I was one,—
Hating to be so,—crossed me in my path,
I felt myself degraded back to them,
And was all clay again. And then I dived,
In my lone wanderings, to the caves of Death, 80
Searching its cause in its effect; and drew
From withered bones, and skulls, and heaped up dust,
Conclusions most forbidden. Then I passed
The nights of years in sciences untaught,
Save in the old-time; and with time and toil, 85
And terrible ordeal, and such penance
As in itself hath power upon the air,
And spirits that do compass air and earth,
Space, and the peopled Infinite, I made
Mine eyes familiar with Eternity,
Such as, before me, did the Magi, and
He who from out their fountain-dwellings raised
Eros and Anteros,[6] at Gadara,
As I do thee;—and with my knowledge grew
The thirst of knowledge, and the power and joy 95
Of this most bright intelligence, until——

    Witch. Proceed.

    Man.   Oh! I but thus prolonged my words,
Boasting these idle attributes, because
As I approach the core of my heart's grief—
But—to my task. I have not named to thee 100
Father or mother, mistress, friend, or being,
With whom I wore the chain of human ties;
If I had such, they seemed not such to me—
Yet there was One——

    Witch.   Spare not thyself—proceed.

    Man. She was like me in lineaments—her eyes— 105
Her hair—her features—all, to the very tone
Even of her voice, they said were like to mine;
But softened all, and tempered into beauty:
She had the same lone thoughts and wanderings,
The quest of hidden knowledge, and a mind 110
To comprehend the Universe: nor these

6. The Neoplatonic philosopher Iambli-
chus (A.D. fourth century) was supposed
to have summoned the deities Eros and
Anteros from a spring in Gadara, Syria,
which bore their names. Eros is the god
of love; Anteros or "anti-love" is the avenging deity of disappointed or betrayed
love.

Alone, but with them gentler powers than mine,
Pity, and smiles, and tears—which I had not;
And tenderness—but that I had for her;
Humility—and that I never had. 115
Her faults were mine—her virtues were her own—
I loved her, and destroyed her!
   Witch.   With thy hand?
   Man. Not with my hand, but heart, which broke her
      heart;
It gazed on mine, and withered. I have shed
Blood, but not hers—and yet her blood was shed; 120
I saw—and could not stanch it.
   Witch.   And for this—
A being of the race thou dost despise—
The order, which thine own would rise above,
Mingling with us and ours,—thou dost forego
The gifts of our great knowledge, and shrink'st back 125
To recreant mortality——Away!
   Man. Daughter of Air! I tell thee, since that hour—
But words are breath—look on me in my sleep,
Or watch my watchings—Come and sit by me!
My solitude is solitude no more, 130
But peopled with the Furies;—I have gnashed
My teeth in darkness till returning morn,
Then cursed myself till sunset;—I have prayed
For madness as a blessing—'tis denied me.
I have affronted Death—but in the war 135
Of elements the waters shrunk from me,
And fatal things passed harmless; the cold hand
Of an all-pitiless Demon held me back,
Back by a single hair, which would not break.
In Fantasy, Imagination, all 140
The affluence of my soul—which one day was
A Croesus[7] in creation—I plunged deep,
But, like an ebbing wave, it dashed me back
Into the gulf of my unfathomed thought.
I plunged amidst Mankind—Forgetfulness 145
I sought in all, save where 'tis to be found—
And that I have to learn—my Sciences,
My long pursued and superhuman art,
Is mortal here: I dwell in my despair—
And live—and live for ever.[8]
   Witch.   It may be 150

7. King of Lydia, 560–546 B.C., reputedly the most fabulously wealthy man in the ancient world; hence, a byword for profligacy.
8. This is one of Byron's most important allusions to the legend of the Wandering Jew, a popular theme of Gothic and Romantic fiction. The Wandering Jew, Ahasuerus, had (according to legend), cursed Christ at the Crucifixion, and was condemned to wander the earth, immortal in his guilt, till the Second Coming. Manfred, like Ahasuerus, is questing for "forgetfulness" or expiation of his crime through oblivion.

That I can aid thee.
    Man.   To do this thy power
Must wake the dead, or lay me low with them.
Do so—in any shape—in any hour—
With any torture—so it be the last.
    Witch. That is not in my province; but if thou   155
Wilt swear obedience to my will, and do
My bidding, it may help thee to thy wishes.
    Man. I will not swear—Obey! and whom? the Spirits
Whose presence I command, and be the slave
Of those who served me—Never!
    Witch.   Is this all?   160
Hast thou no gentler answer?—Yet bethink thee,
And pause ere thou rejectest.
    Man.   I have said it.
    Witch. Enough! I may retire then—say!
    Man.   Retire!
                    [*The* WITCH *disappears.*]
    Man. (*alone*). We are the fools of Time and Terror:
        Days
Steal on us, and steal from us; yet we live,   165
Loathing our life, and dreading still to die.
In all the days of this detested yoke—
This vital weight upon the struggling heart,
Which sinks with sorrow, or beats quick with pain,
Or joy that ends in agony or faintness—   170
In all the days of past and future—for
In life there is no present—we can number
How few—how less than few—wherein the soul
Forbears to pant for death, and yet draws back
As from a stream in winter, though the chill   175
Be but a moment's. I have one resource
Still in my science—I can call the dead,
And ask them what it is we dread to be:
The sternest answer can but be the Grave,
And that is nothing: if they answer not——
The buried Prophet[9] answered to the Hag   180
Of Endor; and the Spartan Monarch[1] drew
From the Byzantine maid's unsleeping spirit
An answer and his destiny—he slew
That which he loved, unknowing what he slew,   185
And died unpardoned—though he called in aid
The Phyxian Jove, and in Phigalia roused

9. Samuel, whom King Saul forced the Witch of Endor (the "Hag") to raise from the dead, and who foretold Saul's death (I Samuel 28).
1. According to Plutarch, Pausanias (king of Sparta) was deceived into killing his bride Cleonice on their wedding night. Overcome with remorse and haunted by Cleonice's ghost, Pausanias had the priests of Jove in Phigalia ("Arcadian Evocators") raise Cleonice, who prophesied that the king's troubles would soon be over. This was an ambiguous prophecy of Pausanias's impending death.

The Arcadian Evocators to compel
The indignant shadow to depose her wrath,
Or fix her term of vengeance—she replied   190
In words of dubious import, but fulfilled.
If I had never lived, that which I love
Had still been living; had I never loved,
That which I love would still be beautiful,
Happy and giving happiness. What is she?   195
What is she now?—a sufferer for my sins—
A thing I dare not think upon—or nothing.
Within few hours I shall not call in vain—
Yet in this hour I dread the thing I dare:
Until this hour I never shrunk to gaze   200
On spirit, good or evil—now I tremble,
And feel a strange cold thaw upon my heart.
But I can act even what I most abhor,
And champion human fears.—The night approaches.
                                              [*Exit.*]

SCENE III.—*The summit of the Jungfrau Mountain.*
            Enter FIRST DESTINY.

The Moon is rising broad, and round, and bright;
And here on snows, where never human foot
Of common mortal trod, we nightly tread,
And leave no traces: o'er the savage sea,
The glassy ocean of the mountain ice,   5
We skim its rugged breakers, which put on
The aspect of a tumbling tempest's foam,
Frozen in a moment—a dead Whirlpool's image:
And this most steep fantastic pinnacle,
The fretwork of some earthquake—where the clouds   10
Pause to repose themselves in passing by—
Is sacred to our revels, or our virgils;
Here do I wait my sisters, on our way
To the Hall of Arimanes—for to-night
Is our great festival—'tis strange they come not.   15

             A *Voice without, singing.*

    The Captive Usurper,
       Hurled down from the throne,
    Lay buried in torpor,
       Forgotten and lone;
    I broke through his slumbers,   20
       I shivered his chain,
    I leagued him with numbers—
       He's Tyrant again!
With the blood of a million he'll answer my care,
With a Nation's destruction—his flight and despair!   25

Second Voice, without,

The Ship sailed on, the Ship sailed fast,
But I left not a sail, and I left not a mast;
There is not a plank of the hull or the deck,
And there is not a wretch to lament o'er his wreck;
Save one, whom I held, as he swam, by the hair,   30
And he was a subject well worthy my care;
A traitor on land, and a pirate at sea—
But I saved him to wreak further havoc for me!

FIRST DESTINY, *answering.*

The City lies sleeping;
    The morn, to deplore it,   35
May dawn on it weeping:
    Sullenly, slowly
The black plague flew o'er it—
    Thousands lie lowly;
Tens of thousands shall perish;   40
    The living shall fly from
The sick they should cherish;
    But nothing can vanquish
The touch that they die from.
    Sorrow and anguish,   45
And evil and dread,
    Envelope a nation;
The blest are the dead,
Who see not the sight
    Of their own desolation;   50
This work of a night—
This wreck of a realm—this deed of my doing—
For ages I've done, and shall still be renewing!

Enter the SECOND *and* THIRD DESTINIES.

The Three.

Our hands contain the hearts of men,
    Our footsteps are their graves;   55
We only give to take again
    The Spirits of our slaves!

First Des. Welcome!—Where's Nemesis?[2]
Second Des.   At some
    great work;
But what I know not, for my hands were full.
    Third Des. Behold she cometh.

2. In classical mythology, the goddess of remorse and vengeance. Here, the hand-maiden of Arimanes.

Enter NEMESIS.

First Des.   Say, where hast thou been?   60
My Sisters and thyself are slow to-night.
    Nem. I was detained repairing shattered thrones—
Marrying fools, restoring dynasties—
Avenging men upon their enemies,
And making them repent their own revenge;   65
Goading the wise to madness; from the dull
Shaping out oracles to rule the world
Afresh—for they were waxing out of date,
And mortals dared to ponder for themselves,
To weigh kings in the balance—and to speak   70
Of Freedom, the forbidden fruit.—Away!
We have outstayed the hour—mount we our clouds!

                                        [*Exeunt.*]

SCENE IV.—*The Hall of Arimanes.—Arimanes on his*
    Throne, a Globe of Fire, surrounded by the Spirits.

Hymn of the SPIRITS.

Hail to our Master!—Prince of Earth and Air!
    Who walks the clouds and waters—in his hand
The sceptre of the Elements, which tear
    Themselves to chaos at his high command!
He breatheth—and a tempest shakes the sea;   5
    He speaketh—and the clouds reply in thunder;
He gazeth—from his glance the sunbeams flee;
    He moveth—Earthquakes rend the world asunder.
Beneath his footsteps the Volcanoes rise;
    His shadow is the Pestilence: his path   10
The comets herald through the crackling skies;
    And Planets turn to ashes at his wrath.
To him War offers daily sacrifice;
    To him Death pays his tribute; Life is his,
With all its Infinite of agonies—   15
    And his the Spirit of whatever is!

Enter the DESTINIES *and* NEMESIS.

First Des. Glory to Airmanes! on the earth
His power increaseth—both my sisters did
His bidding, nor did I neglect my duty!
    Second Des. Glory to Arimanes! we who bow   20
The necks of men, bow down before his throne!
    Third Des. Glory to Arimanes! we await
His nod!
    Nem.   Sovereign of Sovereigns! we are thine,
And all that liveth, more or less, is ours,
And most things wholly so; still to increase   25
Our power, increasing thine, demands our care,

And we are vigilant. Thy late commands
Have been fulfilled to the utmost.

Enter MANFRED.

  A Spirit.   What is here?
A mortal!—Thou most rash and fatal wretch,
Bow down and worship!
  Second Spirit.   I do know the man—   30
A Magian[3] of great power, and fearful skill!
  Third Spirit. Bow down and worship, slave!—What,
    know'st thou not
Thine and our Sovereign?—Tremble, and obey!
  All the Spirits. Prostrate thyself, and thy condemnéd
    clay,
Child of the Earth! or dread the worst.
  Man..   I know it;   35
And yet ye see I kneel not.
  Fourth Spirit.   'Twill be taught thee.
  Man. 'Tis taught already;—many a night on the earth,
On the bare ground, have I bowed down my face,
And strewed my head with ashes; I have known
The fulness of humiliation—for   40
I sunk before my vain despair, and knelt
To my own desolation.
  Fifth Spirit.   Dost thou dare
Refuse to Arimanes on his throne
What the whole earth accords, beholding not
The terror of his Glory?—Crouch! I say.   45
  Man. Bid *him* bow down to that which is above him,
The overruling Infinite—the Maker
Who made him not for worship—let him kneel,
And we will kneel together.
  The Spirits.   Crush the worm!
Tear him in pieces!—
  First Des.   Hence! Avaunt!—he's mine.   50
Prince of the Powers invisible! This man
Is of no common order, as his port
And presence here denote: his sufferings
Have been of an immortal nature—like
Our own; his knowledge, and his powers and will,   55
As far as is compatible with clay,
Which clogs the ethereal essence, have been such
As clay hath seldom borne; his aspirations
Have been beyond the dwellers of the earth,
And they have only taught him what we know—   60
That knowledge is not happiness, and science
But an exchange of ignorance for that
Which is another kind of ignorance.

---

3. Magician, sorcerer.

This is not all—the passions, attributes
Of Earth and Heaven, from which no power, nor being,   65
Nor breath from the worm upwards is exempt,
Have pierced his heart; and in their consequence
Made him a thing—which—I who pity not,
Yet pardon those who pity. He is mine—
And thine it may be; be it so, or not—   70
No other Spirit in this region hath
A soul like his—or power upon his soul.
   Nem. What doth he here then?
   First Des.   Let *him* answer that.
   Man. Ye know what I have known; and without
        power
I could not be amongst ye: but there are   75
Powers deeper still beyond—I come in quest
Of such, to answer unto what I seek.
   Nem. What would'st thou?
   Man.   *Thou* canst not reply to me.
Call up the dead—my question is for them.
   Nem. Great Arimanes, doth thy will avouch   80
The wishes of this mortal?
   Ari.   Yea.
   Nem.   Whom wouldst thou
Uncharnel?
   Man.   One without a tomb—call up
Astarte.[4]

NEMESIS.

Shadow! or Spirit!
   Whatever thou art,   85
Which still doth inherit
   The whole or a part
Of the form of thy birth,
   Of the mould of thy clay,
Which returned to the earth,   90
   Re-appear to the day!
Bear what thou borest,
   The heart and the form,
And the aspect thou worest
   Redeem from the worm.   95
Appear!—Appear!—Appear!
Who sent thee there requires thee here!
  [*The Phantom of* ASTARTE *rises and stands in the
    midst.*]
   Man. Can this be death? there's bloom upon her cheek;
But now I see it is no living hue,

4. Astarte is the name of the Phoenician goddess of love and beauty, equivalent to the Greek Aphrodite and the Roman Venus.

But a strange hectic—like the unnatural red
Which Autumn plants upon the perished leaf.   100
It is the same! Oh, God! that I should dread
To look upon the same—Astarte!—No,
I cannot speak to her—but bid her speak—
Forgive me or condemn me.   105

[handwritten annotation: hasn't done anything to be forgiven for or condemned]

NEMESIS.

By the Power which hath broken
    The grave which enthralled thee,
Speak to him who hath spoken,
    Or those who have called thee!
  Man.   She is silent,
And in that silence I am more than answered.   110
  Nem. My power extends no further. Prince of Air!
It rests with thee alone—command her voice.
  Ari. Spirit—obey this sceptre!
  Nem.   Silent still!
She is not of our order, but belongs
To the other powers. Mortal! thy quest is vain,   115
And we are baffled also.
  Man.   Hear me, hear me—
Astarte! my belovéd! speak to me:
I have so much endured—so much endure—
Look on me! the grave hath not changed thee more
Than I am changed for thee. Thou lovedst me   120
Too much, as I loved thee: we were not made
To torture thus each other—though it were
The deadliest sin to love as we have loved.
Say that thou loath'st me not—that I do bear
This punishment for both—that thou wilt be   125
One of the blesséd—and that I shall die;
For hitherto all hateful things conspire
To bind me in existence—in a life
Which makes me shrink from Immortality—
A future like the past. I cannot rest.   130
I know not what I ask, nor what I seek:
I feel but what thou art, and what I am;
And I would hear yet once before I perish
The voice which was my music—Speak to me!
For I have called on thee in the still night,   135
Startled the slumbering birds from the hushed boughs,
And woke the mountain wolves, and made the caves
Acquainted with thy vainly echoed name,
Which answered me—many things answered me—
Spirits and men—but thou wert silent all.   140
Yet speak to me! I have outwatched the stars,
And gazed o'er heaven in vain in search of thee.

Speak to me! I have wandered o'er the earth,
And never found thy likeness—Speak to me!
Look on the fiends around—they feel for me: 145
I fear them not, and feel for thee alone.
Speak to me! though it be in wrath;—but say—
I reck not what—but let me hear thee once—
This once—once more!
    Phantom of Astarte. Manfred!
    Man.   Say on, say on—
I live but in the sound—it is thy voice!   150
    Phan. Manfred! To-morrow[5] ends thine earthly ills.
Farewell!
    Man. Yet one word more—am I forgiven?
    Phan. Farewell!
    Man.   Say, shall we meet again?
    Phan.   Farewell!
    Man. One word for mercy! Say thou lovest me.
    Phan. Manfred!

                [*The Spirit of* ASTARTE *disappears.*]
    Nem.   She's gone, and will not be recalled: 155
Her words will be fulfilled. Return to the earth.
    A Spirit. He is convulsed—This is to be a mortal,
And seek the things beyond mortality.
    Another Spirit. Yet, see, he mastereth himself, and makes
His torture tributary to his will.   160
Had he been one of us, he would have made
An awful Spirit.
    Nem.   Hast thou further question
Of our great Sovereign, or his worshippers?
    Man. None.
    Nem.   Then for a time farewell.
    Man. We meet then! Where? On the earth?—   165
Even as thou wilt: and for the grace accorded
I now depart a debtor. Fare ye well!

                      [*Exit* MANFRED.]
          (*Scene closes.*)

Act III

SCENE I.—*A Hall in the Castle of Manfred.*
MANFRED *and* HERMAN.

    Man. What is the hour?
    Her.   It wants but one till sunset,
And promises a lovely twilight.
    Man.   Say,
Are all things so disposed of in the tower
As I directed?

---

5. As in the stories of Cleonice and the   fred is the assurance of his own death.
Witch of Endor, Astarte's gift to Man-

    Her.   All, my Lord, are ready:
Here is the key and casket.
    Man.   It is well: 5
Thou mayst retire.   [*Exit* Herman.]
    Man. (*alone*).   There is a calm upon me—
Inexplicable stillness! which till now
Did not belong to what I knew of life.
If that I did not know Philosophy
To be of all our vanities the motliest,   10
The merest word that ever fooled the ear
From out the schoolman's jargon, I should deem
The golden secret, the sought "Kalon,"[6] found,
And seated in my soul. It will not last,
But it is well to have known it, though but once: 15
It hath enlarged my thoughts with a new sense,
And I within my tablets would note down
That there is such a feeling. Who is there?

Re-enter Herman.

    Her. My Lord, the Abbot of St. Maurice craves
To greet your presence.

Enter the Abbot of St. Maurice.

    Abbot.   Peace be with Count Manfred!   20
    Man. Thanks, holy father! welcome to these walls;
Thy presence honours them, and blesseth those
Who dwell within them.
    Abbot.   Would it were so, Count!—
But I would fain confer with thee alone.
    Man. Herman, retire.—What would my reverend guest?   25
    Abbott. Thus, without prelude:—Age and zeal—my
        office—
And good intent must plead my privilege;
Our near, though not acquainted neighbourhood,
May also be my herald. Rumours strange,
And of unholy nature, are abroad,   30
And busy with thy name—a noble name
For centuries: may he who bears it now
Transmit it unimpaired!
    Man.   Proceed,—I listen.
    Abbot. 'Tis said thou holdest converse with the things
Which are forbidden to the search of man;   35
That with the dwellers of the dark abodes,
The many evil and unheavenly spirits
Which walk the valley of the Shade of Death,
Thou communest. I know that with mankind,

---

6. *Tò kalón*, the beautiful, the highest good of Platonic metaphysics.

Thy fellows in creation, thou dost rarely   40
Exchange thy thoughts, and that thy solitude
Is as an Anchorite's[7]—were it but holy.
    Man. And what are they who do avouch these things?
    Abbot. My pious brethren—the scaréd peasantry—
Even thy own vassals—who do look on thee   45
With most unquiet eyes. Thy life's in peril!
    Man. Take it.
    Abbot.   I come to save, and not destroy:
I would not pry into thy secret soul;
But if these things be sooth, there still is time
For penitence and pity: reconcile thee   50
With the true church, and through the church to Heaven.
    Man. I hear thee. This is my reply—whate'er
I may have been, or am, doth rest between
Heaven and myself—I shall not choose a mortal
To be my mediator—Have I sinned   55
Against your ordinances? prove and punish![8]
    Abbot. My son! I did not speak of punishment,
But penitence and pardon;—with thyself
The choice of such remains—and for the last,
Our institutions and our strong belief   60
Have given me power to smooth the path from sin
To higher hope and better thoughts; the first
I leave to Heaven,—"Vengeance is mine alone!"
So saith the Lord, and with all humbleness
His servant echoes back the awful word.   65
    Man. Old man! there is no power in holy men,
Nor charm in prayer, nor purifying form
Of penitence, nor outward look, nor fast,
Nor agony—nor, greater than all these,
The innate tortures of that deep Despair,   70
Which is Remorse without the fear of Hell,
But all in all sufficient to itself
Would make a hell of Heaven[9]—can exorcise
From out the unbounded spirit the quick sense
Of its own sins—wrongs—sufferance—and revenge   75
Upon itself; there is no future pang
Can deal that justice on the self-condemned
He deals on his own soul.
    Abbot.   All this is well;
For this will pass away, and be succeeded
By an auspicious hope, which shall look up   80
With calm assurance to that blessed place,

---

7. Hermit.
8. Following this line, in the original manuscript of *Manfred*, was a broadly comic scene in which Manfred summons the demon Ashtaroth to carry the Abbot off. Byron rewrote the scene as it now appears to satisfy the criticism of his friend William Gifford, who insisted that the slapstick was out of tone with the solemnity of the rest of the drama.
9. See Satan's speech in *Paradise Lost* I (254–255): "The mind is its own place, and in itself / Can make a heaven of Hell, a Hell of Heaven."

Which all who seek may win, whatever be
Their earthly errors, so they be atoned:
And the commencement of atonement is
The sense of its necessity. Say on— 85
And all our church can teach thee shall be taught;
And all we can absolve thee shall be pardoned.
   Man. When Rome's sixth Emperor[1] was near his last,
The victim of a self-inflicted wound,
To shun the torments of a public death 90
From senates once his slaves, a certain soldier,
With show of loyal pity, would have stanched
The gushing throat with his officious robe;
The dying Roman thrust him back, and said—
Some empire still in his expiring glance— 95
"It is too late—is this fidelity?"
   Abbot. And what of this?
   Man.   I answer with the Roman—
"It is too late!"
   Abbot.   It never can be so,
To reconcile thyself with thy own soul,
And thy own soul with Heaven. Hast thou no hope? 100
'Tis strange—even those who do despair above,
Yet shape themselves some fantasy on earth,
To which frail twig they cling, like drowning men.
   Man. Aye—father! I have had those early visions,
And noble aspirations in my youth, 105
To make my own the mind of other men,
The enlightener of nations; and to rise
I knew not whither—it might be to fall;
But fall, even as the mountain-cataract,
Which having leapt from its more dazzling height, 110
Even in the foaming strength of its abyss,
(Which casts up misty columns that become
Clouds raining from the re-ascended skies,)
Lies low but mighty still.—But this is past,
My thoughts mistook themselves.
   Abbot.   And wherefore so? 115
   Man. I could not tame my nature down; for he
Must serve who fain would sway; and soothe, and sue,
And watch all time, and pry into all place,
And be a living Lie, who would become
A mighty thing amongst the mean—and such 120
The mass are; I disdained to mingle with
A herd, though to be leader—and of wolves.
The lion is alone, and so am I.
   Abbot. And why not live and act with other men?
   Man. Because my nature was averse from life; 125
And yet not cruel; for I would not make,

1. Nero.

But find a desolation. Like the Wind,
The red-hot breath of the most lone Simoom,[2]
Which dwells but in the desert, and sweeps o'er
The barren sands which bear no shrubs to blast,   130
And revels o'er their wild and arid waves,
And seeketh not, so that it is not sought,
But being met is deadly,—such hath been
The course of my existence; but there came
Things in my path which are no more.
    Abbot.   Alas!   135
I 'gin to fear that thou art past all aid
From me and from my calling; yet so young,
I still would——
    Man.   Look on me! there is an order
Of mortals on the earth, who do become
Old in their youth, and die ere middle age,   140
Without the violence of warlike death;
Some perishing of pleasure—some of study—
Some worn with toil, some of mere weariness,—
Some of disease—and some insanity—
And some of withered, or of broken hearts;   145
For this last is a malady which slays
More than are numbered in the lists of Fate,
Taking all shapes, and bearing many names.
Look upon me! for even of all these things
Have I partaken; and of all these things,   150
One were enough; then wonder not that I
Am what I am, but that I ever was,
Or having been, that I am still on earth.
    Abbot. Yet, hear me still——
    Man.   Old man! I do respect
Thine order, and revere thine years; I deem   155
Thy purpose pious, but it is in vain:
Think me not churlish; I would spare thyself,
Far more than me, in shunning at this time
All further colloquy—and so—farewell.

                      [*Exit* Manfred.]
    Abbot. This should have been a noble creature: he   160
Hath all the energy which would have made
A goodly frame of glorious elements,
Had they been wisely mingled; as it is,
It is an awful chaos—Light and Darkness—
And mind and dust—and passions and pure thoughts   165
Mixed, and contending without end or order,—
All dormant or destructive. He will perish—
And yet he must not—I will try once more,
For such are worth redemption; and my duty
Is to dare all things for a righteous end.   170

2. The hot wind of the desert. See *The Giaour*, lines 282–284, note.

I'll follow him—but cautiously, though surely.

[*Exit* ABBOT.]

SCENE II.—*Another Chamber.*

MANFRED *and* HERMAN.

Her. My lord, you bade me wait on you at sunset:
He sinks behind the mountain.
  Man.   Doth he so?
I will look on him.
                  [MANFRED *advances to the* Window *of the* Hall.]
Glorious Orb! the idol[3]
Of early nature, and the vigorous race
Of undiseased mankind, the giant sons   5
Of the embrace of Angels, with a sex
More beautiful than they, which did draw down
The erring Spirits who can ne'er return.—
Most glorious Orb! that wert a worship, ere
The mystery of thy making was revealed!   10
Thou earliest minister of the Almighty,
Which gladdened, on their mountain tops, the hearts
Of the Chaldean[4] shepherds, till they poured
Themselves in orisons! Thou material God!
And representative of the Unknown—   15
Who chose thee for his shadow! Thou chief Star!
Centre of many stars! which mak'st our earth
Endurable, and temperest the hues
And hearts of all who walk within thy rays!
Sire of the seasons! Monarch of the climes,   20
And those who dwell in them! for near or far,
Our inborn spirits have a tint of thee
Even as our outward aspects;—thou dost rise,
And shine, and set in glory. Fare thee well!
I ne'er shall see thee more. As my first glance   25
Of love and wonder was for thee, then take
My latest look: thou wilt not beam on one
To whom the gifts of life and warmth have been
Of a more fatal nature. He is gone—
I follow.

[*Exit* MANFRED.]

SCENE III.—*The Mountains—The Castle of Manfred at some dis-*
        tance—A Terrace before a Tower.—Time, Twilight.
    HERMAN, MANUEL, *and other dependants of* MANFRED.

  Her. 'Tis strange enough! night after night, for years,
He hath pursued long vigils in this tower,

---

3. Of the following lines Byron wrote to
John Murray, July 9, 1817: "Pray, was
Manfred's speech to *the Sun* still retained in Act third? I hope so: it was
one of the best in the thing, and better
than the Colosseum."
4. The ancient Semitic people who
founded Babylon, and who were renowned astronomers.

Without a witness. I have been within it,—
So have we all been oft-times; but from it,
Or its contents, it were impossible   5
To draw conclusions absolute, of aught
His studies tend to. To be sure, there is
One chamber where none enter: I would give
The fee of what I have to come these three years,
To pore upon its mysteries.
    Manuel.   'Twere dangerous;   10
Content thyself with what thou know'st already.
  Her. Ah! Manuel! thou art elderly and wise,
And couldst say much; thou hast dwelt within the castle—
How many years is't?
I served his father, whom he nought resembles.   15
    Manuel.   Ere Count Manfred's birth,
  Her. There be more sons in like predicament!
But wherein do they differ?
    Manuel.   I speak not
Of features or of form, but mind and habits;
Count Sigismund was proud, but gay and free,—
A warrior and a reveller; he dwelt not   20
With books and solitude, nor made the night
A gloomy vigil, but a festal time,
Merrier than day; he did not walk the rocks
And forests like a wolf, nor turn aside
From men and their delights.
    Her.   Beshrew the hour,   25
But those were jocund times! I would that such
Would visit the old walls again; they look
As if they had forgotten them.
    Manuel.   These walls
Must change their chieftain first. Oh! I have seen
Some strange things in them, Herman.
    Her..   Come, be friendly;   30
Relate me some to while away our watch:
I've heard thee darkly speak of an event
Which happened hereabouts, by this same tower.
    Manuel. That was a night indeed! I do remember
'Twas twilight, as it may be now, and such   35
Another evening:—yon red cloud, which rests
On Eigher's[5] pinnacle, so rested then,—
So like that it might be the same; the wind
Was faint and gusty, and the mountain snows
Began to glitter with the climbing moon;   40
Count Manfred was, as now, within his tower,—
How occupied, we knew not, but with him
The sole companion of his wanderings
And watchings—her, whom of all earthly things

---

5. The "Grosse Eiger," a mountain east of the Jungfrau.

That lived, the only thing he seemed to love,— 45
As he, indeed, by blood was bound to do,
The Lady Astarte, his[6]——

        Hush! who comes here?

Enter the ABBOT.

Abbot. Where is your master?
Her.   Yonder in the tower.
Abbot. I must speak with him.
Manuel.   'Tis impossible;
He is most private, and must not be thus   50
Intruded on.
  Abbot.   Upon myself I take
The forfeit of my fault, if fault there be—
But I must see him.
  Her.   Thou hast seen him once
This eve already.
  Abbot.   Herman! I command thee,
Knock, and apprize the Count of my approach. 55
Her. We dare not.
  Abbot.   Then it seems I must be herald
Of my own purpose.
  Manuel.   Reverend father, stop—
I pray you pause.
  Abbot. Why so?
  Manuel.   But step this way,
And I will tell you further.   [*Exeunt.*]

SCENE IV.—*Interior of the Tower.*

MANFRED *alone.*

The stars are forth, the moon above the tops
Of the snow-shining mountains.—Beautiful!
I linger yet with Nature, for the Night
Hath been to me a more familiar face
Than that of man; and in her starry shade   5
Of dim and solitary loveliness,
I learned the language of another world.
I do remember me, that in my youth,
When I was wandering,—upon such a night
I stood within the Coliseum's wall,   10
'Midst the chief relics of almighty Rome;
The trees which grew along the broken arches
Waved dark in the blue midnight, and the stars
Shone through the rents of ruin; from afar
The watch-dog bayed beyond the Tiber;[7] and 15
More near from out the Cæsars' palace came
The owl's long cry, and, interruptedly,

6. At this point in the original manuscript there followed a final scene in which the servants discovered the dead body of Manfred. Byron revised it at the suggestion of William Gifford.
7. The river of Rome.

Of distant sentinels the fitful song
Begun and died upon the gentle wind.
Some cypresses beyond the time-worn breach   20
Appeared to skirt the horizon, yet they stood
Within a bowshot. Where the Cæsars dwelt,
And dwell the tuneless birds of night, amidst
A grove which springs through levelled battlements,
And twines its roots with the imperial hearths,   25
Ivy usurps the laurel's place of growth;
But the gladiators' bloody Circus stands,
A noble wreck in ruinous perfection,
While Cæsar's chambers, and the Augustan halls,
Grovel on earth in indistinct decay.—   30
And thou didst shine, thou rolling Moon, upon
All this, and cast a wide and tender light,
Which softened down the hoar austerity
Of rugged desolation, and filled up,
As 'twere anew, the gaps of centuries;   35
Leaving that beautiful which still was so,
And making that which was not—till the place
Became religion, and the heart ran o'er
With silent worship of the Great of old,—
The dead, but sceptred, Sovereigns, who still rule   40
Our spirits from their urns.

                               'Twas such a night!
'Tis strange that I recall it at this time;
But I have found our thoughts take wildest flight
Even at the moment when they should array
Themselves in pensive order.

                     Enter the ABBOT.

  Abbot.   My good Lord!   45
I crave a second grace for this approach;
But yet let not my humble zeal offend
By its abruptness—all it hath of ill
Recoils on me; its good in the effect
May light upon your head—could I say *heart*—   50
Could I touch *that*, with words or prayers, I should
Recall a noble spirit which hath wandered,
But is not yet all lost.
  Man.   Thou know'st me not;
My days are numbered, and my deeds recorded:
Retire, or 'twill be dangerous—Away!   55
  Abbot. Thou dost not mean to menace me?
  Man.   Not I!
I simply tell thee peril is at hand,
And would preserve thee.
  Abbot.   What dost thou mean?
  Man.   Look there!

What dost thou see?
    Abbot.   Nothing.
    Man.   Look there, I say,
And steadfastly;—now tell me what thou seest?   60
    Abbot. That which should shake me,—but I fear it not:
I see a dusk and awful figure rise,
Like an infernal god, from out the earth;
His face wrapt in a mantle, and his form
Robed as with angry clouds: he stands between   65
Thyself and me—but I do fear him not.
    Man. Thou hast no cause—he shall not harm thee—but
His sight may shock thine old limbs into palsy.
I say to thee—Retire!
    Abbot.   And I reply—
Never—till I have battled with this fiend:—   70
What doth he here?
    Man.   Why—aye—what doth he here?
I did not send for him,—he is unbidden.
    Abbot. Alas! lost Mortal! what with guests like these
Hast thou to do? I tremble for thy sake:
Why doth he gaze on thee, and thou on him?   75
Ah! he unveils his aspect: on his brow
The thunder-scars are graven; from his eye
Glares forth the immortality of Hell—
Avaunt!—
    Man.   Pronounce—what is thy mission?
    Spirit.   Come!
    Abbot. What art thou, unknown being? answer!—
        speak!   80
    Spirit. The genius[8] of this mortal.—Come! 'tis time.
    Man. I am prepared for all things, but deny
The Power which summons me. Who sent thee here?
    Spirit. Thou'lt know anon—Come! come!
    Man.   I have commanded
Things of an essence greater far than thine,   85
And striven with thy masters. Get thee hence!
    Spirit. Mortal! thine hour is come—Away! I say.
    Man. I knew, and know my hour is come, but not
To render up my soul to such as thee:
Away! I'll die as I have lived—alone.   90
    Spirit. Then I must summon up my brethren—Rise!
                      [*Other Spirits rise up.*]
    Abbot. Avaunt! ye evil ones!—Avaunt! I say,—
Ye have no power where Piety hath power,
And I do charge ye in the name—
    Spirit.   Old man!
We know ourselves, our mission, and thine order;   95
Waste not thy holy words on idle uses,

8. Guardian—or, here, persecuting—spirit.

It were in vain: this man is forfeited.
Once more—I summon him—Away! Away!
   Man. I do defy ye,—though I feel my soul
Is ebbing from me, yet I do defy ye;   100
Nor will I hence, while I have earthly breath
To breathe my scorn upon ye—earthly strength
To wrestle, though with spirits; what ye take
Shall be ta'en limb by limb.
   Spirit.   Reluctant mortal!
Is this the Magian who would so pervade   105
The world invisible, and make himself
Almost our equal? Can it be that thou
Art thus in love with life? the very life
Which made thee wretched?
   Man.   Thou false fiend, thou liest!
My life is in its last hour,—*that* I know,   110
Nor would redeem a moment of that hour;
I do not combat against Death, but thee
And thy surrounding angels; my past power
Was purchased by no compact with thy crew,
But by superior science—penance, daring,   115
And length of watching, strength of mind, and skill
In knowledge of our Fathers—when the earth
Saw men and spirits walking side by side,
And gave ye no supremacy; I stand
Upon my strength—I do defy—deny—   120
Spurn back, and scorn ye!—
   Spirit.   But thy many crimes
Have made thee——
   Man.   What are they to such as thee?
Must crimes be punished but by other crimes,
And greater criminals?—Back to thy hell!
Thou hast no power upon me, *that* I feel;   125
Thou never shalt possess me, *that* I know:
What I have done is done; I bear within
A torture which could nothing gain from thine:
The Mind which is immortal makes itself
Requital for its good or evil thoughts,—   130
Is its own origin of ill and end—
And its own place and time: its innate sense,
When stripped of this mortality, derives
No colour from the fleeting things without,
But is absorbed in sufferance or in joy,   135
Born from the knowledge of its own desert.
Thou didst not tempt me, and thou couldst not tempt me;
I have not been thy dupe, nor am thy prey—
But was my own destroyer, and will be
My own hereafter.—Back, ye baffled fiends!   140
The hand of Death is on me—but not yours!
                         [*The Demons disappear.*]

Abbot. Alas! how pale thou art—thy lips are white—
And thy breast heaves—and in thy gasping throat
The accents rattle: Give thy prayers to Heaven—
Pray—albeit but in thought,—but die not thus.
    Man. 'Tis over—my dull eyes can fix thee not;
But all things swim around me, and the earth
Heaves as it were beneath me. Fare thee well—
Give me thy hand.
    Abbot.   Cold—cold—even to the heart—
But yet one prayer—Alas! how fares it with thee?   150
    Man. Old man! 'tis not so difficult to die.[9]
                                        [MANFRED *expires.*]
    Abbot. He's gone—his soul hath ta'en its earthless
        flight;
Whither? I dread to think—but he is gone.

[handwritten margin note: abbot has no conception of manfred]

The Vision of Judgment

Robert Southey (1774–1843), along with Wordsworth and Coleridge, was
a member of the so-called "Lake School" of poetry. A radical in his youth,
Southey turned conservative (as did his two greater friends), and in 1813
was made poet laureate of England.

Byron hated Southey both for the quality of his poetry and, more importantly, the quality of his turncoat politics, and had attacked him as early as
1809 in his satire, *English Bards* and *Scotch Reviewers.* The attack became
stronger in the 1819 Dedication of *Don Juan,* and culminated in 1822 in
The Vision of Judgment. When George III died in 1820, Southey had
written *A Vision of Judgment,* a celebration of the king which verged on
idolatry, describing his triumphal entry into heaven and the presence of
God himself. Furthermore, in the preface to his *Vision,* Southey had levelled a vituperative attack on Byron, describing him as a "Satanic" poet, a
corrupter of morals and a threat to national spiritual health. Byron's reply
was his own *Vision of Judgment,* originally published under the name
"Quevedo Redivivus"—that is, "Quevedo Reborn" (Quevedo was a seventeenth century Spanish satirist). John Murray was afraid that the poem
might be legally actionable slander, so Byron published it in the journal,
The Liberal, which he and John Hunt (brother of Leigh Hunt) were edit-
ing at the time.

I

SAINT PETER[1] sat by the celestial gate:
    His keys were rusty, and the lock was dull,
So little trouble had been given of late;
    Not that the place by any means was full,

---

9. In the first edition, again at Gifford's
urging, John Murray omitted this line.
Byron was enraged, and had it reinserted
in subsequent editions.

1. Christ gave Peter the "keys of the
Kingdom of Heaven" (Matthew 16 : 17–
19) when He appointed Peter chief of
His disciples.

But since the Gallic era "eighty-eight"[2]
    The Devils had ta'en a longer, stronger pull,
And "a pull altogether," as they say
    At sea—which drew most souls another way.

II

The Angels all were singing out of tune,
    And hoarse with having little else to do,
Excepting to wind up the sun and moon,
    Or curb or runaway young star or two,
Or wild colt of a comet, which too soon
    Broke out of bounds o'er the ethereal blue,
Splitting some planet with its playful tail,
As boats are sometimes by a wanton whale.

III

The Guardian Seraphs[3] had retired on high,
    Finding their charges past all care below;
Terrestrial business filled nought in the sky
    Save the Recording Angel's black bureau;
Who found, indeed, the facts to multiply
    With such rapidity of vice and woe,
That he had stripped off both his wings in quills,
And yet was in arrear[4] of human ills.

IV

His business so augmented of late years,
    That he was forced, against his will, no doubt,
(Just like those cherubs,[5] earthly ministers,)
    For some resource to turn himself about,
And claim the help of his celestial peers,
    To aid him ere he should be quite worn out
By the increased demand for his remarks:
Six Angels and twelve Saints were named his clerks.

V

This was a handsome board—at least for Heaven;
    And yet they had even then enough to do,
So many Conquerors' cars[6] were daily driven,
    So many kingdoms fitted up anew;
Each day, too, slew its thousands six or seven,
    Till at the crowning carnage, Waterloo,[7]
They threw their pens down in divine disgust—
The page was so besmeared with blood and dust.

VI

This by the way; 'tis not mine to record
    What Angels shrink from: even the very Devil
On this occasion his own work abhorred,
    So surfeited with the infernal revel:

2. In 1788 Louis XVI was forced to call a meeting of the Estates General to discuss France's economic crisis; this was the congress that led to the French Revolution in 1789.
3. One of the nine traditional choirs or orders of angels.
4. That is, he could not keep up with recording all the evil done by men.
5. Another of the orders of angels.
6. Triumphal processions of the conquerors.
7. Scene of Napoleon's defeat by the Duke of Wellington on June 18, 1815.

Though he himself had sharpened every sword,
  It almost quenched his innate thirst of evil.
(Here Satan's sole good work deserves insertion—
'Tis, that he has both Generals in reversion.)[8]

VII

Let's skip a few short years of hollow peace,
  Which peopled earth no better, Hell as wont,
And Heaven none—they form the tyrant's lease,
  With nothing but new names subscribed upon 't;
'Twill one day finish: meantime they increase,
  "With seven heads and ten horns,"[9] and all in front,
Like Saint John's foretold beast; but ours are born
Less formidable in the head than horn.[1]

VIII

In the first year of Freedom's second dawn[2]
  Died George the Third; although no tyrant, one
Who shielded tyrants, till each sense withdrawn
  Left him nor mental nor external sun:[3]
A better farmer[4] ne'er brushed dew from lawn,
  A worse king never left a realm undone!
He died—but left his subjects still behind,
One half as mad—and t'other no less blind.

IX

He died! his death made no great stir on earth:
  His burial made some pomp; there was profusion
Of velvet—gilding—brass—and no great dearth
  Of aught but tears—save those shed by collusion;[5]
For these things may be bought at their true worth;
  Of elegy there was the due infusion—
Bought also; and the torches, cloaks and banners,
Heralds, and relics of old Gothic manners,

X

Formed a sepulchral melodrame. Of all
  The fools who flocked to swell or see the show,
Who cared about the corpse? The funeral
  Made the attraction, and the black the woe,
There throbbed not there a thought which pierced the
    pall;[6]
  And when the gorgeous coffin was laid low,

---

8. A legal term meaning the return of an estate to its original owner after the interest granted on its loan expires. Byron means that the Devil will have both generals of Waterloo, Napoleon and Wellington, after they have died. In fact, Napoleon died May 5, 1821, two days after Byron began writing *The Vision of Judgment*—though the news did not reach Europe till some time later.
9. The description of the Beast of Apocalypse in Revelations 17:3-4—a book traditionally assumed to be the work of St. John the Apostle. The Beast himself symbolizes the coming end of the world.

1. An obscene joke.
2. The year 1820, the year of George III's death, was also the year in which revolutionary activity in Italy began to grow serious. Byron himself was involved in many of these revolutionary movements.
3. George III in his last illness was both deranged and blind.
4. George III, who deliberately espoused conventionally modest English habits and values, was referred to during his reign as "farmer George."
5. Insincere tears.
6. Coffin.

It seemed the mockery of hell to fold
The rottenness of eighty years in gold.

XI

So mix his body with the dust! It might
    Return to what it *must* far sooner, were
The natural compound left alone to fight
    Its way back into earth, and fire, and air;
But the unnatural balsams[7] merely blight
    What Nature made him at his birth, as bare
As the mere million's base unmummied clay—
Yet all his spices but prolong decay.

XII

He's dead—and upper earth with him has done;
    He's buried; save the undertaker's bill,
Or lapidary scrawl,[8] the world is gone
    For him, unless he left a German will:[9]
But where's the proctor[1] who will ask his son?
    In whom his qualities are reigning still,
Except that household virtue, most uncommon,
Of constancy to a bad, ugly woman.[2]

XIII

"God save the king!" It is a large economy
    In God to save the like; but if he will
Be saving, all the better; for not one am I
    Of those who think damnation better still:
I hardly know too if not quite alone am I
    In this small hope of bettering future ill
By circumscribing, with some slight restriction,
The eternity of Hell's hot jurisdiction.

XIV

I know this is unpopular; I know
    'Tis blasphemous; I know one may be damned
For hoping no one else may e'er be so;
    I know my catechism; I know we're crammed
With the best doctrines till we quite o'erflow;
    I know that all save England's Church have shammed.
And that the other twice two hundred churches
And synagogues have made a *damned* bad purchase.[3]

XV

God help us all! God help me too! I am,
    God knows, as helpless as the Devil can wish,
And not a whit more difficult to damn,
    Than is to bring to land a late-hooked fish,

---

7. The embalming fluids.
8. The tombstone inscription.
9. George II had hidden the "German will" of his father, George I. There was, in fact, a rumor abroad at the time that George IV had done the same with George III's will.
1. Official examiner of the validity of wills in probate court.
2. George IV was notorious for his many extramarital affairs, and for his constant bickering with his wife, Queen Caroline, a very ugly and very promiscuous woman whom he finally brought to trial for adultery in 1820.
3. Bargain.

Or to the butcher to purvey the lamb;
   Not that I'm fit for such a noble dish,
As one day will be that immortal fry
Of almost every body born to die.

XVI

Saint Peter sat by the celestial gate,
   And nodded o'er his keys: when, lo! there came
A wondrous noise he had not heard of late—
   A rushing sound of wind, and stream, and flame;
In short, a roar of things extremely great,
   Which would have made aught save a Saint exclaim;
But he, with first a start and then a wink,
Said, "There's another star gone out, I think!"

XVII

But ere he could return to his repose,
   A Cherub flapped his right wing o'er his eyes—
At which Saint Peter yawned, and rubbed his nose:
   "Saint porter," said the angel, "prithee rise!"
Waving a goodly wing, which glowed, as flows
   An earthly peacock's tail, with heavenly dyes:
To which the saint replied, "Well, what's the matter?
"Is Lucifer come back with all this clatter?"

XVIII

"No," quoth the Cherub: "George the Third is dead."
   "And who *is* George the Third?" replied the apostle:
"*What George? what Third?*" "The King of Eng-
      land," said
The angel. "Well! he won't find kings to jostle
   Him on his way; but does he wear his head?
Because the last[4] we saw here had a tustle,
   And ne'er would have got into Heaven's good graces,
Had he not flung his head in all our faces.

XIX

"He was—if I remember—King of France;
   That head of his, which could not keep a crown
On earth, yet ventured in my face to advance
   A claim to those of martyrs—like my own:
If I had had my sword, as I had once[5]
   When I cut ears off, I had cut him down;
But having but my *keys*, and not my brand,
I only knocked his head from out his hand.

XX

"And then he set up such a headless howl,
   That all the Saints came out and took him in;
And there he sits by Saint Paul, cheek by jowl;

4. Louis XVI of France, who was beheaded in 1793.
5. When Christ was arrested on the eve
of the Crucifixion, Peter in a rage cut
off the ear of one of the arresting
officers (Matthew 26 : 50–52).

That fellow Paul—the parvenu![6] The skin
   Of Saint Bartholomew,[7] which makes his cowl
     In heaven, and upon earth redeemed his sin,
So as to make a martyr, never sped[8]
Better than did this weak and wooden head.

XXI

"But had it come up here upon its shoulders,
   There would have been a different tale to tell:
The fellow-feeling in the Saint's beholders
     Seems to have acted on them like a spell;
And so this very foolish head Heaven solders
   Back on its trunk: it may be very well,
And seems the custom here to overthrow
Whatever has been wisely done below."

XXII

The Angel answered, "Peter! do not pout:
   The King who comes has head and all entire,
And never knew much what it was about—
     He did as doth the puppet—by its wire,
And will be judged like all the rest, no doubt:
   My business and your own is not to inquire
Into such matters, but to mind our cue—
Which is to act as we are bid to do."

XXIII

While thus they spake, the angelic caravan,
   Arriving like a rush of mighty wind,
Cleaving the fields of space, as doth the swan
     Some silver stream (say Ganges, Nile, or Inde,
Or Thames, or Tweed), and midst them an old man
   With an old soul, and both extremely blind,
Halted before the gate, and, in his shroud,
Seated their fellow-traveller on a cloud.

XXIV

But bringing up the rear of this bright host
   A Spirit of a different aspect waved
His wings, like thunder-clouds above some coast
     Whose barren beach with frequent wrecks is paved;
His brow was like the deep when tempest-tossed;
   Fierce and unfathomable thoughts engraved
Eternal wrath on his immortal face,
And *where* he gazed a gloom pervaded space.

XXV

As he drew near, he gazed upon the gate
   Ne'er to be entered more by him or Sin,

---

6. The word means "newly rich." Byron
imagines St. Peter resenting St. Paul because the latter was converted only after
being, in his early years, a persecutor of
Christians—and then rapidly became the
most influential of early members of the
faith.
7. One of the Apostles, who was martyred by being flayed alive. His skin,
then, is his "cowl" or hood of dignity in
Heaven.
8. Succeeded.

With such a glance of supernatural hate,
   As made Saint Peter wish himself within;
He pottered with his keys at a great rate,
   And sweated through his Apostolic skin:
Of course his perspiration was but ichor,[9]
   Or some such other spiritual liquor.

XXVI

The very Cherubs huddled all together,
   Like birds when soars the falcon; and they felt
A tingling to the tip of every feather,
   And formed a circle like Orion's belt[1]
Around their poor old charge; who scarce knew whither
   His guards had led him, though they gently dealt
With royal Manes (for by many stories,
And true, we learn the Angels all are Tories).[2]

XXVII

As things were in this posture, the gate flew
   Asunder, and the flashing of its hinges
Flung over space an universal hue
   Of many-coloured flame, until its tinges
Reached even our speck of earth, and made a new
   Aurora borealis[3] spread its fringes
O'er the North Pole; the same seen, when ice-bound,
By Captain Parry's crew, in "Melville's Sound."[4]

XXVIII

And from the gate thrown open issued beaming
   A beautiful and mighty Thing of Light,
Radiant with glory, like a banner streaming
   Victorious from some world-o'erthrowing fight:
My poor comparisons must needs be teeming
   With earthly likenesses, for here the night
Of clay[5] obscures our best conceptions, saving
Johanna Southcote,[6] or Bob Southey raving.

XXIX

'Twas the Archangel Michael:[7] all men know
   The make of Angels and Archangels, since
There's scarce a scribbler has not one to show,
   From the fiends' leader to the Angels' Prince.
There also are some altar-pieces,[8] though
   I really can't say that they much evince

---

9. In Homer, the blood of the gods on Mount Olympus.
1. The constellation Orion.
2. Royalists.
3. The Northern Lights.
4. An inlet in Greenland where in 1819 the English explorer William Edward Parry (1790–1855) established winter quarters on one of his voyages.
5. Mortal flesh.
6. Or Joanna Southcott (1750–1814), English religious fanatic—espoused by some of the more apocalyptic English radicals—who claimed that she would give birth in 1814 to a new messiah. Her "pregnancy" turned out to be a dropsical condition from which she died.
7. The greatest of the archangels, who defeated Lucifer/Satan when he rebelled against God.
8. A painted screen behind or above the altar, common in Catholic churches of the Middle Ages and Renaissance.

One's inner notions of immortal spirits;
But let the connoisseurs[9] explain *their* merits.

XXX

Michael flew forth in glory and in good;
   A goodly work of him from whom all Glory
And Good arise; the portal past—he stood;
   Before him the young Cherubs and Saints hoary—
   (I say *young*, begging to be understood
   By looks, not years; and should be very sorry
To state, they were not older than St. Peter,
But merely that they seemed a little sweeter).

XXXI

The Cherubs and the Saints bowed down before
   That arch-angelic Hierarch,[1] the first
Of Essences angelical who wore
   The aspect of a god; but this ne'er nursed
Pride in his heavenly bosom, in whose core
   No thought, save for his Maker's service, durst
Intrude, however glorified and high;
He knew him[2] but the Viceroy[3] of the sky.

XXXII

He and the sombre, silent Spirit met—
   They knew each other both for good and ill;
Such was their power, that neither could forget
   His former friend and future foe; but still
There was a high, immortal, proud regret
   In either's eye, as if 'twere less their will
Than destiny to make the eternal years
Their date of war, and their "Champ Clos"[4] the spheres.

XXXIII

But here they were in neutral space: we know
   From Job,[5] that Satan hath the power to pay
A heavenly visit thrice a-year or so;
   And that the "Sons of God," like those of clay,
Must keep him company; and we might show
   From the same book, in how polite a way
The dialogue is held between the Powers
Of Good and Evil—but t'would take up hours.

XXXIV

And this is not a theologic tract,
   To prove with Hebrew and with Arabic,
If Job be allegory or a fact,
   But a true narrative; and thus I pick
From out the whole but such and such an act

9. Art critics.
1. Ruler.
2. Himself.
3. A ruler or overseer whose authority is delegated by a yet higher lord.
4. An enclosed space for a tournament.

"The "spheres" are the planets.
5. At the beginning of the Book of Job, Satan is described conversing with God about the faithfulness of God's servants on earth, and challenging Him to test the loyalty of the pious man Job.

As sets aside the slightest thought of trick.
'Tis every tittle true, beyond suspicion,
And accurate as any other vision.

XXXV

The spirits were in neutral space, before
    The gate of Heaven; like eastern thresholds[6] is
The place where Death's grand cause is argued o'er,
    And souls despatched to that world or to this;
And therefore Michael and the other wore
    A civil aspect: though they did not kiss,
Yet still between his Darkness and his Brightness
There passed a mutual glance of great politeness.

XXXVI

The Archangel bowed, not like a modern beau,[7]
    But with a graceful oriental bend,
Pressing one radiant arm just where below
    The heart in good men is supposed to tend;
He turned as to an equal, not too low,
    But kindly; Satan met his ancient friend
With more hauteur, as might an old Castilian[8]
Poor Noble meet a mushroom[9] rich civilian.

XXXVII

He merely bent his diabolic brow
    An instant; and then raising it, he stood
In act to assert his right or wrong, and show
    Cause why King George by no means could or should
Make out a case to be exempt from woe
    Eternal, more than other kings, endued
With better sense and hearts, whom History mentions,
Who long have "paved Hell with their good intentions."[1]

XXXVIII

Michael began: "What wouldst thou with this man,
    Now dead, and brought before the Lord? What ill
Hath he wrought since his mortal race began,
    That thou canst claim him? Speak! and do thy will,
If it be just: if in this earthly span
    He hath been greatly failing to fulfil
His duties as a king and mortal, say,
And he is thine; if not—let him have way."

XXXIX

"Michael!" replied the Prince of Air, "even here
    Before the gate of Him thou servest, must

6. In the cities of the Near East, the gates of the city were the normal places for the dispensation of justice.
7. In the parlance of the early nineteenth century, a dandified or affectedly elegant gentleman.
8. Native of Castile, one of the most ancient provinces of Spain.
9. Newly sprung up.

1. This phrase, by now a cliché, was first uttered by the great eighteenth century critic, Dr. Samuel Johnson (1709–84)—a writer intensely admired by Byron—and was recorded in the monumental *Life of Samuel Johnson* (1791) by Johnson's friend James Boswell (1740–95).

I claim my subject: and will make appear
  That as he was my worshipper in dust,
So shall he be in spirit, although dear
  To thee and thine, because nor wine nor lust
Were of his weaknesses; yet on the throne
He reigned o'er millions to serve me alone.

XL

"Look to *our* earth, or rather *mine*; it was,
  Once, more thy master's: but I triumph not
In this poor planet's conquest; nor, alas!
  Need he thou servest envy me my lot:
With all the myriads[2] of bright worlds which pass
  In worship round him, he may have forgot
Yon weak creation of such paltry things:
I think few worth damnation save their kings,

XLI

"And these but as a kind of quit-rent,[3] to
  Assert my right as Lord: and even had
I such an inclination, 'twere (as you
  Well know) superfluous; they are grown so bad,
That Hell has nothing better left to do
  Than leave them to themselves: so much more mad
And evil by their own internal curse,
Heaven cannot make them better, nor I worse.

XLII

"Look to the earth, I said, and say again:
  When this old, blind, mad, helpless, weak, poor worm
Began in youth's first bloom and flush to reign,
  The world and he both wore a different form,
And much of earth and all the watery plain
  Of Ocean called him king: through many a storm
His isles had floated on the abyss of Time;
For the rough virtues chose them for their clime.

XLIII

"He came to his sceptre young; he leaves it old:
  Look to the state in which he found his realm,
And left it; and his annals too behold,
  How to a minion[4] first he gave the helm;
How grew upon his heart a thirst for gold,
  The beggar's vice, which can but overwhelm
The meanest hearts; and for the rest, but glance
Thine eye along America and France.

XLIV

" 'Tis true, he was a tool from first to last
  (I have the workmen safe); but as a tool
So let him be consumed. From out the past

---

2. Thousands.
3. A small sum paid to a landlord to satisfy the legal conditions of rental.
4. Petty servant: a reference to John

Stuart, prime minister 1762–63 (George III came to the throne in 1760).

Of ages, since mankind have known the rule
Of monarchs—from the bloody rolls amassed
   Of Sin and Slaughter—from the Cæsars' school,[5]
Take the worst pupil; and produce a reign
More drenched with gore, more cumbered[6] with the slain.

XLV

"He ever warred with freedom and the free:
   Nations as men, home subjects, foreign foes,
So that they uttered the word 'Liberty!'
   Found George the Third their first opponent. Whose
History was ever stained as his will be
   With national and individual woes?
I grant his household abstinence; I grant
His neutral virtues, which most monarchs want;

XLVI

"I know he was a constant consort; own
   He was a decent sire, and middling lord.
All this is much, and most upon a throne;
   As temperance, if at Apicius'[7] board,
Is more than at an anchorite's[8] supper shown.
   I grant him all the kindest can accord;
And this was well for him, but not for those
Millions who found him what Oppression chose.

XLVII

"The New World shook him off; the Old yet groans
   Beneath what he and his prepared, if not
Completed: he leaves heirs on many thrones
   To all his vices, without what begot
Compassion for him—his tame virtues; drones
   Who sleep, or despots who have now forgot
A lesson which shall be re-taught them, wake
Upon the thrones of earth; but let them quake!

XLVIII

"Five millions of the primitive, who hold
   The faith which makes ye great on earth, implored
A *part* of that vast *all* they held of old,—
   Freedom to worship—not alone your Lord,
Michael, but you, and you, Saint Peter! Cold
   Must be your souls, if you have not abhorred
The foe to Catholic participation[9]
In all the license[1] of a Christian nation.

XLIX

"True! he allowed them to pray God; but as
   A consequence of prayer, refused the law

---

5. The line of Roman emperors, many of whom were remarkable for their cruelty.
6. Encumbered.
7. Famous Roman voluptuary of the first century A.D.
8. Religious hermit. An anchorite's table would have only the simplest fare.
9. The cause of Catholic Emancipation —allowing Catholics to hold office in Parliament, etc.—was squelched by George III in 1795, in 1801, and again in 1807.
1. Liberty.

Which would have placed them upon the same base
   With those who did not hold the Saints in awe."
But here Saint Peter started from his place
   And cried, "You may the prisoner withdraw:
Ere Heaven shall ope her portals to this Guelph,[2]
While I am guard, may I be damned myself!

L

"Sooner will I with Cerberus[3] exchange
   My office (and *his* is no sinecure)[4]
Than see this royal Bedlam[5] bigot range
   The azure fields of Heaven, of that be sure!"
"Saint!" replied Satan, "you do well to avenge
   The wrongs he made your satellites endure;
And if to this exchange you should be given,
I'll try to coax *our* Cerberus up to Heaven!"

LI

Here Michael interposed: "Good Saint! and Devil!
   Pray, not so fast; you both outrun discretion.
Saint Peter! you were wont to be more civil:
   Satan! excuse this warmth of his expression,
And condescension to the vulgar's level:
   Even Saints sometimes forget themselves in session.
Have you got more to say?"—"No."—"If you please,
I'll trouble you to call your witnesses."

LII

Then Satan turned and waved his swarthy hand,
   Which stirred with its electric qualities
Clouds farther off than we can understand,
   Although we find him sometimes in our skies;
Infernal thunder shook both sea and land
   In all the planets—and Hell's batteries
Let off the artillery, which Milton[6] mentions
As one of Satan's most sublime inventions.

LIII

This was a signal unto such damned souls
   As have the privilege of their damnation
Extended far beyond the mere controls
   Of worlds past, present, or to come; no station
Is theirs particularly in the rolls
   Of Hell assigned; but where their inclination
Or business carries them in search of game,

---

2. This is the family name of the House of Hanover, to which George belonged. But it is possible that Byron (or St. Peter) is confusing Guelphs with Ghibellines: in medieval Italy and Germany the Guelph party defended the sovereignty of the Pope against the German emperors, while the Ghibellines supported the cause of the emperors.
3. The triple-headed dog who was guardian of the classical underworld; thus, St. Peter's hellish opposite number.
4. Position for which one is paid but does no work; an easy job.
5. Madhouse, from "Bedlam" or the Hospital of St. Mary of Bethlehem, the famous London asylum.
6. In *Paradise Lost* VI (484 ff.) Milton describes Satan and the rebellious angels inventing gunpowder.

They may range freely—being damned the same.

LIV

They are proud of this—as very well they may,
  It being a sort of knighthood, or gilt key
Stuck in their loins; or like to an "entré"[7]
  Up the back stairs, or such free-masonry.[8]
I borrow my comparisons from clay,
  Being clay myself. Let not those spirits be
Offended with such base low likenesses;
We know their posts are nobler far than these.

LV

When the great signal ran from Heaven to Hell—
  About ten million times the distance reckoned
From our sun to its earth, as we can tell
  How much time it takes up, even to a second,
For every ray that travels to dispel
  The fogs of London, through which, dimly beaconed,
The weathercocks are gilt some thrice a year,
If that the *summer* is not too severe:

LVI

I say that I can tell—'twas half a minute;
  I know the solar beams take up more time
Ere, packed up for their journey, they begin it;
  But then their Telegraph[9] is less sublime,
And if they ran a race, they would not win it
  'Gainst Satan's couriers bound for their own clime.
The sun takes up some years for every ray
To reach its goal—the Devil not half a day.

LVII

Upon the verge of space, about the size
  Of half-a-crown, a little speck appeared
(I've seen a something like it in the skies
  In the Ægean,[1] ere a squall); it neared,
And, growing bigger, took another guise;
  Like an aërial ship it tacked, and steered,
Or *was* steered (I am doubtful of the grammar
Of the last phrase, which makes the stanza stammer;

LVIII

But take your choice): and then it grew a cloud;
  And so it was—a cloud of witnesses.
But such a cloud! No land ere saw a crowd
  Of locusts numerous as the heavens saw these;

---

7. A gold key worn in the belt was one
of the insignia of the Lord Chamberlain
and other court officials, and was thus
an *entré* or badge of membership in a
select circle.
8. The secret society of Freemasons, dating back to the Middle Ages, was celebrated for its elaborate and arcane sym-
bols of membership.

9. Byron is probably not referring to the
electric telegraph, although the invention
was in its infancy at the time. There was
then a more famous "telegraph" or net-
work of semaphore signaling from London to Portsmouth, and this is what he
probably means.
1. The Aegean Sea, the arm of the Mediterranean between Greece and Turkey.

They shadowed with their myriads Space; their loud
    And varied cries were like those of wild geese,
(If nations may be likened to a goose),
And realised the phrase of "Hell broke loose."

LIX

Here crashed a sturdy oath of stout John Bull,[2]
    Who damned away his eyes as heretofore:[3]
There Paddy[4] brogued "By Jasus!"—"What's your wull?"
    The temperate Scot exclaimed: the French ghost swore
In certain terms I shan't translate in full,
    As the first coachman will; and 'midst the war,
The voice of Jonathan[5] was heard to express,
"*Our* President is going to war, I guess."

LX

Besides there were the Spaniard, Dutch, and Dane;
    In short, an universal shoal of shades
From Otaheite's isle to Salisbury Plain,[6]
    Of all climes and professions, years and trades,
Ready to swear against the good king's reign,
    Bitter as clubs in cards are against spades:
All summoned by this grand "subpoena," to
Try if kings mayn't be damned like me or you.

LXI

When Michael saw this host, he first grew pale,
    As Angels can; next, like Italian twilight,
He turned all colours—as a peacock's tail,
    Or sunset streaming through a Gothic skylight
In some old abbey, or a trout not stale,
    Or distant lightning on the horizon *by* night,
Or a fresh rainbow, or a grand review
Of thirty regiments in red, green, and blue.

LXII

Then he addressed himself to Satan: "Why—
    My good old friend, for such I deem you, though
Our different parties make us fight so shy,
    I ne'er mistake you for a *personal* foe;
Our difference is *political*, and I
    Trust that, whatever may occur below,
You know my great respect for you: and this
Makes me regret whate'er you do amiss—

LXIII

"Why, my dear Lucifer, would you abuse
    My call for witnesses? I did not mean
That you should half of Earth and Hell produce;
    'Tis even superfluous, since two honest, clean,

2. The popular national symbol of the blunt, straightforward Englishman.
3. As he did in life—an allusion to the notorious English penchant for profanity.
4. An Irishman. "Wull" is his slurred (brogue) pronunciation of "will."

5. A Jew. Byron's joke is that the Devil is "President" of the Jews—a distasteful but, for his time, common bit of anti-Semitism.
6. Otaheite is Tahiti. Salisbury Plain is the Stonehenge area of England.

True testimonies are enough: we lose
  Our Time, nay, our Eternity, between
The accusation and defence: if we
Hear both, 'twill stretch our immortality."

LXIV

Satan replied, "To me the matter is
  Indifferent, in a personal point of view:
I can have fifty better souls than this
  With far less trouble than we have gone through
Already; and I merely argued his
  Late Majesty of Britain's case with you
Upon a point of form: you may dispose
Of him; I've kings enough below, God knows!"

LXV

Thus spoke the Demon (late called "multifaced"
  By multo-scribbling[7] Southey). "Then we'll call
One or two persons of the myriads placed
  Around our congress, and dispense with all
The rest," quoth Michael: "Who may be so graced
  As to speak first? there's choice enough—who shall
It be?" Then Satan answered, "There are many;
But you may choose Jack Wilkes[8] as well as any."

LXVI

A merry, cock-eyed, curious-looking Sprite[9]
  Upon the instant started from the throng,
Dressed in a fashion now forgotten quite;
  For all the fashions of the flesh stick long
By people in the next world; where unite
  All the costumes since Adam's, right or wrong,
From Eve's fig-leaf down to the petticoat,
Almost as scanty, of days less remote.

LXVII

The Spirit looked around upon the crowds
  Assembled, and exclaimed, "My friends of all
The spheres, we shall catch cold amongst these clouds;
  So let's to business: why this general call?
If those are freeholders[1] I see in shrouds,
  And 'tis for an election that they bawl,
Behold a candidate with unturned coat!
Saint Peter, may I count upon your vote?"

LXVIII

"Sir," replied Michael, "you mistake; these things
  Are of a former life, and what we do

<hr/>

7. A contemptuous reference to the great size of Southey's literary output. Southey had called the Devil "multifaced" in his own *Vision of Judgment*.
8. John Wilkes (1727–97) the most influential radical opponent of George III. Wilkes was three times elected to Parliament, and in 1774 was elected lord

mayor of London; in his last years, however, he voted consistently against the Whig policies he had done so much to form.
9. Spirit.
1. Independent owners of land or property; hence empowered to vote in an election.

Above is more august: to judge of kings
   Is the tribunal met: so now you know."
"Then I presume those gentlemen with wings,"
   Said Wilkes, "are Cherubs; and that soul below
Looks much like George the Third, but to my mind
A good deal older—bless me! is he blind?"

LXIX

"He is what you behold him, and his doom
   Depends upon his deeds," the Angel said;
"If you have aught to arraign in him, the tomb
   Gives license to the humblest beggar's head
To lift itself against the loftiest."—"Some,"
   Said Wilkes, "don't wait to see them laid in lead,
For such a liberty—and I, for one,
Have told them what I thought beneath the sun."

LXX

"*Above* the sun repeat, then, what thou hast
   To urge against him," said the Archangel. "Why,"
Replied the spirit, "since old scores are past,
   Must I turn evidence? In faith, not I.
Besides, I beat him hollow at the last,
   With all his Lords and Commons:[2] in the sky
I don't like ripping up old stories, since
His conduct was but natural in a prince.

LXXI

"Foolish, no doubt, and wicked, to oppress
   A poor unlucky devil without a shilling;
But then I blame the man himself much less
   Than Bute and Grafton,[3] and shall be unwilling
To see him punished here for their excess,
   Since they were both damned long ago, and still in
Their place below: for me, I have forgiven,
And vote his *habeas corpus*[4] into Heaven."

LXXII

"Wilkes," said the Devil, "I understand all this;
   You turned to half a courtier ere you died,
And seem to think it would not be amiss
   To grow a whole one on the other side
Of Charon's ferry;[5] you forget that *his*
   Reign is concluded; whatsoe'er betide,
He won't be sovereign more: you've lost your labour,
For at the best he will but be your neighbour.

LXXIII

"However, I knew what to think of it,
   When I beheld you in your jesting way,

2. The two houses of the English Parliament.
3. Two ministers of George III and enemies of Wilkes.
4. A writ of law requiring a person to be brought to trial before judge and jury.
5. Charon, in classical mythology, ferried the souls of the dead across the River Styx into Hades.

Flitting and whispering round about the spit
    Where Belial,[6] upon duty for the day,
With Fox's lard was basting William Pitt,[7]
    His pupil; I knew what to think, I say:
That fellow even in Hell breeds farther ills;
    I'll have him *gagged*—'twas one of his own Bills.[8]

LXXIV

"Call Junius!"[9] From the crowd a shadow stalked,
    And at the name there was a general squeeze,
So that the very ghosts no longer walked
    In comfort, at their own aërial ease,
But were all rammed, and jammed (but to be balked,
    As we shall see), and jostled hands and knees,
Like wind compressed and pent within a bladder,
Or like a human colic,[1] which is sadder.

LXXV

The shadow came—a tall, thin, grey-haired figure,
    That looked as it had been a shade on earth;
Quick in its motions, with an air of vigour,
    But nought to mark its breeding or its birth;
Now it waxed little, then again grew bigger,
    With now an air of gloom, or savage mirth;
But as you gazed upon its features, they
Changed every instant—to *what*, none could say.

LXXVI

The more intently the ghosts gazed, the less
    Could they distinguish whose the features were;
The Devil himself seemed puzzled even to guess;
    They varied like a dream—now here, now there;
And several people swore from out the press,
    They knew him perfectly; and one could swear
He was his father; upon which another
Was sure he was his mother's cousin's brother:

LXXVII

Another, that he was a duke, or knight,
    An orator, a lawyer, or a priest,
A nabob,[2] a man-midwife; but the wight
    Mysterious changed his countenance at least
As oft as they their minds: though in full sight
    He stood, the puzzle only was increased;

6. One of the traditional devils in hell (originally simply an alternate Hebrew name for Satan).

7. Charles James Fox (1749–1806) was an important—and very fat—Whig statesman. His lifelong opponent, William Pitt the Younger (1759–1806) was prime minister 1783–1801 and 1804–6, and the agent of highly repressive measures against political dissenters in England.

8. Pitt's so-called "gagging" laws (1795) drastically restricted freedom of the press and of speech.

9. This was the pseudonym used by the author of a series of public letters attacking George III's policies. His identity has never been conclusively determined.

1. In the early nineteenth century this was not a term for the infants' malady, but a generic term for any severe abdominal pain.

2. A very wealthy person.

The man was a phantasmagoria[3] in
Himself—he was so volatile and thin.

LXXVIII

The moment that you had pronounced him *one*,
　　Presto! his face changed, and he was another;
And when that change was hardly well put on,
　　It varied, till I don't think his own mother
(If that he had a mother) would her son
　　Have known, he shifted so from one to t'other;
Till guessing from a pleasure grew a task,
At this epistolary "Iron Mask."[4]

LXXIX

For sometimes he like Cerberus would seem—
　　"Three gentlemen at once" (as sagely says
Good Mrs. Malaprop);[5] then you might deem
　　That he was not even *one*; now many rays
Were flashing round him; and now a thick steam
　　Hid him from sight—like fogs on London days:
Now Burke, now Tooke, he grew to people's fancies,
And certes often like Sir Philip Francis.[6]

LXXX

I've an hypothesis—'tis quite my own;
　　I never let it out till now, for fear
Of doing people harm about the throne,
　　And injuring some minister or peer,
On whom the stigma might perhaps be blown;
　　It is—my gentle public, lend thine ear!
'Tis, that what Junius we are wont to call,
Was *really—truly*—nobody at all.

LXXXI

I don't see wherefore letters should not be
　　Written without hands, since we daily view
Them written without heads; and books, we see,
　　Are filled as well without the latter too;
And really till we fix on somebody
　　For certain sure to claim them as his due,
Their author, like the Niger's mouth,[7] will bother
The world to say if *there* be mouth or author.

LXXXII

"And who and what art thou?" the Archangel said.

3. A whole mob of phantoms.
4. The "Man in the Iron Mask" (it was actually a black velvet mask) was a nobleman imprisoned in the Bastille during the reign of Louis XIV, and died in 1703. His identity, too remains a mystery.
5. A character in Richard Brinsley Sheridan's play *The Rivals* (1775), who has a habit of comically mispronouncing words and scrambling concepts.

6. Edmund Burke (1729–97), the great Irish statesman and political theorist; John Horne Tooke (1736–1812), the English radical; and Sir Philip Francis (1740–1818), an official in the War Office under George III, were all believed at one time or another to be the author of the "Junius" letters.
7. The mouth of the River Niger in west Africa had not yet been discovered.

"For *that* you may consult my title-page,"[8]
Replied this mighty shadow of a shade:
    "If I have kept my secret half an age,
I scarce shall tell it now."—"Canst thou upbraid,"
    Continued Michael, "George Rex,[9] or allege
Aught further?" Junius answered, "You had better
First ask him for *his* answer to my letter:

LXXXIII

"My charges upon record will outlast
    The brass of both his epitaph and tomb."
"Repent'st thou not," said Michael, "of some past
    Exaggeration? something which may doom
Thyself if false, as him if true? Thou wast
    Too bitter—is it not so?—in thy gloom
Of passion?"—"Passion!" cried the phantom dim,
"I loved my country, and I hated him.

LXXXIV

"What I have written, I have written: let
    The rest be on his head or mine!" So spoke
Old "*Nominis Umbra;*" and while speaking yet,
    Away he melted in celestial smoke.
Then Satan said to Michael, "Don't forget
    To call George Washington, and John Horne Tooke,
And Franklin;"—but at this time there was heard
A cry for room, though not a phantom stirred.

LXXXV

At length with jostling, elbowing, and the aid
    Of Cherubim appointed to that post,
The devil Asmodeus[1] to the circle made
    His way, and looked as if his journey cost
Some trouble. When his burden[2] down he laid,
    "What's this?" cried Michael; "why, 'tis not a
        ghost?"
"I know it," quoth the Incubus;[3] but he
Shall be one, if you leave the affair to me.

LXXXVI

"Confound the renegado![4] I have sprained
    My left wing, he's so heavy; one would think
Some of his works about his neck were chained.
    But to the point; while hovering o'er the brink
Of Skiddaw[5] (where as usual it still rained),
    I saw a taper,[6] far below me, wink,

---

8. The title page of each of the Junius letters read: "Letters of Junius, *Stat Nominis Umbra.*" The Latin phrase means "It is the shadow of a name." See LXXXIV, line 3.
9. George the King.
1. One of the traditional devils in Hell.

2. Southey.
3. A male devil.
4. Renegade or outlaw.
5. A mountain in the Lake District of England, near Southey's home.
6. Candle.

And stooping, caught this fellow at a libel—
No less on History—than the Holy Bible.

LXXXVII

"The former is the Devil's scripture, and
    The latter yours, good Michael: so the affair
Belongs to all of us, you understand.
    I snatched him up just as you see him there,
And brought him off for sentence out of hand:
    I've scarcely been ten minutes in the air—
At least a quarter it can hardly be:
I dare say that his wife is still at tea."

LXXXVIII

Here Satan said, "I know this man of old,
    And have expected him for some time here;
A sillier fellow you will scarce behold,
    Or more conceited in his petty sphere:
But surely it was not worth while to fold
    Such trash below your wing, Asmodeus dear:
We had the poor wretch safe (without being bored
With carriage) coming of his own accord.

LXXXIX

"But since he's here, let's see what he has done."
    "Done!" cried Asmodeus, "he anticipates
The very business you are now upon,
    And scribbles as if head clerk to the Fates.
Who knows to what his ribaldry may run,
    When such an ass as this, like Balaam's,[7] prates?"
"Let's hear," quoth Michael, "what he has to say:
You know we're bound to that in every way."

XC

Now the bard, glad to get an audience, which
    By no means often was his case below,
Began to cough, and hawk, and hem, and pitch
    His voice into that awful note of woe
To all unhappy hearers within reach
    Of poets when the tide of rhyme's in flow;
But stuck fast with his first hexameter,[8]
Not one of all whose gouty feet would stir.

XCI

But ere the spavined[9] dactyls could be spurred
    Into recitative,[1] in great dismay
Both Cherubim and Seraphim were heard
    To murmur loudly through their long array;

---

7. In Numbers 22 : 28 the Lord speaks to the priest Balaam through Balaam's ass (beast of burden).
8. Dactyllic hexameter (see XCI, line 1) is the poetic meter of the epics of Homer and Vergil; Southey frequently tried to approximate the rhythm of hexameter in his "epics."
9. Crippled.
1. Portentously intoned or semi-sung verse.

And Michael rose ere he could get a word
    Of all his foundered verses under way,
And cried, "For God's sake stop, my friend! 'twere
    best—
'*Non Di, non homines*'[2]—you know the rest."

XCII

A general bustle spread throughout the throng,
    Which seemed to hold all verse in detestation;
The Angels had of course enough of song
    When upon service; and the generation
Of ghosts had heard too much in life, not long
    Before, to profit by a new occasion:
The Monarch, mute till then, exclaimed, "What!
    what!
Pye[3] come again? No more—no more of that!"

XCIII

The tumult grew; an universal cough
    Convulsed the skies, as during a debate,
When Castlereagh[4] has been up long enough
    (Before he was first minister of state,
I mean—the *slaves hear now*); some cried "Off, off!"
    As at a farce; till, grown quite desperate,
The Bard Saint Peter prayed to interpose
(Himself an author) only for his prose.

XCIV

The varlet was not an ill-favoured knave;
    A good deal like a vulture in the face,
With a hook nose and a hawk's eye, which gave
    A smart and sharper-looking sort of grace
To his whole aspect, which, though rather grave,
    Was by no means so ugly as his case;
But that, indeed, was hopeless as can be,
Quite a poetic felony "*de se*."[5]

XCV

Then Michael blew his trump, and stilled the noise
    With one still greater, as is yet the mode
On earth besides; except some grumbling voice,
    Which now and then will make a slight inroad
Upon decorous silence, few will twice
    Lift up their lungs when fairly overcrowed;
And now the Bard could plead his own bad cause,
With all the attitudes of self-applause.

---

2. *Mediocribus esse poetis / Non homines, non di, non concessere columnae*: "Neither gods nor men can tolerate mediocre poets." From Horace, *The Art of Poetry*, lines 372–373. Horace was Quintus Horatius Flaccus (65–8 B.C.), Rome's greatest lyric poet.

3. Henry James Pye (1745–1813) a notoriously bad poet, poet laureate before Southey.
4. Robert Stewart, Viscount Castlereagh (1769–1822), highly influential Tory statesman and notoriously dull orator.
5. Suicide.

XCVI

He said—(I only give the heads)—he said,
   He meant no harm in scribbling; 'twas his way
Upon all topics; 'twas, besides, his bread,
   Of which he buttered both sides; 'twould delay
Too long the assembly (he was pleased to dread),
   And take up rather more time than a day,
To name his works—he would but cite a few—
"Wat Tyler"—"Rhymes on Blenheim"—"Waterloo."[6]

XCVII

He had written praises of a Regicide;[7]
   He had written praises of all kings whatever;
He had written for republics far and wide,
   And then against them bitterer than ever;
For pantisocracy[8] he once had cried
   Aloud, a scheme less moral than 'twas clever;
Then grew a hearty anti-jacobin[9]—
Had turned his coat—and would have turned his skin.

XCVIII

He had sung against all battles, and again
   In their high praise and glory; he had called
Reviewing "the ungentle craft," and then
   Became as base a critic as e'er crawled—
Fed, paid, and pampered by the very men
   By whom his muse and morals had been mauled:
He had written much blank verse, and blanker prose,
And more of both than any body knows.

XCIX

He had written Wesley's[1] life:—here turning round
   To Satan, "Sir, I'm ready to write yours,
In two octavo[2] volumes, nicely bound,
   With notes and preface, all that most allures
The pious purchaser; and there's no ground
   For fear, for I can choose my own reviewers:
So let me have the proper documents,
That I may add you to my other saints."

C

Satan bowed, and was silent. "Well, if you,
   With amiable modesty, decline
My offer, what says Michael? There are few
   Whose memoirs could be rendered more divine.
Mine is a pen of all work; not so new
   As it was once, but I would make you shine

6. All poems by Southey.
7. Wat Tyler was one of the leaders of the Peasants' Revolt of 1381; Southey's poem celebrating this revolutionary character caused him embarrassment from a number of quarters after his conversion to Tory conservatism.
8. This was the name of the ideal society Southey (with Samuel Taylor Coleridge) had hoped to found in Pennsylvania in 1794.
9. One opposed to the policies of the French Revolution.
1. In 1820 Southey published his *Life of John Wesley* (1703–91) the founder of Methodism.
2. A book size, about six by nine inches.

Like your own trumpet. By the way, my own
Has more of brass in it, and is as well blown.

CI

"But talking about trumpets, here's my 'Vision!'[3]
    Now you shall judge, all people—yes—you shall
Judge with my judgment! and by my decision
    Be guided who shall enter heaven or fall.
I settle all these things by intuition,
    Times present, past, to come—Heaven—Hell—and
        all,
Like King Alfonso.[4] When I thus see double,
I save the Deity some worlds of trouble."

CII

He ceased, and drew forth an MS.;[5] and no
    Persuasion on the part of Devils, Saints,
Or Angels, now could stop the torrent; so
    He read the first three lines of the contents;
But at the fourth, the whole spiritual show
    Had vanished, with variety of scents,
Ambrosial and sulphureous,[6] as they sprang,
Like lightning, off from his "melodious twang."

CIII

Those grand heroics acted as a spell;
    The Angels stopped their ears and plied their pinions;[7]
The Devils ran howling, deafened, down to Hell;
    The ghosts fled, gibbering, for their own dominions—
(For 'tis not yet decided where they dwell,
    And I leave every man to his opinions);
Michael took refuge in his trump—but, lo!
His teeth were set on edge, he could not blow!

CIV

Saint Peter, who has hitherto been known
    For an impetuous saint, upraised his keys,
And at the fifth line knocked the poet down;
    Who fell like Phaeton,[8] but more at ease,
Into his lake, for there he did not drown;
    A different web being by the Destinies
Woven for the Laureate's final wreath, whene'er
Reform shall happen either here or there.

CV

He first sank to the bottom—like his works,
    But soon rose to the surface—like himself;

3. Southey's *Vision of Judgment* (1820).
4. Alfonso X, King of Castile (1221–84).
"King Alfonso, speaking of the Ptolo-
mean system, said, that 'had he been
consulted at the creation of the world,
he would have spared the Maker some
absurdities.' " [*Byron's note.*]
5. Manuscript.
6. Ambrosia is the food of the gods in
Homer; sulphur is among the traditional
ingredients of hell-fire.
7. Wings.
8. In classical mythology Phaeton, son
of the sun god Apollo, attempted to
drive the chariot of the sun across the
heavens for one day, but lost control of
it and was thrown to earth.

For all corrupted things are buoyed like corks,
  By their own rottenness, light as an elf,
Or wisp that flits o'er a morass: he lurks,
  It may be, still, like dull books on a shelf,
In his own den, to scrawl some "Life" or "Vision,"
  As Welborn[9] says—"the Devil turned precisian."

CVI

As for the rest, to come to the conclusion
  Of this true dream, the telescope is gone
Which kept my optics[1] free from all delusion,
  And showed me what I in my turn have shown;
All I saw farther, in the last confusion,
  Was, that King George slipped into Heaven for one;
And when the tumult dwindled to a calm,
I left him practising the hundredth psalm.[2]

Don Juan

There has never been any doubt about *Don Juan*. Whatever the fluctuations of Byron's reputation as a "serious" poet, *Don Juan* has remained one of the few indisputable comic masterpieces of English poetry.

We owe the poem not only to Byron, but to an unassuming, pleasant, second-rate poet named John Hookham Frere. In 1817 Frere published two cantos of a burlesque narrative entitled, alternately, *The Monks and the Giants* or (after Frere's pseudonyn in the volume) *Whistlecraft*. Frere chose for his tale the verse form called in Italian *"ottava rima"*: it is the standard verse form of the Renaissance Italian epic, and in Italian is capable of both comic and highly serious, tragic effect. But Italian abounds in polysyllabic words and in natural rhymes. To write true *ottava rima* in English is to be forced to find at least three rhymes for every stanza, as many of the rhymes as possible consisting of two or three syllables; it means, by the very choice of this form, to write comically. Byron read *Whistlecraft* and found it superb. In 1817 he began experimenting with the form, and in 1818 began writing *Don Juan*.

His initial intent, as he wrote to Thomas Moore on September 19, 1818, was to be "a little quietly facetious upon everything." But it is a question whether Byron could do anything quietly. At any rate his enthusiasm for the poem grew as the poem itself grew, in spite (or because) of strenuous objections from the English press—and from his last mistress, Countess Teresa Guiccioli—about the poem's immorality. Cantos I and II appeared in 1819; III–V in 1821; VI–XIV in 1823; XV and XVI in 1824. Part of canto XVII had been written when the poet died of a fever, in the rain of Missolonghi, April 19, 1824.

9. A Puritan ("precisian") character in Philip Massinger's comedy *A New Way to Pay Old Debts* (1626).
1. Eyes.

2. Probably because Psalm 100 includes the lines (4–5), "Come into his [the Lord's] gates with thanksgiving, / And into his courts with praise!"

FRAGMENT

ON THE BACK OF THE MS. OF CANTO THE FIRST

I WOULD to Heaven that I were so much clay,
    As I am blood, bone, marrow, passion, feeling—
Because at least the past were passed away,
    And for the future—(but I write this reeling,
Having got drunk exceedingly to-day,
    So that I seem to stand upon the ceiling)
I say—the future is a serious matter—
And so—for God's sake—hock[1] and soda-water!

[handwritten margin notes: vitality of body will overcome wisdom of age / SPRING overcoming WINTER / WINTER's coming—FIND SOMETHING ELSE]

DEDICATION

I

BOB SOUTHEY![2] You're a poet—Poet-laureate,
    And representative of all the race;
Although 'tis true that you turned out a Tory at
    Last,—yours has lately been a common case;
And now, my Epic Renegade! what are ye at?
    With all the Lakers, in and out of place?
A nest of tuneful persons, to my eye
Like "four and twenty Blackbirds in a pye;

II

"Which pye being opened they began to sing,"
    (This old song and new simile holds good),
"A dainty dish to set before the King,"
    Or Regent,[3] who admires such kind of food;—
And Coleridge, too, has lately taken wing,
    But like a hawk encumbered with his hood—
Explaining Metaphysics to the nation[4]—
I wish he would explain his Explanation.

[handwritten margin note: Lakers sold out.]

III

You, Bob! are rather insolent, you know,
    At being disappointed in your wish
To supersede all warblers here below,
    And be the only Blackbird in the dish;

1. A dry white wine. Byron refers to a hangover cure, the "hair of the dog."
2. Robert Southey (1774–1843). Southey, along with Wordsworth and Coleridge, was known as one of the "Lake Poets." Liberal in his youth, he became, (like Wordsworth) an enthusiastic Tory, and was made poet laureate in 1813. Byron despised all the "Lakers" for what he conceived to be their opportunistic politics—and Southey in particular because of Southey's solemn, self-righteous attacks upon Byron as a "Satanic" poet.
3. Before he became king, George IV served as Prince Regent from 1811 to 1820 during the insanity of his father George III.
4. Coleridge's *Biographia Literaria*, a narrative of his literary life and philosophical opinions, had been published in 1817.

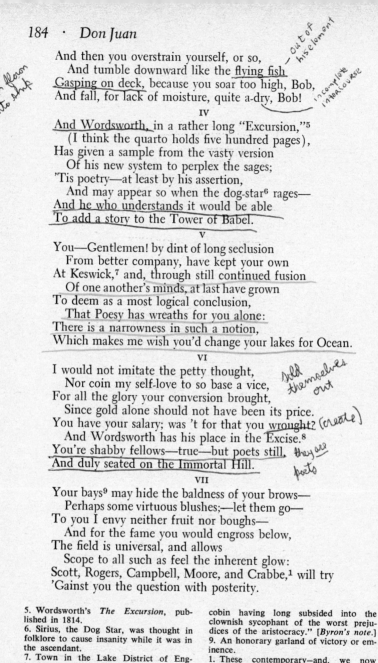

And then you overstrain yourself, or so,
   And tumble downward like the flying fish
Gasping on deck, because you soar too high, Bob,
And fall, for lack of moisture, quite a-dry, Bob!

IV

And Wordsworth, in a rather long "Excursion,"[5]
   (I think the quarto holds five hundred pages),
Has given a sample from the vasty version
   Of his new system to perplex the sages;
'Tis poetry—at least by his assertion,
   And may appear so when the dog-star[6] rages—
And he who understands it would be able
To add a story to the Tower of Babel.

V

You—Gentlemen! by dint of long seclusion
   From better company, have kept your own
At Keswick,[7] and, through still continued fusion
   Of one another's minds, at last have grown
To deem as a most logical conclusion,
   That Poesy has wreaths for you alone:
There is a narrowness in such a notion,
Which makes me wish you'd change your lakes for Ocean.

VI

I would not imitate the petty thought,
   Nor coin my self-love to so base a vice,
For all the glory your conversion brought,
   Since gold alone should not have been its price.
You have your salary; was 't for that you wrought?
   And Wordsworth has his place in the Excise.[8]
You're shabby fellows—true—but poets still,
And duly seated on the Immortal Hill.

VII

Your bays[9] may hide the baldness of your brows—
   Perhaps some virtuous blushes;—let them go—
To you I envy neither fruit nor boughs—
   And for the fame you would engross below,
The field is universal, and allows
   Scope to all such as feel the inherent glow:
Scott, Rogers, Campbell, Moore, and Crabbe,[1] will try
'Gainst you the question with posterity.

5. Wordsworth's *The Excursion*, published in 1814.
6. Sirius, the Dog Star, was thought in folklore to cause insanity while it was in the ascendant.
7. Town in the Lake District of England, near Wordsworth's home.
8. In 1813 Wordsworth had accepted a government sinecure: "the converted Jacobin having long subsided into the clownish sycophant of the worst prejudices of the aristocracy." [*Byron's note.*]
9. An honorary garland of victory or eminence.
1. These contemporary—and, we now feel, minor—Romantic poets were all rated by Byron high above such men as Wordsworth and Coleridge.

VIII

For me, who, wandering with pedestrian Muses,
  Contend not with you on the wingéd steed,[2]
I wish your fate may yield ye, when she chooses,
  The fame you envy, and the skill you need;
And, recollect, a poet nothing loses
  In giving to his brethren their full meed
Of merit—and complaint of present days
Is not the certain path to future praise.

[margin handwriting: knows his limits, doesn't have "starry" poetry. praising other poets doesn't diminish yourself]

IX

He that reserves his laurels for posterity
  (Who does not often claim the bright reversion)
Has generally no great crop to spare it, he
  Being only injured by his own assertion;
And although here and there some glorious rarity
  Arise like Titan[3] from the sea's immersion,
The major part of such appellants go
To—God knows where—for no one else can know.

X

If, fallen in evil days[4] on evil tongues,
  Milton appealed to the Avenger, Time,
If Time, the Avenger, execrates his wrongs,
  And makes the word "Miltonic" mean *"Sublime,"*
He deigned not to belie his soul in songs,
  Nor turn his very talent to a crime;
He did not loathe the Sire to laud the Son,
But closed the tyrant-hater he begun.

XI

Think'st thou, could he—the blind Old Man—arise
  Like Samuel[5] from the grave, to freeze once more
The blood of monarchs with his prophecies,
  Or be alive again—again all hoar
With time and trials, and those helpless eyes,
  And heartless daughters[6]—worn—and pale—and poor;
Would *he* adore a sultan? *he* obey
The intellectual eunuch Castlereagh?[7] *[handwriting: John Mitchell]*

XII

Cold-blooded, smooth-faced, placid miscreant!

2. Pegasus, the winged horse, conventional image of inspiration.
3. The Titan Oceanus, who was bound by Zeus beneath the sea.
4. After the restoration of the monarchy in 1660, Milton was in peril of his life for having supported the Puritan commonwealth. He did not change his politics to praise Charles II, however, and remained a fierce civil libertarian.
5. In I Samuel 28 : 13–21 King Saul summons the ghost of Samuel, the great prophet and judge of Israel, to advise him in his war against the Philistines. But Samuel instead berates Saul for deserting the way of the Lord and becoming a tyrant.
6. Milton's two older daughters are reputed to have defrauded him in his old age.
7. Robert Stewart, Viscount Castelreagh (1769–1822). Castelreagh was a highly influential Tory statesman from 1812 until his madness and suicide in 1822. Byron despised him heartily as a political hypocrite and oppressor.

Dabbling its sleek young hands in Erin's[8] gore,
And thus for wider carnage taught to pant,
    Transferred to gorge upon a sister shore,
    The vulgarest tool that Tyranny could want,
        With just enough of talent, and no more,
    To lengthen fetters by another fixed,
    And offer poison long already mixed.

XIII

An orator of such set trash of phrase
    Ineffably—legitimately vile,
That even its grossest flatterers dare not praise,
    Nor foes—all nations—condescend to smile,—
Nor even a sprightly blunder's spark can blaze
    From that Ixion[9] grindstone's ceaseless toil,
That turns and turns to give the world a notion
Of endless torments and perpetual motion.

XIV

A bungler even in its disgusting trade,
    And botching, patching, leaving still behind
Something of which its masters are afraid—
    States to be curbed, and thoughts to be confined,
Conspiracy or Congress[1] to be made—
    Cobbling at manacles for all mankind—
A tinkering slave-maker, who mends old chains,
With God and Man's abhorrence for its gains.

XV

If we may judge of matter by the mind,
    Emasculated to the marrow *It* (Castlereagh)
Hath but two objects, how to serve, and bind,
    Deeming the chain it wears even men may fit,
Eutropius[2] of its many masters,—blind
    To worth as freedom, wisdom as to wit,
Fearless—because *no* feeling dwells in ice
Its very courage stagnates to a vice.

XVI
chains

Where shall I turn me not to *view* its bonds,
    For I will never *feel* them?—Italy!
Thy late reviving Roman soul desponds
    Beneath the lie[3] this State-thing breathed o'er thee—
Thy clanking chain, and Erin's yet green wounds,
    Have voices—tongues to cry aloud for me.

---

8. Castelreagh was instrumental in defeating the Irish Rebellion of 1798.
9. In Greek myth, Ixion was punished by being eternally bound to a revolving wheel in Hades; hence he is an image of dull, grinding monotony. (Castelreagh was a notoriously bad orator.)
1. The Congress of Vienna (1814–15), called to reapportion Europe after Napoleon's defeat. Castelreagh participated in the Congress, whose decisions were to disrupt European politics for the next century.
2. A eunuch in the court of the Roman emperor Arcadius.
3. Castelreagh at Vienna insisted that Italy was not ready for political freedom.

Europe has slaves—allies—kings—armies still—
And Southey lives to sing them very ill.

XVII

Meantime, Sir Laureate, I proceed to dedicate,
In honest simple verse, this song to you.
And, if in flattering strains I do not predicate,
'Tis that I still retain my "bluff and blue;"[4]
My politics as yet are all to educate:
Apostasy's so fashionable, too,
To keep *one* creed's a task grown quite Herculean;
Is it not so, my Tory, ultra-Julian?[5]

RENUNCIATION

CANTO THE FIRST

DISTANCE FROM BYRON

I

I WANT a hero: an uncommon want,
When every year and month sends forth a new one,
Till, after cloying the gazettes with cant,
The age discovers he is not the true one;
Of such as these I should not care to vaunt,
I'll therefore take our ancient friend Don Juan—
We all have seen him, in the pantomime,[1]
Sent to the Devil somewhat ere his time.

II

Vernon,[2] the butcher Cumberland, Wolfe, Hawke,
Prince Ferdinand, Granby, Burgoyne, Keppel, Howe,
Evil and good, have had their tithe of talk,
And filled their sign-posts[3] then, like Wellesley now;
Each in their turn like Banquo's monarchs[4] stalk,
Followers of Fame, "nine farrow" of that sow:
France, too, had Buonaparté and Dumourier
Recorded in the Moniteur and Courier.[5]

III

Barnave, Brissot, Condorcet, Mirabeau,
Petion, Clootz, Danton, Marat, La Fayette
Were French, and famous people, as we know;
And there were others, scarce forgotten yet,
Joubert, Hoche, Marceau, Lannes, Desaix, Moreau,

4. The colors of the liberal Whig party.
5. Julian the Apostate (331–63), emperor of Rome, renounced his Christianity to reinstigate pagan worship.
1. Pantomimes and puppet shows of the eighteenth and early nineteenth centuries frequently dealt with the damnation of Don Juan.
2. The catalogue of English military leaders here, like the catalogue of French generals and revolutionaries in stanza III, is intended to be confusing. Byron's point is that the age provides so many instant heroes that their identities become meaningless, a mere list of famous names.
3. A reference to the habit of naming streets and squares for the hero of the hour. For Wellesley (the Duke of Wellington) see Don Juan IX, stanza I.
4. In *Macbeth* IV. i. 109 ff., the three witches show Macbeth a procession of the Kings of Scotland who will be the issue of Banquo, whom Macbeth has killed. The "nine farrow" of the following line is a quotation from the witches' chant, *Macbeth* IV. i. 65.
5. French newspapers.

With many of the military set,
Exceedingly remarkable at times,
But not at all adapted to my rhymes.

IV

Nelson[6] was once Britannia's god of War,
    And still should be so, but the tide is turned;
There's no more to be said of Trafalgar,
    'Tis with our hero quietly inurned;
Because the army's grown more popular,
    At which the naval people are concerned;
Besides, the Prince[7] is all for the land-service,
Forgetting Duncan, Nelson, Howe, and Jervis.

V

Brave men were living before Agamemnon[8]
    And since, exceeding valorous and sage,
A good deal like him too, though quite the same none;
    But then they shone not on the poet's page,
And so have been forgotten:—I condemn none,
    But can't find any in the present age
Fit for my poem (that is, for my new one);
So, as I said, I'll take my friend Don Juan.

VI

Most epic poets plunge *"in medias res"*[9]
    (Horace makes this the heroic turnpike road),
And then your hero tells, whene'er you please
    What went before—by way of episode,
While seated after dinner at his ease,
    Beside his mistress in some soft abode,
Palace, or garden, paradise, or cavern,
Which serves the happy couple for a tavern.

VII

That is the usual method, but not mine—
    My way is to begin with the beginning;
The regularity[1] of my design
    Forbids all wandering as the worst of sinning,
And therefore I shall open with a line
    (Although it cost me half an hour in spinning),
Narrating somewhat of Don Juan's father,
And also of his mother, if you'd rather.

VIII

In Seville was he born, a pleasant city,
    Famous for oranges and women,—he

---

6. Horatio, Lord Nelson (1758–1805), England's greatest naval hero, who defeated Napoleon's navy at Trafalgar, 1805.
7. George IV, who between 1811 and 1820 served as Prince Regent during the insanity of his father, George III. One of George IV's controversial policies was to allot greater funds to the army than to the navy. "Duncan" and the others in line 8 are British naval figures.
8. Leader of the Greek army in the Trojan War.
9. The prescription of Horace in the *Art of Poetry* for beginning an epic "in the middle of events."
1. Ironic, of course.

Who has not seen it will be much to pity,
    So says the proverb—and I quite agree;
Of all the Spanish towns is none more pretty,
    Cadiz perhaps—but that you soon may see;—
Don Juan's parents lived beside the river,
A noble stream, and called the Guadalquivir.

IX

His father's name was José—*Don*, of course,—
    A true Hidalgo,[2] free from every stain
Of Moor or Hebrew blood, he traced his source
    Through the most Gothic gentlemen of Spain;
A better cavalier ne'er mounted horse,
    Or, being mounted, e'er got down again,
Than José, who begot our hero, who
Begot—but that's to come——Well, to renew:

X

His mother was a learnéd lady, famed
    For every branch of every science known—
In every Christian language ever named,
    With virtues equalled by her wit alone:
She made the cleverest people quite ashamed,
    And even the good with inward envy groan,
Finding themselves so very much exceeded,
In their own way, by all the things that she did.

XI

Her memory was a mine: she knew by heart
    All Calderon and greater part of Lopé,[3]
So, that if any actor missed his part,
    She could have served him for the prompter's copy;
For her Feinagle's[4] were an useless art,
    And he himself obliged to shut up shop—he
Could never make a memory so fine as
That which adorned the brain of Donna Inez.

XII

Her favourite science was the mathematical,
    Her noblest virtue was her magnanimity,
Her wit (she sometimes tried at wit) was Attic[5] all,
    Her serious sayings darkened to sublimity;
In short, in all things she was fairly what I call
    A prodigy—her morning dress was dimity,[6]
Her evening silk, or, in the summer, muslin,
And other stuffs, with which I won't stay puzzling.

2. Spanish nobleman: Don Jose's nobility is such that he has no Moorish blood
(the Moors being the African Moslems
who controlled much of Spain during the
medieval and renaissance centuries), nor
any Hebrew or Jewish blood.
3. Pedro Calderón de la Barca (1600–
81) and Lope de Vega (1562–1635), the
great originators of classical Spanish
drama.
4. Gregor von Feinagle (1765–1819) developed a system, popular in Byron's
day, for improving the memory.
5. Greek. "Attic wit" was proverbially
learned, sarcastic—and not very funny.
6. A thin cotton fabric.

Smattering of education

XIII

She knew the Latin—that is, "the Lord's prayer,"
　　And Greek—the alphabet—I'm nearly sure;
She read some French romances here and there,
　　Although her mode of speaking was not pure;
For native Spanish she had no great care,
　　At least her conversation was obscure;
Her thoughts were theorems, her words a problem,
As if she deemed that mystery would ennoble 'em.

XIV

She liked the English and the Hebrew tongue,
　　And said there was analogy between 'em;
She proved it somehow out of sacred song,
　　But I must leave the proofs to those who've seen 'em;
But this I heard her say, and can't be wrong,
　　And all may think which way their judgments lean 'em,
" 'T is strange—the Hebrew noun[7] which means 'I am,'
The English always use to govern d—n."

XV

Some women use their tongues—she *looked* a lecture,
　　Each eye a sermon, and her brow a homily,
An all-in-all sufficient self-director,
　　Like the lamented late Sir Samuel Romilly,[8]
The Law's expounder, and the State's corrector,
　　Whose suicide was almost an anomaly—
One sad example more, that "All is vanity,"[9]—
(The jury brought their verdict in "Insanity!")

Irregularity

XVI

In short, she was a walking calculation,
　　Miss Edgeworth's[1] novels stepping from their covers,
Or Mrs. Trimmer's books on education,[2]
　　Or "Coelebs' Wife"[3] set out in quest of lovers,
Morality's prim personification,
　　In which not Envy's self a flaw discovers;
To others' share let "female errors fall,"[4]
For she had not even one—the worst of all.

XVII

Oh! she was perfect past all parallel—
　　Of any modern female saint's comparison;
So far above the cunning powers of Hell,
　　Her Guardian Angel had given up his garrison;

7. God names Himself "I am" in Exodus 3 : 14. Thus, the English never say "God" without adding "damn." The English penchant for profanity has always been proverbial in Europe.
8. Samuel Romilly (1757–1818), a liberal reformer, originally represented Byron in his separation from Lady Byron, but later shifted loyalty to the Lady. Romilly committed suicide after the death of his wife; Byron's continued hatred of him is not one of the poet's most admirable traits.
9. Ecclesiastes 1 : 2.
1. Maria Edgeworth (1767–1849), author of sentimental novels.
2. Sarah Trimmer (1741–1810), author of tracts on moral education.
3. *Coelebs in Search of a Wife* was a book of moral instruction by the bluestocking Hannah Moore (1745–1833).
4. Pope's *The Rape of the Lock*, II, 17.

Even her minutest motions went as well
  As those of the best time-piece made by Harrison:[5]
In virtues nothing earthly could surpass her,
Save thine "incomparable oil," Macassar![6]

XVIII

BORING

pattern of fall.

Perfect she was, but as perfection is
  Insipid in this naughty world of ours,
Where our first parents never learned to kiss
  Till they were exiled from their earlier bowers,
Where all was peace, and innocence, and bliss,
  (I wonder how they got through the twelve hours),
Don José, like a lineal son of Eve,
Went plucking various fruit without her leave.

XIX

He was a mortal of the careless kind,
  With no great love for learning, or the learned,
Who chose to go where'er he had a mind,
  And never dreamed his lady was concerned;
The world, as usual, wickedly inclined
  To see a kingdom or a house o'erturned,
Whispered he had a mistress, some said *two*.
But for domestic quarrels *one* will do.

XX

Now Donna Inez had, with all her merit,
  A great opinion of her own good qualities;
Neglect, indeed, requires a saint to bear it,
  And such, indeed, she was in her moralities;
But then she had a devil of a spirit,
  And sometimes mixed up fancies with realities,
And let few opportunities escape
Of getting her liege lord into a scrape.

XXI

sets 'em up

This was an easy matter with a man
  Oft in the wrong, and never on his guard;
And even the wisest, do the best they can,
  Have moments, hours, and days, so unprepared,
That you might "brain them with their lady's fan;"[7]
  And sometimes ladies hit exceeding hard,
And fans turn into falchions[8] in fair hands,
And why and wherefore no one understands.

XXII

'Tis pity learnéd virgins ever wed
  With persons of no sort of education,
Or gentlemen, who, though well born and bred,
  Grow tired of scientific conversation:
I don't choose to say much upon this head,

5. John Harrison (1693–1776), famous English watchmaker.
6. Hair oil from the Isle of Macassar was a popular commodity, advertised as possessing all manner of healthful qualities.
7. 1 *Henry IV*, II. iii. 20–21.
8. Swords.

I'm a plain man, and in a single station,
But—Oh! ye lords of ladies intellectual,
Inform us truly, have they not hen-pecked you all?

XXIII

Don José and his lady quarrelled—*why*,
    Not any of the many could divine,
Though several thousand people chose to try,
    'Twas surely no concern of theirs nor mine;
I loathe that low vice—curiosity;
    But if there's anything in which I shine,
'Tis in arranging all my friends' affairs,
Not having, of my own, domestic cares.

XXIV

And so I interfered, and with the best
    Intentions, but their treatment was not kind;
I think the foolish people were possessed,
    For neither of them could I ever find,
Although their porter afterwards confessed—
    But that's no matter, and the worst's behind
For little Juan o'er me threw, down stairs,
A pail of housemaid's water unawares.

XXV

A little curly-headed, good-for-nothing,
    And mischief-making monkey from his birth;
His parents ne'er agreed except in doting
    Upon the most unquiet imp on earth;
Instead of quarreling, had they been but both in
    Their senses, they'd have sent young master forth
To school, or had him soundly whipped at home,
To teach him manners for the time to come.

XXVI

Don José and the Donna Inez led
    For some time an unhappy sort of life,
Wishing each other, not divorced, but dead;
    They lived respectably as man and wife,
Their conduct was exceedingly well-bred,
    And gave no outward signs of inward strife,
Until at length the smothered fire broke out,
And put the business past all kind of doubt.

XXVII[9]

For Inez called some druggists and physicians,
    And tried to prove her loving lord was *mad*,
But as he had some lucid intermissions,
    She next decided he was only *bad*;
Yet when they asked her for her depositions,
    No sort of explanation could be had,

9. During the separation proceedings, Lady Byron frequently claimed that Byron was clinically insane. There are, indeed, many points of similarity between the character of Dona Inez and that of Byron's wife.

Save that her duty both to man and God
Required this conduct—which seemed very odd.

XXVIII

She kept a journal, where his faults were noted,
　　And opened certain trunks of books and letters,
All which might, if occasion served, be quoted;
　　And then she had all Seville for abettors,
Besides her good old grandmother (who doted);
　　The hearers of her case became repeaters,
Then advocates, inquisitors, and judges,
Some for amusement, others for old grudges.

XXIX

And then this best and meekest woman bore
　　With such serenity her husband's woes,
Just as the Spartan[1] ladies did of yore,
　　Who saw their spouses killed, and nobly chose
Never to say a word about them more—　*slander*
　　Calmly she heard each calumny that rose,
And saw *his* agonies with such sublimity,
That all the world exclaimed, "What magnanimity!"

XXX

No doubt this patience, when the world is damning us,
　　Is philosophic in our former friends;
'Tis also pleasant to be deemed magnanimous,
　　The more so in obtaining our own ends;
And what the lawyers call a "*malus animus*"[2]
　　Conduct like this by no means comprehends:
Revenge in person's certainly no virtue,
But then 't is not *my* fault, if *others* hurt you.

XXXI

And if our quarrels should rip up old stories,
　　And help them with a lie or two additional,
I'm not to blame, as you well know—no more is
　　Any one else—they were become traditional;
Besides, their resurrection aids our glories
　　By contrast, which is what we just were wishing all:
And Science profits by this resurrection—
Dead scandals form good subjects for dissection.

XXXII

Their friends had tried at reconciliation,
　　Then their relations, who made matters worse.
('Twere hard to tell upon a like occasion
　　To whom it may be best to have recourse—
I can't say much for friend or yet relation):
　　The lawyers did their utmost for divorce,
But scarce a fee was paid on either side
Before, unluckily, Don José died.

1. The detail is literally true. The natives of Sparta, in ancient Greece, were renowned for their stoic impassivity to grief.
2. Bad intent.

XXXIII

He died: and most unluckily, because,
    According to all hints I could collect
From Counsel learnéd in those kinds of laws,
    (Although their talk's obscure and circumspect)
His death contrived to spoil a charming cause;
    A thousand pities also with respect
To public feeling, which on this occasion
Was manifested in a great sensation.

XXXIV

But ah! he died; and buried with him lay
    The public feeling and the lawyers' fees:
His house was sold, his servants sent away,
    A Jew took one of his two mistresses,
A priest the other—at least so they say:
    I asked the doctors after his disease—
He died of the slow fever called the tertian,[3]
And left his widow to her own aversion.

XXXV

Yet José was an honourable man,
    That I must say, who knew him very well;
Therefore his frailties I'll no further scan,
    Indeed there were not many more to tell:
And if his passions now and then outran
    Discretion, and were not so peaceable
As Numa's (who was also named Pompilius),[4]
He had been ill brought up, and was born bilious.[5]

XXXVI

Whate'er might be his worthlessness or worth,
    Poor fellow! he had many things to wound him.
Let's own—since it can do no good on earth—
    It was a trying moment that which found him
Standing alone beside his desolate hearth,
    Where all his household gods lay shivered round him:
No choice was left his feelings or his pride,
Save Death or Doctors' Commons[6]—so he died.

XXXVII

Dying intestate, Juan was sole heir
    To a chancery[7] suit, and messuages,[8] and lands,
Which, with a long minority and care,
    Promised to turn out well in proper hands:
Inez became sole guardian, which was fair,
    And answered but to Nature's just demands;
An only son left with an only mother
Is brought up much more wisely than another.

---

3. A fever which recurs every other day.
4. Early king of Rome, legendary for patience and moderation.
5. Of an angry disposition.

6. Divorce court.
7. Court which tried legacy disputes.
8. Dwelling places (legalism).

XXXVIII

Sagest of women, even of widows, she
　　Resolved that Juan should be quite a paragon,
And worthy of the noblest pedigree,
　　(His Sire was of Castile, his Dam from Aragon):[9]
Then, for accomplishments of chivalry,
　　In case our Lord the King should go to war again,
He learned the arts of riding, fencing, gunnery,
And how to scale a fortress—or a nunnery.

XXXIX

But that which Donna Inez most desired,
　　And saw into herself each day before all
The learnéd tutors whom for him she hired,
　　Was, that his breeding should be strictly moral:
Much into all his studies she inquired,
　　And so they were submitted first to her, all,
Arts, sciences—no branch was made a mystery
To Juan's eyes, excepting natural history.

XL

The languages, especially the dead,
　　The sciences, and most of all the abstruse,
The arts, at least all such as could be said
　　To be the most remote from common use,
In all these he was much and deeply read:
　　But not a page of anything that's loose,
Or hints continuation of the species,
Was ever suffered, lest he should grow vicious.

XLI

His classic studies made a little puzzle,
　　Because of filthy loves of gods and goddesses,
Who in the earlier ages raised a bustle,
　　But never put on pantaloons or bodices;
His reverend tutors had at times a tussle,
　　And for their Æneids, Iliads, and Odysseys,
Were forced to make an odd sort of apology,
For Donna Inez dreaded the Mythology.

XLII[1]

Ovid's a rake, as half his verses show him,
　　Anacreon's morals are a still worse sample,

9. The two great noble houses of Spain.
1. In this and the next stanza Byron indicates his own veneration for the genius and frankness of the great Greek and Latin poets, and at the same time mocks the foolish prudery of Dona Inez's "culture." Ovid (Publius Ovidius Naso, 43 B.C.–A.D. 17) wrote the *Art of Love* and the highly erotic *Metamorphoses*; Catullus (Gaius Valerius Catullus, 84–54 B.C.) and Anacreon (570–485 B.C.) were passionately sexual lyric poets; Sappho (sixth century B.C.) created an erotic masterpiece in her *Ode to Aphrodite*; Longinus (died A.D. 273) in his treatise *On the Sublime* praised Sappho's *Ode*; Vergil's Fourth Eclogue (*Formosum pastor*) is a lyric of homosexual love. Lucretius (Titus Lucretius Carus, 100–55 B.C.) in *On the Nature of Things* argued for a materialistic and Epicurean world view; Juvenal (Decimus Iunius Iuvenalis, A.D. 60–140) and Martial (Marcus Valerius Martialis, A.D. 40–104) were the most vitriolic satirists of ancient Rome.

Catullus scarcely has a decent poem,
  I don't think Sappho's Ode a good example,
Although Longinus tells us there is no hymn
  Where the Sublime soars forth on wings more ample;
But Virgil's songs are pure, except that horrid one
Beginning with *"Formosum Pastor Corydon."*

XLIII

Lucretius' irreligion is too strong
  For early stomachs, to prove wholesome food;
I can't help thinking Juvenal was wrong,
  Although no doubt his real intent was good,
For speaking out so plainly in his song,
  So much indeed as to be downright rude;
And then what proper person can be partial
To all those nauseous epigrams of Martial?

XLIV

Juan was taught from out the best edition,
  Expurgated[2] by learnéd men, who place,
Judiciously, from out the schoolboy's vision,
  The grosser parts; but, fearful to deface
Too much their modest bard by this omission,
  And pitying sore his mutilated case,
They only add them all in an appendix,
Which saves, in fact, the trouble of an index;

XLV

For there we have them all "at one fell swoop,"
  Instead of being scattered through the pages;
They stand forth marshalled in a handsome troop,
  To meet the ingenuous youth of future ages,
Till some less rigid editor shall stoop
  To call them back into their separate cages,
Instead of standing staring all together,
Like garden gods[3]—and not so decent either.

XLVI

The Missal[4] too (it was the family Missal)
  Was ornamented in a sort of way
Which ancient mass-books often are, and this all
  Kinds of grotesques illumined; and how they,
Who saw those figures on the margin kiss all,
  Could turn their optics[5] to the text and pray,
Is more than I know—but Don Juan's mother
Kept this herself, and gave her son another.

XLVII

Sermons he read, and lectures he endured,
  And homilies, and lives of all the saints;

---

2. "Fact! There is, or was, such an edition, with all the obnoxious epigrams of Martial placed by themselves at the end." [*Byron't note.*]

3. The statues of gods assembled in a classical English garden.
4. Roman Catholic liturgical text.
5. Eyes.

To Jerome and to Chrysostom[6] inured,
    He did not take such studies for restraints;
But how Faith is acquired, and then insured,
    So well not one of the aforesaid paints
As Saint Augustine[7] in his fine Confessions,
Which make the reader envy his transgressions.

XLVIII

This, too, was a sealed book to little Juan—
    I can't but say that his mamma was right,
If such an education was the true one.
    She scarcely trusted him from out her sight;
Her maids were old, and if she took a new one,
    You might be sure she was a perfect fright;
She did this during even her husband's life—
I recommend as much to every wife.

XLIX

Young Juan waxed in goodliness and grace;
    At six a charming child, and at eleven
With all the promise of as fine a face
    As e'er to Man's maturer growth was given:
He studied steadily, and grew apace,
    And seemed, at least, in the right road to Heaven,
For half his days were passed at church, the other
Between his tutors, confessor,[8] and mother.

L

At six, I said, he was a charming child,
    At twelve he was a fine, but quiet boy;
Although in infancy a little wild,
    They tamed him down amongst them: to destroy
His natural spirit not in vain they toiled,
    At least it seemed so; and his mother's joy
Was to declare how sage, and still, and steady,
Her young philosopher was grown already.

LI

I had my doubts, perhaps I have them still,
    But what I say is neither here nor there:
I knew his father well, and have some skill
    In character—but it would not be fair
From sire to son to augur good or ill:
    He and his wife were an ill-sorted pair—
But scandal's my aversion—I protest
Against all evil speaking, even in jest.

LII

For my part I say nothing—nothing—but
    This I will say—my reasons are my own—

6. St. Jerome (348–420) and St. John
Chrysostom (345–407) were two important fathers of the early Christian
church.
7. St. Augustine (345–430), one of the
greatest figures in church history. His
Confessions (ca. 397) describe in detail
his dissolute life before his conversion.
8. The priest who served as his spiritual
advisor.

That if I had an only son to put
    To school (as God be praised that I have none),
'Tis not with Donna Inez I would shut
    Him up to learn his catechism alone,
No—no—I'd send him out betimes to college,
For there it was I picked up my own knowledge.

LIII

For there one learns—'tis not for me to boast,
    Though I acquired—but I pass over *that*,
As well as all the Greek I since have lost:
    I say that there's the place—but *"Verbum sat,"*[9]
I think I picked up too, as well as most,
    Knowledge of matters—but no matter *what*—
I never married—but, I think, I know
That sons should not be educated so.

LIV

Young Juan now was sixteen years of age,
    Tall, handsome, slender, but well knit: he seemed
Active, though not so sprightly, as a page;
    And everybody but his mother deemed
Him almost man; but she flew in a rage
    And bit her lips (for else she might have screamed)
If any said so—for to be precocious
Was in her eyes a thing the most atrocious.

LV

Amongst her numerous acquaintance, all
    Selected for discretion and devotion,
There was the Donna Julia, whom to call
    Pretty were but to give a feeble notion
Of many charms in her as natural
    As sweetness to the flower, or salt to Ocean,
Her zone to Venus,[1] or his bow to Cupid,
(But this last simile is trite and stupid.)

LVI

The darkness of her Oriental eye
    Accorded with her Moorish[2] origin;
(Her blood was not all Spanish; by the by,
    In Spain, you know, this is a sort of sin;)
When proud Granada fell, and, forced to fly,
    Boabdil[3] wept: of Donna Julia's kin
Some went to Africa, some stayed in Spain—
Her great great grandmamma chose to remain.

LVII

She married (I forget the pedigree)
    With an Hidalgo, who transmitted down

9. Enough said.
1. The "zone" (belt) of Venus, goddess of love, was believed to give its wearer the power of instilling passion in others.
2. The Moors, African Moslems, dominated much of Spain from the eighth to the fifteenth centuries, and deeply influenced its culture.
3. When the Moors were driven from Granada in 1492, the warrior prince Boabdil wept at leaving the city.

His blood less noble than such blood should be;
　At such alliances his sires would frown,
In that point so precise in each degree
　That they bred *in and in*, as might be shown,
Marrying their cousins—nay, their aunts, and nieces,
Which always spoils the breed, if it increases.

LVIII

This heathenish cross restored the breed again,
　Ruined its blood, but much improved its flesh;
For from a root the ugliest in Old Spain
　Sprung up a branch as beautiful as fresh;
The sons no more were short, the daughters plain:
　But there's a rumour which I fain would hush,
'Tis said that Donna Julia's grandmamma
Produced her Don more heirs at love than law.

LIX

However this might be, the race went on
　Improving still through every generation,
Until it centred in an only son,
　Who left an only daughter; my narration
May have suggested that this single one
　Could be but Julia (whom on this occasion
I shall have much to speak about), and she
Was married, charming, chaste, and twenty-three.

LX

Her eye (I'm very fond of handsome eyes)
　Was large and dark, suppressing half its fire
Until she spoke, then through its soft disguise
　Flashed an expression more of pride than ire,
And love than either; and there would arise
　A something in them which was not desire,
But would have been, perhaps, but for the soul
Which struggled through and chastened down the whole.

LXI

Her glossy hair was clustered o'er a brow
　Bright with intelligence, and fair, and smooth;
Her eyebrow's shape was like the aërial bow,
　Her cheek all purple with the beam of youth,
Mounting, at times, to a transparent glow,
　As if her veins ran lightning; she, in sooth,
Possessed an air and grace by no means common:
Her stature tall—I hate a dumpy woman.

LXII

Wedded she was some years, and to a man
　Of fifty, and such husbands are in plenty;
And yet, I think, instead of such a ONE
　'Twere better to have TWO of five-and-twenty,
Especially in countries near the sun:
　And now I think on 't, *"mi vien in mente,"*[4]

4. It comes to my mind.

Ladies even of the most uneasy virtue
Prefer a spouse whose age is short of thirty.

LXIII

'Tis a sad thing, I cannot choose but say,
  And all the fault of that indecent sun,
Who cannot leave alone our helpless clay,
  But will keep baking, broiling, burning on,
That howsoever people fast and pray,
  The flesh is frail, and so the soul undone:
What men call gallantry, and gods adultery,
Is much more common where the climate's sultry.

LXIV

Happy the nations of the moral North!
  Where all is virtue, and the winter season
Sends sin, without a rag on, shivering forth
  ('Twas snow that brought St. Anthony[5] to reason);
Where juries cast up what a wife is worth,
  By laying whate'er sum, in mulct,[6] they please on
The lover, who must pay a handsome price,
Because it is a marketable vice.

LXV

Alfonso was the name of Julia's lord,
  A man well looking for his years, and who
Was neither much beloved nor yet abhorred:
  They lived together as most people do,
Suffering each other's foibles by accord,
  And not exactly either *one* or *two*;
Yet he was jealous, though he did not show it,
For Jealousy dislikes the world to know it.

LXVI

Julia was—yet I never could see why—
  With Donna Inez quite a favourite friend;
Between their tastes there was small sympathy,
  For not a line had Julia ever penned:
Some people whisper (but, no doubt, they lie,
  For Malice still imputes some private end)
That Inez had, ere Don Alfonso's marriage,
Forgot with him her very prudent carriage;

LXVII

And that still keeping up the old connection,
  Which Time had lately rendered much more chaste,
She took his lady also in affection,
  And certainly this course was much the best:
She flattered Julia with her sage protection,
  And complimented Don Alfonso's taste;

---

5. "For the particulars of St. Anthony's recipe for hot blood in cold weather, see Mr. Alban Butler's 'Lives of the Saints' [*Byron's note*]. Byron later remembered that it was St. Francis of As- sisi who used this method of curbing the passions.
6. A fine. Byron refers to alimony for adultery.

And if she could not (who can?) silence scandal,
At least she left it a more slender handle.

LXVIII

I can't tell whether Julia saw the affair
    With other people's eyes, or if her own
Discoveries made, but none could be aware
    Of this, at least no symptom e'er was shown;
Perhaps she did not know, or did not care,
    Indifferent from the first, or callous grown:
I'm really puzzled what to think or say,
She kept her counsel in so close a way.

LXIX

Juan she saw, and, as a pretty child,
    Caressed him often—such a thing might be
Quite innocently done, and harmless styled,
    When she had twenty years, and thirteen he;
But I am not so sure I should have smiled
    When he was sixteen, Julia twenty-three;
These few short years make wondrous alterations,
Particularly amongst sun-burnt nations.

LXX

Whate'er the cause might be, they had become
    Changed; for the dame grew distant, the youth shy,
Their looks cast down, their greetings almost dumb,
    And much embarrassment in either eye;
There surely will be little doubt with some
    That Donna Julia knew the reason why,
But as for Juan, he had no more notion
Than he who never saw the sea of Ocean.

LXXI

Yet Julia's very coldness still was kind,
    And tremulously gentle her small hand
Withdrew itself from his, but left behind
    A little pressure, thrilling, and so bland
And slight, so very slight, that to the mind
    'Twas but a doubt; but ne'er magician's wand
Wrought change with all Armida's[7] fairy art
Like what this light touch left on Juan's heart.

LXXII

And if she met him, though she smiled no more,
    She looked a sadness sweeter than her smile,
As if her heart had deeper thoughts in store
    She must not own, but cherished more the while
For that compression in its burning core;
    Even Innocence itself has many a wile,
And will not dare to trust itself with truth,
And Love is taught hypocrisy from youth.

7. Sorceress and temptress in Tasso's epic *Jerusalem Delivered* (1575).

LXXIII

But passion most dissembles, yet betrays
 Even by its darkness; as the blackest sky
Fortells the heaviest tempest, it displays
 Its workings through the vainly guarded eye,
And in whatever aspect it arrays
 Itself, 'tis still the same hypocrisy;
Coldness or Anger, even Disdain or Hate,
Are masks it often wears, and still too late.

LXXIV

Then there were sighs, the deeper for suppression,
 And stolen glances, sweeter for the theft,
And burning blushes, though for no transgression,
 Tremblings when met, and restlessness when left;
All these are little preludes to possession,
 Of which young Passion cannot be bereft,
And merely tend to show how greatly Love is
Embarrassed at first starting with a novice.

LXXV

Poor Julia's heart was in an awkward state;
 She felt it going, and resolved to make
The noblest efforts for herself and mate,
 For Honour's, Pride's, Religion's, Virtue's sake:
Her resolutions were most truly great,
 And almost might have made a Tarquin[8] quake:
She prayed the Virgin Mary for her grace,
As being the best judge of a lady's case.

LXXVI

She vowed she never would see Juan more,
 And next day paid a visit to his mother,
And looked extremely at the opening door,
 Which, by the Virgin's grace, let in another;
Grateful she was, and yet a little sore—
 Again it opens, it can be no other,
'Tis surely Juan now—No! I'm afraid
That night the Virgin was no further prayed.

LXXVII

She now determined that a virtuous woman
 Should rather face and overcome temptation,
That flight was base and dastardly, and no man
 Should ever give her heart the least sensation,
That is to say, a thought beyond the common
 Preference, that we must feel, upon occasion,
For people who are pleasanter than others,
But then they only seem so many brothers.

LXXVIII

And even if by chance—and who can tell?
 The Devil's so very sly—she should discover

8. Legendary early Roman king, famous for his rigor and cruelty.

That all within was not so very well,
    And, if still free, that such or such a lover
Might please perhaps, a virtuous wife can quell
    Such thoughts, and be the better when they're over;
And if the man should ask, 'tis but denial:
I recommend young ladies to make trial.

LXXIX

And, then, there are such things as Love divine,
    Bright and immaculate, unmixed and pure,
Such as the angels think so very fine,
    And matrons, who would be no less secure,
Platonic,[9] perfect, "just such love as mine;"
    Thus Julia said—and thought so, to be sure;
And so I'd have her think, were *I* the man
On whom her reveries celestial ran.

LXXX

Such love is innocent, and may exist
    Between young persons without any danger.
A hand may first, and then a lip be kissed;
    For my part, to such doings I'm a stranger,
But *hear* these freedoms form the utmost list
    Of all o'er which such love may be a ranger:
If people go beyond, 'tis quite a crime,
But not my fault—I tell them all in time.

LXXXI

Love, then, but Love within its proper limits,
    Was Julia's innocent determination
In young Don Juan's favour, and to him its
    Exertion might be useful on occasion;
And, lighted at too pure a shrine to dim its
    Ethereal lustre, with what sweet persuasion
He might be taught, by Love and her together—
I really don't know what, nor Julia either.

LXXXII

Fraught with this fine intention, and well fenced
    In mail of proof[1]—her purity of soul—
She, for the future, of her strength convinced,
    And that her honour was a rock, or mole,
Exceeding sagely from that hour dispensed
    With any kind of troublesome control;
But whether Julia to the task was equal
Is that which must be mentioned in the sequel.

LXXXIII

Her plan she deemed both innocent and feasible,
    And, surely, with a stripling of sixteen

9. Byron ridicules the idea (not Plato's at all) of a "pure," sexless love—one of the great clichés of Western sentimentality. See *Don Juan* V, I.
1. Strong armor. The exaggeration of this epic image is deliberate, and parodies the habit, in Catholic devotional tracts, of referring to the soul as a "warrior of purity."

Not Scandal's fangs could fix on much that's seizable,
    Or if they did so, satisfied to mean
Nothing but what was good, her breast was peaceable—
    A quiet conscience makes one so serene!
Christians have burnt each other, quite persuaded
That all the Apostles would have done as they did.

LXXXIV

And if in the mean time her husband died,
    But Heaven forbid that such a thought should cross
Her brain, though in a dream! (and then she sighed)
    Never could she survive that common loss;
But just suppose that moment should betide,
    I only say suppose it—*inter nos*:[2]
(This should be *entre nous*, for Julia thought
In French, but then the rhyme would go for nought.)

LXXXV

I only say, suppose this supposition:
    Juan being then grown up to man's estate
Would fully suit a widow of condition,
    Even seven years hence it would not be too late;
And in the interim (to pursue this vision)
    The mischief, after all, could not be great,
For he would learn the rudiments of Love,
I mean the *seraph*[3] way of those above.

LXXXVI

So much for Julia! Now we'll turn to Juan.
    Poor little fellow! he had no idea
Of his own case, and never hit the true one;
    In feelings quick as Ovid's Miss Medea,[4]
He puzzled over what he found a new one,
    But not as yet imagined it could be a
Thing quite in course, and not at all alarming,
Which, with a little patience, might grow charming.

LXXXVII

Silent and pensive, idle, restless, slow,
    His home deserted for the lonely wood,
Tormented with a wound he could not know,
    His, like all deep grief, plunged in solitude:
I'm fond myself of solitude or so,
    But then, I beg it may be understood,
By solitude I mean a Sultan's (not
A Hermit's), with a haram for a grot.

LXXXVIII

"Oh Love! in such a wilderness as this,
    Where Transport and Security entwine,

---

2. "Just between us."
3. The highest order of angels.
4. Ovid describes Medea's passion for Jason in the *Art of Love* I, 11. But the image is more complex. It reminds us of the "passion" which Dona Inez has tried to expunge from Juan's education—and also that Medea, far from being "Miss" Medea, is one of the most violently sexual and murderous figures in classical mythology.

Here is the Empire of thy perfect bliss,
  And here thou art a God indeed divine."
The bard[5] I quote from does not sing amiss,
  With the exception of the second line,
For that same twining "Transport and Security"
Are twisted to a phrase of some obscurity.

LXXXIX

The Poet meant, no doubt, and thus appeals
  To the good sense and senses of mankind,
The very thing which everybody feels,
  As all have found on trial, or may find,
That no one likes to be disturbed at meals
  Or love.—I won't say more about "entwined"
Or "Transport," as we knew all that before,
But beg "Security" will bolt the door.

XC

Young Juan wandered by the glassy brooks,
  Thinking unutterable things; he threw
Himself at length within the leafy nooks
  Where the wild branch of the cork forest grew;
There poets find materials[6] for their books,
  And every now and then we read them through,
So that their plan and prosody are eligible,
Unless, like Wordsworth, they prove unintelligible.

XCI

He, Juan (and not Wordsworth), so pursued
  His self-communion with his own high soul,
Until his mighty heart, in its great mood,
  Had mitigated part, though not the whole
Of its disease; he did the best he could
  With things not very subject to control,
And turned, without perceiving his condition,
Like Coleridge, into a metaphysician.[7]

XCII

He thought about himself, and the whole earth,
  Of man the wonderful, and of the stars,
And how the deuce they ever could have birth;
  And then he thought of earthquakes, and of wars,
How many miles the moon might have in girth,
  Of air-balloons, and of the many bars
To perfect knowledge of the boundless skies;—
And then he thought of Donna Julia's eyes.

XCIII

In thoughts like these true Wisdom may discern
  Longings sublime, and aspirations high,

---

5. "[Thomas] Campbell's *Gertrude of Wyoming*—(I think)—the opening of Canto Second—but quote from memory." [*Byron's note.*]
6. In the double sense that poets are supposed to be inspired by the forests, and also that the paper from which their books are made is from trees (though not usually cork trees).
7. In the next three stanzas Byron jokingly rehearses the great speculative themes of Romantic metaphysics—and attributes them all to adolescent sexual anxiety.

Which some are born with, but the most part learn
   To plague themselves withal, they know not why:
'Twas strange that one so young should thus concern
   His brain about the action of the sky;
If *you* think 'twas Philosophy that this did,
I can't help thinking puberty assisted.

XCIV

He poured upon the leaves, and on the flowers,
   And heard a voice in all the winds; and then
He thought of wood-nymphs and immortal bowers,
   And how the goddesses came down to men:
He missed the pathway, he forgot the hours,
   And when he looked upon his watch again,
He found how much old Time had been a winner—
He also found that he had lost his dinner.

XCV

Sometimes he turned to gaze upon his book,
   Boscan, or Garcilasso;[8]—by the wind
Even as the page is rustled while we look,
   So by the poesy of his own mind
Over the mystic leaf his soul was shook,
   As if 'twere one whereon magicians bind
Their spells, and give them to the passing gale,
According to some good old woman's tale.

XCVI

Thus would he while his lonely hours away
   Dissatisfied, not knowing what he wanted;
Nor glowing reverie, nor poet's lay,
   Could yield his spirit that for which it panted,
A bosom whereon he his head might lay,
   And hear the heart beat with the love it granted,
With——several other things, which I forget,
Or which, at least, I need not mention yet.

XCVII

Those lonely walks, and lengthening reveries,
   Could not escape the gentle Julia's eyes;
She saw that Juan was not at his ease;
   But that which chiefly may, and must surprise,
Is, that the Donna Inez did not tease
   Her only son with question or surmise;
Whether it was she did not see, or would not,
Or, like all very clever people, could not.

XCVIII

This may seem strange, but yet 'tis very common;
   For instance—gentlemen, whose ladies take
Leave to o'erstep the written rights of Woman,
   And break the——Which commandment[9] is 't they break?
(I have forgot the number, and think no man

---

8. Juan Boscan Almugaver (1490–1542) and Garcilasso de la Vega (1503–36), Spanish lyric poets.

9. The sixth, "Thou shalt not commit adultery."

Should rashly quote, for fear of a mistake;)
I say, when these same gentlemen are jealous,
They make some blunder, which their ladies tell us.

XCIX

A real husband always is suspicious,
    But still no less suspects in the wrong place,
Jealous of some one who had no such wishes,
    Or pandering blindly to his own disgrace,
By harbouring some dear friend extremely vicious;
    The last indeed's infallibly the case:
And when the spouse and friend are gone off wholly,
He wonders at their vice, and not his folly.

C

Thus parents also are at times short-sighted:
    Though watchful as the lynx, they ne'er discover,
The while the wicked world beholds delighted,
    Young Hopeful's mistress, or Miss Fanny's lover,
Till some confounded escapade has blighted
    The plan of twenty years, and all is over;
And then the mother cries, the father swears,
And wonders why the devil he got heirs.

CI

But Inez was so anxious, and so clear
    Of sight, that I must think, on this occasion,
She had some other motive much more near
    For leaving Juan to this new temptation,
But what that motive was, I sha'n't say here;
    Perhaps to finish Juan's education,
Perhaps to open Don Alfonso's eyes,
In case he thought his wife too great a prize.

nasty Donna Inez

CII

It was upon a day, a summer's day;—
    Summer's indeed a very dangerous season,
And so is spring about the end of May;
    The sun, no doubt, is the prevailing reason;
But whatsoe'er the cause is, one may say,
    And stand convicted of more truth than treason,
That there are months which nature grows more merry in,—
March has its hares, and May must have its heroine.

CIII

'Twas on a summer's day—the sixth of June:
    I like to be particular in dates,
Not only of the age, and year, but moon;
    They are a sort of post-house, where the Fates
Change horses, making History change its tune,
    Then spur away o'er empires and o'er states,
Leaving at last not much besides chronology,
Excepting the post-obits[1] of theology.

---

1. Literally, legal bonds or responsibilities entailed after a death—for example, by the executor of a will. Byron refers to the questionable promise of an afterlife.

CIV

'Twas on the sixth of June, about the hour
 Of half-past six—perhaps still nearer seven—
When Julia sate within as pretty a bower
 As e'er held houri[2] in that heathenish heaven
Described by Mahomet, and Anacreon Moore,[3]
 To whom the lyre and laurels have been given
With all the trophies of triumphant song—
He won them well, and may he wear them long!

CV

She sate, but not alone; I know not well
 How this same interview had taken place,
And even if I knew, I should not tell—
 People should hold their tongues in any case;
No matter how or why the thing befell,
 But there were she and Juan, face to face—
When two such faces are so, 'twould be wise,
But very difficult, to shut their eyes.

CVI

How beautiful she looked! her conscious heart
 Glowed in her cheek, and yet she felt no wrong:
Oh Love! how perfect is thy mystic art,
 Strengthening the weak, and trampling on the strong!
How self-deceitful is the sagest part
 Of mortals whom thy lure hath led along!—
The precipice she stood on was immense,
So was her creed in her own innocence.

CVII

She thought of her own strength, and Juan's youth,
 And of the folly of all prudish fears,
Victorious Virtue, and domestic Truth,
 And then of Don Alfonso's fifty years:
I wish these last had not occurred, in sooth,
 Because that number rarely much endears,
And through all climes, the snowy and the sunny,
Sounds ill in love, whate'er it may in money.

CVIII

When people say, "I've told you *fifty* times,"
 They mean to scold, and very often do;
When poets say, "I've written *fifty* rhymes,"
 They make you dread that they'll recite them too;
In gangs of *fifty*, thieves commit their crimes;
 At *fifty* love for love is rare, 'tis true,
But then, no doubt, it equally as true is,
A good deal may be bought for *fifty* Louis.[4]

2. Paradisiacal concubine promised to the chosen in the Koran.
3. Byron's friend Thomas Moore (1779–1852) had translated the lyrics of Anacreon (see note to *Don Juan* I, XLII) and in *Lalla Rookh* (1817) had written a tale of Oriental romance and mythology.
4. The louis d'or, French coin of the eighteenth century.

CIX

Julia had honour, virtue, truth, and love
  For Don Alfonso; and she inly swore,
By all the vows below to Powers above,
  She never would disgrace the ring she wore,
Nor leave a wish which wisdom might reprove;
  And while she pondered this, besides much more,
One hand on Juan's carelessly was thrown,
Quite by mistake—she thought it was her own;

CX

Unconsciously she leaned upon the other,
  Which played within the tangles of her hair;
And to contend with thoughts she could not smother
  She seemed by the distraction of her air.
'Twas surely very wrong in Juan's mother
  To leave together this imprudent pair,
She who for many years had watched her son so—
I'm very certain *mine* would not have done so.

CXI

The hand which still held Juan's, by degrees
  Gently, but palpably confirmed its grasp,
As if it said, "Detain me, if you please;"
  Yet there's no doubt she only meant to clasp
His fingers with a pure Platonic squeeze;
  She would have shrunk as from a toad, or asp,
Had she imagined such a thing could rouse
A feeling dangerous to a prudent spouse.

CXII

I cannot know what Juan thought of this,
  But what he did, is much what you would do;
His young lip thanked it with a grateful kiss,
  And then, abashed at its own joy, withdrew
In deep despair, lest he had done amiss,—
  Love is so very timid when 'tis new:
She blushed, and frowned not, but she strove to speak,
And held her tongue, her voice was grown so weak.

CXIII

The sun set, and up rose the yellow moon:
  The Devil's in the moon for mischief; they
Who called her CHASTE, methinks, began too soon
  Their nomenclature; there is not a day,
The longest, not the twenty-first of June,
  Sees half the business in a wicked way,
On which three single hours of moonshine smile—
And then she looks so modest all the while!

CXIV

There is a dangerous silence in that hour,
  A stillness, which leaves room for the full soul
To open all itself, without the power

Of calling wholly back its self-control;
The silver light which, hallowing tree and tower,
    Sheds beauty and deep softness o'er the whole,
Breathes also to the heart, and o'er it throws
A loving languor, which is not repose.

CXV

And Julia sate with Juan, half embraced
    And half retiring from the glowing arm,
Which trembled like the bosom where 'twas placed;
    Yet still she must have thought there was no harm,
Or else 'twere easy to withdraw her waist;
    But then the situation had its charm,
And then——God knows what next—I can't go on;
I'm almost sorry that I e'er begun.

CXVI

Oh Plato! Plato! you have paved the way,
    With your confounded fantasies, to more
Immoral conduct by the fancied sway
    Your system feigns o'er the controlless core
Of human hearts, than all the long array
    Of poets and romancers:—You're a bore,
A charlatan, a coxcomb⁵—and have been,
At best, no better than a go-between.

[marginalia: healthy distrust of philosophy can't deny human functions]

CXVII

And Julia's voice was lost, except in sighs,
    Until too late for useful conversation;
The tears were gushing from her gentle eyes,
    I wish, indeed, they had not had occasion;
But who, alas! can love, and then be wise?
    Not that Remorse did not oppose Temptation;
A little still she strove, and much repented,
And whispering "I will ne'er consent"—consented.

CXVIII

'Tis said that Xerxes⁶ offered a reward
    To those who could invent him a new pleasure:
Methinks the requisition's rather hard,
    And must have cost his Majesty a treasure:
For my part, I'm a moderate-minded bard,
    Fond of a little love (which I call leisure);
I care not for new pleasures, as the old
Are quite enough for me, so they but hold.

CXIX

Oh Pleasure! you're indeed a pleasant thing,
    Although one must be damned for you, no doubt:
I make a resolution every spring
    Of reformation, ere the year run out,
But somehow, this my vestal⁷ vow takes wing,

---

5. Vain person, fop.
6. Fifth century B.C. Persian king, and a famous voluptuary.

7. In Rome, the priestesses of the goddess Vesta took a vow of virginity.

Yet still, I trust, it may be kept throughout:
I'm very sorry, very much ashamed,
And mean, next winter, to be quite reclaimed.

CXX

Here my chaste Muse a liberty must take—
    Start not! still chaster reader—she'll be nice hence
Forward, and there is no great cause to quake;
    This liberty is a poetic licence,
Which some irregularity may make
    In the design, and as I have a high sense
Of Aristotle[8] and the Rules, 'tis fit
To beg his pardon when I err a bit.

CXXI

This licence is to hope the reader will
    Suppose from June the sixth (the fatal day,
Without whose epoch my poetic skill
    For want of facts would all be thrown away),
But keeping Julia and Don Juan still
    In sight, that several months have passed; we'll say
'Twas in November, but I'm not so sure
About the day—the era's more obscure.

CXXII

We'll talk of that anon.—'Tis sweet to hear
    At midnight on the blue and moonlit deep
The song and oar of Adria's[9] gondolier,
    By distance mellowed, o'er the waters sweep;
'Tis sweet to see the evening star appear;
    'Tis sweet to listen as the night-winds creep
From leaf to leaf; 'tis sweet to view on high
The rainbow, based on ocean, span the sky.

[handwritten marginalia: what's beautiful & sweet]

CXXIII

'Tis sweet to hear the watch-dog's honest bark
    Bay deep-mouthed welcome as we draw near home;
'Tis sweet to know there is an eye will mark
    Our coming, and look brighter when we come;
'Tis sweet to be awakened by the lark,
    Or lulled by falling waters; sweet the hum
Of bees, the voice of girls, the song of birds,
The lisp of children, and their earliest words.

CXXIV

Sweet is the vintage, when the showering grapes
    In Bacchanal[1] profusion reel to earth,
Purple and gushing: sweet are our escapes
    From civic revelry to rural mirth;
Sweet to the miser are his glittering heaps,
    Sweet to the father is his first-born's birth,
Sweet is revenge—especially to women—
Pillage to soldiers, prize-money to seamen.

8. A reference to Aristotle's *Poetics*, the basis of the "rules" of neoclassical criticism.

9. Venice (on the Adriatic Sea).
1. A drunken revel or orgy; from Bacchus, Roman god of wine.

CXXV

Sweet is a legacy, and passing sweet
  The unexpected death of some old lady,
Or gentleman of seventy years complete,
  Who've made "us youth" wait too—too long already,
For an estate, or cash, or country seat,
  Still breaking, but with stamina so steady,
That all the Israelites[2] are fit to mob its
Next owner for their double-damned post-obits.

CXXVI

'Tis sweet to win, no matter how, one's laurels,
  By blood or ink; 'tis sweet to put an end
To strife; 'tis sometimes sweet to have our quarrels,
  Particularly with a tiresome friend:
Sweet is old wine in bottles, ale in barrels;
  Dear is the helpless creature we defend
Against the world; and dear the schoolboy spot
We ne'er forget, though there we are forgot.

CXXVII

But sweeter still than this, than these, than all,
  Is first and passionate Love—it stands alone,
Like Adam's recollection of his fall;
  The Tree of Knowledge has been plucked—all's known—
And Life yields nothing further to recall
  Worthy of this ambrosial sin, so shown,
No doubt in fable, as the unforgiven
Fire which Prometheus[3] filched for us from Heaven.

CXXVIII

Man's a strange animal, and makes strange use
  Of his own nature, and the various arts,
And likes particularly to produce
  Some new experiment to show his parts;
This is the age of oddities let loose,
  Where different talents find their different marts;
You'd best begin with truth, and when you've lost your
Labour, there's a sure market for imposture.

CXXIX

What opposite discoveries we have seen!
  (Signs of true genius, and of empty pockets.)
One makes new noses, one a guillotine,
  One breaks your bones, one sets them in their sockets;
But Vaccination certainly has been
  A kind antithesis to Congreve's rockets,[4]
With which the Doctor[5] paid off an old pox,
By borrowing a new one from an ox.

---

2. Byron was unfortunately not immune to the popular prejudice against Jews as grasping usurers.
3. In classical mythology the Titan Prometheus stole the gift of fire from the gods on Olympus to share it with mankind.

4. Sir William Congreve (1772–1828) perfected a military rocket which was used in 1813 in the Battle of Leipzig.
5. Edward Jenner (1749–1823) developed a vaccine against smallpox which utilized the innards of infected cattle.

CXXX
Bread has been made (indifferent) from potatoes:
    And Galvanism[6] has set some corpses grinning,
But has not answered like the apparatus
    Of the Humane Society's[7] beginning,
By which men are unsuffocated gratis:
    What wondrous new machines have late been spinning!
I said the small-pox has gone out of late;
Perhaps it may be followed by the great.[8]

CXXXI
'Tis said the great came from America;[9]
    Perhaps it may set out on its return,—
The population there so spreads, they say
    'Tis grown high time to thin it in its turn,
With war, or plague, or famine—any way,
    So that civilisation they may learn;
And which in ravage the more loathsome evil is—
Their real *lues*,[1] or our pseudo-syphilis?

CXXXII
This is the patent age of new inventions
    For killing bodies, and for saving souls,
All propagated with the best intentions;
    Sir Humphry Davy's[2] lantern, by which coals
Are safely mined for in the mode he mentions,
    Tombuctoo travels, voyages to the Poles
Are ways to benefit mankind, as true,
Perhaps, as shooting them at Waterloo.

CXXXIII
Man's a phenomenon, one knows not what,
    And wonderful beyond all wondrous measure;
'Tis pity though, in this sublime world, that
    Pleasure's a sin, and sometimes Sin's a pleasure;
Few mortals know what end they would be at,
    But whether Glory, Power, or Love, or Treasure,
The path is through perplexing ways, and when
The goal is gained, we die, you know—and then——

CXXXIV
What then?—I do not know, no more do you—
    And so good night.—Return we to our story;
'Twas in November, when fine days are few,
    And the far mountains wax a little hoary,
And clap a white cape on their mantles blue;
    And the sea dashes round the promontory,

6. Luigi Galvani (1737–98) discovered that motion could be induced in dead bodies by passing an electric current through them. His theory of "animal electricity" exerted immense influence on nineteenth century physiology and poetry.
7. The Royal Humane Society was founded in 1774, to resuscitate drowning persons—"free of charge," as Byron ironically notes.
8. The "great pox" was syphilis.
9. A popular legend—still current—was that syphilis was brought to Europe by Columbus's sailors, who had caught it from the American Indians.
1. *Lues venerea*, syphilis.
2. Davy (1778–1829) invented the safety lamp for coal miners.

And the loud breaker boils against the rock,
And sober suns must set at five o'clock.

CXXXV

'Twas, as the watchmen say, a cloudy night;
  No moon, no stars, the wind was low or loud
By gusts, and many a sparkling hearth was bright
    With the piled wood, round which the family crowd;
There's something cheerful in that sort of light,
    Even as a summer sky's without a cloud:
I'm fond of fire, and crickets, and all that,
A lobster salad, and champagne, and chat.

CXXXVI

'Twas midnight—Donna Julia was in bed,
  Sleeping, most probably,—when at her door
Arose a clatter might awake the dead,
  If they had never been awoke before,
And that they have been so we all have read,
  And are to be so, at the least, once more;[3]—
The door was fastened, but with voice and fist
First knocks were heard, then "Madam—Madam—hist!

CXXXVII

"For God's sake, Madam—Madam—here's my master,
  With more than half the city at his back—
Was ever heard of such a curst disaster!
  'Tis not my fault—I kept good watch—Alack!
Do pray undo the bolt a little faster—
  They're on the stair just now, and in a crack
Will all be here; perhaps he yet may fly—
Surely the window's not so *very* high!"

CXXXVIII

By this time Don Alfonso was arrived,
  With torches, friends, and servants in great number;
The major part of them had long been wived,
  And therefore paused not to disturb the slumber
Of any wicked woman, who contrived
  By stealth her husband's temples[4] to encumber:
Examples of this kind are so contagious,
Were *one* not punished, *all* would be outrageous.

CXXXIX

I can't tell how, or why, or what suspicion
  Could enter into Don Alfonso's head;
But for a cavalier of his condition
  It surely was exceedingly ill-bred,
Without a word of previous admonition,
  To hold a levee[5] round his lady's bed,
And summon lackeys, armed with fire and sword,
To prove himself the thing he most abhorred.

3. The Second Coming of Christ, at which all the dead would awaken.
4. To cuckold him. Cuckolds were referred to as having been given horns by their unfaithful wives.
5. An "arising": morning reception of callers on a celebrated personage, often held in the bedroom.

CXL

Poor Donna Julia! starting as from sleep,
  (Mind—that I do not say—she had not slept),
Began at once to scream, and yawn, and weep;
  Her maid, Antonia, who was an adept,
Contrived to fling the bed-clothes in a heap,
  As if she had just now from out them crept:
I can't tell why she should take all this trouble
To prove her mistress had been sleeping double.

CXLI

But Julia mistress, and Antonia maid,
  Appeared like two poor harmless women, who
Of goblins, but still more of men afraid,
  Had thought one man might be deterred by two,
And therefore side by side were gently laid,
  Until the hours of absence should run through,
And truant husband should return, and say,
"My dear,—I was the first who came away."

CXLII

Now Julia found at length a voice, and cried,
  "In Heaven's name, Don Alfonso, what d' ye mean?
Has madness seized you? would that I had died
  Ere such a monster's victim I had been!
What may this midnight violence betide,
  A sudden fit of drunkenness or spleen?
Dare you suspect me, whom the thought would kill?
Search, then, the room!"—Alfonso said, "I will."

CXLIII

He searched, they searched, and rummaged everywhere,
  Closet and clothes' press, chest and window-seat,
And found much linen, lace, and several pair
  Of stockings, slippers, brushes, combs, complete,
With other articles of ladies fair,
  To keep them beautiful, or leave them neat:
Arras they pricked and curtains with their swords,
And wounded several shutters, and some boards.

CXLIV

Under the bed they searched, and there they found—
  No matter what[6]—it was not that they sought;
They opened windows, gazing if the ground
  Had signs or footmarks, but the earth said nought;
And then they stared each others' faces round:
  'Tis odd, not one of all these seekers thought,
And seems to me almost a sort of blunder,
Of looking *in* the bed as well as under.

CXLV

During this inquisition Julia's tongue
  Was not asleep—"Yes, search and search," she cried,
"Insult on insult heap, and wrong on wrong!

6. Probably a chamber pot.

It was for this that I became a bride!
For this in silence I have suffered long
    A husband like Alfonso at my side;
But now I'll bear no more, nor here remain,
If there be law or lawyers in all Spain.

CXLVI

"Yes, Don Alfonso! husband now no more,
    If ever you indeed deserved the name,
Is't worthy of your years?—you have threescore—
    Fifty, or sixty, it is all the same—
Is't wise or fitting, causeless to explore
    For facts against a virtuous woman's fame?
Ungrateful, perjured, barbarous Don Alfonso,
How dare you think your lady would go on so?

CXLVII

"Is it for this I have disdained to hold
    The common privileges of my sex?
That I have chosen a confessor so old
    And deaf,[7] that any other it would vex,
And never once he has had cause to scold,
    But found my very innocence perplex
So much, he always doubted I was married—
How sorry you will be when I've miscarried!

CXLVIII

"Was it for this that no Cortejo[8] e'er
    I yet have chosen from out the youth of Seville?
Is it for this I scarce went anywhere,
    Except to bull-fights, mass, play, rout, and revel?
Is it for this, whate'er my suitors were,
    I favoured none—nay, was almost uncivil?
Is it for this that General Count O'Reilly,[9]   *military*
Who took Algiers, declares I used him vilely?

CXLIX

aristocracy

"Did not the Italian *Musico* Cazzani[1]
    Sing at my heart six months at least in vain?
Did not his countryman, Count Corniani,[2]
    Call me the only virtuous wife in Spain?
Were there not also Russians, English, many?
    The Count Strongstroganoff I put in pain,
And Lord Mount Coffeehouse, the Irish peer,
Who killed himself for love (with wine) last year.

---

7. If her confessor was deaf, Doña Julia would have to shout her confession; thus, she had committed no sins which she was afraid of having overheard by others.
8. Spanish term for an accepted, semi-public adulterous lover to a noble lady.
9. Alexander O'Reilly (1722–94), a Spanish general of Irish parentage. "Donna Julia here made a mistake.

Count O'Reilly did not take Algiers—but Algiers very nearly took him: he and his army and fleet retreated with great loss, and not much credit, from before that city, in the year 1775." [*Byron's note.*]
1. A made-up name. *Cazzo* was Italian slang for penis.
2. Again, made-up. *Cornuto*, "horned," refers to cuckoldry.

CL

"Have I not had two bishops at my feet?
  The Duke of Ichar, and Don Fernan Nunez; *church & law*
And is it thus a faithful wife you treat?
  I wonder in what quarter now the moon is:
I praise your vast forbearance not to beat
  Me also, since the time so opportune is—
Oh, valiant man! with sword drawn and cocked trigger,
Now, tell me, don't you cut a pretty figure?

CLI

"Was it for this you took your sudden journey,
  Under pretence of business indispensable
With that sublime of rascals your attorney,
  Whom I see standing there, and looking sensible
Of having played the fool? though both I spurn, he
  Deserves the worst, his conduct's less defensible,
Because, no doubt, 'twas for his dirty fee,
And not from any love to you nor me.

CLII

"If he comes here to take a deposition,
  By all means let the gentleman proceed;
You've made the apartment in a fit condition:—
  There's pen and ink for you, sir, when you need—
Let everything be noted with precision,
  I would not you for nothing should be fee'd—
But, as my maid's undressed, pray turn your spies out."
"Oh!" sobbed Antonia, "I could tear their eyes out."

CLIII

"There is the closet, there the toilet, there
  The antechamber—search them under, over;
There is the sofa, there the great arm-chair,
  The chimney—which would really hold a lover.
I wish to sleep, and beg you will take care
  And make no further noise, till you discover
The secret cavern of this lurking treasure—
And when 'tis found, let me, too, have the pleasure.

CLIV

"And now, Hidalgo! now that you have thrown
  Doubt upon me, confusion over all,
Pray have the courtesy to make it known
  Who is the man you search for? how d' ye call
Him? what's his lineage? let him but be shown—
  I hope he's young and handsome—is he tall?
Tell me—and be assured, that since you stain
My honour thus, it shall not be in vain.

CLV

"At least, perhaps, he has not sixty years,
  At that age he would be too old for slaughter,
Or for so young a husband's jealous fears—
  (Antonia! let me have a glass of water.)

I am ashamed of having shed these tears,
    They are unworthy of my father's daughter;
My mother dreamed not in my natal hour,
That I should fall into a monster's power.

CLVI

"Perhaps 'tis of Antonia you are jealous,
    You saw that she was sleeping by my side,
When you broke in upon us with your fellows:
    Look where you please—we've nothing, sir, to hide;
Only another time, I trust, you'll tell us,
    Or for the sake of decency abide
A moment at the door, that we may be
Dressed to receive so much good company.

CLVII

"And now, sir, I have done, and say no more;
    The little I have said may serve to show
The guileless heart in silence may grieve o'er
    The wrongs to whose exposure it is slow:—
I leave you to your conscience as before,
    'Twill one day ask you *why* you used me so?
God grant you feel not then the bitterest grief!—
Antonia! where's my pocket-handkerchief?"

CLVIII

She ceased, and turned upon her pillow; pale
    She lay, her dark eyes flashing through their tears,
Like skies that rain and lighten; as a veil,
    Waved and o'ershading her wan cheek, appears
Her streaming hair; the black curls strive, but fail
    To hide the glossy shoulder, which uprears
Its snow through all;—her soft lips lie apart,
And louder than her breathing beats her heart.

CLIX

The Senhor Don Alfonso stood confused;
    Antonia bustled round the ransacked room,
And, turning up her nose, with looks abused
    Her master, and his myrmidons, of whom
Not one, except the attorney, was amused;
    He, like Achates,[3] faithful to the tomb,
So there were quarrels, cared not for the cause,
Knowing they must be settled by the laws.

CLX

With prying snub-nose, and small eyes, he stood,
    Following Antonia's motions here and there,
With much suspicion in his attitude;
    For reputations he had little care;
So that a suit or action were made good,
    Small pity had he for the young and fair,

---

3. Fidus Achates, "Faithful Achates," Aeneas's trusty companion in Vergil's *Aeneid*.

And ne'er believed in negatives, till these
Were proved by competent false witnesses.

CLXI

But Don Alfonso stood with downcast looks,
    And, truth to say, he made a foolish figure;
When, after searching in five hundred nooks,
    And treating a young wife with so much rigour,
He gained no point, except some self-rebukes,
    Added to those his lady with such vigour
Had poured upon him for the last half-hour,
Quick, thick, and heavy—as a thunder-shower.

CLXII

At first he tried to hammer an excuse,
    To which the sole reply was tears, and sobs,
And indications of hysterics, whose
    Prologue is always certain throes, and throbs,
Gasps, and whatever else the owners choose:
    Alfonso saw his wife, and thought of Job's;[4]
He saw too, in perspective, her relations,
And then he tried to muster all his patience.

CLXIII

He stood in act to speak, or rather stammer,
    But sage Antonia cut him short before
The anvil of his speech received the hammer,
    With "Pray, sir, leave the room, and say no more,
Or madam dies."—Alfonso muttered, "D—n her,"
    But nothing else, the time of words was o'er;
He cast a rueful look or two, and did,
He knew not wherefore, that which he was bid.

CLXIV

With him retired his *"posse comitatus,"*[5]
    The attorney last, who lingered near the door
Reluctantly, still tarrying there as late as
    Antonia let him—not a little sore
At this most strange and unexplained *"hiatus"*[6]
    In Don Alfonso's facts, which just now wore
An awkward look; as he revolved the case,
The door was fastened in his legal face.

CLXV

No sooner was it bolted, than—Oh Shame!
    Oh Sin! Oh Sorrow! and Oh Womankind!
How can you do such things and keep your fame,
    Unless this world, and t'other too, be blind?
Nothing so dear as an unfilched good name!
    But to proceed—for there is more behind:
With much heartfelt reluctance be it said,
Young Juan slipped, half-smothered, from the bed.

4. Job's wife was proverbial as a nagging woman.
5. Literally, the Latin phrase for a "posse"—a group of citizens empowered to act as temporary enforcers of the law.
6. Gap or pause.

CLXVI

He had been hid—I don't pretend to say
　How, nor can I indeed describe the where—
Young, slender, and packed easily, he lay,
　No doubt, in little compass, round or square;
But pity him I neither must nor may
　His suffocation by that pretty pair;
'Twere better, sure, to die so, than be shut
With maudlin Clarence[7] in his Malmsey butt.

CLXVII

And, secondly, I pity not, because
　He had no business to commit a sin,
Forbid by heavenly, fined by human laws;—
　At least 'twas rather early to begin,
But at sixteen the conscience rarely gnaws
　So much as when we call our old debts in
At sixty years, and draw the accompts of evil,
And find a deuced balance with the Devil.

CLXVIII

Of his position I can give no notion:
　'Tis written in the Hebrew Chronicle,[8]
How the physicians, leaving pill and potion,
　Prescribed, by way of blister,[9] a young belle,
When old King David's blood grew dull in motion,
　And that the medicine answered very well;
Perhaps 'twas in a different way applied,
For David lived, but Juan nearly died.

CLXIX

What's to be done? Alfonso will be back
　The moment he has sent his fools away.
Antonia's skill was put upon the rack,
　But no device could be brought into play—
And how to parry the renewed attack?
　Besides, it wanted but few hours of day:
Antonia puzzled; Julia did not speak,
But pressed her bloodless lip to Juan's cheek.

CLXX

He turned his lip to hers, and with his hand
　Called back the tangles of her wandering hair;
Even then their love they could not all command,
　And half forgot their danger and despair:
Antonia's patience now was at a stand—
　"Come, come, 'tis no time now for fooling there,"
She whispered, in great wrath—"I must deposit
This pretty gentleman within the closet:

CLXXI

"Pray, keep your nonsense for some luckier night—

---

7. In *Richard III* I. iv. 276, the Duke of
Clarence is drowned in a cask of malmsey wine.

8. I Kings 1 : 1–3.
9. Cure or treatment.

Who can have put my master in this mood?
What will become on 't—I'm in such a fright,
     The Devil's in the urchin, and no good—
Is this a time for giggling? this a plight?
     Why, don't you know that it may end in blood?
You'll lose your life, and I shall lose my place,
My mistress all, for that half-girlish face.

CLXXII

"Had it but been for a stout cavalier
     Of twenty-five or thirty—(come, make haste)
But for a child, what piece of work is here!
     I really, madam, wonder at your taste—
(Come, sir, get in)—my master must be near:
     There, for the present, at the least, he's fast,
And if we can but till the morning keep
Our counsel—(Juan, mind, you must not sleep.)"

CLXXIII

Now, Don Alfonso entering, but alone,
     Closed the oration of the trusty maid:
She loitered, and he told her to be gone,
     An order somewhat sullenly obeyed;
However, present remedy was none,
     And no great good seemed answered if she staid:
Regarding both with slow and sidelong view,
She snuffed the candle, curtsied, and withdrew.

CLXXIV

Alfonso paused a minute—then begun
     Some strange excuses for his late proceeding;
He would not justify what he had done,
     To say the best, it was extreme ill-breeding;
But there were ample reasons for it, none
     Of which he specified in this his pleading:
His speech was a fine sample, on the whole,
Of rhetoric, which the learned call *"rigmarole."*

CLXXV

Julia said nought; though all the while there rose
     A ready answer, which at once enables
A matron, who her husband's foible knows,
     By a few timely words to turn the tables,
Which, if it does not silence, still must pose,—
     Even if it should comprise a pack of fables;
'Tis to retort with firmness, and when he
Suspects with *one*, do you reproach with *three*.

CLXXVI

Julia, in fact, had tolerable grounds,—
     Alfonso's loves with Inez were well known;
But whether 'twas that one's own guilt confounds—
     But that can't be, as has been often shown,
A lady with apologies abounds;—
     It might be that her silence sprang alone

From delicacy to Don Juan's ear,
To whom she knew his mother's fame was dear.

CLXXVII

There might be one more motive, which makes two;
  Alfonso ne'er to Juan had alluded,—
Mentioned his jealousy, but never who
  Had been the happy lover, he concluded,
Concealed amongst his premises; 'tis true,
  His mind the more o'er this its mystery brooded;
To speak of Inez now were, one may say,
Like throwing Juan in Alfonso's way.

CLXXVIII

A hint, in tender cases, is enough;
  Silence is best: besides, there is a *tact*—
(That modern phrase appears to me sad stuff,
  But it will serve to keep my verse compact)—
Which keeps, when pushed by questions rather rough,
  A lady always distant from the fact:
The charming creatures lie with such a grace,
There's nothing so becoming to the face.

CLXXIX

They blush, and we believe them; at least I
  Have always done so; 'tis of no great use,
In any case, attempting a reply,
  For then their eloquence grows quite profuse;
And when at length they're out of breath, they sigh,
  And cast their languid eyes down, and let loose
A tear or two, and then we make it up;
And then—and then—and then—sit down and sup.

CLXXX

Alfonso closed his speech, and begged her pardon,
  Which Julia half withheld, and then half granted,
And laid conditions he thought very hard on,
  Denying several little things he wanted:
He stood like Adam lingering near his garden,
  With useless penitence perplexed and haunted;
Beseeching she no further would refuse,
When, lo! he stumbled o'er a pair of shoes.

CLXXXI

A pair of shoes!—what then? not much, if they
  Are such as fit with ladies' feet, but these
(No one can tell how much I grieve to say)
  Were masculine; to see them, and to seize,
Was but a moment's act—Ah! well-a-day!
  My teeth begin to chatter, my veins freeze!
Alfonso first examined well their fashion,
And then flew out into another passion.

CLXXXII

He left the room for his relinquished sword,
  And Julia instant to the closet flew.

"Fly, Juan, fly! for Heaven's sake—not a word—
　　The door is open—you may yet slip through
The passage you so often have explored—
　　Here is the garden-key—Fly—fly—Adieu!
Haste—haste! I hear Alfonso's hurrying feet—
　　Day has not broke—there's no one in the street."

CLXXXIII

None can say that this was not good advice,
　　The only mischief was, it came too late;
Of all experience 'tis the usual price,
　　A sort of income-tax laid on by fate:
Juan had reached the room-door in a trice,
　　And might have done so by the garden-gate,
But met Alfonso in his dressing-gown,
Who threatened death—so Juan knocked him down.

CLXXXIV

Dire was the scuffle, and out went the light;
　　Antonia cried out "Rape!" and Julia "Fire!"
But not a servant stirred to aid the fight.
　　Alfonso, pommelled to his heart's desire,
Swore lustily he'd be revenged this night;
　　And Juan, too, blasphemed an octave higher;
His blood was up: though young, he was a Tartar,[1]
And not at all disposed to prove a martyr.

CLXXXV

Alfonso's sword had dropped ere he could draw it,
　　And they continued battling hand to hand,
For Juan very luckily ne'er saw it;
　　His temper not being under great command,
If at that moment he had chanced to claw it,
　　Alfonso's days had not been in the land
Much longer.—Think of husbands', lovers' lives!
And how ye may be doubly widows—wives!

CLXXXVI

Alfonso grappled to detain the foe,
　　And Juan throttled him to get away,
And blood ('twas from the nose) began to flow;
　　At last, as they more faintly wrestling lay,
Juan contrived to give an awkward blow,
　　And then his only garment quite gave way;
He fled, like Joseph, leaving it; but there,
I doubt, all likeness ends between the pair.

CLXXXVII

Lights came at length, and men, and maids, who found
　　An awkward spectacle their eyes before;
Antonia in hysterics, Julia swooned,
　　Alfonso leaning, breathless, by the door;
Some half-torn drapery scattered on the ground,
　　Some blood, and several footsteps, but no more:

1. Tartars were Moslems from the area of Mongolia, renowned for their ferocity as warriors.

Juan the gate gained, turned the key about,
And liking not the inside, locked the out.

CLXXXVIII

Here ends this canto.—Need I sing, or say,
  How Juan, naked, favoured by the night,
Who favours what she should not, found his way,
  And reached his home in an unseemly plight?
The pleasant scandal which arose next day,
  The nine days' wonder which was brought to light,
And how Alfonso sued for a divorce,
Were in the English newspapers, of course.

CLXXXIX

If you would like to see the whole proceedings,
  The depositions, and the Cause at full,
The names of all the witnesses, the pleadings
  Of Counsel to nonsuit, or to annul,
There's more than one edition, and the readings
  Are various, but they none of them are dull:
The best is that in short-hand ta'en by Gurney,[2]
Who to Madrid on purpose made a journey.

CXC

But Donna Inez, to divert the train
  Of one of the most circulating scandals
That had for centuries been known in Spain,
  At least since the retirement of the Vandals,[3]
First vowed (and never had she vowed in vain)
  To Virgin Mary several pounds of candles;
And then, by the advice of some old ladies,
She sent her son to be shipped off from Cadiz.

CXCI

She had resolved that he should travel through
  All European climes, by land or sea,
To mend his former morals, and get new,
  Especially in France and Italy—
(At least this is the thing most people do.)
  Julia was sent into a convent—she
Grieved—but, perhaps, her feelings may be better
Shown in the following copy of her Letter:—

CXCII

"They tell me 'tis decided you depart:
  'Tis wise—'tis well, but not the less a pain;
I have no further claim on your young heart,
  Mine is the victim, and would be again:
To love too much has been the only art
  I used;—I write in haste, and if a stain
Be on this sheet, 'tis not what it appears;
My eyeballs burn and throb, but have no tears.

2. William Gurney, a famous shorthand reporter frequently employed by the English press.
3. The Vandals, a Germanic tribe, ravaged Spain in the fifth century A.D., and have since become a byword for wanton destructiveness.

CXCIII

"I loved, I love you, for this love have lost
   State, station, Heaven, Mankind's, my own esteem,
And yet can not regret what it hath cost,
   So dear is still the memory of that dream;
Yet, if I name my guilt, 'tis not to boast,
   None can deem harshlier of me than I deem:
I trace this scrawl because I cannot rest—
I've nothing to reproach, or to request.

CXCIV

"Man's love is of man's life a thing apart,
   'Tis a Woman's whole existence; Man may range
The Court, Camp, Church, the Vessel, and the Mart;
   Sword, Gown, Gain, Glory, offer in exchange
Pride, Fame, Ambition, to fill up his heart,
   And few there are whom these can not estrange;
Men have all these resources, We but one,
To love again, and be again undone.

[handwritten margin note: 19th cent. woman as sexual victim]

CXCV

"You will proceed in pleasure, and in pride,
   Beloved and loving many; all is o'er
For me on earth, except some years to hide
   My shame and sorrow deep in my heart's core:
These I could bear, but cannot cast aside
   The passion which still rages as before,—
And so farewell—forgive me, love me—No,
That word is idle now—but let it go.

CXCVI

"My breast has been all weakness, is so yet;
   But still I think I can collect my mind;
My blood still rushes where my spirit's set,
   As roll the waves before the settled wind;
My heart is feminine, nor can forget—
   To all, except one image, madly blind;
So shakes the needle, and so stands the pole,
As vibrates my fond heart to my fixed soul.

CXCVII

"I have no more to say, but linger still,
   And dare not set my seal upon this sheet,
And yet I may as well the task fulfil,
   My misery can scarce be more complete;
I had not lived till now, could sorrow kill;
   Death shuns the wretch who fain the blow would meet
And I must even survive this last adieu,
And bear with life, to love and pray for you!"

CXCVIII

This note was written upon gilt-edged paper
   With a neat little crow-quill, slight and new;
Her small white hand could hardly reach the taper,[4]

4. Candle, for hot wax with which to seal the letter.

It trembled as magnetic needles do,
  And yet she did not let one tear escape her;
    The seal a sun-flower; *"Elle vous suit partout,"*[5]
The motto cut upon a white cornelian;
The wax was superfine, its hue vermilion.

CXCIX

This was Don Juan's earliest scrape; but whether
  I shall proceed with his adventures is
Dependent on the public altogether;
  We'll see, however, what they say to this:
Their favour in an author's cap's a feather,
  And no great mischief's done by their caprice;
And if their approbation we experience,
Perhaps they'll have some more about a year hence.

CC

My poem's epic, and is meant to be
  Divided in twelve books; each book containing,
With Love, and War, a heavy gale at sea,
  A list of ships, and captains, and kings reigning,
New characters; the episodes are three:
  A panoramic view of Hell's in training,
After the style of Virgil and of Homer,
So that my name of Epic's no misnomer.

CCI

All these things will be specified in time,
  With strict regard to Aristotle's rules,
The *Vade Mecum*[6] of the true sublime,
  Which makes so many poets, and some fools:
Prose poets like blank-verse, I'm fond of rhyme,
  Good workmen never quarrel with their tools;
I've got new mythological machinery,
And very handsome supernatural scenery.

CCII

There's only one slight difference between
  Me and my epic brethren gone before,
And here the advantage is my own, I ween
  (Not that I have not several merits more,
But this will more peculiarly be seen);
  They so embellish, that 'tis quite a bore
Their labyrinth of fables to thread through,
Whereas this story's actually true.

CCIII

If any person doubt it, I appeal
  To History, Tradition, and to Facts,
To newspapers, whose truth all know and feel,

---

5. "She follows you everywhere." Byron himself had a seal with this motto.
6. Literally, "Go with me"—a popular catch phrase for a book which one finds indispensable (and therefore carries everywhere). Byron is ridiculing the obsession of neoclassical critics and poets with observing Aristotle's "rules" for poetry as laid down in his *Poetics*.

To plays in five, and operas in three acts;
All these confirm my statement a good deal,
    But that which more completely faith exacts
Is, that myself, and several now in Seville,
Saw Juan's last elopement[7] with the Devil.

CCIV

If ever I should condescend to prose,
    I'll write poetical commandments, which
Shall supersede beyond all doubt all those
    That went before; in these I shall enrich
My text with many things that no one knows,
    And carry precept to the highest pitch:
I'll call the work "Longinus[8] o'er a Bottle,
Or, Every Poet his *own* Aristotle."

"10 'Commandments

CCV

Thou shalt believe in Milton, Dryden, Pope;
    Thou shalt not set up Wordsworth, Coleridge, Southey;
Because the first is crazed beyond all hope,
    The second drunk, the third so quaint and mouthy:
With Crabbe[9] it may be difficult to cope,
    And Campbell's Hippocrene is somewhat drouthy:
Thou shall not steal from Samuel Rogers, nor
Commit—flirtation with the muse of Moore.

CCVI

Thou shall not covet Mr. Sotheby's[1] Muse,
    His Pegasus, nor anything that's his;
Thou shalt not bear false witness like "the Blues"[2]—
    (There's *one*, at least, is very fond of this);
Thou shalt not write, in short, but what I choose:
    This is true criticism, and you may kiss—
Exactly as you please, or not,—the rod;
But if you don't, I'll lay it on, by G—d!

CCVII

If any person should presume to assert
    This story is not moral, first, I pray,
That they will not cry out before they're hurt,
    Then that they'll read it o'er again, and say

7. In the popular legends and pantomimes concerning Don Juan (and in Mozart's great opera of 1787, *Don Giovanni*), Don Juan at the end of his life was carried off to hell by a demon.
8. Dionysius Longinus, third century A.D. Greek rhetorician whose treatise *On the Sublime* exerted immense influence upon the theoreticians of Romanticism.
9. The poets George Crabbe (1754–1832), Thomas Campbell (1777–1814), and Samuel Rogers (1763–1855) were all minor Romantics whom Byron generally rated high above Wordsworth and the "Lakers": but here he devalues even these poets when judged against the standard of "Milton, Dryden, Pope." "Hippocrene" of line 6 is a spring on Mount Helicon sacred to the Muses; so in saying Campbell's Hippocrene is "drouthy" or dry, Byron means that Campbell is a generally uninspired poet. For Moore, see note to *Don Juan* I, CIV.
1. William Sotheby (1757–1833), a minor poet whom Byron despised.
2. Byron's contempt for "bluestockings" —intellectual ladies—was lifelong, particularly after his marriage to the eminent "blue" Annabella Milbanke (the *"one"* of line 4).

(But, doubtless, nobody will be so pert)
    That this is not a moral tale, though gay
Besides, in Canto Twelfth, I mean to show
The very place where wicked people go.

CCVIII

If, after all, there should be some so blind
    To their own good this warning to despise,
Led by some tortuosity of mind,
    Not to believe my verse and their own eyes,
And cry that they "the moral cannot find,"
    I tell him, if a clergyman, he lies;
Should captains the remark, or critics, make,
They also lie too—under a mistake.

CCIX

The public approbation I expect,
    And beg they'll take my word about the moral,
Which I with their amusement will connect
    (So children cutting teeth receive a coral);
Meantime they'll doubtless please to recollect
    My epical pretensions to the laurel:
For fear some prudish readers should grow skittish,
I've bribed my Grandmother's Review—the British.[3]

CCX

I sent it in a letter to the Editor,
    Who thanked me duly by return of post—
I'm for a handsome article his creditor;
    Yet, if my gentle Muse he please to roast,
And break a promise after having made it her,
    Denying the receipt of what it cost,
And smear his page with gall instead of honey,
All I can say is—that he had the money.

CCXI

I think that with this holy *new* alliance
    I may ensure the public, and defy
All other magazines of art or science,
    Daily, or monthly, or three monthly; I
Have not essayed to multiply their clients,
    Because they tell me 'twere in vain to try,
And that the Edinburgh Review and Quarterly
Treat a dissenting author very martyrly.

CCXII

"*Non ego hoc ferrem calidus juventâ*
    Consule Planco,"[4] Horace said, and so

3. *The British Review* had mounted a strong attack upon Byron's "immorality." With customary myopia the *Review* took the joke of this stanza seriously, and made a public denial of the bribe. Byron was delighted.
4. "I would not have stood for this when I was a hot youth, during the consulship of Plancus." Horace, *Odes* III, 14 : 27–28. Quintus Horatius Flaccus (65–8 B.C.) was Rome's greatest lyric poet, and one of the poets most venerated by Byron.

Say I; by which quotation there is meant a
   Hint that some six or seven good years ago
(Long ere I dreamt of dating from the Brenta)[5]
   I was most ready to return a blow,
And would not brook at all this sort of thing
In my hot youth—when George the Third was King.

CCXIII

But now at thirty years my hair is grey—
   (I wonder what it will be like at forty?
I thought of a peruke[6] the other day—)
   My heart is not much greener; and, in short, I
Have squandered my whole summer while 'twas May,
   And feel no more the spirit to retort; I
Have spent my life, both interest and principal,
And deem not, what I deemed—my soul invincible.

CCXIV

No more—no more—Oh! never more on me
   The freshness of the heart can fall like dew,
Which out of all the lovely things we see
   Extracts emotions beautiful and new,
Hived in our bosoms like the bag o' the bee.
   Think'st thou the honey with those objects grew?
Alas! 'twas not in them, but in thy power
To double even the sweetness of a flower.

CCXV

No more—no more—Oh! never more, my heart,
   Canst thou be my sole world, my universe!
Once all in all, but now a thing apart,
   Thou canst not be my blessing or my curse:
The illusion's gone for ever, and thou art
   Insensible, I trust, but none the worse,
And in thy stead I've got a deal of judgment,
Though Heaven knows how it ever found a lodgment.

CCXVI

My days of love are over; me no more
   The charms of maid, wife, and still less of widow,
Can make the fool of which they made before,—
   In short, I must not lead the life I did do;
The credulous hope of mutual minds is o'er,
   The copious use of claret is forbid too,
So for a good old-gentlemanly vice,
I think I must take up with avarice.

CCXVII

Ambition was my idol, which was broken
   Before the shrines of Sorrow, and of Pleasure;
And the two last have left me many a token

5. Venetian river. Byron was "dating"— now resided in Venice.
i.e., writing—from the Brenta, since he 6. Wig.

O'er which reflection may be made at leisure:
Now, like Friar Bacon's Brazen Head, I've spoken,
   "Time is, Time was, Time's past:"⁷—a chymic treasure
Is glittering Youth, which I have spent betimes—
My heart in passion, and my head on rhymes.

CCXVIII

What is the end of Fame? 'tis but to fill
   A certain portion of uncertain paper:
Some liken it to climbing up a hill,
   Whose summit, like all hills, is lot in vapour;
For this men write, speak, preach, and heroes kill,
   And bards burn what they call their "midnight taper,"
To have, when the original is dust,
A name, a wretched picture and worse bust.

CCXIX

What are the hopes of man? Old Egypt's King
   Cheops erected the first Pyramid
And largest, thinking it was just the thing
   To keep his memory whole, and mummy hid;
But somebody or other rummaging,
   Burglariously broke his coffin's lid:
Let not a monument give you or me hopes,
Since not a pinch of dust remains of Cheops.

CCXX

But I, being fond of true philosophy,
   Say very often to myself, "Alas!
All things that have been born were born to die,
   And flesh (which Death mows down to hay) is grass;
You've passed your youth not so unpleasantly,
   And if you had it o'er again—'twould pass—
So thank your stars that matters are no worse,
And read your Bible, sir, and mind your purse."

CCXXI

But for the present, gentle reader! and
   Still gentler purchaser! the Bard—that's I—
Must, with permission, shake you by the hand,
   And so—"your humble servant, and Good-bye!"
We meet again, if we should understand
   Each other; and if not, I shall not try
Your patience further than by this short sample—
'Twere well if others followed my example.

CCXXII

"Go, little Book, from this my solitude!
   I cast thee on the waters—go thy ways!
And if, as I believe, thy vein be good,
   The World will find thee after many days."

7. Speech of the Brazen Head in *Friar Bacon and Friar Bungay*, by the Elizabe- than dramatist Robert Greene. *Chymic* means "alchemistic", or magic.

When Southey's read, and Wordsworth understood,
  I can't help putting in my claim to praise—
The four first rhymes[8] are Southey's every line:
  For God's sake, reader! take them not for mine.

CANTO THE SECOND

Juan, after being exiled from Spain for his affair with Julia, is caught in a storm at sea. He endures a terrible ordeal in an open lifeboat, and is finally cast up on a Mediterranean island which is the stronghold of the ferocious pirate, Lambro. Juan struggles on to the shore and collapses, half dead, where he is found by Lambro's beautiful daughter, Haidée. Haidée and her servant Zoe carry Juan to a cave where they can tend him without his being discovered by her violent father.

CXLI

And Haidée met the morning face to face;
  Her own was freshest, though a feverish flush
Had dyed it with the headlong blood, whose race
  From heart to cheek is curbed into a blush,
Like to a torrent which a mountain's base,
  That overpowers some Alpine river's rush,
Checks to a lake, whose waves in circles spread;
Or the Red Sea—but the sea is not red.

CXLII

And down the cliff the island virgin came,
  And near the cave her quick light footsteps drew,
While the Sun smiled on her with his first flame,
  And young Aurora[1] kissed her lips with dew,
Taking her for a sister; just the same
  Mistake you would have made on seeing the two,
Although the mortal, quite as fresh and fair,
Had all the advantage, too, of not being air.

CXLIII

And when into the cavern Haidée stepped
  All timidly, yet rapidly, she saw
That like an infant Juan sweetly slept;
  And then she stopped, and stood as if in awe
(For sleep is awful), and on tiptoe crept
  And wrapped him closer, lest the air, too raw,
Should reach his blood, then o'er him still as Death
Bent, with hushed lips, that drank his scarce-drawn breath.

CXLIV

And thus like to an Angel o'er the dying
  Who die in righteousness, she leaned; and there
All tranquilly the shipwrecked boy was lying,
  As o'er him lay the calm and stirless air:

8. Literally true; Byron quotes the first four lines ("rhymes") from Southey's *Epilogue to the Lay of the Laureate.*
1. The Roman goddess of dawn.

But Zoe the meantime some eggs was frying,
   Since, after all, no doubt the youthful pair
Must breakfast—and, betimes, lest they should ask it,
She drew out her provision from the basket.

CXLV

She knew that the best feelings must have victual,
   And that a shipwrecked youth would hungry be;
Besides, being less in love, she yawned a little,
   And felt her veins chilled by the neighbouring sea;
And so, she cooked their breakfast to a tittle;
   I can't say that she gave them any tea,
But there were eggs, fruit, coffee, bread, fish, honey,
With Scio[2] wine,—and all for love, not money.

CXLVI

And Zoe, when the eggs were ready, and
   The coffee made, would fain have wakened Juan;
But Haidée stopped her with her quick small hand,
   And without word, a sign her finger drew on
Her lip, which Zoe needs must understand;
   And, the first breakfast spoilt, prepared a new one,
Because her mistress would not let her break
That sleep which seemed as it would ne'er awake.

CXLVII

For still he lay, and on his thin worn cheek
   A purple hectic[3] played like dying day
On the snow-tops of distant hills; the streak
   Of sufferance yet upon his forehead lay,
Where the blue viens looked shadowy, shrunk, and weak;
   And his black curls were dewy with the spray,
Which weighed upon them yet, all damp and salt,
Mixed with the stony vapours of the vault.

CXLVIII

And she bent o'er him, and he lay beneath,
   Hushed as the babe upon its mother's breast,
Drooped as the willow when no winds can breathe,
   Lulled like the depth of Ocean when at rest,
Fair as the crowning rose of the whole wreath,
   Soft as the callow cygnet in its nest;
In short, he was a very pretty fellow,
Although his woes had turned him rather yellow.

CXLIX

He woke and gazed, and would have slept again,
   But the fair face which met his eyes forbade
Those eyes to close, though weariness and pain
   Had further sleep a further pleasure made:
For Woman's face was never formed in vain
   For Juan, so that even when he prayed
He turned from grisly saints, and martyrs hairy,
To the sweet portraits of the Virgin Mary.

---

2. An island in the Aegean sea.   3. Flush of fever.

CL

And thus upon his elbow he arose,
  And looked upon the lady, in whose cheek
The pale contended with the purple rose,
  As with an effort she began to speak;
Her eyes were eloquent, her words would pose,
  Although she told him, in good modern Greek,
With an Ionian accent, low and sweet,
That he was faint, and must not talk, but eat.

CLI

Now Juan could not understand a word,
  Being no Grecian; but he had an ear,
And her voice was the warble of a bird,
  So soft, so sweet, so delicately clear,
That finer, simpler music ne'er was heard;
  The sort of sound we echo with a tear,
Without knowing why—an overpowering tone,
Whence Melody descends as from a throne.

CLII

And Juan gazed as one who is awoke
  By a distant organ, doubting if he be
Not yet a dreamer, till the spell is broke
  By the watchman, or some such reality,
Or by one's early valet's curséd knock;
  At least it is a heavy sound to me,
Who like a morning slumber—for the night
Shows stars and women in a better light.

CLIII

And Juan, too, was helped out from his dream,
  Or sleep, or whatsoe'er it was, by feeling
A most prodigious appetite; the steam
  Of Zoe's cookery no doubt was stealing
Upon his senses, and the kindling beam
  Of the new fire, which Zoe kept up, kneeling,
To stir her viands, made him quite awake
And long for food, but chiefly a beef-steak.

CLIV

But beef is rare within these oxless isles;
  Goat's flesh there is, no doubt, and kid, and mutton,
And, when a holiday upon them smiles,
  A joint upon their barbarous spits they put on:
But this occurs but seldom, between whiles,
  For some of these are rocks with scarce a hut on;
Others are fair and fertile, among which
This, though not large, was one of the most rich.

CLV

I say that beef is rare, and can't help thinking
  That the old fable of the Minotaur[4]—

4. In Greek myth Queen Pasiphae, wife of Minos of Crete, conceived a sexual passion for a white bull. Disguising herself as a cow, she had intercourse with him and gave birth to the Minotaur—half man, half bull.

From which our modern morals, rightly shrinking,
  Condemn the royal lady's taste who wore
A cow's shape for a mask—was only (sinking
  The allegory) a mere type, no more,
That Pasiphae promoted breeding cattle,
To make the Cretans bloodier in battle.

CLVI

For we all know that English people are
  Fed upon beef—I won't say much of beer,
Because 'tis liquor only, and being far
  From this my subject, has no business here;
We know, too, they are very fond of war,
  A pleasure—like all pleasures—rather dear;
So were the Cretans—from which I infer,
That beef and battles both were owing to her.

CLVII

But to resume. The languid Juan raised
  His head upon his elbow, and he saw
A sight on which he had not lately gazed,
  As all his latter meals had been quite raw,[5]
Three or four things, for which the Lord he praised,
  And, feeling still the famished vulture gnaw,
He fell upon whate'er was offered, like
A priest, a shark, an alderman, or pike.

CLVIII

He ate, and he was well supplied; and she,
  Who watched him like a mother, would have fed
Him past all bounds, because she smiled to see
  Such appetite in one she had deemed dead:
But Zoe, being older than Haidée,
  Knew (by tradition, for she ne'er had read)
That famished people must be slowly nurst,
And fed by spoonfuls, else they always burst.

CLIX

And so she took the liberty to state,
  Rather by deeds than words, because the case
Was urgent, that the gentleman, whose fate
  Had made her mistress quit her bed to trace
The sea-shore at this hour, must leave his plate,
  Unless he wished to die upon the place—
She snatched it, and refused another morsel,
Saying, he had gorged enough to make a horse ill.

CLX

Next they—he being naked, save a tattered
  Pair of scarce decent trowsers—went to work,
And in the fire his recent rags they scattered,
  And dressed him, for the present, like a Turk,

---

5. An understatement. During their time
in the open boat, Juan and his starving
companion had been forced to resort to
cannibalism.

Or Greek—that is, although it not much mattered,
   Omitting turban, slippers, pistol, dirk,[6]—
They furnished him, entire, except some stitches,
   With a clean shirt, and very spacious breeches.

CLXI

And then fair Haidée tried her tongue at speaking,
   But not a word could Juan comprehend,
Although he listened so that the young Greek in
   Her earnestness would ne'er have made an end;
And, as he interrupted not, went eking
   Her speech out to her protégé and friend,
Till pausing at the last her breath to take,
She saw he did not understand Romaic.[7]

CLXII[8]

And then she had recourse to nods, and signs,
   And smiles, and sparkles of the speaking eye,
And read (the only book she could) the lines
   Of his fair face, and found, by sympathy,
The answer eloquent, where the Soul shines
   And darts in one quick glance a long reply;
And thus in every look she saw expressed
A world of words, and things at which she guessed.

CLXIII

And now, by dint of fingers and of eyes,
   And words repeated after her, he took
A lesson in her tongue; but by surmise,
   No doubt, less of her language than her look:
As he who studies fervently the skies
   Turns oftener to the stars than to his book,
Thus Juan learned his *alpha beta* better
From Haidée's glance than any graven letter.

CLXIV

'Tis pleasing to be schooled in a strange tongue
   By female lips and eyes—that is, I mean,
When both the teacher and the taught are young,
   As was the case, at least, where I have been;
They smile so when one's right, and when one's wrong
   They smile still more, and then there intervene
Pressure of hands, perhaps even a chaste kiss;—
I learned the little that I know by this:

CLXV

That is, some words of Spanish, Turk, and Greek,
   Italian not at all, having no teachers;[9]

---

6. Dagger.
7. Modern Greek.
8. This stanza introduces an important theme. Since Haidée and Juan cannot talk to each other, they cannot lie to or mislead each other; and therefore, ironically, their love is the most faithful and the most idyllic of any in Byron's narra-tive poetry.
9. The original line was "Italian rather more, having more teachers." The revi-sion is ironic, and probably also a grace-ful capitulation to Countess Teresa Guic-cioli, Byron's mistress at the time, who disapproved of the "immorality" of *Don Juan*.

Much English I cannot pretend to speak,
    Learning that language chiefly from its preachers,
Barrow,[1] South, Tillotson, whom every week
    I study, also Blair—the highest reachers
Of eloquence in piety and prose—
I hate your poets, so read none of those.

CLXVI

As for the ladies, I have nought to say,
    A wanderer from the British world of Fashion,
Where I, like other "dogs, have had my day,"
    Like other men, too, may have had my passion—
But that, like other things, has passed away,
    And all her fools whom I *could* lay the lash on:
Foes, friends, men, women, now are nought to me
But dreams of what has been, no more to be.

CLXVII

Return we to Don Juan. He begun
    To hear new words, and to repeat them; but
Some feelings, universal as the Sun,
    Were such as could not in his breast be shut
More than within the bosom of a nun:
    He was in love,—as you would be, no doubt,
With a young benefactress,—so was she,
Just in the way we very often see.

CLXVIII

And every day by daybreak—rather early
    For Juan, who was somewhat fond of rest—
She came into the cave, but it was merely
    To see her bird reposing in his nest;
And she would softly stir his locks so curly,
    Without disturbing her yet slumbering guest,
Breathing all gently o'er his cheek and mouth,
As o'er a bed of roses the sweet South.[2]

CLXIX

And every morn his colour freshlier came,
    And every day helped on his convalescence;
'Twas well, because health in the human frame
    Is pleasant, besides being true Love's essence,
For health and idleness to Passion's flame
    Are oil and gunpowder; and some good lessons
Are also learnt from Ceres[3] and from Bacchus,
Without whom Venus will not long attack us.

CLXX

While Venus fills the heart, (without heart really
    Love, though good always, is not quite so good,)
Ceres presents a plate of vermicelli,—

---

1. Barrow, South, and Tillotson were theologians and preachers. Hugh Blair wrote *Lectures on Rhetoric.*
2. The gentle south wind.
3. Ceres, goddess of grain, and Bacchus, god of wine, contribute to the rites of Venus, goddess of love.

For Love must be sustained like flesh and blood,—
While Bacchus pours out wine, or hands a jelly:
    Eggs, oysters, too, are amatory food;
But who is their purveyor from above
Heaven knows,—it may be Neptune, Pan, or Jove.

CLXXI

When Juan woke he found some good things ready,
    A bath, a breakfast, and the finest eyes
That ever made a youthful heart less steady,
    Besides her maid's, as pretty for their size;
But I have spoken of all this already—
    A repetition's tiresome and unwise,—
Well—Juan, after bathing in the sea,
Came always back to coffee and Haidée.

CLXXII

Both were so young, and one so innocent,
    That bathing passed for nothing; Juan seemed
To her, as 'twere, the kind of being sent,
    Of whom these two years she had nightly dreamed,
A something to be loved, a creature meant
    To be her happiness, and whom she deemed
To render happy; all who joy would win
Must share it,—Happiness was born a Twin.

CLXXIII

It was such pleasure to behold him, such
    Enlargement of existence to partake
Nature with him, to thrill beneath his touch,
    To watch him slumbering, and to see him wake:
To live with him for ever were too much;
    But then the thought of parting made her quake;
He was her own, her ocean-treasure, cast
Like a rich wreck—her first love, and her last.

CLXXIV

And thus a moon rolled on, and fair Haidée
    Paid daily visits to her boy, and took
Such plentiful precautions, that still he
    Remained unknown within his craggy nook;
At last her father's prows put out to sea,
    For certain merchantmen upon the look,
Not as of yore to carry off an Io,[4]
But three Ragusan vessels, bound for Scio.

CLXXV

Then came her freedom, for she had no mother,
    So that, her father being at sea, she was
Free as a married woman, or such other
    Female, as where she likes may freely pass,
Without even the encumbrance of a brother,

---

4. The maiden Io was carried off by Pheonician merchants. *Ragusa* is the Italian for Dubrovnik, capital of Yugoslavia.

The freest she that ever gazed on glass:
I speak of Christian lands in this comparison,
Where wives, at least, are seldom kept in garrison.

CLXXVI

Now she prolonged her visits and her talk
  (For they must talk), and he had learnt to say
So much as to propose to take a walk,—
  For little had he wandered since the day
On which, like a young flower snapped from the stalk,
  Drooping and dewy on the beach he lay,—
And thus they walked out in the afternoon,
And saw the sun set opposite the moon.

CLXXVII

It was a wild and breaker-beaten coast,
  With cliffs above, and a broad sandy shore,
Guarded by shoals and rocks as by an host,
  With here and there a creek, whose aspect wore
A better welcome to the tempest-tost;
  And rarely ceased the haughty billow's roar,
Save on the dead long summer days, which make
The outstretched Ocean glitter like a lake.

CLXXVIII

And the small ripple spilt upon the beach
  Scarcely o'erpassed the cream of your champagne,
When o'er the brim the sparkling bumpers reach,
  That spring-dew of the spirit! the heart's rain!
Few things surpass old wine; and they may preach
  Who please,—the more because they preach in vain,—
Let us have Wine and Woman, Mirth and Laughter,
Sermons and soda-water the day after.

CLXXIX

Man, being reasonable, must get drunk;
  The best of Life is but intoxication:
Glory, the Grape, Love, Gold, in these are sunk
  The hopes of all men, and of every nation;
Without their sap, how branchless were the trunk
  Of Life's strange tree, so fruitful on occasion!
But to return,—Get very drunk, and when
You wake with headache—you shall see what then!

CLXXX

Ring for your valet—bid him quickly bring
  Some hock and soda-water, then you'll know
A pleasure worthy Xerxes[5] the great king;
  For not the blest sherbet, sublimed[6] with snow,
Nor the first sparkle of the desert-spring,
  Nor Burgundy in all its sunset glow,
After long travel, Ennui, Love, or Slaughter,
Vie with that draught of hock and soda-water!

---

5. King of Persia (519–465 B.C.), renowned for his opulence.

6. Sherbet was kept cool by being packed and served in a mold of snow.

CLXXXI

The coast—I think it was the coast that I
    Was just describing—Yes, it *was* the coast—
Lay at this period quiet as the sky,
    The sands untumbled, the blue waves untossed,
And all was stillness, save the sea-bird's cry,
    And dolphin's leap, and little billow crossed
By some low rock or shelve, that made it fret
Against the boundary it scarcely wet.

CLXXXII

And forth they wandered, her sire being gone,
    As I have said, upon an expedition;
And mother, brother, guardian, she had none,
    Save Zoe, who, although with due precision
She waited on her lady with the Sun,
    Thought daily service was her only mission,
Bringing warm water, wreathing her long tresses,
And asking now and then for cast-off dresses.

CLXXXIII

It was the cooling hour, just when the rounded
    Red sun sinks down behind the azure hill,
Which then seems as if the whole earth it bounded,
    Circling all Nature, hushed, and dim, and still,
With the far mountain-crescent half surrounded
    On one side, and the deep sea calm and chill
Upon the other, and the rosy sky
With one star sparkling through it like an eye.

CLXXXIV

And thus they wandered forth, and hand in hand,
    Over the shining pebbles and the shells,
Glided along the smooth and hardened sand,
    And in the worn and wild receptacles
Worked by the storms, yet worked as it were planned
    In hollow halls, with sparry roofs and cells,
They turned to rest; and, each clasped by an arm,
Yielded to the deep Twilight's purple charm.

CLXXXV

They looked up to the sky, whose floating glow
    Spread like a rosy Ocean, vast and bright;
They gazed upon the glittering sea below,
    Whence the broad Moon rose circling into sight;
They heard the waves' splash, and the wind so low,
    And saw each other's dark eyes darting light
Into each other—and, beholding this,
Their lips drew near, and clung into a kiss;

CLXXXVI

A long, long kiss, a kiss of Youth, and Love,
    And Beauty, all concentrating like rays
Into one focus, kindled from above;
    Such kisses as belong to early days,

Where Heart, and Soul, and Sense, in concert move,
  And the blood's lava, and the pulse a blaze,
Each kiss a heart-quake,—for a kiss's strength,
I think, it must be reckoned by its length.

CLXXXVII

By length I mean duration; theirs endured
  Heaven knows how long—no doubt they never
    reckoned;
And if they had, they could not have secured
  The sum of their sensations to a second:
They had not spoken, but they felt allured,
  As if their souls and lips each other beckoned,
Which, being joined, like swarming bees they clung—
Their hearts the flowers from whence the honey sprung.

CLXXXVIII

They were alone, but not alone as they
  Who shut in chambers think it loneliness;
The silent Ocean, and the starlight bay,
  The twilight glow, which momently grew less,
The voiceless sands, and dropping caves, that lay
  Around them, made them to each other press,
As if there were no life beneath the sky
Save theirs, and that their life could never die.

CLXXXIX

They feared no eyes nor ears on that lone beach;
  They felt no terrors from the night; they were
All in all to each other: though their speech
  Was broken words, they *thought* a language there,—
And all the burning tongues the Passions teach
  Found in one sigh the best interpreter
Of Nature's oracle—first love,—that all
Which Eve has left her daughters since her fall.

CXC

Haidée spoke not of scruples, asked no vows,
  Nor offered any; she had never heard
Of plight and promises to be a spouse,
  Or perils by a loving maid incurred;
She was all which pure Ignorance allows,
  And flew to her young mate like a young bird;
And, never having dreamt of falsehood, she
Had not one word to say of constancy.

CXCI

She loved, and was belovéd—she adored,
  And she was worshipped after Nature's fashion—
There intense souls, into each other poured,
  If souls could die, had perished in that passion,—
But by degrees their senses were restored,
  Again to be o'ercome, again to dash on;
And, beating 'gainst *his* bosom, Haidée's heart
Felt as if never more to beat apart.

[handwritten margin note: Stasis of is land causes their love to degenerate into stasis (decay)]

CXCII

[handwritten: "A thing of beauty / I's A joy foRever"]

[handwritten left margin: Through intensity give both pleasure & pain.]

Alas! they were so young, so beautiful,
    So lonely, loving, helpless, and the hour
Was that in which the Heart is always full,
    And, having o'er itself no further power,
Prompts deeds Eternity can not annul,
    But pays off moments in an endless shower *[handwritten: (IRONY)]*
Of hell-fire—all prepared for people giving
Pleasure or pain to one another living.

CXCIII.

Alas! for Juan and Haidée! they were
    So loving and so lovely—till then never,
Excepting our first parents, such a pair
    Had run the risk of being damned for ever:
And Haidée, being devout as well as fair,
    Had, doubtless, heard about the Stygian[7] river,
And Hell and Purgatory—but forgot
Just in the very crisis she should not.

CXCIV

They look upon each other, and their eyes
    Gleam in the moonlight; and her white arm clasps
Round Juan's head, and his around her lies
    Half buried in the tresses which it grasps;
She sits upon his knee, and drinks his sighs,
    He hers, until they end in broken gasps;
And thus they form a group that's quite antique,
Half naked, loving, natural, and Greek.

CXCV

And when those deep and burning moments passed,
    And Juan sunk to sleep within her arms,
She slept not, but all tenderly, though fast,
    Sustained his head upon her bosom's charms
And now and then her eye to Heaven is cast,
    And then on the pale cheek her breast now warms,
Pillowed on her o'erflowing heart, which pants
With all it granted, and with all it grants.

CXCVI

An infant when it gazes on a light,
    A child the moment when it drains the breast,
A devotee when soars the Host in sight,
    An Arab with a stranger for a guest,
A sailor when the prize has struck in fight,
    A miser filling his most hoarded chest,
Feel rapture; but not such true joy are reaping
As they who watch o'er what they love while sleeping.

CXCVII

For there it lies so tranquil, so beloved,
    All that it hath of Life with us is living;

---

7. The River Styx bordered the classical underworld.

So gentle, stirless, helpless, and unmoved,
    And all unconscious of the joy 'tis giving;
All it hath felt, inflicted, passed, and proved,
    Hushed into depths beyond the watcher's diving:
There lies the thing we love with all its errors
And all its charms, like Death without its terrors.

CXCVIII

The Lady watched her lover—and that hour
    Of Love's, and Night's, and Ocean's solitude
O'erflowed her soul with their united power;
    Amidst the barren sand and rocks so rude
She and her wave-worn love had made their bower,
    Where nought upon their passion could intrude,
And all the stars that crowded the blue space
Saw nothing happier than her glowing face.

CXCIX

Alas! the love of Women! it is known
    To be a lovely and a fearful thing;
For all of theirs upon that die is thrown,
    And if 'tis lost, Life hath no more to bring
To them but mockeries of the past alone,
    And their revenge is as the tiger's spring,
Deadly, and quick, and crushing; yet, as real
Torture is theirs—what they inflict they feel.

CC

They are right; for Man, to man so oft unjust,
    Is always so to Women: one sole bond
Awaits them—treachery is all their trust;
    Taught to conceal their bursting hearts despond
Over their idol, till some wealthier lust
    Buys them in marriage—and what rests beyond?
A thankless husband—next, a faithless lover—
Then dressing, nursing, praying—and all's over.

CCI

Some take a lover, some take drams or prayers,
    Some mind their household, others dissipation,
Some run away, and but exchange their cares,
    Losing the advantage of a virtuous station;
Few changes e'er can better their affairs,
    Theirs being an unnatural situation,
From the dull palace to the dirty hovel:
Some play the devil, and then write a novel.[8]

CCII

Haidée was Nature's bride, and knew not this;
    Haidée was Passion's child, born where the Sun
Showers triple light, and scorches even the kiss

---

8. Lady Caroline Lamb, with whom Byron had had a tempestuous affair in 1812, depicted Byron as a diabolical seducer in her novel *Glenarvon* (1816).

Of his gazelle-eyed daughters; she was one
Made but to love, to feel that she was his
   Who was her chosen: what was said or done
Elsewhere was nothing. She had nought to fear,
Hope, care, nor love, beyond,—her heart beat *here*.

CCIII

And oh! that quickening of the heart, that beat!
   How much it costs us! yet each rising throb
Is in its cause as its effect so sweet,
   That Wisdom, ever on the watch to rob
Joy of its alchemy, and to repeat
   Fine truths; even Conscience, too, has a tough job
To make us understand each good old maxim,
So good—I wonder Castlereagh don't tax 'em.

CCIV

And now 'twas done—on the lone shore were plighted
   Their hearts; the stars, their nuptial torches, shed
Beauty upon the beautiful they lighted:
   Ocean their witness, and the cave their bed,
By their own feelings hallowed and united,
   Their priest was Solitude, and they were wed:
And they were happy—for to their young eyes
Each was an angel, and earth Paradise.

CCV[9]

Oh, Love! of whom great Cæsar was the suitor,
   Titus the master, Antony the slave,
Horace, Catullus, scholars—Ovid tutor—
   Sappho the sage blue-stocking, in whose grave
All those may leap who rather would be neuter—
   (Leucadia's rock still overlooks the wave)—
Oh, Love! thou art the very God of evil,
For, after all, we cannot call thee Devil.

CCVI

Thou mak'st the chaste connubial state precarious,
   And jestest with the brows of mightiest men:
Cæsar and Pompey, Mahomet, Belisarius,[1]
   Have much employed the Muse of History's pen:
Their lives and fortunes were extremely various,
   Such worthies Time will never see again;
Yet to these four in three things the same luck holds,
They all were heroes, conquerors, and cuckolds.

9. This stanza is a mini-history of classical attitudes toward love. Julius Caesar was the "suitor" of the young Cleopatra; the emperor Titus "mastered" his passion for Berenice, wife of King Herod of Chalcis, and refused to wed her; Marc Antony was the "slave" of a rather older Cleopatra. The poetess Sappho conducted a school for girls on the Island of Lesbos (hence she was a "blue-stocking"), and reputedly leaped to her death on the Island of Leucadia after having been jilted by a lover.

1. The wives of all these men were suspected of infidelity.

CCVII

Thou mak'st philosophers; there's Epicurus[2]
  And Aristippus, a material crew!
Who to immortal courses would allure us
  By theories quite practicable too;
If only from the Devil they would insure us,
  How pleasant were the maxim (not quite new),
"Eat, drink, and love, what can the rest avail us?"
So said the royal sage Sardanapalus.[3]

CCVIII

But Juan! had he quite forgotten Julia?
  And should he have forgotten her so soon?
I can't but say it seems to me most truly a
  Perplexing question; but, no doubt, the moon
Does these things for us, and whenever newly a
  Strong palpitation rises, 'tis her boon,
Else how the devil is it that fresh features
Have such a charm for us poor human creatures?

CCIX

I hate inconstancy—I loathe, detest,
  Abhor, condemn, abjure the mortal made
Of such quicksilver clay that in his breast
  No permanent foundation can be laid;
Love, constant love, has been my constant guest,
  And yet last night, being at a masquerade,
I saw the prettiest creature, fresh from Milan,
Which gave me some sensations like a villain.

CCX

But soon Philosophy came to my aid,
  And whispered, "Think of every sacred tie!"
"I will, my dear Philosophy!" I said,
  "But then her teeth, and then, oh, Heaven! her eye!
I'll just inquire if she be wife or maid,
  Or neither—out of curiosity."
"Stop!" cried Philosophy, with air so Grecian,
(Though she was masqued then as a fair Venetian;)

CCXI

"Stop!" so I stopped.—But to return: that which
  Men call inconstancy is nothing more
Than admiration due where Nature's rich
  Profusion with young beauty covers o'er
Some favoured object; and as in the niche
  A lovely statue we almost adore,
This sort of adoration of the real
Is but a heightening of the *beau ideal*.[4]

---

2. Third century B.C. Greek philosopher, who held that pleasure is the highest goal of life. Aristippus, a fourth century B.C. thinker, held much the same view.
3. Ninth century B.C. warrior king of As-syria who was also a famous voluptuary. In 1821 Byron was to make him the subject of a classical drama, *Sardanapalus*.
4. The concept of the lofty or the beautiful.

CCXII

'Tis the perception of the Beautiful,
  A fine extension of the faculties,
Platonic, universal, wonderful,
  Drawn from the stars, and filtered through the skies,
Without which Life would be extremely dull;
  In short, it is the use of our own eyes,
With one or two small senses added, just
To hint that flesh is formed of fiery dust.[5]

fire & clay
no split between
body & soul.

CCXIII

Yet 'tis a painful feeling, and unwilling,
  For surely if we always could perceive
In the same object graces quite as killing
  As when she rose upon us like an Eve,
'Twould save us many a heartache, many a shilling,
  (For we must get them anyhow, or grieve),
Whereas if one sole lady pleased for ever,
How pleasant for the heart, as well as liver!

CCXIV

The Heart is like the sky, a part of Heaven,
  But changes night and day, too, like the sky;
Now o'er it clouds and thunder must be driven,
  And Darkness and Destruction as on high:
But when it hath been scorched, and pierced, and riven,
  Its storms expire in water-drops; the eye
Pours forth at last the Heart's blood turned to tears,
Which make the English climate of our years.

CCXV

The liver is the lazaret[6] of bile,
  But very rarely executes its function,
For the first passion stays there such a while,
  That all the rest creep in and form a junction,
Like knots of vipers on a dunghill's soil—
  Rage, fear, hate, jealousy, revenge, compunction—
So that all mischiefs spring up from this entrail,
Like Earthquakes from the hidden fire called "central."

CCXVI

In the mean time, without proceeding more
  In this anatomy, I've finished now
Two hundred and odd stanzas as before,
  That being about the number I'll allow
Each canto of the twelve, or twenty-four;
  And, laying down my pen, I make my bow,
Leaving Don Juan and Haidée to plead
For them and theirs with all who deign to read.

5. The first draft read, "ticklish dust."

6. A lazaret is a quarantine building. Byron's point is that, physiologically, the liver isolates "bile"—which was believed to cause anger, jealousy, etc.—but that because of the complexity of human emotions, nothing can really prevent outbursts of our most violent feelings.

CANTO THE FIFTH

Lambro, Haidée's father, returns to the island, finds Juan with Haidée, and drives him out. Juan eventually finds himself in Turkey, where he is taken captive and, as this canto opens, is about to be sold into slavery.

I

WHEN amatory poets sing their loves
   In liquid lines mellifluously bland,
And pair their rhymes as Venus yokes her doves,
   They little think what mischief is in hand;
The greater their success the worse it proves,
   As Ovid's[1] verse may give to understand;
Even Petrarch's self, if judged with due severity,
Is the Platonic pimp of all posterity.

II

I therefore do denounce all amorous writing,
   Except in such a way as not to attract;
Plain—simple—short, and by no means inviting,
   But with a moral to each error tacked,
Formed rather for instructing than delighting,
   And with all passions in their turn attacked;
Now, if my Pegasus should not be shod ill,
This poem will become a moral model.

III

The European with the Asian shore
   Sprinkled with palaces—the Ocean stream
Here and there studded with a seventy-four,[2]
   Sophia's[3] Cupola with golden gleam,
The cypress groves, Olympus high and hoar,
   The twelve isles, and the more than I could dream,
Far less describe, present the very view
Which charmed the charming Mary Montagu.[4]

IV

I have a passion for the name of "Mary,"[5]
   For once it was a magic sound to me;
And still it half calls up the realms of Fairy,
   Where I beheld what never was to be;
All feelings changed, but this was last to vary,
   A spell from which even yet I am not quite free:

1. Publius Ovidius Naso (43 B.C.–A.D. 17) wrote the highly erotic *Metamorphoses* and the *Art of Love*. Petrarch, or Francesco Petrarca (1304–74), one of the greatest Italian poets, established the conventions of the love sonnet. Byron's irreverent point in this stanza is that the great lyric celebrations of love by poets all reduce, finally, to the same undignified and basically physical passion.
2. A warship.
3. The dome of St. Sophia, the splendid Byzantine church of Constantinople (Istanbul).
4. Lady Mary Wortley Montagu (1689–1762), a brilliant literary figure of the eighteenth century and sometime friend of Alexander Pope.
5. Byron's youthful love for Mary Chaworth was to remain, in his memory, one of the most passionate experiences of his life. See his letter to Francis Hodgson November 3, 1808.

But I grow sad—and let a tale grow cold,
Which must not be pathetically told.

V

The wind swept down the Euxine,[6] and the wave
    Broke foaming o'er the blue Symplegades;[7]
'Tis a grand sight from off "the Giant's Grave"[8]
    To watch the progress of those rolling seas
Between the Bosphorus, as they lash and lave
    Europe and Asia, you being quite at ease:
There's not a sea the passenger e'er pukes in,
Turns up more dangerous breakers than the Euxine.

VI

'Twas a raw day of Autumn's bleak beginning,
    When nights are equal, but not so the days;
The Parcæ[9] then cut short the further spinning
    Of seamen's fates, and the loud tempests raise
The waters, and repentance for past sinning
    In all, who o'er the great deep take their ways:
They vow to amend their lives, and yet they don't;
Because if drowned, they can't—if spared, they won't.

VII

A crowd of shivering slaves of every nation,
    And age, and sex, were in the market ranged;
Each bevy with the merchant in his station:
    Poor creatures! their good looks were sadly changed.
All save the blacks seemed jaded with vexation,
    From friends, and home, and freedom far estranged;
The negroes more philosophy displayed,—
Used to it, no doubt, as eels are to be flayed.

VIII

Juan was juvenile, and thus was full,
    As most at his age are, of hope, and health;
Yet I must own, he looked a little dull,
    And now and then a tear stole down by stealth;
Perhaps his recent loss of blood might pull
    His spirit down; and then the loss of wealth,
A mistress, and such comfortable quarters,
To be put up for auction amongst Tartars,

IX

Were things to shake a Stoic; ne'ertheless,
    Upon the whole his carriage was serene:
His figure, and the splendour of his dress,
    Of which some gilded remnants still were seen,
Drew all eyes on him, giving them to guess
    He was above the vulgar by his mien;

6. The Black Sea.
7. The "Wandering Rocks" of classical legend, a formation in the Bosporus.
8. "The 'Giant's Grave' is a height on the Asiatic shore of the Bosphorus, much frequented by holiday parties; like Harrow and Highgate." [*Byron's note.*]
9. The classical Fates.

And then, though pale, he was so very handsome;
And then—they calculated on his ransom.

X

Like a backgammon board the place was dotted
    With whites and blacks, in groups on show for sale,
Though rather more irregularly spotted:
    Some bought the jet, while others chose the pale.
It chanced amongst the other people lotted,
    A man of thirty, rather stout and hale,
With resolution in his dark grey eye,
Next Juan stood, till some might choose to buy.

XI

He had an English look; that is, was square
    In make, of a complexion white and ruddy,
Good teeth, with curling rather dark brown hair,
    And, it might be from thought, or toil, or study,
An open brow a little marked with care:
    One arm had on a bandage rather bloody;
And there he stood with such *sang froid*,[1] that greater
Could scarce be shown even by a mere spectator.

XII

But seeing at his elbow a mere lad,
    Of a high spirit evidently, though
At present weighed down by a doom which had
    O'erthrown even men, he soon began to show
A kind of blunt compassion for the sad
    Lot of so young a partner in the woe,
Which for himself he seemed to deem no worse
Than any other scrape, a thing of course.

XIII

"My boy!"—said he, "amidst this motley crew
    Of Georgians, Russians, Nubians[2] and what not,
All ragamuffins differing but in hue,
    With whom it is our luck to cast our lot,
The only gentlemen seem I and you;
    So let us be acquainted, as we ought:
If I could yield you any consolation,
'Twould give me pleasure.—Pray, what is your nation?"

XIV

When Juan answered—"Spanish!" he replied,
    "I thought, in fact, you could not be a Greek;
Those servile dogs are not so proudly eyed:
    Fortune has played you here a pretty freak,
But that's her way with all men, till they're tried;
    But never mind,—she'll turn, perhaps, next week;
She has served me also much the same as you,
Except that I have found it nothing new."

1. Cold blood.
2. Georgia was a nation of Caucasia, on the edge of the Black Sea. Nubia is the area of the present-day Sudan.

XV

"Pray, sir," said Juan, "if I may presume,
  W*hat* brought you here?"—"Oh! nothing very rare—
Six Tartars and a drag-chain———"—"To this doom
  But what conducted, if the question's fair,
Is that which I would learn."—"I served for some
  Months with the Russian army here and there;
And taking lately, by Suwarrow's[3] bidding,
A town, was ta'en myself instead of Widdin."

XVI

"Have you no friends?"—"I had—but, by God's blessing,
  Have not been troubled with them lately. Now
I have answered all your questions without pressing,
  And you an equal courtesy should show."
"Alas!" said Juan, " 'twere a tale distressing,
  And long besides."—"Oh! if 'tis really so,
You're right on both accounts to hold your tongue;
A sad tale saddens doubly when 'tis long.

XVII

"But droop not: Fortune at your time of life,
  Although a female moderately fickle,
Will hardly leave you (as she's not your wife)
  For any length of days in such a pickle.
To strive, too, with our fate were such a strife
  As if the corn-sheaf should oppose the sickle:
Men are the sport of circumstances, when
The circumstances seem the sport of men."

XVIII

" 'Tis not," said Juan, "for my present doom
  I mourn, but for the past;—I loved a maid:"—
He paused, and his dark eye grew full of gloom;
  A single tear upon his eyelash staid
A moment, and then dropped; "but to resume,
  'Tis not my present lot, as I have said,
Which I deplore so much; for I have borne
Hardships which have the hardiest overworn,

XIX

"On the rough deep. But this last blow—" and here
  He stopped again, and turned away his face.
"Aye," quoth his friend, "I thought it would appear
  That there had been a lady in the case;
And these are things which ask a tender tear,
  Such as I, too, would shed if in your place:
I cried upon my first wife's dying day,
And also when my second ran away:

XX

"My third———"—"Your third!" quoth Juan, turning round;

<hr/>

3. Russian Field Marshall Suvarov (1729–1800) had led a campaign against Napoleon in Eastern Europe in 1789. Widdin was one of the towns contested in the campaign.

"You scarcely can be thirty: have you three?"
"No—only two at present above ground:
    Surely 'tis nothing wonderful to see
One person thrice in holy wedlock bound!"
    "Well, then, your third," said Juan; "what did she?
She did not run away, too,—did she, sir?"
    "No, faith."—"What then?"—"I ran away from her."

XXI

"You take things coolly, sir," said Juan. "Why,"
    Replied the other, "what can a man do?
There still are many rainbows in your sky,
    But mine have vanished. All, when Life is new,
Commence with feelings warm, and prospects high;
    But Time strips our illusions of their hue,
And one by one in turn, some grand mistake
Casts off its bright skin yearly like the snake.

XXII

" 'Tis true, it gets another bright and fresh,
    Or fresher, brighter; but the year gone through,
This skin must go the way, too, of all flesh,
    Or sometimes only wear a week or two;—
Love's the first net which spreads its deadly mesh;
    Ambition, Avarice, Vengeance, Glory, glue
The glittering lime-twigs⁴ of our latter days,
Where still we flutter on for pence or praise."

XXIII

"All this is very fine, and may be true,"
    Said Juan; "but I really don't see how
It betters present times with me or you."
    "No?" quoth the other; "yet you will allow
By setting things in their right point of view,
    Knowledge, at least, is gained; for instance, now,
We know what slavery is, and our disasters
May teach us better to behave when masters."

XXIV

"Would we were masters now, if but to try
    Their present lessons on our Pagan friends here,"
Said Juan,—swallowing a heart-burning sigh:
    "Heaven help the scholar, whom his fortune sends here!"
"Perhaps we shall be one day, by and by,"
    Rejoined the other, "when our bad luck mends here;
Meantime (yon old black eunuch seems to eye us)
I wish to G—d that somebody would buy us.

XXV

"But after all, what *is* our present state?
    'Tis bad, and may be better—all men's lot:

4. Small branches or twigs were smeared with birdlime, a sticky substance prepared from holly or mistletoe, to catch birds; hence, a "lime-twig" is a snare or trap.

Most men are slaves, none more so than the great,
    To their own whims and passions, and what not;
Society itself, which should create
    Kindness, destroys what little we had got:
To feel for none is the true social art
Of the world's Stoics—men without a heart."

XXVI

Just now a black old neutral personage
    Of the third sex[5] stepped up, and peering over
The captives seemed to mark their looks and age,
    And capabilities, as to discover
If they were fitted for the purposed cage:
    No lady e'er is ogled by a lover,
Horse by a blackleg, broadcloth by a tailor,
Fee by a counsel, felon by a jailor,

XXVII

As is a slave by his intended bidder.
    'Tis pleasant purchasing our fellow-creatures;
And all are to be sold, if you consider
    Their passions, and are dext'rous; some by features
Are brought up, others by a warlike leader,
    Some by a place—as tend their years or natures:
The most by ready cash—but all have prices,
From crowns to kicks, according to their vices.

XXVIII

The eunuch, having eyed them o'er with care,
    Turned to the merchant, and began to bid
First but for one, and after for the pair;
    They haggled, wrangled, swore, too—so they did!
As though they were in a mere Christian fair,
    Cheapening an ox, an ass, a lamb, or kid;
So that their bargain sounded like a battle
For this superior yoke of human cattle.

XXIX

At last they settled into simple grumbling,
    And pulling out reluctant purses, and
Turning each piece of silver o'er, and tumbling
    Some down, and weighing others in their hand,
And by mistake sequins with paras[6] jumbling,
    Until the sum was accurately scanned,
And then the merchant giving change, and signing
Receipts in full, began to think of dining.

XXX

I wonder if his appetite was good?
    Or, if it were, if also his digestion?
Methinks at meals some odd thoughts might intrude,
    And Conscience ask a curious sort of question,
About the right divine how far we should

---

5. A eunuch.   6. Turkish coins.

Sell flesh and blood. When dinner[7] has oppressed one,
I think it is perhaps the gloomiest hour
Which turns up out of the sad twenty-four.

XXXI

Voltaire[8] says "No:" he tells you that Candide
   Found life most tolerable after meals;
He's wrong—unless man were a pig, indeed,
   Repletion rather adds to what he feels,
Unless he's drunk, and then no doubt he's freed
   From his own brain's oppression while it reels.
Of food I think with Philip's son[9] or rather
Ammon's (ill pleased with one world and one father);

XXXII

I think with Alexander, that the act
   Of eating, with another act or two,
Makes us feel our mortality in fact
   Redoubled; when a roast and a ragout,
And fish, and soup, by some side dishes backed,
   Can give us either pain or pleasure, who
Would pique himself on intellects, whose use
Depends so much upon the gastric juice?

XXXIII

The other evening ('twas on Friday last)—
   This is a fact, and no poetic fable—
Just as my great coat was about me cast,
   My hat and gloves still lying on the table,
I heard a shot—'twas eight o'clock scarce past
   And, running out as fast as I was able,[1]
I found the military commandant
Stretched in the street, and able scarce to pant.

XXXIV

Poor fellow! for some reason, surely bad,
   They had slain him with five slugs; and left him there
To perish on the pavement: so I had
   Him borne into the house and up the stair,
And stripped, and looked to,—— But why should I add
   More circumstances? vain was every care;
The man was gone—in some Italian quarrel
Killed by five bullets from an old gun-barrel.

---

7. Byron suffered from a metabolic tendency to overweight, and throughout his life engaged in murderous fasts to keep himself slim. Dinner—especially a heavy dinner—was often literally a depressing, gloomy time for him.
8. François Marie Arouet de Voltaire (1644–1778), the most brilliant satirist of the French Enlightenment. His *Candide* (1759) is a bitter attack upon philosophical optimism: the book's hero, the innocent, trusting Candide, is one of the important literary ancestors of Byron's

Juan.
9. Alexander the Great (356–323 B.C.), the conqueror of the ancient world, son of Philip of Macedon. In the course of his conquests, Alexander claimed (for political reasons) descent from Ammon or Amen, the high god of Egypt.
1. "The assassination alluded to took place on the 8th of December, 1820, in the streets of Ravenna, not a hundred paces from the residence of the writer. The circumstances were as described." [*Byron's note.*]

XXXV

I gazed upon him, for I knew him well;
  And though I have seen many corpses, never
Saw one, whom such an accident befell,
  So calm; though pierced through stomach, heart, and liver,
He seemed to sleep,—for you could scarcely tell
  (As he bled inwardly, no hideous river
Of gore divulged the cause) that he was dead:
So as I gazed on him, I thought or said—

XXXVI

"Can this be Death? then what is Life or Death?
  Speak!" but he spoke not: "Wake!" but still he slept:—
"But yesterday and who had mightier breath?
  A thousand warriors by his word were kept
In awe: he said, as the Centurion[2] saith,
  'Go,' and he goeth; 'come,' and forth he stepped.
The trump and bugle till he spake were dumb—
And now nought left him but the muffled drum."

XXXVII

And they who waited once and worshipped—they
  With their rough faces thronged about the bed
To gaze once more on the commanding clay
  Which for the last, though not the first, time bled;
And such an end! that he who many a day
  Had faced Napoleon's foes until they fled,—
The foremost in the charge or in the sally,
Should now be butchered in a civic alley.

XXXVIII

The scars of his old wounds were near his new,
  Those honourable scars which brought him fame;
And horrid was the contrast to the view——
  But let me quit the theme; as such things claim
Perhaps even more attention than is due
  From me: I gazed (as oft I have gazed the same)
To try if I could wrench aught out of Death
Which should confirm, or shake, or make a faith;

XXXIX

But it was all a mystery. Here we are,
  And there we go:—but *where*? five bits of lead,
Or three, or two, or one, send very far!
  And is this blood, then, formed but to be shed?
Can every element our elements mar?
  And Air—Earth—Water—Fire live—and we dead?
We, whose minds comprehend all things? No more;
But let us to the story as before.

XL

The purchaser of Juan and acquaintance

2. In Matthew 8 : 5–9, a Roman centurion humbly asks Christ to cure his sick servant, and describes a centurion's military role to Christ in these words: "And I tell one to go, and he goes, and another to come, and he comes. . . ."

Bore off his bargains to a gilded boat,
Embarked himself and them, and off they went thence
    As fast as oars could pull and water float;
They looked like persons being led to sentence,
    Wondering what next, till the caïque[3] was brought
Up in a little creek below a wall
O'ertopped with cypresses, dark-green and tall.

XLI

Here their conductor tapping at the wicket
    Of a small iron door, 'twas opened, and
He led them onward, first through a low thicket
    Flanked by large groves, which towered on either hand:
They almost lost their way, and had to pick it—
    For night was closing ere they came to land.
The eunuch made a sign to those on board,
Who rowed off, leaving them without a word.

XLII

As they were plodding on their winding way
    Through orange bowers, and jasmine, and so forth:
(Of which I might have a good deal to say,
    There being no such profusion in the North
Of oriental plants, *et cetera*,
    But that of late your scribblers think it worth
Their while to rear whole hotbeds in *their* works,
Because *one* poet travelled 'mongst the Turks:)

XLIII

As they were threading on their way, there came
    Into Don Juan's head a thought, which he
Whispered to his companion:—'twas the same
    Which might have then occurred to you or me.
"Methinks,"—said he,—"it would be no great shame
    If we should strike a stroke to set us free;
Let's knock that old black fellow on the head,
And march away—'twere easier done than said."

XLIV

"Yes," said the other, "and when done, what then?
    How get out? how the devil got we in?
And when we once were fairly out, and when
    From Saint Bartholomew[4] we have saved our skin,
To-morrow'd see us in some other den,
    And worse off than we hitherto have been;
Besides, I'm hungry, and just now would take,
Like Esau,[5] for my birthright a beef-steak.

XLV

"We must be near some place of man's abode;—
    For the old negro's confidence in creeping,

---

3. A light Turkish rowboat, usually ornamented.
4. This early saint was supposed to have been martyred by being flayed to death.

5. In Genesis 25 : 29–34, Esau, firstborn of the patriarch Isaac, sells his birthright to his brother Jacob for a bowl of stew.

With his two captives, by so queer a road,
  Shows that he thinks his friends have not been sleeping;
A single cry would bring them all abroad:
  'Tis better therefore looking before leaping—
And there, you see, this turn has brought us through,
By Jove, a noble palace!—lighted too."

XLVI

It was indeed a wide extensive building
  Which opened on their view, and o'er the front
There seemed to be besprent a deal of gilding
  And various hues, as is the Turkish wont,—
A gaudy taste; for they are little skilled in
  The arts of which these lands were once the font:
Each villa on the Bosphorus looks a screen
New painted, or a pretty opera-scene.

XLVII

And nearer as they came, a genial savour
  Of certain stews, and roast-meats, and pilaus,
Things which in hungry mortals' eyes find favour,
  Made Juan in his harsh intentions pause,
And put himself upon his good behaviour:
  His friend, too, adding a new saving clause,
Said, "In Heaven's name let's get some supper now,
And then I'm with you, if you're for a row."

XLVIII

Some talk of an appeal unto some passion,
  Some to men's feelings, others to their reason;
The last of these was never much the fashion,
  For Reason thinks all reasoning out of season:
Some speakers whine, and others lay the lash on,
  But more or less continue still to tease on,
With arguments according to their "forte:"
But no one ever dreams of being short.—

XLIX

But I digress: of all appeals,—although
  I grant the power of pathos, and of gold,
Of beauty, flattery, threats, a shilling,—no
  Method's more sure at moments to take hold
Of the best feelings of mankind, which grow
  More tender, as we every day behold,
Than that all-softening, overpowering knell,
The Tocsin[6] of the Soul—the dinner-bell.

L

Turkey contains no bells, and yet men dine;
  And Juan and his friend, albeit they heard
No Christian knoll to table, saw no line
  Of lackeys usher to the feast prepared,

6. A heavy bell used to sound an alarm.

Yet smelt roast-meat, beheld a huge fire shine,
    And cooks in motion with their clean arms bared,
And gazed around them to the left and right,
With the prophetic eye of appetite.

LI

And giving up all notions of resistance,
    They followed close behind their sable guide,
Who little thought that his own cracked existence
    Was on the point of being set aside:
He motioned them to stop at some small distance,
    And knocking at the gate, 'twas opened wide,
And a magnificent large hall displayed
The Asian pomp of Ottoman[7] parade.

LII

I won't describe; description is my "forte,"
    But every fool describes in these bright days
His wondrous journey to some foreign court,
    And spawns his quarto, and demands your praise—
Death to his publisher, to him 'tis sport;
    While Nature, tortured twenty thousand ways,
Resigns herself with exemplary patience
To guide-books, rhymes, tours, sketches, illustrations.

LIII

Along this hall, and up and down, some, squatted
    Upon their hams, were occupied at chess;
Others in monosyllable talk chatted,
    And some seemed much in love with their own dress;
And divers smoked superb pipes decorated
    With amber mouths of greater price or less;
And several strutted, others slept, and some
Prepared for supper with a glass of rum.

LIV

As the black eunuch entered with his brace
    Of purchased Infidels, some raised their eyes
A moment, without slackening from their pace;
    But those who sate ne'er stirred in any wise:
One or two stared the captives in the face,
    Just as one views a horse to guess his price;
Some nodded to the negro from their station,
But no one troubled him with conversation.

LV

He leads them through the hall, and, without stopping,
    On through a farther range of goodly rooms,
Splendid, but silent, save in *one*, where dropping
    A marble fountain echoes through the glooms
Of night which robe the chamber, or where popping
    Some female head most curiously presumes
To thrust its black eyes through the door or lattice,

7. Turkish.

As wondering what the *devil* noise that is!

LVI

Some faint lamps gleaming from the lofty walls
  Gave light enough to hint their farther way,
But not enough to show the imperial halls
  In all the flashing of their full array;
Perhaps there's nothing—I'll not say appals,
  But saddens more by night as well as day,
Than an enormous room without a soul
To break the lifeless splendour of the whole.

LVII

Two or three seem so little, *one* seems nothing:
  In deserts, forests, crowds, or by the shore,
There Solitude, we know, has her full growth in
  The spots which were her realms for evermore;
But in a mighty hall or gallery, both in
  More modern buildings and those built of yore,
A kind of Death comes o'er us all alone,
Seeing what's meant for many with but one.

LVIII

A neat, snug study on a winter's night,
  A book, friend, single lady, or a glass
Of claret, sandwich, and an appetite,
  Are things which make an English evening pass—
Though *certes*[8] by no means so grand a sight
  As is a theatre lit up by gas—
I pass my evenings in long galleries solely,
And that's the reason I'm so melancholy.

LIX

Alas! Man makes that great which makes him little—
  I grant you in a church 'tis very well:
What speaks of Heaven should by no means be brittle,
  But strong and lasting, till no tongue can tell
Their names who reared it; but huge houses fit ill,
  And huge tombs, worse, Mankind—since Adam fell:
Methinks the story of the tower of Babel
Might teach them this much better than I'm able.

LX

Babel was Nimrod's[9] hunting-box, and then
  A town of gardens, walls, and wealth amazing,
Where Nabuchadonosor,[1] King of men,
  Reigned, till one summer's day he took to grazing,

---

8. "To be sure."
9. **Legendary** king, described as "a mighty hunter before the Lord," who in Genesis 11 : 1–9 attempted to build the Tower of Babel. Byron's irreverent description suggests that Nimrod built the Tower simply as a "hunting-box," or platform from which to shoot at game.
1. Nebuchadnezzar, king of Babylon (sixth century B.C.) and conqueror of Jerusalem. The Book of Daniel tells how Nebuchadnezzar punished the prophet Daniel for Daniel's refusal to abjure the God of Israel; for this impiety Nebuchadnezzar was driven mad (Daniel 4 : 1–37) and forced to eat grass like the beasts of the field.

And Daniel tamed the lions in their den,
  The people's awe and admiration raising;
'Twas famous, too, for Thisbe and for Pyramus,[2]
And the calumniated queen Semiramis[3]—

LXI

That injured Queen, by chroniclers so coarse,
  Has been accused (I doubt not by conspiracy)
Of an improper friendship for her horse
  (Love, like Religion, sometimes runs to heresy):
This monstrous tale had probably its source
  (For such exaggerations here and there I see)
In writing "Courser" by mistake for "Courier:"
I wish the case could come before a jury here.[4]

LXII

But to resume,—should there be (what may not
  Be in these days?) some infidels, who don't,
Because they can't find out the very spot
  Of that same Babel, or because they won't
(Though Claudius Rich,[5] Esquire, some bricks has got,
  And written lately two memoirs upon 't),
Believe the Jews, those unbelievers, who
Must be believed, though they believe not you:

LXIII

Yet let them think that Horace[6] has expressed
  Shortly and sweetly the masonic folly
Of those, forgetting the great place of rest,
  Who give themselves to Architecture wholly;
We know where things and men must end at best:
  A moral (like all morals) melancholy,
And "Et sepulchri immemor struis domos"[7]
Shows that we build when we should but entomb us.

LXIV

At last they reached a quarter most retired,
  Where Echo woke as if from a long slumber;
Though full of all things which could be desired,
  One wondered what to do with such a number
Of articles which nobody required;
  Here Wealth had done its utmost to encumber
With furniture an exquisite apartment,
Which puzzled Nature much to know what Art meant.

LXV

It seemed, however, but to open on

---

2. Two star-crossed lovers, the Romeo and Juliet of Babylon.
3. The legendary queen-founder of Babylon; "calumniated" for reasons discussed in the next stanza.
4. Unlike the legendary Semiramis, Queen Caroline, the scandal-prone wife of George IV, was in 1820 brought to public trial for adultery with her chamberlain.

5. Claudius James Rich, Esq., published two volumes attempting to establish the location of the ruins of Babylon, 1815 and 1818.
6. Quintus Horatius Flaccus (65–8 B.C.), the Roman lyric poet.
7. Loosely, "While we yet live we should not worry about our funeral monuments."

A range or suite of further chambers, which
Might lead to Heaven knows where; but in this one
   The moveables were prodigally rich:
Sofas 'twas half a sin to sit upon,
   So costly were they; carpets every stitch
Of workmanship so rare, they made you wish
You could glide o'er them like a golden fish.

LXVI

The black, however, without hardly deigning
   A glance at that which wrapped the slaves in wonder,
Trampled what they scarce trod for fear of staining,
   As if the milky way their feet was under
With all its stars; and with a stretch attaining
   A certain press or cupboard niched in yonder,
In that remote recess which you may see—
Or if you don't the fault is not in me,—

LXVII

I wish to be perspicuous—and the black,
   I say, unlocking the recess, pulled forth
A quantity of clothes fit for the back
   Of any Mussulman,[8] whate'er his worth;
And of variety there was no lack—
   And yet, though I have said there was no dearth,—
He chose himself to point out what he thought
Most proper for the Christians he had bought.

LXVIII

The suit he thought most suitable to each
   Was, for the elder and the stouter, first
A Candiote[9] cloak, which to the knee might reach,
   And trousers not so tight that they would burst,
But such as fit an Asiatic breech;
   A shawl, whose folds in Cashmire had been nursed,
Slippers of saffron, dagger rich and handy;
In short, all things which form a Turkish Dandy.

LXIX

While he was dressing, Baba, their black friend,
   Hinted the vast advantages which they
Might probably attain both in the end,
   If they would but pursue the proper way
Which Fortune plainly seemed to recommend;
   And then he added, that he needs must say,
"'Twould greatly tend to better their condition,
If they would condescend to circumcision.[1]

LXX

"For his own part, he really should rejoice
   To see them true believers, but no less

---

8. Moslem.
9. Cretan, native to the island of Crete (Candia), southeast of Greece, in the Mediterranean.
1. A necessary part of the ritual for becoming a Moslem.

Would leave his proposition to their choice."
　The other, thanking him for this excess
Of goodness, in thus leaving them a voice
　In such a trifle, scarcely could express
"Sufficiently" (he said) "his approbation
Of all the customs of this polished nation.

LXXI

"For his own share—he saw but small objection
　To so respectable an ancient rite;
And, after swallowing down a slight refection,
　For which he owned a present appetite,
He doubted not a few hours of reflection
　Would reconcile him to the business quite."
"Will it?" said Juan, sharply: "Strike me dead,
But they as soon shall circumcise my head!

LXXII

"Cut off a thousand heads, before——"—"Now, pray,"
　Replied the other, "do not interrupt:
You put me out in what I had to say.
　Sir!—as I said, as soon as I have supped,
I shall perpend if your proposal may
　Be such as I can properly accept;
Provided always your great goodness still
Remits the matter to our own free-will."

LXXIII

Baba eyed Juan, and said, "Be so good
　As dress yourself—" and pointed out a suit
In which a Princess with great pleasure would
　Array her limbs; but Juan standing mute,
As not being in a masquerading mood,
　Gave it a slight kick with his Christian foot;
And when the old negro told him to "Get ready,"
Replied, "Old gentleman, I'm not a lady."

LXXIV

"What you may be, I neither know nor care,"
　Said Baba; "but pray do as I desire:
I have no more time nor many words to spare."
　"At least," said Juan, "sure I may inquire
The cause of this odd travesty?"—"Forbear,"
　Said Baba, "to be curious; 'twill transpire,
No doubt, in proper place, and time, and season:
I have no authority to tell the reason."

LXXV

"Then if I do," said Juan, "I'll be——"—"Hold!"
　Rejoined the negro, "pray be not provoking;
This spirit's well, but it may wax too bold,
　And you will find us not too fond of joking."
"What, sir!" said Juan, "shall it e'er be told
　That I unsexed my dress?" But Baba, stroking

The things down, said, "Incense me, and I call
Those who will leave you of no sex at all.

LXXVI

"I offer you a handsome suit of clothes:
 A woman's, true; but then there is a cause
Why you should wear them."—"What, though my soul loathes
 The effeminate garb?"—thus, after a short pause,
Sighed Juan, muttering also some slight oaths,
 "What the devil shall I do with all this gauze?"
Thus he profanely termed the finest lace
Which e'er set off a marriage-morning face.

LXXVII

And then he swore; and, sighing, on he slipped
 A pair of trousers of flesh-coloured silk;
Next with a virgin zone² he was equipped,
 Which girt a slight chemise as white as milk;
But tugging on his petticoat, he tripped,
 Which—as we say—or as the Scotch say, *whilk,*
(The rhyme obliges me to this; sometimes
Monarchs are less imperative than rhymes)—

LXXVIII

Whilk, which (or what you please), was owing to
 His garment's novelty, and his being awkward:
And yet at last he managed to get through
 His toilet, though no doubt a little backward:
The negro Baba helped a little too,
 When some untoward part of raiment stuck hard;
And, wrestling both his arms into a gown,
He paused, and took a survey up and down.

LXXIX

One difficulty still remained—his hair
 Was hardly long enough; but Baba found
So many false long tresses all to spare,
 That soon his head was most completely crowned,
After the manner then in fashion there;
 And this addition with such gems was bound
As suited the *ensemble* of his toilet,
While Baba made him comb his head and oil it.

LXXX

And now being femininely all arrayed,
 With some small aid from scissors, paint, and tweezers,
He looked in almost all respects a maid,
 And Baba smilingly exclaimed, "You see, sirs,
A perfect transformation here displayed;
 And now, then, you must come along with me, sirs.
That is—the Lady:" clapping his hands twice,
Four blacks were at his elbow in a trice.

2. **Belt.**

LXXXI

"You, sir," said Baba, nodding to the one,
  "Will please to accompany those gentlemen
To supper; but you, worthy Christian nun,
  Will follow me: no trifling, sir; for when
I say a thing, it must at once be done.
  What fear you? think you this a lion's den?
Why, 'tis a palace; where the truly wise
Anticipate the Prophet's paradise.

LXXXII

"You fool! I tell you no one means you harm."
  "So much the better," Juan said, "for them;
Else they shall feel the weight of this my arm,
  Which is not quite so light as you may deem.
I yield thus far; but soon will break the charm,
  If any take me for that which I seem:
So that I trust for every body's sake,
That this disguise may lead to no mistake."

LXXXIII

"Blockhead! come on, and see," quoth Baba; while
  Don Juan, turning to his comrade, who
Though somewhat grieved, could scarce forbear a smile
  Upon the metamorphosis in view,—
  "Farewell!" they mutually exclaimed: "this soil
  Seems fertile in adventures strange and new;
One's turned half Mussulman, and one a maid,
By this old black enchanter's unsought aid."

LXXXIV

"Farewell!" said Juan: "should we meet no more,
  I wish you a good appetite."—"Farewell!"
Replied the other; "though it grieves me sore:
  When we next meet, we'll have a tale to tell:
We needs must follow when Fate puts from shore.
  Keep your good name; though Eve herself once fell."
"Nay," quoth the maid, "the Sultan's self shan't carry me,
Unless his Highness promises to marry me."

LXXXV

And thus they parted, each by separate doors;
  Baba led Juan onward, room by room,
Through glittering galleries, and o'er marble floors,
  Till a gigantic portal through the gloom,
Haughty and huge, along the distance lowers;
  And wafted far arose a rich perfume:
It seemed as though they came upon a shrine,
For all was vast, still, fragrant, and divine.

LXXXVI

The giant door was broad, and bright, and high,
  Of gilded bronze, and carved in curious guise;
Warriors thereon were battling furiously;
  Here stalks the victor, there the vanquished lies;

There captives led in triumph droop the eye,
   And in perspective many a squadron flies:
It seems the work of times before the line
Of Rome transplanted fell with Constantine.[3]

LXXXVII

This massy portal stood at the wide close
   Of a huge hall, and on its either side
Two little dwarfs, the least you could suppose,
   Were sate, like ugly imps, as if allied
In mockery to the enormous gate which rose
   O'er them in almost pyramidic pride:
The gate so splendid was in all its *features*,[4]
You never thought about those little creatures,

LXXXVIII

Until you nearly trod on them, and then
   You started back in horror to survey
The wondrous hideousness of those small men,
   Whose colour was not black, nor white, nor grey,
But an extraneous mixture, which no pen
   Can trace, although perhaps the pencil may;
They were mis-shapen pigmies, deaf and dumb—
Monsters, who cost a no less monstrous sum.

LXXXIX

Their duty was—for they were strong, and though
   They looked so little, did strong things at times—
To ope this door, which they could really do,
   The hinges being as smooth as Rogers' rhymes;
And now and then, with tough strings of the bow,
   As is the custom of those Eastern climes,
To give some rebel Pacha a cravat[5]—
For mutes are generally used for that.

XC

They spoke by signs—that is, not spoke at all;
   And looking like two Incubi,[6] they glared
As Baba with his fingers made them fall
   To heaving back the portal folds: it scared
Juan a moment, as this pair so small,
   With shinking serpent optics on him stared;
It was as if their little looks could poison
Or fascinate whome'er they fixed their eyes on.

XCI

Before they entered, Baba paused to hint
   To Juan some slight lessons as his guide:

3. The last great Roman emperor, A.D. 288–337. In Constantine's time the capital of the empire was no longer Rome, but had been "transplanted" to Constantinople ("the City of Constantine") where the action of this Canto takes place.
4. One of Castelreagh's most notorious mixed metaphors was the phrase, "the feature upon which this question hinges." Byron's mention of the "features" of a door is an allusion to his adversary's blunder.
5. Necktie; i.e., the dwarves are sometimes employed to strangle rivals of the Sultan.
6. Male devils.

"If you could just contrive," he said, "to stint
  That somewhat manly majesty of stride,
'Twould be as well, and—(though there's not much in 't)
  To swing a little less from side to side,
Which has at times an aspect of the oddest;—
And also could you look a little modest,

XCII

"'Twould be convenient; for these mutes have eyes
  Like needles, which may pierce those petticoats;
And if they should discover your disguise,
  Your know how near us the deep Bosphorus floats;
And you and I may chance, ere morning rise,
  To find our way to Marmora[7] without boats,
Stitched up in sacks—a mode of navigation
A good deal practised here upon occasion."

XCIII

With this encouragement he led the way
  Into a room still nobler than the last;
A rich confusion formed a disarray
  In such sort, that the eye along it cast
Could hardly carry anything away,
  Object on object flashed so bright and fast;
A dazzling mass of gems, and gold, and glitter,
Magnificently mingled in a litter.

XCIV

Wealth had done wonders—taste not much; such things
  Occur in Orient palaces, and even
In the more chastened domes of Western kings
  (Of which I have also seen some six or seven),
Where I can't say or gold or diamond flings
  Great lustre, there is much to be forgiven;
Groups of bad statues, tables, chairs, and pictures,
On which I cannot pause to make my strictures.

XCV

In this imperial hall, at distance lay
  Under a canopy, and there reclined
Quite in a confidential queenly way,
  A lady; Baba stopped, and kneeling signed
To Juan, who though not much used to pray,
  Knelt down by instinct, wondering in his mind
What all this meant; while Baba bowed and bended
His head, until the ceremony ended.

XCVI

The lady rising up with such an air
  As Venus rose with from the wave, on them
Bent like an antelope a Paphian[8] pair

7. Or Marmara, the sea connected by
the Bosporus with the Black Sea.
8. The island of Paphos was sacred to
Aphrodite, goddess of love. Hence,

"Paphian" came to refer to illicit love
and prostitution. See *Childe Harold* I,
VII, 7.

Of eyes, which put out each surrounding gem;
And raising up an arm as moonlight fair,
   She signed to Baba, who first kissed the hem
Of her deep purple robe, and, speaking low,
Pointed to Juan who remained below.

XCVII

Her presence was as lofty as her state;
   Her beauty of that overpowering kind,
Whose force Description only would abate:
   I'd rather leave it much to your own mind,
Than lessen it by what I could relate
   Of forms and features; it would strike you blind
Could I do justice to the full detail;
So, luckily for both, my phrases fail.

XCVIII

Thus much however I may add,—her years
   Were ripe, they might make six-and-twenty springs,
But there are forms which Time to touch forbears
   And turns aside his scythe to vulgar things:
Such as was Mary's, Queen of Scots;[9] true—tears
   And Love destroy; and sapping Sorrow wrings
Charms from the charmer, yet some never grow
Ugly; for instance—Ninon de l'Enclos.[1]

XCIX

She spake some words to her attendants, who
   Composed a choir of girls, ten or a dozen,
And were all clad alike; like Juan, too,
   Who wore their uniform, by Baba chosen:
They formed a very nymph-like looking crew,
   Which might have called Diana's[2] chorus "cousin,"
As far as outward show may correspond—
I won't be bail for anything beyond.

C

They bowed obeisance and withdrew, retiring,
   But not by the same door through which came in
Baba and Juan, which last stood admiring,
   At some small distance, all he saw within
This strange saloon, much fitted for inspiring
   Marvel and praise; for both or none things win;
And I must say, I ne'er could see the very
Great happiness of the "Nil admirari."[3]

CI

"Not to admire is all the art I know
   (Plain truth, dear Murray, needs few flowers of speech)—
To make men happy, or to keep them so"

9. Mary Stuart (1542–87), queen of Scotland. She was imprisoned and later beheaded by her half sister and rival for power, Queen Elizabeth I.
1. Ninon (1620–1705) was the most celebrated courtesan of the seventeenth century.
2. Roman goddess of the hunt and patroness of young virgins.
3. "Show surprise at nothing."

(So take it in the very words of Creech)[4]—
Thus Horace wrote we all know long ago;
　And thus Pope quotes the precept to re-teach
From his translation; but had *none admired*,
Would Pope have sung, or Horace been inspired?

CII

Baba, when all the damsels were withdrawn,
　Motioned to Juan to approach, and then
A second time desired him to kneel down,
　And kiss the lady's foot; which maxim when
He heard repeated, Juan with a frown
　Drew himself up to his full height again,
And said, "It grieved him, but he could not stoop
To any shoe, unless it shod the Pope."

CIII

Baba, indignant at this ill-timed pride,
　Made fierce remonstrances, and then a threat
He muttered (but the last was given aside)
　About a bow-string—quite in vain; not yet
Would Juan bend, though 'twere to Mahomet's bride:
　There's nothing in the world like *etiquette*
In kingly chambers or imperial halls,
As also at the Race and County Balls.

CIV

He stood like Atlas, with a world of words
　About his ears, and nathless would not bend;
The blood of all his line's Castilian lords
　Boiled in his veins, and, rather than descend
To stain his pedigree, a thousand swords
　A thousand times of him had made an end;
At length perceiving the *"foot"* could not stand,
Baba proposed that he should kiss the hand.

CV

Here was an honourable compromise,
　A half-way house of diplomatic rest,

---

4. The first four lines of this stanza—indeed, the entire stanza—represent a complicated joke and a two- (or three-) part quotation. Horace had uttered the formula *Nil admirari* in the Sixth Epistle of his first Book of Epistles. Thomas Creech (1659–1701) in his 1684 *Translation of Horace* rendered the relevant lines as "Not to admire, as most are wont to do, / Is the only method that I know, / To make Men happy and to keep 'em so." Alexander Pope (1688–1744) in his 1738 translation of the same Horatian poem began by quoting Creech: " 'Not to Admire, is all the Art I know, / To make men happy, and to keep them so.' / (Plain Truth, dear MURRAY, needs no flow'rs of speech, / So take it in the very words of Creech.)"

The "Murray" Pope addresses is Lord Mansfield, to whom his translation is dedicated. And Byron, in this stanza, both quotes and rearranges Pope's quotation and rearrangement of Creech's translation of Horace's original lines—and incidentally translates Pope's "Murray" into his own "Murray," his publisher John Murray—precisely to demonstrate that the sentiment *Nil admirari* is all wrong anyway; for if no one "admired," or showed wonder at the state of the universe, neither Horace nor Creech nor Pope would have written poetry in the first place.

Where they might meet in much more peaceful guise;
    And Juan now his willingness expressed
To use all fit and proper courtesies,
    Adding, that this was commonest and best,
For through the South, the custom still commands
The gentleman to kiss the lady's hands.

CVI

And he advanced, though with but a bad grace,
    Though on more *thorough-bred* or fairer fingers
No lips e'er left their transitory trace:
    On such as these the lip too fondly lingers,
And for one kiss would fain imprint a brace,
    As you will see, if she you love shall bring hers
In contact; and sometimes even a fair stranger's
An almost twelvemonth's constancy endangers.

CVII

The lady eyed him o'er and o'er, and bade
    Baba retire, which he obeyed in style,
As if well used to the retreating trade;
    And taking hints in good part all the while,
He whispered Juan not to be afraid,
    And looking on him with a sort of smile,
Took leave, with such a face of satisfaction,
As good men wear who have done a virtuous action.

CVIII

When he was gone, there was a sudden change:
    I know not what might be the lady's thought,
But o'er her bright brow flashed a tumult strange,
    And into her clear cheek the blood was brought,
Blood-red as sunset summer clouds which range
    The verge of Heaven; and in her large eyes wrought,
A mixture of sensations might be scanned,
Of half voluptuousness and half command.

CIX

Her form had all the softness of her sex,
    Her features all the sweetness of the Devil,
When he put on the Cherub to perplex
    Eve, and paved (God knows how) the road to evil;
The Sun himself was scarce more free from specks
    Than she from aught at which the eye could cavil;
Yet, somehow, there was something somewhere wanting,
As if she rather *ordered* than was *granting.*—

CX

Something imperial, or imperious, threw
    A chain o'er all she did; that is, a chain
Was thrown as 'twere about the neck of you,—
    And Rapture's self will seem almost a pain
With aught which looks like despotism in view;
    Our souls at least are free, and 'tis in vain

We would against them make the flesh obey—
    The spirit in the end will have its way.

CXI

Her very smile was haughty, though so sweet;
    Her very nod was not an inclination;
There was a self-will even in her small feet,
    As though they were quite conscious of her station—
They trod as upon necks; and to complete
    Her state (it is the custom of her nation),
A poniard decked her girdle, as the sign
She was a Sultan's bride (thank Heaven, not mine!).

CXII

"To hear and to obey" had been from birth
    The law of all around her; to fulfil
All phantasies which yielded joy or mirth,
    Had been her slaves' chief pleasure, as her will;
Her blood was high, her beauty scarce of earth:
    Judge, then, if her caprices e'er stood still;
Had she but been a Christian, I've a notion
We should have found out the "perpetual motion."

CXIII

Whate'er she saw and coveted was brought;
    Whate'er she did *not* see, if she supposed
It might be seen, with diligence was sought,
    And when 'twas found straightway the bargain closed:
There was no end unto the things she bought,
    Nor to the trouble which her fancies caused;
Yet even her tyranny had such a grace,
The women pardoned all except her face.

CXIV

Juan, the latest of her whims, had caught
    Her eye in passing on his way to sale;
She ordered him directly to be bought,
    And Baba, who had ne'er been known to fail
In any kind of mischief to be wrought,
    At all such auctions knew how to prevail:
She had no prudence, but he had—and this
Explains the garb which Juan took amiss.

CXV

His youth and features favoured the disguise,
    And should you ask how she, a Sultan's bride,
Could risk or compass such strange phantasies,
    This I must leave sultanas to decide:
Emperors are only husbands in wives' eyes,
    And kings and consorts oft are mystified,
As we may ascertain with due precision,
Some by experience, others by tradition.

CXVI

But to the main point, where we have been tending:—

She now conceived all difficulties past,
And deemed herself extremely condescending
    When, being made her property at last,
Without more preface, in her blue eyes blending
    Passion and power, a glance on him she cast,
And merely saying, "Christian, canst thou love?"
Conceived that phrase was quite enough to move.

CXVII

And so it was, in proper time and place;
    But Juan, who had still his mind o'erflowing
With Haidée's isle and soft Ionian face,
    Felt the warm blood, which in his face was glowing
Rush back upon his heart, which filled apace,
    And left his cheeks as pale as snowdrops blowing:
These words went through his soul like Arab spears,
So that he spoke not, but burst into tears.

CXVIII

She was a good deal shocked; not shocked at tears,
    For women shed and use them at their liking;
But there is something when man's eye appears
    Wet, still more disagreeable and striking;
A woman's tear-drop melts, a man's half sears,
    Like molten lead, as if you thrust a pike in
His heart to force it out, for (to be shorter)
To them 'tis a relief, to us a torture.

CXIX

And she would have consoled, but knew not how:
    Having no equals, nothing which had e'er
Infected her with sympathy till now,
    And never having dreamt what 'twas to bear
Aught of a serious, sorrowing kind, although
    There might arise some pouting petty care
To cross her brow, she wondered how so near
Her eyes another's eye could shed a tear.

CXX

But Nature teaches more than power can spoil,
    And, when a *strong* although a strange sensation
Moves—female hearts are such a genial soil
    For kinder feelings, whatso'er their nation,
They naturally pour the "wine and oil,"
    Samaritans in every situation;
And thus Gulbeyaz, though she knew not why,
Felt an odd glistening moisture in her eye.

CXXI

But tears must stop like all things else; and soon
    Juan, who for an instant had been moved
To such a sorrow by the intrusive tone
    Of one who dared to ask if "he *had* loved,"
Called back the Stoic to his eyes, which shone

Bright with the very weakness he reproved;
And although sensitive to beauty, he
Felt most indignant still at not being free.

CXXII

Gulbeyaz, for the first time in her days,
　　Was much embarrassed, never having met
In all her life with aught save prayers and praise;
　　And as she also risked her life to get
Him whom she meant to tutor in love's ways
　　Into a comfortable tête-à-tête,
To lose the hour would make her quite a martyr,
And they had wasted now almost a quarter.

CXXIII

I also would suggest the fitting time
　　To gentlemen in any such like case,
That is to say in a meridian clime—
　　With us there is more law given to the chase,
But here a small delay forms a great crime:
　　So recollect that the extremest grace
Is just two minutes for your declaration—
A moment more would hurt your reputation.

CXXIV

Juan's was good; and might have been still better,
　　But he had got Haidée into his head:
However strange, he could not yet forget her,
　　Which made him seem exceedingly ill-bred.
Gulbeyaz, who looked on him as her debtor
　　For having had him to her palace led,
Began to blush up to the eyes, and then
Grow deadly pale, and then blush back again.

CXXV

At length, in an imperial way, she laid
　　Her hand on his, and bending on him eyes
Which needed not an empire to persuade,
　　Looked into his for love, where none replies:
Her brow grew black, but she would not upbraid,
　　That being the last thing a proud woman tries;
She rose, and pausing one chaste moment threw
Herself upon his breast, and there she grew.

CXXVI

This was an awkward test, as Juan found,
　　But he was steeled by Sorrow, Wrath, and Pride:
With gentle force her white arms he unwound,
　　And seated her all drooping by his side,
Then rising haughtily he glanced around,
　　And looking coldly in her face he cried,
"The prisoned eagle will not pair, nor I
Serve a Sultana's sensual phantasy.

CXXVII

"Thou ask'st, if I can love? be this the proof

How much I *have* loved—that I love not *thee!*
In this vile garb, the distaff, web, and woof,[5]
    Were fitter for me: Love is for the free!
I am not dazzled by this splendid roof:
    Whate'er thy power, and great it seems to be,
Heads bow, knees bend, eyes watch around a throne,
And hands obey—our hearts are still our own."

                    CXXVIII
This was a truth to us extremely trite;
    Not so to her, who ne'er had heard such things:
She deemed her least command must yield delight,
    Earth being only made for Queens and Kings.
If hearts lay on the left side or the right
    She hardly knew, to such perfection brings
Legitimacy its born votaries, when
Aware of their due royal rights o'er men.

                    CXXIX
Besides, as has been said, she was so fair
    As even in a much humbler lot had made
A kingdom or confusion anywhere,
    And also, as may be presumed, she laid
Some stress on charms, which seldom are, if e'er,
    By their possessors thrown into the shade:
She thought hers gave a double "right divine;"
And half of that opinion's also mine.

                    CXXX
Remember, or (if you can not) imagine,
    Ye! who have kept your chastity when young,
While some more desperate dowager has been waging
    Love with you, and been in the dog-days stung
By your refusal, recollect her raging!
    Or recollect all that was said or sung
On such a subject; then suppose the face
Of a young downright beauty in this case!

                    CXXXI
Suppose,—but you already have supposed,
    The spouse of Potiphar, the Lady Booby,
Phædra,[6] and all which story has disclosed
    Of good examples; pity that so few by
Poets and private tutors are exposed,
    To educate—ye youth of Europe—you by!
But when you have supposed the few we know,
You can't suppose Gulbeyaz' angry brow.

                    CXXXII
A tigress robbed of young, a lioness,

---

5. The "distaff" is a tool for spinning thread. "Web" (or "warp") and "woof" are the vertical and lateral patterns of a woven fabric. Juan is saying that, in his nostalgia for Haidée, he is fitter for women's work than for making love to Gulbeyaz.

6. For Potiphar's wife, see *Don Juan* I, CLXXXVI, 7. Lady Booby unsuccessfully attempts to seduce the hero of Fielding's *Joseph Andrews* (1742). Phaedra, wife of Theseus, fell tragically in love with her stepson Hippolytus.

Or any interesting beast of prey,
Are similes at hand for the distress
　　Of ladies who can *not* have their own way;
But though my turn will not be served with less,
　　These don't express one half what I should say:
For what is stealing young ones, few or many,
To cutting short their hope of having *any?*

CXXXIII

The love of offspring's Nature's general law,
　　From tigresses and cubs to ducks and ducklings;
There's nothing whets the beak, or arms the claw
　　Like an invasion of their babes and sucklings;
And all who have seen a human nursery, saw
　　How mothers love their children's squalls and chucklings:
This strong extreme effect (to tire no longer
Your patience) shows the cause must still be stronger.

CXXXIV

If I said fire flashed from Gulbeyaz' eyes,
　　'Twere nothing—for her eyes flashed always fire;
Or said her cheeks assumed the deepest dyes,
　　I should but bring disgrace upon the dyer,
So supernatural was her passion's rise;
　　For ne'er till now she knew a checked desire:
Even ye who know what a checked woman is
(Enough, God knows!) would much fall short of this.

CXXXV

Her rage was but a minute's, and 'twas well—
　　A moment's more had slain her; but the while
It lasted 'twas like a short glimpse of Hell:
　　Nought's more sublime than energetic bile,
Though horrible to see, yet grand to tell,
　　Like Ocean warring 'gainst a rocky isle;
And the deep passions flashing through her form
Made her a beautiful embodied storm.

CXXXVI

A vulgar tempest 'twere to a typhoon
　　To match a common fury with her rage,
And yet she did not want to reach the moon,
　　Like moderate Hotspur[7] on the immortal page;
Her anger pitched into a lower tune,
　　Perhaps the fault of her soft sex and age—
Her wish was but to "kill, kill, kill," like Lear's,[8]
And then her thirst of blood was quenched in tears.

CXXXVII

A storm it raged, and like the storm it passed,
　　Passed without words—in fact she could not speak;
And then her sex's shame broke in at last,

---

7. Henry Percy, the irascible claimant to
the English throne in I *Henry IV*.
　　8. See *King Lear*, IV. vi. 185–86.

A sentiment till then in her but weak,
But now it flowed in natural and fast,
    As water through an unexpected leak;
For she felt humbled—and humiliation
Is sometimes good for people in her station.

CXXXVIII

It teaches them that they are flesh and blood,
    It also gently hints to them that others,
Although of clay, are yet not quite of mud;
    That urns and pipkins are but fragile brothers,
And works of the same pottery, bad or good,
    Though not all born of the same sires and mothers;
It teaches—Heaven knows only what it teaches,
But sometimes it may mend, and often reaches.

CXXXIX

Her first thought was to cut off Juan's head;
    Her second, to cut only his—acquaintance;
Her third, to ask him where he had been bred;
    Her fourth, to rally him into repentance;
Her fifth, to call her maids and go to bed;
    Her sixth, to stab herself; her seventh, to sentence
The lash to Baba:—but her grand resource
Was to sit down again, and cry—of course.

CXL

She thought to stab herself, but then she had
    The dagger close at hand, which made it awkward;
For Eastern stays are little made to pad,
    So that a poniard pierces if 'tis struck hard:
She thought of killing Juan—but, poor lad!
    Though he deserved it well for being so backward,
The cutting off his head was not the art
Most likely to attain her aim—his heart.

CXLI

Juan was moved: he had made up his mind
    To be impaled, or quartered as a dish
For dogs, or to be slain with pangs refined,
    Or thrown to lions, or made baits for fish,
And thus heroically stood resigned,
    Rather than sin—except to his own wish:
But all his great preparatives for dying
Dissolved like snow before a woman crying.

CXLII

As through his palms Bob Acres'[9] valour oozed,
    So Juan's virtue ebbed, I know not how;
And first he wondered why he had refused;
    And then, if matters could be made up now;
And next his savage virtue he accused,
    Just as a friar may accuse his vow,

---

9. Character in Sheridan's *The Rivals*, whose "courage" is his perspiration.

Or as a dame repents her of her oath,
Which mostly ends in some small breach of both.

CXLIII

So he began to stammer some excuses;
    But words are not enough in such a matter,
Although you borrowed all that e'er the Muses
    Have sung, or even a Dandy's dandiest chatter,
Or all the figures Castlereagh abuses;
    Just as a languid smile began to flatter
His peace was making, but, before he ventured
Further, old Baba rather briskly entered.

CXLIV

"Bride of the Sun! and Sister of the Moon!"
    ('Twas thus he spake,) "and Empress of the Earth!
Whose frown would put the spheres all out of tune,
    Whose smile makes all the planets dance with mirth,
Your slave brings tidings—he hopes not too soon—
    Which your sublime attention may be worth:
The Sun himself has sent me like a ray,
To hint that he is coming up this way."

CXLV

"Is it," exclaimed Gulbeyaz, "as you say?
    I wish to heaven he would not shine till morning!
But bid my women form the milky way.
    Hence, my old comet! give the stars due warning—
And, Christian! mingle with them as you may,
    And as you'd have me pardon your past scorning——"
Here they were interrupted by a humming
Sound, and then by a cry, "The Sultan's coming!"

CXLVI

First came her damsels, a decorous file,
    And then his Highness' eunuchs, black and white;
The train might reach a quarter of a mile:
    His Majesty was always so polite
As to announce his visits a long while
    Before he came, especially at night;
For being the last wife of the Emperor,
She was of course the favourite of the four.

CXLVII

His Highness was a man of solemn port,
    Shawled to the nose, and bearded to the eyes,
Snatched from a prison to preside at court,
    His lately bowstrung brother caused his rise;
He was as good a sovereign of the sort
    As any mentioned in the histories
Of Cantemir, or Knölles, where few shine[1]
Save Solyman,[2] the glory of their line.

---

1. Cantemir and Knölles were eighteenth century historians of the Turkish Empire.

2. Suleiman the Magnificent (A.D. 1520–66), most renowned of all the Sultans of Turkey.

CXLVIII

He went to mosque in state, and said his prayers
    With more than "Oriental scrupulosity;"
He left to his vizier all state affairs,
    And showed but little royal curiosity:
I know not if he had domestic cares—
    No process proved connubial animosity;
Four wives and twice five hundred maids, unseen,
Were ruled as calmly as a Christian queen.

CXLIX

If now and then there happened a slight slip,
    Little was heard of criminal or crime;
The story scarcely passed a single lip—
    The sack and sea had settled all in time,
From which the secret nobody could rip:
    The public knew no more than does this rhyme;
No scandals made the daily press a curse—
Morals were better, and the fish no worse.

CL

He saw with his own eyes the moon was round,
    Was also certain that the earth was square,
Because he had journeyed fifty miles, and found
    No sign that it was circular anywhere;
His empire also was without a bound:
    'Tis true, a little troubled here and there,
By rebel pachas, and encroaching giaours,
But then they never came to "the Seven Towers;"

CLI

Except in shape of envoys, who were sent
    To lodge there when a war broke out, according
To the true law of nations, which ne'er meant
    Those scoundrels, who have never had a sword in
Their dirty diplomatic hands, to vent
    Their spleen in making strife, and safely wording
Their lies, yclept[3] despatches, without risk or
The singeing of a single inky whisker.

CLII

He had fifty daughters and four dozen sons,
    Of whom all such as came of age were stowed,
The former in a palace, where like nuns
    They lived till some Bashaw[4] was sent abroad,
When she, whose turn it was, was wed at once,
    Sometimes at six years old—though this seems odd,
'Tis true; the reason is, that the Bashaw
Must make a present to his sire-in-law.

CLIII

His sons were kept in prison, till they grew

---

3. Called.
4. Pasha, an honorary title given a high-ranking Turk.

Of years to fill a bowstring or the throne,
One or the other, but which of the two
   Could yet be known unto the fates alone;
Meantime the education they went through
   Was princely, as the proofs have always shown;
So that the heir apparent still was found
No less deserving to be hanged than crowned.

CLIV

His Majesty saluted his fourth spouse
   With all the ceremonies of his rank,
Who cleared her sparkling eyes and smoothed her brows,
   As suits a matron who has played a prank;
These must seem doubly mindful of their vows,
   To save the credit of their breaking bank:
To no men are such cordial greetings given
As those whose wives have made them fit for Heaven.

CLV

His Highness cast around his great black eyes,
   And looking, as he always looked, perceived
Juan amongst the damsels in disguise,
   At which he seemed no whit surprised nor grieved,
But just remarked with air sedate and wise,
   While still a fluttering sigh Gulbeyaz heaved,
"I see you've bought another girl; 'tis pity
That a mere Christian should be half so pretty."

CLVI

This compliment, which drew all eyes upon
   The new-bought virgin, made her blush and shake.
Her comrades, also, thought themselves undone:
   Oh! Mahomet! that his Majesty should take
Such notice of a giaour, while scarce to one
   Of them his lips imperial ever spake!
There was a general whisper, toss, and wriggle,
But etiquette forbade them all to giggle.

CLVII

The Turks do well to shut—at least, sometimes—
   The women up—because, in sad reality,
Their chastity in these unhappy climes
   Is not a thing of that astringent quality
Which in the North prevents precocious crimes,
   And makes our snow less pure than our morality;
The Sun, which yearly melts the polar ice,
Has quite the contrary effect—on vice.

CLVIII

Thus in the East they are extremely strict,
   And wedlock and a padlock mean the same:
Excepting only when the former's picked
   It ne'er can be replaced in proper frame;
Spoilt, as a pipe of claret is when pricked:

But then their own polygamy's to blame;
Why don't they knead two virtuous souls for life
Into that moral centaur, man and wife?

CLIX

Thus far our chronicle; and now we pause,
    Though not for want of matter; but 'tis time,
According to the ancient epic laws,
    To slacken sail, and anchor with our rhyme.
Let this fifth canto meet with due applause,
    The sixth shall have a touch of the sublime;
Meanwhile, as Homer sometimes sleeps,[5] perhaps
You'll pardon to my muse a few short naps.

CANTO THE NINTH

Juan escapes from the Sultan and Gulbeyaz, and makes his way to the siege
of Ismail, a city of the Turks which the Russian army attacked in 1790.
Enlisting under Marshall Suvarov, the Russian commander, Juan distinguishes himself in the battle, and is sent back to St. Petersburg to give
news of the Russian victory to the czarina, Catherine the Great. Catherine,
who ruled Russia from 1762 to 1796, was one of the most extraordinary
figures of the eighteenth century: mannish, exuberant, sensual, and ferocious, she was a female version of what most fascinated and repelled Byron
in the figure of Napoleon, a political tyrant with heroic force of will. As the
canto opens, Juan is on his way to deliver the dispatch to the czarina.

I

OH, Wellington![1] (or "Villainton"—for Fame
    Sounds the heroic syllables both ways;
France could not even conquer your great name,
    But punned it down to this facetious phrase—
Beating or beaten she will laugh the same,)
    You have obtained great pensions and much praise:
Glory like yours should any dare gainsay,
Humanity would rise, and thunder "Nay!"[2]

II

I don't think that you used Kinnaird[3] quite well
    In Marinèt's affair—in fact, 'twas shabby,

5. Pope in his *Essay on Criticism* (1711) had discussed the occasional lapses or dullnesses of even great poetry by writing: "Those oft are *Stratagems* which *Errors* seem, / Nor is it *Homer Nods*, but *We* that *Dream*" (179–80).
1. Arthur Wellesley, Duke of Wellington (1769–1852), victor of Waterloo. Byron's hatred of Wellington is motivated by the fact that, in defeating Napoleon, Wellington ensured the reestablishment of repressive monarchies throughout Europe, endangering the cause of populist revolution. "Villainton" was a popular French satirical pronunciation of his name (*vilain* means "villain" or lowborn person).
2. "Query, *Ney*?–Printer's Devil" [*Byron's note*.] Marshall Michel Ney (1769–1815) was one of the bravest and most brilliant of Napoleon's generals. A "printer's devil" is an apprentice in a printing office who often becomes black with ink—hence the name "devil."
3. In 1818, a Frenchman named Marinet tried to assassinate Wellington. Lord Kinnaird had warned Wellington of the attempt; but, since Kinnaird refused to divulge the identity of his informant, Wellington accused him of treason.

And like some other things won't do to tell
   Upon your tomb in Westminster's old Abbey.
Upon the rest 'tis not worth while to dwell,
   Such tales being for the tea-hours of some tabby;
But though your years as *man* tend fast to zero,
In fact your Grace is still but a *young Hero*.[4]

III

Though Britain owes (and pays you too) so much,
   Yet Europe doubtless owes you greatly more:
You have repaired Legitimacy's crutch,[5]
   A prop not quite so certain as before:
The Spanish, and the French, as well as Dutch,
   Have seen, and felt, how strongly you *restore*;
And Waterloo has made the world your debtor
(I wish your bards would sing it rather better).

IV

You are "the best of cut-throats:"—do not start;
   The phrase is Shakespeare's,[6] and not misapplied:—
War's a brain-spattering, windpipe-slitting art,
   Unless her cause by right be sanctified.
If you have acted *once* a generous part,
   The World, not the World's masters, will decide,
And I shall be delighted to learn who,
Save you and yours, have gained by Waterloo?

V

I am no flatterer—you've supped full of flattery:
   They say you like it too—'tis no great wonder.
He whose whole life has been assault and battery,
   At last may get a little tired of thunder;
And swallowing eulogy much more than satire, he
   May like being praised for every lucky blunder,
Called "Saviour of the Nations"—not yet saved,—
And "Europe's Liberator"—still enslaved.

VI

I've done. Now go and dine from off the plate
   Presented by the Prince of the Brazils,
And send the sentinel before your gate
   A slice or two from your luxurious meals:
He fought, but has not fed so well of late.
   Some hunger, too, they say the people feels:—
There is no doubt that you deserve your ration,
But pray give back a little to the nation.

VII

I don't mean to reflect—a man so great as
   You, my lord Duke! is far above reflection:

---

4. Wellington achieved eminence in his middle age and—Byron suggests—quite undeservedly.
5. England had restored the tottering Bourbon monarchy, in the person of Louis XVIII, to the throne of France.
6. In Macbeth III. iv. 17, Macbeth tells the murderer he has hired to kill Banquo that he is "the best o' the cut-throats."

The high Roman fashion, too, of Cincinnatus,[7]
  With modern history has but small connection:
Though as an Irishman you love potatoes,
  You need not take them under your direction;
And half a million for your Sabine[8] farm
Is rather dear!—I'm sure I mean no harm.

VIII

Great men have always scorned great recompenses:
  Epaminondas[9] saved his Thebes, and died,
Not leaving even his funeral expenses:
  George Washington had thanks, and nought beside,
Except the all-cloudless glory (which few men's is)
  To free his country: Pitt[1] too had his pride,
And as a high-souled Minister of state is
Renowned for ruining Great Britain gratis.

IX

Never had mortal man such opportunity,
  Except Napoleon, or abused it more:
You might have freed fallen Europe from the unity
  Of Tyrants, and been blest from shore to shore:
And *now*—what *is* your fame? Shall the Muse tune it ye?
  Now—that the rabble's first vain shouts are o'er?
Go! hear it in your famished country's cries!
Behold the World! and curse your victories!

X

As these new cantos touch on warlike feats,
  To *you* the unflattering Muse deigns to inscribe
Truths, that you will not read in the Gazettes,
  But which 'tis time to teach the hireling tribe
Who fatten on their country's gore, and debts,
  Must be recited—and without a bribe.
You *did great* things, but not being *great* in mind,
Have left *undone* the *greatest*—and mankind.

XI

Death laughs—Go ponder o'er the skeleton
  With which men image out the unknown thing
That hides the past world, like to a set sun
  Which still elsewhere may rouse a brighter spring—
Death laughs at all you weep for!—look upon
  This hourly dread of all! whose *threatened sting*
Turns Life to terror, even though in its sheath:
Mark! how its lipless mouth grins without breath!

7. Roman general and dictator (519–439 B.C.), renowned for his humility and courage.
8. The reference is to a region of central Italy where Cincinnatus owned a farm until summoned to leadership by the Roman senators.
9. Theban general and philosopher (418–362 B.C.) who helped save Greece from a Persian invasion, 371 B.C.
1. William Pitt the Younger (1759–1806), twice prime minister (1783–1801 and 1804–6), who in the years following the French Revolution adopted extremely repressive measures against political dissenters in England.

XII

Mark! how it laughs and scorns at all you are!
  And yet *was* what you are; from *ear* to *ear*
It *laughs not*—there is now no fleshy bar
  So called; the Antic long hath ceased to *hear*,
But still he *smiles*; and whether near or far,
  He strips from man that mantle (far more dear
Than even the tailor's), his incarnate skin,
White, black, or copper—the dead bones will grin.

XIII

And thus Death laughs,—it is sad merriment,
  But still it *is* so; and with such example
Why should not Life be equally content
  With his Superior, in a smile to trample
Upon the nothings which are daily spent
  Like bubbles on an Ocean much less ample
Than the Eternal Deluge, which devours
Suns as rays—worlds like atoms—years like hours?

XIV

"To be, or not to be? *that* is the question,"
  Says Shakespeare, who just now is much in fashion.
I am neither Alexander[2] nor Hephæstion,
  Nor ever had for *abstract* fame much passion;
But would much rather have a sound digestion
  Than Buonaparte's cancer:—could I dash on
Through fifty victories to shame or fame—
Without a stomach what were a good name?

XV

"*O dura ilia messorum!*"—"Oh
  Ye rigid guts of reapers!" I translate
For the great benefit of those who know
  What indigestion is—that inward fate
Which makes all Styx through one small liver flow.
  A peasant's sweat is worth his lord's estate:
Let *this* one toil for bread—*that* rack for rent,
He who sleeps best may be the most content.

XVI

"To be, or not to be?"—Ere I decide,
  I should be glad to know that which *is being*.
'Tis true we speculate both far and wide,
  And deem, because we *see*, we are *all-seeing*:
For my part, I'll enlist on neither side,
  Until I see both sides for once agreeing.
For me, I sometimes think that Life is Death,
Rather than Life a mere affair of breath.

---

2. Alexander the Great. Hephaestion (died 324 B.C.) was Alexander's most skillful general and his closest friend.

3. "Ah, the tough flanks of harvesters!" Horace, *Epodes* III.

XVII

"*Que scais-je?*"[4] was the motto of Montaigne,
    As also of the first academicians:
That all is dubious which man may attain,
    Was one of their most favourite positions.
There's no such thing as certainty, that's plain
    As any of Mortality's conditions;
So little do we know what we're about in
This world, I doubt if doubt itself be doubting.

XVIII

It is a pleasant voyage perhaps to float,
    Like Pyrrho,[5] on a sea of speculation;
But what if carrying sail capsize the boat?
    Your wise men don't know much of navigation;
And swimming long in the abyss of thought
    Is apt to tire: a calm and shallow station
Well nigh the shore, where one stoops down and gathers
Some pretty shell, is best for moderate bathers.

XIX

"But Heaven," as Cassio says, "is above all—[6]
    No more of this, then, let us pray!" We have
Souls to save, since Eve's slip and Adam's fall,
    Which tumbled all mankind into the grave,
Besides fish, beasts, and birds, "The sparrow's fall
    Is special providence," though how *it* gave
Offence, we know not; probably it perched
Upon the tree which Eve so fondly searched.

XX

Oh! ye immortal Gods! what is Theogony?
    Oh! thou, too, mortal man! what is Philanthropy?
Oh! World, which was and is, what is Cosmogony?
    Some people have accused me of Misanthropy;
And yet I know no more than the mahogany
    That forms this desk, of what they mean;—*Lykanthropy*[7]
I comprehend, for without transformation
Men become wolves on any slight occasion.

XXI

But I, the mildest, meekest of mankind,
    Like Moses, or Melancthon,[8] who have ne'er
Done anything exceedingly unkind,—
    And (though I could not now and then forbear
Following the bent of body or of mind)
    Have always had a tendency to spare,—

4. "What do I know?" Michel Eyquem de Montaigne (1533–92), the great French essayist and skeptic, was highly esteemed by Byron.
5. Greek philosopher of absolute skepticism (365–275 B.C.), a major influence upon Montaigne.
6. The speaker of these optimistic lines from *Othello* II. iii. 95–96—Cassio—is drunk when he utters them, and about to be duped by Iago into causing Othello to kill his bride, Desdemona.
7. Werewolfism.
8. Philipp Melanchthon (1497–1560), German Protestant reformer, friend of Luther, and a man renowned for his mildness.

Why do they call me Misanthrope? Because
    They hate me, not I them:—and here we'll pause,

XXII

'Tis time we should proceed with our good poem,—
    For I maintain that it is really good,
Not only in the body but the proem,
    However little both are understood
Just now,—but by and by the Truth will show 'em
    Herself in her sublimest attitude:
And till she doth, I fain must be content
To share her beauty and her banishment.

XXIII

Our hero (and, I trust, kind reader! yours)
    Was left upon his way to the chief city
Of the immortal Peter's polished boors,
    Who still have shown themselves more brave than witty.
I know its mighty Empire now allures
    Much flattery—even Voltaire's,[9] and that's a pity.
For me, I deem an absolute autocrat
Not a barbarian, but much worse than that.

XXIV

And I will war, at least in words (and—should
    My chance so happen—deeds), with all who war
With Thought;—and of Thought's foes by far most rude,
    Tyrants and sycophants have been and are.
I know not who may conquer: if I could
    Have such a prescience, it should be no bar
To this my plain, sworn, downright detestation
Of every despotism in every nation.

XXV

It is not that I adulate the people:
    Without *me*, there are demagogues enough,
And infidels, to pull down every steeple,
    And set up in their stead some proper stuff.
Whether they may sow scepticism to reap Hell,
    As is the Christian dogma rather rough,
I do not know;—I wish men to be free
As much from mobs as kings—from you as me.

XXVI

The consequence is, being of no party,
    I shall offend all parties:—never mind!
My words, at least, are more sincere and hearty
    Than if I sought to sail before the wind.
He who has nought to gain can have small art: he
    Who neither wishes to be bound nor bind,
May still expatiate freely, as will I,
Nor give my voice to slavery's jackal cry.

9. Voltaire had praised Catherine's brilliance effusively. After the French Revolution, however, Catherine forbade the printing or circulation of Voltaire's books in Russia.

XXVII

That's an appropriate simile, *that jackal;*[1]—
 I've heard them in the Ephesian ruins howl
By night, as do that mercenary pack all,
 Power's base purveyors, who for pickings prowl,
And scent the prey their masters would attack all.
 However, the poor jackals are less foul
(As being the brave lions' keen providers)
Than human insects, catering for spiders.

XXVIII

Raise but an arm! 'twill brush their web away,
 And without *that*, their poison and their claws
Are useless. Mind, good people! what I say—
 (Or rather Peoples)—*go on* without pause!
The web of these Tarantulas each day
 Increases, till you shall make common cause:
None, save the Spanish Fly and Attic Bee,
As yet are strongly stinging to be free.

XXIX

Don Juan, who had shone in the late slaughter,
 Was left upon his way with the despatch,
Where blood was talked of as we would of water:
 And carcasses that lay as thick as thatch
O'er silenced cities, merely served to flatter
 Fair Catherine's pastime—who looked on the match
Between these nations as a main of cocks,
Wherein she liked her own to stand like rocks.

XXX

And there in a *kibitka* he rolled on,
 (A curséd sort of carriage without springs,
Which on rough roads leaves scarcely a whole bone,)
 Pondering on Glory, Chivalry, and Kings,
And Orders, and on all that he had done—
 And wishing that post-horses had the wings
Of Pegasus, or at the least post-chaises
Had feathers, when a traveller on deep ways is.

XXXI

At every jolt—and they were many—still
 He turned his eyes upon his little charge,[2]
As if he wished that she should fare less ill
 Than he, in these sad highways left at large
To ruts, and flints, and lovely Nature's skill,
 Who is no paviour, nor admits a barge
On *her* canals, where God takes sea and land,
Fishery and farm, both into his own hand.

XXXII

At least he pays no rent, and has best right

---

1. "In Greece I never saw or heard these animals; but among the ruins of Ephesus I have heard them by hundreds." [*Byron's note.*]

2. Leila, an orphan girl Juan has saved at the battle for Ismail.

To be the first of what we used to call
  "Gentlemen farmers"—a race worn out quite,
    Since lately there have been no rents at all,
  And "gentlemen" are in a piteous plight,
    And "farmers" can't raise Ceres from her fall:
  She fell with Buonaparte,—What strange thoughts
  Arise, when we see Emperors fall with oats!

XXXIII

But Juan turned his eyes on the sweet child
  Whom he had saved from slaughter—what a trophy
Oh! ye who build up monuments, defiled
  With gore, like Nadir Shah,[3] that costive Sophy,
Who, after leaving Hindostan a wild,
  And scarce to the Mogul a cup of coffee
To soothe his woes withal, was slain, the sinner!
Because he could no more digest his dinner;—

XXXIV

Oh ye! or we! or he! or she! reflect,
  That *one* life saved, especially if young
Or pretty, is a thing to recollect
  Far sweeter than the greenest laurels sprung
From the manure of human clay, though decked
  With all the praises ever said or sung:
Though hymned by every harp, unless within
Your heart joins chorus, Fame is but a din.

XXXV

Oh! ye great authors luminous, voluminous!
  Ye twice ten hundred thousand daily scribes!
Whose pamphlets, volumes, newspapers, illumine us!
  Whether you're paid by government in bribes,
To prove the public debt is not consuming us—
  Or, roughly treading on the "courtier's kibes"
With clownish heel your popular circulation
Feeds you by printing half the realm's starvation;—

XXXVI

Oh, ye great authors!— *A propos des bottes,*[4]—
  I have forgotten what I meant to say,
As sometimes have been greater sages' lots;—
  'Twas something calculated to allay
All wrath in barracks, palaces, or cots:
  Certes it would have been but thrown away,
And that's one comfort for my lost advice,
Although no doubt it was beyond all price.

3. Turkish general (1688–1747) who invaded India. Having gone violently mad (perhaps as a result of chronic indigestion), he was assassinated by his own soldiers. "Sophy" is another name for Turk, and the "Mogul" is one of the Mongolian emperors of India, who ruled the country from 1526 to 1857.
4. "Speaking of boots." Byron jokingly free-associates with the "courtier's kibes" or "heels" of the preceding stanza. Or, perhaps, not so jokingly. *Botte* in French refers expecially to the military jack boot called in England the "Wellington boot." The theme of these stanzas continues to contrast liberal humanitarianism with Wellington's style of militant imperialism.

XXXVII

But let it go:—it will one day be found
   With other relics of "a former World,"
When this World shall be *former*, underground,
   Thrown topsy-turvy, twisted, crisped, and curled,
Baked, fried, or burnt, turned inside-out, or drowned,
   Like all the worlds before, which have been hurled
First out of, and then back again to chaos—
The superstratum which will overlay us.

XXXVIII

So Cuvier says:[5]—and then shall come again
   Unto the new creation, rising out
From our old crash, some mystic, ancient strain
   Of things destroyed and left in airy doubt;
Like to the notions we now entertain
   Of Titans, giants, fellows of about
Some hundred feet in height, *not* to say *miles*,
And mammoths, and your wingéd crocodiles.

XXXIX

Think if then George the Fourth should be dug up!
   How the new worldlings of the then new East
Will wonder where such animals could sup!
   (For they themselves will be but of the least:
Even worlds miscarry, when too oft they pup,
   And every new creation hath decreased
In size, from overworking the material—
Men are but maggots of some huge Earth's burial.)

XL

How will—to these young people, just thrust out
   From some fresh Paradise, and set to plough,
And dig, and sweat, and turn themselves about,
   And plant, and reap, and spin, and grind, and sow,
Till all the arts at length are brought about,
   Especially of War and taxing,—*how*,
I say, will these great relics, when they see 'em,
Look like the monsters of a new Museum!

XLI

But I am apt to grow too metaphysical:
   "The time is out of joint,"[6]—and so am I;
I quite forget this poem's merely quizzical,
   And deviate into matters rather dry.
I ne'er decide what I shall say, and this I call
   Much too poetical: men should know why
They write, and for what end; but, note or text,
I never know the word which will come next.

5. Baron Georges Cuvier (1769–1832), French scientist who theorized that the world had been destroyed and recreated a number of times, each time on a smaller scale.
6. *Hamlet* I. v. 189.

XLII

So on I ramble, now and then narrating,
　　Now pondering:—it is time we should narrate.
I left Don Juan with his horses baiting—
　　Now we'll get o'er the ground at a great rate:
I shall not be particular in stating
　　His journey, we've so many tours of late:
Suppose him then at Petersburgh; suppose
That pleasant capital of painted snows;

XLIII

Suppose him in a handsome uniform—
　　A scarlet coat, black facings, a long plume,
Waving, like sails new shivered in a storm,
　　Over a cocked hat in a crowded room,
And brilliant breeches, bright as a Cairn Gorme,[7]
　　Of yellow casimire we may presume,
White stockings drawn uncurdled as new milk
O'er limbs whose symmetry set off the silk;

XLIV

Suppose him sword by side, and hat in hand,
　　Made up by Youth, Fame, and an army tailor—
That great enchanter, at whose rod's command
　　Beauty springs forth, and Nature's self turns paler,
Seeing how Art can make her work more grand
　　(When she don't pin men's limbs in like a gaoler),—
Behold him placed as if upon a pillar! He
Seems Love turned a Lieutenant of Artillery!

XLV

His bandage slipped down into a cravat—
　　His wings subdued to epaulettes—his quiver
Shrunk to a scabbard, with his arrows at
　　His side as a small sword, but sharp as ever—
His bow converted into a cocked hat—
　　But still so like, that Psyche[8] were more clever
Than some wives (who make blunders no less stupid),
If she had not mistaken him for Cupid.

XLVI

The courtiers stared, the ladies whispered, and
　　The Empress smiled: the reigning favourite frowned—
I quite forget which of them was in hand
　　Just then, as they are rather numerous[9] found,
Who took, by turns, that difficult command
　　Since first her Majesty was singly crowned:[1]
But they were mostly nervous six-foot fellows,
All fit to make a Patagonian[2] jealous.

7. Smoky quartz, a gem-like mineral found in Scotland.
8. In Greek myth, the beloved of Cupid, god of love.
9. Catherine's sexual appetite was notorious. She died, at age sixty-seven, perhaps from her exertions with the last of her lovers.
1. Catherine was crowned Czarina of all the Russians in 1762, after the death of her moronic husband, Czar Peter III.
2. From "Patagonia" (Argentina) fabled to be inhabited by giants.

XLVII

Juan was none of these, but slight and slim,
    Blushing and beardless; and, yet, ne'ertheless,
There was a something in his turn of limb,
    And still more in his eye, which seemed to express,
That, though he looked one of the Seraphim,
    There lurked a man beneath the Spirit's dress.
Besides, the Empress sometimes liked a boy,
And had just buried the fair-faced Lanskoi.[3]

XLVIII

No wonder then that Yermoloff, or Momonoff,
    Or Scherbatoff, or any other *off*
Or *on*, might dread her Majesty had not room enough
    Within her bosom (which was not too tough),
For a new flame; a thought to cast of gloom enough
    Along the aspect, whether smooth or rough,
Of him who, in the language of his station,
Then held that "high official situation."

XLIX

O gentle ladies! should you seek to know
    The import of this diplomatic phrase,
Bid Ireland's Londonderry's Marquess[4] show
    His parts of speech, and in the strange displays
Of that odd string of words, all in a row,
    Which none divine, and every one obeys,
Perhaps you may pick out some queer *no* meaning,—
Of that weak wordy harvest the sole gleaning.

L

I think I can explain myself without
    That sad inexplicable beast of prey—
That Sphinx, whose words would ever be a doubt,
    Did not his deeds unriddle them each day—
That monstrous hieroglyphic—that long spout
    Of blood and water—leaden Castlereagh!
And here I must an anecdote relate,
But luckily of no great length or weight.

LI

An English lady asked of an Italian,
    What were the actual and official duties
Of the strange thing some women set a value on,
    Which hovers oft about some married beauties,
Called "Cavalier Servente?"[5]—a Pygmalion[6]
    Whose statues warm (I fear, alas! too true 'tis)
Beneath his art:—the dame, pressed to disclose them,
Said—"Lady, I beseech you to *suppose them*."

3. Lanskoi, Yermoloff, and the others named in the next stanza—all were accepted lovers of Catherine's.
4. Castlereagh: see *Don Juan*, Dedication, XI, 8.
5. In Italian society, a semipublicly accepted lover to a married lady.
6. In Greek myth, the sculptor Pygmalion fell in love with the female statue he had created, and the gods, granting his prayers, brought the statue to life.

LII

And thus I supplicate your supposition,
　And mildest, matron-like interpretation,
Of the imperial favourite's condition.
　'Twas a high place, the highest in the nation
In fact, if not in rank; and the suspicion
　Of any one's attaining to his station,
No doubt gave pain, where each new pair of shoulders,
If rather broad, made stocks rise—and their holders.

LIII

Juan, I said, was a most beauteous boy,
　And had retained his boyish look beyond
The usual hirsute seasons which destroy,
　With beards and whiskers, and the like, the fond
Parisian aspect, which upset old Troy
　And founded Doctors' Commons:—I have conned
The history of divorces, which, though chequered,
Calls Ilion's the first damages on record.[7]

LIV

And Catherine, who loved all things (save her Lord,
　Who was gone to his place), and passed for much,
Admiring those (by dainty dames abhorred)
　Gigantic gentlemen, yet had a touch
Of sentiment: and he she most adored
　Was the lamented Lanskoi, who was such
A lover as had cost her many a tear,
And yet but made a middling grenadier.

LV

Oh thou *"teterrima causa"*[8] of all *"belli"*—
　Thou gate of Life and Death—thou nondescript!
Whence is our exit and our entrance,—well I
　May pause in pondering how all souls are dipped
In thy perennial fountain:—how man *fell* I
　Know not, since Knowledge saw her branches stripped
Of her first fruit; but how he *falls* and rises
Since,—*thou* hast settled beyond all surmises.

LVI

Some call thee "the *worst* cause of War," but I
　Maintain thou art the *best*: for after all,
From thee we come, to thee we go, and why
　To get at thee not batter down a wall,
Or waste a World? since no one can deny
　Thou dost replenish worlds both great and small:
With—or without thee—all things at a stand
Are, or would be, thou sea of Life's dry land!

7. Byron wryly reflects on divorce proceedings (tried in Doctors' Commons),
and associates them with the fall of Troy
("Ilion"), since the Greeks were seeking
"damages" for the elopment of Helen
from her older husband, Menelaus.
8. "The foulest cause" of wars (*belli*).

LVII

Catherine, who was the grand Epitome
    Of that great cause of War, or Peace, or what
You please (it causes all the things which be,
    So you may take your choice of this or that)—
Catherine, I say, was very glad to see
    The handsome herald, on whose plumage sat
Victory; and, pausing as she saw him kneel
With his despatch, forgot to break the seal.

LVIII

Then recollecting the whole Empress, nor
    Forgetting quite the Woman (which composed
At least three parts of this great whole), she tore
    The letter open with an air which posed
The Court, that watched each look her visage wore,
    Until a royal smile at length disclosed
Fair weather for the day. Though rather spacious,
Her face was noble, her eyes fine, mouth gracious.

LIX

Great joy was hers, or rather joys: the first
    Was a ta'en city, thirty thousand slain:
Glory and triumph o'er her aspect burst,
    As an East Indian sunrise on the main:—
These quenched a moment her Ambition's thirst—
    So Arab deserts drink in Summer's rain:
In vain!—As fall the dews on quenchless sands,
Blood only serves to wash Ambition's hands!

LX

Her next amusement was more fanciful;
    She smiled at mad Suwarrow's rhymes, who threw
Into a Russian couplet rather dull
    The whole gazette of thousands whom he slew:
Her third was feminine enough to annul
    The shudder which runs naturally through
Our veins, when things called Sovereigns think it best
To kill, and Generals turn it into jest.

LXI

The two first feelings ran their course complete,
    And lighted first her eye, and then her mouth:
The whole court looked immediately most sweet,
    Like flowers well watered after a long drouth:—
But when on the Lieutenant at her feet
    Her Majesty, who liked to gaze on youth
Almost as much as on a new despatch,
Glanced mildly,—all the world was on the watch.

LXII

Though somewhat large, exuberant, and truculent,
    When *wroth*—while *pleased*, she was as fine a figure
As those who like things rosy, ripe, and succulent,

Would wish to look on, while they are in vigour.
She could repay each amatory look you lent
    With interest, and, in turn, was wont with rigour
To exact of Cupid's bills the full amount
At sight, nor would permit you to discount.

LXIII

With her the latter, though at times convenient,
    Was not so necessary; for they tell
That she was handsome, and though fierce *looked* lenient,
    And always used her favourites too well.
If once beyond her boudoir's precincts in ye went,
    Your "fortune" was in a fair way "to swell
A man" (as Giles says);[9] for though she would widow all
Nations, she liked Man as an individual.

LXIV

What a strange thing is Man! and what a stranger
    Is Woman! What a whirlwind is her head,
And what a whirlpool full of depth and danger
    Is all the rest about her! Whether wed,
Or widow—maid—or mother, she can change her
    Mind like the wind: whatever she has said
Or done, is light to what she'll say or do;—
The oldest thing on record, and yet new!

LXV

Oh Catherine! (for all interjections,
    To thee both *oh*! and *ah*! belong, of right,
In Love and War) how odd are the connections
    Of human thoughts, which jostle in their flight!
Just now *yours* were cut out in different sections:
    First Ismail's capture caught your fancy quite;
Next of new knights, the fresh and glorious batch:
And *thirdly* he who brought you the despatch!

LXVI

Shakespeare[1] talks of "the herald Mercury
    New lighted on a heaven-kissing hill:"
And some such visions crossed her Majesty,
    While her young herald knelt before her still.
'Tis very true the hill seemed rather high,
    For a Lieutenant to climb up; but skill
Smoothed even the Simplon's[2] steep, and by God's blessing
With Youth and Health all kisses are "Heaven-kissing."

LXVII

Her Majesty looked down, the youth looked up—
    And so they fell in love;—she with his face,
His grace, his God-knows-what: for Cupid's cup
    With the first draught intoxicates apace,

---

9. Sir Giles Overreach, in Philip Massinger's Elizabethan comedy, *A New Way to Pay Old Debts*.

1. In *Hamlet* III. iv. 58–59.
2. Mountain in the Alps.

A quintessential laudanum or "Black Drop,"
    Which makes one drunk at once, without the base
Expedient of full bumpers; for the eye
    In love drinks all Life's fountains (save tears) dry.

LXVIII

He, on the other hand, if not in love,
    Fell into that no less imperious passion,
Self-love—which, when some sort of thing above
    Ourselves, a singer, dancer, much in fashion,
Or Duchess—Princess—Empress, "deigns to prove"
    ('Tis Pope's[3] phrase) a great longing, though a rash one,
For one especial person out of many,
Make us believe ourselves as good as any.

LXIX

Besides, he was of that delighted age
    Which makes all female ages equal—when
We don't much care with whom we may engage,
    As bold as Daniel in the lions' den,
So that we can our native sun assuage
    In the next ocean, which may flow just then—
To make a *twilight* in, just as Sol's heat is
Quenched in the lap of the salt sea, or Thetis.[4]

LXX

And Catherine (we must say thus much for Catherine),
    Though bold and bloody, was the kind of thing
Whose temporary passion was quite flattering,
    Because each lover looked a sort of King,
Made up upon an amatory pattern.
    A royal husband in all save the *ring*—
Which, (being the damnedest part of matrimony,)
Seemed taking out the sting to leave the honey:

LXXI

And when you add to this, her Womanhood
    In its meridian, her blue eyes or gray—
(The last, if they have soul, are quite as good,
    Or better, as the best examples say:
Napoleon's, Mary's (Queen of Scotland), should
Lend to that colour a transcendent ray;
And Pallas[5] also sanctions the same hue,
Too wise to look through optics black or blue)—

LXXII

Her sweet smile, and her then majestic figure,
    Her plumpness, her imperial condescension,
Her preference of a boy to men much bigger
    (Fellows whom Messalina's[6] self would pension),

---

3. In his *Eloisa to Abelard* (1717).
4. Sea-nymph in Homer's *Iliad*, mother of the warrior Achilles.
5. Pallas Athena, Greek goddess of wisdom, often referred to by Homer as "gray-eyed Athena."
6. Wife of the Roman emperor Claudius (died A.D. 48), a particularly bloodthirsty, violent woman.

Her prime of life, just now in juicy vigour,
  With other *extras*, which we need not mention,—
All these, or any one of these, explain
Enough to make a stripling very vain.

LXXIII

And that's enough, for Love is vanity,
  Selfish in its beginning as its end,
Except where 'tis a mere insanity,
  A maddening spirit which would strive to blend
Itself with Beauty's frail inanity,
  On which the Passion's self seems to depend;
And hence some heathenish philosophers
Make Love the main-spring of the Universe.

LXXIV

Besides Platonic love,[7] besides the love
  Of God, the love of sentiment, the loving
Of faithful pairs—(I needs must rhyme with dove,
  That good old steam-boat which keeps verses moving
'Gainst reason—Reason ne'er was hand-and-glove
  With rhyme, but always leant less to improving
The sound than sense)—besides all these pretences
To Love, there are those things which words name senses;

LXXV

Those movements, those improvements in our bodies
  Which make all bodies anxious to get out
Of their own sand-pits, to mix with a goddess,
  For such all women are at first no doubt.
How beautiful that moment! and how odd is
  That fever which precedes the languid rout
Of our sensations! What a curious way
The whole thing is of clothing souls in clay!

LXXVI

The noblest kind of love is love Platonical,
  To end or to begin with; the next grand
Is that which may be christened love canonical,
  Because the clergy take the thing in hand;
The third sort to be noted, in our chronicle
  As flourishing in every Christian land,
Is when chaste matrons to their other ties
Add what may be called *marriage in disguise*.

LXXVII

Well, we won't analyse—our story must
  Tell for itself: the Sovereign was smitten,
Juan much flattered by her love, or lust;—
  I cannot stop to alter words once written,
And the *two* are so mixed with human dust,
  That he who *names one*, both perchance may hit on:

7. See *Don Juan* V, I.

But in such matters Russia's mighty Empress
Behaved no better than a common sempstress.

LXXVIII

The whole court melted into one wide whisper,
    And all lips were applied unto all ears!
The elder ladies' wrinkles curled much crisper
    As they beheld; the younger cast some leers
One one another, and each lovely lisper
    Smiled as she talked the matter o'er; but tears
Of rivalship rose in each clouded eye
Of all the standing army who stood by.

LXXIX

All the ambassadors of all the powers
    Inquired, Who was this very new young man,
Who promised to be great in some few hours?
    Which is full soon (though Life is but a span).
Already they beheld the silver showers
    Of rubles rain, as fast as specie can,
Upon his cabinet, besides the presents
Of several ribands, and some thousand peasants.[8]

LXXX

Catherine was generous,—all such ladies are:
    Love—that great opener of the heart and all
The ways that lead there, be they near or far,
    Above, below, by turnpikes great or small,—
Love—(though she had a curséd taste for War,
    And was not the best wife unless we call
Such Clytemnestra,[9] though perhaps 'tis better
That one should die—than two drag on the fetter)—

LXXXI

Love had made Catherine make each lover's fortune,
    Unlike our own half-chaste Elizabeth,[1]
Whose avarice all disbursements did importune,
    If History, the grand liar, ever saith
The truth; and though grief her old age might shorten,
    Because she put a favourite to death,
Her vile, ambiguous method of flirtation,
And stinginess, disgrace her sex and station.

LXXXII

But when the levée rose, and all was bustle
    In the dissolving circle, all the nations'
Ambassadors began as 'twere to hustle
    Round the young man with their congratulations.
Also the softer silks were heard to rustle

8. "A Russian estate is always valued by the number of the slaves upon it." [*Byron's note.*]
9. After the Trojan War, Clytemnestra murdered her husband Agamemnon when he returned to Argos.
1. Queen Elizabeth I had several lovers, but was extremely discreet about them—unlike Catherine.

Of gentle dames, among whose recreations
It is to speculate on handsome faces,
Especially when such lead to high places.

LXXXIII

Juan, who found himself, he knew not how,
  A general object of attention, made
His answers with a very graceful bow,
  As if born for the ministerial trade.
Though modest, on his unembarrassed brow
  Nature had written "Gentleman!" He said
Little, but to the purpose; and his manner
Flung hovering graces o'er him like a banner.

LXXXIV

An order from her Majesty consigned
  Our young Lieutenant to the genial care
Of those in office: all the world looked kind,
  (As it will look sometimes with the first stare,
Which Youth would not act ill to keep in mind,)
  As also did Miss Protasoff[2] then there,
Named from her mystic office "l'Eprouveuse,"
A term inexplicable to the Muse.

LXXXV

With *her* then, as in humble duty bound,
  Juan retired,—and so will I, until
My Pegasus shall tire of touching ground.
  We have just lit on a "heaven-kissing hill,"
So lofty that I feel my brain turn round,
  And all my fancies whirling like a mill;
Which is a signal to my nerves and brain,
To take a quiet ride in some green lane.

CANTO THE SIXTEENTH

Juan becomes Catherine's favorite at the Russian court. But when he falls
seriously ill, Catherine decides that it will be good for his health to send
him on a special ambassadorial mission to England. There he becomes
entangled with three ladies: the vivacious and sensible Aurora Raby, the
arrogant Adeline Amundeville, and the mysterious Countess Fitz-Fulke. As
canto XVI opens, Juan is a guest of Lord Henry Amundeville, Adeline's
husband, at whose country house the three ladies are also members of the
party. Lord Henry's country house shows certain striking resemblances to
Byron's own ancestral dwelling place, Newstead Abbey.

I

THE antique Persians taught three useful things,
  To draw the bow, to ride, and speak the truth.
This was the mode of Cyrus,[1] best of kings—

2. An actual member of Catherine's
court. "L'Eprouveuse" means "the
tester" or "the tryer-out."

1. Cyrus the Great (558–529 B.C.), founder of the Persian empire.

A mode adopted since by modern youth.
Bows have they, generally with two strings;
   Horses they ride without remorse or ruth;
At speaking truth perhaps they are less clever,
But draw the long bow better now than ever.

II

This cause of this effect, or this defect,—
   "For this effect defective comes by cause,"—[2]
Is what I have not leisure to inspect;
   But this I must say in my own applause,
Of all the Muses that I recollect,
   Whate'er may be her follies or her flaws
In some things, mine's beyond all contradiction
The most sincere that ever dealt in fiction.

III

And as she treats all things, and ne'er retreats
   From anything, this Epic will contain
A wilderness of the most rare conceits,
   Which you might elsewhere hope to find in vain.
'Tis true there be some bitters with the sweets,
   Yet mixed so slightly, that you can't complain,
But wonder they so few are, since my tale is
"De rebus cunctis et quibusdam aliis."[3]

IV

But of all truths which she has told, the most
   True is that which she is about to tell.
I said it was a story of a ghost—
   What then? I only know it so befell.
Have you explored the limits of the coast,
   Where all the dwellers of the earth must dwell?
'Tis time to strike such puny doubters dumb as
The sceptics who would not believe Columbus.

V

Some people would impose now with authority,
   Turpin's or Monmouth Geoffry's[4] Chronicle;
Men whose historical superiority
   Is always greatest at a miracle.
But Saint Augustine[5] has the great priority,
   Who bids all men believe the impossible,
Because 'tis so. Who nibble, scribble, quibble, he
Quiets at once with "quia *impossible*."

VI

And therefore, mortals, cavil not at all;
   Believe:—if 'tis improbable, you *must*,
And if it is impossible, you *shall*:

2. *Hamlet* II. ii. 103.
3. "About all things, and a few other things."
4. Medieval historians.
5. It was not St. Augustine but the theologican Tertullian (A.D. 160–230) who uttered the famous profession of faith, *Credo quia impossibile est* ("I believe it, because it is impossible").

'Tis always best to take things upon trust.
   I do not speak profanely to recall
      Those holier Mysteries which the wise and just
   Receive as Gospel, and which grow more rooted,
   As all truths must, the more they are disputed:

VII

I merely mean to say what Johnson[6] said,
   That in the course of some six thousand years,
All nations have believed that from the dead
   A visitant at intervals appears:
And what is strangest upon this strange head,
   Is, that whatever bar the reason rears
'Gainst such belief, there's something stronger still
In its behalf—let those deny who will.

VIII

The dinner and the *soirée* too were done,
   The supper too discussed, the dames admired,
The banqueteers had dropped off one by one—
   The song was silent, and the dance expired:
The last thin petticoats were vanished, gone
   Like fleecy clouds into the sky retired,
And nothing brighter gleamed through the saloon
Than dying tapers—and the peeping moon.

IX

The evaporation of a joyous day
   Is like the last glass of champagne, without
The foam which made its virgin bumper gay;
   Or like a system coupled with a doubt;
Or like a soda bottle when its spray
   Has sparkled and let half its spirit out;
Or like a billow left by storms behind,
Without the animation of the wind;

X

Or like an opiate, which brings troubled rest,
   Or none; or like—like nothing that I know
Except itself;—such is the human breast;
   A thing, of which similitudes can show
No real likeness,—like the old Tyrian vest
   Dyed purple, none at present can tell how,
If from a shell-fish or from cochineal.
So perish every Tyrant's robe piece-meal![7]

XI

But next to dressing for a rout or ball,
   Undressing is a woe; our *robe de chambre*[8]

---

6. Dr. Samuel Johnson (1709–84), the great literary critic of the late eighteenth century, throughout his life retained an open mind on the possibility of supernatural visitations.
7. "The composition of the old Tyrian purple, whether from a shell-fish, or from cochineal, or from kermes, is still an article of dispute; and even its colour —some say purple, others scarlet: I say nothing." [*Byron's note.*]
8. Dressing gown. Nessus was the centaur whose blood was used to poison the shirt which killed Hercules.

May sit like that of Nessus, and recall
    Thoughts quite as yellow, but less clear than amber.
Titus exclaimed, "I've lost a day!"[9] Of all
    The nights and days most people can remember,
(I have had of both, some not to be disdained,)
I wish they'd state how many they have gained.

XII

And Juan, on retiring for the night,
    Felt restless, and perplexed, and compromised:
He thought Aurora Raby's eyes more bright
    Then Adeline (such is advice) advised;
If he had known exactly his own plight,
    He probably would have philosophised:
A great resource to all, and ne'er denied
Till wanted; therefore Juan only sighed.

XIII

He sighed;—the next resource is the full moon,
    Where all sighs are deposited; and now
It happened luckily, the chaste orb shone
    As clear as such a climate will allow;
And Juan's mind was in the proper tone
    To hail her with the apostrophe—"O thou!"
Of amatory egotism the *Tuism*,[1]
Which further to explain would be a truism.

XIV

But Lover, Poet, or Astronomer—
    Shepherd, or swain—whoever may behold,
Feel some abstraction when they gaze on her;
    Great thoughts we catch from thence (besides a cold
Sometimes, unless my feelings rather err);
    Deep secrets to her rolling light are told;
The Ocean's tides and mortals' brains she sways,
And also hearts—if there be truth in lays.

XV

Juan felt somewhat pensive, and disposed
    For contemplation rather than his pillow:
The Gothic chamber, where he was enclosed,
    Let in the rippling sound of the lake's billow,
With all the mystery by midnight caused:
    Below his window waved (of course) a willow;
And he stood gazing out on the cascade
That flashed and after darkened in the shade.

XVI

Upon his table or his toilet,[2]—*which*
    Of these is not exactly ascertained,—

9. The emperor Titus exclaimed this, according to Suetonius (*The Lives of the Twelve Caesars*), when once he realized that he had let a day go by without acting on the petitions of any of his suppliants.
1. Use of the intimate form of address, "thou" (French *tu*).
2. Dressing table.

(I state this, for I am cautious to a pitch
   Of nicety, where a fact is to be gained,)
A lamp burned high, while he leant from a niche,
   Where many a Gothic ornament remained,
In chiselled stone and painted glass, and all
That Time has left our fathers of their Hall.

XVII

Then, as the night was clear though cold, he threw
   His chamber door wide open—and went forth
Into a gallery of a sombre hue,
   Long, furnished with old pictures of great worth,
Of knights and dames heroic and chaste too,
   As doubtless should be people of high birth;
But by dim lights the portraits of the dead
Have something ghastly, desolate, and dread.

XVIII

The forms of the grim Knight and pictured Saint
   Look living in the moon; and as you turn
Backward and forward to the echoes faint
   Of your own footsteps—voices from the Urn
Appear to wake, and shadows wild and quaint
   Start from the frames which fence their aspects stern,
As if to ask how you can dare to keep
A vigil there, where all but Death should sleep.

XIX

And the pale smile of Beauties in the grave,
   The charms of other days, in starlight gleams,
Glimmer on high; their buried locks still wave
   Along the canvas; their eyes glance like dreams
On ours, or spars within some dusky cave,
   But Death is imaged in their shadowy beams.
A picture is the past; even ere its frame
Be gilt, who sate hath ceased to be the same.

XX

As Juan mused on Mutability,
   Or on his Mistress—terms synonymous—
No sound except the echo of his sigh
   Or step ran sadly through that antique house;
When suddenly he heard, or thought so, nigh,
   A supernatural agent—or a mouse,
Whose little nibbling rustle will embarrass
Most people as it plays along the arras.

XXI

It was no mouse—but lo! a monk, arrayed
   In cowl and beads, and dusky garb, appeared,
Now in the moonlight, and now lapsed in shade,
   With steps that trod as heavy, yet unheard;
His garments only a slight murmur made;

He moved as shadowy as the Sisters weird,[3]
But slowly; and as he passed Juan by,
Glanced, without pausing, on him a bright eye.

XXII

Juan was petrified; he had heard a hint
    Of such a Spirit in these halls of old,
But thought, like most men, that there was nothing in't
    Beyond the rumour which such spots unfold,
Coined from surviving Superstition's mint,
    Which passes ghosts in currency like gold,
But rarely seen, like gold compared with paper.
And did he see this? or was it a vapour?

XXIII

Once, twice, thrice passed, repassed—the thing of air,
    Or earth beneath, or Heaven, or t'other place;
And Juan gazed upon it with a stare,
    Yet could not speak or move; but, on its base
As stands a statue, stood: he felt his hair
    Twine like a knot of snakes around his face;
He taxed his tongue for words, which were not granted,
To ask the reverend person what he wanted.

XXIV

The third time, after a still longer pause,
    The shadow passed away—but where? the hall
Was long, and thus far there was no great cause
    To think his vanishing unnatural:
Doors there were many, through which, by the laws
    Of physics, bodies whether short or tall
Might come or go; but Juan could not state
Through which the Spectre seemed to evaporate.

XXV

He stood—how long he knew not, but it seemed
    An age—expectant, powerless, with his eyes
Strained on the spot where first the figure gleamed
    Then by degrees recalled his energies,
And would have passed the whole off as a dream,
    But could not wake; he was, he did surmise,
Waking already, and returned at length
Back to his chamber, shorn of half his strength.

XXVI

All there was as he left it: still his taper
    Burned, and not *blue*,[4] as modest tapers use,
Receiving sprites with sympathetic vapour;
    He rubbed his eyes, and they did not refuse
Their office: he took up an old newspaper;
    The paper was right easy to peruse;

3. The three witches in *Macbeth*.
4. In Gothic fiction and in folklore, the presence of ghosts caused candles to burn blue.

He read an article the King attacking,
And a long eulogy of "Patent Blacking."[5]

XXVII

This savoured of this world; but his hand shook:
  He shut his door, and after having read
A paragraph, I think about Horne Tooke,[6]
  Undressed, and rather slowly went to bed.
There, couched all snugly on his pillow's nook,
  With what he had seen his phantasy he fed;
And though it was no opiate, slumber crept
Upon him by degrees, and so he slept.

XXVIII

He woke betimes; and, as may be supposed,
  Pondered upon his visitant or vision,
And whether it ought not to be disclosed,
  At risk of being quizzed for superstition.
The more he thought, the more his mind was posed:
  In the mean time, his valet, whose precision
Was great, because his master brooked no less,
Knocked to inform him it was time to dress.

XXIX

He dressed; and like young people he was wont
  To take some trouble with his toilet, but
This morning rather spent less time upon 't;
  Aside his very mirror soon was put;
His curls fell negligently o'er his front,
  His clothes were not curbed to their usual cut,
His very neckcloth's Gordian knot[7] was tied
Almost an hair's breadth too much on one side.

XXX

And when he walked down into the Saloon,
  He sate him pensive o'er a dish of tea,
Which he perhaps had not discovered soon,
  Had it not happened scalding hot to be,
Which made him have recourse unto his spoon;
  So much *distrait* he was, that all could see
That something was the matter—Adeline
The first—but *what* she could not well divine.

XXXI

She looked, and saw him pale, and turned as pale
  Herself; then hastily looked down, and muttered
Something, but what's not stated in my tale.
  Lord Henry said, his muffin was ill buttered;
The Duchess of Fitz-Fulke played with her veil,

5. Juan reads a rhymed advertisement for shoe polish.
6. John Horne Tooke (1736–1812), English radical and supporter of the American and French revolutions.
7. An extremely complicated knot. (In legend, the Gordian knot was an elaborate knot of which it was said that the man who loosed it would rule the world; Alexander the Great loosed it by cutting it in half with his sword.)

And looked at Juan hard, but nothing uttered.
Aurora Raby with her large dark eyes
Surveyed him with a kind of calm surprise.

XXXII

But seeing him all cold and silent still,
  And everybody wondering more or less,
Fair Adeline inquired, "If he were ill?"
  He started, and said, "Yes—no—rather—yes."
The family physician had great skill,
  And being present, now began to express
His readiness to feel his pulse and tell
The cause, but Juan said, he was "quite well."

XXXIII

"Quite well; yes,—no."—These answers were mysterious,
  And yet his looks appeared to sanction both,
However they might savour of delirious;
  Something like illness of a sudden growth
Weighed on his spirit, though by no means serious:
  But for the rest, as he himself seemed loth
To state the case, it might be ta'en for granted
It was not the physician that he wanted.

XXXIV

Lord Henry, who had now discussed his chocolate,
  Also the muffin whereof he complained,
Said, Juan had not got his usual look elate,
  At which he marvelled, since it had not rained;
Then asked her Grace what news were of the Duke of late?
  Her Grace replied, *his* Grace was rather pained
With some slight, light, hereditary twinges
Of gout, which rusts aristocratic hinges.

XXXV

Then Henry turned to Juan, and addressed
  A few words of condolence on his state:
"You look," quoth he, "as if you had had your rest
  Broke in upon by the Black Friar[8] of late."
"What Friar?" said Juan; and he did his best
  To put the question with an air sedate,
Or careless; but the effort was not valid
To hinder him from growing still more pallid.

XXXVI

"Oh! have you never heard of the Black Friar?
  The Spirit of these walls?"—"In truth not I."
"Why Fame—but Fame you know's sometimes a liar—
  Tells an odd story, of which by and by:
Whether with time the Spectre has grown shyer,
  Or that our Sires had a more gifted eye
For such sights, though the tale is half believed,
The Friar of late has not been oft perceived.

8. There was a legend about such a ghostly monk haunting Newstead Abbey.

XXXVII

"The last time was—" —"I pray," said Adeline—
  (Who watched the changes of Don Juan's brow,
And from its context thought she could divine
  Connections stronger than he chose to avow
With this same legend)—"if you but design
  To jest, you'll choose some other theme just now,
Because the present tale has oft been told,
And is not much improved by growing old."

XXXVIII

"Jest!" quoth Milor; "why, Adeline, you know
  That we ourselves—'twas in the honey moon—
Saw——"—"Well, no matter, 'twas so long ago;
  But, come, I'll set your story to a tune."
Graceful as Dian when she draws her bow,
  She seized her harp, whose strings were kindled soon
As touched, and plaintively began to play
The air of " 'Twas a Friar of Orders Gray."

XXXIX

"But add the words," cried Henry, "which you made;
  For Adeline is half a poetess,"
Turning round to the rest, he smiling said.
  Of course the others could not but express
In courtesy their wish to see displayed
  By one *three* talents, for there were no less—
The voice, the words, the harper's skill, at once,
Could hardly be united by a dunce.

XL

After some fascinating hesitation,—
  The charming of these charmers, who seem bound,
I can't tell why, to this dissimulation,—
  Fair Adeline, with eyes fixed on the ground
At first, then kindling into animation,
  Added her sweet voice to the lyric sound,
And sang with much simplicity,—a merit
Not the less precious, that we seldom hear it.

1

Beware! beware! of the Black Friar,
  Who sitteth by Norman stone,
For he mutters his prayer in the midnight air,
  And his mass of the days that are gone.
When the Lord of the Hill, Amundeville,
  Made Norman Church his prey,
And expelled the friars, one friar still
  Would not be driven away.

2

Though he came in his might, with King Henry's right,
  To turn church lands to lay,

With sword in hand, and torch to light
    Their walls, if they said nay;
A monk remained, unchased, unchained,
    And he did not seem formed of clay,
For he's seen in the porch, and he's seen in the church,
    Though he is not seen by day.

3

And whether for good, or whether for ill,
    It is not mine to say;
But still with the house of Amundeville
    He abideth night and day.
By the marriage-bed of their lords, 'tis said,
    He flits on the bridal eve;
And 'tis held as faith, to their bed of Death
    He comes—but not to grieve.

4

When an heir is born, he's heard to mourn,
    And when aught is to befall
That ancient line, in the pale moonshine
    He walks from hall to hall.
His form you may trace, but not his face,
    'Tis shadowed by his cowl;
But his eyes may be seen from the folds between,
    And they seem of a parted soul.

5

But beware! beware! of the Black Friar,
    He still retains his sway,
For he is yet the Church's heir,
    Whoever may be the lay.
Amundeville is Lord by day,
    But the monk is Lord by night;
Nor wine nor wassail could raise a vassal
    To question that Friar's right.

6

Say nought to him as he walks the Hall,
    And he'll say nought to you;
He sweeps along in his dusky pall,
    As o'er the grass the dew.
Then grammercy! for the Black Friar;
    Heaven sain him! fair or foul,—
And whatsoe'er may be his prayer,
    Let ours be for his soul.

XLI

The lady's voice ceased, and the thrilling wires
    Died from the touch that kindled them to sound;
And the pause followed, which when song expires
    Pervades a moment those who listen round;
And then of course the circle much admires,

Nor less applauds, as in politeness bound,
The tones, the feeling, and the execution,
To the performer's diffident confusion.

XLII

Fair Adeline, though in a careless way,
　As if she rated such accomplishment
As the mere pastime of an idle day,
　Pursued an instant for her own content,
Would now and then as 'twere *without* display,
　Yet *with* display in fact, at times relent
To such performances with haughty smile,
To show she *could*, if it were worth her while.

XLIII

Now this (but we will whisper it aside)
　Was—pardon the pedantic illustration—
Trampling on Plato's pride with greater pride,
　As did the Cynic on some like occasion;
Deeming the sage would be much mortified,
　Or thrown into a philosophic passion,
For a spoilt carpet—but the "Attic Bee"
Was much consoled by his own repartee.[9]

XLIV

Thus Adeline would throw into the shade
　(By doing easily, whene'er she chose,
What dilettanti do with vast parade)
　Their sort of *half profession*; for it grows
To something like this when too oft displayed;
　And that it is so, everybody knows,
Who have heard Miss That or This, or Lady T'other,
Show off—to please their company or mother.

XLV [1]

Oh! the long evenings of duets and trios!
　The admirations and the speculations;
The "Mamma Mia's!" and the "Amor Mio's!"
　The "Tanti palpiti's" on such occasions:
The "Lasciami's," and quavering "Addio's,"
　Amongst our own most musical of nations!
With "Tu mi chamas's" from Portingale,
To soothe our ears, lest Italy should fail.

XLVI

In Babylon's *bravuras*—as the Home-
　Heart-Ballads of Green Erin or Grey Highlands,

9. The Cynic philosopher Diogenes is supposed once to have stamped upon Plato's couch, exclaiming, "So much for the pride of Plato!" Plato (the "Attic Bee") replied, "And how much for the pride of Diogenes?" The point of the anecdote is that proclaiming one's contempt of arrogance is often the highest form of arrogance.

1. The Italian phrases in this stanza are to represent opening lines of pieces sung by the *dilettanti* or amateurs. Their opening lines—"My mother," "My love!" "So many heartbeats," "Leave me" and "Farewell"—indicate that they are sentimental love songs. "Tu mi chamas" is a Portugese song which Byron translated in one of his own lyrics.

That bring Lochaber[2] back to eyes that roam
 O'er far Atlantic continents or islands,
The calentures[3] of music which o'ercome
 All mountaineers with dreams that they are nigh lands,
No more to be beheld but in such visions—
Was Adeline well versed, as compositions.

XLVII

She also had a twilight tinge of *"Blue,"*[4]
 Could write rhymes, and compose more than she wrote,
Made epigrams occasionally too
 Upon her friends, as everybody ought.
But still from that sublimer azure hue,[5]
 So much the present dye, she was remote;
Was weak enough to deem Pope a great poet,
And what was worse, was not ashamed to show it.

XLVIII

Aurora—since we are touching upon taste,
 Which now-a-days is the thermometer
By whose degrees all characters are classed—
 Was more Shakespearian, if I do not err.
The worlds beyond this World's perplexing waste
 Had more of her existence, for in her
There was a depth of feeling to embrace
Thoughts, boundless, deep, but silent too as Space.

XLIX

Not so her gracious, graceful, graceless Grace,
 The full-grown Hebe[6] of Fitz-Fulke, whose mind,
If she had any, was upon her face,
 And that was of a fascinating kind.
A little turn for mischief you might trace
 Also thereon,—but that's not much; we find
Few females without some such gentle leaven,
For fear we should suppose us quite in Heaven.

L

I have not heard she was at all poetic,
 Though once she was seen reading the *Bath Guide,*[7]
And Hayley's *Triumphs,* which she deemed pathetic,
 Because she said *her temper* had been tried
So much, the bard had really been prophetic
 Of what she had gone through with—since a bride.
But of all verse, what most ensured her praise
Were sonnets to herself, or *bouts rimés.*[8]

2. Lochinvar, romantic hero of Scottish ballads, celebrated by Sir Walter Scott in *Marmion* (1808).
3. Violent fevers, usually associated with delirium of one sort or another. Byron's point is that the delights of romantic song may be hallucinatory and dangerous.
4. She was at least partly a "bluestocking," or priggishly intellectual female.
5. Adeline was not an enthusiast about Romantic poetry: a point in her favor, from Byron's point of view.
6. Classical goddess of youth and beauty, and bride of Hercules.
7. Christopher Anstey's *New Bath Guide* (1766) was a series of lightly humorous verse-letters. William Hayley's *The Triumphs of Temper* (1781) was a popular exercise in overemotional vacuity.
8. Stylized rhymed verse.

LI

'Twere difficult to say what was the object
    Of Adeline, in bringing this same lay
To bear on what appeared to her the subject
    Of Juan's nervous feelings on that day.
Perhaps she merely had the simple project
    To laugh him out of his supposed dismay;
Perhaps she might wish to confirm him in it,
Though why I cannot say—at least this minute.

LII

But so far the immediate effect
    Was to restore him to his self-propriety,
A thing quite necessary to the elect,
    Who wish to take the tone of their society:
In which you cannot be too circumspect,
    Whether the mode be persiflage or piety,
But wear the newest mantle of hypocrisy,
On pain of much displeasing the gynocracy.[9]

LIII

And therefore Juan now began to rally
    His spirits, and without more explanation
To jest upon such themes in many a sally.
    Her Grace, too, also seized the same occasion,
With various similar remarks to tally,
    But wished for a still more detailed narration
Of this same mystic friar's curious doings,
About the present family's deaths and wooings.

LIV

Of these few could say more than has been said;
    They passed as such things do, for superstition
With some, while others, who had more in dread
    The theme, half credited the strange tradition;
And much was talked on all sides on that head:
    But Juan, when cross-questioned on the vision,
Which some supposed (though he had not avowed it)
Had stirred him, answered in a way to cloud it.

LV

And then, the mid-day having worn to one,
    The company prepared to separate;
Some to their several pastimes, or to none,
    Some wondering 'twas so early, some so late.
There was a goodly match too, to be run
    Between some greyhounds on my Lord's estate,
And a young race-horse of old pedigree,
Matched for the spring, whom several went to see.

LVI

There was a picture-dealer who had brought
    A special Titian,[1] warranted original,

---

9. Rule by women.
1. Tiziano Vecellio (1477–1576), the great Italian painter.

So precious that it was not to be bought,
  Though Princes the possessor were besieging all—
The King himself had cheapened it, but thought
  The civil list he deigns to accept (obliging all
His subjects by his gracious acceptation)—
Too scanty, in these times of low taxation.

LVII

But as Lord Henry was a connoisseur,—
  The friend of Artists, if not Arts,—the owner,
With motives the most classical and pure,
  So that he would have been the very donor,
Rather than seller, had his wants been fewer,
  So much he deemed his patronage an honour,
Had brought the *capo d'opera*,[2] not for sale,
But for his judgment—never known to fail.

LVIII

There was a modern Goth, I mean a Gothic
  Bricklayer of Babel, called an architect,
Brought to survey these grey walls which, though so thick,
  Might have from Time acquired some slight defect;
Who, after rummaging the Abbey through thick
  And thin, produced a plan whereby to erect
New buildings of correctest conformation,
And throw down old—which he called *restoration*.

LIX

The cost would be a trifle—an "old song,"
  Set to some thousands ('tis the usual burden
Of that same tune, when people hum it long)—
  The price would speedily repay its worth in
An edifice no less sublime than strong,
  By which Lord Henry's good taste would go forth in
Its glory, through all ages shining sunny,
For Gothic daring shown in English money.

everything is levelled

LX

There were two lawyers busy on a mortgage
  Lord Henry wished to raise for a new purchase;
Also a lawsuit upon tenures burgage,[3]
  And one on tithes, which sure as Discord's torches,
Kindling Religion till she throws down *her* gage,
  "Untying" squires "to fight against the churches:"[4]
There was a prize ox, a prize pig, and ploughman,
For Henry was a sort of Sabine showman.

Everything is valued by how much it's worth

LXI

There were two poachers caught in a steel trap,
  Ready for gaol, their place of convalescence;

2. Masterpiece.
3. Royal ownership of farmland. "Tithe," in the next line, refers to a tax of ten per cent of the produce of a farm which the royal owner could charge.

4. The quotation is from *Macbeth* IV. i. 50–52, where Macbeth conjures the three witches to answer him even if they "untie the winds, and let them fight / Against the churches."

There was a country girl in a close cap
    And scarlet cloak (I hate the sight to see, since—
Since—since—in youth, I had the sad mishap—
    But luckily I have paid few parish fees[5] since):
That scarlet cloak, alas! unclosed with rigour,
Presents the problem of a double figure.

LXII

A reel within a bottle is a mystery,
    One can't tell how it e'er got in or out;
Therefore the present piece of natural history
    I leave to those who are fond of solving doubt;
And merely state, though not for the Consistory,
    Lord Henry was a Justice, and that Scout
The constable, beneath a warrant's banner,
Had bagged this poacher upon Nature's manor.

LXIII

Now Justices of Peace must judge all pieces
    Of mischief of all kinds, and keep the game
And morals of the country from caprices
    Of those who have not a licence for the same;
And of all things, excepting tithes and leases,
    Perhaps these are most difficult to tame:
Preserving partridges and pretty wenches
Are puzzles to the most precautious benches.

LXIV

The present culprit was extremely pale,
    Pale as if painted so; her cheek being red
By nature, as in higher dames less hale
    'Tis white, at least when they just rise from bed.
Perhaps she was ashamed of seeming frail,
    Poor soul! for she was country born and bred,
And knew no better in her immorality
Than to wax white—for blushes are for quality.

LXV

Her black, bright, downcast, yet *espiègle*[6] eye,
    Had gathered a large tear into its corner,
Which the poor thing at times essayed to dry,
    For she was not a sentimental mourner
Parading all her sensibility,
    Nor insolent enough to scorn the scorner,
But stood in trembling, patient tribulation,
To be called up for her examination.

LXVI

Of course these groups were scattered here and there,
    Not nigh the gay saloon of ladies gent.
The lawyers in the study; and in air
    The prize pig, ploughman, poachers: the men sent

---

5. For the support of an illegitimate child.   6. Arch, mischievous.

From town, viz. architect and dealer, were
    Both busy (as a General in his tent
Writing despatches) in their several stations,
Exulting in their brilliant lucubrations.

LXVII

But this poor girl was left in the great hall,
    While Scout, the parish guardian of the frail,
Discussed (he hated beer yclept the "small")
    A mighty mug of *moral* double ale.
She waited until Justice could recall
    Its kind attentions to their proper pale,
To name a thing in nomenclature rather
Perplexing for most virgins—a child's father.

LXVIII

You see here was enough of occupation
    For the Lord Henry, linked with dogs and horses.
There was much bustle too, and preparation
    Below stairs on the score of second courses;
Because, as suits their rank and situation,
    Those who in counties have great land resources
Have "public days," when all men may carouse,
Though not exactly what's called "open house."

LXIX

But once a week or fortnight, *un*invited
    (Thus we translate a *general invitation*)
All country gentlemen, esquired or knighted,
    May drop in without cards, and take their station
At the full board, and sit alike delighted
    With fashionable wines and conversation;
And, as the isthmus of the grand connection,
Talk o'er themselves the past and next election.

LXX

Lord Henry was a great electioneerer,
    Burrowing for boroughs like a rat or rabbit.
But county contests cost him rather dearer,
    Because the neighbouring Scotch Earl of Giftgabbit
Had English influence, in the self-same sphere here;
    His son, the Honourable Dick Dicedrabbit,
Was member for the "other interest" (meaning
The same self-interest, with a different leaning).

LXXI

Courteous and cautious therefore in his county,
    He was all things to all men, and dispensed
To some civility, to others bounty,
    And promises to all—which last commenced
To gather to a somewhat large amount, he
    Not calculating how much they condensed;
But what with keeping some, and breaking others,
His word had the same value as another's.

LXXII

A friend to Freedom and freeholders—yet
  No less a friend to Government—he held,
That he exactly the just medium hit
  'Twixt Place and Patriotism—albeit compelled,
Such was his Sovereign's pleasure, (though unfit,
  He added modestly, when rebels railed,)
To hold some sinecures he wished abolished,
But that with them all Law would be demolished.

LXXIII

He was "free to confess"—(whence comes this phrase?
  Is't English? No—'tis only parliamentary)
That Innovation's spirit now-a-days
  Had made more progress than for the last century.
He would not tread a factious path to praise,
  Though for the public weal disposed to venture high;
As for his place, he could but say this of it,
That the fatigue was greater than the profit.

LXXIV

Heaven, and his friends, knew that a private life
  Had ever been his sole and whole ambition;
But could he quit his King in times of strife,
  Which threatened the whole country with perdition?
When demagogues would with a butcher's knife
  Cut through and through (oh! damnable incision!)
The Gordian or the Geordi-an knot, whose strings
Have tied together Commons, Lords, and Kings.

LXXV

Sooner "come Place into the Civil List
  And champion him to the utmost[7]—" he would keep it,
Till duly disappointed or dismissed:
  Profit he cared not for, let others reap it;
But should the day come when Place ceased to exist,
  The country would have far more cause to weep it:
For how could it go on? Explain who can!
He gloried in the name of Englishman.

LXXVI

He was as independent—aye, much more—
  Than those who were not paid for independence,
As common soldiers, or a common——shore,
  Have in their several arts or parts ascendance
O'er the irregulars in lust or gore,
  Who do not give professional attendance.
Thus on the mob all statesmen are as eager
To prove their pride, as footmen to a beggar.

LXXVII

All this (save the last stanza) Henry said,

7. *Macbeth* III. i. 70–71. The original is "come, Fate, into the list / And champion me to the utterance," spoken by Macbeth as he resolves to murder Banquo.

And thought. I say no more—I've said too much;
For all of us have either heard or read—
    Off—or *upon* the hustings[8]—some slight such
Hints from the independent heart or head
    Of the official candidate. I'll touch
No more on this—the dinner-bell hath rung,
And grace is said; the grace I *should* have sung—

LXXVIII

But I'm too late, and therefore must make play.
    'Twas a great banquet, such as Albion old
Was wont to boast—as if a glutton's tray
    Were something very glorious to behold.
But 'twas a public feast and public day,—
    Quite full—right dull—guests hot, and dishes cold,—
Great plenty, much formality, small cheer,—
And everybody out of their own sphere.

LXXIX

The squires familiarly formal, and
    My Lords and Ladies proudly condescending;
The very servants puzzling how to hand
    Their plates—without it might be too much bending
From their high places by the sideboard's stand—
    Yet, like their masters, fearful of offending;
For any deviation from the graces
Might cost both man and master too—their *places*.

LXXX

There were some hunters bold, and coursers keen,
    Whose hounds ne'er erred, nor greyhounds deigned to lurch;
Some deadly shots too, Septembrizers,[9] seen
    Earliest to rise, and last to quit the search
Of the poor partridge through his stubble screen.
    There were some massy members of the church,
Takers of tithes, and makers of good matches,
And several who sung fewer psalms than catches.[1]

LXXXI

There were some country wags too—and, alas!
    Some exiles from the Town, who had been driven
To gaze, instead of pavement, upon grass,
    And rise at nine in lieu of long eleven.
And lo! upon that day it came to pass,
    I sate next that o'erwhelming son of Heaven,
The very powerful parson, Peter Pith,[2]
The loudest wit I e'er was deafened with.

8. Platforms erected for campaign speakers.
9. The Septembrists were those who took part in the bloody massacre of the royal inmates in the Bastille, September 1792. Byron, in applying this hated name to pheasant hunters, voices his lifelong love of wild animals and equally lifelong hatred of hunting for sport.
1. Drinking songs.
2. Perhaps a reference to Sidney Smith (1771–1845), a classic example of the wealthy, venal—and irreligious—English country Parson.

LXXXII

I knew him in his livelier London days,
    A brilliant diner-out, though but a curate,
And not a joke he cut but earned its praise,
    Until Preferment, coming at a sure rate,
(O Providence! how wondrous are thy ways!
    Who would suppose thy gifts sometimes obdurate?)
Gave him, to lay the Devil[3] who looks o'er Lincoln,
A fat fen vicarage, and nought to think on.

LXXXIII

His jokes were sermons, and his sermons jokes;
    But both were thrown away amongst the fens;
For Wit hath no great friend in aguish[4] folks.
    No longer ready ears and short-hand pens
Imbibed the gay bon-*mot*,[5] or happy hoax:
    The poor priest was reduced to common sense,
Or to coarse efforts very loud and long,
To hammer a hoarse laugh from the thick throng.

LXXXIV

There *is* a difference, says the song, "between
    A beggar and a Queen," or *was* (of late
The latter worse used of the two we've seen—
    But we'll say nothing of affairs of state);
A difference " 'twixt a Bishop and a Dean,"
    A difference between crockery ware and plate,
As between English beef and Spartan broth—
And yet great heroes have been bred by both.

LXXXV

But of all Nature's discrepancies, none
    Upon the whole is greater than the difference
Beheld between the Country and the Town,
    Of which the latter merits every preference
From those who have few resources of their own,
    And only think, or act, or feel, with reference
To some small plan of interest or ambition—
Both which are limited to no condition.

LXXXVI

But *En avant!*[6] The light loves languish o'er
    Long banquets and too many guests, although
A slight repast makes people love much more,
    Bacchus and Ceres[7] being, as we know,
Even from our grammar upwards, friends of yore
    With vivifying Venus, who doth owe
To these the invention of champagne and truffles:
Temperance delights her, but long fasting ruffles.

---

3. A striking gargoyle atop the tower of
Lincoln Cathedral.
4. Feverish, because of the inhospitable
climate of the fens (marshes).

5. Witty saying.
6. "Forward!"
7. See note to *Don Juan* II, CLXIX, 7.

LXXXVII

Dully passed o'er the dinner of the day;
  And Juan took his place, he knew not where,
Confused, in the confusion, and *distrait*,[8]
  And sitting as if nailed upon his chair:
Though knives and forks clanked round as in a fray,
  He seemed unconscious of all passing there,
Till some one, with a groan, expressed a wish
(Unheeded twice) to have a fin of fish.

LXXXVIII

On which, at the *third* asking of the banns,[9]
  He started; and perceiving smiles around
Broadening to grins, he coloured more than once,
  And hastily—as nothing can confound
A wise man more than laughter from a dunce—
  Inflicted on the dish a deadly wound,
And with such hurry, that, ere he could curb it,
He had paid his neighbour's prayer with half a turbot.

LXXXIX

This was no bad mistake, as it occurred,
  The supplicator being an amateur;
But others, who were left with scarce a third,
  Were angry—as they well might, to be sure,
They wondered how a young man so absurd
  Lord Henry at his table should endure;
And this, and his not knowing how much oats
Had fallen last market, cost his host three votes.

XC

They little knew, or might have sympathized,
That he the night before had seen a ghost,
A prologue which but slightly harmonized
  With the substantial company engrossed
By matter, and so much materialised,
  That one scarce knew at what to marvel most
Of two things—*how* (the question rather odd is)
Such bodies could have souls, or souls such bodies!

XCI

But what confused him more than smile or stare
  From all the 'squires and 'squiresses around,
Who wondered at the abstraction of his air,
  Especially as he had been renowned
For some vivacity among the fair,
  Even in the country circle's narrow bound—
(For little things upon my Lord's estate
Were good small talk for others still less great)—

8. Distraught, preoccupied.
9. In the Anglican Church, a couple would have to announce their intention to marry (the "banns" of marriage) three times on three successive weeks before the wedding could take place—so as to allow anyone having a legitimate objection to the marriage time to come forward.

XCII

Was, that he caught Aurora's eye on his,
  And something like a smile upon her cheek.
Now this he really rather took amiss;
  In those who rarely smile, their smile bespeaks
A strong external motive; and in this
  Smile of Aurora's there was nought to pique,
Or Hope, or Love—with any of the wiles
Which some pretend to trace in ladies' smiles.

XCIII

'Twas a mere quiet smile of contemplation,
  Indicative of some surprise and pity;
And Juan grew carnation with vexation,
  Which was not very wise, and still less witty,
Since he had gained at least her observation,
  A most important outwork of the city—
As Juan should have known, had not his senses
By last night's Ghost been driven from their defences.

XCIV

But what was bad, she did not blush in turn,
  Nor seem embarrassed—quite the contrary;
Her aspect was as usual, still—*not* stern—
  And she withdrew, but cast not down, her eye,
Yet grew a little pale—with what? concern?
  I know not; but her colour ne'er was high—
Though sometimes faintly flushed—and always clear,
As deep seas in a sunny atmosphere.

XCV

But Adeline was occupied by fame
  This day; and watching, witching, condescending
To the consumers of fish, fowl, and game,
  And dignity with courtesy so blending,
As all must blend whose part it is to aim
  (Especially as the sixth year[1] is ending)
At their lord's son's, or similar connection's
Safe conduct through the rocks of re-elections.

XCVI

Though this was most expedient on the whole
  And usual—Juan, when he cast a glance
On Adeline while playing her grand *rôle*,
  Which she went through as though it were a dance,
Betraying only now and then her soul
  By a look scarce perceptibly askance
(Of weariness or scorn), began to feel
Some doubt how much of Adeline was *real*;

XCVII

So well she acted all and every part

---

1. Lord Henry's Parliamentary term is   help him stand for reelection.
ending. He has invited these guests to

By turns—with that vivacious versatility,
Which many people take for want of heart.
　They err—'tis merely what is called mobility,
A thing of temperament and not of art,
　Though seeming so, from its supposed facility;
And false—though true; for, surely, they're sincerest
Who are strongly acted on by what is nearest.

excessive susceptibility to the present. Role-playing- Responding to what's nearest while at the same time w/o losing your self-expression. Don Juan w/ Heidee while still recalling Julia.

XCVIII

This makes your actors, artists, and romancers,
　Heroes sometimes, though seldom—sages never:
But speakers, bards, diplomatists, and dancers,
　Little that's great, but much of what is clever;
Most orators, but very few financiers,
　Though all Exchequer Chancellors[2] endeavour,
Of late years, to dispense with Cocker's[3] rigours,
And grow quite figurative with their figures.

XCIX

The poets of Arithmetic are they
　Who, though they prove not two and two to be
Five, as they might do in a modest way,
　Have plainly made it out that four are three,
Judging by what they take, and what they pay:
　The Sinking Fund's[4] unfathomable sea,
That most unliquidating liquid, leaves
The debt unsunk, yet sinks all it receives.

C

While Adeline dispensed her airs and graces,
　The fair Fitz-Fulke seemed very much at ease;
Though too well bred to quiz[5] men to their faces,
　Her laughing blue eyes with a glance could seize
The ridicules of people in all places—
　That honey of your fashionable bees—
And store it up for mischievous enjoyment;
And this at present was her kind employment.

CI

However, the day closed, as days must close;
　The evening also waned—and coffee came.
Each carriage was announced, and ladies rose,
　And curtsying off, as curtsies country dame,
Retired: with most unfashionable bows
　Their docile Esquires also did the same,
Delighted with their dinner and their Host,
But with the Lady Adeline the most.

CII

Some praised her beauty: others her great grace;
　The warmth of her politeness, whose sincerity

2. Treasurers.
3. Cocker's *Arithmetic* (1677) was still a standard textbook in Byron's day.
4. A scheme to eliminate the British na-
tional debt, which proved a financial disaster.
5. Mock.

Was obvious in each feature of her face,
  Whose traits were radiant with the rays of verity.
Yes; *she* was truly worthy *her* high place!
  No one could envy her deserved prosperity.
And then her dress—what beautiful simplicity
Draperied her form with curious felicity!

CIII

Meanwhile sweet Adeline deserved their praises,
  By an impartial indemnification
For all her past exertion and soft phrases,
  In a most edifying conversation,
Which turned upon their late guests' miens and faces,
  Their families, even to the last relation;
Their hideous wives, their horrid selves and dresses,
And truculent distortion of their tresses.

CIV

True, *she* said little—'twas the rest that broke
  Forth into universal epigram;
But then 'twas to the purpose what she spoke:
  Like Addison's[6] "faint praise," so wont to damn,
Her own but served to set off every joke,
  As music chimes in with a melodrame.
How sweet the task to shield an absent friend!
I ask but this of mine, to——*not* defend.

CV

There were but two exceptions to this keen
  Skirmish of wits o'er the departed; one,
Aurora, with her pure and placid mien;
  And Juan, too, in general behind none
In gay remark on what he had heard or seen,
  Sate silent now, his usual spirits gone:
In vain he heard the others rail or rally,
He would not join them in a single sally.

CVI

'Tis true he saw Aurora look as though
  She approved his silence; she perhaps mistook
Its motive for that charity we owe
  But seldom pay the absent, nor would look
Farther—it might or it might not be so.
  But Juan, sitting silent in his nook,
Observing little in his reverie,
Yet saw this much, which he was glad to see.

CVII

The Ghost at least had done him this much good,
  In making him as silent as a ghost,
If in the circumstances which ensued
He gained esteem where it was worth the most;

6. In Pope's *Prologue to the Satires*, he describes the essayist Joseph Addison's uncharitableness in the lines, "Damn with faint praise, assent with civil leer, / And without sneering, teach the rest to sneer" (201–2).

And, certainly, Aurora had renewed
  In him some feelings he had lately lost,
Or hardened; feelings which, perhaps ideal,
Are so divine, that I must deem them real:—

CVIII

The love of higher things and better days;
  The unbounded hope, and heavenly ignorance
Of what is called the World, and the World's ways;
  The moments when we gather from a glance
More joy than from all future pride or praise,
  Which kindle manhood, but can ne'er entrance
The Heart in an existence of its own,
Of which another's bosom is the zone.

CIX

Who would not sigh Ἀι ἀι τὰν Κυθερειαν[7]
  That *hath* a memory, or that *had* a heart?
Alas! *her* star must fade like that of Dian:
  Ray fades on ray, as years on years depart.
Anacreon[8] only had the soul to tie an
  Unwithering myrtle round the unblunted dart
Of Eros: but though thou hast played us many tricks,
Still we respect thee, "*Alma Venus Genetrix!*"[9]

CX

And full of sentiments, sublime as billows
  Heaving between this World and Worlds beyond,
Don Juan, when the midnight hour of pillows
  Arrived, retired to his; but to despond
Rather than rest. Instead of poppies, willows
  Waved o'er his couch; he meditated, fond
Of those sweet bitter thoughts which banish sleep,
And make the worldling sneer, the youngling weep.

CXI

The night was as before: he was undrest,
  Saving his night-gown, which is an undress;
Completely *sans culotte*,[1] and without vest;
  In short, he hardly could be clothed with less:
But apprehensive of his spectral guest,
  He sate with feelings awkward to express
(By those who have not had such visitations),
Expectant of the Ghost's fresh operations.

CXII

And not in vain he listened;—Hush! what's that?
  I see—I see—Ah, no!—'tis not—yet 'tis—

---

7. *Aí, aí, tàn Kythérian.* "Alas, alas for Cytherea (Aphrodite)." From Bion's *Lament for Adonis*. Bion (c. 100 B.C.) was an early Greek pastoral poet, and his elegy for Adonis (the young man whom Aphrodite loved, who died, and whom she brought back to life as a god) set the pattern for the pastoral elegy.

8. Greek poet (570–480 B.C.), author of drinking and erotic songs.

9. The opening words of Lucretius's first century B.C. philosophical poem, *On the Nature of Things*: "Hail, life-giving, beneficent Venus!"

1. Trouserless.

Ye powers! it is the—the—the—Pooh! the cat!
    The Devil may take that stealthy pace of his!
So like a spiritual pit-a-pat,
    Or tiptoe of an amatory Miss,
Gliding the first time to a *rendezvous,*
And dreading the chaste echoes of her shoe.

CXIII

Again—what is 't? The wind? No, no,—this time
    It is the sable Friar as before,
With awful footsteps regular as rhyme,
    Or (as rhymes may be in these days) much more.
Again through shadows of the night sublime,
    When deep sleep fell on men, and the World wore
The starry darkness round her like a girdle
Spangled with gems—the Monk made his blood curdle.

CXIV

A noise like to wet fingers drawn on glass,
    Which sets the teeth on edge; and a slight clatter,
Like showers which on the midnight gusts will pass,
    Sounding like very supernatural water,
Came over Juan's ear, which throbbed, alas!
    For Immaterialism's a serious matter;
So that even those whose faith is the most great
In Souls immortal, shun them *tête-à-tête.*

CXV

Were his eyes open?—Yes! and his mouth too.
    Surprise has this effect—to make one dumb,
Yet leave the gate which Eloquence slips through
    As wide as if a long speech were to come.
Nigh and more nigh the awful echoes drew,
    Tremendous to a mortal tympanum:
His eyes were open, and (as was before
Stated) his mouth. What opened next?—the door.

CXVI

It opened with a most infernal creak,
    Like that of Hell. "Lasciate ogni speranza,
Voi, ch' entrate!"[2] The hinge seemed to speak,
    Dreadful as Dante's *rima,*[3] or this stanza;
Or—but all words upon such themes are weak:
    A single shade's sufficient to entrance a
Hero—for what is Substance to a Spirit?
Or how is 't *Matter* trembles to come near it?

CXVII

The door flew wide, not swiftly,—but, as fly
    The sea-gulls, with a steady, sober flight—

2. The words written over the Gate of
Hell in Dante's *Inferno* (III, 9): "Abandon all hope, ye who enter here."
3. The *terza rima,* the distinctive verse

form of the *Divine Comedy* of Dante. It
is "dreadful" in that Dante's poem ex-
plores the dreadful or awe-inspiring
themes of hell, purgatory, and heaven.

And then swung back; nor close—but stood awry,
  Half letting in long shadows on the light,
Which still in Juan's candlesticks burned high,
  For he had two, both tolerably bright,
And in the doorway, darkening darkness, stood
The sable Friar in his solemn hood.

CXVIII

Don Juan shook, as erst he had been shaken
  The night before; but being sick of shaking,
He first inclined to think he had been mistaken;
  And then to be ashamed of such mistaking;
His own internal ghost began to awaken
  Within him, and to quell his corporal quaking—
Hinting that Soul and Body on the whole
Were odds against a disembodied Soul.

CXIX

And then his dread grew wrath, and his wrath fierce,
  And he arose, advanced—the Shade retreated;
But Juan, eager now the truth to pierce,
  Followed, his veins no longer cold, but heated,
Resolved to thrust the mystery *carte* and *tierce*,[4]
  At whatsoever risk of being defeated:
The Ghost stopped, menaced, then retired, until
He reached the ancient wall, then stood stone still.

CXX

Juan put forth one arm—Eternal powers!
  It touched no soul, nor body, but the wall,
On which the moonbeams fell in silvery showers,
  Chequered with all the tracery of the Hall;
He shuddered, as no doubt the bravest cowers
  When he can't tell what 'tis that doth appal.
How odd, a single hobgoblin's nonentity
Should cause more fear than a whole host's identity!

CXXI

But still the Shade remained: the blue eyes glared,
  And rather variably for stony death;
Yet one thing rather good the grave had spared,
  The Ghost had a remarkably sweet breath:
A straggling curl showed he had been fair-haired;
  A red lip, with two rows of pearls beneath,
Gleamed forth, as through the casement's ivy shroud
The Moon peeped, just escaped from a grey cloud.

CXXII

And Juan, puzzled, but still curious, thrust
  His other arm forth—Wonder upon wonder!
It pressed upon a hard but glowing bust,
  Which beat as if there was a warm heart under.
He found, as people on most trials must,

---

4. Positions of attack in fencing.

That he had made at first a silly blunder,
And that in his confusion he had caught
Only the wall, instead of what he sought.

CXXIII

The Ghost, if Ghost it were, seemed a sweet soul
    As ever lurked beneath a holy hood:
A dimpled chin, a neck of ivory, stole
    Forth into something much like flesh and blood;
Back fell the sable frock and dreary cowl,
    And they revealed—alas! that e'er they should!
In full, voluptuous, but *not o'er*grown bulk,
The phantom of her frolic Grace—Fitz-Fulke![5]

---

5. **Byron** wrote fourteen stanzas of the seventeenth canto, but they do not carry the action of the poem beyond this point.

Byron's
Letters and Journals

Byron's prose was by and large confined to his correspondence and his diaries, which he kept at odd times during his life. There were some critical essays published during his lifetime, some speeches in the House of Lords —even an attempt at a novel, which never got beyond the first ten pages. But as a writer of intensely private prose, Byron is perhaps unequaled among the Romantics—or, indeed, in his whole century.

Some recent critical estimates of the poet indeed have argued that while the poetry may not be of a consistently high order, Byron's letters display an energy, a wit, a range of tone, and an exuberance for life and for writing which elevate him to true greatness among stylists in English. One thinks of *Don Juan*, the great improvisation, as the only real analogue to the spirit of the letters in Byron's poetry.

To His Mother

Harrow-on-the-Hill, Sunday, May 1st, 1803

* * * I am sorry to say that Mr. Henry Drury[1] has behaved himself to me in a manner I neither *can* nor *will bear*. He has seized now an opportunity of showing his resentment towards me. To day in church I was talking to a Boy who was sitting next me; *that* perhaps was not right, but hear what followed. After Church he spoke not a word to me, but he took this Boy to his pupil room, where he abused me in a most violent manner, called me *blackguard*, said he *would* and *could* have me expelled from the School, and bade me thank his *Charity* that *prevented* him; this was the Message he sent me, to which I shall return no answer, but submit my case to *you* and those you may think *fit* to *consult*. Is this fit usage for any body! had I *stole* or behaved in the most *abominable* way to him, his language could not have been more outrageous. What must the boys think of me to hear such a Message ordered to be delivered to me by a *Master*? Better let him take away my life than ruin my *Character*. My Conscience acquits me of ever *meriting* expulsion at this School; I have been *idle* and I certainly ought not to talk in church, but I have never done a mean action at this School to him or *any one*. If I had done anything so *heinous*, why should he allow me to stay at the school? Why should he himself be so *criminal* as to overlook faults which merit the *appellation* of a *blackguard*? If he had had it in his power to have me expelled, he would long ago have *done* it; as it is, he has done *worse*. If I am treated in this Manner, I will not stay at this *School*. I write you that I will not as yet appeal to Dr. Drury; his son's influence is more than mine and *justice* would be *refused* me. Remember I told you, when I *left* you at *Bath*, that he would seize every means and opportunity of

1. Rev. Henry Joseph Drury was Byron's tutor at Harrow, and the son of Joseph Drury (the "Dr. Drury" mentioned later in this letter), the school's headmaster. After the row described in this letter, Byron and Drury became affectionate friends.

revenge, not for leaving him so much as the mortification he suffered, because I begged you to let me leave him. * * * If you do not take notice of this, I will leave the School myself; but I am sure *you* will not see me *ill treated*; better that I should suffer anything than this. I believe you will be tired by this time of reading my letter, but, if you love me, you will now show it. Pray write me immediately. I shall ever remain,

> Your affectionate Son,
> BYRON

To Francis Hodgson[2]

Newstead Abbey, Notts, Nov. 3, 1808

* * * We dined the other day with a neighbouring Esquire. . . . I was seated near a woman,[3] to whom, when a boy, I was as much attached as boys generally are, and more than a man should be. I knew this before I went, and was determined to be valiant, and converse with *sang froid*;[4] but instead I forgot my valour and my nonchalance, and never opened my lips even to laugh, far less to speak, and the lady was almost as absurd as myself, which made both the object of more observation than if we had conducted ourselves with easy indifference. You will think all this great nonsense; if you had seen it, you would have thought it still more ridiculous. What fools we are!

To William Harness[5]

8 St. James's Street, March 18th, 1809

* * * I am going abroad, if possible, in the spring, and before I depart I am collecting the pictures if my most intimate school-fellows; I have already a few, and shall want yours, or my cabinet will be incomplete. I have employed one of the first miniature painters of the day to take them, of course, at my own expense, as I never allow my acquaintance to incur the least expenditure to gratify a whim of mine. To mention this may seem indelicate; but when I tell you a friend of ours first refused to sit, under the idea that he was to disburse on the occasion, you will see that it is necessary to state these preliminaries to prevent the recurrence of any similar mistake. I shall see you in time, and will carry you to the *limner*.[6] It will be a tax on your patience for a week; but pray excuse it, as it is possible the resemblance may be the sole trace I shall be able to

2. Hodgson was a close friend of Byron's until 1816, himself a writer and a resident tutor at Cambridge while Byron was there.
3. Mary Chaworth, perhaps Byron's most passionate attachment.
4. French, meaning "cold blood."
5. William Harness was a friend of Byron's at Harrow; he later became a fairly well-known editor of Shakespeare.
6. Painter.

preserve of our friendship and acquaintance. Just now it seems foolish enough; but in a few years, when some of us are dead, and others are separated by inevitable circumstances, it will be a kind of satisfaction to retain in these images of the living the idea of our former selves, and, to contemplate, in the resemblances of the dead, all that remains of judgment, feeling and a host of passions. But all this will be dull enough for you, and so good night; and, to end my chapter, or rather my homily,

Believe me, my dear H., yours most affectionately.

To Henry Drury

Salsette frigate, May 3, 1810

* * * This morning I swam from *Sestos* to *Abydos*.[7] The immediate distance is not above a mile, but the current renders it hazardous;—so much so that I doubt whether Leander's conjugal affection must not have been a little chilled in his passage to Paradise. I attempted it a week ago, and failed,—owing to the north wind, and the wonderful rapidity of the tide,—though I have been from my childhood a strong swimmer. But, this morning being calmer, I succeeded, and crossed the 'broad Hellespont' in an hour and ten minutes.

Well, my dear sir, I have left my home, and seen part of Africa and Asia, and a tolerable portion of Europe. I have been with generals and admirals, princes and pashas, governors and ungovernables, —but I have not time or paper to expatiate . . .

I like the Greeks, who are plausible rascals,—with all the Turkish vices, without their courage. However, some are brave, and all are beautiful, very much resembling the busts of Alcibiades;[8]—the women not quite so handsome. I can swear in Turkish; but, except one horrible oath, and 'pimp' and 'bread', and 'water', I have got no great vocabulary in that language. They are extremely polite to strangers of any rank, properly protected * * *

I am like the Jolly Miller, caring for nobody, and not cared for. All countries are much the same in my eyes. I smoke, and stare at mountains, and twirl my mustachios very independently. I miss no comforts, and the mosquitoes that rack the morbid frame of H.[9] have, luckily for me, little effect on mine, because I live more temperately. * * *

My paper is full, and my ink ebbing—good afternoon! If you address to me at Malta, the letter will be forwarded wherever I may be. H. greets you; he pines for his poetry,—at least, some tidings of

7. See the lyric "On Swimming from Sestos to Abydos."
8. Alcibiades (450–404 B.C.) was an Athenian statesman and general.

9. "H." is John Cam Hobhouse, Byron's lifelong friend, and his companion on approximately the first half of this journey.

it. I almost forgot to tell you that I am dying for love of three Greek girls at Athens, sisters, I lived in the same house. Teresa, Mariana, and Katinka, are the names of these divinities,—all of them under fifteen.

Your ταπεινοτατοσ δουλοσ,[1]

BYRON

To Francis Hodgson[2]

Newstead Abbey, Sept. 3, 1811

My dear Hodgson,

I will have nothing to do with your immortality; we are miserable enough in this life, without the absurdity of speculating upon another. If men are to live, why die at all? and if they die, why disturb the sweet and sound sleep that 'knows no waking'? 'Post Mortem nihil est, ipsaque Mors nihil . . . quaeris quo jaceas post obitum loco? Quo *non* Nata jacent.'[3]

As to revealed religion, Christ came to save men; but a good Pagan will go to heaven, and a bad Nazarene to hell; 'Argal' (I argue like the gravedigger[4]) why are not all men Christians? or why are any? If mankind may be saved who never heard or dreamt, at Timbuctoo, Otaheite, Terra Incognita, etc., of Galilee and its Prophet, Christianity is of no avail: if they cannot be saved without, why are not all orthodox? It is a little hard to send a man preaching to Judaea, and leave the rest of the world—Negers and what not—*dark* as their complexions, without a ray of light for so many years to lead them on high; and who will believe that God will damn men for not knowing what they were never taught? I hope I am sincere; I was so at least on a bed of sickness in a far-distant country, when I had neither friend, nor comforter, nor hope, to sustain me. I looked to death as a relief from pain, without a wish for an after-life, but a confidence that the God who punishes in this existence had left that last asylum for the weary.

Ὁν ὁ θεός ἀγαπαει ἀποθνήσχει νέοσ

I am no Platonist, I am nothing at all; but I would sooner be a Paulician, Manichean, Spinozist, Gentile, Pyrrhonian, Zoroastrian, than one of the seventy-two villainous sects who are tearing each other to pieces for the love of the Lord and hatred of each other.

1. *Tapeinotatos doulos*, "most humble servant."
2. Hodgson, like many, was to profess shock at the apparent immorality of *Childe Harold* when it was published the year after this letter—and expressed concern to Byron over the latter's spiritual state.
3. From the *Troades* of the Roman tragedian Seneca. "After death there is no-thing, and death itself is nothing * * * you ask, where shall you lie after your death? In the same place where those *not yet born* lie."
4. In *Hamlet* V. i. 21 the gravedigger, speaking to Hamlet, uses "Argal" for the Latin "Ergo" ("therefore").
5. *Hon ho theos agapáei apothnéskei néos*: "He whom the god loves dies young."

Talk of Galileeism? Show me the effects—are you better, wiser, kinder by your precepts? I will bring you ten Mussulmans shall shame you in all goodwill towards men, prayer to God, and duty to their superiors. And is there a Talapoin, or a Bonze, who is not superior to a fox-hunting curate? But I will say no more on this endless theme; let me live, well if possible, and die without pain. The rest is with God, who assuredly, had He *come* or *sent*, would have made Himself manifest to nations, and intelligible to all.

I shall rejoice to see you. My present intention is to accept Scrope Davies's[6] invitation; and then, if you accept mine, we shall meet *here* and *there*. Did you know poor Matthews?[7] I shall miss him much at Cambridge.

To John Murray[8]

Newstead Abbey, Sept. 5, 1811

Sir,—

The time seems to be past when (as Dr. Johnson said) a man was certain to 'hear the truth from his bookseller', for you have paid me so many compliments, that, if I was not the veriest scribbler on earth, I should feel affronted. As I accept your compliments, it is but fair I should give equal or greater credit to your objections, the more so as I believe them to be well founded. With regard to the political and metaphysical parts, I am afraid I can alter nothing; but I have high authority for my Errors in that point, for even the *Aeneid* was a *political* poem, and written for a *political* purpose; and as to my unlucky opinions on Subjects of more importance, I am too sincere in them for recantation. On Spanish affairs I have said what I saw, and every day confirms me in that notion of the result formed on the Spot; and I rather think honest John Bull[9] is beginning to come round again to that Sobriety which Massena's retreat[1] had begun to reel from its centre—the usual consequence of *un*usual success. So you perceive I cannot alter the Sentiments; but if there are any alterations in the structure of the versification you would wish to be made, I will tag rhymes and turn stanzas as much as you please. As for the 'Orthodox', let us hope they will buy, on purpose to abuse—you will forgive the one, if they will do the other. You are aware that any thing from my pen must expect

---

6. Scrope Davies was a Cambridge friend of Byron's, a relatively notorious high liver.
7. Charles Matthews, one of Byron's close friends, drowned in 1811.
8. John Murray was Byron's publisher. This letter concerns the objections Murray and Byron's friend R. C. Dallas had raised to the moral attitudes of *Childe*

Harold I and II.
9. "John Bull" is the popular caricature of the portly, bluff, straightforward Englishman.
1. Napoleon's general, Massena, had been forced to retreat from Portugal in 1811 after meeting severe resistance from the English army under Wellington and widespread Portuguese guerilla action.

no quarter, on many accounts; and as the present publication is of a nature very different from the former, we must not be sanguine.

You have given me no answer to my question—tell me fairly, did you show the MS. to some of your corps?—I sent an introductory stanza to Mr. Dallas, that it might be forwarded to you; the poem else will open too abruptly. The Stanzas had better be numbered in Roman characters, there is a disquisition on the literature of the modern Greeks, and some smaller poems to come in at the close. These are now at Newstead, but will be sent in time. If Mr. D. has lost the Stanza and note annexed to it, write, and I will send it myself.—You tell me to add two cantos, but I am about to visit my *Collieries* in Lancashire on the 15th instant, which is so *unpoetical* an employment that I need say no more.

I am, sir, your most obedient, etc, etc.,

BYRON

To Lady Caroline Lamb[2]

May 1st, 1812

My Dear Lady Caroline,—

I have read over the few poems of Miss Milbank[3] with attention. They display fancy, feeling, and a little practice would very soon induce facility of expression. Though I have an abhorrence of Blank Verse, I like the lines on Dermody[4] so much that I wish they were in rhyme. The lines in the Cave at Seaham have a turn of thought which I cannot sufficiently commend, and here I am at least candid as my own opinions differ upon such subjects. The first stanza is very good indeed, and the others, with a few slight alterations might be rendered equally excellent. The last are smooth and pretty. But these are all, has she no others? She certainly is a very extraordinary girl; who would imagine so much strength and variety of thought under that placid Countenance? It is not necessary for Miss M. to be an authoress, indeed I do not think publishing at all creditable either to men or women, and (though you will not believe me) very often feel ashamed of it myself; but I have no hesitation in saying that she has talents which, were it proper or requisite to indulge, would have led to distinction.

A friend of mine (fifty years old, and an author, but not *Rogers*) has just been here. As there is no name to the MSS I shewed them to him, and he was much more enthusiastic in his praises than I

2. Lady Caroline Lamb, wife of William Lamb (who, as Lord Melbourne, was to be Queen Victoria's first prime minister), had a passionate and scandalous affair with Byron in 1812.
3. Annabella Milbanke, who was to become Byron's wife.

4. Thomas Dermody (1775–1802) was a minor Irish poet.
5. Joseph Blacket (died 1810) was a cobbler's son in the village of Seaham, and a self-taught lyric poet of brief and minor reputation.

have been. He thinks them beautiful; I shall content myself with observing that they are better, much better, than anything of Miss M's protegee Blacket.[5] You will say as much of this to Miss M. as you think proper. I say all this very sincerely. I have no desire to be better acquainted with Miss Milbank; she is too good for a fallen spirit to know, and I should like her more if she were less perfect.

Believe me, yours ever most truly, **B**

From His Journal, November 1813 to April 1814

Nov. 14

* * * At five-and-twenty, when the better part of life is over, one should be *something*;—and what am I? nothing but five-and-twenty —and the odd months. What have I seen? the same man all over the world,—ay, and woman too. Give *me* a Mussulman who never asks questions, and a she of the same race who saves one the trouble of putting them. But for this same plague—yellow fever—and New-stead delay, I should have been by this time a second time close to the Euxine.[6] * * *

No more reflections,—Let me see—last night I finished 'Zuleika',[7] my second Turkish Tale. I believe the composition of it kept me alive—for it was written to drive my thoughts from the recollection of—

Dear sacred name, rest ever unreveal'd.[8]

At least, even here, my hand would tremble to write it. This afternoon I have burnt the scenes of my commenced comedy. I have some idea of expectorating a romance, or rather a tale in prose;— but what romance could equal the events—* * *

Nov. 17

* * * I wish I could settle to reading again,—my life is monotonous, and yet desultory. I take up books, and fling them down again. I began a comedy, and burnt it because the scene ran into *reality*—a novel;—for the same reason. In rhyme, I can keep more away from facts; but the thought always runs through, through . . . yes, yes, through. I have had a letter from Lady Melbourne[9]—the best friend I ever had in my life, and the cleverest of women. * * *

November 23
Tuesday morning

* * * If I had any views in this country, they would probably be parliamentary. But I have no ambition; at least, if any, it would be

6. The Black Sea.
7. The first title of Byron's *The Bride of Abydos*.
8. The quote is from Alexander Pope's *Eloisa to Abelard*. This is probably a reference to Byron's affair with his half sister Augusta.
9. Lady Melbourne, Caroline Lamb's mother-in-law and Annabella Milbanke's aunt, was one of Byron's closest and most trusted friends until her death in 1818.

aut Caesar aut nihil.[1] My hopes are limited to the arrangement of my affairs, and settling either in Italy or the East (rather the last), and drinking deep of the languages and literature of both. Past events have unnerved me; and all I can now do is to make life an amusement, and look on while others play. After all, even the highest game of crowns and sceptres, what is it? *Vide* Napoleon's last twelvemonth. It has completely upset my system of fatalism. I thought, if crushed, he would have fallen, when *fractus illabitur orbis*,[2] and not have been pared away to gradual insignificance; that all this was not a mere *jeu*[3] of the gods, but a prelude to greater changes and mightier events. But men never advance beyond a certain point; and here we are, retrograding, to the dull, stupid old system,—balance of Europe—poising straws upon kings' noses, instead of wringing them off! Give me a republic, or a despotism of one, rather than the mixed government of one, two, three. A republic! —look in the history of the Earth—Rome, Greece, Venice, France, Holland, America, our short (eheu!)[4] Commonwealth, and compare it with what they did under masters. The Asiatics are not qualified to be republicans, but they have the liberty of demolishing despots, which is the next thing to it. To be the first man—not the Dictator—not the Sylla, but the Washington or the Aristides—the leader in talent and truth—is next to the Divinity! Franklin, Penn, and, next to these, either Brutus or Cassius—even Mirabeau —or St. Just.[5] I shall never be any thing, or rather always be nothing. The most I can hope is, that some will say, 'He might, perhaps, if he would.'

To Lady Melbourne

January 7th, 1815

* * * I got a wife and a cold on the same day, but have got rid of the last pretty speedily. I don't dislike this place, it is just the spot for a moon; there is my only want, a *library*, and thus I can always amuse myself, even if alone. I have great hopes this match will turn out well. I have found nothing as yet that I could wish changed for the better; but time does wonders, so I won't be too hasty in my happiness.

I will tell you all about the ceremony when we meet. It went off

1. "Either Caesar or nothing": if one cannot be a truly great figure, there is no use in being anything at all.
2. "When the world itself is broken apart."
3. Jest.
4. "Alas!"
5. In the flurry of examples with which this entry concludes, Byron expresses his wish to be remembered as one of the liberators, rather than oppressors, of mankind. "Sylla" or, more often, Sulla, was dictator of Rome from 82 to 79 B.C. Aristides (530–486 B.C.), called "the Just," was an Athenian statesman and general. Brutus and Cassius were the leaders of the plot to kill Julius Caesar, 44 B.C., in the name of Republican libertarianism. Honoré Riqueti, Count de Mirabeau (1749–91) and Louis Antoine Léon de Saint-Just (1767–94) were influential leaders of the French Revolution.

very pleasantly, all but the cushions, which were stuffed with peach-stones I believe, and made me make a face which passed for piety.

My love to all my relatives; by the way, what do they mean to give *me*? I will compromise, provided they let me choose what I will have instead of their presents, nothing but what they could very well spare.

Ever Aunt, thine dutifully,
B.

To Lady Byron

February 8th, 1816

* * *

All I can say seems useless—and all I could say might be no less unavailing—yet I still cling to the wreck of my hopes, before they sink for ever. Were you, then, *never* happy with me? Did you never at any time or times express yourself so? Have no marks of affection of the warmest and most reciprocal attachment passed between us? or did in fact hardly a day go down without some such on one side, and generally on both? Do not mistake me: I have not denied my state of mind—but you know its causes—and were those deviations from calmness never followed by acknowledgments and repentance? Was not the last that recurred more particularly so? and had I not —had we not the days before and on the day we parted—every reason to believe that we loved each other? that we were to meet again? Were not your letters kind? Had I not acknowledged to you all my faults and follies—and assured you that some had not and could not be repeated? I do not require these questions to be answered to me, but to your own heart. * * * It is torture to correspond thus, and there are things to be settled and said which cannot be written.

You say it is my disposition to deem what I have worthless. Did I deem *you* so? Did I ever so express myself to you, or of you to others? You are much changed within these twenty days or you would never have thus poisoned your own better feelings and trampled on mine.

Ever your most truly and affectly.

To John Murray

September 15, 1817

Dear Sir,

I enclose a sheet[6] for correction, if ever you get to another edition. You will observe that the blunder in printing makes it appear

6. Of *The Prisoner of Chillon*.

as if the Chateau was *over* St. Gingo, instead of being on the opposite shore of the Lake, over Clarens. So, separate the paragraphs,
otherwise my *to*pography will seem as inaccurate as your *ty*pography
on this occasion.

The other day I wrote to convey my proposition with regard to
the 4th and concluding canto.[7] I have gone over and extended it to
one hundred and fifty stanzas. * * * I look upon *Childe Harold* as
my best; and as I begun, I think of concluding with it. But I make
no resolutions on that head, as I broke my former intention with
regard to *The Corsair*. However, I fear that I shall never do better;
and yet, not being thirty years of age, for some moons to come, one
ought to be progressive as far as Intellect goes for many a good year.
But I have had a devilish deal of wear and tear of mind and body in
my time, besides having published too often and much already. * * *

With regard to poetry in general, I am convinced, the more I
think of it, that [Moore] and *all* of us—Scott, Southey, Wordsworth, Moore, Campbell,[8] I,—are all in the wrong, one as much as
another; that we are upon a wrong revolutionary poetical system, or
systems, not worth a damn in itself, and from which none but
Rogers and Crabbe[9] are free; and that the present and next generations will finally be of this opinion. I am the more confirmed in this
by having lately gone over some of our classics, particularly *Pope*,
whom I tried in this way,—I took Moore's poems and my own and
some others, and went over them side by side with Pope's, and I
was really astonished (I ought not to have been so) and mortified
at the ineffable distance in point of sense, harmony, effect, and even
Imagination, passion and *Invention*, between the little Queen
Anne's man, and us of the Lower Empire. * * *

To Thomas Moore

Venice, February 2, 1818

* * * I don't much care what the wretches of the world think of
me—all *that's* past. But I care a good deal what *you* think of me,
and, so say what you like. You *know* that I am not sullen; and, as
to being *savage*, such things depend on circumstances. However, as
to being in good humour in *your* society, there is no great merit in
that, because it would be an effort, or an insanity, to be otherwise.

I don't know what Murray may have been saying or quoting.[1] I
called Crabbe and Sam the fathers of present Poesy; and said, what
I thought—except them—*all* of '*us youth*' were on a wrong tack.
But I never said that we did not sail well. Our fame will be hurt by

7. Of *Childe Harold's Pilgrimage*.
8. Sir Walter Scott (1771–1832), Robert
Southey (1774–1843), William Wordsworth (1770–1850), Thomas Moore
(1779–1852), and Thomas Campbell
(1777–1814).
9. Samuel Rogers (1763–1855) and
George Crabbe (1754–1832).
1. Byron's letter to John Murray, September 15, 1817.

admiration and *imitation*. When I say *our*, I mean *all* (Lakers[2] included), except the postscript of the Augustans. The next generation (from the quantity and facility of imitation) will tumble and break their necks off our Pegasus, who runs away with us; but we keep the *saddle*, because we broke the rascal and can ride. But though easy to mount, he is the devil to guide; and the next fellows must go back to the riding-school and the manège, and learn to ride the 'great horse.' * * *

To John Cam Hobhouse and the Honorable Douglas Kinnaird[3]

Venice, January 19th, 1819

Dear H. and Dear K.,

I approve and sanction all your legal proceedings with regard to my affairs, and can only repeat my thanks and approbation. If you put off the payments of debts 'till *after* Lady Noel's[4] death,' it is well; if till *after* her damnation, better, for that will last for ever; yet I hope not; for her sake as well as the creditors I am willing to believe in purgatory.

With regard to the Poeshie, I will have no 'cutting and slashing,' as Perry calls it; you may omit the stanzas on Castelreagh, indeed it is better, and the two *'Bobs'* at the end of the 3rd stanza of the dedication, which will leave 'high' and 'a-dry' good rhymes without any *'double* (or single) entendre,' but no more.[5] I appeal, not 'to Philip fasting,' but to Alexander drunk; I shall appeal to Murray at his ledger, to the people, in short, Don Juan shall be an entire horse, or none. If the objection be to the indecency, the Age which applauds the 'Bath Guide,' and Little's poems, and reads Fielding and Smollett still, may bear with that. If to the poetry, I will take my chance. I will not give away to all the cant of Christendom. I have been cloyed with applause, and sickened with abuse; at present I care for little but the copy-right; I have imbibed a great love for money, let me have it; if Murray loses this time, he won't the next; he will be cautious, and I shall learn the decline of his customers by his epistolary indications. But in no case will I submit to have the poem mutilated. There is another Canto written, but not copied, in two hundred and odd Stanzas, if this succeeds; as to the prudery of the present day, what is it? Are we more moral than when Prior[6] wrote? Is there anything in 'Don Juan' so strong as in Ariosto,[7] or Voltaire, or Chaucer? . . .

2. The "Lake" poets (Wordsworth, Southey, and Coleridge) so-called because they lived in the Lake District of England.
3. Kinnaird (1788–1830) was Bryon's close friend and his banker.
4. That is, his wife, Lady George Noel Gordon Byron.

5. Byron ultimately refused even these "mutilations" of *Don Juan.*
6. Matthew Prior (1664–1721), English lyric amatory poet.
7. Ludovico Ariosto (1474–1537), Italian epic poet who celebrated the passionate variety of love.

To the Honorable Douglas Kinnaird

Venice, Octr 26, 1819

* * * As to 'Don Juan,' confess, confess—you dog and be candid that it is the sublime of *that there* sort of writing it may be bawdy but is it not good English? It may be profligate but is it not *life*, is it not *the thing*? Could any man have written it who has not lived in the world? and —ooled[8] in a post-chaise? in a hackney coach? in a gondola? against a wall? in a court carriage? in a vis à vis? on a table? and under it? I have written about a hundred stanzas of a third Canto, but it is a damned modest—the outcry has frighted me. I have such projects for the Don but the Cant is so much stronger than the ——,[9] nowadays, that the benefit of experience in a man who had well weighed the worth of both monosyllables must be lost to despairing posterity. * * *

You are right about *income*. I must have it all. How the devil do I know that I may live a year, or a month? I wish I knew, that I might regulate my spending in more ways than one.[1] As it is, one always thinks that there is but a span. A man may as well break, or be damned for a large sum as a small one. I should be loth to pay the devil, or any other creditor more than six pence in the pound.

Yours, B.

From His "Detached Thoughts," October 1821 to May 1822[2]

Octr 15th, 1821

* * * My Mother, before I was twenty, would have it that I was like Rousseau, and Madame de Staël[3] used to say so too in 1813, and the *Edinʰ Review* has something of the sort in its critique on the 4ᵗʰ Canto of *Chᵉ Haᵈ*. I can't see any point of resemblance: he wrote prose, I verse: he was of the people, I of the Aristocracy: he was a philosopher, I am none: he published his first work at forty, I mine at eighteen: his first essay brought him universal applause, mine the contrary: he married his house-keeper, I could not keep house with my wife: he thought all the world in a plot against

---

8. The first letter in the word is illegible, but must be either *T*, making the word "tooled" (driven grandly) or *F*, making it "fooled" (made love). The conjectures of various editors as to which is the first letter say a good deal about their respective attitudes toward Byron's personality.

9. Expletive deleted: obviously it is "cunt."

1. Another bawdy pun. In the nineteenth century, "to spend" could also mean "to ejaculate in sexual intercourse."

2. What Byron called his "Detached Thoughts" was a reflective journal—a kind of philosophical diary—he kept for nearly a year.

3. Jean-Jacques Rousseau (1712–78) was the great philosopher of early French Romanticism. Madame de Staël (Anne Louise Germaine Necker, Baroness de Staël, 1766–1817), writer and friend of writers, is one of the important figures in the social and intellectual life of the early nineteenth century.

him, my little world seems to think *me* in a plot against it, if I may judge by their abuse in print and coterie: he liked Botany, I like flowers, and herbs, and trees, but know nothing of their pedigrees: he wrote Music, I limit my knowledge of it to what I catch by *Ear* —I could never learn any thing by *study,* not even a language, it was all by rote and ear and memory: he had a bad memory, I *had* at least an excellent one . . . he wrote with hesitation and care, I with rapidity and rarely with pains: he could never ride nor swim 'nor was cunning of fence,' *I* am an excellent swimmer, a decent though not at all a dashing rider (having staved in a rib at eighteen in the course of scampering), and was sufficient of fence—particularly of the Highland broadsword. * * *

Altogether, I think myself justified in thinking the comparison not well founded. I don't say this out of pique, for Rousseau was a great man, and the thing if true were flattering enough; but I have no idea of being pleased with a chimera. . . .

33

I have a notion that Gamblers are as happy as most people, being always *excited.* Women, wine, fame, the table, even Ambition, sate[4] now and then; but every turn of the card, and cast of the dice, keeps the Gamester alive: besides one can Game ten times longer than one can do any thing else.

I was very fond of it when young, that is to say, of 'Hazard'; for I hate all *Card* Games, even Faro. When Macco (or whatever they spell it) was introduced, I gave up the whole thing; for I loved and missed the *rattle* and *dash* of the box and dice, and the glorious uncertainty, not only of good luck or bad luck, but of *any luck at all,* as one had sometimes to throw *often* to decide at all. * * *

53

In general, I do not draw well with literary men; not that I dislike them, but I never know what to say to them after I have praised their last publication. There are several exceptions, to be sure; but then they have either been men of the world, such as Scott, and Moore, etc., or visionaries out of it, such as Shelley, etc.: but your literary every day man and I never went well in company —especially your foreigner, whom I never could abide. * * *

66

One of my notions, different from those of my contemporaries, is, that the present is not a high age of English Poetry: there are *more* poets (soi-disant)[5] than ever there were, and proportionally *less* poetry.

This *thesis* I have maintained for some years, but, strange, to say, it meeteth not with favour from my brethren of the Shell. Even Moore shakes his head, and firmly believes that it is the grand Era of British Poetry. * * *

4. Cloy.   5. Self-serving.

96

Of the Immortality of the Soul, it appears to me that there can be little doubt, if we attend for a moment to the action of Mind. It is in perpetual activity. I used to doubt of it, but reflection has taught me better. It acts also very independent of body; in dreams for instance incoherently and madly, I grant you; but still it is *Mind*, and much more *Mind* than when we are awake. Now, that *this* should not act *separately*, as well as jointly, who can pronounce? The Stoics, Epictetus and Marcus Aurelius,[6] call the present state 'a Soul which drags a Carcase': a heavy chain, to be sure; but all chains, being material, may be shaken off. * * *

A *material* resurrection seems strange, and even absurd, except for purposes of punishment; and all punishment, which is to *revenge* rather than *correct*, must be *morally wrong*. And *when* the *World is at an end*, what moral or warning purpose *can* eternal tortures answer? Human passions have probably disfigured the divine doctrines here, but the whole thing is inscrutable. It is useless to tell me *not* to *reason*, but to *believe*. You might as well tell a man not to wake but *sleep*. And then to *bully* with torments! and all that; I cannot help thinking that the *menace* of Hell makes as many devils, as the severe penal codes of inhuman humanity make villains.

Man is born *passionate* of body, with an innate though secret tendency to the love of Good in his Mainspring of Mind. But God help us all! It is at present a sad jar of atoms. * * *

To the Honorable Augusta Leigh

Cephalonia S^{bre} *12*th *1823*

* * * You ask why I came up amongst the Greeks? It was stated to me that my so doing might tend to their advantage in some measure in their present struggle for independence, both as an individual and as a member for the Committee now in England. How far this may be realised I cannot pretend to anticipate, but I am willing to do what I can. They have at length found leisure to quarrel among themselves, after repelling their other enemies, and it is no very easy part that I may have to play to avoid appearing partial to one or other of their factions. They have turned out Mavrocordato,[7] who was the only *Washington* or *Kosciusko*[8] kind of man amongst them, and they have not yet sent their deputies to

6. The Stoic school of classical philosophy taught that a resigned, intellectual detachment from the cares of existence was the highest good to which man could attain, and that a truly enlightened man would not allow himself to be moved to outward signs of emotion by even the most violent events. Epictetus (A.D. 60–120), a Greek philosopher living in Rome, and Marcus Aurelius (A.D. 121–180), Emperor of Rome from 161 till his death, were important expositors of Stoicism.
7. Alexander Mavrocordato, Greek patriot and sometime leader of the revolution against Turkish rule, who had first solicited Byron's involvement in the war.

London to treat for a loan, nor in short done themselves so much good as they might have done. I have written to Mr. Hobhouse three several times with a budget of documents on the subject, from which he can extract all the present information for the Committee. I have written to their Gov^t. at Tripolizza and Salamis, and am waiting for instructions *where* to proceed, for things are in such a state amongst them, that it is difficult to conjecture where one could be useful to them, if at all. However, I have some hopes that they will see their own interest sufficiently not to quarrel till they have received their national independence, and then they can fight it out among them in a domestic manner—and welcome. You may suppose that I have something to *think* of at least, for you can have no idea what an intriguing cunning unquiet generation they are, and as emissaries of all parties come to me at present, and I must act impartially, it makes me exclaim, as Julian[9] did at his military exercises, 'Oh! Plato, what a task for a Philosopher!'

However, *you* won't think much of *my philosophy*: nor do I, *entre nous*.[1] * * *

To Mr. Mayer, English Consul at Prevesa

[Undated]

Sir,

Coming to Greece, one of my principal objects was to alleviate as much as possible the miseries incident to a warfare so cruel as the present. When the dictates of humanity are in question, I know no difference between Turks and Greeks. It is enough that those who want assistance are men, in order to claim the pity and protection of the meanest pretender to humane feelings. I have found here twenty-four Turks, including women and children, who have long pined in distress, far from the means of support and the consolations of their home. The Government has consigned them to me; I transmit them to Prevesa, whither they desire to be sent. I hope you will not object to take care that they may be restored to a place of safety, and that the Governor of your town may accept of my present. The best recompense I can hope for would be to find that I had inspired the Ottoman commanders with the same sentiments towards those unhappy Greeks who may hereafter fall into their hands. I beg you to believe me, etc.

N. BYRON

8. Thaddeus Kosciusko (1746–1817), Polish patriot and general in the American Revolution.
9. Julian, called "the Apostate" (331–363) was Emperor of Rome from 361 till his death, and attempted to reintroduce the old pagan gods in place of Christianity.
1. "Just between us."

Criticism

BERGEN EVANS

Lord Byron's Pilgrimage†

"There is no sterner moralist than pleasure," Byron wrote towards the end of his life. And certainly few men have ever been in a better position to know. One of the world's great hedonists, gifted in profusion with all that all men desire—genius, beauty, wealth, social position, high spirits, and the power to charm all he met, men and women—and freed (though humiliated and tormented) by his deformity from the restriction of conventional values, he drained "life's enchanted cup" only to tell us that it "but sparkles near the brim."

If prudence, playing it safe, and seeking one's material advantage are signs of sanity, if the ultimate test is the rat in the maze, then of course the man was mad. And the descendant of madmen.

Through his mother he was one of the Gordons of Gight, border reavers who "lived a life of storm and strife and died of treachery."

Through his father he came of an even wilder strain. At the time of his birth the family titles and estates were in the possession of the fifth Lord Byron, called "the Wicked Lord" because he had killed a neighbor in a duel, was rumored to have murdered his wife, and stabled his horses in his chapel. In lighter moments he chopped down trees and emptied his neighbors' fish ponds at night. To prevent retaliation he built a fort on his own fish pond and supplemented the fort with a small navy in the form of an armed raft—though this may also have been intended to repel any invasion by his younger brother, the redoubtable Admiral John Byron, known in the service as "Foul-weather Jack."

It was the admiral's eldest son, "Mad Jack" Byron, who fathered the poet. At the age of twenty Jack persuaded Lady Carmarthen, one of the wealthiest women of the day, to desert her husband and three children and elope with him to France. There he married her and spent as much of her money as he could get his hands on. They had one child, Augusta.

Lady Carmarthen died in 1784 and for his next heiress he had to come down to Kitty Gordon, who was not very pretty and, worse, not very rich. However, he got her to convert whatever she had to cash, squandered that within a year, and deserted her. So that by the time her child was born (1788) she was a ruined and abandoned woman, with a violent temper and a broken heart, living in lodgings in Aberdeen.

And, as an extra blow, her child was lame. Though his feet were

† Professor Evans's lecture is here printed for the first time, with his kind permission.

seemingly normal, he was unable to put his whole foot to the ground and walked, or rather teetered, on his toes. This deformity may have been due to the mother's excessive prudery at the time of her delivery. At least Byron always thought so.

The baby grew up to be an affectionate and intelligent child, but emotionally unstable, subject to fits of rage and sullenness, proud, obstinate, rebellious, and passionate. And all this was made worse by a stupid nurse who stuffed his head full of superstitions of hell-fire and God's wrath. When she wasn't engaged in these pious activities, or drunk, she instructed him in certain mundane practices which the curious will find fully described in Kinsey and Kraft-Ebbing.

Then, when the boy was ten, came a piece of good luck. Or perhaps it was an added piece of bad luck. It's hard to say. Foul-weather Jack had transferred his pennant to the Waters above the Firmament in 1786 and Mad Jack had made good his sobriquet by committing suicide. So that when, in 1798, the Devil belatedly got around to picking up the Wicked Lord, the child found himself Lord Byron, Baron Rochdale, a peer of the realm and the possessor of vast, romantic (and heavily mortgaged) estates. His teachers, his schoolfellows, his mother and even the amorous, alcoholic, pious nurse addressed him as "my lord." Very gratifying, no doubt, to one who but the day before had been the "lame brat," but very dangerous, too.

Kitty hurried south but found the estate submerged in debt and, thanks to the genius of the Wicked Lord, totally uninhabitable. So it was lodgings once more, the more humiliating in that they were this time in Nottingham, at the very gates of Newsteal Abbey, the family seat.

And there was more than humiliation. The child was put into the hands of a sadistic charlatan who professed to be able to cure his lameness and tortured him for years with various therapeutic boots that caused him great pain and served no purpose other than to drive home, in anguish, the realization that he could not be like other people.

He was sent to Harrow where, after the usual preliminary pre-school cruelties, he became accepted and admired. Despite his misfortune, he was athletic and became a good boxer and an excellent swimmer. He was also a marksman, and for the rest of his days he was never without loaded pistols. Plainly, he did not intend to be pushed around. Nor did he intend, so far as he could help it, to permit those whom he liked to be pushed around. He set himself up as the champion of the smaller boys when they were persecuted.

The estates had been rented to a Lord Gray and in his long vacation Byron visited Gray, living as a guest in his own house. But he wasn't there much of the time because he had fallen in love with Mary Chaworth, the granddaughter of the man the Wicked Lord had killed. The estates adjoined and the old enmity made the association doubly romantic. She was seventeen and he was fourteen, ages which made the affair ludicrous to her but tragic to him. She was actually in love with Jack Musters, a local fox-hunting clod and the ardent, wild boy who galloped over every day and announced his arrival by discharging his pistols into the oaken front door was to her only a diversion. But to *him, she* was no diverson. He always insisted that this was the deepest, most passionate love affair of his life.

At the end of the vacation he refused to return to school and moved in with the Chaworths. But the accidental overhearing of a contemptuous remark by Mary about his lameness brought him sufficiently to his senses to lead him to return to Harrow the following term.

In 1805 he went up to Cambridge, to Trinity College, where, to his scrimping mother's rage, he began squandering in a manner worthy of his father, blithely borrowing on the estates at one hundred percent interest. These transactions, which left him at graduation in debt to about the modern equivalent of two hundred thousand dollars, were necessitated in part by an entourage of trulls and pugilists with which, as a young aristocrat, he felt it proper to be surrounded. Among the esoterica in his train was a tame bear for which, he said, he had applied for a Fellowship. The brute was probably maintained for the sake of the joke.

At his majority he returned to Newstead. Lord Gray had left the place almost as run down as the Wicked Lord had left it, but Byron enjoyed the dilapidation, cultivated melancholy and wrote verses about Mary Chaworth—who was now Mrs. Musters and wishing she wasn't.

Then, as a sort of graduate course, he decided to see something of the world and simply ordered his startled agent to sell the estates in order to finance his travels.

Before he set out for the East he had his Cambridge friends up for a farewell house party. Since Newstead had formerly been an abbey, the motif was monastic. The guests dressed as monks, Byron as the abbot, though conventual discipline was relaxed in many particulars, especially in regard to the housemaids. They drank from a skull which had been found in the garden and which Byron had had mounted as a wassail bowl. Years later, when the Byronic legend had flowered, several French biographers asserted that the skull was that of one of his former mistresses.

From 1809 to 1811 he traveled in the Mediterranean, diversifying pleasant idleness with various amours (including, probably, some homosexuality) and the writing of a sort of rimed travelogue which on his return to England was published as the first two cantos of *Childe Harold's Pilgrimage.*

It was an immediate and enormous popular success. He awoke, as he said, one morning to find himself famous.

More famous, perhaps, than any man up to that time had ever been. No Englishman has ever enjoyed (or suffered) greater popularity than Byron did in the following year. Everything combined to make him the lion of 1812. His beauty, his nobility, his genius, his aloofness, his deformity—not content with all these, rumor heaped surmise on conjecture and added mystery to fascination. It was known that he lived in a great ruined abbey in the north where he indulged in criminal debauches of unspeakable voluptuousness which, none the less, failed to move his cold, cold heart.

This unfailing aphrodisiac prescription has never been more successfully mixed. The women went wild. They obstructed traffic before his lodgings. They deluged him with fan mail. They threw themselves at his feet. Older women threw younger women. An Irish mother, combining lewdness and thrift, urged him to buy her daughter for a hundred pounds, assuring him that "with dilicaci everything may be made asy."

One admirer outdid the rest. And this was Lady Caroline Lamb, the young wife of that William Lamb who, as Lord Melbourne, was later to exercise a wise and affectionate control over the young Queen Victoria.

From the first, Lady Caroline had been frantic to meet the man of the hour and when she finally met him he proved to be all that she had imagined and more. Or, rather, she was able to project onto the actual man wilder fantasies than those with which she had endowed his mere name and reputation. "Mad, bad, and dangerous to know," she confided breathlessly to her diary, and added: "That beautiful pale face will be my destiny."

Whether he was her destiny or not, she was certainly his. She offered him her all, including her jewels. Byron declined the jewels and soon wished he had declined everything else. For she was passionate and moody and jealous and made scenes—public scenes. And public scenes were something that Byron, with his secret loathing of his lameness, could not endure. The whole thing culminated in a hysterical outburst at a ball in which a glass was broken and her wrist cut. Whether it was a serious attempt at suicide, or merely exhibitionism, or simply an accident, Byron had had enough and was eager to be rid of her. It wasn't easy, but by joining with her husband and her mother-in-law they got her packed off to Ireland where he wrote her that he was willing to protest his love to her to any degree that was necessary to keep her from coming back.

She relieved the tedium of her exile and the rancor of her rejection by writing a novel, *Glenarvon,* in which, under the most transparent of veils and in the most strained and turgid of language she depicted their love affair as she saw it. Naturally she was eager to hear *his* opinion of it and he expressed it in a sort of books-of-the-month-in-review jingle which remains, in the history of book-reviewing, as a masterpiece of forceful concision:

> I read "Glenarvon," too, by Caro Lamb
> God damn!

Scarcely had he time, however, to congratulate himself on escaping the clutches of this Scylla than he was sucked into the Charybdis of marriage. He had been toying with the idea of matrimony for some time and had written his half sister Augusta, "When I can find a woman rich enough to suit me and foolish enough to have me, I'll give her leave to make me miserable if she can."

And he thought he had found such a woman—as, far more than he knew, he had!—in Annabella Milbanke, a cousin of Lady Caroline's. She was a serious, chaste young woman who dabbled in mathematics and poetry, was icily religious and self-righteous to the verge of paranoia. She was allured not merely by Byron's reputed wickedness—always fascinating to those whose piety has corroded their normal impulses into prurience—but by a firm conviction that she could "save" him.

Byron knew that it was all a mistake even before the ceremony and tried in every way to get her to wriggle out of it, and when she failed to take his hints, went through with it and then sought vengeance by attacking her. They had been married less than an hour before he told her that he would seek a separation. The honeymoon was a nightmare. He attacked her religion. He entertained her with accounts of his various love affairs and stalked about the bedroom at night brandishing the loaded pistols he always kept beneath his pillow.

She might have laughed it off and by gaiety have won him over —for, as he had told Augusta, he was a great creature of habit and might very easily fall in love with his wife. But gaiety was the one thing she didn't have. That, and even a chemical trace of humility. High moral earnestness in belligerent abundance, absolute assurance that she knew all the ultimate answers to the riddle of the universe, and an evangelical zeal to subdue others for her convictions—these she had; but tenderness, laughter, playfulness, helplessness, absurdity, affection—the things Byron liked and needed in a woman— these she had not.

They returned to London where Byron—married—was no longer the rage. It had been said that the wives forgot him and the husbands remembered. Then his political opinions were as unpopular as his expression of them was indiscreet. He admired Napoleon, England's arch enemy, and said so. His publisher begged him not to express such ideas openly, but Byron said that his political opinions were to him what a mistress is to an old man: the sillier they were, the more he liked them!

Annabella was pregnant. Byron said that the only thing about her having a child that pleased him was that it would make his mother-in-law a grandmother. He cordially detested Lady Milbanke. In a letter to a friend he wrote that his mother-in-law had been dangerously ill but was now dangerously well again.

Oscar Wilde said that the only way a woman can ever reform a man is by boring him so completely that he loses all interest in life. Byron was too intensely alive to lose interest in life, but he was monstrously bored with domesticity and vastly irritated by the relentless pressure of accusing virtue. He grew morose, drank to excess, took laudanum, and carried on with several very dull young ladies.

But Annabella wasn't bored. She was vibrant with grief, self-pity, and indignation and, increasingly, with horror and high-minded resolution. Under Byron's pose of wickedness she had discovered, or thought she had discovered, *real* wickedness and perceived, with mounting excitement (and some satisfaction), that the moral task to which God had assigned her was no such minor reform as He would have relegated to an ordinary woman. It was enormous!

Nothing less, indeed, than incest! She believed that Byron had had a child by Augusta!

And maybe he had. Thirty to forty years ago it was taken for granted that the half-incest was a proven fact but scholars are now hedging. Nowhere is there indisputable confirmation. Annabella's own conviction grew as she sought self-justification for the separation that ensued, and the most recent investigations make it plain that her chief informant was Lady Caroline Lamb, who had escaped from Ireland and was seeking vengeance. And even Lady Caroline's words are vague and mysterious. Byron had confided something to her about his private life that was unspeakable, dreadful, revolting, and shocking! But just what, we don't know. Some think it may have been a homosexual experience. Some think it may have been much more trifling. Others believe that Annabella's conjecture—for it was never more than a conjecture—was true.

That he loved Augusta—that poor, confused, addleheaded, gay, charming, sympathetic "Goose" held a deeper and more lasting place in his heart than any other woman he ever knew—is beyond doubt. It is attested in his will and in a hundred tender and amusing letters. And that she loved him in return is equally indisputable, attested in her absurd, misspelled letters, her endless solicitude for him, and the pathetic memorial that she—and she alone—erected to his memory. And there may have been incest. It was certainly charged, in veiled terms, and it can't be disproved. But it certainly has not been definitely proved.

But, at any rate, there was no more Annabella. She passed quickly from horror to hatred and devoted the rest of her long life to virtuous malignance, furious to see the world honoring Byron and neglecting her. Until finally, in her last years, the glorious young man that she might have loved having long been dead and the splendor of his verse now acknowledged as part of the greatness of civilization, she revealed her bitter, gnawing secret to Harriet Beecher Stowe, who with lascivious zeal published it in—of all places!—the *Atlantic Monthly*. But it boomeranged. Not out of humanity but out of even more obdurate righteousness. Cancellations poured in on the luckless magazine and it was twenty-five years before the subscription list fully recovered. How Byron would have laughed!

But at the time of separation there was no laughter. Fantastic as it may seem, Byron was grief-stricken at her leaving him. And all appeals to her to return were not merely coldly rejected but cunningly exploited to his disadvantage. Society sniffed a really juicy scandal and was fed just enough to keep the rumors multiplying. Byron was now as detested as he had formerly been admired, and left England for ever.

He swept across Europe in tumultuous despair, bearing, as Matthew Arnold said, "the pageant of his bleeding heart" before him. He paused at Waterloo to lament for the dead, senselessly slaughtered, and at the ruined castles on the Rhine and on the Bridge of Sighs in Venice and in the Colisseum at Rome to bewail the loveliness and cruelty of the past. He was the Pilgrim of Eternity, the wandering outlaw of his own dark mind who had found that the broken heart lives on ("For it were as nothing did we die") and that life, like to the fabled Dead Sea fruit, was all ashes at the core.

Though there remained, of course, a certain amount of fizzing in the enchanted cup, even if the sparkle was abating. The women still pursued him and he enjoyed both flight and counterattack. "I have been more ravished than anybody since the Trojan war," he wrote to Augusta.

One of the ravishers was Claire Clairmont, Mary Shelley's half sister. Byron and Shelley met on the shore of Lake Geneva and spent long evening hours together, rowing and talking. Years later Mary Shelley remembered those hours in the boat as among the most memorable of her life and heard in her mind as long as she lived the thrilling cadences of the men's excited voices. Shelley came to have an ascendancy over Byron and under his influence Byron wrote his noblest poetry, the soaring, throbbing Third Canto of *Childe Harold*.

But it was the old, old story. Claire became pregnant and troublesome and her demands made Byron irritable. He agreed to care for the child when it should be born but only on condition that she promise never to enter any city in which he might be. She consented but Shelley disliked the whole business and they parted.

From Geneva Byron moved on to Venice whose melancholy and splendid decadence suited his own. The dying city pleased him. Then his lameness was not so obvious where there were no streets. He was becoming very wealthy, too. Not from his verse—he scorned to make money from that. The proposed purchase of Newstead had fallen through, with the forfeiture, in his favor, of a huge option. Then coal had been discovered under his land and there were enormous royalties.

He need deny himself nothing and lived in princely grandeur in the palace of the Lanfranchi on the Grand Canal. It was rumored that he maintained the Nine Muses, but this was largely the imagination of the Italians working on fascinating possibilities. The realities were more prosaic. He established a comfortable relationship with a complacent baker's wife, Margarita Cogni. But she was greedy. She sold his gifts and he, with admirable irony, bought them back and gave them to her a second time. Not the least advantage of wealth is that it gives whimsy a wider scope.

Then, in the spring, there was a new love—Teresa Guiccioli, the seventeen-year-old wife of the sixty-year-old Count Guiccioli, an urbane nobleman who was believed to have had his first wife's lover assassinated. At the first sign of danger the count whisked his youthful bride off to Ravenna, but she was unhappy and became very sick. Byron went to visit her, living in the palace with them (and paying the count a good, stiff rent for his apartment), and found himself deeply and sincerely in love. And she returned his love.

He was amused at the absurdity of it, but deeply touched and grateful to her for moving him to such unexpected tenderness. "Never, never more on me" he had written, "the freshness of the heart will fall like dew." But here it was, all dewy and tremulous, the more delightful for the multifarious debaucheries that enabled him to know how fresh and innocent it was. He offered to get a divorce and marry her, but she was shocked at the suggestion: she was religious and divorce was wicked! He was faithful to her. They lived, he said, "in the strictest adultery."

It was very much like marriage. Too much, as a matter of fact, and marriage, as he himself had written

> . . . from love, like vinegar from wine—
> A sad, sour, sober beverage—by time
> Is sharpened from its high celestial flavor
> Down to a very homely household savor.

After a year or so it became boring and he became restless. Making love and writing poetry, he felt, were not enough. He wanted to do something more manly, more worth-while. The cursed lameness taunted him.

So he took to dabbling in Italian revolutionary politics and began to store guns in the palace of the Guiccioli. And that exasperated the count; a milord was above the law, but the count wasn't and *he* would be held responsible. There was a quarrel and, finally, the pope granted the Guicciolis a separation. But this, instead of giving Byron more freedom, gave him a great deal less. For the mores did not permit a man to live with his mistress unless she were living with her husband and, furthermore, it was now expected of Byron that he would be faithful to her the rest of his life. "In their extra-marital relations," Byron wailed, the Italian women "have the most *awful* notions of constancy."

The child Allegra, his daughter by Claire Clairmont, died in the convent school in which he had placed her. Then Shelley was drowned. Though but thirty-six, Byron felt that "his days were in the yellow leaf, the flowers and fruit of love were gone," and "The worm, the canker, and the grief were his alone." Teresa had lost her appeal and was losing her beauty. Leigh Hunt said she waddled like a duck and had a complexion like boiled pork. Hunt was competing with Teresa for Byron's favor and his malice makes him an unreliable witness, but there are others who supply supporting testimony.

There was one great field of manly delight he had never experienced—the military. He had known love and fame and wealth, but what of glory? He hated the reactionaries who governed Europe since the Congress of Vienna. Why not strike a blow for liberty? And why not strike it in Greece itself—still bathed for him in the eternal summer of his young manhood—which was struggling to free itself from Turkey?

A committee had been formed in London to further the cause of Greek independence. Byron offered them his services and the full purchase price of Rochdale, which had just been sold, and, to his innocent satisfaction, both were immediately accepted. He fitted out a ship with arms and money, engaging as a sort of admiral a byronic ruffian, Trelawny, who had attached himself to him and secretly despised him. Two magnificent swords were forged and two glittering brass helmets with horsehair streamers and "Crede Biron," the family motto ("Trust Byron"), engraved on them. Teresa was persuaded to return to the count. It took a lot of persuading but was finally accomplished without any of what Byron called "Carolinization."

On the way Byron was in high spirits, indulging in practical jokes and horseplay. But once in Greece there was very little fun or romance in the business. The smell of milord's money brought patriots into camp on the double, but far more pugnacity went into the internal struggle for the money than was directed against the enemy. Byron said that he had "the best army that ever quarreled under one banner." He could impose no discipline. His fleet dispersed. He had to bribe his men to fight the enemy, bribe them still more not to fight each other and, eventually, bribe them most of all to disband and go home.

He was surrounded by treachery, spying, and intrigue. It soon became apparent that the expedition was a fiasco that would serve not to rehabilitate him but only to arm hatred with ridicule.

His health sank. It rained, rained, rained. His headquarters, at Missolonghi, was in a marsh. He caught a fever. Around his sickbed there was confusion and greedy struggle for advantage. Of his four attendants two spoke only Italian and two only English. None of them spoke Greek; they had to wait for the sick man's conscious intervals for him to serve as interpreter. The soldiers chose this moment to mutiny, and despite his protests the doctors insisted on bleeding him. They took from him two quarts of blood in two days and so made good their gloomiest prognostics. For on the following day, April 19, 1824, he died.

It was a splendid exit. Childe Harold had made his last pilgrimage: "The last and lingering troubadour to whom the bird has sung, / That once went singing southward when all the world was young." He had once been liberty's champion but had long been thought of as sunk in cynicism and debauchery. But suddenly this had been revealed as a mask hiding the old aspirations. A shudder of excitement passed over Europe. Young men wore mourning and began planning barricades.

The body was brought home. Burial in Westminster Abbey was sternly refused and he was buried in the little church of Hucknall-Torkard, near Newstead. The only memorial over him was a small tablet erected by Augusta. He left her his fortune but it was all spent in hushing up various memoirs and "revelations." It was not her doing; she was pressured into it by Lady Byron. It was the old story of the virtuous trying to force the world into their own sterile mold. But it did no good; the soaring vitality, the flashing wit, the passion and tenderness of the poetry could not be suppressed.

JOHN D. JUMP

Byron: The Historical Context

Early Regency England

It could be argued that economic developments in Britain during the twenty-two years of war were more truly revolutionary than were the political developments in France that precipitated the struggle. This is no place to describe in any detail matters of which Byron had apparently little knowledge and no first-hand experience. In general, it may be said that the industrial exploitation of new inventions facilitated an expansion of production and of trade that led at once to rapid urban growth and in the long run to a predominance of industry over agriculture.

Industrialization brought material benefits for many, and it promised more of them for all. But there were grave drawbacks. The regimentation of labour that goes with factory life could provoke a violent hostility towards the machines that made factory life possible. Moreover, at particular times and in particular places the introduction of new machines could threaten the very livelihood of those employed in an industry. Forbidden by law to organize themselves in trade unions for their protection, the workers were tempted in such circumstances to resort to illegal action.

Towards the end of 1811, economically the worst year of the war for Britain, outbreaks of organized machine-smashing occurred in Nottinghamshire. The trouble spread to Derbyshire, Leicestershire, Staffordshire, Lancashire, and Yorkshire. The government reacted by making such sabotage, and even the taking of a Luddite[1] oath, punishable by death. In his maiden speech in the House of Lords in 1812, Byron resisted this. He emphasized the 'squalid wretchedness' of the working people, ascribed it to 'the destructive warfare of the last eighteen years', and denounced the bill as unjust, inefficient, and inhumane (*Letters and Journals*, ii. pp. 424–30). The Whigs welcomed him as a promising recruit.

Despite executions and transportations, Luddism outlasted the war and became one of many factors contributing to the social unrest of the first five years or so of peace. But Byron left England for the last time only ten months after Waterloo. The England he knew as an adult was the England of the years from 1811 to 1816, and it is this early Regency England that calls for the closest attention now.

---

1. The Luddites (so called after Ned Ludd, an eighteenth-century English workman who originated the idea) were bands of English laborers who, between 1811 and 1816, attempted to destroy industrial machinery in the belief that such machinery tended to reduce employment. [*Editor.*]

George III lapsed into madness towards the end of 1810 and never recovered sufficiently to resume his duties as King. The Prince of Wales became Regent a few weeks later, and on his father's death in 1820 he succeeded to the throne as George IV.

The middle-aged aesthete who came to power in 1811 had a lively if shallow intelligence and considerable social gifts. At the same time, he was vain, idle, and self-indulgent. Leigh Hunt, poet and Radical journalist, went to gaol for describing him as 'a libertine over head and ears in debt and disgrace, a despiser of domestic ties, the companion of gamblers and demireps,[2] a man who has just closed half a century without one single claim on the gratitude of his country or the respect of posterity'.

But the Prince still retained for some—for 'Monk' Lewis, the terror novelist, for example—the charm that had once won him the regard of many. As a young man he had, like previous Hanoverian heirs, opposed the King. Politics as well as a fondness for similar amusements had made him Fox's[3] companion, and when he became Regent the Foxites naturally expected him to favour them.

They were to be disappointed. The Prince had grown into agreement with the Tories. He thought the war ought to be fought with vigour, he was in no hurry about Catholic Emancipation, and he felt little enthusiasm for Reform. So the Whigs remained in opposition, convinced that their friend had betrayed them. Thomas Moore, the Irish poet, voiced their resentment in verse. The two opening stanzas of his 'King Crack and his Idols' are typical:

King Crack was the best of all possible Kings
  (At least, so his Courtiers would swear to you gladly,)
But Crack now and then would do het'rodox things,
  And, at last, took to worshipping *image*s sadly.

Some broken-down Idols, that long had been plac'd
  In his father's old *Cabinet*, pleas'd him so much,
That he knelt down and worshipp'd, though—such was his taste!—
  They were monstrous to look at, and rotten to touch.

Nor did the poets in opposition spare his physical characteristics. In 'The Devil's Walk', Shelley commented upon his enormous corpulence:

For he is fat,—his waistcoat gay,
When strained upon a levee day,
  Scarce meets across his princely paunch;
And pantaloons are like half-moons
  Upon each brawny haunch.

2. People of questionable or shady reputation. [*Editor*.]

3. Charles James Fox (1749–1806) was a Whig orator and statesman. [*Editor*.]

The Whigs took an active revenge for his neglect of them by espousing the cause of his wife, Princess Caroline, whom he heartily detested. It was a far from immaculate cause. If he had been promiscuous, she had been indiscreet; if he was pampered and self-centred, she was loud and sluttish. Nevertheless, the Whigs gave her their somewhat interested backing, and Byron went along with them. This backing was extended to her unruly daughter, Princess Charlotte, whom the Whigs knew irreverently as 'the young'un' and who was the next in succession to the throne after her father. Princess Caroline had also the boisterous support of the populace, and her husband its contempt.

The country of which he was, so to speak, the acting constitutional monarch was still a mainly agricultural country, and it was still a country of wide though not insuperable class distinctions. Its turbulent and freedom-loving people responded to the leadership of a ruling class which knew how to inspire and evoke their obedience. The men of this class prided themselves on being gentlemen and received admiration for being gentlemen. As such, they placed a high valuation upon a personal honour that would have been sullied by a lie, an act of cowardice, or a failure to face the consequences of any of their deeds; and they recognized an obligation to behave with generosity. They might be Philistines, and they were often selfish. But they did take seriously the values which their code of honour existed to defend. A duel could follow an affront to a gentleman's honour. Pitt, Castlereagh, Canning, Wellington, and Peel all become involved in such encounters. Byron and Moore would probably have taken a shot at each other but for an accidental failure in communications.

In their stately country houses, surrounded by their terraces, gardens, lawns, avenues, and parks, they lived a life which Byron presents mockingly in the final cantos of *Don Juan* but which a popular twentieth-century historian, Arthur Bryant, records in more favourable terms. 'The gentlemen hunted, raced, shot, fished, read, played at billiards, cards and *écarté*, looked after their estates, sat on the Bench, and rode, danced and joined in charades with the ladies; the latter gossiped, sketched, made scrapbooks, embroidered stools, looked at engravings, walked in the gardens and inspected the greenhouses, played with their children in the nursery wings, devoured the novels of Walter Scott or Lady Morgan, constantly dressed and redressed, and displayed their elegant accomplishments to the gentlemen.' They were attended by an army of servants.

Since egalitarian notions had not yet penetrated far, masters remained masters, and servants servants. But their relationship was a personal one, and there were many activites in which both happily shared. Sporting activities were prominent among these. Hunting, for example, provided rôles for both, and on the cricket field the sole superiority was that established by greater skill.

The country was rich. Despite periods of economic peril, such as that already mentioned as having occurred around 1811, it was emerging from the war richer than it had entered it. Trade had expanded, industry had grown, farming had flourished. The hard work of a rapidly growing population—about thirteen millions by 1815, five millions more than in the seventeen-eighties—was achieving extraordinary results. These seemed even more extraordinary when compared with the results on the Continent of the long wasteful period of war.

The more affluent classes aspired to elegance in their dress, their furniture, their conveyances, their gardens, and their buildings. In all things the fashionable Regency style was graceful and just a little showy. The dandies were its most skilful exponents, and G. B. Brummell, the famous Beau, was the chief of the dandies. No mere fop, he dressed with exquisite propriety and scrupulous cleanliness. Aesthete and bantering wit, accomplished dancer and singer, and inveterate gambler, he was at the height of his prosperity during Byron's years in England. Friendship with the Prince Regent gave him, like other dandies, an influential position in society. Lady Hester Stanhope left a vivid record of his appearance 'riding in Bond Street, with his bridle between his fore-finger and thumb, as if he held a pinch of snuff'. Expressing a fondness for the dandies, Byron observed: 'they were always very civil to *me*, though in general they disliked literary people' ('Detached Thoughts', 29).

The social life of these men, and of the great ladies who gave the balls and routs in London's West End during the season, was glittering and extravagant. It could also be narrow and snobbish. Vulgarity was often closely attendant upon the most elegant Regency achievements.

High society shone most brilliantly during 'the summer of the sovereigns', 1814. Napoleon had just been overthrown for the first time, after the Russian, Prussian, and Austrian armies from the east, and the British army from across the Pyrénées, had successfully invaded France. In June, the Tsar of Russia and the King of Prussia arrived in London, accompanied by the Prussian Field Marshal von Blücher and the Chancellor of the Austrian Empire, Prince Metternich, among others. They dined in splendour at Carlton House with the Prince Regent. Three weeks of ceremony and pageantry followed, three weeks of balls, dinners, and visits to the Opera, to Hyde Park, and to Ascot. Byron sympathized with Napoleon rather than with these representatives of the old régimes. Nevertheless, he threw himself wholeheartedly into the festivities of this summer gala.

Few of those who attended the balls, masquerades, and routs

knew much about the other Britain that the Industrial and Agrarian Revolutions were bringing into existence. Factory production in the growing towns of the Midlands and the North, and the larger-scale farming made possible by the enclosure of common land, were expanding the numbers and changing the nature of the urban and rural proletariats. Conditions in the growing towns—Manchester increased its population by 70 per cent in the first two decades of the century—were often nothing less than horrifying. Low-quality housing, inadequate drainage, excessive hours of work in unhealthy and dangerous conditions, and an absence of social amenities made for distressed and eventually resentful workers. The tyranny of individual bosses could aggravate these ills; surviving sets of factory rules seem to us today to be very harsh. Nor was life in the slums in the East End of London any better than life in the least savoury of the industrial areas.

The well-to-do were not all of them ignorant or forgetful of these things. The Wesleyan and Evangelical religious revival had among other effects that of strengthening humanitarian feeling generally. Action was taken not only to abolish the slave trade but also to alleviate domestic evils. Charitable persons visited the poor, provided them with comforts, and instructed their children in the Christian faith. They established Sunday schools, benefit societies, and soup and clothing clubs. They tried to reform prisoners and to protect children against undue exploitation in industry. When particular calamities occurred, they subscribed to the funds that were opened to mitigate them.

Nevertheless, the evils seemed still to grow. A post-war recession, which would in any case have been difficult to avoid, was turned into a disaster by the government's ill-judged economic and financial measures. Moreover, the harvest of 1816 was the worst in living memory. The consequent widespread and acute distress provoked Luddite and other riots to such an extent that Shelley, writing to Byron in Italy on 20 November 1816, declared:

The whole fabric of society presents a most threatening aspect. What is most ominous of an approaching change is the strength which the popular party have suddenly acquired, and the importance which the violence of demagogues has assumed. But the people appear calm and steady even under situations of great excitement; and reform may come without revolution . . . I earnestly hope that, without such an utter overthrow as should leave us the prey of anarchy, and give us illiterate demagogues for masters, a most radical reform of the institutions of England may result from the approaching contest.

For about five years, protest was urgent and reaction sharp. Mass meetings and demonstrations occurred. The so-called Blanketeers in 1817 set off to march from Manchester to London. The Habeas

Corpus Act was suspended, and the leaders were imprisoned. Two years later, a crowd of between fifty and sixty thousand persons assembled to hear Henry Hunt in St Peter's Field, Manchester, and came into violent collision with the Lancashire Yeomanry. Nine men and two women were killed and many were injured, with the result that the encounter became known as the massacre of Peterloo. The government which had defeated the French revolutionaries was not going to succumb to English revolutionaries. It introduced the notorious Six Acts against arming and drilling, seditious meetings, and inflammatory political journals. With the failure of the wild Cato Street assassination plot against members of the Cabinet in the following year, 1820, the agitation subsided, to mount again in a more constitutional form ten years later.

There was a continuity between these later movements and those stimulated by the French Revolution in its first phase. Some of the new leaders were disciples of the old, and some of the old leaders reappeared; ideas and methods often corresponded closely with those of the Reform clubs of the seventeen-nineties. At the same time, conditions were changing. Increasing industrialization was bringing new troubles. While most men continued to think in terms of political remedies even for their economic ills, a few of them were beginning to look for economic remedies; and some of them were thinking that they might have to use physical force.

Nationalism: Italy and Greece

From the start of the twenty-two years' war, the advanced 'Foxite' Whigs had been less convinced of its necessity than were those composing the conservative governments that were almost uninterruptedly in power. The Terror did not make Fox withdraw his early praise of the Revolution; instead, he blamed the admitted evils of the French régime on the enmity of the more reactionary European powers. His disciple Charles Grey asserted in 1797 that the Revolution 'in the end . . . would tend to the diffusion of liberty and rational knowledge all over the world.' Napoleon's career shook this faith in some and shattered it in others. From the time of the brief Peace of Amiens (1802–3), Grey conceded that the war was just and necessary.

In 1806, during the last few months of his life, Fox was Foreign Secretary. In the previous year, Austerlitz had made Napoleon master of Europe, but Trafalgar had destroyed his hopes of invading England. Fox negotiated to end hostilities. The insatiability of Napoleon's demands forced him to acknowledge that Grey was right. Nine years later, during the hundred days that preceded Waterloo, Grey himself and Whitbread[4] were recommending the recog-

4. Samuel Whitbread, a minor Whig or-   ator. [*Editor.*]

nition and acceptance of the newly reinstated French Emperor, but they could not even carry with them all the members of their own group.

The dramatic spectacle of Napoleon's career dazzled many who were by no means wholly in sympathy with the political forces it represented—or misrepresented. Byron, an advanced Whig with certain limited Radical sympathies, assuredly felt its fascination. His attitude, as expressed in *Childe Harold's Pilgrimage*, III, was too ambivalent to satisfy a Bonapartist as fervent as Hazlitt, but it sufficed to sharpen Byron's own animosity towards two Tories who had contributed greatly to Napoleon's downfall: Viscount Castlereagh, Foreign Secretary from 1812 to 1822, and Arthur Wellesley, from 1814 Duke of Wellington, who had commanded the victorious British forces in the Peninsular campaign and at Waterloo.

Wellington combined aristocratic pride with a painstaking professionalism as a soldier and ruthless honesty as a man. Byron saw him as the stiff-necked agent of European reaction. He believed Castlereagh to be one of the promoters of that reaction. Nor was he alone in this belief. Most Englishmen of his political complexion shared it, not least Shelley, who wrote in *The Mask of Anarchy*, after receiving news of Peterloo:

> I met Murder on the way—
> He had a mask like Castlereagh—
> Very smooth he looked, yet grim;
> Seven blood-hounds followed him.
>
> (ll. 5–8)

Undoubtedly, Castlereagh acquiesced in the restoration of the old régimes after 1815 in France, Italy, and elsewhere. On what except the principle of legitimacy could a sincere Tory hope to found a stable peace at that date? But Castlereagh was no extremist. The highly reactionary Holy Alliance of Russia, Austria, and Prussia excited his derision as 'this piece of sublime mysticism and nonsense'. He knew well the strength of the new democratic and nationalist faith (quoted by J. Steven Watson, p. 569):

> It is impossible not to believe a great moral change coming on in Europe, and that the principles of freedom are in full operation. The danger is that the transition may be too sudden to ripen into anything likely to make the world better or happier . . . I am sure that it is better to retard than accelerate the operation of this most hazardous principle which is abroad.

By accelerating the operation, the French had inflicted on Europe a quarter-century of bloodshed, war, and tyranny. Castlereagh wished to retard it by adjusting the new faith and the old legitimacy to each other; he laboured to persuade the restored Louis XVIII to see himself as a constitutional monarch.

He differed sharply from the devious Austrian statesman, Metternich, with whom he found it expedient to associate himself at times while the peace treaty was being negotiated. Metternich offered an unqualified resistance to the new faith. Just as the Austrian Empire, with its Teutons, Czechs, Magyars, Italians, Serbs, Croats, and Poles, by its very existence denied the principle of nationalism, so its leading negotiator was prepared to re-define European frontiers without respect for it. Nor did his fellow-negotiators in Vienna regard it with anything like the favour that was to be shown to it at Versailles following the First World War.

As a result of their negotiations, the Austrian Empire expanded into Italy as far south as the river Po, the cities of Milan, Verona, and Venice thus coming into its possession. In 1817, the Piedmontese ambassador at St. Petersburg described the resulting situation in a memorandum submitted to the Tsar:

> Austria, possessing the richest and most fertile regions of the peninsula, besides nearly a quarter of the total Italian population, and also holding sway over Tuscany, Parma, and Modena through princes of her ruling House, cuts Italy in half and is its actual mistress. On the one hand, by the re-establishment of the entire temporal domain of the Pope, two and a half millions of Italians have been plunged afresh into a state of absolute nullity, and the King of Naples, relegated to the end of the peninsula, has no longer any means of contributing to the defence of Italy; while on the other hand Austria threatens the King of Piedmont on his flank, pressing upon him with all her weight, and by merely calling up her garrisons in Lombardy could sweep down upon him, reach his capital in a couple of marches, and destroy his resources.

Nationalism was a growing force and was eventually to compel the unification of Italy. But it was still weak during these postwar years. Metternich himself observed sardonically to his Emperor in 1817: 'I have for some time been certain of the existence in Italy of several secret fraternities, which, under different names, foster a spirit of excitement, discontent, and opposition. . . . In design and principle divided among themselves, these sects change every day and on the morrow may be ready to fight against one another. . . . I believe . . . that the surest method of preventing any of them from becoming too powerful is to leave these sects to themselves.' The most important of them was the Carboneria.

In 1820, elements of the Neapolitan army, in which the secret fraternities were especially strong, forced King Ferdinand to accept a constitution. Early in the following year, an Austrian force restored his absolute power. Elsewhere in Italy some of the more fervent and sanguine of the nationalists hoped that events in Naples would spark off a general rising. Byron, who had become a Carbonaro and had determined to play an active part in any such rising, did not believe that it could succeed. At all events, it did not occur.

During this same period, there were related stirrings in Piedmont and in Spain. But more successful than any of the movements directed against régimes newly restored by the Congress of Vienna was the struggle in Greece against a Turkish domination that had lasted for centuries. The Greek War of Independence began on 25 March 1821 and ended in effect six-and-a-half years later when the British, French, and Russians destroyed the Turkish and Egyptian fleets at Navarino.

After a slow start, a number of groups in Britain began to organize assistance for the Greeks in their fight for freedom. In March 1823 a London Greek committee was established. Evangelicals, Dissenters, Whigs, and Benthamite Radicals became members. The elderly Jeremy Bentham himself brought his clear and incisive mind and blithe inexperience to its service, and one of his disciples became secretary. J. C. Hobhouse, who had accompanied Byron on much of his Mediterranean grand tour of 1809–11 and who was now a Member of Parliament, gave Byron the first notification that the committee meant to appeal to him to serve as its agent in Greece.

Meanwhile, it was raising funds. Eventually it collected well over £11,000. It spent £4,000 on war supplies; nearly £1,800 on such nonmilitary items as medical supplies and printing-presses; £500 on a plan of Bentham's to educate eight Greek children in England; about £4,000 on advertising, freight and insurance fees, and the expense accounts of representatives in Greece; and almost £750 on 'sundry minor expenses'.

Byron never saw these accounts. If he had, he would surely have protested against the nature and size of some of the items. Even without seeing them, he had to warn the committee against sending articles that were completely useless to the Greek insurgents: mathematical instruments, for example, and trumpets. His well-informed realism constantly conflicted with the committee's high-minded progressivism, and this conflict became acute when a devoted Benthamite, Colonel Leicester Stanhope, was sent out to join him. Byron wished to talk about gunpowder and field guns, but Stanhope was more interested in education and the Press. Byron chose to support the moderate Greek leader, Alexander Mavrokordatos, but Stanhope favoured the unreliable Odysseus, who pleased him by voicing Radical views. The subsequent history of the struggle for Greek independence proved the correctness of Byron's judgment.

Of the matters surveyed here, Byron knew about some by hearsay, he had the opportunity of partially observing others, and he commented at one time or another upon most. * * *

In two important general respects he bore the imprint of his epoch. First, he was a Regency aristocrat, for a time in his youth a dandy, and he retained to the end an affection for a style of life that he came to deride but never quite outgrew. Second, though too young to share the enthusiasm that many felt initially for the French Revolution, he was old enough to witness, and to react strongly against, the repressive policies at home and abroad that conservative governments adopted in their anger and fright at the course it took. A hater of war, which he could tolerate only when fought by a subject people against its oppressors—by the Spaniards against the Napoleonic armies, for example, or the Greeks against the Turks—and a downright opponent of every kind of despotism, political, religious, or moral, he was in many respects a representative Whig aristocrat with certain Radical sympathies, but, it must be said, with little sympathy with Radicals who had risen from the lower orders. This, however, is only the man in so far as he was a product of his age. Like everyone else, Byron must also be seen as a unique individual.

MICHAEL G. COOKE

Byron and the Romantic Lyric†

* * *

A substantial proportion of Byron's lyrical output will not at first blush rate the romantic cachet; and no one will expect to discover, in his unmethodical writing in prose, any principle to rectify this view, to "create taste." Perhaps the lyrics not summarily eliminated seem as obviously out of harmony with the romantic type. But many of them, though judged to be "of relative superficial character and value,"[1] will reward the kind of ungrudging scrutiny that has discovered the power of an "elemental" lyric by Blake or Wordsworth.[2] They are romantic lyrics and frequently commenda-

† References in this essay to *LJ* are to *The Works of Lord Byron: Letters and Journals*, ed. Rowland Prothero (London: John Murray, 1898–1901). References to *Letters* are to *Collected Letters of Samuel Taylor Coleridge*, ed. E. L. Griggs (London: Oxford University Press, 1956–71). [*Editor.*]

1. Ward Pafford, "Byron and the Mind of Man: *Childe Harold* III–IV and *Manfred*," *SiR*, I (Winter, 1962), 105. A comparable opinion seems to underlie the brief remarks of Northrop Frye who, while expressing lukewarm praise of the rhythm of some of Byron's lyrics, deprecates the flat diction and conventionality of the lyrics as a whole (*Fables of Identity: Studies in Poetic Mythology*, New York, 1963, pp. 174ff.). The "faint praise" of Byron's lyrical rhythms goes back at least to H. J. C. Grierson, *The Background of English Literature*, London, 1925, pp. 84–85, and *Lyrical Poetry from Blake to Hardy*, London, 1928, p. 45, and is discernible as an undertone in George Saintbury's *A History of English Prosody*, New York, 1961, III, 95–102. For frank dispraise of Byron's "harmony," one should consult Swinburne's essay, "Wordsworth and Byron" (*The Complete Works*, ed. Edmund Gosse and T. J. Wise, London, 1926, XIV, 162).

2. Though not concerned with Byron's lyrics as such, George M. Ridenour illustrates the kind of scrutiny I mean in his discussion of the "Ode to a Lady whose Lover was Killed by a Ball" (*The Style of Don Juan*, New Haven, 1960, pp. 51ff.).

ble ones as well. In a typical romantic way they can be shown to encase in a plain, cryptic exterior finely wrought personal positions on time, memory, nature, will, culture, knowledge, and essential being. They reward study, too, as a capsule history of Byron's experience of the romantic vision, which he at first in a manner of speaking blindly recites, then positively enjoys and celebrates, then willy-nilly sees drift into a detached area of memory.

Many of Byron's lyrical positions turn out to bear comparison with those of Wordsworth, who it may be recalled was not unsympathetic to *Hours of Idleness.* "On a Distant View of the Village and School of Harrow on the Hill," though most readily associated with Gray's "Ode on a Distant Prospect of Eton College," is more meaningfully seen in relation to "Tintern Abbey"—the poem Wordsworth felt Byron had laboriously used and "spoiled" in *Childe Harold*—or Coleridge's "Sonnet to the River Otter." Gray's "Ode" offers an ironic view of the "paradise" of "careless childhood," a flat and generally pessimistic opposition between "the little victims" and "men." As Patricia Meyer Spacks says, in this poem "we are offered the opposition, most dreadful of all, between youth and age, between the ignorance which provides hope and the wisdom which reveals futility, an opposition for which, in the nature of things, no reconciliation can be possible."[3] This is an attitude not unknown to Byron. But he is not guilty of it in "On a Distant View," which like "Tintern Abbey" loves and *trusts* the recollections of the past; they are "dreams . . . of boyhood" because he cannot now *realize* them—the temporal gap—and because he wishes he could, but *not* because he has misgivings as to their original reality. Again like Wordsworth, Byron laments the loss in actuality of boyhood's "pleasures," and asserts their immortality in "ne'er fading remembrance." Though less systematically than Wordsworth, Byron also finds in memory the possibility of partial recovery, partial redemption of present loss: "Since darkness o'ershadows the prospect before me, / More dear is the beam of the past to my soul." The past for Byron is, perhaps typically, more social than for Wordsworth, as he includes not only the natural scene of hills and stream and field, but also the school and the churchyard and even particular theatrical shows (sts. 5–6) which lead to an unWordsworthian humor: "I regard myself as a Garrick revived." Also, unlike the older poet, Byron hints at the opening up of "new scenes of pleasure" which may match the "scenes . . . of childhood." The poem is effectively tenacious of childhood joys, failing to balance its affirmative philosophy of childhood with anything like Wordsworth's affirmative philosophy of maturity.[4]

Still, "On a Distant View" looks forward with Wordsworth-Col-

3. " 'Artful Strife': Conflict in Gray's Poetry," *PMLA*, LXXXI (1966), 69.
4. This failing, found also in Coleridge's

"Sonnet to the River Otter," in no way adulterates the romanticism of the poem.

eridge rather than backward to Gray. This, it need hardly be said, is a judgment of its content and mood; as poetry the piece can be summarized in words applied to Addison's verse by Johnson: "it has not often those felicities of diction which give lustre to sentiments, or that vigor of sentiment that animates diction." The crucial point, however, is that the eighteen-year-old Byron, with no great finesse or feeling as a poet, correctly and sensitively carries out a romantic exercise, and concocts a Wordsworthian flavor. This gives a peculiar extension to a verdict he later passed on himself: "My earlier poems are the thoughts of one at least ten years older than the age at which they were written: I don't mean for their solidity, but their Experience" (*LJ*, V, 450). A natural aptitude, a receptivity on Byron's part to certain central terms of romanticism first manifests itself here.

Byron's assimilation of romantic tendencies of thought comes out in a most unexpected place, namely, in his relation to Pope. That relation has been gradually turning into a problematical one, with Eliot substituting Dunbar, John Wain substituting Burns, and Paul West substituting Diogenes for Pope as a positive influence on Byron, and with Ridenour curiously asserting Byron's "pious" devotion to the Augustans while demonstrating his "startling" divergence from the ways of Pope and Horace in the supposed act of following them (*The Style of Don Juan*, pp. 7, 36–38). Byron, as in his repeated demands for a poetry of truth, a poetry that was profitable to society, logical, and moral, seems typically to have made over the terms he undeniably borrowed from the Enlightenment. Truth for him carries little of the idea of tradition and authority, of standard and systematic values which are available and beneficial to the individual; it means candor and resolution in facing the voluminous problems of knowledge and experience. This is a cardinal and pervasive distinction. As regards the moral burden of literature, for example, when advised to suppress the early cantos of *Don Juan* on grounds of taste and morality, Byron bridled that it was "the first time" he had heard the word morality "from any body who was not a rascal that used it for a purpose" (*LJ*, IV, 479). One recognizes an opportunity to transfix him with an *argumentum ad hominem*,[5] but it may be better to take another tack. Morality for Byron is not found in orthodox, behavioristic ways; in that sense, Donna Inez ranks high among the "moral," and it becomes necessary even to grant the horrendous "morality" of Glory and War. Byron's sense of morality is peculiarly epistemological, and rests on his conviction of the inscrutability of the universe, so that instead of formal obedience and a goal-directed self-discipline he appears to

5. "Argument against the man": that is, an attack upon the personality, rather than the ideas, of one's adversary. [*Editor*.]

espouse self-honesty, personal generosity and if necessary self-sacrifice, spontaneity and inclusiveness of experience, and equilibrium in the face of human imperfection and incertitude. A harder and stricter style appears in his early works, such as *English Bards*, but in my judgment we see here his impulsive and even impure dislikes, not his considered moral view. We do not sufficiently stress the fact that he outgrew *English Bards*, a fairly shallow tyro's effort (*LJ*, III, 227 passim). To be sure he confessed to following a "wrong revolutionary poetical system" (*LJ*, V, 169). But if he called Gifford,[6] whom he somewhat uncritically conceived of as an authentic upholder of Popean traditions, his "literary father," he also termed himself his "prodigal son" (*LJ*, VI, 329, 333), with no prospect of a homecoming.

How clearly then did Byron apprehend the difference between the wrong and the right poetical systems? We know that, far from insisting on the dichotomy of romanticism and classicism, he made a somewhat awkward, and "inconsistent" effort to scoff it out of existence:

'Classical' and 'Romantic' . . . were not subjects of classification in England . . . when I left it four or five years ago. Some of the English Scribblers, it is true, abused Pope and Swift, . . . but nobody thought them worth making a sect of. Perhaps there may be something of the kind sprung up lately, but . . . it would be such bad taste that I should be very sorry to believe it.
(*LJ*, V, 104)

More important yet, Byron found nothing intrinsically wrong with contemporary poetry, and did not denounce it outright. He was principally afraid of its effects on unwary successors, anticipating that "the next generation (from the quantity and facility of imagination) will tumble and break their necks off our Pegasus, who runs away with us; but we keep the *saddle*, because we broke the rascal and can ride. But though easy to mount, he is the devil to guide" (*LJ*, IV, 197).

This relatively mild attitude gives way to an animated depreciation of contemporary verse in the course of the defenses of Pope. But is Byron's basic position therefore altered? He did, after all, act as defender and not as crusader—in fact he seems to have been drawn into the controversy by Bowles's[7] gratuitous invocation of his name; and one may observe that he is less inclined to reconcile his contemporaries to Pope than to reconcile Pope's poetry with contemporary preferences.

6. William Gifford (1756–1826), minor verse satirist. [*Editor.*]
7. Rev. William Lisle Bowles (1762–1850) was a country parson and a minor, if pleasant, poet. In 1807 Bowles published an edition of Pope in which he accused Pope of want of vision; this inflamed Byron. [*Editor.*]

For Byron's favorites among Pope's poems (e.g., *Eloisa to Abelard*) were typical of his day, and he liked the qualities typically liked: softness, purity, passion, beauty, and holiness (*LJ*, V, 581–582). He may have appreciated Pope as a poet of reason, but he urged his countrymen not to let this quality get in the way of their appreciation of Pope's imagination and passion. Rarely is he concerned, in discussing the Augustan poet, with the Augustan standards of judgment, sense, propriety, moral, and design in poetry. He is concerned with emotion, and with emotion that borders on the indiscriminate. He speaks glowingly of the "imagery" of the *Epistle to Dr. Arbuthnot*, but shows withal little sense of Pope's aim. "The subject," he asserts, "is of no consequence (whether it be Satire or Epic)"—as if he conceived of Pope as merely seeking to put down lines "from which," as he himself puts it, "a painting might . . . be made" (*LJ*, V, 259–260). Even in *English Bards*, that ostensibly neo-Augustan poem, Pope is the writer whose "pure strain / Sought the rapt soul to charm, nor sought in vain." Byron holds up before detractors as a poet of "imagination" the man who had defined himself as having "stoop'd to Truth," and who had written to Swift on 19 December 1734:

> My system is a short one, and my circle narrow. Imagination has no limits, and that is a sphere in which you may move on to eternity; but where one is confined to truth, or, to speak more like a human creature, to the appearance of truth, we soon find the shortness of our tether.

Byron's romanticizing of Pope was hardly unique; it was the way of his age to praise Pope's command of "pathos" and "the moral sublime," to redefine in order to reclaim the naoclassical author. It is crucial to remember the vagaries of the Regency reception of the Augustan age, as shown by Mark Van Doren in his study of *John Dryden* and more extensively by Upali Amarasinghe in his *Dryden and Pope in the Early Nineteenth Century*. As things went, Augustan genius could be accommodated while Augustan correctness was cut away. If Pope defied rehabilitation, there was always Dryden to satisfy the craving for "orthodox" license.

In the final analysis Byron espouses a "classicism" so genial and so adventurous as to arrive at a near kinship with less extreme forms of romanticism, a classicism full of passion, sublimity, imagination, and individual genius. It is uncodified, uncrystallized, largely nominal classicism and no more makes Byron Popean (or, for that matter, Drydenesque), than his experiments with classical drama make him Greek. The fact that he championed Pope must, as far as major romantic poets go, remain singular, though we may recall Coleridge hesitating to condemn Pope comprehensively and Keats

going to school to Dryden for the composition of *Lamia*. The
reason that he championed him has something to do with sentimental associationism (he got his Pope young, and had a lifelong tendency to be fond of things of his youth); and something to do with
romantic experimentalism, with his social suspicions of Wordsworth, and, as I have tried to show, with his declassicizing, unwit-
tingly subversive conception of Pope.

How materially Byron developed a natural romantic aptitude can
be seen in such poems as "To Edward Noel Long, Esq.," "Epistle
to Augusta," and "I Would I Were a Careless Child." The first of
these, by a certain arch self-consciousness in the fourth and in parts
of the fifth stanza, perhaps betrays itself to be another product of
Byron's "infant Muse." But this disability is more than offset as the
poem demonstrates a deeper and more sensitive use of nature, and
of poetic language and structure, than "On a Distant View," as
well as a more elaborate knowledge of the links between past and
present joys.

> Dear Long, in this sequester'd scene
> While all around in slumber lie,
> The joyous days which ours have been
> Come rolling fresh on Francy's eye. . . .
>
> . . . .
>
> Though Youth has flown on rosy pinion,
> And Manhood claims his stern dominion—
> Age will not every hope destroy,
> But yield some hours of sober joy.

The spirit as well as the ring of these lines, bating the problematical
"Fancy," will almost inevitably conjure up thoughts of Wordsworth. We sense the world of "Tintern Abbey" where the "wild
ecstasies" of youth mature "into a sober pleasure." Byron has
"sequestration" to Wordsworth's "seclusion." He writes, "all
around in slumber lie"; Wordsworth, in his more intricately woven
work, accumulates the evidence of slumber all around with his "soft
inland murmur," "quiet of the sky," "repose," and "silence." Both
poets make seclusion and repose not only a setting for actors but
also a vital condition for reflection and insight. Both also qualify
their solitude by use of an alter ego,[8] contriving thereby to give na-

8. Long is used fairly straightforwardly
by Byron as a companion in the past
and a sure present corroborator of its
truth: "Yes, as you knew me in the
days / O'er which Rememberance yet
delays, / Still may I rove, untutored,
wild. / And even in age at heart a
child."
  Byron here suggests not only the
Wordsworthian paradox of wishing to
combine memory with an untutored, unaffected state, and be "even in age at
heart a child," but also the poignant
blending of energy and radical self-doubt
in such a wish. "Still may I rove" is simultaneously a statement of permission
or liberty and a confession of disability,
a wish.

ture a "human center," a human fulfillment. At the end of his poem Byron again turns farther than Wordsworth in a social direction; his version of a removal from youthful purity seems to be the picture of "daliaunce and fayre langage" in the fourth stanza. But he does not lose his sense of identification with Long or of *their* involvement with memory and nature. The rest of the faceless festive crew in which they "mingle" presumably do not have the same *spiritual* experience as they.[9] The moon, for them, is no casual factor. It is a redeeming agent whose light chases away "the gloom profound" that is at once literal and metaphysical—darkness in the first stanza is definitely associated with the present, and with day, as "clouds the darken'd noon deform"; and this association appears again at the close of the poem when the propitious moon fades and one is caught in "the mist [the unreliable light] of morn." Byron's "sacred intellectual shower," social in context as it is, remains a personal, mystical phenomenon under the aegis of the moon which in nature transcends and for us rescinds awhile time's natural consequences:

> . . . Ere yon silver lamp of night
> Has thrice perform'd her stated round,
> Has thrice retraced her path of light,
> And chased away the gloom profound,
> I trust that we, my gentle friend,
> Shall see her rolling orbit wend
> Above the dear-loved peaceful seat
> Which once contained our youth's retreat;
>
> .   .   .   .
>
> And all the flow of souls shall pour
> The sacred intellectual shower,
> Nor cease till Luna's waning horn
> Scarce glimmers through the mist of morn.

The influence not only of the mist of morn but of the darkened and cloud-deformed noon was not always to be denied in Byron's experience. Memory and nature, without losing their powers, lose their efficacy; we find them curiously inert in the "Epistle to Augusta," which is significantly the latest of the poems under discussion. Here the redemption of time appears incalculably remote. Byron, less wise and less passive than Wordsworth, has brought on his own alienation: "I have been cunning in my overthrow, / The

---

9. An arresting picture of Byron's aloof participation in festivity and also of his burdened sense of privations of age is provided in his "Detached Thoughts": "I mingled with, and dined and supped, etc., with them [companions at Cambridge]; but, I know not how, it was one of the deadliest and heaviest feelings of my life to feel that I was no longer a boy. From that moment I began to grow old in my own esteem; and in my esteem age is not estimable" (*LJ*, V, 445).

careful pilot of my proper woe." His knowledge that his woe is
deserved (one meaning of "proper") in no way leads toward
redemption. Even his knowledge of the way of redemption through
nature and memory (sts. 7–8) proves futile. But that knowledge
possesses all the poignancy and stature of Coleridge's "I see, not
feel, how beautiful they are!" The poem, as Oliver Elton states, "is
grave and beautiful in finish";[1] that finish serves to bring home and
clinch, esthetically, the dark emotional and moral burden of the
"Epistle." Byron goes beyond Coleridge and Wordsworth in recognizing the will, the individual's conscious deeds, as thwarting the
potential reconciliation between man and nature, man and his existence in altering time. This recognition constitutes a special contribution to the philosophy of the romantic lyric, or indeed to romantic philosophy.

The lyric "I Would I Were a Careless Child" also centers
around the possibility of fusing knowledge, memory, and nature
into a philosophical recovery of the losses of time. That possibility
is not negated here, but neither is it fully realized. The poem occupies the middle ground between "To Edward Noel Long, Esq." and
the "Epistle to Augusta." It shows not will, but sheer circumstances
upsetting man's innocence. It presents not a scene of recovery, but
a state of desire. The subjunctive mood with which it begins ("I
would I were . . .") effectively controls its amplitude. A "festive
crew" appears in a light very different from that in "To Edward
Noel Long, Esq."

> Though gay companions o'er the bowl
> Dispel awhile the sense of ill;
> Though pleasure stirs the maddening soul,
> The heart—the heart—is lonely still.

The poem, it may be useful to note, commences from the point
at which Coleridge's "Sonnet to the River Otter" ends:

> I would I were a careless child,
> Still dwelling in my Highland cave,
> Or roving through the dusky wild,
> Or bounding o'er the dark blue wave;[2]
> The cumbrous pomp of Saxon pride
> Accords not with the freeborn soul,
> Which loves the mountain's craggy side,
> And seeks the rocks where billows roll.

But the gifts of nature, original innocence and spontaneous belong-

---

1. "Byron," in *A Survey of English Literature*: 1780–1880, Vol. II, New York,
1920, 159.
2. The obscurity common to the three
settings, "cave" and "dusky wild" and
"dark blue wave," bears noticing; it

must be distinguished from the "gloom"
that "may suit" the speaker's now "darken'd mind." There is nothing pat or
mechanical about Byron's use of the
image of darkness here, or elsewhere in
his poetry.

ing in nature, have been supplanted by the gifts of fortune. What is gained seems worthless beside what is lost, and the poem poignantly cries to fortune to revoke its own gifts and restore those of nature. The eight-line stanza is divided equally betwen the two wishes, with an almost perfect antithesis between the halves: present vs. past, "cultured lands" vs. "the rocks," hate vs. love, slaves ceaselessly cringing around vs. freedom to rove, a "name of splendid sound" vs. the sound of the wild Ocean.

> Fortune! take back these cultured lands,
> Take back this name of splendid sound!
> I hate the touch of servile hands,
> I hate the slaves that cringe around.
> Place me among the rocks I love,
> Which sound to Ocean's wildest roar;
> I ask but this—again to rove
> Through scenes my youth hath known before.

Clearly the stanza is dealing with loss of liberty on various levels, for more is at stake than "the license to roam at will."[3] The boy who was free to rove with *the* free ("wild") Ocean as setting and standard finds himself a man limited to his lands and implicitly hemmed in by the very servants who, in the "cultured" context, should release him from care. Worse than this, in his attendants (or flatterers, perhaps) he beholds undisguised the last implications of being without liberty. They are not servants but "servile," "slaves that cringe." To hate their degraded condition—he does not hate them in themselves—is to keep in some degree free from culture, or corruption. But, unfortunately, not to be free.

The menace of the cultured context, it develops, can have positive benefits. For just as Wordsworth at Cambridge, under a challenge to his natural possession of liberty and unity in nature, is obliged to comprehend and affirm that possession, the speaker in "I Would I Were a Careless Child" must face his assumptions and define his position. He learns, like Wordsworth, that he "was not for that hour, / Nor for that place" (*The Prelude* IV, 81–82). Simultaneously he learns the essential quality of the hour and place he *was* for, but which he will not know again. Byron's lines seem remarkably close to the "Ode: Intimations of Immortality":[4]

> Few are my years, and yet I feel
> The world was ne'er design'd for me:
> Ah! why do dark'ning shades conceal

3. Bernard Blackstone, *The Lost Travellers: A Romantic Theme with Variations*, London, 1962, p. 189
4. For a review of the prompt and profound influence of this poem on the poetry and thinking of the first half of the nineteenth century, the reader is referred to Barbara Garlitz' "The Immortality Ode: Its Cultural Progeny," *SEL*, VI (1966), 639–649. [*Studies in English Literature—Editor.*]

> The hour when man must cease to be?
> Once I beheld a splendid dream,
> A visionary scene of bliss:
> Truth!—wherefore did thy hated beam
> Awake me to a world like this?

Here truth, like fortune above, is the ironic and antipathetic concept. Its beam is no better than "dark'ning shades," the world it reveals is "design'd" not created, formal not free: "Reality's dark dream."

Two factors prevent a resolution of the speaker's dilemma: the absence of a Long or Dorothy[5] to engage him and turn him from his present desolation toward the continuing viability of the past, and the inability of the solitary will to serve the turn. For though man must diligently lay hold of what he has in nature, he must also keep time with the rhythm with which nature freely gives; there is no ordering a custom model of experience, pat to the singular heart's desire. "Dejection: An Ode" bears witness to the inefficacy of mere will. So do Wordsworth's empirical faith in "wise passiveness" and his definition of beatitude of being as a state with no *particular* will. It is typical of romanticism that the function of the will proves injurious in the "Ode: Intimations of Immortality" (st. vi), and is beneficial accidentally, not intrinsically, in such as the rowboat scene and the Mt. Snowdon episode in *The Prelude*: the unanticipated educative gift of nature counters or cuts across Wordsworth's purposes in each case. A precocious sense of the imperviousness of circumstances to the play of the will emerges from "I Would I Were a Careless Child" The speaker, confined to "cultured lands," and doubly portcullised from the liberty of nature by "servile hands" and "slaves that cringe around," predictably ends on a note of sorrowing velleity:

> Fain would I fly the haunts of men—
> I seek to shun, not hate mankind;
> My breast requires the sullen glen,
> Whose gloom may suit a darken'd mind.
> Oh! that to me the wings were given
> Which bear the turtle to her nest!
> Then would I cleave the vault of heaven,
> To flee away, and be at rest.

The poems just considered begin, I think, to give color to the conception of Byron as a romantic lyrist, showing him at once more spontaneously and more richly concerned with the problems of time, memory, knowledge, and nature than he is usually given credit for. He did not, of course, recover his place and poise in

5. Dorothy Wordsworth, William's sister. In *Tintern Abbey* Wordsworth describes himself turning to Dorothy for solace and reinforcement in his poem. [*Editor*.]

nature. Of those who agonized over the loss, only Wordsworth recovered, and he only with laborious patience and self-dedication. By and large the desire for "the sullen glen, / Whose gloom may suit a darken'd mind" gets its literary fulfillment in Byron. The attitude we see in his desire to "shun, not hate mankind" curdles into *Manfred* with its disdainful view of man and exalted view of the very will which in the "Epistle to Augusta" denaturalizes man. When Manfred speaks of "My Mother Earth," it is fair to say that he is indulging in a name of splendid sound. Byron's passing ejaculations of reunion with nature, as for example in *Childe Harold* III, quite fail to bridge the practical abyss between faith in nature as a vital power and mere acknowledgment of nature as a potentially vital power. And Byron was fully aware of this. He is ready to profess himself "a lover of Nature and an admirer of Beauty," but no less prompt in admitting that "neither the music of the Shepherd, the crashing of the Avalanche, nor the torrent, the mountain, the Glacier, the Forest, nor the Cloud, have for one moment lightened the weight upon my heart, nor enabled me to lose my own wretched identity in the majesty, and the power, and the Glory, around, above, and beneath me" (*LJ*, III, 364). Fortune, and that skepticism which took hold in his mind and inhibited his ability to derive conviction from commitment, usually shut nature off for Byron as a serene and generous home.[6]

But of course that exclusion, or loss, is entirely in keeping with the pattern of romantic experience of nature. For the latter does not merely replace the old classical (and largely limited and horizontal) formality of response to nature with a mystical (and frequently limitless, vertical) concentration; it also shows, instead of the axiological clarity and assurance of the classical response, a new sense of the precariousness of nature's powers, or at least of man's fruitful perception thereof. Finders of something new in nature, the romantics were less than successful keepers.

A substantial conception of nature and of the mind, and of their mutual relation in the modifying circumstances of time and place has been seen as the radical content of a number of Byron's lyrics. In *Hebrew Melodies* one finds that conception tacitly assumed and applied, and also significantly complemented with a philosophy of art. "The Harp the Monarch Minstrel Swept" may be taken as exemplary. The poem, which may appear merely atavistic as a type of *encomium musicae*,[7] is remarkable as a cogent revival and transformation of that venerable fashion. The ordinary distinction between king and musician, to which Dryden lends his authority, is canceled in the oxymoron of "monarch minstrel"; here excellence in

---

6. A full-scale treatment of Byron's deteriorated responses to nature is provided by Ernest J. Lovell, Jr., in *Byron: The Record of a Quest*, Austin, Texas, 1949.

7. "The praise of music," a common motif for seventeenth-century poetry. [*Editor.*]

music is to surpass and cap excellence in arms: "David's Lyre grew mightier than his Throne." Similarly the power of music proves to be less than a virtuoso one, able to make men match its own gamut of emotions.[8] It does produce contradictions, but within a definite humane or ethical system of values: "It soften'd men of iron mould, / It gave them virtues not their own." In a cryptic paradox combining secular power and divine favor, David is at once "The King of men" and "the loved of Heaven"; and his music, the poem's music, is "hallow'd" rather than aesthetic or cosmic. So wholly does David act within a universal moral context that, when his music tells of "the triumphs of our King," he is as much the King as Christ, under whom he is king. In a quiet and decisive way, Byron is reversing the historical pattern which had led to the "minimization of the cosmological significance of the music of the spheres.[9]

Still, it is clear that Byron's view of music is less religious than prototypal. The focus of the poem becomes the sacred and unique moment hypostatized in music, and its relation to a time obscurely reflecting back on that moment. David's music embodies immortality in music. That immortality, lost in fact, is preserved somehow in memory, which thereby serves as a defense against the experience of mortality. "The Harp" is thus revealed as a special parallel to the poem "To Edward Noel Long, Esq." The parallel gets significantly extended as "The Harp" contrives, by a sort of semi-synaesthesia, to transfer the idealized musical context into the visual terms of light and dark, the more typical vehicle for its near-mystical statement:

> Since then,[1] though heard on earth no more,
> Devotion and her daughter Love
> Still bid the bursting spirit soar
> To sounds that seem as from above,
> In dreams that day's broad light can not remove.

The failure of daylight to remove the dreams[2] amounts to the failure of mortality to get the better of immortality. The music, after

8. Instead of making men feel everything, music makes all men feel: "No ear so full, no soul so cold,/That felt not, fired not to the tone, / Till David's Lyre grew mightier than his Throne."

9. John Hollander, *The Untuning of the Sky: Ideas of Music in English Poetry, 1500–1700*, Princeton, New Jersey, 1961, p. 358.

1. The sound of the harp, the poem has said, "aspired to Heaven and there abode."

2. Another of the *Hebrew Melodies*, "She Walks in Beauty," also disparages daylight ("gaudy day") and favors instead the night of "cloudless climes and starry skies." Such a night, like the "aspect" and "eyes" of the poem's subject, embraces "All that's best of dark and bright." The fusion of the opposites of dark and bright is matter-of-factly stated, but it is a mysterious thing. Only the "best of dark and bright" comes into play, so that neither term really has its natural meaning: they are idealized terms. Something timeless, preternatural hangs about the night and the lady alike. The "beauty" *in* which she is said to walk is also essential and timeless. That "beauty," "the night" and "she" interpenetrate and become interchangeable in an uncanny identification of a human being with a phenomenal state and an abstraction. The ostensibly simple rhetoric asserts nature, achieves mysticism.

all, only *seems* "as from above." It is partly with us yet. For "dreams" must carry the definition enunciated by Coleridge, the "semblance of some unknown past, like to a dream, and not 'a semblance *presented* in a dream'" (*Letters*, I, 167). The bursting spirit soars *up towards*, but also in *direct response to* the music, for if it is ideal it is also somehow familiar: something we have known. Indeed, it appears that we first created it, even if it was to make "Heaven" its "abode." Byron spends a relatively large proportion of the poem's twenty verses on Orphic[3] music and heavenly music, but without making these his chief concern. They are forms of the first human excellence, which was not infused, but implicit. Its "chords are riven," of course; yet memory and language effectively revive and consecrate it, unto eternity, in the very teeth of the materialistic assumption of a strict, finite succession of things, of a past that is gone and done with. The truth of memory puts down the nihilistic suppositions of logic; the truth of "dreams" withstands "day's broad light," as the poem posits an extra-scientific theory that experience is not destroyed but translated into invisible but still available terms. Mythic in impulse, it humanizes and romanticizes its classical and Christian myths. Its "dreams" are of a perfectly human past, and latently also, I think, of a like future.[4] Like poetry, music offers "the feeling of a Former world and a Future" (*LJ*, V, 189).

The little span from dreams to daylight repeats in miniature the considerable span of time between "then" and "since." History is imaged in less than a natural day, and in turn both general history and singular day image and are implicitly imaged in a third span: that of the single life going, as in "Tintern Abbey" or "To Edward Noel Long, Esq.," from integrated youth to alienated manhood. Like nature in those poems, art, ideally conceived, reveals to us and preserves for us knowledge of our place outside of mutable time, whose light is obscurity. More than this, art withstands time for us;

3. In Greek mythology, Orpheus was the supreme poet, who through the power of his song brought his bride Eurydice out of Hades. Thus, "Orphic" music is music imagined as a spiritual or semidivine force. [*Editor.*]
4. Even allowing for Byron's usual fluency in composition, his prompt and flawless execution of these last five lines of the poem, which bring us "down again" from Heaven (Isaac Nathan, *Fugitive Pieces*, London, 1828, p. 30), may well betoken the ripeness of the humanistic idea in his mind. Nor is such a human orientation out of place; it is by inertia that Byron's lyrics retain the general title of Hebrew Melodies, with which their association was never very close or profound. As E. H. Coleridge points out, less than half of the pieces were composed in accordance with Byron's agreement to provide lyrics for music scored by Isaac Nathan and to be sung by John Braham (*PW*, III, 375). The reviewers of the *Analectic Magazine*, VI (1815), 292–294 and of the *Christian Observer*, XIV (1815), 542–549 found the poems at best vaguely scriptural. But then neither poet nor musician labored under an illusion about the matter. When Nathan asked Byron how "Oh! Snatch'd Away in Beauty's Bloom" might "refer to any scriptural subject," Byron "appeared for a moment affected," then fudged an answer: "Every mind must make its own reference" (Nathan, p. 30). [*PW* refers to the E. H. Coleridge edition of Byron's *Poetical Works—Editor.*]

we withstand time through it, and are restored, albeit partially and temporarily, to our extratemporal place.

Such a view of art underlies yet another of the *Hebrew Melodies*, "My Soul Is Dark," which also involves the semi-synaesthesia of a vision created by a sound. But critical details have changed. Instead of the abstract, almost communal voice of "The Harp," this poem offers a vividly self-conscious speaker who knows better things then he has.

> My soul is dark—Oh! quickly string
> The harp I yet can brook to hear;
> And let thy gentle fingers fling
> Its melting murmurs o'er mine ear.
> If in this heart a hope be dear,
> That sound shall charm it forth again:
> If in these eyes there lurk a tear,
> 'Twill flow, and cease to burn my brain.
>
> But bid the strain be wild and deep,
> Nor let thy notes of joy be first:
> I tell thee, minstrel, I must weep,
> Or else this heavy heart will burst;
> For it hath been by sorrow nursed,
> And ached in sleepless silence long;
> And now 'tis doom'd to know the worst,
> And break at once—or yield to song.

It is left uncertain whether he is saved from darkness and suffering by the harp. He certainly expects, and urgently desires, to be. No doubt arises as to the power of the harp, and little doubt is encouraged as to the receptivity of the speaker. The crucial element in the poem would once again appear to be the will. The hearer knows his state, and its danger, both emotional and intellectual (burning brain, overladen heart). He knows he "must weep," must lose himself to save himself emotionally and intellectually for some imaginable future: "If in this heart a hope be dear. . . ." The implication is that something will necessarily follow "if the stated condition is met. The precondition embodied in music is compounded (but bid the strain be wild . . .) and further compounded (nor let the notes of joy be first); and then, when it would seem that so precise a formulation must guarantee success, we come upon the possibility of its being altogether too late: his heart may be "doom'd" to "break." This sort of practical uncertainty is bound up with a pair of philosophical paradoxes in "My Soul Is Dark," with its dramatization of the will to surrender the will, of the self-conscious mind striving to yield away the self. Add to these the paradox of the dream which is truer than day, and a radical problem of knowledge and belief appears.

The title of the poem suggests a pre-mystical state, but it is an arrested pre-mysticism, at once too analytically conscious and too doubtful of the means to a saving self-transcendence. The present material reality—the power of pain—is locked at a point of crisis with the immanent, timeless reality of the power of music (and it may offer a presage of the future that this conflict of two realities or schemes of knowledge remains unresolved; Byron will again be caught between the claims of actuality and hope). Music and pain, both undeniable, cannot both survive, but the poem cannot settle the issue. Its palpable instrument is will, which we see as isolating and incapable of redeeming itself, though the definite fear that the present could negate the immanent places the poem on the side of the angels.

The want of a definite solution in "My Soul Is Dark" is perhaps supplied in "The Destruction of Sennacherib," where the pervasive similes suggest that nature, or a general will, favors innocence as an ordained state over the contingent state of terror. Naïve and mechanically "Biblical" though they may seem in terms of today's literary predilections, these similes subtly define the universe of the poem. First they suggest a certain ordinariness or typicality in nature: "The Assyrian came down like the wolf on the fold," "And the gleam of their [his cohorts'] spears was like stars on the sea, / When the blue wave rolls nightly. . . ." A sort of delayed tension, developing with the apprehension that it is war which gets defined as ordinary or "natural," is both reflected and reinforced in the conflict of the natural trope: the wolf vs. the fold. Tension in nature recurs in the second stanza, between "leaves of the forest when Summer is green" and "leaves of the forest when Autumn hath blown." But a crucial reorientation takes place here. The activity and purpose involved in the wolf-fold metaphor give way to the passivity of the cycling leaves, a passivity emphasized in the static and passive phrasing: "are seen" and "lay wither'd and strown." Moreover, the metaphor of the leaves refers *in both instances* to the Assyrian host, who in the first stanza so fiercely "came down" on the lamb-like enemy. Still in a pattern of nature, they find their activity and will superseded by a higher and less momentary principle. The more or less horizontal tension, wolf vs. fold, is revised into a vertical one, leaves (raised banners) vs. leaves (fallen host), or rather into an abstract tension between the partial present and an eternal perfection, between self-will and the implicit will of Nature; a certain quality of ignorance and presumption in the Assyrians is revealed when they are called "sleepers." The subjection of the agressor to Nature appears graphically as the erstwhile rider "lay . . . distorted and pale,[5] / With the *dew* on his brow and the

5. No longer does he gleam "in purple and gold."

rust on his mail" (italics added). The negation of his activity reveals itself in "the lances *unlifted*, the trumpet *unblown*" (italics added); the participles, as a contemporary reviewer felt, make "lagging lazy words."[6] It is noticeable, too, that his enemy, though successful, is no more active, as the Gentile falls "unsmote by the sword." Nature itself in the form of the "blast," as something exceeding and superseding human agency, is what fells the Gentiles. Actually the natural manifests the supernatural. But to the last the poem's rhetoric orients us toward the natural world:

> And the might of the Gentile, unsmote by the sword,
> Hath *melted like snow* in the glance of the Lord.

Rhetorically it is in terms of, and through, a complex but consistent nature that the supernatural occurrence unfolds and has meaning. The similes are not ornamental but instrumental, serving to inform the simple if strange story with a philosophy that is complex, yet clear.[7]

In the light of the readings set forth here, a significant number of Byron's lyrics would take a place in the romantic category. They do so not only in terms of philosophy, but also in terms of rhetoric, with an ostensibly naive surface of form and language manifesting an essentially knowledgeable and complex position. Perhaps Byron's lyrics have "suffered" more than those of his major contemporaries from what Earl R. Wasserman sees as a typical crux of the romantic lyric, "the superficial appearance of not requiring an intensive metaphysical reading"; for it proves true often enough with the uncelebrated Byron, as with the rest, that "it is . . . not merely in the overt statements, often disarmingly simple, but especially in the inner subtleties of [the] language . . . that we must seek the articulation of" a poem's fullest meaning.[8]

It would bear stressing, however, that such lyrics stand in no pat relation to the great body of Byron's work. He articulates no propaedeutic[9] *Prelude*. He does not, like Wordsworth, have an "Old Cumberland Beggar" to clarify a cryptic line ("Stop here, or gently pass') in "The Solitary Reaper." His poetic manifesto, if the "Reply to *Blackwood's*" can be so called, tends to obfuscate the issues it pretends to define: his own poetic principles, Pope's poetry, and contemporary poetic philosophy and prejudice. In a special way Byron's romantic lyrics stand alone.

6. "Hebrew Melodies, by Lord Byron," *Christian Observer*, XIV (1815), 547.
7. The reader should compare G. Wilson Knight's suggestive, if fulsome reading of this poem in his *Byron and Shakespeare*, New York, 1966, pp. 13–15, and Robert F. Gleckner's reading, in *Byron and the*

Ruins of Paradise, with its isolating focus on a "landscape of death" and "victory hollow and wintry," Baltimore, Maryland, 1967, p. 209.
8. *The Subtler Language*, Baltimore, Maryland, 1959, p. 252.
9. Introductory. [*Editor.*]

FRANCIS BERRY

The Poet of *Childe Harold*†

* * *

'*Alles Grosses bildet*', Goethe said of Byron: 'every great *thing* is
a portent, an active embodying representative; it is more than a
symbol of the moment because it is active, predictive of the future,
its immediate agent. Byron was such a thing, an it.' Now that all
sounds very one-time German, Goethian and pompous, but not
therefore always false. As on many other occasions—this was in
December 1816—Goethe was right.

In 1827, three years after Byron's death, Goethe referred to his
Helena, that vast Act III of the second part of *Faust*, written in his
old age. In that Act, Faust consummates his nuptials with Helen of
Greece, and from that union is born Euphorion, whom Goethe
acknowledged to be Byron. 'You were right to present him with
that immortal monument of love in *The Helena*,' said Eckermann.
The younger man was deferential, but he was not a toady. He could
have asked: Why, your Excellency, do you attach such importance
to the late Lord Byron as to bring him in *Faust*, Part II, as Euphorion? But Goethe explained. For he declared: 'I could not . . . make
use of any man as the representative of the modern poetical era
except him, who undoubtedly is the greatest genius of our century.'
Again Byron is 'neither Antique [classical] nor Romantic but like
the present day—itself:' to understand, to realise what the moment
in 1827 *is*, and what its tomorrow will be, understand and realise
what Byron is.

Which is, of this poet if of no other, to realise beyond the poetry
and understand the life. Goethe said he had intended a different
conclusion to *The Helena*: 'then this conclusion with Lord Byron
and Missolonghi was suggested to me by the events of the day
[Byron's death in 1824 in Greece] and I gave up all the rest.' The
issue of the marriage between Faust and Helena died in Greece.
How luckily for an old and famous author, seeking for a conclusion
exactly right for this part of his masterpiece, that this should
happen. But it did. And Byron too was lucky that it should happen
that he died then and there, perhaps.

A more specifically literary-critical remark by Goethe. Speaking of
one of Byron's plays (*The Two Foscari*) he exclaimed: 'Admirable!
every word is strong, significant, and subservient to the aim—there
are no weak lines in Byron.' No weak lines in 'Byron'—and no
waste! But it is possible that he had only this play particularly in

† From *Byron: A Symposium*, ed. John D. Jump (London: Macmillan, 1965),
pp. 35–51.

mind. In his introduction to *The Two Foscari*, Byron had written: 'The simplicity of plot is intentional and the avoidance of *rant* also, as also the compression of the speeches in the most severe situations.'

Be that as it may, whatever Byron's merits as a poet, as specified by Goethe, they are not surely—except perhaps for 'strong'—the ones recognized in the twentieth century. For T. S. Eliot, until lately our century's representative poet and critic, wrote in 1937:

> Byron would seem the most nearly remote from the sympathies of every living critic . . . The bulk of Byron's verse is distressing in proportion to its quality . . . We have come to expect poetry to be something very concentrated, something distilled; but if Byron had distilled his verse, there would have been nothing whatever left.

Against the 'strong, significant, and subservient to the aim . . . there are no weak lines' (compactness, all meaningful, organic unity, no waste) of Goethe, we have Eliot's: 'Byron has been admired for his most ambitious efforts to be poetic: and these attempts turn out on examination to be fake; nothing but sonorous affirmations of the commonplace.' It can be exactly understood what the Christian critic means: by 1937 the 'sonorous affirmations' had become 'commonplace'. But they had become *déjà vu*[1] to Byron himself when he wrote the stanza which provoked the comment. The affirmations of Gray's *Elegy*, less sonorous, equally publicly addressed, are also commonplace.

The critics between Goethe and Eliot foresaw the weakness, not original but which time has brought; to Matthew Arnold 'Byron was a child as soon as he began to think.' Nevertheless he was the one English poet who realised the essential need for 'action', for 'subject matter', in poetry, and Arnold clearly recognised Byron as in this respect the first poet of—what was still—their shared age. Yes, the Victorians had their reservations, and George Eliot could style Byron 'a vulgar genius'. Of course to her he was vulgar ('a vulgar patrician', T. S. Eliot was to call him), but there was no doubt as to the genius. 'Whereas', as Auden was to remark in his 'Letter to Lord Byron':

> Whereas T. S. Eliot, I am sad to find,
> Damns you with an uninteresting mind.

It is a clash between the poetics and the theologies of two periods. Both twentieth-century poetics and Eliot's theology probably inclined him to admit, even assert, as against the earlier poetry, the merits of *Don Juan*, that great *déjà vu* testament. Here Eliot admits a 'raffish honesty'—Byron could detachedly look at himself—

---

1. "Already seen," i.e., commonplace and outworn. [*Editor.*]

whereas the earlier diabolism and the postures of defiance had been spurious. *Scrutiny*[2] too had exempted (though no theology or merely a very grey one had been involved) *Don Juan* in its dismissal of an *oeuvre*,[3] all largely of a period. We now should recognize *Don Juan* as the one supreme comic poem in English. Even so, of the whole output, early or late, not excluding the comic epic, there is this summarising: 'Of Byron one can say, as of no other English poet of his eminence, that he added nothing to the language, that he discovered nothing in the sound, and develops nothing in the meaning of individual words.' And this verdict: he 'might have been an accomplished foreigner writing in English'. Not much later another critic, an admirable and interesting critic, remote in theology (he had none) and politics, and in poetics, from Eliot, yet near in human sympathies—Herbert Read—was to declare that Byron's verse showed no 'true voice of feeling' unlike Keats's verse, but that Byron's words were poured *ti-tum, ti-tum, ti-tum* into pre-cast frames.

I grew up at a time when Eliot's prestige as a poet approached that of Byron a hundred years earlier, though Eliot's was more hardly won; and when Eliot's criticism (the auxiliary to his poems, and always working towards the making of a 'climate of opinion' favourable to the acceptance of his poems, creating the critical taste necessary for the enjoyment of his own poems) had an extraordinarily persuasive authority, even hold. How could the young man of the early thirties answer such a carefully argued case demonstrating Byron's incapacity for original thought or his insensitivity towards the English language? Or fail to agree with Herbert Read, that Byron's metrics were duly mechanical? There were answers, but what were they? Were there answers without resorting to the Life? Or to the Letters and Journals, so close to the Life but still, then, an under-read and under-appreciated area of the poet's writing?

It can take years before one can outgrow views and opinions conditioned by the views and opinions of the great and respected; to outgrow while still respecting, while gaining an understanding of the reason or reasons for the formation of the views and opinions of the conditioner. In the case of Eliot the views and opinions of the critic were essential—and inevitable—to the growth and maturation of Eliot the poet. To at least understand that; and then to further realise that such views and opinions ought not to govern, either with regard to Byron or to another poet, one's own individual feelings—this is a result of ageing, and a result, too, of noting that the most eminent poet-critics can modify, if not reverse, earlier opinions

2. The highly influential English journal of literary criticism (1932–53), guided by the critic F. R. Leavis and responsible for many early twentieth-century literary attitudes, including the reversion of taste against romanticism. [*Editor.*]
3. A complete, coherent body of works. [*Editor.*]

which their generation and their temperament and their ambitions dictated. This is simply a warning that it is damaging to read, say, an introduction or preface to a collected or a selected edition of a poet unless its writer delights in that poet. Eliot knew this, and his preface to his choice of Kipling serves as an example. Nevertheless, in the *Selected Essays* he drew the young reader towards the Jacobean dramatists; he repelled him from the Romantics. This was perhaps right and necessary at the time—though time is a 'whirligig' —except in so far as it ministered to the pride of belief that it was unnecessary to read Byron before accepting a judgement on him.

Anyway, it is now 1974, and times have changed for Byron, and Eliot, and for the readers of both. The positive homage of Goethe, the negating strictures of Eliot, respectively, provoke endorsement and expansion or resistance at the present.

In the interim, during the thirties, in a series of letters in the delightfully entertaining *Letters from Iceland* by W. H. Auden and Louis MacNeice, the former, with wit and high-spirited brilliance, saluted, in verses derived from *ottava rima*, the 'inventor' of a style; Byron was 'the master of the airy manner'. And in a volume originally entitled *The Burning Oracle*, but now republished as *Poets of Action*, G. Wilson Knight stood firm as the champion not only of the *Beppo–Don Juan* group but of the whole vast and magnificent Byronic achievement, an achievement that included, but was not confined to, the creation of a poetry which galvanised the poets of several languages of Europe.

To declare my position: I have come, and not a moment too soon, to accept Byron's poetry with enormous pleasure and admiration, and to receive, when I read him, an intense kind of driving excitement, vigour and assurance not found elsewhere in nineteenth-century English poetry. And with what consequence? With this: he alone would seem to combine a propulsive revolutionary blaze, an expanding of sympathies, with an equally strong blaze—or passion—for metrical and stanzaic, and a larger constructional, order. In the present age of fervour but near anarchy in life and in letters, Byron is the wholesome model for poets writing today, and tomorrow. He admired Dryden; he admired Pope. Yet he was liberal; more than that, a liberator; and he understood himself. He can help tomorrow's lives as well as tomorrow's poets.

Byron's drive, vigour, assurance! But 'We have come to expect poetry to be very concentrated, something distilled . . .' And not only concentrated, but diffident—as diffident as Mr Prufrock[4] is diffident. This was generally true of expectations in the 1920s and the 1930s and the 1940s. It would have been agreed that a mind,

4. The ineffectual, self-doubting hero of J. Alfred Prufrock" (1919). [*Editor.*]
Eliot's early poem, "The Love Song of

and its moods, are nearly infinitely subtle, that the language was tired, and that the grand gestures of rhetoric were outdated because they were expressive of certainties, and the educated man, the civilised man (the descendant of Henry James's people), the sensitive man, was incapable of the callow, or shallow; of the untested assumption; of all those forms of rhetoric which could only be the utterance of a crude insensibility—which insensibility was expressive of little except a lack of awareness of the complexities of modern life. Certainties! look for them to Mussolini, for 'The best lack all conviction . . .' while it is 'the worst' who are full 'of passionate intensity'.[5] The poet's job was to be aware of these complexities, of the proper diffidences that attended such awareness, and to render them. The citation from F. H. Bradley, in the Notes to *The Waste Land*, is a sufficient indication that not only the transmutation of an experience but the experience itself, any experience, must be peculiar to the individual. That tree, that bus, is *there*, but to no two among all the millions is it the same tree, the same bus. Or are tree and bus really not there? Realise, then, what a task, a tricky one, it is to write a poem—a genuine one. Or to address others in a common understanding in any mode or mood. 'I gotta use words when I talk to you,' declared the hero, Sweeney.[6] Whether he communicated or not meant 'nothing'.

Hence the *symboliste*, and later the Eliotic, and all the sub- or post-Eliotic postulates, or lack of them, and they companion, or presuppose, most assuredly a profound—a so profound as to be fundamental—scepticism of the worth of heroic action, of 'heroes' and of 'action', of rhetoric or thumping discourse.

Now what are the striking qualities of Byron's verse? So striking, as they were, that they shook London and agitated Europe?

Besides being politically revolutionary with a passion for rigorously stable artistic form and forms, he was, of all poets, 'a man speaking to men'. This was Wordsworth's definition of the poet in the exercise of his office. But with Wordsworth it was a *desideratum;*[7] Byron spoke clearly and boldly not *for* peasants—but *to* all men (and women) with an interest in public affairs, in human behaviour, and with a real or affected interest in what used to be called the passions. Historic events are not superseded by those occurring later. Unashamedly, I quote lines in evidence of this, because they are so well known:

> There was a sound of revelry by night,
> And Belgium's Capital had gathered then
> Her Beauty and her Chivalry—and bright

5. These lines are from W. B. Yeats's poem of apocalyptic vision, "The Second Coming." [*Editor.*]
6. An archetypally vulgar, brutal character in some of Eliot's early poems. [*Editor.*]
7. Something to be desired. [*Editor.*]

The lamps shone o'er fair women and brave men;
A thousand hearts beat happily; and when
Music arose with its voluptuous swell,
Soft eyes looked love to eyes which spake again,
And all went merry as a marriage-bell;
But hush! hark! a deep sound strikes like a rising knell!

(*Childe Harold's Pilgrimage*, III.xxi)

Of course this is rhetoric, or public address; certainly the poet could count on that audience being interested in the Battle of Waterloo, and the hours before that battle. He could take it for granted that the audience were as wholly with him here, as he could take it for granted that there was some opposition when he had used prose oratory in the House of Lords on behalf of the Nottinghamshire stocking-frame breakers.[8] This consciousness and confidence of an audience—in the tradition of Dryden and Pope—sets Byron apart 'from all the Lakers in and out of season' and from Keats. Words-worth, the recluse, would murmur to himself, 'I wandered lonely as a cloud' (albeit he was with his sister); Keats, in solitariness, assumed a sympathetic overhearer, when *he* murmured about the condition of his heart and his sense:

My heart aches, and a drowsy numbness pains
My sense as though of hemlock I had drunk—

but Byron is addressing an assured audience about an event of public importance to the British then and to our partners in the Common Market now. This is not to suggest that Wordsworth or Keats are to be despised (nor indeed that they are either inferior or superior), but it is to point to the strong difference in kind between Byron and them, and to suggest why Byron did, to some degree, genuinely look down on them. He, like Keats, to be sure complained about his heart, indeed paraded 'the pageant of his bleeding heart' across Europe, but he related those pangs to the settings of histori-cal events that fairly claimed the interest of his assured audience in London and in the countries of Europe. He made the landscapes of Europe vivid and vibrative with memories for the Europeans. He became, and still is, the Common Market poet. He displayed an interest in Europe, and Europe has repaid the compliment, as Wilson Knight pointed out: but since 'Common' has its demeaning significance ('a common lodging house'), let us say he is the poet of Our Shared Europe. Along with insurance, freight charges and capital investments, Byron ranks high among our 'invisible exports',

8. In 1811 a group of Nottinghamshire weavers, angered at their replacement by industrial weaving machines, broke and burned a number of these "stocking frames." Byron, in one of his speeches in the House of Lords, eloquently de-fended the frustration and anger (though not the actions) of the frame breakers, and urged the imposition of only a light penalty for their crime. [*Editor.*]
9. The opening lines of Keats's "Ode to a Nightingale." [*Editor.*]

however deplorable the figures of our balance of trade. But, of course, he shared himself particularly with Italy and with Greece.

We can notice, in that 'eve before the Battle of Waterloo' stanza, its lucidity combined with, or in despite of, its packing of detail—detail observed, detail heard. It has the Byronic charge, the drive of confidence. He composed hurriedly, chancing the luck of his enormous talent. Well, he had luck, and could justify his aristocratic contempt for those who toiled, strained and revised in composition. He possessed the Renaissance *sprezzatura*.[1] And he could manage the swell—and the check. And he had a virtuosity in the management of stops. The whole rising surge of social grand ball-room gaiety is checked by that last line which is, appropriately, an alexandrine 'dragging its slow length along'. The stanza is a prescription for a score of historical painters submitting their pictures of 'the night before Waterloo.'

In the happy violence of such verse, Byron has re-tuned the Spenserian stanza to suit his own nature. The stanza in *The Faerie Queene*, for all its grace, was disposed to languor, moving, as Coleridge expressed it, 'with the moon's soft pace', a stanza with a pulse beat agreeable to Thomson's celebration of lassitude in *The Castle of Indolence* but remote from the strength and pace of the Byronic pulse. Traces of this inherited languor and distancing are discernible in the early stanzas of *Childe Harold*, with their slowing and softening 'sooths to say', their 'wights', 'hights' and 'swains', and the stanza, on account of its name (what other stanza is named after its founder?), and its original purpose—pilgrimages, questing knights or apprentice knights—provided Byron with the bold 'plan'. And as he acquired the knack (as later he was to acquire the knack of the *ottava rima* and then transform that) he came to subdue it to his own masterful temperament, to direct it. Still a connection between the two poets remains because of that stanza. Following *Childe Harold*, Shelley and Keats wrote poems in the Spenserian stanza. They are derivatives of *Childe Harold*'s fame more than Spenser's. *The Faerie Queene* and Byron's poem are connected but contrasted: each expresses its age. In this way they were both originals and epoch-making.

In *The Faerie Queene* it is the spiritual contests and the interior landscapes that primarily signify, but in *Childe Harold* it is the outward, veritable, evidential fact that is registered—the fact in the past, the fact in the now—and signifies. And let the observer, the knower, digest it as he can, adjusting his sensibility's capacity to absorb the shock. Hence no apology again for invoking the bullfight which fascinates the British tourists today in their thousands, even

1. The quality of doing everything, even difficult tasks, with ease and nonchal-   ance. [*Editor.*]

as they condemn it, as it did the few travellers who watched it in 1809. The poet, early tourist (and it is here, I suspect, that the poet first positively breaks with the 'slow pace' of Spenser, whose jousting knights are seen in slow motion through shimmering gauze), hears:

> Hushed is the din of tongues . . .

and sees:

> on gallant steeds . . .
> Four cavaliers prepare . . .

The picadors' lances are to break the muscles of the neck so that the matador may finally confront the exhausted animal with its head lowered sufficiently for him to poise and bring his blade down vertically to the heart. Next Byron observes that the peons with their athletic nimbleness have planted their 'clinging' darts with ribbons or streamers attached to weaken and enrage; have skipped out of the way just in time.

> On foams the Bull, but not unscathed he goes;
> Streams from his flank the crimson torrent clear;
> He flies, he wheels, distracted with his throes;
> Dart follows dart; . . .

A horse, carrying a lancer, is gored and 'unseamed appears':

> His gory chest unveils life's panting source . . .

The horse is down on its haunches, but it gets up:

> Though death-struck, still his feeble frame he rears:
> Staggering, but stemming all, his Lord [his rider]
> unharmed he bears.

The matador makes his kill:

> Where his vast neck just mingles with the spine,
> Sheathed in his form the deadly weapon lies.
> He [the bull] stops—he starts—disdaining to decline:
> Slowly he falls, amidst triumphant cries . . .

The carcass needs to be cleared from the ring before the next fight, the sand must be spread over the blood, so

> The decorated car appears—on high
> The corse is piled—sweet sight for vulgar eyes—
> Four steeds that spurn the rein, as swift as shy,
> Hurl the dark bulk along, scarce seen in dashing by.

The poet, and he is a young poet, has made vividly real in words the drama (but is that the word since a drama runs to a preordained text?), or sport, or high ceremony, of the bullfight. And since he was in Spain he could scarcely have done otherwise than poetically realise—act by act, or round by round—a ceremony which, in its blood-spill, passion, excitement and skill, is so poignantly eloquent of the country. And rereading the stanzas (*Childe Harold's Pilgrimage*, I. lxxii–lxxx), I find it evident how open Byron was, and how he shared, like a good poet, the experience: the excitement, the passion, the blood, the death—consequences of daring skill. Yet, also like a good poet, because he is of inclusive sympathies, after giving himself to the experience, vivid and gleaming with violence, he could, absorbing it, judge that the 'sport' was 'ungentle':

> Such the ungentle sport that oft invites
> The Spanish maid, and cheers the Spanish swain . . .

But 'ungentle' the grandees and dames? The *thing*, the event or ceremony, requires an explanation, and this is to be had by recourse to the Spaniard's history; his genius (if so it can be called) for 'pain' must be referred to the *vendetta*:

> Nurtured in blood betimes, his heart delights
> In vengeance, gloating on another's pain . . .

No excuse, we say, to be case-hardened to cruelty. No excuse, but an attempt at an understanding. Where else, but by an investigation of the past, of history, can we obtain an understanding which is sympathetic, not indictory?

Here it is opportune to remark on Byron's use of words. Eliot, we recall, charged Byron with 'an imperceptiveness to the English word', and Auden referred to 'his lack of reverence for words'; and Byron's wife (none other, as Auden notes) declared that her husband used words 'as Bonaparte did lives, for conquest without regard to their value'.

All poets 'use words'—in different ways. If Byron used words to sway the large and important audience he commanded, and which he succeeded in swaying, then he was honourably exercising poetic rhetoric as have other great poets of the past. In the following lines,

> Four steeds that spurn the rein, as swift as shy,
> Hurl the dark bulk along, scarce seen in dashing by,

there are four syntactic units, 'Four . . . rein', 'as . . . shy', 'Hurl . . . along', 'scarce . . . by.' All are functional ('not a word wasted"), but the elements that tell most are the verb 'Hurl' and the adjective 'dark'. 'Hurl', at the head of the line, creates its emphatic effect of rapid and abruptly strenuous action instantly. 'Dark', on the other hand, might be objected to as being too general, therefore weak: for nothing characterises contemporary verse practice so much as the individual adjective. But the 'dark' has multiple meanings—as against 'Hurl'—which reverberate beyond the stanza. An instant effect combined with impressions that linger is typical of the Byronic rhetoric.

'Dark'. An obvious, quick, lazy adjective to describe immediately the carcass of the dead bull? Yes, and no. 'Dark'. The arena by now may have been in shadow, or partly so? The bull may have been, like most fighting bulls, black? The thrilling but terrible killing may have impressed as a dark deed? Or, and everyone should have noted this, sweat poured out by man or beast in outbursts of energy or agony darkens skin or the hide? On our first hearing we may not notice the alternatives. But in the rapidity of the statement they are not alternatives. The 'dark' is not *in*tensive ambiguity, but an *ex*tensive release of significances, in their plurality, because of the scope —as well as the purpose, if scope can be separated from purpose— of the composition. And the delicately 'swift' and 'shy' *hurl* the dead 'dark' thing, on its drag, out of the arena, so quickly that it is hardly seen. One understands that the spectators wish to clear their minds of the object. 'The din of tongues' can rise before the next contest. Quite. But the characteristic 'Hurl', and the phrases concerning the 'Four steeds . . . shy' and 'scarce seen in dashing by' play on that 'dark'. The events happen rapidly, an effect is immediate, but the simple word 'dark' is *ex*tensive.

The suffering of the bull, the struggle of the gladiator, the agonies of the Childe, of the Byronic heroes of the Tales. Discussing torture in *The Two Foscari* with Eckermann, Goethe saw clearly that here Byron was 'just in his element . . . he was always a self-tormentor', suffering was 'his darling theme'. '*Self*-tormentor': this is probably a pointer to something nearer the truth than the wilful showmanship suggested by 'the pageant of his bleeding heart' or Eliot's 'groomed himself for the rôle of travelling tragedian'. Byron was subjected to early Calvinist influence; he may have been deeply wronged, but he was not entirely guiltless; he may obscurely have wished himself to be wronged, and deeply—and he was guilty of others' hurts if he had so wished to think he was. Like many, he had an impulse towards self-punishment. This is a grim subject, but central to an understanding of Byron. Christians, Calvinists included—a quarter or a fifth of the population of the world—profess, if they understand it, that everyone deserved death for disobedience in eating a fruit. And Byron was prophetic. If the British have exchanged Christianity for an agnostic humanism, they now insist on feeling guilty for their history, for that empire they once had.

The Byronic hero of the Tales drew on his creator's sense of guilt as if it were an abundant capital, and made of infamy a darkly lustrous thing. But the poet was 'more sinned against than sinning'. To complain about being wronged can lead to the charge of self-

386 · *Francis Berry*

pity, which is undignified. Indignation even if justified is hardly noble unless it is subsumed by forgiveness—and the woe is related to the woe of others.

In Canto IV he says in the preface, 'I recur from fiction to truth', and Byron speaks in his own person the lines:

> And if my voice break forth, 'tis not that now
> I shrink from what is suffered: let him speak
> Who hath beheld decline upon my brow,
> Or seen my mind's convulsion leave it weak;
> But in this page a record will I seek.
> Not in the air shall these my words disperse,
> Though I be ashes; a far hour shall wreak
> The deep prophetic fulness of this verse,
> And pile on human heads the mountain of my curse!
> That curse shall be Forgiveness.—Have I not—
> Hear me, my mother Earth! behold it, Heaven!—
> Have I not had to wrestle with my lot?
> Have I not suffered things to be forgiven?
> Have I not had my brain seared, my heart riven,
> Hopes sapped, name blighted, Life's life lied away? . . .
>
> But I have lived, and have not lived in vain.

> (*Childe Harold's Pilgrimage*, IV.
> cxxxiv–cxxxvii)

Now compare this with the following:

> I am, but what I am, who cares or knows?
> My friends forsake me like a memory lost.
> I am the self-consumer of my woes;
> They rise and vanish, an oblivious host,
> Like shades in love and death's oblivion lost;
> And yet I am, and *live* with shadows tossed
>
> Into the nothingness of scorn and noise,
> Into the living sea of waking dream . . .

That poem by Clare[2] is fine, though one is the more indulgent to the poem through an acquaintance with the biography of the poet. But it is 'Byronic'; it would not have been written but for Byron. Byron provided an example for the other poet to feed on his woe and deliver the touching lament of misery. But there is a difference: Byron fuses—as Clare does not—his misery, or agony, with a contemplation of actualities of agonies and griefs of others outside himself, griefs that must be accepted just as history is accepted. The

> Have I not had my brain seared, my heart riven?
> Hopes sapped, name blighted, Life's life lied away? . . .
>
> But I have lived, and have not lived in vain:

2. John Clare (1793–1864), a talented   but minor, later romantic poet. [*Editor.*]

leads into the famous and concretely realised scene of the dying
gladiator in the Coliseum of Imperial Rome (cxl–cxli). Byron
relates his own woes to those of other men. Like the poet, the gladiator is an exile, separated from his wife and offspring, his fate invoking the 'inhuman shout' of the uncompassionating mob. It was
argued, some years ago, that an education in the humanities, if it
did not make a man morally better than others, at least gave him a
resource denied to others: his training in history or the literatures
gave him access to a wide context of collective experience in time
and space to which he could refer his personal sufferings. Such a
man would at least be spared the vanity of supposing himself a
unique victim. Byron had that resource, among others, and draws
on it in *Childe Harold* (and vicariously so in *The Prisoner of Chillon* or *The Lament of Tasso*), and it is this more-than-personal
spread of grief or melancholy which makes Byron's lament noble or,
as Francis Jeffrey said, in his review of Canto IV in 1818, 'majestic'
and 'sublime'. And the compassion for men extends beyond them
—for things, the ruins of Athens or the ruins of Rome. The beautiful and Byronic poem of John Clare, for all its acute pathos, is not
'noble'; it expresses some self-pity and we respond by sharing it.

Scott and Byron, we remember, were the two poets of vast repute
in 1817; Byron accounting Scott the head and summit of Mount
Parnassus, and Scott turning to the prose of the Waverley novels
when—whatever the other reasons—he felt he was no longer able
to compete in rivalry with Byron. There is that amusing passage in
Jane Austen's *Persuasion*:

> . . . having talked of poetry, the richness of the present age, and
> gone through a brief comparison of opinion as to the first-rate
> poets, trying to ascertain whether *Marmion* or *The Lady of the
> Lake* were to be preferred, and how ranked *The Giaour* and *The
> Bride of Abydos*, and moreover how *The Giaour* was to be pro-
> nounced, he [Captain Benwick, R. N.] showed himself so inti-
> mately acquainted with all the tenderest songs of the one poet,
> and all the impassioned descriptions of hopeless agony of the
> other; he repeated, with such tremulous feeling, the various lines
> which imaged a broken heart, or a mind destroyed by wretched-
> ness, . . . that she [Anne] ventured to hope he did not always
> read only poetry . . .

So Anne recommended a strong dose of prose, the works 'of our
best moralists'

> as calculated to rouse and fortify the mind by the highest pre-
> cepts, and the strongest examples of moral and religious endur-
> ances.

(Ch. XI)

Young Captain Benwick had been bereaved of his fiancée, and I
dare say there is a danger of sensitive young men over-indulging

their emotions by reading of verse—or by the writing of it—and identifying themselves with the suffering personae of the poets. In which case, I can see, there was more temptation to identify with the Giaour ('however that is to be pronounced') in 1817, or with Childe Harold, then with Mr Prufrock or Gerontion[3] in 1974. Remote from the age and life-style of the prim and timid Mr Prufrock, the present generation finds itself in an age of eloquent violence, 'full of passionate intensity', and active with corsairs and giaours—hijackers, if not 'water-thieves'. These may, or may not, be 'the worst', for not lacking 'all conviction', but their style is Byronic, except that they do not in their actions invariably display the chivalry of the heroes of Byron's Tales. Nevertheless, like those heroes, the new desperadoes are neither timid nor doubting; nor are they less than certain about the value of their political, or other, opinions, or less than proud of the figures they cut. In such a world it would be strange if it could be said that, of the Romantic poets, Byron 'seemed the most nearly remote from the sympathies of every living critic'.

Nearer to readers, and critics, in 1974 then in 1937, Byron would be of more *use* to poets writing today or tomorrow. The poems by Scott and Byron, which so affected Captain Benwick in *Persuasion*, were narrative poems. In the telling of a story, verse can do things which prose cannot do, irrespective of the current health or decline of the novel, and the advantage of verse extends beyond concentration to include the choice of actions—in Arnold's sense of the term, and to Arnold all-important—outside the range and control of prose. Byron, as a master of the narrative poem, offers himself as an examplar of a *genre* long-neglected but one most likely to render, and interpret, contemporary experience.

I share the view that *Don Juan*, the one great comic poem in our language, is possibly the supreme achievement. But my concern has been mainly with *Childe Harold*, scarcely less great, no less honest, in its own kind, and a necessary stage in the development; for a capacity to develop—or simply to change—is, we recollect, one of the qualities of the major poet.

For *Childe Harold's Pilgrimage* was written from a tragic cast of mind. The comic possibilities of *ottava rima* had still to be discovered; so had the sometimes droll status of *cavalier servente* and the possessive devotion of Teresa Guiccoli. The beyond-the-tragic mood of the lines,

> I would to Heaven that I were so much clay
> As I am blood, bone, marrow, passion, feeling—
> Because at least the past were passed away,

---

3. Gerontion, whose name means "little old man," is the title character in an- other of Eliot's earlier poems on the exhaustion of western culture. [*Editor.*]

And for the future—(but I write this reeling,
Having got drunk exceedingly to-day,
So that I seem to stand upon the ceiling)
I say—the future is a serious matter—
And so—for God's sake—hock and soda-water,

had not yet been reached.

ROBERT F. GLECKNER

The Giaour as Experimental Narrative†

* * *

The history of the composition of *The Giaour* is complex, and we do not know all of it. Byron first mentions it in a letter to Murray of May 13, 1813, accompanying a "corrected, and, I hope, amended copy of the lines for the 'fragment' already sent this evening," with instructions to burn the original copy.[1] That original was 407 lines long and is what Byron called some days later "the first sketch";[2] but as the above letter suggests, almost immediately it was added to and refurbished, so that the first published edition ran to 685 lines. This is the edition Byron refers to in his letters to Hodgson of June 6 and June 8, 1813, where he says he added "ten pages, *text* and *margin* . . . which render it a little less unfinished (but more unintelligible) than before"—additions "to the tune of 300 lines or so towards the end."[3] These "ten pages" or "300 lines" constitute the 224-line first version of the Giaour's long speech to the Monk and 54 lines scattered elsewhere in the poem. The former is a significant addition, giving notice immediately that the poem is to be not merely an exciting narrative but a narrative with some sort of commentary.

The basic plot is extraordinarily simple: it is all contained in the original "sketch" of the poem. Byron's main interest, however, was not in the plot (*Childe Harold* I and II should have warned us against this assumption) but rather in the conflicting points of view from which that plot could be viewed. The sketch is, as it were, a piece of sculpture around which the viewer walks in order to see it in different lights and shadows, the eye building up a structure of fragmentary apperceptions, disjointed by virtue of their temporal and spatial discontinuity, but all tending toward a unified imaginative perception of the whole and its "meaning." More exactly, it is

† From Robert F. Gleckner, *Byron and the Ruins of Paradise* (Baltimore: The Johns Hopkins Press, 1967), pp. 96–117.
1. *LJ*, II, 204. [Byron's *Letters and Journals*, ed. Rowland Prothero (London: John Murray, 1898–1901)—*Editor.*]
2. Ltr. to Hodgson, 6 June 1813, in *LJ*, II, 215.
3. *LJ*, II, 214–15.

like a piece of sculpture surrounded by a number of viewers, each of whom sees it and interprets it in his own light. By focusing not on the sculpture (the plot) but on the beholder or beholders (the speakers) and by juxtaposing their various spatial-temporal views, Byron gradually builds, in the final version of the poem, an interpretation of the "human condition" to which all the viewers contribute, while at the same time he maintains the limited and proper partisanship of each of the separate views.

The first additions to the "sketch," then, provide the initial material for one of the major points of view, that of the Giaour himself, for before this he is represented only at a distance in a third-person narrative, and briefly at the end of the poem in his Manfred-like refusal of aid from the Monk. This basic consistency in Byron's original handling of the Giaour is surely the reason why, in the only other first-edition passage in which he speaks, Byron has him speak of himself in the third as well as the first person (ll. 675–88[4]). It is Byron's early recognition that the Giaour is both an actor in the plot and a commentator on (or an embodiment of a point of view toward) that same plot.

The *editio princeps*,[5] then, sketches as much of the plot as we need to know and introduces the several speakers: the poet-traveler (not necessarily Byron), whose point of view is always larger and fuller than the others; the fisherman, a partisan Moslem and storyteller, whose voice carries the bulk of the narrative in which he himself is a sometime participant; Hassan, who speaks only in the drowning scene and in the battle with the Giaour's band; and the Giaour himself. Of these, the fisherman dominates the poem—as participant, narrator, and commentator. Byron's last footnote to the first edition explains the source of this conception: "The story in the text is one told of a young Venetian many years ago, and now nearly forgotten. I heard it by accident recited by one of the coffeehouse storytellers who abound in the Levant, and sing or recite their narratives. The additions and interpolations by the translator will be easily distinguished from the rest by the want of Eastern imagery. . . ."[6] This conscious attempt to distinguish between storyteller and "translator" (what I have called "the poet" above) represents a noteworthy advance over the technique of *Childe Harold* I and II, where the points of view are distinguished only by voice, attitude, tone, and the like. Dissatisfied with that more subtle, difficult, and finally confusing technique, Byron in *The Giaour* attempts the same thing but assigns to the voices, attitudes, and

4. All line number references will be to the seventh edition, after which Byron made no further changes in the poem. [The "seventh edition" of *The Giaour* is the poem as we now have it—*Editor*.]

5. First version. [*Editor*.]

6. *P*, III, 145n. [The E. H. Coleridge edition of Byron's *Poetical Works*—*Editor*.]

tones a realizable personality and being. Further, rather than merely suggesting vaguely, as he did in *Childe Harold,* that Harold has a companion (or companions) on his tour of the Mediterranean, in *The Giaour* Byron openly announces two narrators, one who speaks the initial, apparently extraneous, lines on Greece and introduces the fisherman, the other the fisherman-storyteller himself. Still, if the poem was not to be merely a narrative with interpolated comments but rather a thematic study of the "human condition" which subsumes all individual and limited views, additional points of view, attitudes, and comments had to be created or enlarged and the role of the controlling poet expanded to the point where he could see the fundamental similarity of man's eternal predicament on earth.

That predicament is simply the inevitability of man's fall. I do not speak here of the archetypal Fall, though Ridenour's argument for this in *The Style of "Don Juan"* is persuasive indeed, and it is at least possible that the Calvinistically trained Byron was more fully aware of the analogies he created in his poems than we are willing to give him credit for. I speak rather of the fundamental (and romantic) ironies of man's finite existence, which are nowhere expressed so succinctly as in *Manfred*:

> Half dust, half deity, alike unfit
> To sink or soar, with our mixed essence make
> A conflict of its elements, and breathe
> The breath of degradation and of pride,
> Contending with low wants and lofty will,
> Till our Mortality predominates,
> And men are—what they name not to themselves,
> And trust not to each other.
>
> (I, ii, 40–47)

Or, even better, the Abbott's speech in Act III, Scene i:

> This should have been a noble creature: he
> Hath all the energy which would have made
> A goodly frame of glorious elements,
> Had they been wisely mingled; as it is,
> It is an awful chaos—Light and Darkness—
> And mind and dust—and passions and pure thoughts
> Mixed, and contending without end or order,—
> All dormant or destructive. He will perish.
>
> (160–67)

This pessimism, or "fatalism," as Byron preferred to call it,[7] is con-

7. Only recently have critics come to see that Byron's "fatalism" is essentially pessimism, neither cynical nor predestinarian. See * * * Alvin B. Kernan's chapter on *Don Juan* in his *The Plot of Satire* (New Haven and London, 1965), Brian Wilkie's chapter on *Don Juan* in his *The Romantic Poets and Epic Tradition* (Madison and Milwaukee, Wis., 1965), and Gilbert Highet's interesting little essay, "The Poet and His Vulture," in *A Clerk at Oxenford* (New York, 1954).

stant in his work and in his life. Man's violence ultimately produces his own defeat or decay, but what is more important is that man's virtues—courage, pride, love, loyalty—also lead him to destruction. As Ridenour says of the Haidée episode in *Don Juan*, "as violence and disorder lurk behind the most winning manifestations of tranquillity and harmony, the tranquil and harmonious are fated inevitably to dissolve again in the violent and chaotic. This is an apparently immutable law of Byron's world."[8] And it is this "immutable law" which Byron seeks to dramatize for the first time in *The Giaour*, whose world is one of love and death, beauty and death, freedom and death, nature and death, man's human and heroic virtues and death. It is not a poem, then, which simply seeks to glorify "the outlaw, the rebel, the renegade, the Ishmaelite, the bold bad man," as Andrew Rutherford[9] and a host of others before him have insisted. Nor is it primarily a poem of self-dramatization (however clearly some of the details of Byron's life seem to obtrude) or an orgiastic indulgence in a vaguely misanthropic melancholy. That these elements, and other similar ones, exist in the poem and in the other tales in varying proportions is obvious; and even if the Giaour is in a distinct *dramatic* and literary tradition, as Bertrand Evans and Peter Thorslev, among others, have shown,[1] what I am concerned with here is Byron's "elaborately coherent" vision of the human condition and his earnest though self-deprecated efforts to achieve a form, a structure, a technique for embodying that vision in his art. The elements repreatedly singled out for critical comment must be seen as the result of partial failures to embody the vision—failures blown out of proportion by the prevailing and almost irresistible penchant of critics (from Byron's day to ours) to read the poems as biography. "My figures are not portraits," Byron cried vainly; and while reveling personally in the notoriety of his figures, he could still attack, with elaborate egotism but abundant justification, those "who, by perversely persisting in referring fiction to truth, and tracing poetry to life, and regarding characters of imagination as creatures of existence, have made me personally responsible for almost every poetical delineation which fancy and a particular bias of thought, may have tended to produce."[2]

That "bias of thought" produced the poet-figure in *The Giaour* as much as the Giaour himself, a vision of human life as well as the fisherman's story—but not without considerable persistence and labor on Byron's part, in which he was perhaps inspired by recalling that his idol, Pope, *"added to the 'Rape of the Lock,'* but did not

8. *The Style of "Don Juan,"* p. 45.
9. *Byron: A Critical Study*, p. 43.
1. Bertrand Evans, *Gothic Drama from Walpole to Shelley* (Berkeley, Calif., 1947), and "Manfred's Remorse and Dramatic Tradition," *PMLA*, LXII (1947), 752–73; Peter Thorslev, *The By-* ronic Hero.
2. Byron's reply to an article in Blackwood's *Edinburgh Magazine*, XXIX (August, 1819), attacking him for *Don Juan*, in *LJ*, IV, 477. See also Byron's complaint in *Detached Thoughts*, in *LJ*, V, 407–8.

reduce it."[3] As usual, his own comments on his progress are facetious: it is his "bravura"; it is a "snake of a poem, which has been lengthening its rattles every month"; and twice, with perhaps a wry look at his own snake image, he writes to Murray that he is "bitten again" and has "quantities for other parts" of the poem.[4] The nature of the additions, however, belies this lightness, for almost all of them bolster existing points of view, add others, or elaborate on the overriding themes.

In the second edition, published about a month after the first, the puzzling six lines on Greece that opened the first edition are supplemented in order to introduce the country's Edenic past, "where every season smiles / Benignant o'er those blessèd isles" (ll. 7–8). The poet-speaker then goes on, in another new passage, to elaborate this idea by linking "Nature" and the "Gods" within "the Paradise" of this "fairy land" (ll. 46ff.). Into this Edenic world "man, enamoured of distress," enters and mars

> it into wilderness,
> And trample[s], brute-like, o'er each flower
> That tasks not one laborious hour;
>
> .   .   .   .   .
>
> Strange—that where all is Peace beside,
> There Passion riots in her pride,
> And Lust and Rapine wildly reign
> To darken o'er the fair domain.
> It is as though the Fiends prevailed
> Against the Seraphs they assailed.
>
> (ll. 51–53, 58–63)

This is followed by the oft-quoted passage beginning "He who hath bent him o'er the dead," which likens present-day Greece to the "mild angelic air" and "rapture of repose" on the face of the newly dead: "Hers is the loveliness in death."[5] The otherwise puzzling six lines that open the poem are thus given a context: the idea of home and safety to the fisherman in his skiff and the beauty and serenity of the land and sea are both shrouded in the gloom of "the Athenian's grave," the grave of the hero set in a land of ruin and death.

The poet's bewailing the loss of this hero (Byron suggests he is Themistocles) is also significant in the light of the presentation of

3. Ltr. to Murray, 18 Sept. 1820, in *LJ*, V, 120. This is the famous letter in which Byron describes himself as a "tyger (in poesy), if I miss the first Spring, I go growling back to my jungle. There is no second." This is his general argument for not revising, refurbishing, correcting; but his approval, in the same context, of addition and interpolation is seldom noted.

4. Ltrs. to Murray, 10 and 26 Aug. and 29 Sept. 1813, in *LJ*. II. 244, 252, 268.

5. Ll. 68–102. Typical of the praise accorded the lines is that of Ethel C. Mayne (Byron [2 vols.; New York, 1912], I, 262). Her phrase, "that strange, slipshod loveliness," seems to me precisely right. Thomas Noon Talfourd's contemporary criticism sets the style for all later misconceptions of the passage (see William A. Coles, "Thomas Noon Talfourd on Byron and the Imagination," *Keats-Shelley Journal*, IX [1960], 108).

Hassan and the Giaour. They, too, are heroes, but of a different mold somehow: as fallen, finite men, betrayed by their own passions, they destroy rather than create or sustain peace and love and beauty. "Spark[s] of that flame, perchance of heavenly birth" (l. 101), they love intensely—and destroy the object of that love as well as each other. To accent the point, as well as to place the Grecian passages and the narrative in proper perspective through the eyes of the poet, Byron, in another passage added in the second edition (ll. 620–54), has his poet comment on the battle between Hassan and the Giaour. Echoing the juxtaposition of Themistocles' grave and idyllic Grecian landscape, the battle takes place in a peaceful vale "More suited to the shepherd's tale"; and the personal clash of the two heroic figures is seen, with terrible irony, as an embrace stronger than that of lovers.

Finally, Byron's third addition to this state of the poem (ll. 999–1023) has the Giaour himself comment on the difference between his own finite, "human" heroism that leads to destruction and death and the kind of heroism represented by Themistocles, "The slave of Glory, not of Love." And Hassan was the same, as the Giaour recognizes:

> Yet did he but what I had done
> Had she been false to more than one.
>
> (ll. 1062–63)

What he does not recognize is the waste of it all, the noble passion that miscarries, the irony of his own strength and singlemindedness. "Love will find its way," he persists in thinking,

> Through paths where wolves would fear to prey;
> And if it dares enough, 'twere hard
> If Passion met not some reward.
>
> (ll. 1048–51)

Yet almost in the same breath he brands his own brow with the curse of Cain (ll. 1057–59). The point is made again some lines later, when the Giaour describes his love in terms of "scorching vein, / Lips taught to writhe, but not complain" (ll. 1105–6), "bursting heart, and maddening brain" (l. 1106), "daring deed, and vengeful steel" (l. 1107):

> I knew but to obtain or die.
> I die—but first I have possessed,
> And come what may, I *have been* blessed.[6]
>
> (ll. 1113–15)

The irony is double-edged here, for his blessing is Cain's curse and his own death (cf. the "blesséd isles" of the opening passage on Greece); further, the very passion which the poet bewails as missing

6. Aside from the passages added in the second edition, all of the passages quoted in the foregoing analysis were present in the first edition.

in present-day enslaved Greece *does* exist, but only to despoil and destroy. The heart of man, "that all / Which Tyranny can ne'er enthrall" (ll. 1068–69), becomes in this world inevitably a tyrant itself. Byron's heroes are consistently slaves of their passions,[7] of love, which presumably in some earlier age led to harmony and peace. Love in this world of men, however, is either destroyed by the world (as Haidée's and Juan's is for example) or by itself. It is ironically, as the Giaour says in a fifth-edition enlargement of his final speech,

> light from Heaven;
> A spark of that immortal fire
> With angels shared, by Alla given,
> To lift from earth our low desire.
> Devotion wafts the mind above,
> But Heaven itself descends in Love;
> A feeling from the Godhead caught,
> To wean from self each sordid thought;
> A ray of Him who formed the whole;
> A Glory circling round the soul!
>
> (ll. 1131–40)

Yet his experience has also given him a certain wisdom in the ways of the world: "I grant *my* love imperfect" (l. 1141)—and Byron implies continually that all mankind's love is imperfect, and hence lost. That is the human condition.[8]

Conscious of this evolving pattern, in the third edition, issued less than a month after the second, Byron inserts in the poet's opening hymn to Greece a portrait of ideal love in a prelapsarian world:

> there the Rose, o'er crag or vale,
> Sultana of the Nightingale,
> The maid for whom his melody,
> His thousand songs are heard on high,
> Blooms blushing to her lover's tale:
> His queen, the garden queen, his Rose,
> Unbent by winds, unchilled by snows,
> Far from the winters of the west,
> By every breeze and season blest,
> Returns the sweets by Nature given
> In softest incense back to Heaven;
> And grateful yields that smiling sky
> Her fairest hue and fragrant sigh.
>
> (ll. 21–33)

7. Bostetter's otherwise excellent analysis of Byron in *The Romantic Ventriloquists* is too heavily dependent on this one point; for example, ". . . under the melodramatic posturings [in *Childe Harold* I and II] there are genuine pessimism and fatalism based on observation of his own sexual nature" (p. 266).

8. This reading of the passage is reinforced by the manuscript version in *P*, III, 137n.

And, in order to forge more solidly the thematic link between this passage on Greece and the Turkish-Christian narrative, he also adds a passage to the fisherman's account of Leila, "armed with beauty," moving on earth as "The cygnet nobly walks the water" (ll. 512, 504). In the lines prior to these, present in the first edition, the fisherman is willing to swear "By Alla" (l. 481) that her form was more than "breathing clay" (l. 482), "That through her eye the Immortal shone" (l. 492), and that

> her feet
> Gleamed whiter than the mountain sleet
> Ere from the cloud that gave it birth
> It fell, and caught one stain of earth.
>
> (ll. 500–3)

Thus Byron carefully identities pristine Greece with an unstained Leila (the flower images in the description of the latter, for example, are precisely parallel to the flower imagery in the Greece passage). But she is also present-day Greece, still lovely but a slave to Hassan, and the Giaour thus becomes an emancipator—paradoxically, in the act of emancipation, her destroyer. As a result, Hassan is dead, his palace and grounds (a refuge of "Courtesy and Pity" afforded to travelers) ruined and decayed, love and beauty and purity dead, and the Giaour left amid these ruins with no faith (in a Moslem or a Christian God), no object, courting death.

The total picture cheers no heroes, advances no cause (private or public), asserts no values. It is a completely depressing, pessimistic, even nihilistic view of man and the world. The only survivors are Hassan's mother (who is fated to greet her son as a corpse rather than a bridegroom), the fisherman (who presumably goes on telling his tale without fully understanding), and the Monk and his brethren (who are helpless to do anything about anything).

With this total picture emerging more clearly in his mind, Byron fills out his presentation of desolation in the fourth, fifth, and seventh editions (only minor verbal changes were made in the sixth) and expands the number of points of view to show more fully the hopelessness of human aspirations and endeavor. In the fourth edition (August, 1813) in a substantial insertion the ruins of Hassan's hall are described at length by the fisherman and contrasted to the idyllic setting it once was (ll. 288–351). Spiders, bats, owls, wild dogs have taken over, and, like the dried-up stream bed on the field of Hassan's and the Giaour's battle, "the stream has shrunk from its marble bed, / Where the weeds and the desolate dust are spread" (ll. 297–98). Luxurious coolness, clear air and stars, music, beauty, childhood innocence, and maternal love have all yielded now to total desolation and death:

> And here no more shall human voice
> Be heard to rage, regret, rejoice.
> The last sad note that swelled the gale
> Was woman's wildest funeral wail:
> That quenched in silence, all is still,
> But the lattice that flaps when the wind is shrill.
>
> (ll. 320–25)

Equally devastating, perhaps even more so because it is more inti-mate and movingly human, is the shrewd insertion in this fourth edition of the section recounting the reception by Hassan's mother of the news of her son's death (ll. 689–722). Again, as in the open-ing passage on Greece and those on Leila's beauty and Hassan's childhood, Byron sets the grimness of death and destruction against an idyllic background:

> The browsing camels' bells are tinkling:
> His mother looked from her lattice high—
> She saw the dews of eve besprinkling
> The pasture green beneath her eye,
> She saw the planets faintly twinkling.
>
> (ll. 688–92)

If it is too much to see the word "lattice" here as a recollection of the ghostly flapping lattice of Hassan's ruined palace, it is clear that from earth to heaven all is peace and beauty, as Hassan's palace once was. Into this scene comes the bloody lone survivor of the battle, bringing death with him in the form of "Hassan's cloven crest" (l. 716). Byron intensifies the blackness of the scene almost unbearably: the mother, expecting her son as bridegroom, about to achieve the fulfillment, joy and beauty of love, receives the news that "a fearful bride [her] Son hath wed." But perhaps even more horrible is the suggestion that the "gift" he promised to bring in celebration of his attainment of love's heights is the cloven crest of the Giaour. Death as the only "true" bride is insisted upon here, just as earlier the fisherman notes that Hassan, on leaving his palace so hurriedly, was thought to be going "to woo a bride / More true than her who left his side" (ll. 533–34), and then comments later on the horror of the fatal destructive embrace, stronger than that of lovers, of Hassan and the Giaour on the battlefield (ll. 645–54).

The additional point of view of the mother is also of importance, adding as it does another piece to Byron's depressing jigsaw puzzle of the total human predicament of high and low, innocent and guilty alike. That Byron was conscious of his expansion of the range of points of view is evident from his rewriting of the first five lines of the mother's section in order to attribute more clearly to her an angle of vision integrally her own. Originally the passage read (in the fourth edition):

> The browzing camel's bells are tinkling,
> The dews of Eve the pasture sprinkling,
> And rising planets faintly twinkling:
> His Mother looked from her lattice high,
> With throbbing breast and eager eye.[9]

By shifting the order of the lines slightly in the fifth edition, and by avoiding statement of fact without reference to the mother's vision of the scene, Byron establishes clearly a physical point of view that he can then shade off into an attitude or moral point of view. The line beginning "His Mother looked," becomes the second line in the passage, and the phrase "She saw" is added in two different places; the fifth line above is wisely dropped as awkwardly descriptive of an attitude and point of view that it would be more proper to dramatize.

The fifth edition also establishes the poet fully as the pilgrim-like poet of *Childe Harold*, who, having no heroic themes as in the past "on which the Muse might soar" (l. 144), must make what he can of present desolation set against the memory of what once was, of the "nameless pyramid" or "tomb" from which the "general doom / Hath swept the column" (ll. 129–30) framed by

> The mountains of their native land!
> There points thy Muse to stranger's eye
> The graves of those that cannot die!
>
> (ll. 133–35)

The transition from Greece to the fisherman and his story is only superficially mechanical, for it has already been made—from the poet-bard of the heroic, epic past to the fisherman-gossip-storyteller of the modern human condition; from the epic form, stately in its order, which mirrors the artistic control of human passions, to the fragments of a vision, presented with a violent curse, with the need for vengeance, and with only partial understanding.

Finally, in the fifth edition, aside from adding the Giaour's poem to love as "light from heaven" (ll. 1131ff.), which was commented upon above, Byron introduced the friend to whom the Giaour sends a pledge (ll. 1218–56). He is voiceless in the poem, though we should recognize the narrator's reasonable voice of *Childe Harold* I and II in his silent accents. His is the voice of prudence, of reason and restraint, of the prophecy of doom for the passion-directed man. He is the ordinary man, like the chamois hunter of *Manfred*, who pursues his ordinary business, but who also suffers in the general loss. As such, he represents one more point of view, that of the bystander snared in a trap not of his own making, that of the inno-

9. Coleridge's transcription of this pas-   ate (*P*, III, 118n).
sage from the fourth edition is inaccur-

cent who suffers merely because all men are born to suffer. The Giaour's

> withered frame, the ruined mind,
> The wrack by passion left behind,
> A shrivelled scroll, a scattered leaf,
> Seared by the autumn blast of Grief!
>
> (ll. 1253–56)

is the same figure, intensified a hundredfold. For Byron's "heroes" are no heroes in the ordinary sense; they are not participants in tragedy, yet they still retain some of the stature of the tragic hero. Like the tragic hero, they are man magnified, macrocosmic, titanic —yet nevertheless small, insignificant, and lost. They are not merely victims, nor are they tyrants; they are a mixture of both, half dust, half deity, at war constantly. The loser, of course, is always self.[1]

The Giaour is, finally, in an addition appearing first in the seventh edition, "like the bird whose pinions quake, / But cannot fly the gazing snake" (ll. 842–43). But only the poet can see this. The fisherman marvels at his eye and mien, and recalls the monastery that

> once I saw that face, yet then
> It was so marked with inward pain,
> I could not pass it by again;
> It breathes the same dark spirit now,
> As death were stamped upon his brow.
>
> (ll. 793–97)

But while death and the mark of Cain are there, the spirit is not all dark. The glance of the "evil angel" which half frightens the Friar and leads him to pray to Saint Francis to

> keep him from the shrine!
> Else may we dread the wrath divine
> Made manifest by awful sign
>
> (ll. 909–11)

reveals to the poet the remnants of the whole man, the face of Greece before the fall into slavery and degradation, the face of the newly dead

> (Before Decay's effacing fingers
> Have swept the lines where Beauty lingers,)
>
> (ll. 72–73)

the face of Leila, on whose

> fair cheek's unfading hue

---

1. Pertinent here is Herbert J. Muller's reminder that "the ultimate source of tragedy, historically and psychologically, is indeed the simple fact that man must die" (*The Spirit of Tragedy* [New York, 1956], p. 3).

> The young pomegranate's blossoms strew
> Their bloom in blushes ever new,
>
> (ll. 493–95)

the face of "A noble soul, and lineage high" (l. 869). Only to the poet is it *sad* to trace

> What once were feelings in that face:
> Time hath not yet the features fixed,
> But brighter traits with evil mixed;
> And there are hues not always faded,
> Which speak a mind not all degraded
> Even by the crimes through which it waded:
> The common crowd but see the gloom
> Of wayward deeds, and fitting doom.
>
> (ll. 860–67)

If the "common crowd" can see only waywardness and "fitting doom," Byron is careful not to make this mistake. To the Moslem fisherman the doom is just, even if it is not quite the fulfillment of his terrible curse; to the Monk, to Hassan's mother, and to the Moslem and the Christian world, in neither of which the Giaour has a place, his end is fitting and proper. But this is the kind of poetic justice Byron eschews. For him man is "no vulgar tenement / To which . . . lofty gifts were lent" (ll. 872–73), and yet those lofty gifts are given in vain. In imagery that he clearly drew upon for this passage in *The Giaour*, Byron earlier summed up the human condition in *Childe Harold*:

> Remove yon skull from out the scattered heaps:
> Is that a Temple where a God may dwell?
> Why ev'n the Worm at last disdains her shattered cell!
>
> Look on its broken arch, its ruined wall,
> Its chambers desolate, and portals foul:
> Yes, this was once Ambition's airy hall,
> The Dome of Thought, the Palace of the Soul:
> Behold through each lack-lustre, eyeless hole,
> The gay recess of Wisdom and of Wit
> And Passion's host, that never brooked control:
> Can all Saint, Sage, or Sophist ever writ,
> People this lonely tower, this tenement refit?
>
> (II, v–vi)

The answer, of course, is no. It is not a matter of refitting or not; the world is simply so. The gifts are real and the tenement is real; but the world and its chaos of destructive passions are even more real.

A final word needs to be said about the method and structure of the poem. I cannot agree with William Marshall that the final version does "not constitute a whole that can be pieced together" and that "any consideration of the structure or imagery of 'The Giaour' should begin with this proposition."[2] That there are inconsistencies of character, an occasional confusion as to the identity of the speaker of certain lines, and perhaps an unnecessary mystery about the whole business one must admit. Yet, having admitted this, we can still admire what Byron has attempted in the structure of the poem—in addition to the converging points of view and the themes I have discussed above.

The narrative itself is carried almost completely by the fisherman, although there are times when a more objective voice is heard to set a scene or "swell a progress." This fisherman is at once a Moslem, garrulous but neither unimaginative nor inarticulate, a collector of gossip and stories, a fierce partisan of Hassan, an eye-witness to several of the scenes and incidents, and, finally, a participant in at least two major events in the story. As such, it is natural for him to blurt out first (to the poet I assume) what he knows best, that is, what he has actually seen—the initial appearance of the Giaour during the Moslem feast (ll. 180–256). That startling sight leads him to jump ahead too quickly, by way of contrast, to the present ruined state of Hassan's palace and its earlier idyllic beauty (ll. 277–351). Immediately following this sequence of death images, he turns naturally, by association, to the scene of death in which he participated, the drowning of Leila (ll. 352–87). From this point to his reappearance at the monastery, the fisherman narrates only what he has gathered from various sources, with the exception of the first-hand descriptions of Leila herself (ll. 473–518) and of Hassan's grave (ll. 723–46).[3] In the first section of his second-hand narrative (ll. 739–72), he even makes a point of saying that he does not know everything:

> Doth Leila there no longer dwell?
> That tale can only Hassan tell:

2. "The Accretive Structure of Byron's 'The Giaour,' " *MLN*, LXXVI (1961), 502. M. K. Joseph is perhaps the only critic to give Byron credit for a serious "concern for the form of the poem"—though he does not say anything about that form other than that it is a fragmentary (*Byron the Poet* [London, 1964], p. 37).

3. One of the most acute comments on the fisherman-narrator is one of the earliest, George Ellis' remark on ll. 288ff.: ". . . this part of the narrative is managed with unusual taste. The fisherman has, hitherto, related nothing more than the extraordinary phenomenon which had excited his curiosity, and of which it is his immediate object to explain the cause to his hearers; but instead of proceeding to do so, he stops to vent his execrations on the Giaour, to describe the solitude of Hassan's once luxurious haram [sic], and to lament the untimely death of the owner, and of Leila, together with the cessation of that hospitality which they had uniformly exercised. He reveals, as if unintentionally and unconsciously, the catastrophe of his story; but he thus prepares his appeal to the sympathy of his audience, without much diminishing of their suspense." Review of *The Giaour* and *The Bride of Abydos, Quarterly Review*, X (1814), 336–37.

See also the intelligent but inconclusive analysis of the structure of *The Giaour* by Clement T. Goode, "Byron's Early Romances: A Study" (unpublished Ph.D. dissertation, Vanderbilt University, 1959), pp. 153–64.

> Strange rumours in our city say
> Upon that eve she fled away
> When Rhamazan's last sun was set.
>
> (ll. 445-49)

From these rumors, from "the tale his [Hassan's] Nubians tell, / Who did not watch their charge too well" (ll. 465-66), from what "others say" about that night (l. 467), and from his own remembrance of the Giaour's mysterious ride into the area, the fisherman pieces the whole story together—Hassan's sudden departure "deck'd for war," the battle (obviously told originally by the lone survivor who reports to Hassan's mother), and the scene with Hassan's mother.

The fisherman, then, is one of the poet-pilgrim's two major sources, the other of course being the Giaour himself. Thus we have the public guesses, so to speak, as to what happened, the soldier's account, the fisherman's absorption of these with interpolations of his own first-hand knowledge, the Giaour's account, the Monk's account of the Giaour—all subsumed under the vision of the poet. To these accounts the poet adds his own impressions of the Giaour, as well as, by manipulation of their tone and gestures, his impressions of all the other characters, his interpretation of the story as he pieced it together, and his commentary on its significance in the light of what he knows of the past and sees in the present. Each of the other points of view is limited to the bias of the beholder; and consequently each of these interpretations is incorrect —or at most only partially correct. For the fisherman, his curse on the Giaour is deserved, and

> This broken tale was all we knew
> Of her he loved, or him he slew.
>
> (ll. 1333-34)

But it was not all. For Hassan's mother, it meant the loss of a son; for Hassan's palace and entourage it meant ruin; for the Monk and the other friars it meant the triumph of evil; and for the Giaour it meant rage at Hassan, despair and remorse, enduring his hell within, isolation from the world and mankind (and, on a shallower level, "one mate, and one alone" man should take). For the poet, the "broken tale" meant all of these separately, but corporately it meant the world, man's present, on which converges a bitter as well as a sweet Edenic past and a hope (though ultimately a vain one) for the future.

> And they who listen may believe,
> Who heard it first had cause to grieve.
>
> (ll. 166-67)

The basic method by which the poet achieves this composite is simple: he extrapolates and generalizes upon the particulars of the story as he receives them, and often comments on their significance, implications, or connections with scenes, characters, and events seemingly extraneous to the business at hand. Thus, after the fisherman's narrative of the Giaour's mysterious appearance in the beginning of the poem, Byron, using fundamentally the same technique he used in *Childe Harold*, slides almost imperceptibly from the fisherman's point of view to the poet's:

> O'er him who loves, or hates, or fears,
> Such moment pours the grief of years:
> What felt *he* then, at once opprest
> By all that most distracts the breast?
> That pause, which pondered o'er his fate,
> Oh, who its dreary length shall date!
> Though in Time's record nearly nought,
> It was Eternity to Thought!
> For infinite as boundless space
> The thought that Conscience must embrace,
> Which in itself can comprehend
> Woe without name, or hope, or end.
>
> (ll. 265–76)

That Byron was consciously shifting gears here is shown not only by the wide-ranging universalization of this passage (a third edition insertion) but also by a late rewrite, for the seventh edition, of a couplet which precedes it. Instead of the present lines 257–58, he originally wrote, with an eye to his poet-pilgrim's narration,

> 'Twas but an instant, though so long
> When thus dilated in my song.[4]

Precisely where the transition from fisherman to poet occurs is impossible to pin-point, and this problem reflects Byron's continuing difficulty with transitions from voice to voice, as in *Childe Harold*. Yet the total effect is of one voice fading out, as if reflecting its finite limitations, while the other more universal, inclusive voice of the poet grows stronger. Simiarly, after the fisherman describes the drowning of Leila (ll. 352ff.), the poet expatiates on the futility of the quest for beauty, the fragility of mortal life, the cruelty of one's fellow man, and the power of remorse (ll. 388ff.) —sentiments which are echoed by the Giaour in his death-bed speech. Again, in the battle scene, the particularity of the fisherman's account—

> The foremost Tartar bites the ground!
> Scarce had they time to check the rein,
> Swift from their steeds the riders bound;
> But three shall never mount again:
> Unseen the foes that gave the wound
>
> (ll. 573–77)

—which concludes with the ballad-like choral refrain that Byron used several times, in varying forms, in the fisherman's narrative (ll. 351, 518, 536, 619, 722, 745, 786), yields to the non-partisan objectivity of the poet's account, with its focus on the significance of the battle in terms of the over-all theme of the poem (ll. 620–54). Once more, after the Monk's first speech, in which his fear and bias lead him to say,

> But were I Prior, not a day
> Should brook such stranger's further stay,
> Or pent within our penance cell
> Should doom him there for aye to dwell,
>
> (ll. 818–21)

the poet comments on the decay of the noble soul of man (ll. 832ff.). And in the dialogue immediately following these comments (ll. 883–970), while the Monk sees the Giaour as a creature of neither "earth nor heaven," the poet interprets the plight of man (in the person of the Giaour) in terms of love, bravery, and human passion, seeing the Giaour's particular situation properly in terms of the desolation of Greece, Hassan's palace, and the "vacant bosom's wilderness."

Thus our sense of the whole clearly depends almost entirely on the ability of the poet-pilgrim to maneuver us into the position of seeing all the points of view represented at once. Though "accretive" is a proper word to use in describing the poem's evolution, its structure is more accurately seen as vertical. The tension between the horizontality toward which each segment of the narrative tends and the coinstantaneous thrust of the poet's generalizations, interpretations, and analogies is what gives the poem its peculiar effect and interest. If a modern analogy is not misleading, Faulkner's *The Sound and the Fury*, though a more consummate work of art and more subtly achieved, does very much what Byron was attempting.

JAMES R. THOMPSON

Byron's Plays and *Don Juan*†

The major problem shared by artists from Blake to the present has been the difficulty in finding an orientation for their work. Whatever despair the thinker may allow himself in contemplating the general disorientation, the artist must create, and to create he needs some frame in which to work; hence the modern preoccupation with mythmaking. The impulse to provide a viable myth in

† From *Bucknell Review*, 15, no. 3 (1967), pp. 22–38.

place of one invalidated by contemporary experience may be basically religious in origin, but for the poet who must write it is, more
immediately, an aesthetic concern. Poets like X. J. Kennedy and W.
D. Snodgrass may cry in mock despair, "Somebody stole my
myths," but their very parody illustrates the widespread and enduring modern concern. A major work (for instance the long poem)
demands some orientation—cosmic, social, psychic—to give it shape
and significance. Blake and Yeats are classic examples of artists who
felt this need.

The Romantics reacted in their several ways to the inheritance of
a bankrupt spiritual and aesthetic orientation. Whatever else we
may say about them we must admit the heroic proportions of the
Romantics' attempt to reorder the world in which they lived. Any
annoyance with Blake's obscurity or Wordsworth's alleged self-repu-
diation must be reconciled with the bulk of their accomplishment.
That their myths did not permanently sustain themselves in no way
invalidates the artistic achievements made under the temporary
equilibrium provided by these orientations.

Insofar as Byron reacted to the fragmentation of values and the
resultant mythic vacuum, he simply faced the dilemma of modern
man and modern artist. However, there is in Byron a rather interesting duality of approach to this spiritual-creative problem. This duality—found in his use of the traditional genres, drama and epic—is
the subject of this essay.

Byron's *Don Juan* and his group of eight plays differ so much
that, were either anonymous, it would be difficult to assign them to
the same author.[1] As Edward E. Bostetter suggests, it is possible to
find a common "existential attitude" in these works, but this attitude can be clearly seen in much modern literature.[2] More important, the plays and the comic epic manifest Byron's concern with
genre. The relationship between the choice of form and the myth
employed in these very different works is so close that one might say
that in these works form itself functions as myth.

Despite his tremendous respect for Pope and his world, Byron
could not, either as a man or as a poet, accept the world he inherited. While Blake began almost at once to construct a powerful and
elaborate myth which was to sustain his creativity until the end,
Byron's early work either imitated the amorous-satiric role of the
gentleman poet or made popular poetry out of contemporary alienation. The immediate social disorientation produced by his exile,

1. Byron's plays and the years they were
written are: *Manfred: A Dramatic Poem*
(1816), *Marino Faliero, Doge of
Venice: An Historical Tragedy* (1820),
Sardanapalus: A Tragedy (1821), *The
Two Foscari: An Historical Tragedy*
(1821), *Cain: A Mystery* (1821),
Heaven and Earth: A Mystery (1821),
Werner; or the Inheritance: A Tragedy
(1821–22), *The Deformed Transformed:
A Drama* (1822).
2. Edward E. Bostetter, *The Romantic
Ventriloquists* (Seattle, Wash., 1963), p.
254.

however, acted as a catalyst; beginning in 1816 a rapid maturation developed in Byron's work. Desiring belief but unable to accept the traditional forms or their modern substitutes, by 1816 Byron was forced into a desperate confrontation with what seemed to him an increasingly meaningless universe. The results of this confrontation —two very different responses to this meaninglessness—are to be found in the plays on one hand and *Don Juan* on the other. The creation of these two groups of poems was simultaneous, not sequential; they are alternate methods of dealing with the absurdity of modern experience.

The writing of the plays was, for Byron, an attempt at reconstruction. In a world demythologized by science and purged of evil by such men as Rousseau, Byron struggled to create a workable myth of the individual and his necessary autonomy in a hostile universe controlled by an omnipotent tyrant. It is not difficult to accept his conclusion that "the Prometheus . . . has always been so much in my head, that I can easily conceive its influence over all or anything that I have written."[3] The figure of Prometheus stands behind his characters (with the important exception of Don Juan) because for Byron, as for Shelley, Prometheus symbolized the single, isolated will in conflict with tyrannical power in the universe. His ode "Prometheus" serves as a prologue to *Manfred* and the plays; in it he compares the Promethean rebellion, defiance and "impenetrable spirit," with man's ability to assert his element of immortality in the face of his mortality. From Prometheus "a mighty lesson we inherit":

> Thou art a symbol and a sign
>   To mortals of their fate and force;
> Like thee, Man is in part divine,
>   A troubled stream from a pure source;
> And Man in portions can foresee
> His own funereal destiny;
> His own wretchedness, and his resistance,
> And his sad unallied existence:
> To which his Spirit may oppose
> Itself—and equal to all woes—
>   And a firm will, and a deep sense,
> Which even in torture can descry
>   Its own concentered recompense,
> Triumphant where it dares defy,
> And making death a Victory.[4]

The recognition here of the tragic duality of man's nature—his "fate" on one hand and his "force" on the other, his "wretched-

3. *The Works of Lord Byron. Letters and Journals*, ed. R. E. Prothero (London, 1898–1901), IV, 174–175.

4. *The Works of Lord Byron. Poetry*, ed. E. H. Coleridge (London, 1898–1904), IV, 51.

ness" and his "resistance," his share of divinity and his "funereal destiny"—points to the concept of "half dust, half deity" which controls the theme of *Manfred* and *Cain* and lies, in a more general way, behind all the plays, realistic and symbolic.

Byron's peculiar adaptation of the Promethean myth is greatly strengthened by the figure of Faust, and, to a lesser extent, by the figure of Satan, both quite appropriate for the construction of a post-Enlightenment myth. From Faust Byron takes limitless aspiration but rejects the idea of a voluntary compact with evil. It is the potentiality of the human will that fascinates and haunts him. In Satan Byron finds the myth of ultimate rebellion and the concept of guilt. Satan's rather than Adam's guilt provides Byron with a symbol of the human condition.

Whether in the cosmic, social or psychic sphere, each tragic protagonist attempts to assert his autonomy; each of the six complete dramas attempts with widely varying success to sketch the conflict of the individual will with the forces of necessity. In the best of Byron's self-termed "metaphysical" or symbolic plays, in which he is freed from the uncomfortable limitations of his own attempt at a neoclassical reform of the drama, the myth of the Promethean man comes closest to fulfillment; *Manfred* and *Cain* have more genuine tragic force than do the traditional realistic plays (*Marino Faliero, Sardanapalus,* and *The Two Foscari*). Just as Byron could not successfuly reclaim the couplet and was forced to find a new vehicle for his satire, so he found it necessary in making his most powerful tragic statements to ignore the classical restraint he thought he admired. But all the plays are infused with the same myth.

The important point is, however, that for Byron drama as a genre represents the very shape of value; it is the concrete embodiment of belief. Byron was unable to master traditional dramatic structure, and in addition significant stylistic differences exist between the "metaphysical" plays and the neoclassical plays. The latter share a modern structural quality with *Don Juan*. But this quality is subordinate to choice of genre; for Byron the drama as a literary form is a structure which can be produced where a vital myth exists. Temporarily, he may even have hoped that the very employment of the genre was sufficient to vitalize the myth. No other major Romantic had a closer association with the stage or made a more vigorous attempt to reestablish the lost genre. However, though drama meant to Byron a genre that reflected earlier mythic and spiritual stability, it was to give way before the new form of *Don Juan*, just as the classical couplet yielded to ottava rima. In Byron there was a struggle between his admiration for the close adherence to generic norms of the early eighteenth century and his naturally romantic assumption that, like artists, works of art are unique. *Don Juan* is a kind of generic explosion produced by the nineteenth-century pressure to redefine form in highly personal terms.

Very little of the optimism of major romantic myth exists in these plays—none of the joy of a "Tintern Abbey" or the exultation of a *Prometheus Unbound.* Some of the great energy found in Byron's contemporaries is, however, evident in these plays; there is a good deal of power in the moving victory, albeit grim, of Manfred in death and Cain in exile. Drama, which to Byron usually meant serious drama, had traditionally been the vehicle for man's tragic success, the form in which man projected his potential victory, even in death. However, since Byron's dramas are really modern tragedies of existential revolt, they could only assert the value of the rebellion itself; no traditional restoration follows the catastrophe and there is no real way to build a larger structure out of the several heroic acts. The Promethean revolt led, in short, to an aesthetic dead end; the freedom Byron wished to assert resisted being structured into a mythic complex like that of Blake. The dramatic genre and the myth of the Promethean man failed to sustain Byron; without significant modification traditional form would not serve for an attack on tradition. In part, the value of the plays lies in the fact that they illustrate by contrast the nature of the aesthetic, as well as philosophic, choice made in *Don Juan.*

Another probable reason for the failure of the plays may be found in Byron's ingrained suspicion of the abstract. He might, given the world he faced, have said with Blake's Los, "I must Create a System, or be enslaved by another Man's," but recognizing, as he says in *Don Juan,* that "one system eats another up" (XIV.1) he rejects his own mythic complex. *Don Juan* reverses the myth and form of the plays: it rejects system for freedom, coherence for diversity.

Byron's dramatic attempts end before *Don Juan* hits its main stride and it is clear that Byron recognized both the generic mythic failure of the plays and the success of *Don Juan.* In what he called his "epic satire" Byron turned also to a traditional genre, one more venerable even than the drama. But whereas the drama appealed to his desire to believe in the stability of some positive value—even if limited to the human will in revolt—Byron saw that the epic could be employed for quite opposite purposes. He found it a most useful tool for coming to grips with the fragmentation that made the position of even his heroes of revolt untenable. He transformed this classic genre into a modern, non-Aristotelean form capable of handling the relativistic view of the world which his observation had forced him to accept. *Don Juan* was, as Paul Elmer More so perceptively suggested, "in its actual form . . . the only epic manner left for a poet of the nineteenth century to adopt with the power of conviction. . . . It is the epic of modern life."[5] Byron not only transforms the epic genre, but, as we will see later, the choice of the "non-form" of *Don Juan* also involves a deliberate transformation of satire as mode.

Byron shared with other Romantics the realization of disorientation and the resultant crisis over myth, but his attitude toward the problem resembles those of the post-World War One artists more than those of his own generation. Wallace Stevens' statement about our age perfectly describes the point of view out of which *Don Juan* emerges: "The spirit of negation" has come to control man's attitude: "All the great things have been denied and we live in an intricacy of new and local mythologies, political, economic, poetic, which are asserted with an ever-enlarging incoherence. This is accompanied by an absence of any authority except force, operative or imminent."[6] Some modern myth may retain the expansive optimism of, say, *Prometheus Unbound*, but more typically human possibilities are vastly reduced. This same reduction is seen in *Don Juan*. Whereas Coleridge might write his "Dejection: An Ode" treating personal failure—the loss of vision—Byron writes in *Don Juan* of absence of vision: "the great things have been denied," found impossible, not their loss lamented. And there is, unquestionably, a sympathetic current between the readers of our age and the Byron of *Don Juan* that is not found in his plays or earlier works. (In the hands of a few critics Byron has even become the hero of English Romanticism; see, for instance, Edward Bostetter's *The Romantic Ventriloquists*.) Byron's appeal to the present is, at least in part, the result of this kinship in stance; it is the anti-heroic *Don Juan* rather than the plays with their Promethean myth that survives Byron's own aesthetic test. Indeed, *Don Juan* satirizes Byron's own Prometheanism and, through its structure, rejects the generic manifestation of that myth.[7]

Many critics have searched for some principle of unity in *Don Juan*. George Ridenour, in his excellent study, *The Style of Don Juan*, has attempted to prove that "the ruling structural principles" consist of three patterns: "the metaphor of the fall, the use of the *persona*, and the idea of epic satire." He describes these motifs as "constituting the proper plot of *Don Juan*."[8] The difficulty comes in using the word *plot* to describe a poem "structured" only by the poet's attitude and habitual literary mannerisms. As Andras Horn says, "none of the seven episodes [of *Don Juan*] . . . points beyond itself, none of them has a function, in the sense of further-

5. *The Complete Poetical Works of Byron,* ed. Paul Elmer More (Cambridge, Mass., 1933), p. 744.
6. Wallace Stevens, "The Noble Rider and the Sound of Words," in *The Nec-*

essary Angel: Essays on Reality and the Imagination (New York, 1965), p. 17.
7. Harold Bloom, *The Visionary Company* (London, 1961), p. 254.
8. New Haven, Conn., 1960, p. 144.

ing a plot and bringing us nearer to a denouement."⁹ Unlike
Ridenour, however, Horn is thinking of plot in a traditional sense
and this will suffice for neither Byron nor many of his contemporaries. Byron deliberately gives to *Don Juan* an "elastic shape," as Virginia Woolf shrewdly noted, "which will hold whatever you choose
to put into it."¹ She might well have said whatever grows out of it,
for the structure of *Don Juan* is Byron's manifestation of Romantic
organicism.

Ernest J. Lovell, one of those critics who believe the poem to be
unified on a thematic basis, describes most aptly the principle of
unity as "the basically ironic theme of appearance versus reality, the
difference between what things seem to be (or are said or thought
to be) and what they actually are."² This is a most useful generalization if we remember that irony is a mode, not a concrete structure. It is Byron's essentially, but far from exclusively, ironical attitude that gives the poem its stability.

We see the poem's deliberate formlessness and ambiguity quite
clearly in its evolution. Byron has no comprehensive plan, no beginning, middle and end, and we watch him from canto to canto
making decisions regarding the direction the poem should take.
Although Byron as narrator ironically claims that "the regularity of
my design / Forbids all wandering as the worst of sinning" (1.7)³
we see his tentative groping for subject, plot and even style:

> I don't pretend that I quite understand
> My own meaning when I would be very fine;
>   But the fact is that I have nothing plann'd,
> Unless it were to be a moment merry,
> A novel word in my vocabulary.
>
> (IV.5)

> .   .   .   .

> I ne'er decide what I shall say, and this I call
>   Much too poetical. Men should know why
> They write, and for what end; but, note or text,
>   I never know the word which will come next.

> .   .   .   .

> So now I ramble, now and then narrating,
>   Now pondering:—it is time we should narrate.
>
> (IX.41–42)

> .   .   .   .

9. Andras Horn, *Byron's Don Juan and
the Eighteenth-Century English Novel*
(Bern, 1962), p. 50.
1. *A Writer's Diary*, ed. Leonard Woolf
(New York, 1954), p. 3.
2. Ernest J. Lovell, "Irony and Image in
Byron's *Don Juan*," in *The Major English Romantic Poets: A Symposium in*
Reappraisal, ed. Clarence D. Thorpe, et
al. (Carbondale, Ill., 1957), p. 132.
3. References to *Don Juan* are given by
canto and stanza. The edition used is
Byron's Don Juan: A Variorum Edition,
ed. Truman Guy Steffan and Willis W.
Pratt, 4 vols. (Austin, Texas, 1957).

Recognizing the fragmentary nature of his work, he again grows ironic:

> However, 'tis no time to chat
> On general topics: poems must confine
> Themselves to Unity, like this of mine.
>
> (XI.44)

Of course, lack of traditional unity is no disadvantage for Byron. The frequency of his digressions accounts for much of the poem's interest and peculiar charm. It is an empirical poem, a poem of Byron's exploration rather than Juan's—and the "structure" must embody the exploration. The poem's shaping force is what R. A. Foakes calls one of the two most important "structural images" of romantic literature, "the image of life as a journey in time."[4]

It is important to remind ourselves here, as Auden has recently pointed out, that the narrative voice of the poem is the same as that of Byron's letters, journals and recorded conversations.[5] It is a mistake to seek a fully realized *persona* separate from the author himself and still more fallacious to find multiple speakers in the poem.[6] Just as in *Childe Harold* the narrator and protagonist move toward each other until all pretense of Harold is dropped—Byron having become, he said, "weary of drawing a line which everyone seemed determined not to perceive"[7]—so in *Don Juan* the narrator rapidly loses his separate identity and becomes a fictional version of Byron. While we may, for a canto or two, accept a created speaker, Byron himself (and not the melodramatic "Byronic mask" of earlier work) soon emerges; when in the final cantos the action moves to England we are almost painfully aware that Byron is going home in the poem. Byron stands in approximately the same relationship to *Don Juan* that Pope stands to the "Epistle to Dr. Arbuthnot." The dividing line between fictionalized speaker and poet is very indistinct in both poems. In the preface to Cantos I and II of *Childe Harold* Byron claimed that "a fictitious character is introduced for the sake of giving some connection to the piece." The poem improved considerably in Cantos III and IV when Byron himself provided the "connection"; in *Don Juan*, having found his true voice, Byron very quickly recognized that his sensibility was the true center and organizing force in the poem. That force is the real "unity, like this of mine."

Hence the reason for the amorphous nature of *Don Juan* is not far to seek, and comparison with the plays is again illuminating. Despite his "epic intentions" Byron claims that the story of Don

4. R. A. Foakes, *The Romantic Assertion* (London, 1958), p. 50.
5. W. H. Auden, "Byron: The Making of a Comic Poet," *New York Review of Books* (August 18, 1966), p. 14.
6. George M. Ridenour. "The Mode of Byron's *Don Juan*," *PMLA*, LXXIX (1964), 442–446.
7. *Poetry*, II, 323.

Juan is "actually true" (I.202). He argues that he is describing, not creating:

> But then the fact's a fact—and 'tis the part
> Of a true poet to escape from fiction
> Whene'er he can; for there is little art
> In leaving verse more free from the restriction
> Of truth than prose, unless to suit the mart
> For what is sometimes called poetic diction,
> And that outrageous appetite for lies
> Which Satan angles with for souls, like flies.
>
> (VIII.86)

> It is an awful topic—but 'tis not
> My cue for any time to be terrific:
> For checquered as is seen our human lot
> With good, and bad, and worse, alike prolific
> Of melancholy merriment, to quote
> Too much of one sort would be soporific;—
> Without, or with, offence to friends or foes,
> I sketch your the world exactly as it goes.
>
> (VIII.89)

Byron insists that he intends "to show things really as they are, / Not as they ought to be" (XII.40). This is precisely the reverse of the plays; in them Byron portrays Romantic man demonstrating the individual's potential greatness—that is, the world as it "ought to be." The rightness of individual will and autonomy is the "value" behind the plays—the supreme good—and the structure, paradoxically, represents belief in that absolute good. However, in *Don Juan* Byron conceives of his role as that of "a mere spectator" (XIII.7), not as a definer of myth in the same sense as a tragic dramatist. As a spectator the poet appears to wander almost aimlessly through the world of fact, speculation and Stevens' "local mythologies"; the only control over that journey is his desire to experience reality. The observed reality is not structured and therefore neither can his poem be structured: "But if a writer should be quite consistent, / How could he possibly show things existent?" (XV.87). However, Byron recognized that tragic drama demands consistency; creating a world of value is not the same as describing a world devoid of value. For Byron the traditional dramatic form helped to create and celebrate that consistency.

However, poetic drama demands the marriage of poetry and speech. Ironically, it is only in *Beppo* and *Don Juan* that Byron's talent for colloquial verse is finally released; one seldom hears the rhythms of actual speech in the plays. There is a kind of generic inversion in this fact; the plays lack the necessary dramatic language and have instead speeches reminiscent of epic poetry, while the so-callld "epic" makes use of colloquial idiom. Byron was well aware that it was now his speaking voice and not the often stilted oratory of the plays that he employed in *Don Juan*: "I rattle on exactly as I talk," he says, and cites his "conversational facility" (XV.19–20).

In the nature of the hero there is also a crucial difference between the plays and *Don Juan*. The protagonist in the plays may be described as the man Byron himself desired to be, a man capable of making a stand. All of Byron's tragic protagonists are committed; they recognize that commitment itself is moral and necessary—they act. Don Juan, on the other hand, is an uncommitted, passive anti-hero dedicated only to living; in one sense Juan is the man Byron actually was. While action in Byron's plays is usually psychological, the wanderings of Don Juan provide only physical action. "I want a hero," Byron states at the outset of the poem, and, rejecting publically acclaimed modern heroes, he decides to take "our ancient friend Don Juan" (I.1), actually Byron's modern man. Byron then leads his protagonist through a variety of adventures—including seductions, adultery, shipwreck, love, slavery, and war. What happens to Juan? Ridenour sees him moving "from innocence to experience,"[8] but it is hard to detect any significant change in him at the end of the poem. Moving from situation to situation he seems to be able to reject the meaning of past experiences almost as fast as they happen. On one occasion he shows innocence or worldliness, on another, kindness or bravery, and on still another, lust or idealism. Essentially, these responses to situations are causally unintegrated; in one sense he is a character of fragments in a poem of narrative fragments. From the protagonist of the plays, committed totally to revolt and death, we move to a character committed only to aimless life. Don Juan is, as Lovell points out, "the exile and wanderer never haunted by a sense of quest."[9] Alienation from a meaningless world leads to rebellion in the plays and to detachment and passivity in Don Juan; Don Juan has more in common with Camus' Meursault[1] than with Manfred or Cain.

This lack of involvement is indicated, for example, in Don Juan's casual acceptance of a place in the Russian army besieging Ismail. It is even more clearly indicated in his role as lover. Byron has rejected the titular myth; named after the world's best-known seducer, Don Juan is always the seduced. Self-deceiving Julia, innocent Haidee, imperious Gulbeyaz, the royal whore Catherine, "her frolic grace" the Duchess Fitz-Fulke—all pursue Juan's passive desirability. He "could be most things to all women," he is "all things unto people of all sorts" (XIV.31) and he has "the art of living in all

---

8. *The Style of Don Juan*, p. 144.
9. "Irony and Image," p. 137.
1. Meursault is the hero and first-person

narrator of Albert Camus's existentialist novel of 1946, *The Stranger*. [*Editor*.]

climes with ease" (XV.11). As Bloom maintains, "the passive Juan
has encountered all these adventures without developing under their
impact. As he falls further into experience, he does not gain in
wisdom."[2] It is still "Juan, with his virgin face" who is being
described in the second to last stanza of the poem (XVII.13).
Caring "not a tobacco-stopper / About philosophy" (X.60), Juan
"was no casuist, nor had pondered / Upon the moral lessons of
mankind" (XII.81). Despite his passivity or perhaps because of it
(and passivity is not here confused with innocence), Don Juan is
capable of surviving all dangerous and humiliating experiences
because he holds no allegiances. Placed in an essentially destructive
situation, Juan always emerges successfully; his particular virtue is
his adaptability. In short, he is not so much a character as an
embodiment of sheer vitality. In this sense, he is the physical manifestation of the narrator's intellectual energy; Don Juan and the
speaker seem to compose a whole.[3] In *Don Juan* Byron passes to a
position beyond rebellion and possibly even beyond choice. Paul
Elmer More spoke of Byron's mind wavering "almost to the end
between the heroic defiance of Prometheus and the cynical defiance
of Don Juan."[4] But there is very little defiance in Don Juan himself. The dramatic protagonists are defiant of society or God; Don
Juan moves easily in the first and simply ignores the second. The
unjust God and social tyranny have been defeated by circumven-
tion.

Let us summarize here some of the major antinomies between
the plays and the satirical epic. The plays are largely structured by
traditional form as well as by theme; *Don Juan* is unstructured by
traditional form or plot. The choice of genre in the plays reflects
the poet's desire to define values; the genre of *Don Juan* reflects
Byron's refusals to pursue that definition. Despite Byron's role-play-
ing, in the plays the choice of genre provides some aesthetic distance; in the satire author and narrator merge early in the poem. In
the plays the protagonist is heroic, committed to action and revolt;
in *Don Juan* the narrative protagonist is unheroic, passive and
acquiescent. The plays are serious; they posit a God and generally
end in purposeful death. *Don Juan* is comic and Godless, ending in
irresistible life. The plays explore the past; *Don Juan* occurs more
nearly in the present. The plays are rhetorical in style; *Don Juan*
lacks the epic style.

These differences emphasize the shift in motive described earlier.
In the plays Byron attempted, through the construction of a personal myth, to find enduring significance in an increasingly valueless
world. In *Don Juan* he abandoned the heroic for the comic vision

2. *The Visionary Company*, p. 259.
3. Leslie A. Marchand sees Don Juan as
Byron's self-portrait. See *Byron's Poetry:*
A Critical Introduction (Boston, 1965),
p. 165.
4. *Poetical Works of Byron*, p. 191.

of "things really as they are." But as a "spectator" observing the world, he insisted, both in the poem and outside it, that the poem was a "moral" work. Many critics have taken this claim to mean that Byron was insisting on a conventional satiric mode for his poem. In fact, scholars have tended to make unqualified generalizations about the satiric side of Byron's nature, often failing to discriminate between various aspects of his negative impulse. The following remark appearing in a popular college anthology voices the usual attitude: "for it happens that Byron had a dual nature; he was a great romanticist, to be sure, but he was a great satirist as well."[5] A brief glance at the couplet satires reminds us that they are not great poetry, and further analysis shows that *Don Juan*, while a great poem, is certainly not only a satire. Further, the epic is just as "romantic" as *Childe Harold* or *Manfred*.

The early satires written in heroic couplets employ Augustan rhetoric and are obviously derivative; they look back to Pope's literary values and techniques. They, along with the neoclassical plays, are products of Byron's admiration for what he felt was the stable world of the early eighteenth century; their remarkable degree of success is an index of that admiration. Our knowledge of this early interest in satire must not lead us to conclude that *Don Juan* is simply the culmination of a lifelong tendency toward conventional satire. Byron could not insist, as it was still possible for Samuel Johnson to claim in *Rasselas*, that the poet "must consider right and wrong in their abstracted and invariable state; he must disregard present laws and opinions, and rise to general and transcendental truths, which will always be the same" (Chapter X, "The Business of the Poet"). When Byron composed *Don Juan*, belief in that coherent structure had crumbled. As Allan Rodway notes, the Romantic satirist is not defending an accepted norm but rather insisting on his individuality.[6] Hence Byron could place no real faith in Dryden's belief that the "true end of satire is the amendment of vices by correction" (Preface to *Absalom and Achitophel*). From neoclassical satire based on universal orientation we have moved to romantic satire based on egocentric orientation.

It is this absence of a traditional and unified value system and hence lack of faith in the therapeutic nature of satire that accounts for the absence of any consistent satiric unity in the poem. Much of the poem is more accurately described as serious comic exploration rather than satire. In addition to satire and comedy it contains genuine pathos and sentiment, sensuousness, meditation, exposition and speculation on a wide range of other concerns. One has only to recall the relentless assaults in *Absalom and Achitophel, An Argu-*

5. *The Literature of England*, ed. George B. Woods, et al. (Fair Lawn, N. J., 1958), pp. 50–51.

6. Allan Rodway, *The Romantic Conflict* (London, 1963), p. 215.

ment Against Abolishing Christianity, or *The Duncaid*, to understand how far we have moved from the Augustan world view and its resultant satiric techniques. Byron's inability to accept the theoretical—the abstraction taken on faith and unverified by the senses or reason—precludes a unified basis for judgment; he rejects all systems because they exclude.

Byron, as his own protagonist, assumes the thinking role that he denies Don Juan. He may speak with contempt of professional philosophers but he is not, like his creation, oblivious to their ideas; he is intensely interested in their sublime and absurd explorations of existence. If Juan "had not pondered / Upon the moral lessons of mankind" the active mind of the poet had pondered, and the narrator's wide-ranging analysis of the human condition is the center of the work:

> My tendency is to philosophize
> On most things, from a tyrant to a tree;
> But still the spouseless virgin *Knowledge* flies.
> What are we? and whence came we? what shall be
> Our *ultimate* existence? what's our present?
> Are questions answerless, and yet incessant.
>
> (VI.63)

Byron's characteristic comic manner does not here disguise his serious preoccupation with questions though answerless, "yet incessant."

It follows, then, that the traditional relationships between the author, his poem and his audience are also lacking. The detachment of the narrator in Byron's poem is markedly different from the detached impersonality of much Augustan satire or epic poetry. Alienated from rather than the spokesman for traditional values, Byron speaks only for himself. The colloquial tone mentioned earlier is a sign of the personal voice. Robson points out that the chatty tone indicated that Byron, unlike many other nineteenth-century poets, is acutely aware that he has a reader: "his sociable tone, his friendship with the reader, is founded on the tacit agreement that he too is a fellow sinner."[7] Or, as John Wain remarks, whereas the Augustan "assumption is the classical one—'I, the satirist, am a better man than you'—his is 'You, the righteous one, are no better than I am.' "[8] What has changed here is what Frye calls the "radical of presentation"—the relationship of poet to audience.[9] Both the traditional role of poet as communal judge (which he attempted in his early couplet satires) and the role of

7. W. W. Robson, "Byron as Improviser," in *Byron: A Collection of Critical Essays*, ed. Paul West (Englewood Cliffs, N. J., 1963), p. 93.
8. John Wain, "The Search for Identity," *The London Magazine*, V, No. 7 (1958), 44–57.
9. Northrop Frye, *Anatomy of Criticism* (Princeton, N. J., 1957), pp. 246–247.

concealed poet (which he experimented with in the closet dramas) are put aside, and the "radical" changes, at least figuratively, from the written to the spoken word.

Nor, of course, is there much similarity between Byron's style and that of his great satirical predecessors. His ottava rima unit with its playful metrics, humorous rhymes, and idiomatic rhythms hardly resembles the polished Augustan couplet with its tight rhetorical form. Ian Jack correctly remarks that Byron's is "an idiom that encouraged expansion and digression rather than compression of the Augustan kind."[1] Byron's greatest poem, then, must not be associated, as it so often has been, with the satiric motivation and techniques of the past. To simply call it satire is to apply a reductive label to a very complex modern poem.

In his book on satire James Sutherland has recently said that "it may well be that the modern poet is too tentative and exploratory . . . to commit himself to satire."[2] As *Don Juan* makes clear, Byron was unable to launch any kind of consistent and total attack. But there is a strong element of satiric force in the poem. Byron can and does call attention to the gulf between what people say they believe and their actual behavior; hypocrisy becomes the main target of his satire. Accordingly, the center of positive value in *Don Juan*, as in the plays, is freedom. His bitterest attack, found in the cantos on the siege of Ismail, is on the false glory of war, any war not fought in freedom's cause. But it is not just political freedom that Byron demands. Like war, "cant"—the voice of hypocrisy—endangers freedom and, as his satiric motive intensifies in the poem, he increasingly sets out to assault that "cant which is the crying sin of this double-dealing and false-speaking time of selfish spoilers."[3] It was this indirect subversion of man's freedom rather than the more direct threat from war that became his chief satiric concern. In modern terms we would describe this preoccupation as a commitment to authenticity, for himself and for others. It is this motive that makes the poem for him a "moral" work. Ironically, the "selfish spoilers" harm not only others but themselves; they are committed to destroying their own freedom. Symbolically, the entire journey—the journey of Byron's mind rather than his hero's adventure—is an assault against that which prevents the assertion of the self: the tyranny of "system," war or hypocritical denial of self.

Hence the great importance of genre to Byron in the discovery of his peculiar mode. What we recognize in *Don Juan* and fail to find in the plays—as did Byron himself—is not a poem of "mature unconviction" as Paul West says,[4] but rather a poem with a new

1. *English Literature 1815–1832* (Oxford, 1963), p. 52.
2. James Sutherland, *English Satire* (Cambridge, 1962), pp. 77–78.
3. *Poetry*, II, 323.
4. *Byron: A Collection of Critical Essays*, p. 5.

kind of conviction. It is not a faith in heroic defiance couched in romantic tragedy, but faith in the endless vitality of the self restlessly questing forth on a journey never to be completed. Only the poet's death can end the poem. Thus the traditional style and structure of the plays are put aside in favor of a generic freedom that could support the mature Byronic myth, a form that in one sense is the myth itself; it is the embodiment of the myth of the unfinished journey. For this reason it is difficult to agree with William Marshall that *"Don Juan* should be regarded as a vast literary joke."[5] Byron could justly ask his critical friends "is it not *life,* is it not the thing?"[6] His own answer demanded not a dead but a living form.

FRANK D. McCONNELL

Byron as Antipoet†

Poetry is willful. It is not an abandonment, a free and gratuitous entry by the senses; it is not to be confused with sensuality, but rather, opposing it, was born, for example, on Saturdays, when, to clean the rooms, housewives put the red velvet chairs, gilded mirrors, and mahogany tables outside, in the nearby meadow.
Jean Genet, *Our Lady of the Flowers.*[1]

E. J. Trelawney records that in 1822 Byron told Shelley of the criticisms John Murray, Byron's publisher, had of his dramas. Murray thought them unstageable and, worse, unmarketable, and urged Byron in the double interest of art and commerce to resume his "Corsair style, to please the ladies." When Shelley reacted with predictable heat and poetic outrage, Byron smiled and replied: "John Murray is right, if not righteous: all I have yet written has been for woman-kind; you must wait until I am forty, their influence will then die a natural death, and I will show the men what I can do."[2]

There is so much of Byron in this anecdote that it might well serve for an emblem of his ambiguous position in English Romanticism, and of his even more ambiguous fate at the hands of his critics. It is useful to try to think in the critical terms current before the generalizing evaluation "Romantic" was coined for these poets. Shelley and Byron, particularly—the so-called "Satanic" school—belong together in a unique and complex imaginative symbiosis that illumines both their works. But a part of that symbiosis is their radical opposition. And here, confronted with the views of his friend

5. William Marshall, *The Structure of Byron's Major Poems* (Philadelphia, 1962), p. 177.
6. *Byron: A Self-Portrait,* ed. Peter Quennell (London, 1950), II, 491.
† Originally published as "Byron's Reductions: 'Much Too Poetical,'" *ELH,* 37, no. 3 (1970), pp. 415–432. (A number of the notes are new in this edition.)
1. New York, 1964, p. 226.
2. E. J. Trelawney, *Recollections of the Last Days of Shelley and Byron* (London, 1858), p. 20.

the apocalyptic prophet and of his friend the bookseller and pay-master, Byron characteristically—and feistily—opts for the absent paymaster. For Byron, there is no doubt that the act of poetry always made more sense as performance rather than prophecy, and his diffident appraisal of his own gift contains a rather subtle germ of aesthetic insight.

Also, there is a curious bit of semantic history involved in Byron's description of Murray as "right" but not "righteous." For the two interlocutors, with their deeply ingrained Protestant background, the word "right," with its minimal connotation of "mere" accuracy, is not nearly as *big* a word as "righteous," with the accumulated weight of a century of dissenting treatises and sermons behind it. That for us the ratio is reversed, and that "righteous" has an inevi-table aura of scorn for hypocrisy about it—we almost never use it without prefixing "self-"—is partly a result precisely of the linguistic energies Byron releases into the modern English and European tra-dition.

Whether or not it is an admirable accomplishment to have released these upsetting energies is, of course, a question that reveals as much about the critic answering as it does about Byron; as does the question whether "writing for the ladies" is Byron's admission of mediocrity or his coy claim to genius. Trelawney's answers to both questions would surely tend toward the negative, just as his mincing animus against Byron makes his whole book a fascinating but unreliable portrait of the man. And the list of critics who have adopted Trelawney's fundamental attitude toward Byron in this century numbers some of our most influential and sensitive appre-ciators of literature, among them Mario Praz, Edmund Wilson, Bertrand Russell, and Harold Bloom.[3] At the heart of this approach lies the formula—venerated by now in uncountable articles and classroom lectures—that Byron was far greater as a myth than as a poet or man, that *Childe Harold, Cain, The Island,* and *Don Juan* itself, not to mention the whole sordid and psychotic life, were less important than the rash of demonic "Byronism" which swept the continent like a highly infectious disease, to break out in such lat-ter-day symptoms as Flaubert's Rudolphe Boulanger, Joyce's young Stephen Dedalus, or—according to Russell at least—Hitler's *Übermensch.*[4]

It is an attitude which offers the critic an instant and intellec-

3. Mario Praz, *The Romantic Agony* (New York, 1963); the essay by Ed-mund Wilson, "Byron in the Twenties," and by Bertrand Russell, "Byron," are conveniently collected in *Byron,* ed. Paul West (New York, 1963), pp. 138–144 and 151–156; Harold Bloom, *The Vision-ary Company* (New York, 1963). There have also been, of course, a number of modern studies which have not only done Byron brilliant justice, but have in-fluenced my own views on the poet: these will be referred to in later foot-notes.

4. Russell, in West, p. 152.

tually pious kind of satisfaction. For it allows him, without ignoring the obvious and massive presence of Byron throughout his century and ours, to eschew the difficulties inherent in treating so cantankerous and problematic a poet as if he were really writing poetry of a high order—which, anyway, he frequently claims not to be doing at all. And this is not mere evasion on the part of the critics. For as this essay will attempt, in part, to demonstrate, Byron *does* write poetry of undeniable power which nevertheless, taken at its own self-evaluation, seems to deny many of our most basic tenets of belief in the nature and efficacy of creative language. Terms like "irony" and "satire" help us a bit to evaluate and identify, but finally even they are inadequate to the range of Byron's reductive imagination; for he ironically calls irony itself into question. It is with a kind of relief that one retreats to a position that makes Byron manageable, while at the same time presenting the illusion of forming delicate distinctions among "life," "art," and "cultural history" which satisfy the rubric of the best modern conventions of New Criticism and the History of Ideas. John Wain gives the prevailing exegesis one of its most graceful articulations when he writes of Byron's interminable posing: "It takes courage, after all, to abandon one's neatly carved *persona* and surrender to the contradictory richness of real life. A little too much defensiveness in one's makeup, and it is impossible."[5]

But we may legitimately ask, is there more undifferentiated "courage" involved in the utter and angry rejection of all roles, or in the dogged insistence on playing out a role, even when its deepest theatricality has been most painfully revealed, to the actor above all? We are back, of course, at the Byronic inversion of "righteous" and "right." But we are also "back" at one of the prime ethical lessons of our most humane modern literature. In a universe where the premeditated and the mediated have become the very stuff of which consciousness is formed, honor—the poet's *or* the critic's—lies not in the direction of an *a priori* mannered confrontation of "the contradictory richness of real life," but rather in the imaginative penetration of the truth at the heart of disguise, in the reductive delineation of the mask itself—be it the mask of thought, feeling, or the body. This seems equally a "point," not only of Byron's poetry, but of the bitter fairy-tales of Henry James, the music-hall tragedies of Samuel Beckett, and the masturbation fantasies of Jean Genet. Genet offers a particularly striking analogue to the sense of poetry I am here concerned with suggesting, since a work like *Our Lady of the Flowers*, with its resolute attempt both completely to objectify the narrative self and completely to devalue the "human dignity" of that self, can be envisaged as the terminal development of a process essentially Byronic.

5. John Wain, "The Search for Identity," in West, p. 160.

The deep undercurrent of weakness or effeminacy in the *form* of these writers' experience is precisely conplementary to the virile and lucid energy of their reductive approach. Byron epitomizes this ambivalent myth of the artist when he writes of the "miser" in *Don Juan*:

> Why call the miser miserable? as
>   I said before; the frugal life is his,
> Which in a saint or cynic ever was
>   The theme of praise: a hermit would not miss
> Canonization for the self-same cause,
>   And wherefore blame gaunt wealth's austerities?
> Because, you'll say, nought calls for such a trial;—
> Then there's more merit in his self-denial.
>
> He is your only poet:—passion pure
>   And sparkling on from heap to heap, displays,
> *Possess'd*, the ore, of which *mere hopes* allure
>   Nations athwart the deep: the golden rays
> Flash up in ingots from the mine obscure:
>   On him the diamond pours its brilliant blaze,
> While the mild emerald's beam shades down the dies
> Of other stones, to soothe the miser's eyes.   (XII. vii–xiii)

It is the miser's *uselessness* which eminently equips him for the role of "only poet." His sainthood is performed in a moral vacuum —sainthood *for* nothing at all, not even God—and is the more ascetic because of the vacuity of its context. The miser is the poet of moral and phenomenal vacuums. For his "art," the art of *possession*, is an anti-poiesis which under the sign of ownership reduces the things of this world to *objects* in their most quantitatively inanimate aspects: the jewels remain the miser's jewels—and therefore the miser remains the miser—only so long as they are not spent, and as the hoards continue to accumulate. Poetry is not creation, but collection, and the collector's impulse is near Byron's deepest sense of his own production.[6]

The man who fulminated against the depredations of Lord Elgin in Greece,[7] and who yet requested Trelawney to save Shelley's skull from the fires for him to make into a drinking-cup was acutely aware of the psychology of collectorship.[8] Byron was in fact a prophetically obsessive collector of scenes, meetings, and memories as well as animals and souvenirs. Reading the letters from his first continental tour, with their tedious cataloguing of places visited and

6. Compare Jean-Paul Sartre's discussion of the destructive thievery of the thief poet Genet: "Outcast of a consuming society, the rites which he celebrates in secret reproduce the cardinal act of the society that excludes him: he sacrifices, he consumes, that is, he destroys." Sartre, *Saint Genet* (New York, 1963), p. 21.

7. In 1808 Lord Elgin brought to England the statues and friezes which had adorned the Parthenon in Athens. In 1816 these "Elgin marbles" were purchased by the government and placed in the British Museum.
8. Trelawney, p. 89.

their *soi-disant*[9] satisfaction at being able to pass everywhere as a peer of the English realm, one is struck by the spiritual brotherhood of Byron and the century of Baedecker[1] (and later Kodak) laden tourists he helped propel around the hemisphere. Rousseau's and Wordsworth's Alpine visions may have suffered a decline into the world of the guided tour and the gift-shop; but Byron's sensibility is only more self-conscious than that of his vacationing progeny. *Only* more self-conscious; but that of course is all the difference. From his first major poem, he was aware of a sinister submerged meaning of "vacation":

> To sit on rocks, to muse o'er flood and fell,
> To slowly trace the forest's shady scene,
> Where things that own not man's dominion dwell,
> And mortal foot hath ne'er or rarely been;
> To climb the trackless mountain all unseen,
> With the wild flock that never needs a fold;
> Alone o'er steeps and foaming falls to lean;
> This is not solitude; 'tis but to hold
> Converse with Nature's charms, and view her stores unroll'd.
>
> But midst the crowd, the hum, the shock of men,
> To hear, to see, to feel, and to possess,
> And roam along, the world's tired denizen,
> With none who bless us, none whom we can bless;
> Minions of splendour shrinking from distress!
> None that, with kindred consciousness endued,
> If we were not, would seem to smile the less,
> Of all that flatter'd, follow'd, sought, and sued;
> This is to be alone; this, this is solitude!
>
> (*Childe Harold*, II. xxv–xxvi)

Vacation is here a transitive concept: not the emptying-out of one's quotidian job of work, but the emptying-out of the world itself in order to sustain one's obsessively self-regarding consciousness. Note the similarity, in the last lines of stanza XXV, between the description of Nature's "charms unroll'd" and the description, in *Don Juan,* of the miser's stored and useless riches. Nature for Byron is not the dynamic welter of nearly-vital phenomena it is for Wordsworth and Shelley, but a set of *objects* whose true "meaning"—or lack of meaning—is only grasped through the effacing, distorting medium of the human consciousness. The stanzas from *Harold* are, in fact, a grim inversion of the key-term "solitude," that patient waiting-before-Nature in which Wordsworth found the condition of his greatest poetry.

For collectorship and tourism are versions of what Paul West has

9. Self-serving.
1. A series of guidebooks for travelers issued by the German Karl Baedecker (1801–59) and his successors.

called Byron's "rage to efface";[2] but they are effacement through the superlatively efficient technique of assimilation. What we own can no longer be the object of desire, and hence can no longer tempt the will or the affections out of the static balance of an assumed role, or impair the integrity of a strenuously fabricated selfhood. But such a role, once assumed, can be neither dropped nor deescalated. As in the miser's hoarding, the "contradictory richness of real life" always presents something new to be assimilated and reduced (*not*, that is, to be confronted in an existential decision); and yet there is no possibility of a single, once-for-all assimilation and reduction of the whole world, since that act itself is a commitment skirting the *real* sainthood of the void rather than the paradoxical sainthood of devalued things—leading to Francis of Assisi rather than Juan of Seville. So that the "fulness of satiety" of Childe Harold (Liv) is not only diagnostic of that character but prognostic for the creator's career. Beginning with *Harold* and extending throughout Byron's entire performance is the sense of the imagination in headlong race to contain and vacate more and more of the world of experience, raising the ante with each new poem so that more may be deliberately lost. It is a reflection, writ large, of what we know of Byron's habits of composition: the hurried peremptory writing of stanzas or large blocks of verse, with the distinctive impulse not so much to shape as to get it over with.

"Getting it over with" is an intensely willed verbal process, the reverse of compulsion. The relatively crude psychologistic error which has infected much of even the best modern Byron criticism, of course, is the assumption that the existential conundrums of the poetry are somehow to be explained as strategies developed from his "real life"—that same "real life" which he is accused of not facing head-on.[3] But the situation is not that simple. Increasingly after *Harold*, the sheerly verbal fabrication of assimilator-reducer attains its own autonomy, clarifying and objectifying rather than being influenced by the "life." For the *pose* of assimilator is itself a radical assimilation of selfhood into the tight confines of that which can be verbalized. Byron writes of his improvisation in *Don Juan*:

> But I am apt to grow too metaphysical:
>   'This time is out of joint'—and so am I;
> I quite forget this poem's merely quizzical,
>   And deviate into matters rather dry.
> I ne'er decide what I shall say, and this I call
>   Much too poetical: men should know why
> They write, and for what end; but, note or text,
> I never know the word which will come next.   (IX. xli)

2. *Byron and the Spoilers' Art* (New York, 1900), p. 17.
3. Wain, in West, p. 158, attributes Byron's psychosexuality—and much of his poetic attitude—to his violation, at age nine, by the governess Mary Gray.

It is impossible to decide whether the first-person verbs in this stanza are simply indicative in mood, or whether they form an idiosyncratic kind of jussive-constitutive subjunctive.[4]

The lines not only announce the speaker's haphazard improvisatory technique, but actually constitute it: the planned deterioration of the rhyme from "metaphysical" to "quizzical" to "this I call," the impossible stanzaic exigency of finding three three-syllable rhymes in English, is the *cause* that the speaker cannot "think as other men." The typical stanza of *Don Juan* (and, to a lesser extent, the verse of *The Island* and *Beppo*) is itself a syntactic metaphor for the process of assimilation-reduction: as the rhymes become more absurdly forced and the rhythm choppier in the course of its eight lines, we see the poet verbalizing another concept, and converting that verbalized concept into another object of *possession*, amenable to all manner of linguistic violence. It is the transmutation of expression into excrescence:

> Oh! she was perfect past all parallel—
>   Of any modern female saint's comparison;
> So far above the cunning powers of hell,
>   Her guardian angel had given up his garrison;
> Even her minutest motions went as well
>   As those of the best time-piece made by Harrison;
> In virtues nothing earthly could surpass her,
> Save thine 'incomparable oil,' Macassar!   (I. xvii)

The language of *Don Juan*, then, does not reflect a disillusioned shift from romance to anti-romantic satire, but an organic and supremely willed outgrowth of his whole career of vacation. For the Byronic relationship of art to "life" is exactly this grim absorption in the transaction between creative and projected or fictive consciousness; and in this line, Juan is as inevitable a product of Harold, Cain, Christian, and Torquil[5] as he is unexpected. For Byron, as both egotist and self-tormentor, plays a continually introverted game with his own projections: a game which follows its own ineluctable arc.

It is the purpose of the remainder of this essay to map some of stages of that arc; but before beginning, it may be useful to suggest its general shape, using a structural analogue from psychology. Jean Piaget, in his seminal *Play, Dreams and Imitation in Childhood*, describes three successive stages of the assimilative play of children, from the second year to the advent of true or "rational" conceptualization. These are *practice games*, involving the performance of sen-

---

4. In Latin, the subjunctive mood of a verb expresses a wish that the action described might occur. The jussive subjunctive expresses this wish as a law or implicit command. A "constitutive" sub- junctive (if the form really existed in Latin) would *codify* the wish expressed as a legal reality.

5. Christian and Torquil are the heroes of Byron's 1823 romance, *The Island*

sory-motor schemas of behavior for the simple sake of performance
(or, in the verbal stage, the stringing together of words or questions
with no apparent motive of real verbal control of reality); *symbolic
games* involving the individual acting-out of symbolic or imitated
actions of others and the substitution of objects for each other (verbally, pretending to be another person or thing); and *games with
rules*, a socialized form of play involving the adaptation of individual play to a group-structure.[6] Without unduly stretching Piaget's
categories, it is possible to regard Byron's career of increasing
absorption in his reductive poetics as a deliberate march backward
along this fundamental line of verbal and ludic development, a
reduction finally of the role of poetry to "language-game" in its
most chillingly autistic aspect. In such a plan, *Childe Harold* and
the other early romances occupy the most "public" position of
games with rules—the rules, among others, of conventional bour-
geois romance—leading to the more individualistic and private operations of a play like *Cain* or a romance like *The Island*, and finally
to that epic of annihilative and repetitive farce which is *Don Juan*.

As early as the Third Canto of *Childe Harold* (1816), Byron
seems to have become fully aware of his peculiar relationship to his
characters and to his fictive world. The artist is public entertainer,
but his creation is singing not only to but for himself:

> Since my young days of passion—joy, or pain,
> Perchance my heart and harp have lost a string,
> And both may jar: it may be, that in vain
> I would essay as I have sung to sing.
> Yet, though a dreary strain, to this I cling;
> So that it wean me from the weary dream
> Of selfish grief or gladness—so it fling
> Forgetfulness around me—it shall seem
> To me, though to none else, a not ungrateful theme.
>
> (III. iv)

This sounds like fairly conventional and fairly dull poetic complaint, until, a stanza later, Byron gives a fuller description of what
this sense of desertion implies:

> 'Tis to create, and in creating live
> A being more intense, that we endow
> With form our fancy, gaining as we give
> The life we imagine, even as I do now.
> What am I? Nothing: but not so art thou,
> Soul of my thought! with whom I traverse earth,
> Invisible but gazing, as I glow
> Mix'd with thy spirit, blended with thy birth,
> And feeling still with thee in my crush'd feelings' dearth.
>
> (III. vi)

6. New York, 1962, p. 110.

It is hard not to see in this passage a Byronic articulation of the Shelleyan idea of the *epipsyche*—that image of perfection and imaginative autonomy which the poet projects and seeks to unite himself with in a high verbal marriage of conception and performance.[7] But while the Shelleyan epipsyche is imaged as the female, quasi-daemonic object of a serious poetic quest, the Byronic projection comes across here as male, as a mirror-reflection of the poet himself, and as a mannikin rather than an Orphic higher soul. What Shelley conceives as a heterosexual, revitalizing activity of the Romantic *vates*,[8] is for Byron an essentially introverted transaction with one's male double, generating not prophecy but an absolute poetic neutrality toward the world outside the maker-*dopplegänger*[9] relationship. What we mentioned before as Byron's indifference to the "new," Romantic sense of a dangerous phenomenal nature can be explained at this point as the result of his profound penetration of the "new" Romantic sense of the epistemological self: the often-cited disappearance of Harold from Cantos III and IV is not a disappearance at all, but the mutual and autistic absorption of poet and persona, which liberates the poet to write his best descriptive poetry, precisely because description has become secondary to the contemplation of actor and role by each other.

This phenomenon is nowhere more evident than in Harold-Byron's famous vision of the Rhine castles in Canto III. xlvi-li. The passage is actually a simultaneous parody of revision of a characteristic Romantic *topos*,[1] the solitary witnessing of the natural sublime (Wordsworth's *Tintern Abbey*, Coleridge's *Hymn Before Sunrise*, Shelley's *Mont Blanc*). Harold raises his eyes from the majestic Rhine to behold—not natural splendor—but the ancient Gothic castles, artifacts degenerating into natural objects where "Ruin greenly dwells" (xlvi). And where Wordsworth and Shelley had contemplated the Power behind natural objects, Byron sees the brutal force of the robber-chieftains who have left their mark in the ruins. Shelley's lines on Mont Blanc were:

> Power dwells apart in its tranquillity,
> Remote, serene, and inaccessible:
> And *this*, the naked countenance of earth,
> On which I gaze, even these primaeval mountains
> Teach the adverting mind. (96–100)

Byron writes of the Rhine castles:

> Beneath those battlements, within those walls,
> Power dwelt amidst her passions; in proud state

7. The best explanation of the Shelleyan epipsyche is probably Carlos Baker's *Shelley's Major Poetry* (New York, 1961) although Bloom's *Visionary Company* adds some important qualifications.

8. Prophet.
1. Double.
1. Any one of the standard devices of classical rhetoric.

> Each robber chief upheld his armed halls,
> Doing his evil will, nor less elate
> Than mightier heroes of a longer date.   (III. xlviii)

And in the final stanza of the vision, as the spectator's eyes return to the river over which the battlements stand, Byron cancels the central Romantic metaphor of mutual reflection of the adverting mind and the phenomena it beholds:

> A thousand battles have assail'd thy banks,
> But these and half their fame have pass'd away,
> And Slaughter heap'd on high his weltering ranks;
> Their very graves are gone, and what are they?
> Thy tide wash'd down the blood of yesterday,
> And all was stainless, and on thy clear stream
> Glass'd, with its dancing light, the sunny ray;
> But o'er the blacken'd blighting dream
> Thy waves would vainly roll, all sweeping as they seem.
>
>   (III. li)

The key word here is "roll"—the kinetic image, in *Tintern Abbey* and *Mont Blanc*, of a problematic but dynamic phenomenology. For Byron, however, the image is appropriate only to the "real" river, and hence ineffectual for the guilt-laden and totally humanized dual role of Byron-Harold. The beginning of the next stanza, 'Thus Harold inly said, and pass'd along," immediately reinforces the self-contemplative absorption of poet and persona which has produced this momentary outward gaze, "collecting" and devaluating the world at the same time.

Byron's relationship with his fictive projections is, I have suggested, introverted. One hesitates to use the franker word, "homosexual" without the qualification that here it is being employed as a primarily *imaginative* value, by analogy with the strongly heterosexual quest-myth of Blake, Shelley, and Keats. Byron's actual penchant for pederasty has as little—or as much—to do with his work in this way as does the sexual practice of Hart Crane or Genet with the tortured rhapsody of *The Bridge* or with the "Divine" and "Darling"—to say nothing of the "Genet"—of *Our Lady of the Flowers*. It is undeniable, however, that homosexuality becomes increasingly crucial for the literature of the post-Romantic imagination, as the perfect analogue, on the metabolic level, to the linguistic impulse toward the devaluation of metaphor and the technical impulse toward conspicuous artifice.

Within this context, the development from *Harold* to the dramas clearly reflects, not an access of high seriousness supplanting the "Corsair style," but an increased—and increasingly committed—command of the art of projective introversion.[2] The explicit manip-

---

2. See James R. Thompson, 'Byron's Plays and *Don Juan*: Genre and Myth," *Bucknell Review*, XV (1967), 22–38, for an excellent discussion of the relationship between the plays and *Don Juan*.

ulation of the characters of the dramas, for example, which has led Paul West to describe them accurately as a manner of puppeteering, is a reduction of personality from three to two dimensions which allows the creator a vastly widened scope for self-contemplation. Far from recognizing the Flaubertian ideal of the dramatist as withdrawn from his characters to the point of disappearance, Byron makes his dramas small parables of his growing involvement with his own assumed personae.

* * *

We have already discussed *Don Juan* as Byron's organically generated final testament: the negative apotheosis of his disruptive gift. Juan himself is, of course, the perfect unconscious hero: critical chestnuts like "character development" aside, it would be difficult to imagine a character who learns less—or is contrived to learn less —from his experience. And counterposed to the unconscious hero is not another conscious *character*, but the narrator himself, whose mind is a riotously proliferating devaluation of thought, insulated even from philosophic nihilism by his refusal to take his own voice seriously. Brian Wilkie, in a perceptive essay on *Don Juan*, has noted the total avoidance of "point" in the so-called "satire" of the poem.[3] It is an inevitable result of the process we have been charting, since in *Don Juan* the annihilative voice of the narrator can issue only in the projection of the ventriloquist's dummy Juan, a projection now devoid of even Harold's or Cain's impulse to look outward. Byron has become "Byron," and the act of poetry has become a complete verbal assimilation—vacation so efficient that it cannot stop vacating itself. For the narrator has assigned himself, finally, the role of repeating interminably the reductive grammar which is language itself, man's negative *fiat*:

> 'Let there be light!' said God, 'and there was light!'
>   'Let there be blood!' says man, and there's a sea!
> The fiat of this spoil'd child of the Night
>   (For Day ne'er saw his merits) could decree
> More evil in an hour, than thirty bright
>   Summers could renovate, though they should be
> Lovely as those which ripen'd Eden's fruit,
> For war cuts up not only branch, but root.   (VII. xli)

One frequently reads or hears comments on Byron's "delight" at his inexhaustibly variable comedy in *Don Juan*:[4] on the contrary, he is literally boring himself to death with the playing of his narrative

3. *Romantic Poets and Epic Tradition* (Madison, 1965).
4. See Guy Steffan, *"Don Juan:* A Thousand Colors," in West, pp. 96–112, and also Northrop Frye's disappointing essay on Byron in *Fables of Identity* (New York, 1963).

role. When he announces, at XII. liv–lv, that his poem is only just beginning and that he plans an additional hundred Cantos or so, it is with a kind of grim recognition that this language-game can only end with the death of the speaker. Like the practice games described by Piaget, here is language proliferating itself for the mere sake of prolonging the action: but the action is the very imaginative life of the poet. It is a grotesque parody of the conventional Augustinian explanation of the Trinity: Father ("Byron") forever contemplating his generated Son (Juan), with no hint of the release of a fructifying and creative Spirit. Words themselves, under the reductive power of the speaking voice, assume a bluntly physical presence which increases their power of sheer metabolic density and denies their power to organize experience. Obscenely punning on the "high official situation" of Catherine the Great's lovers, "Byron" writes:

> Oh, gentle ladies! should you seek to know
>   The import of this diplomatic phrase,
> Bid Ireland's Londonderry Marquess show
>   His parts of speech; and in the strange displays
> Of that odd string of words, all in a row,
>   Which none divine, and every one obeys,
> Perhaps you may pick out some queer *no* meaning,
> Of that weak wordy harvest the sole gleaning.   (IX. xlix)

The welter of educated circumlocution both obscures the gross physicality behind its dead metaphors, and yet reveals it in the very absurdity of its chance collisions—"his parts of speech." And it is with an appropriateness fine beyond irony that the poem ends on a name which—surely intentionally—echoes one of the most venerable obscenities in the language: "The phantom of her frolic Grace —Fitz-Fulke!"

The remarkable shape of the Byronic career—his resolute march into inertia—has led a number of his most successful modern critics to cite his method as an anticipation of the aesthetics and ethics of existentialism.[5] It is a tempting comparison, with more than a minimum of truth in it: one is led to reflect that the three exemplary "absurd men" described in *The Myth of Sisyphus*[6]—the conqueror, the actor, and Don Juan—are a paradigm of the Byronic self-image. But like other attempts to place Byron, in late-Augustan sensibility, or in the European myth of Byron, it tends to displace him from his proper and crucially problematic relationship to the history of the Romantic imagination. For the "existentialist" elements of Byron's career, the election and constant reaffirmation of his role in the face of life, and the firm insistence on *objectifying* his private

5. E.g., West, p. 17, Wilkie, p. 225, and Thompson, p. 32.

6. Albert Camus's 1942 exposition of the philosophy of existentialism.

experience, are perhaps better understood as a variety of anti-existentialism, a resolute denial of conscious freedom which initiates the age which was to lead to the measured affirmations of *La Peste* and *L'Etre et le Néant*. The heroes of Sartre and Camus "elect" death and the final dissolution of meaning because that election itself is a liberation from hope into a limited and hence humanized future. As Jean Tarrou explains the chances for heroism in *La Peste*:

> "What is really *natural* is the microbe. The rest, health, integrity, purity, if you will, is an effect of the will—and of a will which must never let up. The honest man, who contaminates almost nobody, is the man with the least possible distractions. . . . I've heard so many arguments which failed to convince me, but convinced others to consent to murder, that I've learned that all man's unhappiness comes from his not having a clear language. I resolved then to speak and act clearly, to put myself in a good way."[7]

This is the *lucidité* which is the prime value of Camus' humanism. But there is in Byron no sense of an election for life, but rather an election for the role itself which finally, as we have already pointed out, *vacates* life itself to preserve the increasingly verbalized —and verbally *restricted*—persona. With each reconfirmation of the Byronic role, the possibility of a human future becomes more remote, until in *Don Juan* the poet's omnivorous imagination finally turns, in a frozen act of reduction, to the stuff of consciousness itself, his own words:

> AH!—What should follow slips from my reflection;
>   Whatever follows ne'ertheless may be
> As *à-propos* of hope or retrospection,
>   As though the lurking thought had follow'd free.
> All present life is but an interjection,
>   An 'Oh!' or 'Ah!' of joy or misery,
> Or a 'Ha! ha!' or 'Bah!'—a yawn, or 'Pooh!'
>   Of which perhaps the latter is most true.   (XV. i)

So that, once again, the question of "writing for the ladies"— the question of Byron's whole career—assumes its ambivalent nature. *Don Juan* liberated Byron, perhaps, from his obsession with action-in-fiction by forcing on him an absolute disgust with the activity of words—liberated him for the very real heroism of Missolonghi. But it also liberated—or delivered—him *into* a kind of poetry which reflects a dark version of our own central humanistic concerns. Byron is perhaps the first edifying casualty in the battle to achieve wholeness not in spite of but because of the inevitable artificiality

7. Albert Camus, *La Peste* (Paris, 1947), p. 203. My translation.

of all consciousness. In either case, his is a career-in-language which in its full paradox we are the more impoverished and the less self-aware for not understanding.

LESLIE A. MARCHAND

Byron in the Twentieth Century†

Does Byron's poetry have any significant value for us today? The answer depends largely on the depth and catholicity of our concepts of poetry. Poetry can be many things. If we see value in only one kind (as critics have tended to do in every age), we will naturally denigrate all that does not conform to our current taste. If we demand "high seriousness" in poetry, which in Matthew Arnold's use of the term meant a particular moral slant, we will speak disparagingly of Dryden and Pope as poets of "an age of prose and reason"; we will find Chaucer and Burns "poetically unsound" because they lack "the accent of high seriousness." If we demand, as many twentieth century critics do, that poetry embody irony and ambiguity and paradox in a complex and intricate structure of words weighted with symbolic meaning, we shall give short shrift to most other kinds of poetry, and particularly to the work of those poets who, like Byron, seem, in T. S. Eliot's phrase, to have an "imperceptiveness" to words, to be making "sonorous affirmations of the commonplace."[1]

But if we start with a broad definition of poetry as a something plus, a heightened realization of some idea, mood, or meaningful moment, and not something concentrated and distilled according to a single formula, then Byron's best poetry, at least, has merits which can be appreciated by the most fastidious and sophisticated. Such an approach can clear the way for a better understanding and a fairer estimate of the work of a poet whose "sincerity and strength" have impressed critics from Goethe and Matthew Arnold to Eliot himself.

Among his merits are two which are peculiarly Byronic. By sheer genius he could make a statement of the commonplace ricochet past the platitude and lodge memorably in the mind, leaving rever-

† From Leslie A. Marchand, *Byron's Poetry: A Critical Introduction* (Cambridge, Mass.: Harvard University Press, 1968), pp. 1–14.
1. Eliot's essay on "Byron" (*On Poetry and Poets*, 1961; the essay was first published in 1937) is an attempt to separate the good work from the bad, and he ends like most twentieth century critics by lauding *Don Juan*. He grants that in that poem Byron "has the cardinal virtue of being never dull." He praises Byron's "genius for digression," finds his banter and mockery "an admirable antacid to the high-falutin," and sees his ultimate virtue, as many others have, in his "reckless raffish honesty."

berating harmonies of sound and sense. This is a virtue to be found in some stanzas of *Childe Harold* (Eliot notwithstanding) and in some of his tales and shorter lyrics, as well as in his satires. A second and greater merit is his facetious revelation of truths that are too threatening to the self-defensive ego to be presented without a comic mask. Byron was often most serious when he was most waggish. Mockery was the cover for intellectual and emotional honesty in a period solemnly tenacious of its own cant and complacent in its own certainties. When in his self-exile Byron achieved a kind of beyond-the-tomb freedom to speak his mind about all things, he found his true voice in *Don Juan*.

Byron had a sufficient contempt for "system," whether in criticism or poetry. After reading Leigh Hunt's manuscript of *Rimini*, he wrote Moore, "I told him that I deemed it good poetry at bottom, disfigured only by a strange style. His answer was, that his style was a system, or *upon system*, or some such cant; and, when a man talks of system, his case is hopeless."[2] Like most of the Romantics who indulged in the "spontaneous overflow of powerful feelings," Byron wrote many "unpremeditated" and uncorrected poems that cannot be defended. He apologized for them by saying: "I can never *recast* any thing. I am like the Tiger: if I miss the first spring, I go growling back to my jungle again; but if I *do hit*, it is crushing."[3]

For the most part one need not look for verbal subtleties in Byron. His irony is likely to be a brickbat, but hurled with such skill and force that when it does hit, it crushes. Writing to Murray after receiving a plea from his publisher to avoid "approximations to indelicacy" in *Don Juan*, Byron said: ". . . this reminds me of George Lamb's quarrel at Cambridge with Scrope Davies. 'Sir,' said George, 'he *hinted* at my *illegitimacy*.' 'Yes,' said Scrope, 'I called him a damned adulterous bastard'; the approximation and the hint are not unlike."[4]

One of the supposed weaknesses of Byron as a thinker which has lessened his stature among modern critics is his inability, or unwillingness, to adopt a fixed philosophy or permanent point of view. It is the same accusation that was made by Goethe and echoed by Arnold: "The moment he reflects, he is a child." But it may be that that very fact has given him a perennial freshness which makes him more congenial to the twentieth century than those of his contemporaries who adopted a "system" that can no longer answer the questions we perpetually ask about human life and destiny. If Col-

2. *The Works of Lord Byron, Letters and Journals*, ed. R. E. Prothero, IV, 237. Letter of June 1, 1818. (This edition is hereafter cited as *Letters and Journals*).

3. *Letters and Journals*, V, 471. Letter of Nov. 3, 1821.

4. *Letters and Journals*, IV, 304–305. Letter of May 20, 1819.

eridge may be thought a more profound philosopher, it is not because of the acceptance of absolutes and dogmas that made him an apologist for the contemporary orthodoxy in religion and politics. His reputation as a thinker rests rather on those "seminal" thoughts of his journals and conversations that penetrated to individual truths—truths which might have been disquieting to the systems he supported had his rationalizations been less persuasive.

It is probable that the mind that inquires and questions has always expanded philosophic as well as scientific knowledge more than the mind that affirms and accepts. In an era when blood transfusion is as universal a remedy as blood-letting was when Byron died at Missolonghi, it is easy to sympathize with the instinctive skepticism which made him resist the application of leeches. The symbolic significance should not escape us when we consider his skepticism of no less tenaciously held beliefs in other spheres.

In any reassessment of Byron's value to us as a thinker we can do no better than to repeat Professor Fairchild's statement: ". . . one may justly be irritated by the common assumption that a man who refrains from believing in lofty and inspiring ideas for which there is no evidence whatever necessarily has an inferior mind. Although no one would undertake to prove that Byron was a profound thinker, he possessed a quality which many supposedly profound thinkers lack—a sense of the toughness of facts and an inability to dupe himself about them.. . . Beneath all his protective histrionism, his mind possessed a certain desperate integrity which should command respect."[6]

The quality which Lady Blessington[6] and others among his contemporaries saw as a weakness was Byron's real strength: that sensitive response to the impression of the moment without regard to any "system" or principle of unity or consistency. Byron defined the term "mobility" as "an excessive susceptibility of immediate impressions—at the same time without *losing* the past."[7] As his "versified Aurora Borealis . . . flashes o'er a waste and icy clime," he throws the cold light of truth on human smugness. He has been accused, he says, of

> A tendency to under-rate and scoff
> At human power and virtue, and all that.

But, he replies,

> I say no more than hath been said in Dante's
> Verse, and by Solomon and by Cervantes;

5. Hoxie Neale Fairchild, *The Romantic Quest*, 1931, p. 362.
6. The perceptive and charming Marguerite Power, Countess of Blessington (1789–1849) befriended Byron in Genoa in 1823. In 1834 she published *Conversa-tions of Lord Byron*, an important if partial source on the poet's opinions and personality. [*Editor.*]
7. *The Works of Lord Byron, Poetry*, ed. E. H. Coleridge, VI, 600 (Hereafter cited as *Poetry*).

By Swift, by Machiavel, by Rochefoucault,
  By Fénélon, by Luther, and by Plato;
By Tillotson, and Wesley, and Rousseau,
  Who knew this life was not worth a potato.

. . . .

Newton (that proverb of the mind), alas!
  Declared, with all his grand discoveries recent,
That he himself felt only "like a youth
Picking up shells by the great ocean—Truth."
                              (*Don Juan*, VII, 3–5)

In another digression he gives his answer to those who are "hot for certainties":

'Tis true we speculate both far and wide,
  And deem, because we *see*, we are *all-seeing*: . . .

"*Que scais-je?*" was the motto of Montaigne,
  As also of the first academicians:
That all is dubious which man may attain,
  Was one of their most favourite positions.
There's no such thing as certainty, that's plain
  As any of Mortality's conditions. . . .
                              (*Don Juan*, IX, 16–17)

In his disinclination to claim a truth he did not possess, and in his skepticism of absolutes, Byron finds a more sympathetic audience in the twentieth century than he found in the nineteenth. He gives voice to an era that is confused by the increase of knowledge and that no longer has confidence in intellectual leaders who seek easy answers. Byron had the strength to resist the demand for adherence to some creed, for acceptance of some simple and final interpretation of the only partly understood universe. He was aware that to keep an open mind on all subjects required courage.

The consequence is, being of no party,
  I shall offend all parties. . . .   (*Don Juan*, IX, 26)

Keats complained of his friend Dilke—he was nearer to Byron here than either realized—that he was a man "who cannot feel he has a personal identity unless he has made up his mind about everything." That "Negative Capability" which Keats so admired in Shakespeare he might also have seen in Byron had he been able to look under the latter's flippant manner—"that is, when a man is capable of being in uncertainties, mysteries, doubts, without any irritable reaching after fact and reason."

It is easy to see why Byron has frequently been called a romantic paradox. The polarities of his life, opinions, and poetic productions are apparent enough. He was a Deist and free-thinker haunted by a

Calvinistic sense of original sin. He espoused the cause of oppressed peoples in every land and yet was always conscious of his noble ancestry and sometimes displayed a childish aristocratic pride. He liked to think of himself as a Regency Dandy and yet he was sincere in admiration of Shelley's simplicity and unaffected manners. Occasionally with strangers, but seldom with his friends, he struck an attitude, though at bottom he had a "desperate integrity" and a disarming self-honesty. He was a leader of the Romantic revolution in poetry who clung to the literary ideals of Alexander Pope. He was a worshipper of the ideal whose leanings toward realism kept his feet on the ground.

But rightly seen, what appear to be contradictions are in the main only two sides of the same coin. The central problem for Byron, as for most of the Romantics, was to find a satisfying compromise between the demands of the real and the ideal. But with the strong strain of eighteenth century common sense in his nature, Byron's attitude toward the problem was different from that of most other Romantics.

There are several possible attitudes. One may deny that there is any disparity between the real and the ideal, either (a) by saying that the real is ideal (and then he is not a Romantic at all but has taken the so-called common sense view of Pope and the eighteenth century adherents of the "chain of being" philosophy, that seeming imperfections are only a part of the plan, that "all that is, is right"); or (b) by saying that the ideal is real, the only reality, and that the world of sense is only an appearance, an illusion through which the man of perception (let us say the poet) must penetrate in order to get a view of ultimate reality. This latter alternative is the one chosen by all the idealists from Plato to the present. With variations as to the means of perceiving ideal reality, this was the solution to which many of the nineteenth century poets (the so-called transcendental group) turned: Wordsworth, Coleridge, Shelley. Some of them were uneasy in that point of view, and like Wordsworth felt as they grew older that they could only fitfully command the power to see the ideal vision and so asked themselves:

> Whither is fled the visionary gleam?
> Where is it now, the glory and the dream?

This brought on a temporary melancholy, but their "will to believe" was too strong to permit them to rest there.

A second way of viewing the disparity between the real and the ideal is to see the gap as essentially unbridgeable: to come face to face with the necessity of dealing with the real world as real and the ideal world as ideal, as a creation of the mind. Within this possibility are two kinds and many degrees of attitudes: (a) One may be sensible (or insensitive, if you choose to call it so) enough to accept the separation of reality and ideality and feel no particular urge to bridge the gap between them. Such a person is not a Romantic but more nearly what we would call a realist. Or (b) one may be so constituted as to long for the ideal with an uncompromising zeal, and may be consequently disappointed and unhappy because the real fails to measure up to it, yet be too clear-sighted to confuse the two. He may then vary his mental occupations between a dwelling upon the ideal, which is his only true love, and a melancholy or a bitterly mocking reflection upon how disgustingly short of the ideal the real is and must always be. In this last description of an attitude we come as near as can any generalization to fixing the place of Byron among the Romantics. Of course Byron seemed at times to be admiring the classical (or neo-classical) acceptance of the world as it is. But because he was a child of his age, and could not detach himself sufficiently from the romantic longing for what the world does not give, he could seldom achieve the Augustan calm he admired in his idol Pope.

In one mood, that which permeates *Childe Harold*, he displays the melancholy and despair which accompany the recognition of the failure of the real to match the ideal. In another, he presents the comedy, sometimes bitter, sometimes roguishly facetious, of the disparity between real and ideal. With a keen delight he tears away the mask of sentimentalism, of hypocritical self-deception, of mock-ideality, of wishful thinking, and shows the plain or ugly face of reality. This is the mood that dominates much, but by no means all, of *Don Juan*.

We have the feeling now that the satiric Byron found himself, for it is this aspect of his work that most appeals to us. The melancholy Byron belongs more to his own time, though he too may voice a modern (and universal) *Weltschmerz*.[8] But both moods pervade *Don Juan* and alternate in Byron's poetry throughout his career. Professor Fairchild has phrased it most aptly: "Aspiration, melancholy, mockery—the history of a mind too idealistic to refrain from blowing bubbles, and too realistic to refrain from pricking them."[9]

It is a common supposition that Byron began his career as a melancholy Childe Harold, a gloomy egoist, a Conrad (*The Corsair*) brooding over his "one virtue and a thousand crimes." Some biographers have pictured him standing on the sidelines at one of the London balls in his years of fame, wrapped in somber disillusionment and despair, "the wandering outlaw of his own dark mind." But it is just as likely that his curled lip of scorn indicated that he

8. World-weariness. [*Editor.*]   9. *The Romantic Quest*, p. 370.

was about to voice a facetious witticism more appropriate to *Don Juan* than to *Childe Harold*. Judging not only from his letters and the record of his conversations at the time but also from some of the poems he wrote early in his career, the satiric, realistic, mocking vein was strong in Byron from his Cambridge days, or before, until the end of his life. It only tended to be suppressed in his poetry after the success of the first two cantos of *Childe Harold* had fixed the pattern of his poetic production, and the flattering public demand for his tales of "pleasing woe" made it difficult for him to shatter the image of himself he had created.[1]

Though he had written some facetious and realistic (or cynical) verses before he ended his residence at Cambridge, only a very few were ventured upon the public, and those only in the privately printed volume *Fugitive Pieces*, intended to be circulated among friends. After that volume was suppressed and all but four copies destroyed because his parson friend John Becher objected that one of the poems ("To Mary") was "rather too warmly drawn," Byron retained only the more romantic, and less original, verses in his sub- sequent volumes. Many of the moods of *Childe Harold* appeared in *Hours of Idleness*, but no hint was given that the author possessed even at that time much of the mischievious good humor that later found expression in *Beppo*. Perhaps the *Edinburgh Review* critic would have been kinder to *Hours of Idleness* if its mawkishness had been leavened by the lively satire on sentimentalism from *Fugitive Pieces*: "To a Lady Who Presented to the Author a Lock of Hair Braided with His Own, and Appointed a Night in December to Meet Him in the Garden." Some of the lines suggest the mood if not the maturity of *Don Juan*.

> Why should you weep, like *Lydia Languish*,
> And Fret with self-created anguish?
> Or doom the lover you have chosen,
> On winter nights to sigh half frozen. . . .

Byron's next attempt, stimulated rather than initiated by the attack in the *Edinburgh*, as a Popean satire begun at Cambridge under the influence of his friend Hobhouse and encouraged by Francis Hodgson, a translator of Juvenal. *English Bards, and Scotch Reviewers* owes something to the Roman satirist, but more to Pope and Gifford. Byron had read and admired Pope at Harrow, as most schoolboys who had any interest in poetry did at the time. But his

1. I have discussed this point in the In- troduction to my edition of *Don Juan* (Riverside Edition, Houghton Mifflin, 1958). Byron himself was aware of the stamp that *Childe Harold* and other poems in that vein had put upon him. In 1817 he asked Moore to assure Francis Jeffrey "that I was not, and, indeed, am not even *now*, the misanthropical and gloomy gentleman he takes me for, but a facetious companion, well to do with those with whom I am intimate, and as loquacious and laughing as if I were a much cleverer fellow." (*Letters and Journals*, IV, 72–74.)

immediate model was William Gifford, whose clever satires in the *Anti-Jacobin* and in *The Maeviad* and *The Baviad* roused Byron to emulation and to admiration scarcely this side idolatry. He would now try a *Dunciad* of his own: "The cry is up, and scribblers are my game."

Having made a success in this genre, imitative though it was, Byron henceforth felt that this was his forte. It was a style that was generally respected by those he most respected, and it did not bring ridicule on him but praise and admiration, even from some whom his barbs had stung. It was small wonder then that he tried to follow up his success by writing, while he was in Greece, *Hints from Horace* and that whenever he felt the urge to satiric expression he turned to the Popean couplet even when the subject and treatment were far from Pope.

Byron continued throughout his life to have a dual concept of poetry. On the one hand was the poetry of serious moral purpose (as he conceived Pope's to be). This was a poetry that would castigate the errors of the age with stringent wit, would point out deviations from good sense and good taste in brilliant balanced couplets, and would attack the corruptions and injustices in society with Juvenalian fierceness modified by Popean good temper.[2] It was the goal Byron had aimed at in *English Bards, and Scotch Reviewers*. It is significant that he set himself the task in that poem, beyond judging the little wits and poetasters of the day, of bringing "the force of wit" to bear on "Vice" and "Folly" as well as on literary lapses. It is significant too that he admired most the virtues of his models that he felt he could not achieve: the objectivity and the verbal skill that the very nature of his own character and genius made it most difficult for him to attain.

In the middle of his career, after he had finished the fourth canto of *Childe Harold* and thought it his best, he wrote to Murray: "With regard to poetry in general, I am convinced, the more I think of it, that . . . *all* of us—Scott, Southey, Wordsworth, Moore, Campbell, I,—are all in the wrong, one as much as another; that we are upon a wrong revolutionary poetical system, or systems, not worth a damn in itself, and from which none but Rogers and Crabbe[3] are free; and that the present and next generations will finally be of this opinion. I am the more confirmed in this by having lately gone over some of our classics, particularly *Pope*, whom I tried in this way,—I took Moore's poems and my own and

2. A close study of Byron's debt to the Roman satirists Horace and Juvenal has been made by Arthur Kahn (New York University doctoral dissertation). Aside from the obvious parallels in *Hints from Horace* and other poems in the Popean couplet, Kahn has found remarkable echoes of both the subject matter and the style of Horace, but many more and closer parallels with Juvenal in *Don Juan* particularly.

3. See note for Byron's letter of September 15, 1817. [*Editor*.]

some others, and went over them side by side with Pope's, and I was really astonished (I ought not to have been so) and mortified at the ineffable distance in point of sense, harmony, effect, and even *Imagination*, passion, and *Invention*, between the little Queen Anne's man, and us of the Lower Empire. Depend upon it, it is all Horace then, and Claudian now, among us; and if I had to begin again, I would model myself accordingly."[4]

The other concept of poetry that guided Byron's literary performance was the subjective Romantic one born of the impulse to "look in your heart and write." He adopted it perforce, impelled by both his temperament and his environment, but he continued to consider it second best and to speak disparagingly of it, as he did in the letter just quoted. Having a conviction of the lesser nature of the art he was practicing, he found a certain satisfaction in deprecating poetry in general: "If one's years can't be better employed than in sweating poesy, a man had better be a ditcher."[5] It is characteristic of Byron that he could not compromise with his concept of the ideal in writing. He would live in the world, but he would not bend his mind to call its imperfections ideal, even when it concerned his own performance. "If I live ten years longer," he told Moore, "you will see, however, that it is not over with me—I don't mean in literature, for that is nothing; and it may seem odd enough to say, I do not think it my vocation."[6] As late as 1821, when he had found in *Don Juan* a literary style that suited his genius far better than any imitation of Gifford or Pope, he wrote to Moore after the failure of the Neapolitan uprising had blighted his hopes for a similar revolt in the Romagna in which he could take an active part: "And now let us be literary;—a sad falling off, but it is always a consolation. If 'Othello's occupation be gone,' let us take to the next best; and, if we cannot contribute to make mankind more free and wise, we may amuse ourselves and those who like it. . . . I have been scribbling at intervals. . . ."[7]

Even before he had fully accepted his own limitations, Byron found an outlet for his energies and his feelings in poetry of the Romantic category. "All convulsions end with me in Rhyme,"[8] he wrote Moore in 1813. And again he spoke of poetry as "the lava of the imagination whose eruption prevents an earthquake."[9] His reluctance to publish *Childe Harold* was motivated as much by his

4. *Letters and Journals*, IV, 169. Letter of Sept. 15, 1817. Byron would have been flattered and pleased had he seen the note which Gifford, to whom Murray showed the letter, wrote on the manuscript: "There is more good sense, and feeling and judgment in this passage, than in any other I ever read, or Lord Byron wrote."

5. *Letters and Journals*, IV, 284, Letter of April 6, 1819.

6. *Letters and Journals*, IV, 62. Letter of Feb. 28, 1817.

7. *Letters and Journals*, V, 272. Letter of April 28, 1821.

8. *Letters and Journals*, II, 293. Letter of Nov. 30, 1813.

9. *Letters and Journals*, III, 405. Letter of Nov. 10, 1813, to Annabella Milbanke.

anxiety that it would damage his claim as an Augustan wit, which he felt he had already staked out in *English Bards, and Scotch Reviewers,* as by his fear of revealing secrets of his private life and feelings. It would be an acknowledgment that he had enrolled himself in the camp of the Romantics who regarded poetry as nothing more than the safety valve of the emotions.

But the acclaim that greeted *Childe Harold,* together with the circumstances that led to the suppression of *English Bards* and the withdrawal of the manuscript of *Hints from Horace,* caused Byron to accept his role as a Romantic poet without ever giving up his conviction that the only ideal of poetry to which he could give full critical allegiance was that of the school of Pope. Swept along, however, by his phenomenal success in what he considered this lesser genre at a time when, frustrated in his ambition to be a political orator and statesman by the strait jacket of Whig politics, and pressed by the need for emotional relief for the impasses created by his fame and his passions, he succumbed to the poetry of self-expression as other men might to drugs or drink. But still he was from time to time stricken with remorse for having given up the ideal of poetic practice. Henceforth, except in these moments of critical contrition, he thought and spoke of poetry as a simple "lava of the imagination." While he was composing *The Bride of Abydos* he wrote Lady Melbourne: ". . . my mind has been from *late* and *later* events in such a state of fermentation, that as usual I have been obliged to empty it in rhyme, and am in the very heart of another Eastern tale."[1]

Most of what Byron wrote henceforth grew directly or indirectly out of his personal need for emotional release, and through practice of this "inferior" art he became adept in voicing the pangs not only of himself but of his generation. Like "wild Rousseau" he "threw / Enchantment over passion, and from woe / Wrung overwhelming eloquence." In *Childe Harold,* in the Oriental and other tales, and also in shorter lyrics and in pieces with supposedly more objective themes like "The Prisoner of Chillon," personal catharsis of turbulent moods was the dominant motive for composition.[2] Likewise in his speculative dramas, *Manfred, Cain, Heaven and Earth,* and *The Deformed Transformed,* the driving force is always the poet's desire to work out a solution to his own deepest quandaries. And it might be said that whatever merit these poetic dramas have lies in the depth and sincerity of the personal revelation rather than in any resolution of a philosophical problem.

Fidelity to the mood of the moment was Byron's forte, and fail-

---

1. *Lord Byron's Correspondence*, ed. John Murray, I, 214. Letter of Nov. 4, 1813.

2. There is no doubt that Byron's deep hatred of personal restraint as well as of governmental tyranny made the story of Bonivard's imprisonment a subject congenial to him. The passionate interest it aroused in him is best seen in the "Sonnet on Chillon"; "Eternal Spirit of the chainless Mind!"

ure to acknowledge this has befuddled Byron criticism from the time the poems were published until the present day. There has been a persistent refusal to accept Byron's own frankest statements, and to recognize that honesty and self-honesty were almost an obsession with him. Somerset Maugham once wrote a story of a man who got a tremendous reputation for being a humorist merely by telling the simple truth about himself and others. So Byron acquired the reputation of being a great poseur because no one would believe that anyone would be as honest in literature as people may frequently be in private conversation.

Among his contemporaries, those who felt the strong spell of his passionate revelation of the romantic ego, but disapproved of the unconventional conduct or opinions of the hero, were constrained to apologize for Byron by saying that he was not drawing from his own experience but was only assuming a Satanic pose. A typical statement is that of one of the Cambridge "Apostle" editors of the *Athenaeum*, who wrote not long after Byron's death: "Among the states of feeling which he describes with so much intensity, we doubt whether any great proportion were really painted from his own feelings."[3] But recent biographical evidence shows convincingly that no writer was ever more patently autobiographical in the creations of his imagination. In fact, this became so much a habit of his mind and of his composition that even when he deliberately set out to write objectively, as in his historical dramas, in which he prided himself on fidelity to the written records of characters and events, he could not but make the major figures over into personalities like himself with problems that were his own.

Byron's supreme literary achievement, however, was developed almost by accident, though its ingredients had been long heated in the crucible of his own experience and literary practice. When he discovered in the Italian ottava rima the possibilities for both colloquial ease and rhetorical brilliance, for kaleidoscopic but natural shifts from serious to comic, he had found his métier and his medium. When he tried it out in *Beppo* he saw that it offered the freest outlet for all the thoughts and feelings of his mobile personality. The darker moods had already found adequate expression in the third and fourth cantos of *Childe Harold* and in *Manfred*. He had achieved something like calm again in Venice, which, he wrote Moore, "has always been (next to the East) the greenest island of my imagination."[4] At last, he felt freed by his self-exile from the necessity of fitting his life or his verse into an English pattern. By November, 1816, he was already willing to become a citizen of the world. If he could only arrange his financial affairs in England, he told Kinnaird, "you might consider me as *posthumous*,

3. *Athenaeum*, Jan. 23, 1828, p. 55.
4. *Letters and Journals*, IV, 7. Letter of Nov. 17, 1816.

for I would never willingly dwell in the 'tight little Island.' "[5] He could now indulge in literature that facetious and satiric bent which had been largely confined to his letters since *Childe Harold* had diverted his talents into the single track of the "Romantic Agony."

When the success of *Beppo* encouraged him to continue the same style and manner in *Don Juan*, Byron was not fully conscious of the significance of the change that was being wrought not only in his poetic subject matter and style but also in his concept of the poetic function. While he was increasingly aware of the value of *Don Juan* as a production that possessed candor and life and truth more than any other literary work of the day, and while he defended it facetiously against the attacks of his squeamish friends in England, he never fully understood why it engrossed his loyalty more than anything else he had written. The fact was that he had found a genre which satisfied his deepest feelings about the moral function of poetry and at the same time allowed the completest cathartic escape for his feelings, whether serious or comic.

It is true that by the very nature of the medium and the style he had adapted from the ottava rima mock-heroic poems of the Italians, Byron's work has less of the neat compactness of Pope's best couplets. But on the other hand, by following his own genius with a freedom of artistry that forgets art, Byron cuts deeper with his broadsword through the armor of conventional pretenses to the living flesh of the human condition than Pope ever does with his more pointed rapier. Byron swung wildly at times, but in more than half of *Don Juan* he did hit and the blow was crushing.

E. D. HIRSCH, JR.

Byron and the Terrestrial Paradise†

ADAH: Why wilt thou always mourn for Paradise?
       Can we not make another?
CAIN: Where?

Lord Byron, *Cain*, III, i.

The Padre . . . assured me "that the terrestrial
Paradise had been certainly in *Armenia*." I went
seeking it—God knows where.—Did I find it? Umph!
Now and then, for a minute or two.

Lord Byron, *Detached Thoughts*, #55.

Like many others, she [Lady Blessington] could not believe that he was sincere in both his sentimental and his cynical expressions, that his longings and his ironic recognition of the unideal nature of the world and himself were but two sides of the same coin.

L. A. Marchand, *Byron*, vol. 3, p. 1065.

5. *Lord Byron's Correspondence*, II, 24. Letter of Nov. 27, 1816.
† From *From Sensibility to Romanticism: Essays Presented to Frederick A.*
Pottle, edited by Frederick W. Hilles and Harold Bloom (New York: Oxford University Press, 1965), pp. 467–86.

When Swinburne and Arnold praised Byron for his excellence of sincerity and strength they were alluding to *Childe Harold* as well as *Don Juan*; today most critics find Byron's sincerity and strength in the ottava rima poems alone—in *Beppo, The Vision of Judgment,* and *Don Juan.* When we consider that the generality of this opinion is an entirely modern phenomenon (E. H. Coleridge lists forty-six editions of *Childe Harold* before 1900 as against fourteen of *Don Juan*)[1] we may conclude that behind it lies one of those reversals in taste that F. A. Pottle[2] has named "shifts of sensibility." It is a shift that tells us, probably, more about ourselves than about Byron, and has blinded us on occasion to essential qualities in the very poems we like best.

Certainly, the current preference for Byron's satirical over his romantic poetry has sometimes accompanied a notion of his poetic development that does not correspond to the facts. "Only as Don Juan," declared Mr. T. S. Eliot, does Byron "get nearer the truth about himself." "His steady growth to adult sanity . . . can be followed in the ottava rima poems," says Mr. Ronald Bottrall: "In them he exchanged his falsetto for a speaking voice."[3] I think we should understand such remarks as reflections of the critic's preference for one of Byron's two principal styles, rather than as descriptions of his spiritual history. For we are all aware that the two styles existed side by side throughout Byron's career; that the "falsetto" and the "speaking voice" alternated in the juvenilia; that *Beppo* was finished before *Childe Harold* IV; that *Cain* was composed in the midst of *Don Juan*; and that *The Island* (in Grierson's view the best of the romantic tales) was the last major poem that Byron completed.[4] Professor Marchand rightly observed that "Byron did not, as has sometimes been said, abandon Childe Harold entirely when he took up Don Juan. Just as the facetious and satiric vein had continued to flow in his letters when the world knew him only as Childe Harold, so now he carried with him into the new poem many of the moods that belonged to that gloomy egoist."[5] Although it is valid and convenient to distinguish between Byron's early, middle, and late poetry, or to classify individual poems as "romantic" or "satiric," it is not true that the divisions into periods mark off significant changes in Byron's outlook or that the classifica-

1. *The Works of Lord Byron. Poetry,* ed. E. H. Coleridge, 7 vols. (London, 1898–1905), VII, pp. 89–310.
2. Pottle, of Yale University, is a distinguished scholar of English literature of the eighteenth and early nineteenth centuries. [*Editor.*]
3. T. S. Eliot, "Byron," p. 198; Ronald Bottrall, "Byron and the Colloquial Tradition in English Poetry," pp. 212, 216; both in M. H. Abrams, ed., *English Romantic Poets. Modern Essays in Criticism* (New York, 1960).

4. In a letter that requested Murray's opinion of "the new Juans and the translations and the Vision [of Judgment]" Byron called his romantic poem, *The Prophecy of Dante,* "the best thing I ever wrote, if it be not *unintelligible.*" See *The Works of Lord Byron. Letters and Journals,* ed. R. E. Prothero, 6 vols. (London, 1898–1905), IV, p. 422.
5. L. A. Marchand, ed., *Don Juan,* Riverside Edition (Cambridge, Mass., 1958); p. xii.

tions, "romantic" and "satiric" reflect "a sharply contradictory spirit, divided against itself."[6] Byron is the single major romantic poet who in his poetry preserved his early outlook for more than a decade, and, as far as can be judged, he preserved it to his death. Behind Byron's contradictions, there is, I think, a unity and consistency that embraces all his moods and styles. In this essay, which, for convenience, deals largely with *Don Juan*, I shall focus my comments on a few aspects of Byron's work that are fundamental to all his poetry. I shall emphasize the "romantic" elements in *Don Juan* not simply to attack its reputation for up-to-date toughmindedness, but primarily to uncover what seems to me its inner form.

I begin by pointing to the undertone of melancholy that *Don Juan* shares with the rest of Byron's work. Take, as the nearest example, the fragment that introduces the modern editions of *Don Juan*:

> I would to Heaven that I were so much clay,
>   As I am blood, bone, marrow, passion, feeling—
> Because at least the past were passed away,
>   And for the future—(but I write this reeling,
> Having got drunk exceedingly to-day,
>   So that I seem to stand upon the ceiling)
> I say—the future is a serious matter—
> And so—for God's sake—hock and soda-water!

The tone is that of a man on the point of moving from drunkenness to sobriety. He has not yet relinquished the insouciance of drunkenness, yet recognizes that all the gaiety is about to pass. It is a middle point between inebriation and sobriety—musing on both. This kind of structure is central in Byron's poetry: the present moment, if happy, is clouded by the knowledge of an inevitable collapse; if unhappy, it is clouded by the knowledge of some glorious possibility which has been denied to us.[7] In this instance, the moment of drunkenness is a bright instant between a past that Byron wants to forget and a future that *is* a serious matter.[8] (Hock and soda-water is Byron's standard antidote to hangovers.) Presumably the speaker has got drunk to forget the past, because the past was a series of baffled hopes and lapses from momentary perfections. Not being clay, but passion and feeling, he cannot forget these failures, and, as a man of feeling, he cannot be reconciled to them; their pang persists. The undertone of melancholy expresses a constant recognition of the central Byronic experience:

6. W. J. Calvert, *Byron. Romantic Paradox* (Chapel Hill, N.C., 1935), p. 54.
7. Byron defined his "mobility" as "an excessive susceptibility of immediate impressions—at the same time without *losing* the past: and is . . . a most painful and unhappy attribute." See Byron's note to *Don Juan*, XVI, 97.
8. Compare: "The best of Life is but intoxication: / Glory, the Grape, Love, Gold, in these are sunk / The hopes of all men, and of every nation" *Don Juan*, II, 179.

I yet might be most happy. I will clasp thee,
And we *again* will be—
> [the figure vanishes]
> My heart is crushed!
> (*Manfred*, I, i, 190 f. My italics)

If one universalizes this experience, one suffers what the Germans call Weltschmerz,[9] a condition which Professor Rose has defined as "the psychic state that ensues when there is a sharp contrast between a man's ideals and his material environment, and his temperament is such as to eliminate the possibility of any sort of reconciliation between the two."[1] This is a definition that sounds remarkably like Byron's explanation of Cain's state of mind, his "rage and fury against the inadequacy of his state to his conceptions."[2] Cain himself expressed his feelings in Byron's favorite symbol for a man's bafflement: the conflict between "clay" and "spirit":

> But if that high thought were
> Link'd to a servile mass of matter—and,
> Knowing such things, aspiring to such things,
> And science still beyond them, were chained down
> To the most gross and petty paltry wants,
> All foul and fulsome. . . .
> (*Cain*, II, i. 50 ff.)

This Byronic refusal to accept complacently the inadequacy of man's state to his conceptions is an element in *Don Juan* that tends to distinguish the satire in that poem from the satire of Pope. For Pope, man's bafflement is far less serious and far more easily resolved. Here is his version of Cain's dilemma:

> He hangs between; in doubt to act or rest;
> In doubt to deem himself a God or Beast;
> In doubt his mind or body to prefer;
> Born but to die and reas'ning but to err.
> (*An Essay on Man*, II, ll. 7–10.)

The contradictions are acknowledged, but implicitly resolved by the idea of a compromise. "Created half to rise and half to fall," man "hangs between." When Pope leaves man in ignorance "whether he thinks too little or too much" his phrasing implies that man should do neither, that the proper course for a creature in a "middle state" is a middle course—the one course that is not open to Manfred:

> Half dust, half deity, alike unfit
> To sink or soar, with our mixed essence make
> A conflict of its elements and breathe

---

9. World-weariness. [*Editor.*]
1. William Rose, *From Goethe to Byron. The Development of Weltschmerz in German Literature* (London, 1924), p. 5.
2. *Letters and Journals*, V, p. 470.

The breath of degradation and of pride
Contending with low wants and lofty will
Till our mortality predominates

(Manfred, I, ii, ll. 40–45.)

The emphasis is not on man's middle state, but on his double state, on his inevitable inner conflict. There is no middle way, no compromise and no solution except death.

This tendency to reject compromise gives Byron's satires on "the human biped" their special, "melancholy merriment":[3]

Love's a capricous power: I've know it hold
Out through a fever caused by its own heat,
But be much puzzled by a cough and cold,
And find a quinsy very hard to treat;
Against all noble maladies he's bold,
But vulgar illnesses don't like to meet,
Nor that a sneeze should interrupt his sigh,
Nor inflammations redden his blind eye.

But worst of all is nausea, or a pain
About the lower region of the bowels.

(Don Juan II, 22–3.)

This commentary on Juan's seasickness may be supposed to puncture Juan's cant about his not being able to forget Julia, and thus to satirize his hyperboles. But are the hyperboles wrong? Does Byron implicitly admonish us, "love neither too little nor too much"? That is not suggested at the height of the Haidée episode.[4] The tone of these lines is good-humored, but laughter can be a mode of accommodating life when one is not completely reconciled to life. I find that Byron's laughter in *Don Juan* frequently has this melancholy undertone—particularly when the comic disporportion involves, as in this case, that conflict between clay and spirit which preoccupied Manfred and Cain:

And the sad truth that hovers o'er my desk
Turns what was once romantic to burlesque.

And if I laugh at any mortal thing
'Tis that I may not weep; and if I weep,
'Tis that our nature cannot always bring
Itself to apathy.[5]

(Don Juan, IV, 3–4.)

3. See *Letters and Journals*, V, p. 187, and *Don Juan*, VII, 89.
4. Compare *Don Juan*, IV, 26.
5. Compare: "People have wondered at the Melancholy which runs through my writings. Others have wondered at my personal gaiety; but I recollect once, after an hour in which I had been sincerely and particularly gay, and rather brilliant in company, my wife replying to me when I said (upon her remarking my high spirits) "and yet, Bell, I have been called and mis-called Melancholy—you must have seen how falsely, frequently." "No B.," (she answered) "it is not so: at *heart* you are the most melancholy of mankind, and often when apparently gayest." *Letters and Journals*, V, p. 446.

To describe the acceptance of life-as-it-is by the pejorative word "apathy" discloses a deeply rooted unwillingness to accept life-as-it-is. But what can such unwillingness consist of? It can, in moments of pride, imply a shaking of the fist at Providence, as in "Prometheus," or *Cain*, but that is primarily the expression of a *Weltschmerz* that has lost its patience, and is not Byron's most frequent tone—which is melancholic and ironic rather than titanic. I think that Byron's recurrent unwillingness to accept the mixed character of experience is rooted in his special sort of religious faith, the most accurate (if not the most sympathetic) description of which was written by T. E. Hulme in his attack on romantic poetry:

> You don't believe in Heaven, so you begin to believe in a heaven on earth, . . . and as there is always the bitter contrast between what you think you ought to be able to do and what man actually can, [romanticism] always tends, in its later stages at any rate to be gloomy.
> (*Speculations*, London, 1924, pp. 118–19.)

To believe in a heaven on earth is to believe in the *possibility* of an earthly perfection, and this was a faith that Byron never relinquished.

Byron's hopes and values were entirely terrestrial. He shocked some of his contemporaries not only by rejecting the consoling idea of Heaven, but also by rejecting with disdain the trepidations of Hell.[6] When Cain shakes his fist at providence he does so because he disbelieves that his ills will be compensated for in some other world; he knows that what is wrong *ici bas* is totally and ultimately wrong:

> There woos no home, nor hope, nor life,
> save what is here.
> (*Childe Harold*, IV, 105.)[7]

One reason Byron could so vigorously resist posthumous consolations was that he never gave up his hope of the terrestrial paradise. It is true that he often denied such a possibility in *Childe Harold* and *Don Juan*, but his very preoccupation with the discrepancy between life as it is and as it should be, discloses how uncertain such denials were. To the question, "What is poetry?" Byron gave an answer that is valid certainly for his own poetry: "The feeling of a Former world and a Future." The phrase partakes of the Byronic melancholy—the feeling of a past golden age that contrasts bitterly

---

6. As in *Childe Harold* I: "It is the settled, ceaseless gloom / The fabled Hebrew Wanderer bore; / That will not look beyond the tomb, / But cannot hope for rest before."

7. About the ending of his drama *Heaven and Earth* Byron once remarked: "I once thought of conveying the lovers to the moon or one of the planets; but it is not easy for the imagination to make any unknown world more beautiful than this." Quoted from Medwin, *Journal of the Conversations of Lord Byron* (London, 1824) by E. H. Coleridge in *Poetry*, V, p. 321.

with the present. On the other hand, the melancholy does not lapse into apathy because it is sustained by the hope of future perfection: "In all human affairs," Byron added in the journal entry from which I have just quoted, "it is Hope-Hope-Hope."[8]

This positive side of Byron's melancholy needs to be emphasized. Professor Ridenour has brilliantly shown that the metaphors of *Don Juan* persistently refer to a collapse from a former world, a Fall from Eden.[9] While this is the most helpful observation on *Don Juan* that I have encountered in recent criticism it is one that requires a corrective footnote: in all Byron's poetry the periodic recurrence of a Fall is predicated on the periodic recurrence of a Redemption. Byron, for all his protective irony, hated the idea of permanent unregeneracy as much as he hated the idea of a permanent Hell. The notion of a Future Eden is implicit, for example, in the political faith for which he died, and for which, at times, he wrote:

> For I will teach, if possible, the stones
> To rise against Earth's tyrants. Never let it
>   Be said that we still truckle unto thrones;—
> But ye—our children's children! think how we
> Showed *what things were* before the World was free!
>
> That hour is not for us, but 'tis for you:
>   And as, in the great joy of your Millennium,
> You hardly will believe such things were true
>   As now occur, I thought that I would pen you'em;
> But may their very memory perish too!—
>
>   (*Don Juan*, VIII, 135–6.)

Although words like "Eden" and "Paradise" are scattered throughout *Don Juan*, they do not usually refer to a future state of society, but rather to a state of nature or to a perfect love relationship, or, as in the Haidée episode, to both at once. It is generally an Eden from which all trace of guilt or taint has been removed—the guilt of "clay" or the taint of "civilization." Here is the way Byron imagines the life of "General Boone, backwoodsman of Kentucky:"

> He was not all alone: around him grew
>   A sylvan tribe of children of the chase,
> Whose young, unwakened world was ever new,
>   Nor sword nor sorrow yet had left a trace
> On her unwrinkled brow, nor could you view
>   A frown on Nature's or on human face;
> The free-born forest found and kept them free,
> And fresh as is a torrent or a tree.
>
>   (*Don Juan*, VIII, 65)

8. *Letters and Journals*, V, 189–90.
9. G. M. Ridenour, *The Style of* Don Juan (New Haven, 1960), pp. 19–89.

Among all these recurrent visions of Edenic purity and perfection in Byron's poetry, the most important is the vision of a totally self-less and totally fulfilling love relationship. That is the principal earthly paradise in the earliest as well as the latest poetry, from the lines:

> Some portion of paradise still is on earth,
>   And Eden revives in the first kiss of love.
>   (1807, "The First Kiss of Love")

to the lines:

> Paradise was breathing in the sigh
> Of nature's child in nature's ecstasy.
>   (1823, *The Island*, III, 195ff.)

Of this ideal, Byron once remarked in his journal, "My earliest dreams (as most boys dreams are) were martial, but a little later they were all for love and retirement."[1] The association of "love" with "retirement" again suggests the idea of an untainted love: it is a retirement from the world and the world's taint, and from the taint of mere lust or "clay" as well. This impulse shows itself (*pace* Mr. Wilson Knight)[2] in Byron's lifelong male friendships and his fondness for young boys. The attraction was, I believe, less homosexual than trans-sexual. Here was a relationship that was not (at least not consciously) tainted by lust, and therefore could be perfectly selfless and spiritual: "a violent though *pure* love and passion"—that is Byron's phrase for "the then romance of the most romantic period of my life."[3] The same purity distinguishes the love of Juan and Hailee:

> When two pure hearts are pour'd in one another
>   And love too much, and yet cannot love less;
> But almost sanctify the sweet excess
>   By the immortal wish and power to bless. . . .[4]
>   (*Don Juan*, IV, 26.)

Byron's concern to preserve the possibility of genuinely pure love manifests itself in his description of the relationship between Juan

1. *Letters and Journals*, V, p. 426.
2. G. Wilson Knight, in such books as *Lord Byron: Christian Virtues* (1952) has argued that Byron's homosexuality was a consciously adopted, Christian moral attitude. [*Editor.*]
3. *Letters and Journals*, V, p. 168.
4. A particularly striking example of Byron's idealization of love is found in *The Island*, II, ll. 370–97. There as elsewhere Byron uses religious words like "sanctify," "bless," and "heaven," to express the ultimacy of the experience. The lover is compared to a religious devotee: "Is love less potent? No—his path is trod / Alike uplifted gloriously to God; / Or linked to all we know of heaven below." (ll. 374–6).
The third line is more typical than the second. Despite T. E. Hulme's bias against the romantic poets his expression, "spilt religion," seems to me an accurate description of romantic faith. See *Speculations* (London, 1924), p. 118.

and Leila, the orphan girl Juan took to Russia. Indeed, this concern is the most probable reason for her being brought into the story.

> Don Juan loved her, and she loved him, as
>   Nor brother, father, sister, daughter love.—[5]
> I cannot tell exactly what it was;
>   He was not yet quite old enough to prove
> Parental feelings and the other class,
>   Called brotherly affection, could not move
> His bosom,—for he never had a sister:
> Ah! if he had—how much he would have missed her!
> And still less was it sensual;

And here Byron performs one of those brilliant maneuvers by which he manages to salvage his ideal without in the least denying its precariousness:

>   for besides
>   That he was not an ancient debauchee,
> (Who like sour fruit, to stir their veins' salt tides,
>   As acids rouse a dormant alkali,)
> Although (*'twill* happen as our planet guides)
>   His youth was not the chastest that might be,
> There was the purest Platonism at bottom
> Of all his feelings—only he forgot 'em.
>
>   (*Don Juan*, X, 55–54.)

But in this case (as the planet does now and then guide), Juan had not forgot 'em:

> Just now there was no peril of temptation;
>   He loved the infant orphan he had saved,
> As patriots (now and then) may love a nation;
>
>   (*Don Juan*, X, 55.)

It is true that in *Don Juan*, as in all Byron's poems, such ideal relationships fail. That is the "sad truth" which sustains both the undercurrent of melancholy in the poem and its explicit ironies. On the other hand, it is remarkable that *Don Juan* is more protective of such ideals than *Childe Harold* or the early verse romances. For the central figure in those poems had been a melancholy, taciturn figure whose

> early dreams of good outstripped the truth
> And troubled manhood followed baffled youth.
>
>   (*Lara*, ll. 323–4.)

In *Don Juan* on the other hand, the central figure never experiences a genuine betrayal of the heart. Juan's relationship with Haidee is

---

5. Compare: "Juan and Haidée gazed upon each other / With swimming looks of speechless tenderness, / Which mixed all feelings—friend, child, lover, brother." (*Don Juan*, IV, 26).

not betrayed from within, and his dream of good does not outstrip the truth:

> For them to be
> Thus was another Eden; they were never
> Weary, unless when separate.
>
> (*Don Juan*, IV, 10.)

The betrayal comes only from the outside, and that in itself is not a disillusioning experience. There is no disloyalty and no failure of love for Juan; all these melancholy disillusionments are allotted to the narrator of the poem, whose irony and cynicism relieve Juan of any outright cynicism of his own. It seems significant to me that Byron's announced intent to make Juan gradually *"blasé"* and *"gaté"* never comes close to being realized.[6] The closest Juan got to this was in his dalliance with Catherine the Great, and there he preserved the ideal of pure love by becoming literally sick of degraded love, and by remaining loyal to the orphan girl, Leila. Juan never relinquishes his "purest Platonism at bottom."

Finally, in the last episode of the poem, Juan encounters another pure soul whose very name, Aurora, calls up, in the midst of an English houseparty, "the former world":

> In figure, she had something of Sublime
> In eyes which sadly shone, as Seraphs' shine.
>   All Youth—but with an aspect beyond Time;
>   Radiant and grave—as pitying Man's decline;
>   Mournful—but mournful of another's crime,
> She looked as if she sat by Eden's door,
> And grieved for those who could return no more.
>
> (*Don Juan*, XV, 45.)

Why is Aurora introduced into the story? I strongly suspect that she is there for the same reason Leila is there, and Leila serves no important function in the plot. She is there to preserve the possibility of the ideal and to renew the imagination of the hero and the narrator as well:

> And, certainly, Aurora had renewed
>   In him some feelings he had lately lost,
> Or hardened; feelings which, perhaps ideal,
> Are so divine, that I must deem them real:—
>
> The love of higher things and better days:
>   The unbounded hope, and heavenly ignorance
> Of what is called the World, and the World's ways;
>   The moments when we gather from a glance
> More joy than from all future pride or praise,

---

6. See *Letters and Journals*, V, p. 242.

> Which kindle manhood, but can ne'er entrance
> The Heart in an existence of its own,
> Of which another's bosom is the zone.
>
> (*Don Juan*, XVI, 107–8.)

These recurrent visions of an earthly perfection bear witness to the power of Byron's persistent faith in the possibilities of life. It was a faith that suffered from attacks launched continually by his own invincible honesty, but it also prevailed to the end. Byron's chips were all on this world: the great distinction of his epic was that it was "true" and his most approving footnote was "Fact!" But the world on which he staked everything was always one in which spirit could (now and then) conquer clay, where selfless love and genuine heroism were not only possible but were, as his true epic showed, sometimes actually to be found.

II

Of all Byron's poems *Don Juan* is the most Byronic not because it is more honest or less posing than the others (Byron never poses) but because it contains more of his astonishingly varied moods than any other: gloom, ecstasy, flippancy, indignation, pride, self-immersion, self-assertion, guilt, insouciance, sentimentality, nostalgia, optimism, pessimism. In the preceding section I attempted to show that beneath many of these moods resides a melancholy refusal to accept the truth that perfection is impossible in life, and a recurrent impulse to depict momentary fulfillments which confirm and sanction this precarious secular faith. Now my purpose will be to qualify and amplify this general point in order to bring it closer to the incredible variousness of the poetry that Byron actually wrote. The danger in generalizing about the whole corpus of a poet's work is, of course, that the work can become merely a source of data to illustrate the generalization. I hope to convince the reader that my intent is to free Byron's poetry, and particularly *Don Juan*, from generalizations that make it seem more narrow and uniform than it is. Generalizations are necessary tools of criticism: the task is to discover the ones that most nearly fit.

One generalization that emphatically does not fit *Don Juan* is that it preserves a unity of tone. Mr. Andrew Rutherford is surely right (as he so often is) when he observes that Byron frequently evokes both a serious and a frivolous response "to the same event without having any apparent satiric purpose in so doing."[7] The following juxtaposition of tones is not untypical:

> Even Conscience too, has a tough job
> To make us understand each good old maxim,
> So good I wonder Castlereigh don't tax 'em.
>
> And now 'twas done—on the lone shore were plighted

---

7. Andrew Rutherford, *Byron. A Critical Study* (Edinburgh, 1961), p. 161.

Their hearts; the stars their nuptial torches shed
Beauty upon the beautiful they lighted.
                              (*Don Juan*, II, 203–4.)

Hazlitt, among Byron's contemporaries, was the most memorable,
though not the only, critic who found himself unable to admire
these swift changes of tone:

> A classical intoxication is followed by the splashing of soda-water,
> by frothy effusions of ordinary bile. After the lightning and the
> hurricane, we are introduced to the interior of the cabin and the
> contents of wash-hand basins. The solemn hero of tragedy plays
> *Scrub* in the farce. This is 'very tolerable and not to be endured.'
> The Noble Lord is almost the only writer who has prostituted his
> talents in this way. He hallows in order to desecrate; takes a
> pleasure in defacing the images of beauty his hands have
> wrought; and raises our hopes and our belief in goodness only to
> dash them to the earth again, and break them in pieces the more
> effectively from the height they have fallen.
>   (*The Spirit of the Age*, "Lord Byron.")

In a footnote added after Byron's death Hazlitt admitted that
these criticisms were perhaps too strong and were applicable only to
the early parts of *Don Juan*. But despite Hazlitt's exaggerations, his
statement does memorably point to the tonal inconsistencies of
Don Juan. (Yet one does want to reply to Hazlitt that if *Don Juan*
moved only towards deflation, paradox, and satire, and never
towards elevation, hope, and sentimentality, then one could not
complain that one's hopes are always being tricked—and *Don Juan*
would be a far duller poem than it is. The passage from Byron
quoted above illustrates this contrary kind of tonal shift.)

Let it be stated bluntly, then, that *Don Juan*, though in its own
way a unified poem, has no unity of tone. It has no unity of outlook. It has not even unity of theme. I strongly suspect that some
discussions of *Don Juan* "as a poem" have tried to demonstrate its
conformity to standards of unity that are too narrowly formalistic or
conventional. Mr. Lovell, for example, finds a thematic consistency:
"That unifying principle, I suggest, is the principle of thematic unity—here the basically ironic theme of appearance versus reality."[8] So
also finds Mr. Ridenour: "The poet's seemingly most irrelevant
aside or digression is likely to turn out on examination to be
another way of dramatizing his central paradox," i.e., that the means
of grace is an occasion of sin.[9] Mr. Ridenour's comment is closer to
the poem than Mr. Lovell's; indeed, it is valid for the greater part of
Don Juan, and reflects Byron's preoccupation with the conflict of
clay and spirit in man. But there are other times (as I showed in
the preceding section) when Byron expressly rejects this paradox.

8. E. J. Lovell, Jr., "Irony and Image in   9. *The Style of* Don Juan, p. ix.
Don Juan," in Abrams, op. cit. p. 231.

There can be no unity of theme in *Don Juan* because there is no stability of attitude. Thematically, doctrinally, tonally, it is a poem that is founded on contradictions.

If we take the most important theme in Byron's poetry—the theme of love—the nature of these contradictions comes into sharp relief. At one moment love may be "the immortal wish and power to bless"; at another, it may be something quite different:

> And that's enough, for love is vanity
> Selfish in its beginning as its end.
>
> (*Don Juan*, IX, 73.)

And, most frequently, it is the ironic, tragi-comic conflict of selfishness with unselfishness, clay with spirit:

> The Sovereign was smitten;
> Juan much flattered by her love or lust;—
> I cannot stop to alter words once written,
> And the *two* are so mixed with human dust
> That he who *names one*, both perchance may hit on.
>
> (*Don Juan*, IX, 77.)

These are, of course, not merely logical contradictions; they are emotional contradictions—radically different responses to the same event. They reflect Byron's own mobility—his swift changes and contradictions of mood.

That such mobility was one of the most striking characteristics of Byron's temperament is a fact that he commented on more than once, and it was also a characteristic of his imagination both in poetry and prose. In his personal journal one finds precisely the same pattern of conflicting moods as in *Don Juan*. The following two passages from one day's journal entry are found on a single page in the Prothero edition.[1] The first is a typically Juanesque commentary on the mixed character of experience:

> The infinity of wishes lead but to disappointment. All the discoveries which have yet been made have multiplied little but existence. An extirpated disease is succeeded by some new pestilence, and a discovered world has brought little to the old one, except the p[ox] first and freedom afterwards—the latter a fine thing, particularly as they gave it to Europe in exchange for slavery.

At this point Byron paused to receive visitors and listen to some music. He returned to write the following:

> But onward!—it is now the time to act, and what signifies *self*, if a single spark of that which would be worthy of the past can be bequeathed unquenchably to the future! It is not one man, nor a million, but the *spirit* of liberty which must be spread. The waves which dash upon the shore are, one by one, broken, but yet the ocean conquers nevertheless.

1. *Letters and Journals*, V, p. 163.

In the future it will be not freedom *and* the pox, not freedom *and* slavery, but the final defeat of all vitiations of freedom. These same shifts of mood determine Byron's alternating acceptance and rejection of original sin; his waverings on the doctrine of immortality, his use of the same kind of argument to prove and to disprove that the soul is immortal.[2]

The literary question that arises from the tonal contradictions of *Don Juan* is the obvious one: Wherein lies its unity? I believe that its felt unity resides neither in its theme nor its tone but in the *pattern* of its moods. The more precise question would be: How do the divergent moods of *Don Juan* fit together to form an understandable pattern? The unity of *Don Juan* is not logical but psychological; its logic is what the Germans call *Seelenlogik*.[3]

Mr. Rutherford makes the point very concisely when he says of *Don Juan*: "More fundamental is the unity (if one can call it that), the consistency even in inconsistencies that comes from its being unmistakably the product of a single although complex mind."[4] That, as I understand it, is another way of saying that the variety of moods and the inconsistency of ideas in *Don Juan* are exemplifications of Byron's moods and Byron's ideas, that the unity of the poem resides in the unifying idea: Byron.[5] But even when we understand that self-expression is a primary impulse in all of Byron's poetry, and that his own personality constitutes a great deal of its substance, we are still puzzled by the question: "What connects all these moods in Byron himself?"

I ask this question somewhat hesitantly in the face of Professor Ridenour's incisive comments on the importance of the author's "persona" in *Don Juan*.[6] But I think it fair to argue that in most of *Don Juan* the persona and the man himself are so mixed and fused, the "real" Byron and the projected Byron so deliberately identified that it is quite impossible to disentangle them. What are we to make of recurrent asides such as "I have a passion for the name of Mary"? Is not the distinction between that "I" and the person who enunciates it simply the distinction between any real person and the personality he projects in speech?[7] It seems to me that the Byron projected in *Don Juan* is the Byron projected in his conversations, his letters, and his journals; it is, in fact, the only Byron we really know.

How then, do all these clashing moods cohere in Byron's person-

2. See, for instance, *Letters and Journals*, V, p. 211, 456–7.
3. "The logic of the soul." [*Editor.*]
4. *Byron, A Critical Study*, p. 142.
5. The idea is not simply a biographical one; it is also a formal, literary idea, because *Don Juan* belongs to a poetic genre whose chief *formal* intention is self-expression, and whose formal unity resides in its noble author's projected personality. This is an important, By-

ronic element in all Byron's poetry, and we do well to add the adjective "Byronic" to genre classifications of *Don Juan* such as "epic satire."
6. *The Style of* Don Juan, pp. 89–124.
7. See the discussion of the linguistic "dédoublement de la personalité" in Charles Bally, *Linguistique générale et linguistique française*, 2nd ed. (Bern, 1944), p. 39.

ality? I suggest that they are all sponsored by the two central experiences discussed in the first part of this essay: the experience of a fulfillment and the disillusioning experience of its collapse. These are not, of course, peculiarly Byronic experiences, but they are peculiarly romantic ones. Before Byron was born, Goethe had described the archetypal experience in *Werther*:

> Oh, when we rush up to it, when the distant *there* becomes *here*, everything is as it was before and we stand hemmed in by our poverty.
>
> (21 June)

And Byron echoes it in "The Dream:"

> What is it but the telescope of truth
> Which strips the distance of its fantasies
> And brings life near in utter nakedness,
> Making the cold reality too real?
>
> (ll. 181–4)

But this experience of disillusionment would not constantly recur were it not for a recurrence of faith in the distant "there," and this faith, in turn, could not be preserved if one did not (now and then) experience earnests of possible perfection. These ideal visions of the past or the future, and even sometimes of the present, preserve the possibility of disillusionment.

It follows that all the moods of Byron's poetry are so many versions of the three principal moods that arise from these experiences. The three moods are: (1) the ecstatic, corresponding to the vision or experience of perfect fulfillment; (2) the ironic (which may be humorous, melancholic, or both at once) corresponding to the experience of a less than ideal reality; and (3) the cynical, corresponding to the complete failure of the ideal. In the last, relatively infrequent mood, Byron is capable of comments like "*What* are *all* things but a *show?*"[8] But, of course, it is the ironic mood that is central in all his poetry, from beginning to end.

This triadic notion is not so arbitrary as it may at first seem. It reflects, for example, Byron's preoccupation with the conflict of clay and spirit in man, his feeling that at times we are all spirit—and even at times all clay, but that most of the time we are an ironic mixture of both. The triad corresponds to the fluctuations in his attitude to women, whom he regarded in different moments as seraphs, as inscrutable paradoxes, and as "fine animals." This may be seen directly in the character delineations of the women in *Don Juan*. First, we encounter Julia, that mixture of animality and delicacy, loyalty and hypocrisy. The ironic-comic mode in which her

8. *Don Juan*, VII, 2.

love affair is described exemplifies the ironic mood to which she her-self corresponds. The same association of ironic style with a mixed personality is found in the treatment of Lady Adeline at the other end of the story. Then, there is the ecstatic style in which Byron describes the two pure spirits, Haidee and Aurora. Finally, at the lowest ebb of the poem, there is the ironic-sardonic treatment of Catherine the Great, plain clay if it ever existed.

The pattern of *Don Juan* is, then, the pattern of Byron's "mobili-ty"—his unceasing movement from one attitude to a different one. The logic of that pattern is found in the unresolved conflict between the demands of the ideal and the demands of the real, that is, in Byron's refusal to compromise between his honesty and his faith in the terrestrial paradise. Had he been willing to give in entirely to the experience of disillusionment, his attitude and his style would have remained stable and uniform. Thus, Byron's incon-sistency is the mark and measure of his faith, and his mobility pre-serves his loyalty to that faith. For his melancholy, his irony, his sar-donic laughter are capable at any moment of giving way to an ecstasy that sustains and nourishes. But when that occurs the ideal is never for a long period of time defended against actual experi-ence. Byron avoids a decisive battle by surrendering quickly to nos-talgia or irony, and the pattern is then repeated. His own defense of his protective agility in *Don Juan* was an artistic one: it prevented dullness, sponsored honesty, and lent variety.[9] But this conscious defense simply reinforced a deeper impulse in the poem.

Probably the best metaphor for the unity of *Don Juan* is that of a journey. Travel is the structural principle of his two major poems, and the appropriate symbol of his poetry as a whole. It symbolizes the restless movement of the spirit from object to object, as well as the writing of a poem that has no fixed plan. The very unfixedness of the goal permits the pilgrimage to continue: if politics fails there is nature; if love fails there is travel itself; some beckoning Eden always remains intact. Disappointment is never permanent, scorn never completely fatal, and the pilgrimage never comes to an appointed end. *Don Juan* is, in this symbolic sense, a travel poem. Even in its satiric moods it preserves an intensity which Hazlitt called "the great and prominent distinction of Lord Byron's writ-ings." Even in its laughter one detects the melancholy intensity of Byron's "romantic" style:

> unfound the boon—unslaked the thirst,
> Though to the last in verge of our decay,
> Some phantom lures such as we sought at first.
>
> (*Childe Harold*, IV, 124.)

9. See, for instance, *Don Juan*, VIII, 65, 85.

But the laughter itself has a separate power. Just as Byron's melancholy is a reflex of his faith in the possibilities of the actual world, his laughter is an expression of his allegiance to the actual world in spite of its imperfections: "This unriddled wonder, / The world, which at the worst's a *glorious* blunder.[1] That is a typical remark and the italics are Byron's. This gusto of *Don Juan* is the victory of faith over experience, and if I have emphasized the romantic flavor of Byron's faith, that is in part because I find it behind the gusto of all his poetry, including the poetry of *Don Juan*. His laughter is, no doubt, a finer thing than his gloom, but it is the laughter of a man so attached to this life as to be capable of gloom. Out of this immovable commitment to life came his melancholy and his laughter as well as his excellence of sincerity and strength.

1. *Don Juan*, **XI**, 3.

Images of Byron

The short anthology that follows—by no means an exhaustive one—is designed to indicate two things: first, that from his own lifetime to that of the reader, the figure, myth, and poetry of Byron have loomed importantly in the imaginations of many of our most valued and brilliant writers; and second, that a given writer's stand on what some French critics call *"la question Byron"* can often serve as a good index of that writer's own characteristic strengths and weaknesses. Thus, we are not surprised to find that Ralph Waldo Emerson and T. S. Eliot, two great exponents of the higher seriousness, American style, are both annoyed by Byron's triviality and "rhetorical" pose; or that the aesthetic radical Oscar Wilde and the metaphysical radical Albert Camus say very similar things about Byron as an early modern revolutionary—that is, as a *manqué* version of what they both wished to, and did, become; or that Joyce and Nabokov, two of the most self-conscious novelists of our century, both make brilliant use of the "image" of Byron at crucial points in two of their best novels.

But the list—and additions to the list—could go on virtually forever. Byron during his life longed for a career of action rather than words, and lamented the fact that writers, unlike generals and liberators, do not make history. But history itself has had back its ironies at Byron's expense. Few writers of the European tradition have played as formative a role in the mental history of so many of their successors.

FRANCIS JEFFREY

From the *Edinburgh Review* (April 1814) †

* * * Lord Byron has clear titles to applause, in the spirit and beauty of his diction and versification, and the splendour of many of his descriptions: But it is to his pictures of the stronger passions, that he is indebted for the fulness of his fame. He has delineated, with unequalled force and fidelity, the workings of those deep and powerful emotions which alternately enchant and agonize the minds that are exposed to their inroads; and represented, with a terrible energy, those struggles and sufferings and exaltations, by which the spirit is at once torn and transported, and traits of divine inspiration, or demoniacal possession, thrown across the tamer features of humanity. It is by this spell, chiefly, we think, that he has fixed the admiration of the public; and while other poets delight by their vivacity, or enchant by their sweetness, he alone has been able to *command* the sympathy, even of reluctant readers, by the natural magic of his moral sublimity, and the terrors and attractions of those overpowering feelings, the depths and the heights of which he seems to have so successfully explored. All the considerable poets of

† Francis Jeffrey (1773–1850) was a founder and editor of the highly influential *Edinburgh Review*; he was himself one of the most widely read, powerful, and perceptive critics of the Romantic period.

the present age have, indeed, possessed this gift in a greater or lesser degree: but there is no man, since the time of Shakespeare himself, in whom it has been made manifest with greater fulness and splendour, than in the noble author before us. * * *

LADY CAROLINE LAMB

From *Glenarvon* (1816) †

* * * Lord Glenarvon was of a disposition to attend so wholly to those in whose presence he took delight, that he failed to remember those to whom he had once been attached; so that like the wheels of a watch, the chain of his affections might be said to unwind from the absent, in proportion as they twined themselves around the favourite of the moment; and being extreme in all things, he could not sufficiently devote himself to the one, without taking from the other all that he had given.

It were vain to detail the petty instances of barbarity he employed. The web was fine enough, and wove with a skillful hand. He even consulted with Lady Mandeville in what manner to make his inhuman triumph more poignant—more galling; and when he heard that Calantha was irritated even unto madness, and grieved almost unto death, he only mocked at her folly, and despised her still remaining attachment to himself. "Indeed she is ill," said Sophia, in answer to his insulting inquiry, soon after her arrival at Mortanville Priory. "She is even dangerously ill." "And pray may I ask of what malady?" he replied, with a smile of scorn. "Of one, Lord Glenarvon," she answered with equal irony, "which will never endanger your health—of a broken heart." He laughed. * * *

THOMAS LOVE PEACOCK

From *Nightmare Abbey* (1818) †

* * *

Scythrop.—I should have no pleasure in visiting countries that are past all hope of regeneration. There is great hope of our own;

† At the end of the novel, Lady Caroline literally sends Glenarvon-Byron to Hell; for Byron's reaction, see "Versicles." It is interesting that Robert Bolt, in his screenplay *Lady Caroline Lamb* (1972), either echoes or independently arrives at exactly the same ironic line, "of a broken heart," in his treatment of Lady Caroline's death.

In this passage, the fascinating and evil Glenarvon (Byron) has deserted his lover, the beautiful and sensitive Calantha (Lady Caroline Lamb).

† Peacock's satirical novel attacks the strenuous despair and negativity of many Romantic poets. "Scythrop" is his version of his friend Shelley, "Mr. Flosky" is Coleridge, and "Mr. Cypress," of course, is Byron.

In this passage, Mr. Cypress is preparing to leave England.

and it seems to me that an Englishman, who, either by his station in society, or by his genius, or (as in your instance, Mr. Cypress) by both, has the power of essentially serving his country in its arduous struggle with its domestic enemies, yet forsakes his country, which is still so rich in hope, to dwell in others which are only fertile in the ruins of memory, does what none of those ancients, whose fragmentary memorials you venerate, would have done in similar circumstances.

Mr. Cypress.—Sir, I have quarrelled with my wife; and a man who has quarrelled with his wife is absolved from all duty to his country. I have written an ode to tell the people as much, and they may take it as they list. * * * I have no hope for myself or for others. Our life is a false nature; it is not in the harmony of things; it is an all-blasting upas, whose root is earth, and whose leaves are the skies which rain their poison-dews upon mankind. We wither from our youth; we gasp with unslaked thirst for unattainable good; lured from the first to the last by phantoms—love, fame, ambition, avarice—all idle, and all ill—one meteor of many names, that vanishes in the smoke of death[1]

Mr. Flosky.—A most delightful speech, Mr. Cypress. A most amiable and instructive philosophy. You have only to impress its truth on the minds of all living men, and life will then, indeed, be the desert and the solitude. * * *

ROBERT SOUTHEY

From the Preface to His *Vision of Judgment* (1821) †

* * *

The publication of a lascivious book is one of the worst offences which can be committed against the well-being of society. It is a sin, to the consequences of which no limits can be assigned, and those consequences no after repentance in the writer can counteract. Whatever remorse of conscience he may feel when his hour comes (and come it must!) will be of no avail. The poignancy of a death-bed repentance cannot cancel one copy of the thousands which are sent abroad; and as long as it continues to be read, so long is he the pander of posterity, and so long is he heaping up guilt upon his soul in perpetual accumulation.

* * *

The school which they have set up may properly be called the Satanic school; for though their productions breathe the spirit of

1. The latter section of Cypress's speech is actually a parody of two stanzas (124, 126) of *Childe Harold* IV. [*Editor.*]
† For information on Southey, see the notes to the Dedication of *Don Juan*.
Here Southey attacks Byron as an immoral poet, leader of the "Satanic School."

Belial in their lascivious parts, and the spirit of Moloch in those loathsome images of atrocities and horrors which they delight to represent,[2] they are more especially characterized by a Satanic spirit of pride and audacious impiety, which still betrays the wretched feeling of hopelessness wherewith it is allied.

JOHANN WOLFGANG VON GOETHE

From *Conversations with Eckermann* (1822-32) †

* * *

Lord Byron is to be regarded as a man, an Englishman, and as a great genius. His good qualities belong chiefly to the man, his bad to the Englishman and the peer, his talent is incommensurable.

* * *

His high rank as an English peer was very injurious to Byron; for every talent is oppressed by the outer world,—how much more, then, when there is such high birth and so great a fortune. A certain middle rank is much more favorable to talent, on which account we find all great artists and poets in the middle classes. Byron's predilection for the unbounded could not have been nearly so dangerous with more humble birth and smaller means. But as it was, he was able to put every fancy into practice, and this involved him in innumerable scrapes. Besides, how could one of such high rank be inspired with awe and respect by any rank whatever? He expressed whatever he felt, and this brought him into ceaseless conflict with the world.

* * *

I could not make use of any man as the representative of the modern poetical era except him, who undoubtedly is to be regarded as the greatest genius of our century. Byron is neither antique nor romantic, but like the present day itself. This was the sort of man I required. Then he suited me on account of his unsatisfied nature and his warlike tendency, which led to his death at Missolonghi.

Lord Byron is only great as a poet; as soon as he reflects, he is a child.

2. Belial and Moloch are pagan, Babylonian deities traditionally thought to represent, respectively, the sins of lust and murder.
† Goethe's *Conversations with Ecker-* *mann* were published, posthumously, by J. P. Eckermann (1836–48). They are perhaps the most influential set of literary opinions of the nineteenth century.

STENDHAL

Memories of Lord Byron (1829) †

* * * One evening in the autumn of 1816, I entered M. de Brême's box[3] after an excursion on Lake Como; and I discovered something solemn and subdued about the company there. Everyone was silent, and I was listening to the music, when M. de Brême said to me, indicating the man beside me:

"Monsieur Beyle, this is Lord Byron."

He then introduced Lord Byron to me in the same way. I saw a young man whose eyes reflected pride, with an added quality of generosity; he was not at all large. Then I remembered *Lara*.[4] And on second glance I no longer saw Lord Byron as he actually was, but as I imagined the author of *Lara* ought to be. As the conversation was flagging, M. de Brême sought to get me to speak; but it was impossible: I was filled with timidity and tenderness. Had I dared, I would have wept and kissed Lord Byron's hand. Egged on by M. de Brême's interpolations I attempted to speak, and uttered only commonplaces that did nothing to break the silence reigning over the company that evening. Finally Lord Byron asked me—as the only one there who spoke English—what roads he should take walking back to his inn; it was at the other end of the city, near the fortress. I thought that he was wrong to try walking: at that end of Milan, at midnight, all the shops are closed; he would be wandering along solitary, poorly-lit streets, and without knowing a word of the language.[5] So out of solicitude I was foolish enough to advise him to hire a coach. Instantly, an expression of haughtiness appeared on his face; he gave me to understand, with all politeness, that he had asked me for the route, and not for advice on how to travel it. He then left the box, and I understood why he had imposed such silence upon it.

The haughty but perfectly gentlemanly character of the box's owner had met its match. In Lord Byron's presence, no one wished to run the risk to which that man is exposed who, in the midst of seven or eight silent people, proposes a subject of conversation.

Like a child, Lord Byron exposed himself to the attacks of English high society, that aristocracy all-powerful, inexorable, terrible in

---

† From Stendhal, *Oeuvres Complètes*, v. 35, *Journal Littéraire* (tome 3), ed. Victor Del Litto. (Geneva: 1970), Cercle du Bibliophile, pp. 168–71. Translated by Frank D. McConnell. "Stendhal" was the pseudonym of Henri Beyle.

3. At La Scala, the great opera house of Milan. Ludovic de Brême, son of a former minister of Napoleon, was a friend

of Beyle's in Milan.

4. A romance of Byron's published in 1814. [*Editor*.]

5. Later, of course, Byron was to become quite fluent in Italian; as remarked elsewhere, the stanza of *Don Juan* is in part owed to his reading of Renaissance Italian epic. [*Editor*.]

its vengeance, which makes of so many wealthy sots *very respectable*[6] men, but which cannot, without utter loss of self-control, bear the mockery of its children. The fear generated, throughout Europe, by the great nation led by Danton and Carnot[7] has made the English aristocracy what we see today, this body so strong, so morose, so riddled with hypocrisy.

Lord Byron's mockery is bitter in *Childe Harold*; it is the anger of youth; his mockery is only ironic in *Beppo* and in *Don Juan*. But we must not examine this irony too closely; for instead of gaiety and carelessness, hatred and unhappiness are at its heart. Lord Byron knew how to paint only one man: himself. Moreover he was, and knew himself to be, a nobleman; he wanted to appear as such to the world, and yet he was also a great poet and wished to be admired: two incompatible desires, and an immense source of unhappiness for him.

Never, in any country, has the body of wealthy and well-brought-up persons—those people who pride themselves on titles inherited from their ancestors or on patents of nobility earned by themselves—been able to bear the spectacle of a man surrounded by public admiration and enjoying the general favor of society only because he has written a few hundred fine lines of verse. The aristocracy revenges itself upon other poets by complaining, "Such a personality![8] Such manners!" But these two petty complaints could not be used against Lord Byron. Rather, they weighed upon the heart and turned to hatred. This hatred surfaced in a long poem by a M. Southey[9] who, till that time, was known only for the odes which he regularly addressed to the King of England (the paragon of kings, naturally) on the royal birthday. This M. Southey, sponsored by the Quarterly Review, addressed atrocious slanders to Lord Byron, who at one time was on the point of honoring Southey with a pistol shot.

In his ordinary moments, every day of his life, Lord Byron thought of himself as a nobleman; that was the armor which his delicate spirit, deeply vulnerable to insult, put on against the infinite vulgarity of the herd. *Odi profanum vulgus et arceo*.[1] And it must be admitted that the herd, in England, since it also possesses *spleen*[2] by right of birth, is more atrocious than anywhere else.

6. The phrase, underlined and in English in the original, is, of course, ironic. [*Editor.*]

7. Georges Jacques Danton (1759–94) and Lazare Nicolas Marguerite Carnot (1753–1823) were leaders of the French Revolution; Carnot was also an important statesman in the Napoleonic regime. [*Editor.*]

8. The word Stendhal uses is *ton*, an almost untranslatable term for personality, behavior, manners, and general impression. [*Editor.*]

9. Southey's *Vision of Judgment* (1821). [*Editor.*]

1. From Horace: "I hate the vulgar herd and reject it." [*Editor.*]

2. The word, which connotes in English a kind of nasty, brutish moroseness, was adopted by the French throughout the nineteenth century—to describe what they felt to be a distinctively English gloom. [*Editor.*]

On those days when Lord Byron felt braver against vulgarity of word and deed, that is, when he was less sensitive, his affectations of beauty and stylishness were called into play. And finally, two or three times, perhaps, per week, there were moments (lasting five or six hours) when he was a wise man and, often, a great poet. * * *

THOMAS CARLYLE

From *Sartor Resartus* (1838) †

* * *

I asked myself: What is this that, ever since earliest years, thou hast been fretting and fuming, and lamenting and self-tormenting, on account of? Say it in a word: is it not because thou art not HAPPY? Because the THOU (sweet gentleman) is not sufficiently honoured, nourished, soft-bedded, and lovingly cared-for? Foolish soul! What Act of Legislature was there that *thou* shouldst be Happy? A little while ago thou hadst no right to *be* at all. What if thou wert born and predestined not to be Happy, but to be Unhappy! Art thou nothing other than a Vulture, then, that fliest through the Universe seeking after somewhat to *eat*; and shrieking dolefully because carrion enough is not given thee? Close thy *Byron*; open thy *Goethe*.

GUSTAVE FLAUBERT

From His Letters

To Ernest Chevalier, September 13, 1838

Really I profoundly value only two men, Rabelais and Byron, the only two who have written in a spirit of malice toward the human race and with the intention of laughing in its face. What a tremendous position a man occupies who places himself in such a relation to the world!

To Alfred Le Poittevin, May 26, 1845

Two days ago I saw Byron's name written on one of the pillars of the dungeon where the prisoner of Chillon was confined. This sight afforded me great joy. I thought more about Byron than about the

---

† This very famous passage of Carlyle's is one of the first, most influential and most powerful, Victorian indictments of what came to be regarded as Byron's "unhealthy" nihilism and unbelief.

Here Carlyle's mouthpiece character, Teufelsdröckh, is in process of converting himself from Romantic, Byronic self-pity to an assertive, "healthy" frame of mind.

prisoner, and no ideas came to me about tyranny and slavery. All the time I thought of the pale man who one day came there, walked up and down, wrote his name on the stone, and left. One would have to be very daring or very stupid to write one's name in such a place after that.

RALPH WALDO EMERSON

From *Thoughts on Modern Literature* (1840)

* * * All over the modern world the educated and susceptible have betrayed their discontent with the limits of our municipal life, and with the poverty of our dogmas of religion and philosophy. They betray this impatience by fleeing for resource to a conversation with Nature, which is courted in a certain moody and exploring spirit, as if they anticipated a more intimate union of man with the world than has been known in recent ages. Those who cannot tell what they desire or expect still sigh and struggle with indefinite thoughts and vast wishes. The very child in the nursery prattles mysticism, and doubts and philosophizes. A wild striving to express a more inward and infinite sense characterizes the works of every art. The music of Beethoven is said, by those who understand it, to labor with vaster conceptions and aspirations than music has attempted before. This feeling of the Infinite has deeply colored the poetry of the period. This new love of the vast, always native in Germany, was imported into France by De Staël, appeared in England in Coleridge, Wordsworth, Byron, Shelley, * * * and finds a most genial climate in the American mind. Scott and Crabbe, who formed themselves on the past, had none of this tendency; their poetry is objective. In Byron, on the other hand, it predominates; but in Byron it is blind, it sees not its true end—an infinite good, alive and beautiful, a life nourished on absolute beatitudes, descending into Nature to behold itself reflected there. His will is perverted, he worships the accidents of society, and his praise of Nature is thieving and selfish.

HARRIET BEECHER STOWE

From *Uncle Tom's Cabin* (1850)

* * *

St. Clare[3] had one of those natures which could better and more

3. "St. Clare" is the amoral, charming, "Byronic" slaveholder of Mrs. Stowe's famous novel. Mrs. Stowe was later to become the confidante of Lady Byron, and in 1870, in *Lady Byron Vindicated*, she published the most shocking and anti-Byronic version of their unhappy marriage.

clearly conceive of religious things from its own perceptions and instincts, than many a matter-of-fact and practical Christian. The gift to appreciate and the sense to feel the finer shades and relations of moral things, often seems an attribute of those whose whole life shows a careless disregard of them. Hence Moore, Byron, Goethe, often speak words more wisely descriptive of the true religious sentiment, than another man, whose whole life is governed by it. In such minds, disregard of religion is a more fearful treason, a more deadly sin.

* * *

MATTHEW ARNOLD

[Byron] (1881) †

* * * In spite of his prodigious vogue, Byron has never yet, perhaps, had the serious admiration which he deserves. * * * Even of his passionate admirers, how many never got beyond the theatrical Byron, from whom they caught the fashion of deranging their hair, or of knotting their neck-handkerchief, or of leaving their shirt-collar unbuttoned; how few profoundly felt his vital influence, the influence of his splendid and imperishable excellence of sincerity and strength!

His own aristocratic class, whose cynical make-believe drove him to fury; the great middle-class, on whose impregnable Philistinism he shattered himself to pieces,—how little have either of these felt Byron's vital influence! As the inevitable break-up of the old order comes, as the English middle-class slowly awakens from its intellectual sleep of two centuries, as our actual present world, to which this sleep has condemned us, shows itself more clearly,—our world of an aristocracy materialised and null, a middle-class purblind and hideous, a lower class crude and brutal,—we shall turn our eyes again, and to more purpose, upon this passionate and dauntless soldier of a forlorn hope, who, ignorant of the future and unconsoled by its promises, nevertheless waged against the conservation of the old impossible world so fiery battle; waged it till he fell,—waged it with such splendid and imperishable excellence of sincerity and strength.

Wordsworth's value is of another kind. Wordsworth has an insight into permanent sources of joy and consolation for mankind which Byron has not; his poetry gives us more which we may rest upon than Byron's,—more which we can rest upon now, and which men may rest upon always. I place Wordsworth's poetry, therefore,

† Preface to Arnold's edition of Byron's poetry, reprinted in Arnold's *Essays in*   *Criticism, Second Series* (London: Macmillan, 1903).

above Byron's on the whole, although in some points he was greatly Byron's inferior, and although Byron's poetry will always, probably, find more readers than Worlsworth's, and will give pleasure more easily. But these two, Wordsworth and Byron, stand, it seems to me, first and pre-eminent in actual performance, a glorious pair, among the English poets of this century. Keats had probably, indeed, a more consummate poetic gift than either of them; but he died having produced too little and being as yet too immature to rival them. I for my part can never even think of equalling with them any other of their contemporaries;—either Coleridge, poet and philosopher wrecked in a mist of opium; or Shelley, beautiful and ineffectual angel, beating in the void his luminous wings in vain. Wordsworth and Byron stand out by themselves. When the year 1900 is turned, and our nation comes to recount her poetic glories in the century which has just then ended, the first names with her will be these.

OSCAR WILDE

From *The Soul of Man Under Socialism* (1891)

* * *

But it may be asked how Individualism, which is now more or less dependent on the existence of private property for its development, will benefit by the abolition of such private property. The answer is very simple. It is true that, under existing conditions, a few men who have had private means of their own, such as Byron, Shelley, Browning, Victor Hugo, Baudelaire, and others, have been able to realise their personality more or less completely. Not one of these men ever did a single day's work for hire. They were relieved from poverty. They had an immense advantage. The question is whether it would be for the good of Individualism that such an advantage should be taken away. * * * What I mean by a perfect man is one who develops under perfect conditions; one who is not wounded, or worried, or maimed, or in danger. *Most personalities have been obliged to be rebels. Half their strength has been wasted in friction.* Byron's personality, for instance, was terribly wasted in its battle with the stupidity, and hypocrisy, and Philistinism of the English. Such battles do not always intensify strength: they often exaggerate weakness. Byron was never able to give us what he might have given us. Shelley escaped better. Like Byron, he got out of England as soon as possible. But he was not so well known.

GEORGE BERNARD SHAW

Dedicatory Letter to *Man and Superman* (1903)

* * * Byron's hero [Don Juan] is, after all, only a vagabond libertine. And he is dumb: he does not discuss himself with a Sganar-
elle-Leporello or with the fathers or brothers of his mistresses: he
does not even, like Casanova, tell his own story. In fact he is not a
true Don Juan at all; for he is no more an enemy of God than any
romantic and adventurous young sower of wild oats. * * * Byron
was as little of a philosopher as Peter the Great: both were
instances of that rare and useful, but unedifying variation, an energetic genius born without the prejudices or superstitions of his contemporaries. The resultant unscrupulous freedom of thought made
Byron a greater poet than Wordsworth just as it made Peter a
greater king than George III; but as it was, after all, only a negative
qualification, it did not prevent Peter from being an appalling
blackguard and an arrant poltroon, nor did it enable Byron to
become a religious force like Shelley.

* * *

JAMES JOYCE

From *A Portrait of the Artist as a Young Man* (1916) †

— And who do you think is the greatest poet? asked Boland,
nudging his neighbour.

— Byron, of course, answered Stephen.

Heron gave the lead and all three joined in a scornful laugh.

— What are you laughing at? asked Stephen.

— You, said Heron. Byron the greatest poet! He's only a poet for
uneducated people.

* * *

— In any case Byron was a heretic and immoral too.

— I don't care what he was, cried Stephen hotly.

— You don't care whether he was a heretic or not? said Nash.

— What do you know about it? shouted Stephen. You never
read a line of anything in your life except a trans or Boland either.

— I know that Byron was a bad man, said Boland.

† In this passage from Joyce's semiautobiographical novel, the young poet
Stephen Dedalus is being bullied for his
aesthetic taste by his schoolfellows.

— Here, catch hold of this heretic, Heron called out.

In a moment Stephen was a prisoner.

— Tate made you buck up the other day, Heron went on, about the heresy in your essay.

— I'll tell him tomorrow, said Boland.

— Will you? said Stephen. You'd be afraid to open your lips.

— Afraid?

— Ay. Afraid of your life.

— Behave yourself! cried Heron, cutting at Stephen's legs with his cane.

It was the signal for their onset. Nash pinioned his arms behind while Boland seized a long cabbage stump which was lying in the gutter. Struggling and kicking under the cuts of the cane and the blows of the knotty stump Stephen was borne back against a barbed wire fence.

— Admit that Byron was no good.

— No.

— Admit.

— No.

— Admit.

— No. No.

VIRGINIA WOOLF

From *A Writer's Diary*
(Wednesday, August 7, 1918)

Anyhow, I was very glad to go on with my Byron. He has at least the male virtues. In fact, I'm amused to find how easily I can imagine the effect he had upon women—especially upon rather stupid or uneducated women, unable to stand up to him. So many, too, would wish to reclaim him. * * * I'm much impressed by the extreme badness of B.'s poetry—such of it as Moore quotes with almost speechless admiration. Why did they think this Album stuff the finest fire of poetry? It reads hardly better than L.E.L. or Ella Wheeler Wilcox. And they dissuaded him from doing what he knew he could do, which was to write satire. He came home from the East with satires (parodies of Horace) in his bag and *Childe Harold*. He was persuaded that *Childe Harold* was the best poem ever written. But he never as a young man believed in his poetry; a proof, in such a confident dogmatic person, that he hadn't the gift. The Wordsworths and Keatses believe in that as much as they believe in anything. * * * At any rate Byron had superb force; his letters prove it. He had in many ways a very fine nature too; though as no one laughed him out of his affectations he became more like Horace Cole than one could wish. He could only be laughed at by a woman, and they worshipped instead. I haven't yet come to Lady Byron, but I suppose, instead of laughing, she merely disapproved. And so he became Byronic.

WILLIAM BUTLER YEATS

From A *Vision* (1922) †

Phase Nineteen

Will—The Assertive Man.
Mask * * * *True*—Conviction. *False*—Domination.
Creative Mind * * * *True*—Emotional intellect. *False*—The Unfaithful.
Body of fate * * * —Enforced failure of action.
Examples: Gabriele d'Annunzio (perhaps), Oscar Wilde, Byron, a certain actress.

This phase is the beginning of the artificial, the abstract, the fragmentary, and the dramatic. Unity of Being is no longer possible, for the being is compelled to live in a fragment of itself and to dramatise that fragment. * * * When the man lives according to phase, he is now governed by conviction, instead of by a ruling mood, and is effective only in so far as he can find this conviction. * * * He desires to be strong and stable, but as Unity of Being and self-knowledge are both gone, and it is too soon to grasp at another unity through *primary* mind, he passes from emphasis to emphasis. * * * He is doomed to attempt the destruction of all that breaks or encumbers personality, but this personality is conceived of as a fragmentary, momentary intensity.

* * *

Here one finds men and women who love those who rob them or beat them, as though the soul were intoxicated by its discovery of human nature, or found even a secret delight in the shattering of the image of its desire. It is as though it cried, "I would be possessed by" or "I would possess that which is Human. What do I care if it is good or bad?" There is no "disillusionment," for they have found that which they have sought, but that which they have sought and found is a fragment.

† "Phase," "Will," "Mask," etc., are terms relating to Yeats's system for describing the varieties and transformations of human personality and poetic style.

T. E. LAWRENCE

From *Seven Pillars of Wisdom* (1926) †

In my case, the effort for these years to live in the dress of Arabs, and to imitate their mental foundation, quitted me of my English self, and let me look at the West and its conventions with new eyes: they destroyed it all for me. At the same time I could not sincerely take on the Arab skin: it was an affectation only. Easily was a man made an infidel, but hardly might he be converted to another faith. I had dropped one form and not taken on the other, and was become like Mohammed's coffin in our legend, with a resultant feeling of intense loneliness in life, and a contempt, not for other men, but for all they do. Such detachment came at times to a man exhausted by prolonged physical effort and isolation. His body plodded on mechanically, while his reasonable mind left him, and from without looked down critically on him, wondering what that futile lumber did and why. Sometimes these selves would converse in the void; and then madness was very near, as I believe it would be near the man who could see things through the veils at once of two customs, two educations, two environments.

CHARLES DU BOS

Byron and the Need of Fatality (1931) †

An inherent prestige, and perhaps the most intrinsic, the most inalienable of all, attaches to the authentic fatal being; the case of Byron is that which enables us most closely to examine both this notion of prestige and the value of the notion of prestige in general. But let me at once point out what is one of the sources and one of the explanations of that prestige—the fact that a being of this sort is always not only *like* himself, but *equal* to himself; by which I mean that take Byron where we will, how we will, by surprise or otherwise—in a word, a gesture, an act which is to him significant, or on the contrary in those which are essentially quite the reverse— always he gives us himself with the same volume and even, one

† Lawrence does not mention Byron in this passage from his autobiography; but it is difficult not to think of the Giaour, the general figure of the "Byronic outcast," and Byron's own final fight for the liberation of Greece when reading Lawrence's narrative—particularly since Lawrence himself was so profoundly influenced by the traditions of classical and English literature, and by nostalgia for the heroic stature of the epic (in life as well as letters).

† Du Bos was one of the most brilliant French critics of the early twentieth century; and much of the existential urgency and profundity he sees in Byron's life and works has been ratified by more recent English and American commentators.

might say, with the same calibre. * * * At the climax of frenzy he never escapes from himself; his frenzy leaves him where it finds him, his sallies and explosions infallibly come home to roost. That is why, writing solely for relief, though finding that outlet essential to him—for the act of writing more than once in his life represented the only antidote against the temptation of suicide—his sense of relief does not last, does not heal, above all does not liberate; never with Byron is the work liberating, and had it been possible for his nature thus to liberate itself, we feel that he would never have wished it to do so.

MARIO PRAZ

From *The Romantic Agony* (1933) †

What Manfred said of Astarte ('I loved her, and destroy'd her'), what Byron wished to be able to say of Augusta and of Annabella (see the Incantation in *Manfred*), was to become the motto of the 'fatal' heroes of Romantic literature. They diffuse all round them the curse which weighs upon their destiny, they blast, like the simoom, those who have the misfortune to meet with them (the image is from *Manfred*, III. I); they destroy themselves, and destroy the unlucky women who come within their orbit. Their relations with their mistresses are those of an incubus-devil with his victim.

T. S. ELIOT

Byron (1937)

* * *

Of Byron one can say, as of no other English poet of his eminence, that he added nothing to the language, that he discovered nothing in the sounds, and developed nothing in the meaning, of individual words. I cannot think of any other poet of his distinction who might so easily have been an accomplished foreigner writing English. The ordinary person talks English, but only a few people in every generation can write it; and upon this undeliberate collaboration between a great many people talking a living language and a

---

† Praz's book, one of the most celebrated, controversial, and suggestive books about the whole tradition of Romanticism, argues that the center of that imaginative revolution is deeply implicated with pathological psychosexual aberrations, and—Praz argues—Byron and the Marquis de Sade between them define the whole imaginative range of Romanticism.

very few people writing it, the continuance and maintenance of a language depends. Just as an artisan who can talk English beautifully while about his work or in a public bar, may compose a letter painfully written in a dead language bearing some resemblance to a newspaper leader, and decorated with words like "maelstrom" and "pandemonium": so does Byron write a dead or dying language.

ALBERT CAMUS

From *The Rebel* (1951)

Murder, in fact [during the Romantic revolution] is on the way to becoming acceptable * * * Murder, of course, is not recommended for its own sake. But it is implicit in the value—supreme for the romantic—attached to frenzy. Frenzy is the reverse of boredom. * * * The Byronic hero, incapable of love, or capable only of an impossible love, suffers endlessly. He is solitary, languid, his condition exhausts him. If he wants to feel alive, it must be in the terrible exaltation of a brief and destructive action. To love someone whom one will never see again is to give a cry of exultation as one perishes in the flames of passion.

* * *

At the very heart of romanticism, the sterility of this [purely aesthetic, individualist] attitude becomes apparent to a few rebels who provide a transitional type between the eccentrics (or the Incredible) and our revolutionary adventurers. Between the times of the eighteenth-century eccentric and the "conquerors" of the twentieth century, Byron and Shelley are already fighting, though only ostensibly, for freedom. They also expose themselves, but in another way. Rebellion gradually leaves the world of appearances for the world of action, where it will completely commit itself.

VLADIMIR NABOKOV

From *Lolita* (1955) †

I imagined (under conditions of new and perfect visibility) all the casual caresses her mother's husband would be able to lavish on

† From *The Annotated Lolita*, edited by Alfred Appel, Jr. (New York: McGraw-Hill, 1970), p. 72.

The Byron quotation is from *Childe Harold* III, stanza cxvi. Editor Appel notes furthermore (p. 366) that "Byron's works and Byron's Augusta Ada, a gifted girl in her own right resonate in Nabokov's later novel [*Ada*, 1969], as does the "Byronic" * * * theme of incest. * * * Nabokov's deep knowledge of Byron is made evident throughout his *Eugene Onegin* Commentary. . . ."

In this passage from *Lolita*, Humbert Humbert, the narrator, is about to marry the dreadful widow, Charlotte Haze, so that he can be close to his real love, Charlotte's teenage daughter, "Lolita."

his Lolita. I would hold her against me three times a day, every day. All my troubles would be expelled, I would be a healthy man. "To hold thee lightly on a gentle knee and print on thy soft cheek a parent's kiss . . ." Well-read Humbert!

W. H. AUDEN

Byron: The Making of a Comic Poet (1966)

In the history of English poetry before the so-called Romantic Age, comic poetry is comparatively rare: some of Chaucer, some of Dunbar, Skelton, Samuel (*Hudibras*) Butler. Dryden and Pope, though they often write funny lines, cannot be classified as comic poets. But from 1800 onwards, comic poetry has flourished. Byron, Moore (especially in his political poems), Praed, Hood, Barham, Lear, and Carroll (slightly to one side), W. S. Gilbert, J. K. Stephen, Calverly, and in this century the best of Chesterton and Belloc, not to mention the anonymous host of limerick writers, represent a tradition without which English poetry would be very much the poorer, and of them all, Byron is by far the greatest. Whatever its faults, *Don Juan* is the most original poem in English; nothing like it had ever been written before. Speaking for myself, I don't feel like reading it very often, but when I do, it is the only poem I want to read: no other will do.

ANGUS WILSON

Evil in the English Novel (1967)

The figure of Byron was not to be forgotten in the cosy domesticity of the middle-class novel of the Victorian age. Some people were to remember it, and for some novelists it played an important part.

We can see this figure of the Byronic Manfred in Heathcliff, in Mr. Rochester, and in Steerforth;[4] those three characters are, in their different ways, people who forced Dickens and the Brontës to break through the shell of the novel. Dickens, of course, was directly influenced by Gothic novelists of the kind of Ainsworth— criminal novelists. Without their tradition of writing, he would not have found any place for his transcendent and powerful sense of

4. Byronic characters in *Wuthering Heights* by Emily Brontë, *Jane Eyre* by Charlotte Brontë, and *David Copperfield* by Charles Dickens.

5. Imaginary, fantasy-lands which formed the juvenile play of the Brontë children.

evil; he would not have found a way of breaking through. The Brontës began, in the childhood games in "Gondal" and "Angria",[5] with the figures of Byron and Napoleon: the superman and the fallen angel. The greatest of these representations of the fallen angel, the representation that comes directly from the Gothic and gives us a very individual appreciation of transcendent good and evil, is *Wuthering Heights*.

ANTHONY LEWIS

At Last Lord Byron Gets Place in Poets' Corner in Westminster (1968) †

LONDON, May 6—A century and a half after his death, Lord Byron has at last become spiritually acceptable in his homeland. He is to have a plaque in the Poets' Corner of Westminister Abbey.

This quiet revolution has been carried out by the Dean of Westminister, the Very Rev. Eric Abbott. After private approaches, he approved a petition by the Poetry Society for a Byron memorial in the Abbey.

Three similar requests had been turned down. The last attempt was in 1924, when the Dean of the day, Bishop Herbert E. Ryle, wrote:

"Byron, partly by his own openly dissolute life and partly by the influence of licentious verse, earned a worldwide reputation for immorality among English-speaking people. A man who outraged the laws of our Divine Lord, and whose treatment of women violated the Christian principles of purity and honor, should not be commemorated in Westminister Abbey."

An answering letter in Byron's behalf was sent to The Times of London by a group including Thomas Hardy, Rudyard Kipling and three former Prime Ministers—Balfour, Asquith and Lloyd George. But the established church was unmoved.

A Change in Standards

No official reason has been given for the present dean's attitude, but no one would consider Byron's poetry licentious by contemporary standards, and perhaps the Church of England is more charitable now toward eccentric behavior. * * *

†At the time this was written, Anthony Lewis was the London correspondent of the *New York Times*.

Chronology

1788   Born January 22 in London.

1790   Taken by his mother to Aberdeen, Scotland.

1791   Death of his father, Captain John Byron, in France.

1793   Enters his first school, in Aberdeen.

1794–95   Attends Aberdeen Grammar School. In 1794, on the death of his great uncle, becomes heir to the title, Baron Byron of Rochdale.

1798   Is made Lord Byron. Moves with his mother to Newstead Abbey, ancestral home of the Byrons.

1801–5   Attends Harrow School. In 1803 falls in love with Mary Chaworth, his neighbor at Newstead. (The attachment ends when he overhears Mary laugh to her maid, "What! Me care for that lame boy!")

1805   Enters Trinity College, Cambridge.

1806   First volume of poems, *Fugitive Pieces*, privately printed. Upon the Reverend John Becher's objections to certain of the poems, Byron withdraws the volume.

1807   *Poems on Various Occasions*, an expurgated version of *Fugitive Pieces*, privately printed. Later in the year the volume appears in a public printing as *Hours of Idleness*. On March 13, Byron takes his seat in the House of Lords.

1808   *Hours of Idleness* is the subject of a scathing critique in the *Edinburgh Review*. On July 4 Byron receives his A.M. degree from Cambridge.

1809   Publication of *English Bards and Scotch Reviewers*. On July 2, sails from Falmouth for Lisbon with John Cam Hobhouse. Travels through Portugal, Spain, Malta, and Albania, reaching Athens at the end of the year. Writes the first Canto of "Childe Burun" (later *Childe Harold's Pilgrimage*).

1810   Travels through Greece and Turkey. On May 3 swims the Hellespont from Sestos to Abydos. Writes the second canto of "Childe Burun."

1811   Returns to England July 14. Death of Byron's mother and of the Cambridge chorister John Edleston ("Thyrza").

1812   Delivers speeches in the House of Lords. *Childe Harold*, cantos I and II, published in March. First meeting with his wife-to-be, Annabella Milbanke. Affair with Lady Caroline Lamb. Affair with Lady Oxford.

1813   Publication of *The Giaour* (June) and *The Bride of Abydos* (December). Begins affair with his half sister, Augusta Leigh.

1814   Publication of *The Corsair* (January) and *Lara* (August). Byron's daughter, Medora, born to Augusta. Becomes engaged to Annabella Milbanke.

1815   Marries Annabella January 2. Publication of *Hebrew Melodies*. Daughter, Augusta Ada, born to Annabella December 10.

1816   Byron's wife leaves him in January. *The Siege of Corinth* and *Parisina* are published in February. In April the separation from his wife is formalized and Byron leaves England forever on April 24. Arriving in Geneva, he befriends Percy and Mary Shelley and Claire Clairmont, spends the summer with them, and has an affair with Claire. Travels to Venice, has an affair with Marianna Segati, his landlord's wife. At the end of the year, *Childe Harold* canto III and *The Prisoner of Chillon* are published.

1817   Daughter, Allegra, born to Claire Clairmont January 12. Byron travels to Rome with Hobhouse, returns to settle in Venice. Affair with Margarita Cogni, wife of a Venetian baker. Sells Newstead Abbey. *Manfred* published in June.

1818   *Beppo* (satire in the *ottava rima* of *Don Juan*) published in February. The Shelleys come to Italy and are with Byron from March to November. *Childe Harold* canto IV published in April. Allegra comes to Venice.

1819   Beginning of affair with Countess Teresa Guiccioli. *Mazeppa* published in June, *Don Juan* cantos I and II in July. Moves to Ravenna at the end of the year to be near Teresa.

1820   Lives in the Guiccioli palace with his daughter Allegra. Becomes involved in the Carbonari movement, the Italian revolution against Austrian rule. Official separation between Teresa and her husband in July.

1821   Teresa's family, the Gambas, are banished to Pisa after the defeat of the Carbonari movement; Byron moves there with them. *Marino Faliero* published in April, *Don Juan* cantos III–V in August, *Cain*, *The Two Foscari*, and *Sardanapalus* in December. Byron promises Teresa to discontinue *Don Juan*.

1822   Allegra dies in April. Leigh Hunt moves to Byron's house in June, where they collaborate on the journal *The Liberal*. Shelley is drowned July 8 in his boat, the *Don Juan*. *The Vision of Judgment* appears in *The Liberal* in October.

1823   *Don Juan* cantos VI–XIV published. Byron sails for Greece, arriving at Missolonghi December 30.

1824   Catches a chill in the rain on April 9. Dies at Missolonghi April 19. *Don Juan* cantos XV and XVI are published in March. In June Byron is buried in Hucknall Torkard Church, near Newstead Abbey.

Selected Bibliography

EDITIONS

The Works of Lord Byron, Poetry. Edited by E. H. Coleridge. 7 volumes. London, 1898–1904. This is the John Murray edition, still the authoritative text.

The Complete Poetical Works of Lord Byron. Edited by Paul Elmer More, Cambridge Edition of the Poets, Boston, 1905.

Byron: Poetical Works. Edited by F. Page, Oxford Standard Authors, London, 1904 (revised by John D. Jump, 1970).

The Works of Lord Byron, Letters and Journals. Edited by Rowland E. Prothero. 6 volumes. London, 1898–1901. The Murray edition.

Byron's Letters and Journals. Edited by Leslie A. Marchand. London, 1973–74 (a new edition of the Prothero volumes, unexpurgated and containing many previously unpublished letters. Six volumes have appeared so far.)

Byron: A Self-Portrait, Letters and Diaries, 1798 to 1824. Edited by Peter Quennell. 2 volumes. London, 1950.

Lord Byron: Selected Prose. Edited by Peter Gunn. London, 1972.

MEMOIRS BY CONTEMPORARIES

Blessington, Margaret, Countess. *Conversations of Lord Byron.* London, 1834. (Edited by Ernest J. Lovell, Princeton, 1969.)

Guiccioli, Teresa, Countess. *My Recollections of Lord Byron.* London, 1869.

Lovell, Ernest J., ed. *His Very Self and Voice: The Collected Conversations of Lord Byron.* New York, 1954. (Excluding Lady Blessington and Medwin).

Medwin, Thomas. *Journal of the Conversations of Lord Byron.* London, 1824. (Edited by Ernest J. Lovell, Princeton, 1966).

Trelawney, Edward John. *Recollections of the Last Days of Shelley and Byron.* London, 1858.

BIOGRAPHIES AND BIOGRAPHICAL STUDIES

Brent, Peter. *Lord Byron.* London, 1974.

DuBos, Charles. *Byron and the Need of Fatality.* New York, 1932.

Knight, G. Wilson. *Lord Byron: Christian Virtues.* London, 1952.

———. *Lord Byron's Marriage.* London, 1956.

Marchand, Leslie A. *Byron: A Biography.* 3 volumes. New York, 1957.

———. *Byron: A Portrait.* New York, 1971. (A one-volume version of the 3-volume life).

Maurois, André. *Byron.* London, 1930.

CRITICAL DISCUSSIONS

Books marked with an asterisk* contain single chapters or essays on Byron.

*Bloom, Harold. *The Visionary Company.* New York, 1963.

*———, ed. *Romanticism and Consciousness.* New York, 1971.

*Bostetter, Edward E. *The Romantic Ventriloquists.* Seattle, 1963.

*Bowra, C. M. *The Romantic Imagination.* Cambridge, Mass., 1961.

Cooke, Michael G. *The Blind Man Traces the Circle: On the Patterns and Philosophy of Byron's Poetry,* Princeton, 1969.

*Fairchild, Hoxie N. *The Romantic Quest.* New York, 1931.

*Frye, Northrop. *Fables of Identity.* New York, 1963.

Gleckner, Robert F. *Byron and the Ruins of Paradise.* Baltimore, 1967.

Joseph, M. K. *Byron the Poet.* London, 1964.

Jump, John D. *Byron.* London, 1972.

*Kroeber, Karl. *Romantic Narrative Art.* Madison, 1960.

Lovell, Ernest J. *Byron: The Record of a Quest*. Austin, 1950.

Marchand, Leslie A. *Byron's Poetry: A Critical Introduction*. Cambridge, Mass., 1968.

Marshall, William H. *The Structure of Byron's Major Poems*. Philadelphia, 1962.

McGann, Jerome J. *Fiery Dust: Byron's Poetic Development*. Chicago, 1968.

Ridenour, George M. *The Style of Don Juan*. New Haven, 1960.

Rutherford, Andrew. *Byron: A Critical Study*. Palo Alto, 1961.

———, ed. *Byron: The Critical Heritage*. (A collection of essays on Byron dating from the publication of his first poems to the early twentieth century.)

Steffan, Truman Guy. *Don Juan: The Making of a Masterpiece*. Austin, 1957. (Volume 1 of the 4-volume edition of *Don Juan* by Steffan and W. W. Pratt.)

Thorslev, Peter L. *The Byronic Hero: Types and Prototypes*. Minneapolis, 1962.

West, Paul. *Byron and the Spoiler's Art*. New York, 1960.

———, ed. *Byron: A Collection of Critical Essays*. Englewood Cliffs, 1963.

*Wilkie, Brian. *Romantic Poets and Epic Tradition*. Madison, 1965.